ABNORMAL
PSYCHOLOGY

MYTHS OF CRAZY

DREW CURTIS • LESLIE KELLEY

THIRD EDITION

Kendall Hunt
publishing company

Cover image © Shutterstock.com

www.kendallhunt.com
Send all inquiries to:
4050 Westmark Drive
Dubuque, IA 52004-1840

To our loving families.

CONTENTS

AUTHOR BIOGRAPHIES

DR. DREW CURTIS is currently an Associate Professor of Psychology and the Director of the Counseling Psychology Master's Program at Angelo State University in San Angelo, TX. He is also the President for the Southwestern Psychological Association. He earned his BS in Psychology and MA in Clinical Psychology from Sam Houston State University. Dr. Curtis earned his PhD in Counseling Psychology from Texas Woman's University. His clinical experience has been primarily within university counseling centers and private practice, with specific interest and training in treatment of trichotillomania and anxiety disorders. Dr. Curtis completed his pre-doctoral psychology internship at the Career and Counseling Services at the University of Houston Clear Lake in Houston, TX. Dr. Curtis has taught a variety of undergraduate and graduate courses for 12 years at universities and community colleges. Dr. Curtis established the Clinical Science and Deception Lab at ASU. His research has specifically focused on deception: within health

Photo reprinted with permission of Angelo State University Office of Communications and Marketing

care professions, in the context of therapy, pathological lying, intimate relationships, and parental relationships. Other research interests are psychomythology of psychopathology, teaching of psychology and postpartum and perinatal psychology. Dr. Curtis has received several awards for his teaching and research and made various news appearances for Fox and other local news pertaining to his research and textbook.

DR. LESLIE KELLEY is currently an Assistant Professor of Psychology for the Counseling Psychology Master's Program at Angelo State University in San Angelo, TX. He ardently enjoys teaching and challenging his students to think critically about complex and controversial topics, and has taught a wide variety of psychology and philosophy courses over the past 19 years. Dr. Kelley earned his BA and MA degrees in philosophy at Franciscan University of Steubenville, and his MA and PhD in Counseling Psychology at Texas Woman's University. His clinical experience includes individual and group psychotherapy at a residential addiction rehabilitation center, working with students at a college counseling center, and working with clients in private practice and a community mental health center. In 2011, he received the APA Division 17 (Society of Counseling Psychology) Supervision and Training Section Award for his work on the development and evalua-

Photo © 2020 Krista Kelley

tion of a psychotherapy training rating scale. His research interests include psychological integration and frameworks for psychological conceptualization, the intersection of cognition and emotion, and of course, myths of psychopathology.

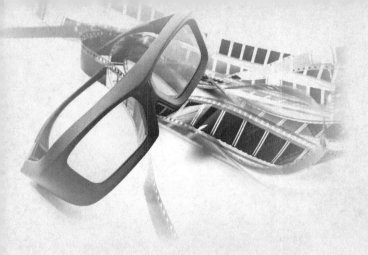

PREFACE

For over a century, movies and media have promoted myths of psychology and psychopathology that have been absorbed into daily perception. Many students entering college possess a number of myths about abnormal psychology and psychopathology (Curtis, 2018). Numerous films attempt to depict forms of psychopathology (Wedding & Niemiec, 2014), however misleading films and media are one of the primary sources that lead to the development of myths (Curtis, 2018; Lilienfeld et al., 2010). Some films may promote the idea that abnormality consists of "crazy" violent killers or deranged individuals who must be isolated from society. One of the goals of this book is to challenge you to reconsider the ideas you have concerning myths of "crazy" and how these ideas developed.

Along with films, personal experiences and cognitive biases may lead to the development of a variety of myths found within the study of abnormal psychology (Lilienfeld et al., 2010). Lilienfeld and colleagues have suggested that debunking myths is useful within psychology courses and positions students to better evaluate psychomythology claims in their everyday life. Assessing and deconstructing myths in abnormal psychology is engaging, involves active learning, and is fun. Further it facilitates critical thinking skills for you beyond the classroom (Lilienfeld et al., 2010).

Goals

This book guides readers in the deconstruction of these myths by a process designed to help formulate a sound approach to abnormality and a thorough understanding of various disorders through the lens of the The Diagnostic and Statistics Manual of Mental Disorders, 5th edition (DSM-5; American Psychiatric Association, 2013). The book will ask you to examine movies, your experiences, talking about differences, and how it relates to what has been learned (MYTH).

In doing this, students are better equipped to discern myths from accurate conceptualization of disorders. Further, students will learn about human error, biases, and how myths shape their social cognitive labels and attitudes toward people with disorders.

Another aim of this text is to promote social awareness of the humanity in mental health over tendencies to be reductionistic or distancing. Students will learn the importance of intentionally directing attention toward the humanity of the individuals who have various disorders, in order to develop more

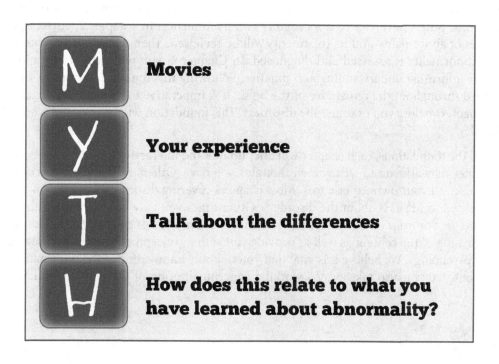

M — Movies

Y — Your experience

T — Talk about the differences

H — How does this relate to what you have learned about abnormality?

accurate perceptions of these individuals. The goal is to reflect on the humanity within abnormality rather than reducing people to a label and stripping them of their humanity. Readers will be confronted with the idea that abnormality is not exemplified by "crazies" in a straitjacket, void of coherent words, or violent characters in film but rather by human persons, who are often suffering, feeling immense pain, or who have impaired functioning in their life.

Along these lines, another goal of this book is to challenge your use of language related to abnormal psychology. Much of our language expresses our thoughts. Seeking to alter our language may assist with our thinking about people who have disorders. Calling someone a schizophrenic may draw a different image for you than stating someone is suffering from schizophrenia. Another general term that we use is the term "crazy." Crazy can paint a variety of pictures for people. Language is a vehicle by which we can influence our thinking about mental health. This book will invite readers to consider the use of their language when referring to various aspects of abnormal psychology.

The book also seeks to provide readers with resources for empirically supported treatments to various disorders. The American Psychological Association Presidential Task Force on Evidence-Based Practice (2006) moved to identify the best evidence-based practices for the psychological treatments of psychological disorders. Many chapters discussing treatments of disorders will provide references to these evidence-based practices.

Structure

Consider the first four chapters as building blocks established on a firm foundation for which to examine the rest of the content. This foundation is pertinent to develop before delving into the different disorders. Chapter 1 will introduce concepts of abnormal psychology, defining abnormality, and discussion of how others have viewed abnormality and its influence. In Chapter 2, current perspectives and theories of abnormality and its treatments will be reviewed. Then Chapter 3 will present readers with how abnormality is assessed and diagnosed. In Chapter 4, you will explore the applications of research for informing understanding and practice. Following this foundation, various disorders will be examined throughout the remainder of the book. It is imperative to have an understanding of the first four chapters before you examine the disorders. This foundation will be revisited when discussing each disorder.

Beyond the foundations, each chapter will offer unique and interactive sections. Some sections such as this chapter may ask you to write down thoughts you have. Others may ask you to consider a case study or reflect on your own experiences. Most chapters covering disorders will ask you to write your thoughts related to MYTHs about the disorders. Other times you may be presented with a case study or asked to reflect on your own experiences. Whichever activity you engage in, the book is designed to promote learning of the content as well as provide you with a conceptualization of abnormality within the field of psychology. We believe it is vital that you not only know some of the information related to a disorder but that you also take away a working conceptualization of the disorder and how it affects people.

Cases

Elements from the case studies were based on the clinical experiences of the authors. Cases do not represent individual clients, but rather the authors' various experiences working with individuals suffering from a particular disorder. If any of these cases seem like they reflect you or someone you know, it may be due to your understanding, empathy, or shared experiences and not due to the details of the case.

We think that this approach to abnormal psychology is beneficial, engaging, and fun. If you're ready to challenge your assumptions and expand your understanding of psychopathology, then crack this "crazy" book open and get to reading!

CHAPTER ONE

UNDERSTANDING ABNORMALITY: A LOOK AT "CRAZY"

LEARNING OBJECTIVES

- ► Examine thoughts about "crazy" and myths of abnormality
- ► Identify goals in studying abnormal psychology
- ► List various myths about abnormality
- ► Define normality and abnormality
- ► Differentiate abnormality and mental illness
- ► Discuss and identify criteria of abnormality
- ► Apply the criteria of abnormality
- ► Examine historical perspectives of abnormality
- ► Explore the connection between understanding and responding to abnormality
- ► Explain the dynamic aspects of abnormality
- ► List various mental health professionals
- ► Recognize the differences between psychologists and psychiatrists

CHAPTER OUTLINE

- ► Thinking About "Crazy"
- ► Some Myths
- ► Defining Abnormality: What Is Normal?
- ► Mental Illness
- ► The 4 Fs of Abnormality: Frequency, Function, Feeling Pain, and Fatal
- ► A Look Into the Part: Historical Perspectives of Abnormality
- ► Releasing the Demons and Evil: Supernatural Perspectives
- ► Releasing Blood and Touching Heads: Biological Perspectives
- ► It's in Your Head: Psychological Perspectives
- ► Are We There Yet? Integrationist Perspectives

► Psychopathology Is Dynamic
► Who Is Involved? Professionals in Mental Health

Thinking About "Crazy"

Think about the craziest thing you have ever seen or experienced. What are the things that made it crazy? Write down the three most abnormal things you have ever seen or experienced and what contributed to them being labeled as abnormal.

You develop many ideas about "crazy" from a variety of sources. We are fascinated with "crazy" but from afar. One of the most common ways that people construct ideas of abnormality is through media (Curtis, 2018). Films provide you with entertainment mediums for which you can observe abnormality, from a distance. There are numerous films that attempt to depict abnormality (Gabbard & Gabbard, 1999; Wedding & Niemiec, 2014) and usually do so with entertaining Hollywood twists. In fact, more and more movies about psychological disorders continue to be produced each year (Schroeder et al., 2019). This conveys a representative view of abnormal psychology, in which it is the study of patients who are locked in a padded room contained in a straitjacket. While abnormal psychology does include the examination of disorders and their occurrence within psychiatric facilities, it encompasses much more.

Myths in Movies

STONEHEARST ASYLUM

The story by Edgar Allan Poe turned into a movie, *Stonehearst Asylum* (Davey et al., 2014), may promote the idea that abnormality consists of violent and homicidal "crazies" who must be isolated from society. The movie depicts scenes of patients who have rallied against the staff and defiantly locked them in the cells meant for the patients.

Reality: Most people with psychological disorders are not confined to psychiatric asylums and do not violently overthrow the asylum.

© Millennium Entertainment/Photofest

HOW ABOUT THESE THINGS? ARE THESE ABNORMAL?

© Jochen Schoenfeld/Shutterstock.com

© Nomad_Soul/Shutterstock.com

© photoschmidt/Shutterstock.com

© Michael Dorausch/Shutterstock.com

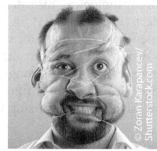
© Zoran Karapancev/Shutterstock.com

© Frenzel/Shutterstock.com

What about these behaviors, thoughts, or feelings?

1. Developing multiple homicidal personalities.
2. Not leaving your apartment because you are worried that a deadly killer will get you.
3. Having visions of dark figures leads to frenzied dance performances and ultimately ends in suicide.
4. Avoid stepping on cracks because it may be bad luck.
5. Lack of emotional expression and repetitively watching the same court show while being able to count, within seconds, the exact number of fallen toothpicks from a full box.

Some of the above-mentioned behaviors are depicted in films. You may enjoy watching films and media of abnormality because it leads to you feeling better about yourself or confirming that you are not "crazy" like other people, deemed social comparison. Social comparison is the social psychology phenomenon in which you compare yourself to others in attempts to elevate your worth or encourage upward change (Festinger, 1954). Thus, watching films may be associated with a normalizing process in which you feel normal when you compare yourself to characters who depict "crazy" in film. One of

Social Comparison

Comparing yourself to others to elevate your worth or motivate upward change

the reasons you may have been interested in taking an abnormal psychology class is to satisfy your curiosity for vicariously experiencing abnormality. Another reason may be to confirm that you are, indeed, normal.

While films are entertaining and may lead us to feel good about our position, they carry a risk of propagating myths and misconceptions. Wedding and Niemiec (2014) suggested that movies are "important in influencing the public perception of mental illness [and] have a greater influence than any other art form" (p. 2). This suggestion has been corroborated within recent research by Curtis (2018), finding that most college students reported movies as having the most influence on deriving information about abnormal psychology and psychological disorders. Interestingly, Curtis found the third person effect (Davison, 1983), in that students believed that movies had more of an effect on others than it had on themselves. Byrne (2009) listed five rules of movie psychiatry and discussed how these have led to cinematic misrepresentations. He strongly urges mental health professionals to actively engage in discussion of film and psychopathology rather than disregarding it or advocating censorship (Byrne, 2009).

Some Myths

There are various myths found within abnormal psychology. Myths come from a variety of sources. Many myths also contribute to a lack of understanding of psychopathology and its treatment. Consider the following list and if you have heard or believe any of these ideas and if they are accurate or inaccurate (some of these were collected from Lilienfeld, Lynn, et al., 2010):

- ▶ There is no such thing as normal.
- ▶ Happiness is the goal of therapy.
- ▶ All therapists practice the same way.
- ▶ People with schizophrenia are likely to harm others.
- ▶ Schizophrenia means having multiple personalities.
- ▶ Autism is on the rise and it's contagious.
- ▶ Bipolar disorder means that you are happy one moment and then completely enraged the next.
- ▶ Suicide is the result of being depressed.
- ▶ Are people who have alcohol-related abuse problems capable of drinking in moderation?
- ▶ Is ADHD real?
- ▶ Do people with depression just need to get over it and go outside?
- ▶ Do psychologists and psychiatrists merely create labels to pathologize people who are normal?

How did you develop these ideas? Did you learn about abnormality through an entertaining film? Did you have experiences with someone who seemed odd (like you noted previously)? As you are presented with information about various psychological disorders, consider how your ideas developed. To assist you in doing this, think of myths. Reflect on movies, media, and your own experiences with regard to how you understand psychological disorders. Then talk with someone or journal about how these movies or experiences have shaped your understanding of abnormal psychology. You will examine your current understanding of psychopathology alongside what you learn about abnormal psychology. Myth-busting has been a successful strategy for educating abnormal psychology students and dispelling myths (Curtis, 2018).

Myths

Stories or constructions of ideas

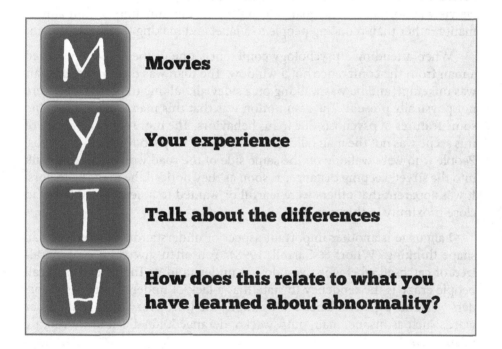

M **Movies**

Y **Your experience**

T **Talk about the differences**

H **How does this relate to what you have learned about abnormality?**

Much of the time our perceptions of people and attributions of their behaviors affect our behaviors and shape our thoughts of abnormality. Attributions are the tendency to seek out and explain the reasons for others' behaviors (Heider, 1958). Social psychology has taught us that we are more likely to make dispositional attributions about others' behaviors (Ross, 1977). Dispositional attributions are used when explaining a person's behaviors by aspects of who they are (Heider, 1958). Thus, when we observe people behaving in a way that we have not seen before, or that fits with the majority of behaviors, do we think about how they are "crazy"? Essentially, are you prone to make dispositional attributions for abnormal behavior and providing people with a general label?

Attributions

Tendency to seek out and explain the reasons for others' behaviors

Dispositional Attributions

Tendency to explain a person's behaviors by aspects of who they are

Psychopathology

Various psychological disorders or atypical illnesses that affect people

Along with challenging the ideas you hold about psychopathology, you will develop an understanding of various disorders. Psychopathology is the examination of various psychological disorders or atypical illnesses that affect people. This term will be used interchangeably with abnormality. You will challenge previously held beliefs about psychopathology and refine your current understanding to achieve more accurate images of individuals who have various disorders.

As you consider influences that shape your understanding of disorders, also think about your attitudes toward people that have disorders. Do you tend to think negatively of people with disorders? Do you tend to avoid someone who you might think has a disorder? Are you fearful that someone with a disorder might harm you? Do you refer to someone suffering with a disorder merely by the label of the disorder? All of these questions get at how we view abnormality. The goal is to reflect on the humanity within abnormality rather than reducing people to a label and making them sub-human.

When attending a psychology conference, one of the authors observed a man from the conference hotel window. The man was disheveled, his hair was unkempt, and he was walking on a sidewalk talking to people who were not physically present. The assumption was that this man was experiencing some features of psychosis due to his behaviors. The more striking feature of this scene was not the man talking to imaginary people but others' reactions. People who were walking on the same side of the road would abruptly walk into the street, keeping distance, as soon as they noticed the man's behaviors. It was apparent that others were fearful or wanted to at least avoid being in close proximity to this man.

Language is another important aspect of understanding. Language can shape thinking (Whorf & Carroll, 1998). You often give things a generalized or catch-all label when you do not understand it. The tendency to call people crazy is the tendency to state that a lack of understanding of disorders warrants a general label. For example, the word crazy, along with other words such as insane, mad, nuts, wacko, deranged, lunatic, and weirdo are misnomers.

Some of these labels have developed from various myths. For example, the label of lunatic comes from the ancient Greek philosopher Aristotle who believed that the brain was affected by the moon, deemed the lunar lunacy effect (Arkowitz & Lilienfeld, 2009). Thus, lunatic became the label for people who display some mental illness or aberrant behaviors due to the influence of the moon. Arkowitz and Lilienfeld discussed how this belief has been perpetuated in movies that display scary or violent behaviors occurring during full-moon nights. This myth has strongly been believed by many people despite evidence from a meta-analysis of 37 studies revealing that the moon does not account for much of people's behavior (Rotton & Kelly, 1985). These labels are potentially detrimental because they often elicit **stigma**, meaning that the labels are used with a derogatory or negative attitude toward individuals suffering from disorders labels. Language can also lead to dehumanization. Dehumanization involves removing human attributes or characteristics that can be in extreme forms of violence or in subtle everyday forms (Haslam et al., 2007). Zimbardo (2007) discusses lessons from his classic Stanford Prison Experiment that led to dehumanization from randomly assigned labels. Labels have the power to strip away humanity and influence our behavior.

Stigma

Negative attitudes associated with a label

When taking a look into abnormality, one of the things that you will notice is that abnormality is not outside of humanity. This means that abnormality is not behaviors that have rarely or never been witnessed, or people who are completely different from you. Rather, with imposed criteria, abnormality is often people who display difficulties in functioning, or stress brought about from behaviors, thoughts, and emotions that are similar to yours. You will be confronted with the idea that abnormality is not exemplified by "crazies" in a straitjacket, void of coherent words, but rather people, with humanity, who are often suffering, feeling immense pain, or have impaired functioning in their life.

Defining Abnormality: What Is Normal?

> [O]ne out of every four people is suffering from a mental illness.
> Look at your three best friends. If they're ok, then it's you.
> —*Susan Musgrave* (1994, p. 47)

Am I normal? This question is one of the reasons that people may struggle with defining abnormality. Sometimes, the difficulty for people in defining abnormality may be due to the cognitive effort to pin down a comprehensive definition. Also, people may avoid defining it because it may lead to them judging others as abnormal and a fear of ostracizing or stigmatizing them. However, many people may avoid defining abnormality because it may challenge how they think of themselves.

To consider abnormality is often reflecting on the status of your normality. Most people ask themselves if they are normal as a common occurrence with developmental phases of life. Specifically, this question is more apparent within the particular developmental stage posed by Erikson (1980), Identity versus Role Confusion. During the adolescent to early adulthood years, people seek to discover their identity in comparison to others, and ask about their

normality while considering their identity. It is the classic teenage stereotypical questions of "Who am I?" and "Am I normal?"

Thus, people may opt out of considering definitions of abnormality and gravitate toward a relativist approach. Relativism is affirming that there are no absolutes and promoting the subjective value of things. Relativism may lend itself to you saying and thinking things such as "What is normal anyway?" or "We are all abnormal in our own way." A popular cliché often used that represents this abandonment of intentionally seeking a definition is that "normal is a setting on a dryer." This approach affirms the notion that abnormality does not exist or that it is relative and unable to be defined. Saying that there is no such thing as normality allows you to avoid its discussion and circumvent answering the initial question, which is whether you are normal.

Defining normal and abnormality does not have to be daunting or even challenge self-perceptions. People throughout time and cultures have sought to explain and understand abnormality. Moreover, how one understands abnormality affects what they do with it. More formally, conceptualization of abnormality affects treatment. Conceptualization is the process of understanding and imagining the various aspects of psychopathology. This will be looked at further when examining historical perspectives of abnormality. For now, let's turn to defining abnormality and looking first at its development.

Mental Illness

One popular view of abnormality was set up as a dichotomy, mentally ill or not. Abnormality might be more simply understood if it were a function of determining whether people were mentally ill. However, abnormal psychology consists of more dimensions than this dichotomous view.

Two opposing popular views have discussed mental illness as a standard for abnormality, Thomas Szasz and David Ausubel (Lilienfeld, 1994). Thomas Szasz vehemently argues that mental illness is a myth. The most pressing case against mental illness is that there are no biological tests that can currently determine if someone is mentally ill. This does not mean that there are no biological tests to determine the levels of neurotransmitters in a person. Neurotransmitters are chemical messengers in the brain that are used in communicating from neurons. This will be discussed further in subsequent chapters. There are ways to determine the levels of neurotransmitters for an individual. However, what this means is that neurotransmitters alone are not sufficient to determine whether an individual has a mental illness. In other words, you are unable to merely provide your blood or urine and someone else determine that you have a mental illness based on that sample.

The difficulty with using mental illness as a criterion is that it offers nothing more than the dichotomous label of either the person being fine mentally or not. The picture of mental illness does not help elicit nomenclature or

Relativism

A view that promotes subjective value

Conceptualization

Process of understanding and imagining the various aspects of psychopathology

Neurotransmitters

The chemical messengers in the brain that are used in communicating from neurons

understanding for individuals who exhibit psychopathology. Thus, there is a necessity to further elaborate on the dimensions of abnormality.

The 4 Fs of Abnormality: Frequency, Function, Feeling Pain, and Fatal

When considering what constitutes abnormality it is crucial to impose four criteria, or the four Fs. The four Fs are concepts that will illuminate the conceptual differences between normative behavior and abnormal behavior as well as the difference between being eccentric and having a disorder. Further, these criteria will be referenced and revisited when considering various disorders.

Other authors have proposed similar criteria for distinguishing between mental disorders and normal behaviors. Nolen-Hoeksema (2007) initially posited that abnormality could be understood and assessed by using three Ds: dysfunction, distress, and deviance. Later, she included a fourth dimension by which mental health professionals use for discerning abnormality: deviance, distress, dysfunction, and danger (Nolen-Hoeksema, 2011, 2014). Frances (2013) noted that definitions of mental disorders consist of features involving distress, disability, dysfunction, dyscontrol, and disadvantage.

One of the commonly referred to instruments used for clinical assessment and understanding of disorders is titled *The Diagnostic and Statistical Manual of Mental Disorders*, 5th edition (DSM-5; American Psychiatric Association; APA, 2013). Due to the prominence of the DSM-5 within the psychotherapeutic profession, it will be referenced throughout this book, especially when considering diagnostic features of various disorders. More discussion of its development and use will be given attention in Chapter 3. The DSM-5 emphasizes that to meet diagnostic criteria for most disorders there is evidence of distress and impairment in social, occupational, or other areas of functioning (APA, 2013). The DSM-5 also indicates that deviance in the frequency of the thoughts, behaviors, or emotions is outside of what may be expected or culturally sanctioned (APA, 2013). The DSM-5 (2013) provides the example that grief experienced from the death of a loved one does not qualify as a mental disorder.

The Diagnostic and Statistical Manual of Mental Disorders

Mental health professionals' instrument used for clinical assessment and understanding of disorders

We propose a definition of normality, in that normal involves behavior, thoughts, and emotions that occur with a relative frequency to the population, assist in daily functioning, do not produce ongoing pain or distress, and do not pose a danger to oneself or others. The four Fs of abnormality: frequency, function, feeling pain, and fatal encompass some of the same conceptual aspects of the dimensions proposed by other authors, though the current labels are more congruent with, and descriptive of, the dimensions. Further, these Fs serve to augment conceptualization of psychopathology by complementing the DSM-5 definition of abnormality and offering imposed

Normal

Behavior, thoughts, and emotions that occur with a relative frequency to the population, assist in daily functioning, do not produce ongoing pain or distress, and do not pose a danger to oneself or others criteria. Specifically, the DSM-5 suggests that behavior that is merely a deviation from social norms is not sufficient to qualify as a disorder; the behavior needs to also result in some impairment in functioning (APA, 2013).

Frequency

In understanding abnormality it is useful to reflect on normality. So, what is normal? How about this?

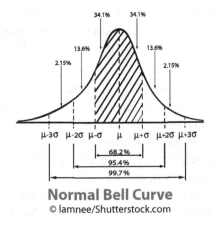

Normal Bell Curve
© Iamnee/Shutterstock.com

If you have taken a statistics class and seen this before, then it will be an imperative to not elicit any further stress that this may be associated with. Let's think through this with the application for abnormality. This picture represents normality and is referred to as a normal bell curve or the normal distribution (Gauss & Davis, 1963). The normal distribution is a statistical perspective of normality that represents a bell-shaped curve.

Normal Distribution

A statistical perspective of normality

So how does this help us understand anything about people and abnormality? The bell curve represents a normal distribution. This represents normality with a frequency distribution. For example, do you wash your hands at least once every day or two? How about at least five times per day? What about 1,000 times per day, most days of the year? This illustrates the ABCs of Frequency: amount of time, behavior, and the curve.

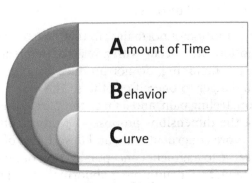

Courtesy of Authors

The first component of frequency is the amount of time that behavior persists. Essentially, how long do the thoughts, feelings, or behavior endure? Washing your hands excessively within one day may not pose any concerns. However, washing your hands a large number of times each day for most days of your life can lead to feeling pain, impaired function, and can even be fatal. Thus, frequency involves the amount of time that the behavior is experienced. For example, feeling intense sadness, pain, and a loss of an appetite shortly after the loss of a loved one may be normative for many people who experience grief. However, if you continue to not eat or barely eat for several months after the loss, then other concerns related to your health may arise.

Next is the frequency of the behavior as an indicator of abnormality. How often does the behavior occur? Abnormality, as discussed before, is not outside of humanity, in that handwashing behaviors represent behavior of a majority of individuals. When imposing the frequency criteria, you may notice that a high frequency of handwashing behaviors (over 100 times per day) to reduce anxiety about thoughts of cleanliness may demonstrate features of a disorder. In fact, you will revisit this disorder in detail in Chapter 8. This example illustrates how a high frequency of behavior is deemed abnormal or disordered. Low frequencies may also serve as indicators. For example, someone who only experiences pleasure from an activity once a year may exhibit a low frequency of behavior. The idea is that many behaviors are normally distributed in terms of their frequency.

Lastly is the curve, the normative bell curve that is. How many people struggle with this issue? When considering the frequency by which people wash their hands, then you may notice a low frequency or small percentage of people engage in washing their hands over 100 times per day. Further, a low percentage of people would be identified who never wash their hands. This depicts the idea of the normative distribution. When you look at the normative distribution, the line in the middle represents average, or the mean. Using this with people, you would be able to state that a majority of people, 68%, fall within one standard deviation of the mean and most people, 96%, fall within two standard deviations of the mean. So, what does it all mean?

Apply the idea of intelligence. The average intelligence quotient (IQ) is 100. An IQ is the score that represents a person's intelligence compared to a normative sample. Many people have an average IQ, ranging between 85–115, one standard deviation. Moreover, most people have an IQ falling between 70–130, two standard deviations. Thus, it would be normative in frequency to have an IQ between 70–130. You could expect 96% of the population to have an IQ within this range. Therefore, it is fewer people that you would expect to have an IQ less than 70, which would be indicative of an intellectual disability.

Intelligence Quotient (IQ)

A score that represents a person's intelligence compared to a normative sample

Much of psychology is concerned with the majority, or the 96% of the normative distribution. Essentially, many psychology experiments look at what affects most people. Abnormal psychology is concerned with the small percentage of the population, the 2% that is two standard deviations below the mean. Abnormal psychology focuses on a smaller number of people or smaller percentage of the population, for example those who wash their hands excessively to mitigate anxiety. However, it is important to note that frequency alone does not completely paint the picture of abnormality or disorder.

Function

How about this picture?

This may be an example of behavior that does not occur often within society, unless you are at a child's *Toy Story*-themed birthday party. Either way, this behavior may not represent the majority of what people do—even at a birthday party. Frequency alone does not provide enough to establish abnormality.

Photo © Rachel Curtis

Let's examine some other "strange" behaviors. Is staring someone in the eyes in an elevator an abnormal behavior? It usually feels uncomfortable for many people because it defies social norms. Social

Social Norms

Implicit instructions for social behavior based on the social situation

norms are implicit instructions for social behavior based on the social situation (Sherif, 1936). For example, when in an elevator there are numerous social norms including facing forward, looking down or up at the floor numbers, and not engaging in lengthy dialogues with others. Bringing a chair from outside an elevator and sitting down in it in the middle of an elevator would defy social norms for elevator behaviors. Thus, behaviors such as these, by default, tend to be rare because they don't align with the majority.

Along with frequency, it is very important to consider functioning as criteria for disorders. Individuals who defy social norms by wearing alien hats on their face or by sitting in a chair in the middle of an elevator do not necessarily show dysfunction resulting from, or related to, their behaviors. Individuals who represent a smaller percentage of the population but evidence no impairment in function may be seen as eccentric or expres-

Eccentric

Behavior that may violate social norms but is not a disorder

sive rather than possessing a disorder or exhibiting abnormality. Eccentric behavior would be behavior that may violate social norms but does not impair function, elicit pain, or carry a likelihood of fatality. Eccentricity is not equivalent to abnormality.

There are times when you engage in behaviors that few other people do, such as sitting in a chair in an elevator or requesting foot-claps when meeting people, as opposed to handshakes. Many people yearn for expressing their identity through attempting to be unique or an iconoclast. Sometimes people will intentionally engage in non-majority behaviors to do this. People may seek a number of methods to express individuality including dying their hair various colors, tattoos, or body modifications. However, if engaging in those behaviors does not impair functioning or other criteria, then you might refer to yourself as eccentric, or the behavior as odd rather than disordered or psychopathological.

© Cora Reed/Shutterstock.com

This is also where there is a need to consider cultural influences. Individuals who have various cultural influences, such as a different ethnicity than the majority need consideration. Some behaviors viewed as normative in a person's ethnicity of origin may be viewed as deviant from behaviors represented by the majority or dominant ethnicity.

These are some of the reasons that deviance as a criteria does not hold by itself and why the DSM-5 suggests that deviance without impaired functioning should not be used to implicate a disorder. An impairment in functioning means that you are unable to fulfill or meet the demands of life or self-established goals. Areas of functioning could include academic, occupational, relational, social, and personal domains. More specifically, this could be seen as not making it to work, being late for a class, failing a class, relationship difficulties, or not taking baths or maintaining personal hygiene.

When people engage in behaviors that are not represented by the high frequency of the distribution, and these behaviors are causing a lack of functioning, then the picture of abnormality is beginning to develop. For example, when someone feels compelled to wash their hands 100 times per day (high frequency) in order to reduce any anxiety which leads to them being late for work and ultimately losing their job, then function has been affected.

Feeling Pain

One of the core features for many individuals who experience a disorder is feeling some pain or distress from their thoughts, behaviors, or emotions. The DSM-5 suggests that there must be evidence of distress for a number of psychological disorders (APA, 2013). This feature of abnormality is extremely important to underscore because it highlights the humanity of people who are suffering from a disorder rather than the "monsters" that we may believe them to be. In fact, most individuals who voluntarily seek mental health professionals are feeling some level of pain brought on by the symptoms or disorder. A number of people who seek counseling might be experiencing great levels of pain because they may have sought other alternatives before therapy.

Feeling pain, in addition to other criteria, reveals that abnormality is not just some eccentric behavior that may lead to someone being late. Feeling pain as a criterion points to the real burden a person is experiencing from the behaviors, thoughts, or emotions. The pain experienced may be a result of physical, emotional, or psychological pain. Newer research examining pain has turned its attention to examining the intersections of cognitive, social, and physical mechanisms of pain (Wasan & Edwards, 2008). Thus, the pain felt from people who have a disorder may be present in any of these areas.

Let's revisit the handwashing behavior. An individual who washes their hands around 100 times per day, leading to functioning being impaired and scarring, may experience significant pain from this behavior. The pain may be experienced as a direct result of the physical pain from the behavior or an emotional pain related to feeling compelled to engage in the behavior.

That being said, there are individuals who may not voluntarily seek mental health services and meet diagnostic criteria for a disorder. For example, an individual who has a specific personality disorder may harm others with a lack of remorse and show no signs of pain from behaviors resultant of their personality. These few exceptions for the criteria of feeling pain indicate that it is not sufficient as a criterion by itself.

Fatal

The last criterion is the one that tends to be perceived as the most dire and immediate. Does the person's thoughts, actions, or emotions place themselves or others in fatal situations? Essentially, is the behavior likely to be fatal to the person displaying the behavior or to others? Fatality can consist of threats to a person's life or health.

Someone who is experiencing a lack of motivation to do anything or get out of bed for most days, resulting in diminished functioning and feeling emotional pain, may threaten their physical health by not eating or not exercising. Another example can be found in someone who is driving and is extremely worried about everything that could go wrong while driving—feeling as though they are putting themselves or others at risk for an automobile accident.

Fatality is also a criterion that is imposed on some behaviors of abnormality where feeling pain may be present. For example, an individual who actively seeks to manipulate or harm others without remorse would meet the criterion for fatality but not necessarily feeling pain. Further, there are some features of disorders where people experience euphoria or great pleasure; however, the feelings influence people to put themselves or others in high-risk situations.

Case Vignette

THE 4 FS

A 22-year-old male, named Felix, who is attending college has recently experienced a relational break-up. His relationship ended due to his girlfriend stating that she was no longer interested in him and wanted to date other people. Felix was deeply upset by this news. He lost his appetite for food and stopped eating. He stopped going to his classes. Felix even stopped taking care of his hygiene by not bathing, brushing his teeth, and wearing the same clothes for several consecutive days. Felix began to drink alcohol more than he ever had. When his friends expressed concern, he stated that he drank so much to just forget about his girlfriend. Felix began to have blackouts from binge drinking. One night, four weeks after the break-up, he went to a party, drank almost two bottles of whiskey and several beers, and then insisted on trying to jump off a two-story ledge. He told his friends that he did not care if he would survive the jump because it would be better than dealing with the pain of losing his girlfriend. Felix later felt embarrassed by this event and slowly retreated from his friends and occasionally drank alcohol by himself. He began to loathe himself and wished that he didn't feel as if he had to drink. Felix was failing his courses, not responding to his friends' attempts to hang out with him, and rarely left his apartment. He carried on drinking alcohol, often several drinks of liquor after an hour of waking up, most days for several months.

Reflect on the case above. According to the criteria of the 4 Fs, would Felix exhibit symptoms of abnormality? If so, which of the Fs are present and how? Write down your responses.

A Look Into the Past: Historical Perspectives of Abnormality

Since there have been humans, abnormality has been found. Abnormality has existed for a long time. Through history, there is documentation of human struggles, how humans have understood their concerns and struggles, and means for alleviating their concerns. Benjamin and Baker (2004) state "one can find evidence of psychological interventions dating to the beginnings of recorded history" (p. 3). Thus, people have understood human struggles and psychopathology and have implemented various interventions taking many forms and labels.

More importantly, how people have understood abnormality is key to realizing how it is dealt with. Examining historical perspectives of abnormality is much more than just filling the pages with how things came to be, rather it greatly informs understanding of abnormality. One of the gems gleaned from studying historical perspectives of abnormality is the understanding of how others viewed abnormality. Why is this important? As mentioned previously, how people view abnormality affects how they respond to it. In other words, how people understand abnormality affects treatment and interventions. This is illustrated in the figure below (see Figure 1.1).

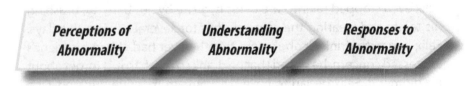

FIGURE 1.1   Understanding Abnormality
Courtesy of Authors

Thus, in reviewing various historical perspectives, attend to how these views influence responses to abnormality. You will notice that people's understanding of abnormality is tied directly to their responses. This foundation will be built upon when considering current psychological perspectives. Historically, people have understood abnormality in a few different contexts: supernatural, biological, and psychological.

Releasing the Demons and Evil: Supernatural Perspectives

In the Stone Age, abnormality was viewed as a source of spiritual possession. People who displayed psychopathology were believed to have had some spirit possess them. As a result, the treatment to cure this abnormality was to rid the person of the spirit. This was done through a practice called trephination. Trephining was a surgical treatment in which a tool was used to drill a hole in the head of a person in an attempt to release the spirit that possessed the person.

Much of trephination understanding is credited to archaeologist Ephraim Squier, and Paul Broca (popularly known for identifying Broca's area in the brain); however, there are early accounts of trephining from Hippocrates (Gross, 1999). Gross discussed the history of trephining as it occurred within Neolithic primitive tribes. Research on the trephined skulls indicated that the skulls were not a result of trauma or accidents but appeared more intentional with evidence supporting that individuals survived the trephination process. In the 17th century, trephination was a procedure implemented to release evil air from the brain or head and was later used as a means to treat mental illness (Gross, 1999).

How people viewed abnormality affected what they did with it. When the source of psychopathology was seen as a spiritual possession, it then made sense to treat the psychopathology with a supernatural treatment, by releasing the spirit from the individual.

Some tribes and groups of people in history had healers, medicine men, or shamans who dealt with issues of mental and physical illness (Frances, 2013). In Frances's discussion of the history of psychiatry he describes the ancient traditions and practices of these shamans. Shamans used magic to assess and diagnose individuals. Diagnoses involved curses and spirits that resulted in some psychopathology. Treatment and healing practices involved chants, dancing, singing, and other means that would challenge the spirits or encourage individuals with

Trephination

A surgical treatment in which a tool is used to drill a hole in the head of a person

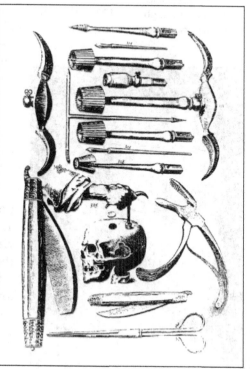

Charles G. Gross, *The Neuroscientist* 5(4) pp. 263–269, copyright © 1999 by SAGE Publications, Inc. Reprinted by Permission of SAGE Publications, Inc.

Reprinted by permission of the Alton Tobey Estate.

psychopathology to enter the magical realms. Thus, once again, the perspective of psychopathology directly leads to how it is treated.

Turning our attention to another historical and cultural reference point, Greeks and Romans, we see more examples of supernatural understandings of psychopathology. Gods and goddesses were at the pinnacle of existence within ancient Greek and Roman culture. Greek mythology contains a variety of stories that depict abnormality through gods, goddesses, and heroes and heroines. These understandings of psychopathology have continued to have an impact on abnormal psychology. One hero in Greek mythology, who is known for being so beautiful that he fell in love with his own reflection, Narcissus (Hamilton, 1942), is referenced as a personality disorder. The personality disorder essentially involves being consumed with one's self.

Releasing Blood and Touching Heads: Biological Perspectives

Have you ever heard or stated that depression was a chemical imbalance? If so, then you have heard of a biological perspective of understanding psychopathology. In fact, this idea of a chemical imbalance is not a new idea, it dates back to Hippocrates. Sticking with the trephination example, from the Hippocratic perspective, it was a process used to release one of the humors, blood (Gross, 1999). Hippocrates viewed the sources of abnormality from a biological lens, in that there was an imbalance of humors: in the body (Frances, 2013). Thus, how you understand psychopathology affects what you do with it. For Hippocrates, a result of abnormality being understood as a biological imbalance of fluids led to treatments such as bloodletting. Trephination was one of these practices where blood was released from an individual's skull to resolve psychopathology.

Phrenology

Practice of assessing abnormality through feeling a person's head

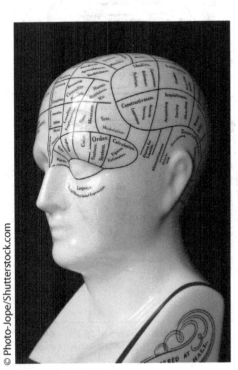

Phrenology Bust

Moving into the 19th century, psychopathology became popularly viewed as the result of brain structural defects. The idea was biological in nature, in that the brain became viewed as the source of abnormality. Franz Gall held to the biological notion that various areas of the brain were related to the different psychological, emotional, and behavioral functioning (Benjamin & Baker, 2004). From this view, structural brain defects would be able to be assessed through inspection of a person's head, due to the idea that the skull would conform to the brain defects. Therefore, people could have psychopathology assessed by having their heads felt by another. Benjamin and Baker (2004) wittily refer to this as "having your head examined" (p. 3). This belief and practice was formally referred to as phrenology.

© Photo-Jope/Shutterstock.com

Phrenology became a popular view and practice. From this, some individuals even established businesses that incorporated phrenology busts to help people become trained in phrenology.

It's in Your Head: Psychological Perspectives

Out of the development of philosophical examination and the movement toward science, a number of psychological perspectives began to emerge. Psychological perspectives sought to explain abnormality as a source of psychological rather than supernatural or natural causes. In other words, psychological perspectives sought to examine psychopathology from the individual rather than religious/spiritual and biological understandings.

Psychology is a newer science. Its formal beginnings get attributed to Wilhelm Wundt with its official year being 1879. From around this time onward, psychological perspectives began taking shape and influencing how people viewed sources of abnormality. Sources of psychopathology were viewed as problems with unconscious conflicts, deficiencies in reinforcement contingencies or schedules of reinforcements, faulty belief systems, inability to express and regulate emotional experiences, and struggles with life's givens or with meaning making. Psychotherapy theories became ever present to explore abnormality and treat it. There are a variety of psychological perspectives and theories that you will read about in the next chapter. Many of these popular perspectives include:

- ► Behavioral
- ► Psychoanalytic
- ► Experiential
- ► Cognitive

You will see how each of these psychological perspectives and theories are tied directly to treatments for psychological disorders. Further, these perspectives have also been integrated and used within integrationist frameworks, meaning that a number of psychological perspectives of abnormality which include one, or more than one, of the abovementioned.

Are We There Yet? Integrationist Perspectives

A number of mental health professionals will operate on integrationist frameworks, such as the biopsychosocial model. The biopsychosocial model was established to move beyond a biomedical framework and toward attending to the humanness of patients (Engel, 1996). The biopsychosocial model allows practitioners to understand psychopathology from the interplay of an individual's biology (e.g., genetics, neurotransmitters), psychology (e.g., thoughts, feelings, behaviors), and social (e.g., relationships, relational

Biopsychosocial Model

A perspective that promoted attending to the humanness of patients patterns) aspects. The idea of accommodating multiple theoretical frameworks can also be found in the DSM-5 (APA, 2013). The DSM-5 indicates that it is used by practitioners and researchers from various theoretical backgrounds and it seeks to use language that is appropriate for any of these perspectives (APA, 2013).

Some areas of integration have not been so readily integrated until recently. Integration of psychological and spiritual perspectives did occur, but they were not given much credence. William James, arguably the father of American psychology, sought to integrate supernatural and psychological perspectives (Benjamin & Baker, 2004). However, the bulk of psychological perspectives did not include supernatural or religious perspectives. Freud, himself, held to this notion. He believed religion was a crutch, though as a crutch, he affirmed that it was helpful for many people (Freud et al., 1900).

Religion and practice are even found on the big screen. The movie titled *The Exorcism of Emily Rose* depicts the tension between psychology and religion. Broadly, the movie sets apart religion and science. The movie setup depicts a priest on trial for performing an exorcism on a woman named Emily Rose, who died (Rosenberg et al., 2005). The trial portrays the priest as a person who understood Emily's behaviors from a spiritual lens of demonic possession, which led to the intervention of an exorcism. A psychiatrist states Emily had displayed signs of schizophrenia and needed to be treated with antipsychotics. Thus, the film depicts the conflict between two seemingly opposing views. Why are they opposing? Evidently, because of how they view the source of abnormality, but also with respect to treatment. The reason the priest is on trial is because of his treatment, not his views. So, does religion and spirituality hold a place in psychology?

Some areas of psychology have recently sought to integrate not only biological perspectives, but also supernatural perspectives, namely religion. This approach to teaching faith with psychological perspectives is done through means such as teaching faith and science, applied integration, or advocacy (Watson & Eveleigh, 2014). A number of therapists deem that religion is important for mental health, even though about 26% of clinical psychologists are not religious (Bergin, 1991). More recently, clinical competencies for working with religion and spirituality have been suggested as a part of clinical training (Vieten et al., 2016). Thus, we see history within the current approaches and movements toward future integrationist models.

The Exorcism of Emily Rose

So, what are your thoughts? Do religious and spiritual understandings hold a place in understanding psychopathology? What about biological perspectives? Do you think that too many people are just prescribed drug cocktails for their problems?

Psychopathology Is Dynamic

Let's revisit the phrase "Depression is a chemical imbalance." As mentioned, this idea is not a newer idea. As you have already read about Hippocrates and Galen, psychopathology was understood to be an imbalance of the four humors. Thus, depression as a chemical imbalance pre-dates current notions. The main difference is that current notions of depression discuss the chemical imbalance of depression due to an imbalance of neurotransmitters.

This statement often comes with unclear understandings about abnormality. When people say this statement they often mean that depression is only the result of an imbalance of neurotransmitters, affirming genetic determinism. Genetic determinism is an idea that individuals and their behaviors are solely the product of their genetics. People may believe that depression is the result of one's genes and therefore there is nothing that they can do to change or escape depression.

Genetic Determinism
The idea that individuals and their behaviors are solely the product of their genetics

The view of psychopathology resultant from only one source is faulty because it is much more dynamic. Examining the neurotransmitter systems related to depression is important but only offers one account of abnormality and is not exclusive from other accounts. When examining depression, there will be some neurotransmitter systems that are involved and related to depression. However, neurotransmitters are one piece of the puzzle (see Figure 1.2).

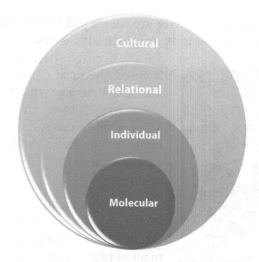

FIGURE 1.2   **Dynamic Aspects of Psychopathology**
Courtesy of Authors

Another aspect of psychopathology is the individual. Psychopathology at the individual level may involve a person's thoughts, feelings, and behaviors. People who experience major depressive disorder will also hold particular beliefs, express certain emotions, and engage is some behaviors more than others. For example, a person with depression may believe that they are the most worthless person, feel sadness, and not leave their bed for much of the day. To illustrate the dynamic aspect, when considering these thoughts, feelings, and behaviors, you may see various neurotransmitters affected.

People are also social creatures. You have a number of relationships, some more close than others. Thus, psychopathology involves relationships. People's thoughts, feelings, and behaviors may affect their relationships and relationships may influence people's thoughts, feelings, and behaviors. For example, a person who was told they were worthless and a failure by his or her parents throughout their childhood, may believe these messages and think these things about him or herself.

Lastly, people are shaped by cultural and societal influences. It may be more acceptable for someone from one ethnicity or gender to express sadness compared to other cultural identities. Thus, the expression or internalization of beliefs may be culturally influenced and can be understood within one's cultural framework.

Therefore, psychopathology is dynamic and not categorically exclusive. As you consider the various disorders, you will be encouraged to reflect on the dynamic pieces that contribute to understanding abnormality.

Who Is Involved? Professionals in Mental Health

There are numerous players in the area of mental health. Some of these professionals include psychologists, psychiatrists, licensed professional counselors, licensed psychological associates, licensed chemical dependency counselors, licensed marriage and family therapists, psychiatric nurses, and social workers. These professionals are frequently working with issues of mental health to varying capacities and within different employment settings.

© Olimpik/Shutterstock.com

Applied psychologists developed subsequently from exclusivity of practice through licensure and the official establishment of psychology as a science to be practiced (Benjamin & Baker, 2004). The role of a therapist was enhanced by the conflict between experimental psychology and applied psychology (Benjamin, 1997). Applied psychologists began to follow a training model known as the Boulder Model, which came about from a synthesis of the experimental and applied psychology (Baker & Benjamin, 2000). The merging of the two areas of psychology allowed for a more unified field. Applied psychology grew by utilizing empirical research to inform its practice and experimental psychology was provided with another area of research questions.

Boulder Model
Training model that synthesized experimental and applied psychology

Psychiatrist or Psychologist? Have you ever been confused about the difference between psychiatrist or psychologist, or have you never really cared? Often, people confuse these two professions or will use the names interchangeably. Applied psychologists have a distinct role as mental health professionals. Clinical and counseling psychologists typically possess a PhD or PsyD, work in mental health settings, and provide assessments, diagnosis, and treatment through psychotherapy. These markers separate psychologists from other mental health providers. Psychologists typically evaluate a client's presenting concern and formulate a treatment tailored to the client's needs. If the treatment required for the client is outside of the scope of psychotherapy, then the psychologist will refer for the appropriate services.

Psychologists
Possess a PhD or PsyD and typically provide psychotherapy

In contrast to clinical and counseling psychologists, psychiatrists are trained as medical doctors, possessing an MD and specializing in the practice of medicine related to psychopathology. Psychiatrists may provide psychotherapy as a treatment, but unlike clinical and counseling psychologists (with the exceptions of New Mexico and Louisiana), psychiatrists are able to prescribe medicine for their patients. As medical doctors, psychiatrists have been traditionally trained in biological understandings and treatment of psychopathology. However, as you read previously, the establishment of the biopsychosocial model encouraged psychiatrists to move toward a dynamic approach to understanding psychopathology.

Psychiatrists
Possess an MD and typically practice medicine related to psychopathology

Conclusion

Understanding abnormality is dynamic and requires you to evaluate a number of preconceived ideas you may have about disorders, psychologists, treatments, and crazy. Learning to critically examine your own beliefs and biases will assist you in correctly understanding psychopathology. Abnormal psychology is not a study of other, but rather a look into many, behaviors that may overlap with your own. The distinction between abnormality lies within the frequency of those behaviors, how behaviors impair functioning, lead to feeling pain, and may result in fatality. These criteria along with the DSM-5, sheds light onto understanding how people may suffer from a mental disorder. Through this understanding, professionals have dedicated years of training and science to provide treatment for these various disorders.

CHAPTER REVIEW

QUESTIONS

1. How do people understand and explain the reasons of others' behaviors? Labeling someone as "crazy" to explain their behavior would be best explained by what kind of attribution?

2. People may possess a number of negative attitudes toward others with mental disorders, which is referred to as? How might this affect relationships or behaviors with people who suffer from a mental disorder?

3. There are four criteria that help distinguish normative behavior from abnormal behavior. What are these four criteria?

4. What is the most commonly used instruments for understanding and classification of disorders?

KEY TERMS

Social Comparison

Myths

Attributions

Dispositional Attributions

Psychopathology

Stigma

Relativism

Conceptualization

Neurotransmitters

The Diagnostic and Statistical Manual of
    Mental Disorders

Normal

Normal Distribution

Intelligence Quotient

Social Norms

Eccentric

Trephination

Phrenology

Biopsychosocial Model

Genetic Determinism

Boulder Model

Psychologists

Psychiatrists

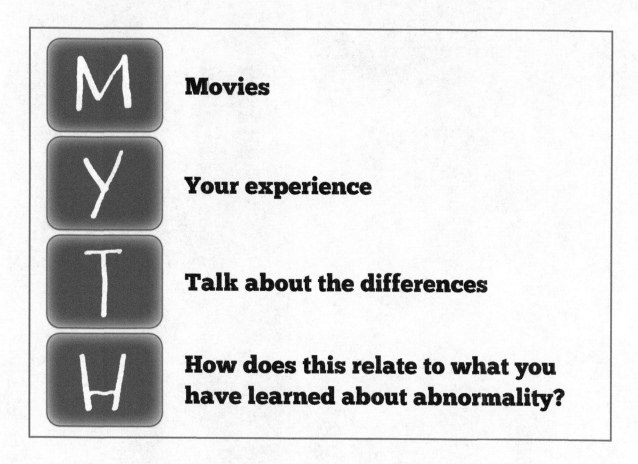

Movies

Your experience

Talk about the differences

How does this relate to what you have learned about abnormality?

CHAPTER TWO

THEORY INFORMS TREATMENT

LEARNING OBJECTIVES

- ► Explore how disorders develop
- ► Examine how theory informs treatment
- ► Identify biological perspectives
- ► Discuss major psychological theoretical perspectives
- ► Explain integrationist perspectives
- ► Recognize common therapeutic factors

CHAPTER OUTLINE

- ► How Do Disorders Develop?
- ► Theory and Treatment
- ► Its in the Genes: Biological Theories and Treatments
- ► Psychological Theories
- ► Psychodynamic and Interpersonal Theories and Treatment
- ► Saliva, Food Pellets, and Dolls: Behavioral Theories and Treatments
- ► What Does It All Mean? Humanistic and Existential Theories and Treatment
- ► If You Think It: Cognitive Theories and Treatments
- ► If You Feel It: Experiential and Emotional Theories and Treatments
- ► It's Not Black and White: Multicultural and Feminist Theories and Treatment
- ► Larger Than One: Systems Theories and Treatment
- ► Putting It All Together: Integrationist Theories and Treatments
- ► Which Is the Best?

How Do Disorders Develop?

Does it all stem from something that happened in childhood? Do you inherit genes from your parents? Do you learn abnormal behaviors? Do you choose to engage in abnormality? Did you get into a bad situation? Is it nature or nurture? The old nature versus nurture debate arises. Take a moment to think about and write down the things you think lead to someone having a psychological disorder. Create two columns to write under, nature and nurture, depending on which it best fits.

LET'S PRACTICE

 NATURE   **NURTURE**

1. _____   1. _____

2. _____   2. _____

3. _____   3. _____

brain © patrice6000/Shutterstock.com and Tree © Mopic/Shutterstock.com

---

So, what does your answer look like? Do you find that your answer mostly has aspects of one's nature or is it mostly an individual's environment? Various films convey images of the etiology of disorders. People may often hold beliefs that psychopathology results from some bad thing that happened in a person's childhood. The idea of some traumatic event leading to the development of psychopathology is largely a theme expressed in films (Hyler, 1988; Wedding & Niemiec, 2014). Aside from the belief that some past trauma leads to psychopathology, Hyler contends that another pervasive misconception in films is that parents are the primary source of abnormality.

So what is the answer? The answer is: it depends. This answer is not an evasive response but one that requires a closer look at the dynamic aspects of psychopathology. As briefly discussed in Chapter 1, psychopathology is dynamic and the etiology of disorders is resultant of a variety of factors. Etiology is the cause or origins of disorders, or how they develop.

Etiology

The cause or origins of a disorder

Diathesis-Stress Model

A model of susceptibility to disorders

One way to examine the etiology of disorders is through the lens of the diathesis-stress model (Zuckerman, 1999). The diathesis-stress model is a model of examining the development of disorders from both the susceptibility facets and the environmental stressors. This model illustrates the role of nature and nurture related to etiology of disorders. Figure 2.1 shows the various components of the diathesis-stress model.

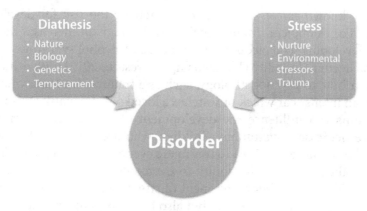

FIGURE 2.1   Diathesis-Stress Model
Courtesy of Authors

The diathesis aspect of the model involves the aspects of the person or dispositional factors that influence the susceptibility to disorders. These include features of one's nature or their biology, genetics, and temperament. People are born with gifts from their biological parents in that they are given 23 chromosomes from each parent. Though at the time of conception your biological parents may not have been consciously thinking about the gifts that they would bestow upon you. So, from conception you inherit genetic features that may predispose you to particular disorders or influence how you interact within your environment. Thus, you may want to thank your parents for this gift, as some people seek to do when assigning culpability for their problematic behaviors.

Some disorders will be more heavily weighted with dispositional influences than others. You will note, when examining schizophrenia, that genetic factors are heavily influential in the etiology of schizophrenia, carrying a 10-fold risk for siblings of individuals with schizophrenia (Maki et al., 2005). On the other hand, the risk for a monozygotic twin with the disorder is only 40 to 50%, suggesting that environment plays an important role as well (Murphy, 2010). Not everyone who has a close relative with schizophrenia is determined to develop schizophrenia, and 85% of persons diagnosed with the disorder have no first-degree relative with the illness (Maki et al., 2005). As mentioned in the previous chapter, people are not genetically determined to develop disorders based on the occurrence of the disorder within a close relative.

Equally, environment plays an important role in the development of psychopathology. The stress aspect of the model involves nurture, environment, and trauma or stressors. Many people will experience environmental stress or trauma throughout their lives. For example, sitting through an abnormal psychology class might induce stress. The stress component of the model includes various aspects of a person's environment. Physical environment may contain chemicals or features that influence the development of psychopathology. In perinatal development the introduction of harmful chemicals

Teratogens

Harmful chemicals or agents that affect perinatal development

or agents, known as teratogens, could increase the risk for developing a disorder. For example, drinking alcohol while pregnant increases the risk of a child developing fetal alcohol syndrome. Fetal alcohol syndrome may lead to an intellectual disability (Blankenship & Weston, 2012). Other life events may contribute to psychopathology, such as a trauma. A person who suffers through an intense car wreck or watches a loved one die may be traumatized. This trauma can influence the development of anxiety disorders or even influence depressive symptoms. Children who are able to self-regulate or self-soothe are more resilient to traumatic events in life (Beeghly & Tronick, 2011). Resilience means the ability to overcome stressful or traumatic life situations. Thus, the other component of stress vulnerability is not only the actual stressor or traumatic event, but also how one perceives the event.

Resilient

Ability to overcome stressful or traumatic life situations

Theory and Treatment

Theory

A unified, organizing, and guiding approach found within a discipline

Remember that how one understands psychopathology affects what one does with it. More formally, theory directly affects treatment. A theory is a unified, organizing, and guiding approach found within a discipline. As noted in the previous chapter, there have been a number of ways that people have understood abnormality throughout history. Currently, there are still a number of ways that mental health professionals understand the etiology of abnormality. These various theoretical perspectives are important because not only do they inform how one thinks about abnormality, they also directly correspond to treatment approaches (see Figure 2.2).

FIGURE 2.2   Theory Informs Treatment
Courtesy of Authors

It's in the Genes: Biological Theories and Treatments

Neurocentrism

A perspective that human behavior can be best explained by the brain

From Hippocrates to modern medicine, the biological view of abnormality is based on viewing the source of abnormality as a function of one's biology. While biological levels of analysis are worthy for understanding psychopathology, keep in mind that it is one level of analysis. As you think about the brain in understanding psychopathology, caution should be exercised against neurocentrism. Neurocentrism is a perspective that human behavior can be explained mostly or exclusively from the analysis of the brain (Satel & Lilienfeld, 2013). Showcasing neurocentrism, people tend to think that articles that include images of brains have better scientific reasoning compared to those without a brain image (McCabe & Castel, 2008).

There are three major components from a biological view of abnormality: brain structure, chemical processes, and genetic influences. These components are viewed as sources where abnormality might occur and, thus, treatment corresponds respectively. In examining brain structure, let's revisit a famous case in psychology, the story of Phineas Gage (see Figure 2.3).

Brain Structure. He was working on the railroad, all the live-long day. Then, all of a sudden, a dynamite blast caused an iron to drive through Phineas Gage's skull, through the frontal lobe of his brain (Garrett, 2009). Figure 2.4 is an example of how the tamping rod went through his head and an example of a psychology-themed Halloween costume. Surprisingly, when you imagine an iron rod going through someone's head such as this, you might not think that they would survive. Phineas Gage lived.

FIGURE 2.3   Phineas Gage
Collection of Jack & Beverly Wilgus

Phineas Gage became very well known in psychology and neuroscience after this incident. He was a case of interest both because he survived the incident, and aspects of his personality changed, in which he became more irresponsible (Garrett, 2009). The Gage laceration contributed to research and investigation of brain structural damage. Hence, the accident of Gage led to understanding that brain damage may lead to psychopathology. Some individuals who have suffered a traumatic brain injury may have subsequent changes in the function of their memory, decision-making, and other areas.

Different areas of your brain have unique functions that contribute to your overall functioning, which is referred to as localization. The brain is classified by four different lobes: frontal, temporal, occipital, and parietal. The frontal lobe regulates executive functions such as decision-making, abstract reasoning, planning, emotion regulation, impulse control, speech production, and voluntary movement (Garrett, 2009). The temporal lobe is primarily involved in processing audition, or sound. The occipital lobe processes visual information, including perception of objects and faces. If you have ever fallen on

FIGURE 2.4   Example of Iron Rod Through a Person's Head
Courtesy of Author

the back of your head and your vision has been blurred or you have seen stars, then this might have been due to acute force to this area. Lastly, your parietal lobe processes sensations, pain, and body movement (Garrett, 2009).

Localization

A perspective that different areas of your brain have unique functions

Chemical Processes. Recall from the previous chapter the discussion of chemical imbalance. Hippocrates posited the claims that abnormality was a source of chemical imbalance in the four humors (Frances, 2013). Modern medicine and biological perspectives still uphold this notion in theory and treatment. However, the imbalance of chemicals is that of neurotransmitters and hormones.

Parts of the Human Brain

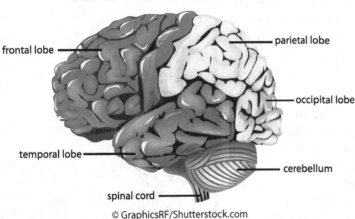

© GraphicsRF/Shutterstock.com

Remember that neurotransmitters are the chemical messengers that come from neurons. Neurons are the vast cells that are in our brain that aid in numerous functions. Neurons work through an electrochemical process. Sodium and potassium channels are opened and closed, an electrical impulse is then sent from the soma down the axon, and out the axon terminal or terminal buttons. Then, the axon terminal releases chemicals into the synapse. Between one neuron's axon terminal and another axon's dendrites is a space referred to as the synapse or synaptic gap. The chemicals released are the neurotransmitters. See Figure 2.5 for the structure of a neuron.

Several things may then happen to the neurotransmitters in the synaptic gap. Many of the neurotransmitters will bind to dendritic receptor sites on

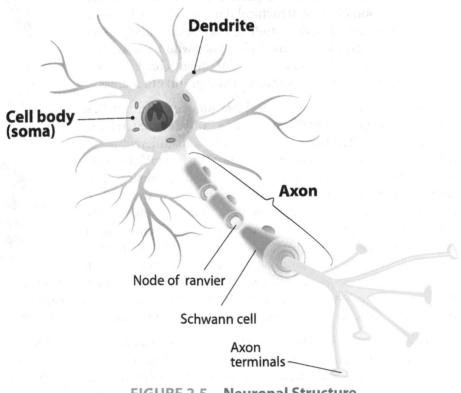

FIGURE 2.5   Neuronal Structure
© Designua/Shutterstock.com

another neuron. To illustrate this, think back to your childhood and toys you may have played with or owned (unless you still have it and play with it). One particular toy involved shape sorting. There are various types and brands of these but the idea was the same for all. There was a sphere or cube with different shaped holes, and blocks of various shapes (e.g., ball, cube). Each shape had a specific hole for it to go into. You might recall that the ball would be able to go into the circle hole. When you made the match, success! However,

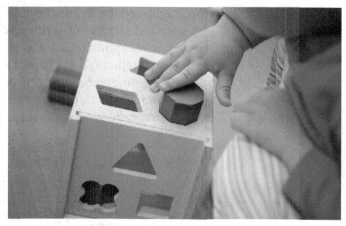

© viki2win/Shutterstock.com

sometimes you might have tried the wrong shape with the wrong hole. For instance, maybe you tried to place a cube in the hole that was cut as a triangle. You might have manipulated the cube but still no success. Think of this as the dendritic receptor sites. Each neurotransmitter has a specific site for it to fit onto.

One of the processes that might happen if neurotransmitters do not go to the dendritic site of another neuron is a process called reuptake. Reuptake means that the neurotransmitters return to the neuron that released them. When people think of chemical imbalance, the imbalance of neurotransmitters may be due to not enough going to dendritic sites of the next neuron and reuptake occurring. Another process that may occur involves enzymes attaching to a neurotransmitter and breaking it down.

Reuptake

A process involving neurotransmitters returning to the neuron that released them

Genetics. As mentioned earlier, you inherit chromosomes from each biological parent. Genes are usually a part of chromosomes. A gene is the biological component that informs cells and contains inherited information. Many genes are made of deoxyribonucleic acid (DNA; Garrett, 2009). Genes provide instruction for proteins, and influence the expression of traits and physical characteristics (Garrett, 2009). Some genes may carry information that influence the development or onset of some diseases, such as Huntington's disease. Schizophrenia has a strong genetic influence and vulnerability, with the most strongly and reliably associated genes being DTNBP1, NRG 1, and CHRNA7 (Garrett, 2009; Tsuang, 2000).

Biological treatments match biological theories. Thus, the treatment depends on the source of abnormality (e.g., chemical imbalance). One of the most common biological treatments is medication or drug therapies. If there is an imbalance of neurotransmitters, then some medications seek to restore that balance. For example, low levels of serotonin have been associated with major depressive disorder. One of the typical medications used for antidepressants is a Selective Serotonin Reuptake Inhibitor (SSRI). So, how does it work? Based on what you know about the process of reuptake, you might deduce its function, in that the medication inhibits or prevents the reuptake process of serotonin. Therefore, the SSRIs increase the levels of serotonin. Some drugs act as agonists and will mimic a neurotransmitter. Thus, you might mold or shape a square into a ball so that it may fit into the circle. Recently glutamate agonists have been examined to treat symptoms of schizophrenia (Garrett, 2009; Patil et al., 2007). Table 2.1 shows examples of typical medications used for some disorders.

TABLE 2.1   Typical Medications for Disorders

Disorder	Medication Class	Some Common Types
Depression	Selective Serotonin Reuptake Inhibitor (SSRI)	Prozac, Zoloft, Paxil, Luvox, Celexa, Lexapro
Depression	Serotonin Norepinephrine Reuptake Inhibitors (SNRI)	Effexor, Pristiq, Cymbalta, Toledomin
Depression	Monoamine Oxidase Inhibitors (MAO-I)	Nardil, Parnate, Marplan, Emsam, Deprenyl, Agilect, Manerix
Depression	Tricyclic Antidepressants	Anafranil, Tryptizol, Adapin, Norpramin, Gamanil
Bipolar Disorder	Classic Mood Stabilizer	Lithium
Bipolar Disorder	Anticonvulsants	Depakote, Lamictal, Gabapentin, Tegretol, Neurontin
Bipolar Disorder	Atypical Antipsychotics	Risperidone, Seroquel, Zyprexa, Abilify, Geodon
Bipolar Disorder	Other Drug Classes	Benzodiazapines, Memantine, Ziprasidone
Anxiety, Panic, PTSD, OCD	Selective Serotonin Reuptake Inhibitor (SSRI)	Prozac, Zoloft, Paxil, Luvox, Celexa, Lexapro
Anxiety, Panic, PTSD	Serotonin Norepinephrine Reuptake Inhibitors (SNRI)	Effexor, Pristiq, Cymbalta, Toledomin
Anxiety, Panic	Benzodiazepines	Ativan, Valium, Clonazepam (Klonopin), Librium, Xanax
Schizophrenia & Psychotic Disorders	Conventional Antipsychotics	Chlorpromazine (Thorazine), Haloperidol (Haldol), Zuclopenthixol (Clopixol)
Schizophrenia & Psychotic Disorders	Atypical Antipsychotics	Risperidone (Risperdal), Clozapine (Clozaril), Olanzapine (Zyprexa), Quetiapine (Seroquel), Ziprasidone (Geodon), Aripiprazole (Abilify)

Some info for this graph was retrieved from Stahl (2011).

In some instances other biological treatments may be considered. Electroconvulsive therapy (ECT) involves providing electricity to the head of a patient in order to produce a seizure (Garrett, 2009). The use of ECT has been controversial because some view the nature of the treatment as being invasive or even inhumane (Garrett, 2009). Because of this view held, some professionals and clients will use ECT in chronic or severe cases only after having tried other forms of treatment. However, ECT has been shown to be efficacious when compared to antidepressants for the treatment of major depressive disorder symptoms (Pagnin et al., 2004). In more rare cases, psychosurgery may be used for treatment (Garrett, 2009). Psychosurgery is the use of surgical procedures to treat psychopathology. An example of psychosurgery that has led to the negative association of psychosurgery has been frontal lobe lobotomies. The procedure for a frontal lobe lobotomy consists of inserting a tool between a patient's eyelid and eyeball, forcing it through the skull with a surgical hammer, and moving the tool to disconnect connections in the prefrontal area of the brain (Garrett, 2009). While this procedure might cause you to tense or elicit some disgust, this is not the only psychosurgical procedure. In some instances, a psychosurgery may be the only method for treatment. For example, in one famous case a man had his corpus callosum severed in a treatment for severe epileptic seizures (Gazzaniga, 1967).

Psychosurgery
The use of surgical procedures to treat psychopathology

Psychological Theories

Psychological theories of abnormality include a wide array of individual factors outside of one's biology. These theories are as rich and diverse as the influence of psychology's history. Psychological theories range from interpersonal conflicts to thought processes and behavioral patterns. There are numerous psychological theories and perspectives for understanding psychopathology. We will review some of the major theoretical approaches.

Psychodynamic and Interpersonal Theories and Treatments

When we think of psychotherapy there is often an iconic image that emerges. This image comes to mind because of its association with the popular psychoanalytic tradition of Freud and psychoanalytic techniques. While the couch fosters one technique rooted in psychoanalysis, psychodynamic and interpersonal theories encompass much more than a couch.

Psychodynamic and interpersonal approaches to abnormality, originating in psychoanalytic treatments, have a long history with many conflicting theories and interventions, often making it difficult for students and psychotherapists alike to conceptualize and treat clients (Kohut, 1977/2009).

Because of this, it will be important for us to focus on what these many and varied perspectives share in common. Summers and Barber (2010) have described the psychodynamic approach as being, "based on a developmental and conflict model of mental life" (p. 23). According to the psychodynamic theory, clients develop unconscious strategies for relating to the world, which aid in their own protection or defense (PDM Taskforce, 2006). These strategies develop into patterns, which lead people to experience the world and relate to the world in a maladaptive manner.

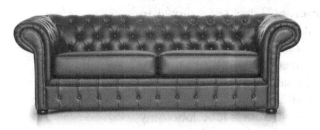

© Petinov Sergey Mihilovich/Shutterstock.com

You all probably remember Freud's concepts of Id, Ego, and Superego. The Id is meant to describe our drive for gratification, the Superego is characterized by the moral ideals we have internalized, and the Ego is ever caught between the two, continually trying to balance the desires of the flesh and the higher ideals one believes. When the conflict between the Id and the Superego becomes intolerable for the Ego; for example, when we strongly desire something we believe is not good for us, the Ego employs defense mechanisms in an attempt to quell the conflict. The most foundational of these defense mechanisms, which is at the heart of all the others, is denial. Repression, suppression, and regression are three other important defense mechanisms which help demonstrate denial as the basis for other defense mechanisms. Repression was understood to occur when someone unconsciously pushes out of their conscious awareness something too difficult to process. Suppression is consciously doing the same thing, which as you probably imagine does not work very well long-term. Whatever you do, don't think of one of the most crucial areas of conflict in your life! Stop it! Regression refers to a return to an earlier stage of development, generally as a means to process some conflict that began during that stage of development. Fixation, or arrested development, is a similar defense, but instead of a return to a childlike means of coping, some personality traits of an individual simply never develop beyond an earlier psychosexual stage of development. While Freud discussed many of these defensive processes, it was his daughter Anna Freud (1936/1993), who in a work entitled *The Ego and the Mechanisms of Defence*, clarified and defined many of these defense mechanisms. See Table 2.2 for a more detailed explanation of each defense mechanism.

Defense Mechanisms

Psychological mechanisms used, most often unconsciously, as a means to reduce mental distress

Psychosexual Stage

Freudian theory describing the development of children based on several stages

Over time, individuals form habits or patterns of utilizing and even specializing in certain defense mechanisms, and so form their own way of negotiating the world and relationships. The formation of these protective patterns is crucial to one's personality development. This formation is done in a more conscious and mature manner with healthy individuals, though Freud was clear to point out that we all have skeletons in our unconscious

TABLE 2.2   Defense Mechanisms

Defense Mechanism	Description	Examples
	Internal conflict, often originating in unresolved issues from childhood, is deflected by . . .	
Denial	Simply pretending that it doesn't exist	A person earnestly holds that cheating on their partner is helping their relationship
Regression	Thinking, feeling, and behaving in a regressed, childlike state to avoid current or past issues	A client who talks like a baby or child when discussing childhood sexual abuse
Repression	The ego unconsciously blocking from awareness traumas, crises, and/or sensual desires that are overwhelming	A person who has been through a trauma or crisis and has trouble or is completely incapable of recalling the events
Fixation	Some personality characteristics being arrested at earlier developmental periods, thereby avoiding crises of a later period	A 30-year-old woman or man who seeks gratification like a child, as this person is an adult, it may be in terms of sex or food (e.g., candy)
Reaction Formation	Taking the exact opposite opinion from what one desires, in order to hide this desire from oneself	Someone who has a deep desire for religious connection rejects all things religious Someone who experiences same-sex attraction being opposed to all things gay
Projection	Attributing one's own thoughts, feelings, or traits to another person to express them but keep some distance from them	Look at Bob, he's really, really attracted to Janet, isn't he? Despite being good at chess, saying, "I wish I was good at chess, like John!"
Displacement	Placing current feelings, often anger, onto a person or object other than the person toward whom they originate	You're pissed at your dad, but you take it out on your boyfriend
Suppression	Consciously pushing out of one's awareness some event or feeling that one does not currently want to deal with	Whatever you do, don't think about the fight you had with your mom yesterday!
Undoing	Thinking about or doing something else to try and undo the events of the past; also called counterfactual thinking	After someone has died, continually thinking about how things could have happened differently so that they did not die
Sublimation	Using the libidinal energy one feels in a different, but healthy manner, sometimes to resolve the conflict	Having a strong desire for sex or revenge, and using that energy to work out or write a letter to the person with whom one's having conflict

For more on defense mechanisms see Freud, A. (1936/1993).

Transference Distortions

Habitual patterns of distorting current events and relationships by unconsciously misperceiving them in light of the experiences of one's past, which is repeatedly transferred or projected onto the present experience

Repetition Compulsions

Habitual patterns of repeating behaviors in an unconscious attempt to resolve crises from earlier in one's life; for example, finding oneself in similar relationship conflicts over and over again, both reliving a crisis and attempting to resolve it

Transference

A form of projection in which a client's early experiences and characteristics of parental figures are transferred or projected onto the therapist

closets! When patterns of defense mechanisms are poorly formed, however, crises of the past, which were never resolved, continue to interfere with present relationships. Book (1997) described two maladaptive defensive patterns, transference distortions and repetition compulsions. Transference occurs when a person transfers or projects experiences from earlier in life onto the present. Has your boyfriend ever seemed an awful lot like your dad? Well, maybe it's just you! Book suggested that if this process becomes a pattern, then a person's very experience of the world may come to be perceived in a distorted manner, only through the lens of transference, that is, transference distortion. On the other hand, a person may also feel a strong need to resolve internal conflict, but without knowing what will actually help. In this case, one may form patterns of compulsively repeating the same behaviors in an attempt to resolve crises from earlier in life. In the case of repetition compulsion, a person's very way of behaviorally responding to the world can become distorted and limited to these compulsions.

Becoming aware of these distorted interpersonal patterns by making the unconscious conscious is the first step toward developing new ways of relating to the world, and only by unsticking the patterns, continually repeated throughout life, can the client experience lasting change, developing a new sense of self and other (Levenson, 2010). Psychodynamic theories suggest that healing from mental illness requires change in terms of

> "how people experience themselves, their relationships, and their world through . . . an empathic close relationship with the therapist that is different from other relationships past and present, and . . . new ways of perceiving old situations that allow them to try new behaviors in response to them." (Summers & Barber, 2010, p. 33)

Several Neo-Freudian researchers developed psychodynamic theories into a multitude of different theoretical veins. Interpersonal psychotherapy was developed in a much different manner. In 1969, Gerald Klerman and Eugene Paykel, along with some other colleagues, were testing new antidepressant medications and wanted to mimic clinical practice as closely as possible (Weissman, 2006). This led them to compare the use of these medications with and without conjoined psychotherapy. To accomplish this, Klerman and Paykel researched psychotherapy, especially the work of Harry Stack Sullivan, Adolf Myers, and John Bowlby, and created a psychotherapy treatment protocol that was believed to encompass the core of psychotherapy as it existed at the time. As Weismann (2006) recounted, the group "did not set out to define a new psychotherapy, but to define what we thought were the important components of good clinical supportive practice with ambulatory patients with depression" (p. 554). In fact, Klerman did not even expect to find an effect for the therapy they created for this drug trial, but instead it was supposed to be functioning more as a control for the study. The results indicated that patients receiving the medication and therapy improved more than patients receiving medications or psychotherapy alone, and that treatment with IPT was as effective as treatment with the antidepressants (Robertson et al., 2008; Weismann, 2006). And so began the race of establishing empirically supported psychotherapy treatments.

Saliva, Food Pellets, and Dolls: Behavioral Theories and Treatments

Imagine a bird that is able to peck a disc in order to receive a food pellet. The bird gets a food pellet every time it pecks. Eventually, the schedule of reinforcement is shifted from continuous (meaning every time) to a variable ratio (meaning the amount of pecks to receive a food pellet changes each time). The bird pecks several times to receive a food pellet. The bird may then peck so much for a food pellet that its beak begins to bleed and break. You can easily see how this progression of behaviors may lead someone to learn behaviors that occur with less frequency than others, lead to feeling pain, impair function, and fatality. Based on this example of a bird, how might it translate to humans learning abnormal behaviors?

We learn many things, including psychopathological behaviors. The tradition of psychology credited with understanding behavioral responses is known as behaviorism. Much of the development of behaviorism was a departure from psychoanalytic approaches and to investigate behaviors with an empirical basis (Corey, 2009). The idea was that psychoanalysis was rooted too much in theory of unseen and unknown. Many of the developers of behaviorism were interested in those things that can be observed, namely environmental stimuli and behavioral responses. At its core are three major concepts and three key individuals that contributed to learning and behavioral theory (see Figure 2.6 on the following page).

Some of the early work of behaviorism came from physiology and not psychology. Recall the famous dog experiments that were conducted by Ivan Pavlov. Pavlov stumbled upon some of the foundational aspects of learning. The dogs learned, via association, that food paired with Pavlov or a sound would produce the same response that is elicited by food itself, in that it produced a salivary response.

Think of your favorite food to eat. Are you there? Picture the food, the smell, and the taste of eating it. Now, wipe off the drool from your face. Whatever food it was that you thought of leads to a natural salivary reflex and this reflex aids in digestion. Now think about where it is that you get that food. Every time that you get that food, you associate that food with a physical building or place. If the food is from a restaurant, then you associate the food with the restaurant. After multiple associations of the food with the restaurant, the restaurant by itself may automatically elicit a drool response or have you at least thinking about that food that you like so much.

FIGURE 2.6   **Concepts and Contributors to Learning Theory**

Classical Conditioning

- Ivan Pavlov
- Learning via Association

Operant Conditioning

- B. F. Skinner
- Learning via Consequences

Social Learning

- Albert Bandura
- Learning via Consequences of Others

Pavlov © Neveshkin Nikolay/Shutterstock.com; Skinner © Omikron/Science Source/Getty Images;
Bandura © Headshot reprinted courtesy of Albert Bandura.

Classical conditioning explains how people develop phobias and many anxiety disorders through their learned associations. Many fearful responses can be understood through John Watson's research based on conditioned emotional responses (Watson & Rayner, 1920). Watson and Rayner exposed a young child, Little Albert, to a variety of stimuli, including rats and other animals. Little Albert did not naturally show fear toward the animals. However, after pairing a loud noise, which naturally produces a startle response for children with the animals, then Little Albert learned to be fearful of rats and some other animals.

Think of something that you may fear. Can you remember a time in your life when that first became fearful? Were there other negative associations to that thing? Sometimes we can pinpoint specific instances. Maybe someone surprises you by yelling (startle response) while throwing a spider on you. Subsequently, you learn to be fearful of spiders and maybe even of the person. In other cases, maybe you remember always being afraid of something without a specific instance or memory of an association. Learning can occur in the absence of a memory and from an early age. As a child, curiosity and exploration of your environment is a natural part of development. Many children may seek to explore their environment by sticking their fingers or other objects into electrical sockets on the walls. While a shock from an electrical outlet would foster learning via an aversive negative response, most parents seek to intervene and provide their own learning. When parents see a child going for an electrical socket the parent may yell "no" or quickly rush to move the child, thereby creating the conditions for learning, in that electrical sockets are bad places to be.

Learning also occurs from consequences of responses. Skinner formalized some of Thorndike's earlier work and established operant conditioning. Through his famous Skinner boxes, Skinner examined organisms in their environment, specifically consequences of their responses. Rats could press a lever in order to receive food pellets. Some of the basic tenets of operant conditioning are the nature of the stimulus, in that the appearance of a stimulus is noted as positive and the removal of a stimulus as negative. Further, reinforcement strengthens a behavioral response and punishment weakens a behavioral response. Hence, giving a student a 100 dollar bill after he or she raised their hand to ask a question would be a positive reinforcement, in that money was given to strengthen hand-raising behavior.

Reinforcement

Strengthens a behavioral response

Punishment

Weakens a behavioral response

Many behaviors may get reinforced and others may not occur because of punishment. Anxiety can, and often does, get reinforced through someone leaving a situation. People who experience anxiety, through sympathetic nervous system arousal and being fearful they might die, will want to be anywhere other than where they are. Thus, they may leave their current environment and negatively reinforce the anxious response. Escape behavior is negatively reinforcing because you have removed the thoughts or sympathetic nervous system arousal, and strengthen escape behavior. The association may have been strong enough that you will even avoid that situation in the future.

Lastly, learning is not only through the direct consequences of our actions, but we also learn through observing the consequences of others. Albert Bandura formally established social learning theory, which posits that learning occurs based on observed consequences of others (Bandura, 1977). Bandura is famously known for his Bobo doll studies, in which children would observe adults interacting with a doll (Bandura et al., 1961). Children who watched adults model aggression with the doll had enacted aggressive acts with the doll as well. Thus, children had learned how to interact with a novel stimulus merely by watching others interact with it. You may observe other people at work to see what they do to get a raise or praise and seek to do the same thing. You learn via observing the consequences of others. How do you think observing others with psychological disorders may shape your learning? How might watching films about people with disorders affect your behavior?

Abnormal behaviors can be modeled and reproduced as well. You may develop a fear of a stimulus by watching someone else respond negatively. If you watched someone confront a snake, yell, and run, then you may have learned that snakes are not animals you want to approach. On the other hand, we may learn to engage in harmful behaviors through observing others. Substance abuse may develop by observing others use a substance and seemingly enjoy the effects of a substance. Therefore, you may desire the same effects and use the substance yourself, or increase your use of a substance.

Extinction

Exposure to a conditioned stimulus that reduces the strength of the conditioned response

Behavioral treatments would involve identifying associations, antecedents, and consequences to behaviors. Upon identifying components that influenced learning, then new learning may occur. For example, people who might have an unwanted fear of spiders may use systematic desensitization and the use of extinction. Extinction is exposure to a conditioned stimulus without the unconditioned stimulus to reduce the strength of the conditioned response. Thus, someone who is scared of spiders would think of a spider or be presented with a spider and be asked to not run away or leave (which would negatively reinforce the response). The goal would be to present the spider (conditioned stimulus) without someone yelling or suddenly throwing it on you (unconditioned stimulus) to reduce the conditioned response or running away behavior. There are a variety of behavioral treatments for various disorders, and each involve understanding how the behavior was learned and reinforced or maintained.

What Does It All Mean? Humanistic and Existential Theories and Treatments

The human need for meaning is a distinguishing factor of human species. One of the criticisms of a behavioral perspective is that much of the research and theory comes from animal learning, and that humans are more complex. Some of the development of humanistic and existential theories was in response to moving away from what was seen as a reductionistic, behavioral view and a purely pathologically-driven approach to understanding humans. This shift away from psychoanalytic and behavioral perspectives was referred to as the "third force" in psychotherapy (Corey, 2009). Humanistic and existential theories focus on meaning-making and positive features of humans or components that foster growth. Two key figures paved the way for the third force in psychotherapy, Abraham Maslow and Carl Rogers.

Abraham Maslow (1943) postulated that humans have a hierarchy of needs. The model was a way to understanding human motivations and desire for growth and change through Maslow's dynamic hierarchy. He believed that people sought first to meet basic physiological needs, such as food, water, and sleep. A person then is motivated to seek other needs, namely safety needs, which include a house or some shelter. Maslow believed that as humans

meet all these needs, they then strive to
self-actualize. Self-actualizing involves
seeking meaning and fulfillment. Maslow
believed that "thwarting of these basic
human goals . . . is considered to be a psychological threat . . . all psychopathology
may be partially traced to such threats"
(1943, p. 395).

In the 1930s and 1940s, Carl Rogers
was developing theories of psychopathology and psychotherapy, which would
stand in contrast to psychoanalytic and
behavioral theories of the time. Roger's
placed a strong focus on the relationship
between the therapist and client, suggesting that the client is the expert of the

Humanistic Psychologist Carl Ransom Rogers

client, and that the answer to the client's problems reside with the client,
rather than the therapist. Rogers believed that humans were able to reach
their full potential and resolve their own conflicts, and that it was crucial for
the therapist to treat them as capable of doing so. This was a radically different approach from psychoanalysis and behaviorism, both of which took the
perspective that the therapist was the expert with all of the answers, and both
of which focused more on therapeutic technique than on the individual.
Appropriately, this approach was called Client-Centered, and later Person-
Centered Psychotherapy (Rogers, 1951, 1961). In a 1975 interview, Rogers
summarized his approach:

> ". . . most important is therapist congruence or genuineness–his
> ability to be a real person with the client. Second is the therapist's
> ability to accept the client as a separate person without judging or
> evaluating him. It is rather an unconditional acceptance—that I'm
> able to accept you as you are. The third condition is a real empathic
> understanding . . . To find that here is a real person who really
> accepts and understands sensitively and accurately perceives just
> the way the world seems to me." (1975, pp. 29–30)

The idea was that a therapist's presence with the client, instead of something
the therapist did, would allow the client to resolve his or her own conflicts.
Instead of doing any specific thing, the therapist was being with the client. Thus, the therapist had specific functions that facilitated being, which
include being genuine, empathic, and providing clients with unconditional
positive regard (acceptance). Unconditional positive regard is accepting
the client as who they are without conditions or based on circumstances.
Interestingly, a myth has evolved around Rogers's theories, such that some
folks have come to believe that emphasis should be placed on acceptance

**Unconditional
Positive Regard**

Accepting the client as
who they are without
conditions or based on
circumstances

over and above therapist genuineness, leading folks to mistakenly believe that Rogers thought we should never strongly challenge or disagree with a client. Rogers (1975) himself clarified this myth by pointing out the need for the therapist to be aware of and express his own genuine feelings in therapy, even if that means telling the client that one is really bored by what the client is saying (Rogers, 1975). Rogers clarifies that this genuineness serves to jolt clients into handling the situation in some way, while reinforcing the importance of clients' genuineness as well as their ability to handle this difficult information (unconditional positive regard).

Genuineness or congruence involves being who you are instead of who you think others may want you to be; for example, playing the role of a therapist or a "good" patient. Being genuine can be difficult for people because it is not necessarily what is popular or conforms to what others are doing. Social responses may pull you to be liked, to go with the crowd, or to follow social convention. Rogers (1975) believed that incongruence "results when the individual's experience is quite discrepant from the way he has organized himself," and when this discrepancy leads to a diminished belief in his ability and self-concept, mental health problems may arise. Empathy is taking on a person's perspective and understanding why she might feel the way she feels and believe the things she believes. Lastly, therapists are to seek unconditional positive regard toward clients. Unconditional positive regard is viewing the client as a person or with humanity regardless of what they have done or what situation they are in. Thus, regarding clients positively and as human is not based on a condition. If someone says "if you love me, then you will . . . " or if a parent told you that you were a bad child because of something you did, this illustrates conditional regard because love or status as a good child is contingent upon performing some action. Rogers (1957) believed that through being genuine with a client, being empathic to their struggles, and always mirroring their unquestionable value as a human person, clients would develop ways to overcome their own problems.

In conjunction to understanding humans' potential and factors that help them become resilient and resourceful, existential theories focus on meaning-making. Baumeister (1991), in his book *Meanings of Life*, elegantly examined, discussed, and utilized empirical research to address the four needs for meaning that humans seek and upon which they rely. The four needs for meaning are purpose, value, efficacy, and self-worth. Humans derive meaning from numerous things including going to work (Baumeister, 1991). Goal-directed behaviors offer purpose for people. Going to work provides people with purpose through completing tasks or seeking achievements. Work can offer value by someone viewing their actions as morally right through contributing to society or a person's family. Work satisfies efficacy because individuals feel as though they can contribute to a job or that they have some control over what is produced. Lastly, work may offer self-worth if an individual believes he or she is the only one that can do the job or do it as well as someone else. The person may gain some sense of worth from the title or position. Therefore, pursuits of humans are in meaning-making.

The deepest level of distress for many people comes from confrontation with the human condition (Yalom, 2002). A confrontation with the human condition can be viewed as an acceptance and understanding of things and situations that occur for humans (Yalom, 2002). For example, all humans are mortal beings. Thus, to deal with one's own biology may mean to come to terms with the emotions or thoughts around the issue of death. Distress around death may come from the dysfunctional thoughts, maladaptive feelings, and ineffective behaviors that are responses and associations with death. A person may experience the loss of a loved one as a loss of meaning or a meaning vacuum (Baumeister, 1991). At whatever level an individual may experience a personal crisis, existential and humanistic theories aim at meeting the client in their crisis, assisting them in developing the ability to face their crisis, and promoting the belief that they are capable and worthy of greater self-actualization.

If You Think It: Cognitive Theories and Treatments

> Men are disturbed, not by things, but by the principles and notions which they form concerning things.
>
> —Epictetus, 55–135 AD

The power of thinking is more powerful than you might think (or typically think). Cognitive theories are built on an idea, similar to the quote of Epictetus, that it is not events that lead to psychopathology but the understanding and thinking about those events. How we think about situations and events greatly influence our behaviors, emotions, and subsequent interpretation of the event. Consider the following scenario:

> As you are going to your next class across the university someone runs into you and spills your coffee.

How might you make sense of this situation? There are several possible interpretations. Think about how each of these interpreted actions might elicit a different emotional or behavioral response.

► That person is a jerk. They weren't even looking where they were going.

► It was just an accident that could have happened to anybody.

© Vitezslav Valka/Shutterstock.com

- ▶ It is my fault, I should have been more careful with my coffee.
- ▶ Ridiculous! I am so stupid and clumsy. I always spill things and make messes of everything.

Each of these possible interpretations may bring about a different response. Even though the event was unchanged, the interpretations and responses can be vastly different. To further illustrate this idea, think about when you or someone you know has experienced death. If someone has said they are sorry for your loss or offers condolences, then one possible response is, "It is okay, I was not that close to them." A person stating this is saying that I am not experiencing intense emotions because the loss of the relationship was not very meaningful to me. Essentially, because the relationship was viewed as not close, then the loss produced little emotional response. In contrast, another potential response to someone offering condolences is, "This is the worst pain I have ever felt." This response may indicate that the relationship was perceived to be very close, which leads to the intense emotional response. These scenarios highlight the power of thinking, which is at the core of cognitive theories.

Cognitive theories are based on how people think and the beliefs they develop. From a very young age we begin to develop beliefs about ourselves and our world. These beliefs are organized into a schema. Schemas are the amalgamation and organization of experiences and how those experiences were understood (Piaget, 1954). Piaget posited that schemas are established based on assimilation and accommodation of experiences. We develop some beliefs from an early age and those beliefs become crystallized through years of experiences, which is often referred to as assimilation of information. Accommodation refers to changing your existing schema for the new information. Usually, people have difficulty accommodating information when the belief is strong.

Let's consider your age-old friend, gravity. If someone was holding a pencil and released it, you would expect it to fall down, right? This is because of the schema you have developed and the experiences in your life that crystallized the concept of gravity. In fact, if a friend were to release a pencil and it did not fall down, then you would probably not renounce the concept of gravity. Instead, you might probably be skeptical that your friend is playing a trick on you.

Psychopathology, understood cognitively, develops the same way. Throughout life, beginning in early childhood, thoughts and ideas about the self, the world, and other people become solidified as intermediate and core beliefs (J. S. Beck, 2011). Intermediate beliefs are composed of attitudes, rules, and assumptions, which serve as a link between core beliefs and automatic thoughts, and influence the construal of and reaction to situations

Schema

Organized beliefs and experiences

Assimilation

The building of beliefs based on congruent experiences

Accommodation

Changing your existing schema for the new information

more directly (J. S. Beck, 2011). Core beliefs, according to J. S. Beck are perceptions or understandings so central and enduring that they are virtually considered to be absolute truths and are often so fundamental that they are not even articulated. These beliefs are at the root of an individual's construal of a situation, and are understood to be highly influential over one's intermediate beliefs, automatic thoughts, and reactions to events. Automatic thoughts stem from core and intermediate beliefs (see Figure 2.7). J. S. Beck (2011) stated that automatic thoughts are the words or pictures that go through our minds and are the most accessible. Automatic thoughts reflect our core beliefs and may influence the crystallization of those beliefs.

Core Beliefs

Cognitive Therapy concept describing the deepest set of values and beliefs held by a person

Let's consider another example of how a person might develop a belief that affects subsequent thinking and psychopathology. A client states that he has a learning disability. You ask the client to tell you more about the learning disability and he states that he has had a difficult time reading since fourth grade, and has seemed to be slower than his peers, evidenced by his turning the pages slower than others when reading. You then ask about his grade point average and find out that he has a 4.0 grade point average. He states that he remembers his fourth grade teacher telling him that he was stupid and slower than the rest of his class. You can see how a belief about being stupid, slow, and incompetent developed. Then, subsequent information (e.g., turning the pages while reading) confirmed the belief even when other information was contrary to the belief (e.g., 4.0 grade point average).

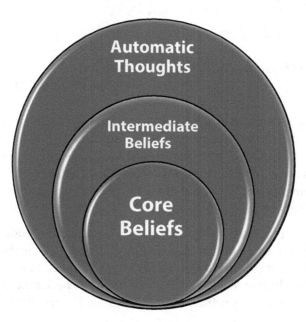

FIGURE 2.7   The Cognitive Model
Courtesy of Authors.

Rooted largely in cognitive theories, Cognitive Behavioral Therapy (CBT) is an integrative approach to therapy based on Aaron Beck's original work in Cognitive Therapy. Beck's original work contained many behavioral principles as well, and later developed into what is now referred to as CBT. Cognitive routes in CBT are means to infiltrate and alter the irrational inferences and premises by which humans operate (Meichenbaum, 1977). The foundational premise of CBT is that cognitive contents and processes are the underlying mechanism of behavioral and affective symptoms (Beck, 1995; DeRubeis et al., 2001).

As previously discussed, how we perceive or interpret an event impacts the manner we respond behaviorally, emotionally, and even biologically to that event. Because of this, awareness of these perceptions is key to psychological change in this therapeutic system. Like Cognitive Therapy, CBT is founded upon this principle. The first goal of CBT, therefore, is to establish patterns of automatic thinking that a client has habituated, and to begin conceptualizing how a client construes these situations (J. S. Beck, 2011). Understanding one's automatic thinking allows therapists to help clients begin to determine which cognitions are dysfunctional, and to learn to challenge these thoughts. Before or concurrent with these early cognitive changes, CBT therapists utilize behaviorally activating techniques to help clients accomplish the scheduling of activities, which is required for the CBT process (J. S. Beck, 2011).

If You Feel It: Experiential and Emotional Theories and Treatments

You could not step twice into the same river.

—Heraclitus as in Plato, *Cratylus*

The quote by Heraclitus indicates that you can only experience things once. Even if you step into the same river a second time you will have a different experience. We live life forward and each moment is a new experience. Some experiences are painful, distressing, or emotionally laden and we may carry those experiences and emotions into the present in the form of regrets or recurrently feeling those emotions.

Experiential therapy may be viewed as an umbrella, under which techniques and strategies of emotion-focused therapy (Greenberg & Paivio, 1997) and Gestalt psychotherapy (Perls et al., 1951) can be found (Brooks-Harris, 2008; Elliot et al., 2004). Contemporary experiential and emotional theories find their roots primarily in the Gestalt Theory of psychotherapy.

Homeostasis

Equilibrium or adaptation to one's surroundings

Gestalt Theory conceives of psychopathology as caused by clients' lack of homeostasis or adaptation to their surroundings resulting in unfulfilled emotional needs (Perls, 1973). Gestalt techniques are implemented within experiential therapy as means to create, build, and foster growth within the psychotherapeutic relationship (Perls et al., 1951). A strategy and feature of Gestalt therapy is to focus attention on the here-and-now moment (Perls et al., 1951). The here-and-now moment intends to raise awareness for the client. Many times people may ruminate on the past and how something has affected them or regrets they have. Similarly, people think of endless future scenarios and possibilities that may cause anxiety. The goal is to focus on the current moment, and to consider whether thinking about the past or future is affecting a person in the current moment.

Gestalt Therapy is also known for its empty-chair technique. Empty-chair dialogues focus on unfinished business with another person, during which this other person is visualized as sitting in an empty chair, and a dialogue is guided by the therapist to resolve these past experiences. Two-chair dialogues, on the other hand, are used to resolve conflicts within the client, during which a person will alternately sit in two different chairs, giving voice to each side of the internal struggle. This dialogue is also guided by the therapist, who helps the client clearly feel and express both sides of the conflict, and resolve it by softening the critical manner in which one or both sides treat each other. Paivio and Greenberg (1995) conducted a study that revealed experiential therapy to be effective in working with clients who have a childhood attachment injury. The study compared the use of the Gestalt empty-chair intervention with psychoeducation and found significantly greater improvements for clients exposed to the empty-chair intervention.

Emotion-Focused Therapy (EFT), a more recent derivative of Gestalt Therapy and Person-Centered Therapy, emphasizes intervening on the level of affect to clarify emotions and modify maladaptive emotional responses (Greenberg, 2002). EFT often conceptualizes clients' problems as a result of maladaptive ways of emotionally responding to their environment and only by recognizing these responses can clients then work toward a healthier emotional life (Greenberg, 2002). Accessing deeper, more primary, and healthier emotions allows clients to come to an awareness of their needs so that they can learn to meet those needs and develop a new narrative for their life

© Fotovika/Shutterstock.com

(Greenberg, 2011). To this end, the therapist works as an emotion coach, challenging and guiding clients through this process (Greenberg, 2011).

Greenberg and Watson (2006) proposed a similar view of the person in a state of conflict such that Emotion-Focused Therapy (EFT) focuses on four principles for processing emotions, including increasing emotional awareness, emotion regulation, reflecting on emotion, and transforming emotion. EFT understands emotion as fundamental to a person's construction of a sense of self and the world, and posits that intervening on the emotional/experiential level is more likely to lead to lasting therapeutic change. EFT generally conceptualizes this change as "the process of one emotion changing into another emotion," that is, the transformation of maladaptive emotion into adaptive emotion (Greenberg & Watson, 2006, p. 85). By guiding a person to feel the emotions they have associated with certain events, they are then able to work through them to more adaptive, healthy emotional responses, which clients can learn to generalize to similar situations in the future. Greenberg (2011) refers to this as the process of transforming one emotion into another. And though we often hear popular myths about not being able to change feelings, or not interfering with others' feelings, or feelings only being information and never being wrong, EFT does suggest that some feelings are maladaptive to some situations and can, and should, be transformed.

It's Not Black and White: Multicultural and Feminist Theories and Treatments

Myth or reality: All feminists are harry-legged hippies who hate men. The term feminism comes with a variety of responses and even controversy. People that think feminism or feminist perspectives may equate feminism to man-hating or some other negative association. There are numerous definitions of feminism and understandings of what it is and should be. At the core of feminist and multicultural theories is understanding the broad social contexts that influence people. Recall from the previous chapter that psychopathology is dynamic and the thoughts, behaviors, and emotions of an individual may be influenced by cultural frameworks.

Culture

The systems of what people know and behaviors that are passed across generations

The DSM-5 (2013) discusses culture at length and provides a comprehensive definition. Culture involves numerous aspects of information, norms, behaviors, and traditions that are learned and shared from generation to generation (American Psychiatric Association, 2013). The American Psychological Association (2002) defines culture as "the belief systems and value orientations that influence customs, norms, practices, and social institutions, including psychological processes and organizations" (p. 380). Further, Markus and Kitayama (2010) suggest that studying culture is not to study a "collection of people . . . but is instead on how psychological processes may be implicitly and explicitly shaped by the worlds, contexts, or sociocultural systems that people inhabit" (p. 422).

Cultural influences are vast. Many times when people think of culture or use the word culture, they may restrictively use the term synonymously with ethnicity. While ethnicity is one aspect of culture, it is not the only component. The following are some additional examples of cultural influences:

- ▶ Gender
- ▶ Religion
- ▶ Socioeconomic Status
- ▶ Class
- ▶ Size
- ▶ Age

Cultural influences are dynamic, overlap, and aspects of cultural influences may be salient depending on the situational context (Enns, 2008). For example, gender may become a salient cultural aspect for a woman when she is alone in a room full of men. Further, an individual may share one cultural aspect but not another; for example, two women who might be the same age and be from the same city, but have different religious beliefs and backgrounds. Thus, making broad conclusions about each person based on understanding of gender may be limiting, and in fact is a myth that some individuals level against multicultural theories. In other words, assuming that both women share the same experiences and beliefs because they are women of similar ages from the same geographic location may lead to inaccuracies and errors. Thus, cultural influences need to be considered in their complexity, and in light of the unique experiences of each client.

Multicultural/feminist views about cultural influences related to psychopathology are divergent. As discussed in the previous chapter, a cultural relativist perspective holds that psychopathology occurs within a culturally constructed context. Others believe that psychopathology exists outside of a relative framework, can be knowable, and culture influences its development and expression. Whether constructed or found across cultures, a central focus from a multicultural/feminist perspective is that culture influences psychopathology or distress, and this idea is held to be true by both multicultural/feminist researchers and researchers from many other perspectives as well.

The influences of culture on psychopathology often involve processes of understanding one's cultural influences and how those influences may not align with others' cultural influences or with the dominant cultural practices. A society that does not hold favorable attitudes toward individuals from a low socioeconomic position might place stress on someone from this position when she or he is seeking employment opportunities. It is important for therapists to consider client cultural influences and considerations for working with clients from diverse backgrounds. The *Guidelines for Psychological Practice with Girls and Women* suggest awareness of inexperience and lack of knowledge when working with women who have experienced trauma (American Psychological Association, 2007). Inexperience and lack of training can reduce the effectiveness of treatment. The APA has additionally published guidelines for working with LGBT persons, older adults, and ethnically and culturally diverse populations as well, to name a few. Each of these guidelines aim at helping therapists meet the unique needs of persons who identify as belonging to each group, based on research highlighting experiences and struggles often faced by members of the respective groups.

Larger Than One: Systems Theories and Treatments

The dog whisperer, Cesar Millan, refers to working with dogs as rehabilitating dogs and training their humans. This idea demonstrates a systems theory. Dogs that are re-trained by one person may go back with their owner and do the same things or behaviors. Why? This is because change has only been made on an individual level, rather than a systemic level.

Systems theories highlight the importance of people within larger contexts and systems. Its history is as rich as its approach, involving several individuals including Norbert Weiner, Gregory Bateson, Murray Bowen, and Carl Whitaker to name a few (Becvar & Becvar, 2009). A system perspective views change from multiple sources. Individual changes can enact changes to a system. The butterfly effect draws on the notion that one small change could lead to vast changes across the world. As a kid, or even now, you may have lined up dominos and knocked over the first one to facilitate a chain reaction. These aspects show how one can affect a system.

© CWA Studios/Shutterstock.com

Similarly, a system can affect an individual. In working with children, a therapist needs to consider the family system as a contributing or maintaining source for psychopathology. Let's consider a child who has been referred for anger management problems. The mother brings the child to therapy and tells a therapist that he needs to work on his aggressive impulses and behaviors, as he has been physically fighting with other children at school. While the child is in therapy, he tells the therapist that he is angry and his dad does not care about him or give him any attention, until he got in trouble at school. The therapist asks the child if his dad would be willing to come to therapy with the child. The child and mother tell the therapist that the child's father has stated that therapy is ridiculous and a waste of time. Thus, even if the child makes changes in reducing or eliminating aggressive behaviors, the child will still not have received attention he desires from his father. In fact, getting in trouble at school has been a way that the child can get attention from his father. Thus, a system has maintained the individual's behaviors.

Gregory Bateson's research group, sometimes referred to as the Palo Alto group, envisioned families as cybernetic systems that preserve homeostasis by means of communication feedback loops (Brooks-Harris, 2008). In a similar manner, Urie Bronfenbrenner's (1979) ecological model described how persons exist in relation to their immediate environments (e.g., family, school, peers), and how these immediate relationships also exist in connection with each other, as well as with community in general, which itself is connected to a larger cultural, political, and economic system, and even a larger historical period. Brooks-Harris envisioned another manner of describing this dynamic systemic interaction, suggesting that individuals form personal narratives within the context of family belief systems, which are influenced by family roles and structures, which are influenced by social and cultural environments. With so much emphasis on cultural and social influences on one's development, you're probably wondering how systems approaches vary from multicultural approaches. While there is a great deal of similarity in terms of their perspective regarding how an individual's identity develops, systemic approaches are more likely to emphasize the importance of intervening on the system as a whole; for example, in the context of family therapy, as opposed to considering these influences as they impact the individual.

Putting It All Together: Integrationist Theories and Treatments

According to Messer (1992), many therapists have moved toward labeling themselves as integrationists or eclectic theorists. Assimilative integrationists are defined as favoring "a firm grounding in any one system of psychotherapy, but with a willingness to incorporate or assimilate, in a considered fashion, perspectives or practices from other schools" (p. 151). Through assimilative integration, a therapist utilizes and recognizes interventions and techniques from other theoretical orientations by the lenses of the therapist's theoretical foundation.

Integration can be composed of as many combinations as there are theories. For example, Cognitive Behavioral Therapy (CBT) is an integrative approach, in that it integrated cognitive theory and behavioral theory. Another example is Cognitive-Behavioral Assimilative Integration (CBAI), which is CBT integrated with experiential therapy (Castonguay et al., 2005). Castonguay and colleagues formally classified the integration of CBT with experiential therapy as cognitive-behavioral assimilative integration. Theories such as CBAI come about through the amalgamation of previous theories based on theoretical views of understanding humans and psychopathology or by some perceived deficit of one theory. For example, traditional

CBT views emotions as a consequence of cognitive labels. The integration of CBAI acknowledges emotion as more than a consequence to be controlled but rather emotions are approached from the idea that they can be experienced, expressed, and understood (Castonguay et al., 2005).

As mentioned above, Emotion-Focused Therapy (EFT) is also understood to be an integration of Gestalt and person-centered therapies (Greenberg, 2002), and experiential and psychodynamic therapies have likewise been integrated in various ways; for example, Accelerated Experiential Dynamic Psychotherapy (AEDP; Fosha & Slowiaczek, 1997). In these cases, integration is occurring on a deeper theoretical level, which Norcross (2005) appropriately called theoretical synthesis. Norcross and Newman (1992) suggested that there are three general routes to integration: Common Factors, Technical Eclecticism, and Theoretical Integration. Other researchers have suggested additional routes to integration, including Assimilative Integration, Multitheoretical Frameworks, and Personal Integration, to name a few (Brooks-Harris, 2008). These forms of integration basically vary in terms of how much emphasis is placed on theory versus technique, factors common to many theories versus specific to certain theories, and the depth at which integration is taking place.

Brooks-Harris (2008) described one model for multitheoretical integration, overviewing many of the major systems of psychotherapy. Multitheoretical Psychotherapy (MTP) "highlights the relative emphasis of different theories and describes a method for deciding how to choose and combine ideas and strategies from different approaches" (Brooks-Harris, 2008, p. 37). Rather than focusing on deeper integration of theoretical principles, MTP recognizes that many therapy modalities work on their own, and therefore emphasizes that therapists should learn, and not only integration, but also when one approach may be more beneficial than another. One may accurately surmise from this approach that psychopathology, and therefore psychological change, may find their origins in many dimensions of the person. Harris and colleagues (2014) described seven focal dimensions that may need to be explored in psychotherapy, emphasizing that MTP regards psychopathology as an interaction occurring between dysfunctional thoughts, feelings, and actions, and that these maladaptive areas are shaped by the contextual dimensions of biology, interpersonal patterns, social systems, and cultural contexts.

In the MTP system of integration, therapeutic modalities are assumed to be complementary, rather than contrary, and are understood as working toward similar goals, albeit from different vantage points (Harris et al., 2014). One example of this complementarity can be recognized in the Key Strategies Training (KST) program developed by Harris and his colleagues, which trains new therapists to integrate therapy modalities that target the three concurrent dimensions: thoughts, feelings, and actions. KST recognizes that cognitive, behavioral, and emotion-focused (as well as many other therapies) share a basic division into two phases of therapy (exploration and transformation). The exploration phase aims at helping clients achieve a deeper awareness, while the transformation phase helps clients progress toward changes deemed important during the exploration phase. KST illustrates parallel processes between cognitive, behavioral, and emotion-focused treatments, within both the exploration and transformation phases. KST recognizes that during the exploration phase these three therapy modalities all focus on their specific dimension of functioning (thoughts, feelings, or actions), followed by an exploration of the context and impact of this dimension, leading to an analysis of the adaptive value of the dimension, and the uncovering of patterns of thinking, feeling, or behaving, of which the person may not be aware. During the transformation phase, these three modalities share intervention processes oriented toward experimenting with different ways of thinking, feeling, or behaving, modifying and solidifying these changes, and ultimately generalizing and consolidating these changes throughout one's life (Harris et al., 2014).

Which Is the Best?

> Everybody has won and all must have prizes!
> —The Dodo Bird, *Alice in Wonderland*

In 1936, Saul Rosenzweig used the above quote to describe the state of psychotherapy at that time, referring to this conclusion as The Dodo Bird Verdict. Since this time, countless questions have been asked and analyzed regarding the effectiveness of psychotherapy. Is it elements specific to certain therapy modalities or factors common to many? Does the relationship of the client and therapist matter more than the therapeutic modality? How much do individual clients' character traits determine which therapies may or may not be effective? Can therapy be harmful to clients? These and a host of other problems have been explored for decades, leading most psychotherapists and researchers to find a niche where they're comfortable, and then hope for the best.

© Morphart Creation/Shutterstock.com

In an effort to determine which therapies have ample research support to be labeled as empirically-supported, the Society of Clinical Psychology (Division 12) of the American Psychological Association have undertaken a review of literature and research on the effectiveness of various therapeutic modalities for various mental health conditions.

Some literature has suggested that no one specific theoretical approach has been greatly advantageous to another (Lambert & Ogles, 2004). However, this is a complex matter because various therapies "require the client to undergo different experiences and to engage in different behaviors" (Lambert & Ogles, 2004, p. 171). There are common factors across theoretical approaches that appear to be effective in eliciting change.

A thorough examination of various meta-analytic reviews pertaining to the success of therapy compared to a placebo or control group found that therapy came out on top (Grissom, 1996). You can think of therapy as "what the chemist calls a catalyst" (Perls et al., 1951, p. 15). People will deal with their feelings of pain, impaired functioning, frequent or infrequent maladaptive behaviors, and fatality. However, psychotherapy aids in this process by helping people to do it more quickly and more effectively.

Conclusion

Therefore, choosing a psychologist or mental health professional is not as simple as playing "eeny meeny miny moe." Just as you would not see a brain surgeon when you have a common cold, you may want to find a therapist that offers a theoretical orientation that is grounded in research and fits well with what you are seeking. With such a wide variety of therapeutic modalities and perspectives on the goals of therapy, carefully selecting a therapist, and knowing how he or she understands therapeutic change to occur, can be of the utmost importance. There is much deliberation and thought that should go into choosing.

© Pavel L Photo and Video/Shutterstock.com

CHAPTER REVIEW

QUESTIONS

1. What model is useful to examine and understand the etiology of psychopathology?

2. What is the importance of learning psychological theories as it pertains to abnormal psychology? What is the importance of theory for a potential client? What are the major theories and key figures for each theory?

3. Which theory is the best?

4. Is therapy effective?

KEY TERMS

Etiology

Diathesis-Stress Model

Teratogens

Resilient

Theory

Neurocentrism

Localization

Reuptake

Psychosurgery

Defense Mechanisms

Psychosexual Stage

Transference Distortions

Repetition Compulsions

Transference

Reinforcement

Punishment

Extinction

Unconditional Positive Regard

Schema

Assimilation

Accommodation

Core Beliefs

Homeostasis

Culture

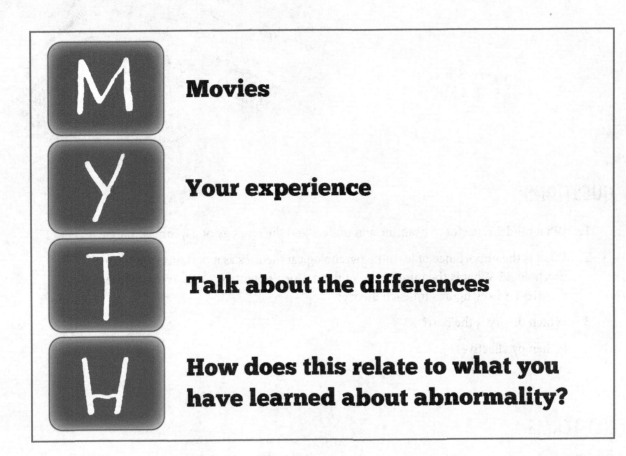

M   Movies

Y   Your experience

T   Talk about the differences

H   How does this relate to what you have learned about abnormality?

CHAPTER THREE

ASSESSMENT AND DIAGNOSIS

LEARNING OBJECTIVES

- ▶ Highlight the importance of assessment and diagnosis
- ▶ Discuss the function of assessment
- ▶ Explain psychometrics
- ▶ Apply reliability, validity, and standardization
- ▶ Review psychological tests
- ▶ Differentiate between objective and projective personality tests
- ▶ Define diagnosis
- ▶ Discuss classification
- ▶ List goals of classification
- ▶ Recognize the benefits and concerns with diagnosis
- ▶ Identify revisions that lead to the DSM-5
- ▶ Review the importance of assessment and diagnosis

CHAPTER OUTLINE

- ▶ Discernment Makes a World of Difference
- ▶ The Function of Assessments
- ▶ Good Tests: Psychometrics
- ▶ Psychological Tests
- ▶ Diagnosis
- ▶ A Historical Overview of the Diagnostic and Statistics Manual of Mental Health
- ▶ DSM-5

Discernment Makes a World of Difference

Years ago, as an adolescent, one of the authors believed that there were some professions that you could not try to trick or which with you could play jokes. These professions included police officers and psychologists. The idea for police officers was that compliance would be the path of least resistance. For example, if you were to get pulled over from a police officer due to speeding and he asked you if you knew how fast you were going, then a compliant response would not be, "Well I was going really fast until I was pulled over." This might make the process a bit lengthier and is ill-advised if you are seeking efficiency and compliance. Similarly, there was a belief that you should maintain a serious demeanor with psychologists. If they thought something negative about you based on a joke, then you would be unable to escape that label. The thinking went something like this, if you jokingly told a psychologist that you were hearing things that were not real and later told her or him that you were not, then it would be too late. You would already be labeled. Subsequently any attempts to escape that label would be futile. You might say, "No, I was just joking, I don't really hear unreal things." The psychologist's response would be that you are merely in denial of your psychopathology. This always seemed daunting to me, that you could be indefinitely labeled as some kind of "monster" or "crazy" person by a psychologist.

© nuvolanevicata/Shutterstock.com

Thankfully, this is just a myth one of the authors believed about psychologists. This is not how the majority, if not all, of psychologists operate. Unfortunately, this was not always the case. Before the author was born and his suspicions of psychologists, another psychologist had very similar thoughts. In 1973, Rosenhan published a seminal article that significantly contributed to psychology, specifically to practitioners. Rosenhan wondered "If sanity and insanity exist, how shall we know them?" (p. 250). He wanted to know if abnormality and normality could be distinguished from each other. In other words, do people actually exhibit symptoms of psychopathology or are these symptoms created by the observers (i.e., psychologists and psychiatrists)? So, Rosenhan developed a study to investigate these questions.

Pseudopatients

Actors playing the role of a patient

Rosenhan (1973) recruited eight pseudopatients to help with the study. Pseudopatients are people with no specific psychological disorders or medical problems who are portraying patients. The eight included three women and five men consisting of a psychology graduate student, three psychologists, a pediatrician, a psychiatrist, a painter, and a housewife. A total of 12 hospitals were sought out and phone calls were made to establish appointments. Upon arrival for the appointment the pseudopatients reported hearing voices. The pseudopatients reported that they heard "unclear [voices] say 'empty,' 'hollow,' and 'thud' [and] the voices were unfamiliar and were of the same sex as the pseudopatient" (p. 251). These symptoms were chosen to simulate existential symptoms. The only other thing that the pseudopatients fabricated was their name and profession; they accurately reported other social history events.

Would the staff and professionals catch them in their attempts to feign symptoms for entry? On the contrary, all were admitted. Once they were admitted, then they ceased reports of symptoms and behaved normally (Rosenhan, 1973). Rosenhan's condition for the pseudopatient to leave was that they would convince the staff that they were sane. In spite of behaving normally, all, except in one case, were diagnosed with schizophrenia. In one case, the person was diagnosed as having manic-depressive psychosis. Psuedopatients remained in the hospital between seven to 52 days, 19 days on average. Upon leaving, all those who were diagnosed with schizophrenia were discharged with the diagnosis of schizophrenia in remission.

© Yannis Ntousiopoulos/Shutterstock.com

Rosenhan's (1973) study highlights several issues for abnormal psychology. One of the main issues is what Rosenhan refers to as the stickiness of labels. Individuals who were diagnosed as having schizophrenia carried that label with them upon discharge, as schizophrenia in remission. Further, the label was the basis for interpreting all other behavior. Rosenhan discussed how one pseudopatient's pacing behavior, out of boredom, was interpreted as nervousness. This was the aforementioned fear of dealing with psychologists, that they might create a label and that label sticks with you. This concern is probably held by the majority of individuals who seek the help of licensed psychologists. Though the deeper concern is that they are given a sticky label that is associated with stigma.

Another issue that arose in Rosenhan's (1973) study was that of mental health provider's attitudes toward patients. Rosenhan asserted that individuals with psychological disorders are viewed by society as lepers. The psuedopatients recorded the interaction of the professionals with the patients and strikingly noted limited time dedicated to interactions. Nurses were seen 11.5 times on average in a shift and physicians were seen on the ward about 6.7 times per day. Further, the pseudopatients were often ignored or invisible. For example, the pseudopatients were administered 2,100 pills and they tossed all but two down the toilet without being caught or noticed. The pseudopatients noted that some of the patients did the same. These

© Lukatme/Shutterstock.com

behaviors went unnoticed as long as the pseudopatients were being cooperative. Thus, cooperation led to invisibility. It is important to note that Rosenhan (1973) stated that the pseudopatients had an overwhelmingly positive impression of the staff, as they were caring, committed, and seemingly intelligent people. The problem was not in the people, per se, but in the environment. The staff were seeking what was wrong with patients rather than employing good assessments.

The last issue stemming from this study might be one of most importance. All patients were diagnosed with a disorder (Rosenhan, 1973). Thus, psychological practitioners inaccurately diagnosed all pseudopatients as exhibiting psychopathology when no symptoms were present, other than hearing empty, thud, and hollow. In other words, psychologically healthy individuals were incorrectly labeled as suffering from a mental disorder.

You might say that the study was not fair because Rosenhan had tricked the staff by having pseudopatients feigning the symptoms. Rosenhan contacted a teaching and research hospital who was aware of these findings and conducted a follow-up study. Rosenhan informed the staff that over 3 months a pseudopatient would seek admittance into their hospital. The results were that out of 193 patients assessed, 41 were deemed to be pseudopatients by a staff member, 23 were suspected by a psychiatrist, and 19 were suspected by one psychiatrist and one staff. So, how many people did Rosenhan send in the 3 months? Rosenhan sent no one.

Misdiagnosis

An incorrect diagnosis

The issue of misdiagnosis or not accurate diagnosing becomes evident with Rosenhan's (1973) study. Misdiagnosis means that the diagnosis provided was not correct. Those who were psychologically healthy had been labeled with a mental disorder and those who very well might have had a disorder were believed to be faking, or pseudopatients. This becomes problematic for potential psychiatric patients as well as providers. For patients to receive treatment, they need to be diagnosed accurately rather than dismissed or provided an incorrect label. These reasons are why it is imperative for practitioners to accurately discern between psychopathology. Accuracy in discernment is the reason that psychologists have moved toward integrating science in practice and reliance of psychometrically sound assessments.

The Function of Assessments

Have you ever broken a bone or had a trip to the emergency room? What do they typically do? Write about a time that you or someone you know has broken a bone. Write about what happened that led to the injury, what happened following the injury? (Did you go to the ER?) What did they do, and how did you or the person leave?

Based on your story, did the medical staff that admitted you begin giving you oral decongestants? Probably not. Nor do most medical professionals just look at you and say, "Well, it looks like you have a broken bone because you are crying and seem to be in pain." Most medical providers will begin with an assessment. If you broke a bone, you probably had that area scanned or had an x-ray. This is referred to as an assessment. An assessment is a formal process of gathering information to make decisions about diagnoses and treatment. So, how do psychologists do this and are they any good at it? Do psychologists merely look at you and make decisions about whether you have a disorder?

Assessment

Formal process of gathering information

The reason that psychologists assess is no different than that of medical professionals or other professions. Auto mechanics assess your car when you are having unusual sounds or performance from your vehicle. Assessments are the starting point. Psychological assessments are tools that prompt diagnosis and inform treatment with clients. We assess so that we can diagnose. Diagnoses are provided so that we can treat (see Figure 3.1). Therefore, accurate assessments and accurate diagnosis lead to effective treatments.

The means by which psychologists and others assess is what matters. Think of the broken bone example above; medical staff do not merely look at you to determine if you broke a bone. Usually, an x-ray is provided, to corroborate that the bone has been broken and to see where the bone has been broken. Then, a diagnosis can be made, in that you broke a bone. Finally, a treatment can be rendered, which might be resetting the bone and placing a cast on the individual. For psychologists, you are given several tests and a clinical interview. Then, a psychologist would determine a diagnosis followed by a treatment.

A poor assessment can lead to a misdiagnosis or even an ineffective or harmful treatment. If you entered the hospital with a broken bone and the medical staff assessed you by merely looking at you and concluded that you have a cold, then you would have a poor assessment leading to a misdiagnosis. The result would likely be poor treatment, in that you would not have

FIGURE 3.1   Process of Psychological Assessment, Diagnosis, and Treatment
Courtesy of Authors

your bone reset in place or a cast, but maybe told to go home, drink plenty of fluids, and get a lot of rest. Similarly, if a mechanic does not provide an accurate assessment of your automobile, then you might receive the wrong diagnosis. Maybe the assessment indicates that the problem is with your battery and you replace your car battery but still have a problem. Thus, the wrong assessment leads to paying money for an ineffective treatment or solution. Psychologists that do not accurately assess, such as in Rosenhan's (1973) study, lead to inaccurate diagnoses, such as schizophrenia, and inappropriate treatment, such as the 2,100 pills.

So, are psychologists any good at it? Paul Meehl (1954) wrote on clinical versus statistical methods of prediction and discussed various studies that supported a conclusion of statistical predictions being more accurate in making predictions compared to clinical methods. Statistical or mechanical methods are psychometric tests or other data combined and "the resultant probability figure which is an empirically determined relative frequency" (p. 3). On the other hand, clinical methods are data obtained, such as from a client's history, and predictions are derived from psychological hypotheses or case conferences. Thus, the results of the studies Meehl analyzed suggested that clinicians were not better at making decisions from data gathered than statistical methods.

Clinical methods may be less accurate in predictions and decisions due to the judgment errors that come with being human. Ruscio (2007) noted the various cognitive limitations and biases a clinician carries, which leads to error. Human information storage, retrieval, and processing speed work much differently than that of computers. Ruscio discussed that these cognitive limitations, along with relying on heuristics, confirmation bias, and hindsight bias, are features of humans that carry over into the work of a clinician. Therefore, it is not surprising that Meehl (1954) discovered statistical methods offering advantages to clinical methods.

Meehl (1954) and Rosenhan's (1973) work led to psychologists using and relying on psychological assessments more heavily than just their own clinical judgments. In doing so, relying on good assessments leads to better measurements and better clinicians (Wood et al., 2007). Psychological assessments are often a component that distinguishes psychologists from other mental health providers (Baker & Benjamin, 2000). An assessment can often be more reliable than clinical judgment alone (Meehl, 1954). Thus, most practicing psychologists (90%) use assessments and spend a moderate amount of time doing so (Watkins et al., 1995).

Assessments encompass any approach of gathering data. One of the most typical ways that this is done for psychologists is the clinical interview. The clinical interview is the process of gathering vast information about a client's history, behavior, emotional expressions, and current life situation through a structured or semi-structured approach of asking questions. This

Clinical Interview

A process of gathering vast information about a client's history, behavior, emotional expressions, and current life situation is one of the most important aspects of an assessment (Groth-Marnat, 2009). The clinical interview provides the foundation for the client's presenting concern and the overall context of what the client is seeking. Groth-Marnat suggests a checklist of questions that a mental health provider may want to ask in a clinical interview.

Other than the clinical interview, a common assessment for psychologists is the use of tests. The word test may elicit a negative or aversive response in you because of your years in educational systems and the negative connotations often associated with tests. Maybe you hear your teacher's voice saying something to the effect of "alright class, let's get ready for your test" or think about the test you took for college admissions. Though you may have negative experiences based on particular tests and their consequences, tests are merely a form of assessment. However, not all tests are created equal, or for that matter, created well.

Good Tests: Psychometrics

If you want to know anything about yourself you can turn to the Internet, social media sites, or magazines. There are a vast number of assessments that will tell you what kind of personality you have, your intelligence, who you should marry, your cleaning type, what psychologist you are most like, how gullible you are, and many more. It may be easy to get caught up in these assessments and even extract meaning from them. So, how do you know if you can rely on these assessments?

One of the things that make psychological assessments distinct from many of the above assessments is that they are grounded in psychometrics. Psychometrics is the scientific study of psychological measures and tests. A psychological assessment is evaluated based on various aspects including whether or not it addresses the referral question/presenting concern, if it's used with the specified normative group, if it is empirically supported, if limitations are understood, and if it is intentional and informative for treatment. Most of the aforementioned Internet or magazine assessments fail in many of these areas.

Psychometrics

The scientific study of psychological measures and tests

Reliability

The consistency in measurement

Reliability. You might be more familiar with psychometrics than you realize. Have you ever stepped upon a scale?

If you have, then you probably have wanted them to exhibit reliability. One way to think of reliability is to think of consistency. Reliability is the consistency in measurement of items and test administrations. For example, you want a scale to tell you how

© Billion Photos/Shutterstock.com

much you weigh, then you want the scale to be consistent. Let's consider getting on and off a scale five times. Your results look like this:

Time 1: 130 lbs

Time 2: 200 lbs

Time 3: 101 lbs

Time 4: 233 lbs

Time 5: 75 lbs

What would you likely do with a scale that gave you these results, throw it in the trash? These results would reveal poor reliability. You would gain little utility from a scale that resulted in the above because of the inconsistency, unless you preferred to see erratic weight fluctuations. Most people seek scales that are reliable. For example, if you weighed 130 lbs, then you would want the scales to provide your weight consistently. Thus, results from a reliable scale would look more like this:

Time 1: 130 lbs

Time 2: 130 lbs

Time 3: 130 lbs

Time 4: 130 lbs

Time 5: 130 lbs

These results illustrate highly reliable weight scales because they produce the same results over several times. This scale would be one that you would probably want to keep around, assuming that it is valid as well, which will be discussed subsequently. Psychologists strive for assessments to demonstrate reliability. Much like wanting consistency in your measurement of weight, psychologists seek consistency in tests or when providing diagnoses.

Reliability in tests will contain some error or random fluctuation (Groth-Marnat, 2009). Error is resultant of human performance and the imprecise measurement of psychological constructs (Groth-Marnat, 2009). Due to these features, there will be error in measurement. The goal then is to reduce error as much as possible. One way to think about reliability is to think of it in terms of error, in that a highly reliable test is one with little error. Consider the following:

$$\text{True Score} = \text{Observed Score} + \text{Error}$$

In this equation, the observed score is the score that you receive on a test. The observed score is not necessarily your true score because the observed score consists of error that is inherent within the test. Thus, your true score is the combination of your observed score and the error of the test. If you reduce the amount of error, then your observed score will more closely approximate your true score. Thus, reliability is reducing testing error as much as possible so that your observed score is closer to your true score.

© vexworldwide/Shutterstock.com

Remember the first example above with the variation of weight measurements from the scale. If you have that much error, you throw the scale in the trash. In that example, the error is so high (i.e., reliability so low) that the observed scores are not getting anywhere near your true weight. However, in the second example, the scores are the same every time, meaning no error. Thus, this would be highly reliable and would indicate your true score, or true weight.

There are various methods to obtain reliability and statistics used for its computation. These methods of reliability are referred to as test-retest reliability, alternate forms, internal consistency, and interrater reliability (Groth-Marnat, 2009). Test-retest is looking at a measurement at two points in time and comparing the two scores. Weighing yourself at one time and immediately a second time and seeing how close the weight measurements are would not be an example of this. For test-retest reliability the time needs to occur in longer intervals than immediately following one test. Thus, measuring weight over two time periods may be difficult to assess the reliability of a measure because weight fluctuates based on diet and exercise. Thus, test-retest is only good to use if the construct is expected to be relatively stable over time. The test-retest approach would be useful in measuring a psychological construct such as intelligence, which is relatively stable over time. A highly reliable intelligence test would produce closely the same scores at two different administrations.

Alternate forms is a method that compares two or more different forms of a test to determine reliability. The greater the correlation between forms means a higher reliability. This approach is often used when wanting to eliminate any **practice effects.** Practice effects are the effects of performance scores increasing due to learning or memorizing items from a test. Thus, an alternate form would reduce this practice effects because the test appears differently the second time it is administered compared to the first. Maybe you took a test in a class where the instructor had you complete form A and other students completed form B, or you had a test that was given in one color and others had a different color. Chances are that your instructor used an alternate forms approach in testing and grading. All the items for each form are the same but may be arranged in a different order. Thus, the first question on form A may be the 14th question on form B. The idea is that if

Practice Effects

The effects of scores increasing due to learning or memorizing items from a test

the order of the items does not matter, then the test should be comparable for both forms. In other words, if the error of the test is minimal, then both forms should correlate highly, demonstrating a high reliability. Sometimes the order of items matter and may influence the performance on subsequent items. For example, if a test began with the question asking you to indicate the percentage of people who fail an entire test based on incorrectly answering the first item, that might introduce stress on subsequent items. However, if this item was situated later in the test, it may not have the same impact on performance. Thus, alternate forms will provide statistical evidence of the consistency of a test.

Internal consistency refers to the relatedness of the items with each other. When items are consistently asking questions then your test would yield a higher coefficient alpha, meaning that the items are demonstrating high internal reliability. For example, a test with a number of questions about anxiety might have a high internal consistency. A test that asks questions about a variety of things might show lower internal consistency because the items would not be as related. This measure of reliability is established based on one testing administration rather than over time, such as that of test-retest or alternate forms.

Interrater reliability is a measurement of consistency between two or more independent raters. For this approach, independent raters will score or provide measurements based on some test or performance. Then, the raters' scores will be analyzed to see how closely related those scores are. The closer the raters' scores are means less error and greater reliability. Think of *American Idol*. People perform and then the judges provide their scores. If one judge's score is completely discrepant from the others, because of being a harsh judge or entertainment factors, then the reliability will be lower. If all judges produce relatively similar scores, then there would be greater consistency. This method might be used anytime you have raters providing their input on a measurement. Another example might be if raters are instructed to watch a therapy session and rate the therapist on a measure of empathy. The more closely the raters' scores are means the more reliable the scores are of the therapists' empathy.

For all of these methods, statistical computations are used to derive a correlation coefficient, which tells you the strength of the relationship between two or more things. Correlation coefficients range from −1 to +1 and the closer to 1, the stronger the correlation. This will be discussed further in the following chapter. However, note that for reliability a high correlation is generally .80 or higher (Groth-Marnat, 2009).

Reliability is an important tool for psychometrics. However, by itself it is not sufficient. In recalling the Rosenhan (1973) study, it could be argued that the psychiatric staff did not completely do a horrible job because they were highly reliable with the diagnosis. Remember that 11 of the 12 diagnosed the pseudopatient as having schizophrenia, indicating a high reliability or consistency. This is important. It could be noted that these results indicated consistent training in the profession that resulted in highly reliable diagnoses. However, the main problem we see with the study is that even though there was a consistency in the diagnosis, the diagnosis was still wrong. Thus, is it any good to be consistent if you are consistently wrong? While reliability is sought after, it is needed in conjunction with another psychometric tool, that is, validity.

Validity. To consider validity, let's revisit those weight scales. Say that your actual weight was 140 lbs and when you stepped on the scale several times, this is what the scale reported:

Time 1: 195 lbs

Time 2: 122 lbs

Time 3: 105 lbs

Time 4: 277 lbs

Time 5: 163 lbs

The scale would not be accurately providing you with your actual weight, which would mean that the scale is not valid. Validity is the accuracy of a test in measuring what it is intended to measure. If the scale is unreliable, or inconsistent, then it would also not be valid. Thus, to have a valid scale you would also need a reliable scale. However, scales might be reliable but not valid. Consider this series of weight measurements:

Validity

The accuracy of a test in measuring what it is intended to measure

Time 1: 194 lbs

Time 2: 194 lbs

Time 3: 194 lbs

Time 4: 194 lbs

Time 5: 194 lbs

In this instance you would have reliability but not validity. Though the scale is consistent in its measurement of 194 lbs, it is not accurately providing you with your actual weight of 140 lbs. Thus, a scale or test can offer consistency but not accuracy. Consistently doing the same wrong thing is not helpful or effective. Practitioners need not only to be consistent, but need to be consistently accurate.

Similar to reliability, there are various empirical methods to derive at the validity of a test or assessment. Some of these methods include content validity, criterion validity, and construct validity (American Educational Research Association, American Psychological Association, & National Council on Measurement in Education, 2014; Groth-Marnat, 2009). Content validity refers to how closely the content of a test is embodying the suggested psychological construct of interest. If you were constructing a test intended to measure depression, then you might ask questions about how sad a person feels and how often they feel this way. These items would be developed with the intent to reflect the construct of depression. Another aspect of content validity is referred to as face validity (Groth-Marnat, 2009). Face validity deals with how much the content appears to measure the intended construct of interest. For example, a test that asks you how much alcohol you drink each day as an item to measure an alcohol-related disorder would demonstrate high face validity. Most people who took such a test would assume that the item is asking about their use and abuse of alcohol. Face validity is nice because individuals can infer the construct being measured based on the content. This validity can also be problematic if someone who abuses alcohol is trying to lie about their use when taking a particular test.

Criterion validity is another method to get at test accuracy. Criterion validity compares test scores to other theoretically related measures (Groth-Marnat, 2009). For example, a test for anxiety might be expected to correlate with people who have been diagnosed with an anxiety disorder. This validity can be gathered by giving two or more tests during the same administration, which is often referred to as concurrent validity. Another option is to gather the information at a future point in time, which is referred to as predictive validity.

Construct validity refers to the accuracy by which a test relates directly to the psychological construct. So, does the test represent what it is intended to represent? For example, a test of depression symptoms should highly correlate with people who exhibit depressive symptoms and not with other symptoms. To get at this you may want to have a test correlate with similar measures, which would be referred to as convergent validity. For example, a new test developed for symptoms of generalized anxiety disorder would be expected to correlate highly with a test that measures symptoms of social anxiety disorder, as these two constructs share some similarities in the construct of anxiety. On the other hand, if the test is representing the construct of anxiety and not to other constructs, then you would expect the test to not correlate as highly with other constructs. Discriminate validity refers to a test being different from other measures or constructs. Thus, a measure of symptoms of anxiety would not be expected to correlate highly with a measure of psychosis.

Standardization. Recall an interview in which people asked you questions about why you deserve the job or position. The interviewers will typically ask you and others the same set of questions. They ask the same set of questions for standardization. Standardization is a procedural approach to a test that is administered similarly to a variety of individuals to establish normative scores and to make comparison of scores based on the normative sample. By standardizing an assessment or interview, you then can make compari-

Standardization

The procedural approach to a test that is administered similarly to a variety of individuals to establish normative scores

sons of responses. For example, if you ask every interviewee the same three questions, then you can compare the responses of all interviewees to aid in making your decision about which individual you want to hire. For psychological tests, the same standard applies. Before providing a test you want to confirm that the test has been standardized on a sample of people that represent characteristics of the person you intend to test. This is important so that you can compare the person's test score to the scores of a sample of individuals who have already been tested. For example, if a test only has normative scores from a sample of individuals who were 40 years old or older, then it would not be useful to give that test to a 6-year-old child. The child's scores would not be compared to peers but to people who were 40 and older. This might be problematic because the test might ask questions that are developmentally unaligned with a child who is 6. Thus, psychometrically strong tests will exhibit standardization, validity, and high reliability.

© Cartoonresource/Shutterstock.com

Psychological Tests

There are numerous psychological tests. The tests will assess intelligence, personality, psychopathology, substance abuse, and more. In fact, there are books that are specifically devoted to discussing the popular assessments in depth (e.g., Groth-Marnat, 2009). Therefore, we will review only some of the most frequently used tests.

These tests fall into categories of objective tests and projective tests. Objective tests are tests that have a concrete response choice set. For example, a multiple-choice exam that you take in college would be an example of this. There are limited choices for a multiple-choice test and scoring is based on those limited choices. Therefore, your score is based on the limited possible choices. For multiple-choice exams, your score is based on a correct or incorrect response. The value of the objective test is that it has clearly defined parameters of choice set, reducing the level of ambiguity or response variation. Thus, reaching a score is done with less ambiguity and more concreteness.

Objective Tests

Tests that elicit a concrete response choice set

Projective tests are tests that allow people to provide a variety of responses. The idea with a projective test is that when given ambiguous stimuli, people will project their thoughts or emotions onto that stimulus. The strength of this approach is that it allows a wide range of individualized responses. On the other hand the drawbacks of such tests are that they introduce more subjectivity.

Projective Tests

Tests that allow people to provide a variety of responses

Minnesota Multiphasic Personality Inventory-2 (MMPI-2). Years ago one of the authors had a friend call and ask if he had ever heard of a test called the MMPI-2. The author said that he did and had studied it fairly extensively throughout graduate training. Following that, the author's friend asked how to take the test. The author's response was "honestly." He was trying to learn how to take the test so that he could secure a specific employment opportunity. As stated earlier, some tests have face validity. If you know what the test is asking, then you could answer according to what you think might give you scores for a specific job. The MMPI-2 does not work the same way as some of these tests used for some job application processes.

Because of the strong research base, the MMPI-2 is one of the most commonly used objective personality tests (Greene, 2000). The original Minnesota Multiphasic Personality Inventory (MMPI) was developed by Hathaway and McKinley (1940) by generating over 1,000 items and then reducing the items to 504 (Greene, 2000). Then, the test was administered to two groups of individuals, a criterion of who met a classification of hypochondriasis, and a normative group of friends or relatives of patients at a hospital in Minnesota (Greene, 2000). The idea was to have two different groups take the test and compare their results. Thus, the test would be built on comparing responses of individuals who exhibited psychopathology compared to those who did not. Many years later the MMPI was re-standardized, which led to the development of the MMPI-2 (Butcher et al., 1989; Greene, 2000).

The MMPI-2 consists of individuals reading 567 items and answering one of three options: "true," "false," or "cannot say" (Greene, 2000). Following the administration of the test, the MMPI-2 is scored and a profile of responses is developed. The profile contains a validity index and 10 clinical scales. The validity index provides information to the clinician regarding the examiners' attitudes toward taking the test and response styles. Thus, if you are trying to paint yourself in a favorable manner, which is referred to as social desirability, then a clinician would be able to see this in the validity index. Further, the validity index would allow a clinician to see scores indicative of lying, or even attempting to fake psychopathology. Once the validity indices have been examined, a clinician will interpret the clinical scales. The clinical scales provide a clinical picture about the client's responses. Clinicians will consider scales that appear to be elevated, which would indicate a higher frequency of item endorsement for that scale compared to what is normative. Figure 3.2 depicts a sample profile of the clinical scales for a male who was in alcohol and drug treatment.

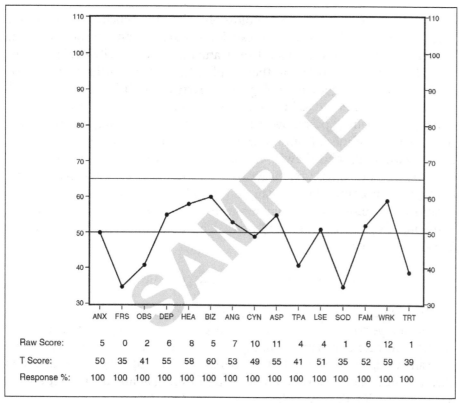

	ANX	FRS	OBS	DEP	HEA	BIZ	ANG	CYN	ASP	TPA	LSE	SOD	FAM	WRK	TRT
Raw Score:	5	0	2	6	8	5	7	10	11	4	4	1	6	12	1
T Score:	50	35	41	55	58	60	53	49	55	41	51	35	52	59	39
Response %:	100	100	100	100	100	100	100	100	100	100	100	100	100	100	100

FIGURE 3.2   Sample MMPI-2 Content Scales Profile

Wechsler Intelligence Scales. When you think of intelligence what comes to mind, this?

What epistemology is to philosophy is intelligence to psychology. Psychologists have long been interested in intelligence and its measurement. The term "mental test" originated from Cattell and later revisited by Spearman, who developed a two-factor theory of intelligence (Guthrie, 2004; von Mayrhauser, 1992), general intelligence, referred to as "g," and specific intelligence abilities, known as "s" (von Mayrhauser, 1992). The early interest in intelligence was in its predictive value (Greene, 2000; von Mayrhauser, 1992). A progression of ideas from a few key individuals, including Alfred Binet, H. H. Goddard, and Lewis Terman, led to the development of the intelligence quotient (von Mayrhauser, 1992). The term intelligence quotient (IQ) was coined by Terman and the idea was to derive a score from a ratio of an individual's mental age to that person's chronological age. Subsequently, this concept was revised by Stanford University (Guthrie, 2004). The ratio looks like this:

Intelligence Quotient

A score from a ratio of an individual's mental age to that person's chronological age

$$IQ = \text{Mental Age} / \text{Chronological Age} \times 100$$

The principle is that an average IQ score would consist of a person's mental age performance matching their chronological age performance. A 10-year-old that performs mentally with that of other 10-year-olds would have an average IQ score of 100. If a person's mental age is greater than their chronological age, then they would be performing at an advanced level and have a higher IQ. For example:

$$120 = 12/10 \times 100$$

A person who has a mental age lower than their chronological age would be mentally performing at a delayed level and have a lower IQ. For example:

$$80 = 8/10 \times 100$$

This concept is what established the foundation for intelligence tests. An IQ falls within a range on a continuum of the normative distribution. Think back to the normal bell curve. The mean IQ score is 100 with a large majority (68%) of people that have an IQ score between one standard deviation of the mean, and most people (96%) fall within two standard deviations of the mean.

Intelligence tests were able to predict academic and occupational performance and used clinically to identify a client's relative cognitive strengths and weaknesses (Greene, 2000). An IQ test will also aid in decision-making for diagnosis, treatment, and educational recommendations. Diagnostic criterion for an intellectual disability requires an IQ test administration (American Psychiatric Association, 2013). Specialists in school psychology may assess children's intelligence and achievement in order to aid the decision-making process regarding recommendations for accommodations or placement. Children who have an intellectual disability, indicated by a lower intelligence quotient score, might be provided a recommendation for special education services.

If you were in public schools and recall being instructed to leave your classroom to follow a stranger into a room where you played with and manipulated blocks, then you might have taken an intelligence test. One of the more popularly used intelligence scales are the Wechsler series that began in 1939 (Groth-Marnat, 2009). The Wechsler Adult Intelligence Scale—Fourth Edition (WAIS-IV) has been normed on adults from

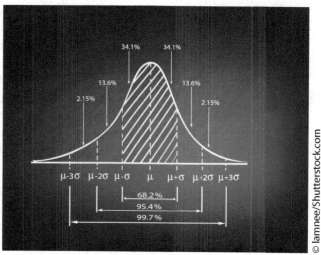

© lamnee/Shutterstock.com

16 to 90 years old (Wechsler, 2008). Alternatively, the Wechsler Intelligence Scale for Children®—Fifth Edition (WISC-V) is designed to test children and adolescents from 6 to 16 years old (Wechsler, 2014). The Wechsler series involves completing several subtests that factor into composites of intelligence (e.g., verbal comprehension, fluid reasoning, processing speed).

Rorschach. Look at this picture and write down what this might be.

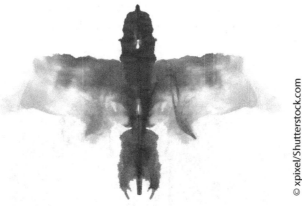

© xpixel/Shutterstock.com

This task represents what individuals would be asked to do if they were administered the Rorschach test. The Rorschach is often referred to as the inkblot test because people are provided with pictures of inkblots, such as the one above. The picture above is not an inkblot from the Rorschach, but would be similar to those on the test. The reason that the Rorschach uses inkblots is because before it was ever a test, it was Friday night entertainment. Many years ago, before Netflix, movie theatres, social media, and football games, people had other means of entertainment. People would put ink on a piece of paper and fold it in half, creating a symmetrical inkblot. Then, you would look at the inkblot and tell a story about what it was. If you are looking for a fun weekend night or party game this is still a hit. In fact, years ago my wife created an inkblot game as a part of my graduation party. The game was to give people a piece of paper with a symmetrical inkblot and the individual states what it was in the picture. Then, the other people had to vote a thumbs-up for a good response or a thumbs-down for an unfavorable response. The majority vote determined your projective success if you won the round.

The inkblot then morphed from a game into a standardized psychological assessment by Hermann Rorschach in 1921 (Groth-Marnat, 2009). The idea was that people might project their thoughts onto the inkblot and reveal aspects of their personality or psychopathology. The Rorschach consists of 10 cards and two phases (Exner, 2001). The Rorschach is controversial in its use, in that there are clinicians who use it frequently and psychologists who are concerned with its scientific merit (Groth-Marnat, 2009; Lilienfeld et al., 2001). Proponents suggest that it taps into conscious resistance, guards against faking, and is easy to administer (Groth-Marnat, 2009). On the other hand, others criticize its subjectivity and scientific merit (e.g., Lilienfeld et al., 2001). Critics suggest that it is still popularly used because of biases, illusory correlations, P. T. Barnum effect, alchemist effect, and clinical tradition (Lilienfeld et al., 2012).

Thematic Apperception Test. Look at this picture and write down what you think is happening here, what the man is thinking and feeling, and what he might do.

© Maria Sbytova/Shutterstock.com

This task represents something similar to what you might be asked to do on the Thematic Apperception Test (TAT). The TAT is a projective test that asks people to view a variety of ambiguous scenes and to respond similarly to the aforementioned. The TAT was formally developed by Henry Murray (1943). The idea of the TAT matches that of the Rorschach, in that a person will project their thoughts onto the scene. Murray thought that it would reveal people's drives, conflicts, and emotions.

The TAT has some strengths and drawbacks. It is one of the most frequently used assessments and it is selected because of the idea that it taps into deep structures of personality (Groth-Marnat, 2009). Similar to the Rorschach it is viewed as a test that is resistant to faking because of the ambiguous nature of the test. The major concerns with the TAT are those that come with any projective, in that it is subjective and may not be empirically sound (Groth-Marnat, 2009). In fact, it has been argued that many of the same reasons that the Rorschach may be popularly used without scientific merit are true for the TAT (Lilienfeld et al., 2012).

Diagnosis

A diagnosis is the pivotal moment of change. It is the answer from assessment and the hope for treatment. Medical television shows capture audiences by inviting them to be a part of diagnosis. If you have ever watched *House, M.D.* then you have probably been a part of this grueling process. The characters spend close to an hour of assessment and throwing out potential diagnoses to solve the case by reaching the diagnosis with minutes to spare for treatment.

CHRONIC FATIG
SORE THROATS
RASHES
PUTRID D/CHARGE
MULT. ABSCESSES – BR
HEARING LOSS

© FOX/Photofest

The world of mental health diagnosis does not match the adrenaline and suspense found in television shows. As mentioned in Chapter 1, the text that guides mental health providers in determining a diagnosis for a client is referred to as The Diagnostic and Statistical Manual of Mental Disorders, 5th edition (DSM-5; American Psychiatric Association, 2013). A diagnosis is merely a label used for symptoms that are typically clustered together. The DSM-5 elaborates on diagnosis to include "symptoms, behaviors, cognitive functions, personality traits, physical signs, syndrome combinations, and durations" (American Psychiatric Association, 2013, p. 5). Further, the American Psychiatric Association (2013) explicitly stated that clinical experience is needed to use the DSM-5 for determining a diagnosis.

Diagnosis

A label used for symptoms that are typically clustered together

LET'S PRACTICE

The use of a label is where things might elicit benefit or detriment. What are some benefits and problems with diagnosis?

BENEFITS	PROBLEMS
1. _____	1. _____
2. _____	2. _____
3. _____	3. _____

What you wrote down may demonstrate how people use and misuse diagnosis as well as reflect myths about diagnosis. There are a variety of benefits and problems that may come from diagnosis, though keep in mind these are not embedded within the diagnosis as much as from people's use of a labeling system. Let's review some of the benefits and problems.

Benefits. One of the major benefits and intended uses of diagnosis is that it is used to inform treatment. Recall that assessment is used to inform diagnosis and diagnosis leads to treatment (Figure 3.1). Accurate and reliable diagnoses are needed to deliver effective treatments. The American Psychiatric Association (2013) encourages reliable diagnoses for treatment and research.

Classification

A system of identification and organization

Other benefits of diagnosis stem from the use of a classification system. Classification is a system of identification and organization. Blashfield and Burgess (2007) claimed that a classification system used in psychopathology is no different than that used in other disciplines (e.g., biology) in that it is central for organization. We classify for a variety of reasons that advance the discipline in science and practice. One of the first influential individuals to do this in the area of psychiatry was Emil Kraepelin, who developed classification of dementia praecox [schizophrenia] and manic depressive (Blashfield & Burgess, 2007; Louter, 2010). Following Kraepelin, Robert Spitzer led the task force for the development of the DSM-III (Blashfield & Burgess, 2007). The DSM-III eventually evolved into its current edition of the DSM-5 and has maintained goals of a classification system described by Blashfield and Burgess. Blashfield and Burgess identify six goals of a classification system.

1. Nomenclature
2. Information Retrieval
3. Description
4. Prediction
5. Concept Formation
6. Sociopolitical

Each of these goals promotes a system of benefit for clinicians, researchers, and clients. The goal of nomenclature is to set up a system of language for mental disorders (Blashfield & Burgess, 2007). This allows clinicians and researchers to establish diagnostic labels. This allows a basic framework for psychological professionals to talk about mental disorders. This is no different than calling a specific element hydrogen or assigning a Greek letter to a mathematical function (Blashfield & Burgess, 2007). Further, naming a disorder can sometimes be very beneficial for clients. Clients who feel pain and impaired functioning but do not know why, may feel relief when they receive a label (diagnosis). Merely having a language for disorders may lead to clients feeling normalized and confident in treatment. Normalization means a process that reduces fear and leads people to believe that they are not alone because of sharing their experience with others.

Normalization

A process that reduces fear and encourages beliefs of shared experience

The language can then be organized and stored for later retrieval (Blashfield & Burgess, 2007). While it is good to have a working knowledge and conceptualization of diagnostic criteria, the DSM-5 has diagnostic criteria stored and can be easily accessed without relying primarily on memory. Many graduate students are thankful for this goal, as looking up diagnostic criteria is much less daunting than expectations of memorizing these criteria.

Beyond language and storing information, classifications provide individuals with an ability to describe the disorder (Blashfield & Burgess, 2007). Descriptions help deepen understanding of the symptoms that cluster together, and how to understand those symptoms. Clinicians are able to learn about the disorder and how treatments may work with specific symptoms. For clients, descriptions may also aid in normalization.

More knowledge about symptoms and names for those co-occurring symptoms fosters predictions (Blashfield & Burgess, 2007). Clinicians and researchers seek to make predictions. Clinicians predict the course and outcome of symptoms for clients based on what is known about the disorder. Also, knowing a disorder allows clinicians to predict effective treatments. Researchers seek to make predictions about the symptoms as well and determine which treatment may be most effective for the symptoms.

Classification can also broadly inform a discipline through theoretical advancement (Blashfield & Burgess, 2007). By classifying many disorders, psychotherapy theories may be refined and base their theory on what is known of the disorders. In other words, by working to classify all mental disorders, theoretical perspectives may be evaluated based on these classifications as a whole. Understanding etiology across all disorders is what informs biopsychosocial, integrationist, and diathesis-stress models.

Lastly, the sociopolitical goal is one of the most important goals for classification. Classification allows mental health providers to exercise their social, political, and economic responsibilities (Blashfield & Burgess, 2007). Blashfield and Burgess stated that one of the sociopolitical concerns of the DSM-IV involved the turf wars between psychiatrists and psychologists, pertaining mostly to understanding psychopathology from a purely biological perspective (former) or psychological and interpersonal perspectives (latter). This goal is a notable goal for mental health professions that may get lost in the trenches. Many practitioners may be so inundated with working with clients that this responsibility falls to the side. One of the reasons that people hold myths about abnormal psychology is from mental health providers not actively practicing this goal. As mental health providers educate the public about the pain that people feel, impaired functioning, fatality, and frequency related to various disorders, then people may be less reluctant to call people crazy and less likely to dehumanize people with disorders. To reduce myths of "crazy," sociopolitical education about the faces and humanity of disorders and the intentionality of diagnosis needs to be in everyday life.

The DSM-5 is not the only classification system of mental disorders. The World Health Organization uses a classification system known as the International Classification of Disorders (ICD). The DSM-5 was revised with the upcoming ICD revision, which will be the ICD-11, expected in 2018, in mind and to harmonize the classifications (American Psychiatric Association, 2013). Currently, the DSM-5 provides the ICD-9 and ICD-10 codes.

Problems. As previously mentioned, there are some problems that stem from diagnosis. However, these problems are generally not problems with diagnosis itself but are brought on by a misconceptions or misuse. A number of these problems were addressed in Rosenhan's (1973) article. He noted that labels can be sticky. An incorrect diagnosis can stick with a client and subsequent information can be interpreted to confirm the label. This issue is a problem with misuse. If a diagnosis is not sought after with accurate assessment practices and with the intent of treatment, then a misdiagnosis can occur. Unfortunately, misdiagnosis occurs within the profession due to mental health professionals having error in decision-making and prediction. Through assessments and the DSM-5, much of the error is reduced. The other issue with sticky labels was that the professional staff had confirmation biases, in that they only used specific information from the pseudopatients to confirm the diagnosis rather than acknowledge information that was contrary to the diagnosis.

Another concern of diagnosis that can be observed in the general public is the desire for self-diagnosis. Sometimes this is done for culpability and other times it may be used to appear "cool" because you have psychological struggles. This can be identified when people say, "It's just my [insert disorder]." Can you think of any disorders that are "cool" disorders? Write down a few.

What did you come up with? How about OCD or ADHD? Some people may frequently tell others how they have either of these disorders, even when never having been diagnosed. Years ago, one of the authors overheard a conversation from some adolescents who were attempting to one-up the other by sharing how pathological each was. One teen stated that he had ADHD. Then, another teen stated, "Oh yeah, well I have depression, bipolar disorder, ADHD, and ADD." It was humorous and saddening to hear these claims. The author's reaction was to laugh at the discrepancy between stating you have ADD and ADHD. Though, the author interjected and asked about a formal diagnosis. None of them had seen a professional, they just knew, in their words. Thus, some disorders are used because they are "cool" disorders. People may claim, "It's just my OCD tendencies" or they might be quick to tell you about their ADHD. However, you never (at least we have never) heard people say, "It's just my schizophrenic tendencies" or ". . . trichotillomania." People do not claim these other disorders because they are not viewed as "cool" disorders. In fact, Curtis (2018) found that college students have said to others "I'm so OCD" and "It's just my ADHD" more than telling others "It's just my schizophrenia." Another large problem with diagnosis that results from public misconceptions and myths of disorders is stigma. Some disorders lead to stigma more than others. As previously mentioned, schizophrenia and trichotillomania are rarely seen as "cool" disorders and are often stigmatized.

Many disorders that get lumped into categories of "cool" or "crazy" are derived from popular media, film, and anecdotal experiences. Think of a few movies that display a disorder, then write whether the disorder was flaunted and respected or stigmatized.

Another issue that often is discussed with diagnosis is social control. It is sometimes thought that the contributors of the DSM-5 are pathologizing normal (Frances, 2013). Public perceptions may be that psychologists and psychiatrists are developing disorders to label everyone as crazy and to stimulate growth in the medicinal marketplace. In response, the American Psychiatric Association invited public and professional opinion for the DSM-IV-TR to DSM-5 change (American Psychiatric Association, 2013).

These concerns can be easily addressed by remembering the sole function of diagnosis. Diagnosis is not created to pathologize normal, but for identifying symptoms that occur together, which ultimately informs treatment. Typically, clinicians do not go into a helping profession so that they can gain the power to get back at a high school bully by providing them with a diagnosis. Nor do clinicians spend many years in education and training to go to grocery stores and popular coffee shops to diagnose people. In fact, mental health professionals are ethically warned against doing so. Psychiatrists follow the Goldwater Rule, established in 1973, which states that professional opinions about the mental states of people who have not been personally and thoroughly evaluated should not be made (Oquendo, 2017). There has been recent controversy over a psychologist, Dr. Gartner, who claimed that Donald Trump meets criteria for malignant narcissism (Caruso, 2017; Gartner, 2017). While many people hold a wide variety of opinions about Donald Trump, the issue has been around the ethics of the Goldwater Rule. The president of the American Psychological Association, Susan McDaniel (2016), in response to another article about professionals weighing in on Trump, stated that though psychologists do not have a Goldwater Rule, the Ethics Code warns against diagnosing public figures. With the exception of a few popularized instances, mental health professionals generally do not seek to diagnose people whom they have not evaluated. Ask most practitioners, especially those who are early in clinical or counseling psychology graduate programs, why they chose their field of study and common responses involve helping people. Diagnosis is designed to inform treatment, and peripheral effects are often developed by myths and mishandlings.

A Historical Overview of the Diagnostic and Statistics Manual of Mental Disorders

The Diagnostic and Statistical Manual of Mental Disorders (DSM) has a rich history. Examining the history of the DSM is critical in understanding mental illness and the influences of mental health professionals (Blashfield, Keeley, et al., 2014; Clegg, 2012). Examining the progression of the DSM also demonstrates how changes in theories of psychopathology have influenced the diagnostic criteria, and how "methodological choices and research preconceptions likely had a strong influence" on diagnostic categories (Blashfield, Keeley, et al., 2014, p. 28). The American Psychiatric Association published its first statistical classification in 1844 of institutionalized mental patients (American Psychiatric Association, 2013). Following World War II, the DSM-I was developed in 1952 (American Psychiatric Association, 1952). After the DSM was originally published it underwent four major editions (2013). Blashfield, Keeley, and colleagues (2014) published a thorough account of the historical progression and influences of the DSM (see Figure 3.3).

DSM-I (1952)

▶ Following World War II, the DSM-I was developed, consisted of 128 diagnostic categories, 132 pages, and cost $3.00.
▶ More theoretical approach than later DSMs, relying heavily on psychodynamic conceptualizations
▶ Generally distinguished organic and functional disorders
▶ Functional disorders divided between psychotic and neurotic

Example Diagnosis
 ▶ Depressive Reaction classified as a neurotic disorder
 ▶ Manic Depressive Reaction & Psychotic Depressive Reaction classified as a psychotic disorder
 ▶ Chronic Depression classified as Cyclothymic Personality—Depressive Subtype

DSM-II (1968)

▶ An emphasis on research, diagnostic reliability, and more integration with other classification systems fueled the development of the DSM-II, which had 119 diagnoses, 119 pages, and cost $3.50.
▶ Slight changes in terminology from DSM-I

DSM-III (1980)

▶ Much of Rosenhan's (1973) research, previously discussed, and Aaron Beck's work with depression was the impetus for the DSM-III, which became a multiaxial system, had 228 diagnoses, contained 494 pages, and was sold for $31.75.
▶ A theoretical approach de-emphasizing psychodynamic conceptualizations
▶ Symptom and Trait based descriptions of diagnoses; Utilization of Inclusion/Exclusion Criteria

Example of Diagnostic Changes
 ▶ All Depressive Disorders categorized as Affective Disorders, and divided into three categories: Major Affective Disorders, Other Specific Affective Disorders, & Atypical Affective Disorders
 ▶ Each diagnosis specified as either bipolar or unipolar, and primary or secondary
 ▶ Bipolar disorder no longer categorized as a psychotic disorder
 ▶ No category for Depressive Personality: Cyclothymia listed as Other Specific Depressive Disorder
 ▶ Elimination of the terms neurosis and psychoneurosis (due to atheoretical approach)

DSM-III-R (1987)

▶ The DSM-III underwent a revision based on more research findings and a newer classification system with some more diagnoses and 567 pages.
▶ No substantial conceptual differences from DSM-III, but some classification differences

Example of Diagnostic Changes: Mood Disorders
 ▶ "Affective Disorders" changed to "Mood Disorders"
 ▶ Two major categories created within Mood Disorders: Depressive Disorders and Bipolar Disorders
 ▶ Depressive Disorders include: Major Depression, Dysthymia, and Depressive Disorder NOS (replaces Atypical)
 ▶ Specifiers Include: melancholic type, chronic type, seasonal pattern, single or recurrent episode
 ▶ Bipolar Disorders include: Bipolar Disorder, Cyclothymia, and Bipolar Disorder NOS (Bipolar II listed as NOS)

- ▶ Specifiers Include: seasonal pattern, single or recurrent episode, recent episode: mixed, manic, or depressed
- ▶ All Mood Disorders designated as mild, moderate, or severe (w/ or w/o psychotic features), or remission status

DSM-IV (1994)

- ▶ Workgroups were initiated, by Allen Frances, to perform literature reviews of diagnostic categories. The DSM-IV consisted of more diagnoses and 886 pages.
- ▶ Language and conceptualization remains similar to DSM-III

Example of Diagnostic Changes: Mood Disorders
- ▶ All Depressive Disorders and Bipolar Disorders retain a single categorization as "Mood Disorders"
- ▶ Depressive Disorders Include: Major Depressive Disorder, Dysthymic Disorder, and Depressive Disorder NOS
- ▶ Bipolar Disorders Include: : Bipolar I, Bipolar II, Cyclothymic Disorder, and Bipolar Disorder NOS
- ▶ Specifers Include: chronic, melancholic features, catatonic features, atypical features, postpartum onset, seasonal pattern, rapid cycling, single or recurrent episode, and with or without interepisode recovery
- ▶ All Mood Disorders designated as mild, moderate, or severe (w/ or w/o psychotic features), or remission status
- ▶ Bipolar I Disorders specified with most recent episode: manic, hypomanic, mixed, or depressed, or unspecified

DSM-IV-TR (2000)

- ▶ The DSM-IV was then revised in 2000 for minor text changes and some changes with paraphilia and tic disorder. It retained the same diagnoses and had 943 pages.

DSM-5 (2013)

- ▶ The DSM-5 was re-organized into a developmental framework, beginning with childhood diagnoses & ending with later life diagnoses. It contains 947 pages and costs $210.
- ▶ Language and conceptualization remain similar, but diagnoses and specifiers expanded.

Example of Diagnostic Changes: Depressive & Bipolar Disorders
- ▶ "Mood Disorders" now divided into distinct categories: Bipolar and Related Disorders and Depressive Disorders
- ▶ New Depressive Diagnoses: Disruptive Mood Dysregulation Disorder, Persistent Depressive Disorder (Dysthymia), Premenstrual Dysphoric Disorder, NOS divided into Specified or Unspecified Depressive Disorder
- ▶ Changes with Bipolar Disorders: Bipolar Disorder NOS changed to Specified or Unspecified Bipolar Disorder
- ▶ New Specifiers for Depressive & Bipolar Disorders: anxious distress, postpartum onset changed to peripartum onset, mixed features added for depressive disorders

FIGURE 3.3   Historical Overview of the DSM
Blashfield, Keeley, et al., (2014); Goldstein & Anthony (1988)

DSM-5

The task force of the DSM-5 made some changes from the DSM-IV-TR that took hundreds of people (not including public forum opinion) over 12 years (American Psychiatric Association, 2013). The goals of the changes were to enhance clinical utility, as the manual is primarily used by clinicians. However, the changes were also aimed to increase the usability within research utility. The DSM-5 was to be more reliable and work toward practice-informing research and research-informing practice.

One of the major goals for the changes made for the DSM-5 was in reliability (American Psychiatric Association, 2013; Blashfield, Keeley, et al., 2014). Previous versions were narrow and resulted in a heavy reliance of Not Otherwise Specified (NOS) categories in determining diagnoses. In response, the task force of the DSM-5 transitioned to a dimensional approach (American Psychiatric Association, 2013). Further, the DSM-5 replaced the NOS category with "other specified disorder" or "unspecified disorder." These changes were to encourage the clinician to communicate a clinical picture of why a client may not fit specific diagnostic criteria. Along with this, the DSM-5 included subtypes and specifiers for some disorders.

Another dimensional change was for the DSM-5 to cluster disorders based on internalizing or externalizing factors (American Psychiatric Association, 2013). Internalizing disorders were those that consisted of depression, anxiety, or somatic symptoms while externalizing disorders include impulse control and substance abuse.

Other changes to the DSM-5 included a reorganization to reflect development and increased attention to culture (American Psychiatric Association, 2013). The DSM-5 is organized in a fashion that parallels the lifespan. The DSM-5 includes a cultural formulation and provides three concepts for understanding cultural influences to psychopathology. These three are:

1. Cultural syndrome
2. Cultural idiom of distress
3. Cultural explanation or perceived cause

Cultural syndromes are clustered symptoms found within a specific cultural group (American Psychiatric Association, 2013). Idioms of distress are terms used by individuals of a cultural group to label their symptoms or even how they feel pain. Cultural explanation is how a label is understood or explained within a cultural framework.

Many of these changes to the DSM-5 were implemented with goals of refinement and increased utility for mental health practitioners. Some people think that many of the DSM-5s did not meet its goals (Blashfield, Keeley, et al., 2014) and there is much more room for development and change. With the changes of specificity, there has been the inclusion of more diagnostic labels. Some have argued that the advances of the DSM to include more diagnostic labels is a movement to pathologize everyone or strip away normality (Frances, 2013). However, others believe that the DSM-5 is a step in the right direction and the changes made have contributed to mental health professions by refining the diagnostic tool. It is important to keep in mind that the identification of newer diagnostic labels is not a creation of more disorders and a desire for practitioners to pathologize normal but rather the development of nomenclature to recognize already existing symptoms. The early Kraepelinian classification system was broad and did not offer much specificity, missing many psychological disorders. A failure to recognize psychological disorders is also a failure to provide treatment, as there can be no treatment for a non-problem. Also, keep in mind that the DSM-5 is a tool for practitioners and it does not diagnose but assists practitioners in determining diagnoses. Thus, equipping competent practitioners with sound assessments and good tools helps with accurate diagnoses.

Conclusion

Psychology as a science, much like that of any science, strives from growth and changes made based on errors made in the past. Meehl (1954) and Rosenhan (1973) did not have ill intentions of single-handedly deconstructing the profession, or attempt to shame their colleagues. The work came about through questions for the profession and attempts for refinement. These individuals wanted to know how effective our profession was and where there was room for improvement. Since their work, mental health providers have sought after more psychometrically sound instruments for use within assessment and empirically driven approaches to accurately make diagnosis. If the goal of mental health professionals is to help people with their functioning, reduce feeling pain, change frequencies of behavior, and decrease fatality, then more accurate assessments and diagnosis are the direction to pursue to make those changes. Clinical and counseling psychology and psychiatry has moved in this direction.

CHAPTER REVIEW

QUESTIONS

1. What did Rosenhan find in his classic study? What are the implications for abnormal psychology and for assessment and diagnosis?

2. What is the need to rely on psychometrically sound instruments?

3. What are subjective assessments? What are some objective assessments?

4. What is the purpose of diagnosis?

KEY TERMS

Pseudopatients

Misdiagnosis

Assessment

Clinical Interview

Psychometrics

Reliability

Practice Effects

Validity

Standardization

Objective Tests

Projective Tests

Intelligence Quotient

Diagnosis

Classification

Normalization

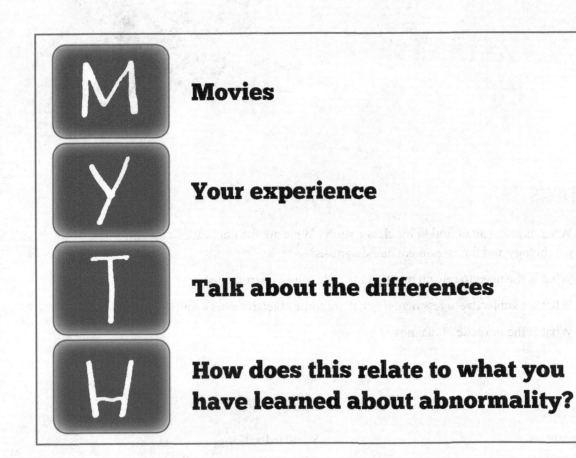

M   Movies

Y   Your experience

T   Talk about the differences

H   How does this relate to what you have learned about abnormality?

CHAPTER FOUR

THE VALUE OF RESEARCH: A GOOD CONSUMER

LEARNING OBJECTIVES

- ▶ Explore claims of research
- ▶ Discuss events related to the role of research
- ▶ Define skepticism within research
- ▶ Explore the impact and consequences of research
- ▶ Explain science as an approach
- ▶ Review philosophies of science
- ▶ Define the scientific method
- ▶ Apply the scientific method
- ▶ Differentiate between independent and dependent variables
- ▶ Discuss psychological constructs
- ▶ Identify the objectives of psychological science
- ▶ Explain research ethics and designs
- ▶ Discern different research designs
- ▶ List benefits of case studies
- ▶ Recognize the role of research and practice

CHAPTER OUTLINE

- ▶ Research, Does It Even Matter?
- ▶ A Horse Is a Horse of Course . . . Unless It is Clever Hans
- ▶ Clever Hands: A Desire to Communicate
- ▶ Science: An Approach and Method
- ▶ Psychological Science Objectives
- ▶ Research Ethics and Designs

Research, Does It Even Matter?

Eating chocolate promotes world peace, says research.

©Brenda Carson/Shutterstock.com

© RTimages/Shutterstock.com

Have you ever heard any claims such as this? Have you ever come across news headlines or newspaper articles that have broad statements such as this example to the left? How do you respond to these headlines? Do you go out and get the biggest chocolate bar you can find? Do you feel better about the chocolate urges you have? Do you scratch your head and read further into the details? How you respond to these headlines might be one of the most important facets of research.

Let's consider a personal story of one of the authors. His 7-month-old son needed surgery to repair a hernia. As a parent, this was very worrisome. The author thought about all the potential scares that might race through many parents' minds, such as death, complications, extended surgery, and every other anxious thought related to negative consequences that could come upon his son. The fact his son was only 7 months old and still a baby made it even worse. His son was viewed as very young and fragile. After coming to terms with the idea that surgery would be best and that it would potentially be more risky for him to not have surgery, then the author had a moment of peace. That was until he was informed that some research has shown that anesthesia can be harmful for children under the age of 4. What? He was informed that some studies indicated anesthesia for young children could impair language development and cognitive abilities.

For a moment he thought that the experts must be correct. Though the author knew little about anesthesia, he felt competent to examine the other aspects of what the research claimed anesthesia supposedly affected; language and cognitive abilities. So, in true nerd fashion, he took a chance and ventured onto academic databases and looked up some of the research. When he looked into the articles, his worry became lessened. He discovered that some of the reported measures were not necessarily the standardized achievement tests used by psychologists or school psychologists. He also noted another very important find that eased his mind. Despite the fact that the most compelling study indicated statistically significant differences, it had some limitations. He knew this in the back of his mind. The voice of his doctoral research mentor and colleague, Dr. Chris Hart, was saying, "There is no perfect research study. All research studies have limitations."

These studies were limited. One of the limitations was that although there were statistically significant differences between two groups: the group of children given anesthesia and the group of children who were not given any, these differences on achievement measures were not clinically or meaningfully different. In other words, the scores were different from each other, but not drastically different from what you would expect to find within the normative range of the population. Another limitation was that the group of children who had anesthesia was not separated, meaning that children could have had multiple surgeries or just one and they were all lumped into this category.

It is imperative to understand that by no means were these studies bad science or poor research. The research was sound. Usually, it is not the research at fault but the mishandling or misunderstanding of research that brings about woe.

Thus, one of the major values of research is that people become good consumers of research. Though it would be a great venture to encourage students to all become researchers, the larger goal is to be able to digest, discuss, and inform others about research. This aspect of research will hold the greatest worth, especially as we consider research related to abnormal psychology.

You will certainly review aspects of research and science. However, before you delve into the jargon of research, let's review a few more examples of your role related to being a good consumer of research. Much of one of the author's understanding of being a good consumer of research is credited to his mentor, Dr. Chris Hart, who discussed two events that paint the picture of our role within research. Let's look at the first one.

A Horse Is a Horse of Course . . . Unless It Is Clever Hans

Have you ever heard of a horse that could do math? Well, a horse by the name of Clever Hans is one such horse. Other talking horses, such as Mr. Ed, could not compare to Clever Hans, as Hans demonstrated superb mathematical abilities.

Clever Hans was able to count things, such as windows on buildings and straw hats that people were wearing (Heinzen et al., 2015; Pfungst & Rosenthal, 1965). He was able to perform mathematical functions that a number of humans might even find challenging. Hans was able to add mathematical fractions and calculate square roots. These were the reasons he was deemed clever. Are you impressed yet?

© Mary Evans Picture Library

Clever Hans performed these feats through various ways. He would often tap his foot on the ground a number of times that corresponded with the answer to the question. For example, if you were to ask Clever Hans to add four plus five, then he would tap his foot nine times. Clever Hans would tap his foot to answer a number of mathematical questions. He also would answer questions by shaking his head and picking up colored scarves with his mouth (Heinzen et al., 2015).

All of this mathematical talent did not naturally flow from Hans. Much of Clever Hans's mathematical ability can be attributed to his teacher, Wilhelm von Osten, who was a retired mathematics teacher (Heinzen et al., 2015). Much like von Osten's dedication to teaching math to humans, he poured his attention into teaching Clever Hans.

It was not long before Clever Hans gained recognition and crowds emerged to watch his mathematical performances (Pfungst & Rosenthal, 1965). A duke, military officers, scientists, professors, and others in the general public were among some of those who Hans drew. Though Clever Hans gained much attention from people and media, his teacher, von Osten, did not utilize this momentum for business gains. He appeared more motivated to contribute to science. Clever Hans gained scientific credibility as a number of scientific and military authorities sent reports to newspapers and scientific organizations (Heinzen et al., 2015).

So, what are your thoughts of Clever Hans? He is fairly clever, right? Are you astounded by the abilities of humans to teach mathematics to horses? Or do you hold another sentiment? Do you think it is all preposterous? Well, if you think that it is absurd, or at least skeptical, then you would be in good company with psychologist Oskar Pfungst. Pfungst approached Clever Hans with skepticism and was unconvinced of Clever Hans's abilities. Skepticism refers to a philosophical approach of initial doubt or a position that seeks corroborative evidence or cogent logical claims. Pfungst wanted more empirical evidence. Empirical evidence refers to experiments designed to gather information about a problem from observation and use of the senses. Thus, Pfungst conducted a series of research trials to test whether Clever Hans was able to demonstrate mathematic ability (Heinzen et al., 2015).

Skepticism

An approach of initial doubt and questioning

Empirical

Gathering information through the senses

Oskar Pfungst devised an experiment in which Clever Hans was shown various numbers on different cards. Then, Clever Hans was to tap out his foot the number of times that equaled the answer to the mathematical problem, as he had been known for doing. However, there were two conditions in which Clever Hans was to do this. In one condition, Clever Hans and the person asking the question could both see the number on the card, and the other condition consisted of only Clever Hans being able to see the number on the card. Clever Hans scored 98% accuracy of correctly identifying the answers to the cards when he and the questioner could see the cards.

TABLE 4.1 Clear Thinking About Clever Hans

It was easy to deceive yourself about Clever Hans if you only paid attention to the shaded cell in the upper right-hand corner labeled "Confirmation Bias." To test whether Hans was being signaled, Pfungst conducted a series of simple tests that he called "With Knowledge" and "Without Knowledge" as outlined below.

Clever Hans	Hans Did Not Tap the Correct Number	Hans Tapped the Correct Number
"WITH KNOWLEDGE"	This happened occasionally but von Osten always had explanations	CONFIRMATION BIAS This happened frequently and got everyone excited about Clever Hans
"WITHOUT KNOWLEDGE"	This happened frequently after Stumpf and Pfungst designed tests that Hans could fail	This never happened except by chance

From "Clever Hans: What a Horse Can Teach Us about Self Deception" by Thomas E. Heinzen, Scott O. Lilienfeld, and Susan A. Nolan, published in *Skeptic 20.1*. Copyright © 2015 by Skeptic. Reprinted by permission.

TABLE 4.2

Method	The Number Displayed on Card	The Number Tapped by Clever Hans
Without knowledge	8	14
With knowledge	8	8
Without knowledge	4	8
With knowledge	4	4
Without knowledge	7	9
With knowledge	7	7
Without knowledge	10	17
With knowledge	10	10
Without knowledge	3	9
With knowledge	3	3

From "Clever Hans: What a Horse Can Teach Us about Self Deception" by Thomas E. Heinzen, Scott O. Lilienfeld, and Susan A. Nolan, published in *Skeptic 20.1*. Copyright © 2015 by Skeptic. Reprinted by permission.

However, when only Clever Hans could see the card, his score fell to only correctly identifying 8%. Further, Pfungst's trials indicated that Clever Hans could only successfully read cards with simple words when the questioner saw the cards too (100%), and was not as successful when only Clever Hans saw the cards (0%); (Heinzen et al., 2015). The tables from Heinzen and colleagues indicate the research design and findings from Pfungst's experiment.

Based on Pfungst's findings, maybe Clever Hans is not as clever as you initially thought or hoped. However, there is much to learn from Clever Hans. First, although he was no Einstein, Clever Hans was not entirely void of ability. In fact, he demonstrated firsthand learning principles of behaviorism. He was able to learn, via classical and operant conditioning, when to stop tapping his foot when he was signaled.

One of the heroes of the story of Clever Hans is that of Pfungst. He was one of the individuals who held a healthy amount of skepticism. Healthy skepticism refers to having doubts about phenomena and seeking further corroboration rather than outright denial and dismissal of any claims. Not only did Pfungst bring his healthy skepticism with him, he also employed aspects of science and research design to the case of Clever Hans. Pfungst highlights the role that we should consider taking when dealing with phenomena and when considering the rationale for the development of research in abnormal psychology.

So, are you thinking, "It's just a horse." This event may have been entertaining and ended with an unexpected twist for von Osten, one that was probably not anticipated when he began teaching Hans. However, this event may not appear to carry many negative consequences, other than for the pride of von Osten. Let's look at another event that also illuminates what role to assume in handling research, and one that reveals more dire consequences.

Clever Hands: A Desire to Communicate

Put yourself into a position in which you have a child that you love immensely. Now, suppose that your child was unable to communicate or speak with you. Throughout much of your child's life you have wondered about having conversations with your child and occasionally yearned for moments of verbal exchanges expressing your love for each other.

You discover that your child's difficulties with speaking are related to Autism Spectrum Disorder (ASD). Symptoms of ASD are deficits in social and emotional domains (American Psychiatric Association, 2013).

After many years of no changes in your child's ability to speak, you stumble upon a new method that claims to help children, such as yours, to communicate. The newer method involves a person who assists non-speaking children with typing so that they can communicate. For the first time in awhile you experience excitement and hope at the new possibility to finally receive an "I love you" from your child.

The Wendrow family was one of many families who were able to pursue facilitated communication to help their daughter, Aislinn, communicate (Alexander, 2009). Facilitated communication was developed out of speech pathology to help non-speaking people communicate by having a facilitator use specific placements on the individual's wrist and arm (Crossley, 1992). Facilitated communication had probably brought some excitement and relief for the Wendrow family until the day when Aislinn and her facilitated communicator typed a message that she had been sexually assaulted by her father (Alexander, 2009). Following this message, there was an investigation and legal proceedings (Alexander, 2009).

Much like Clever Hans, some psychologists and researchers had been skeptical and raised concerns of facilitated communication. Lab studies were conducted which revealed there was no evidence that a person with a disability was able to communicate, but rather the responses appear to come from the facilitated communicator (Fuller & Sparrow, 2003; Green & Shane, 1994; Wegner et al., 2003). For the Wendrow family, the same results surfaced in the courtroom, in which the absence of the facilitated communicator in hearing the questions resulted in Aislinn, by way of the facilitated communicator, only typing random keystrokes (Alexander, 2009). The charges against Mr. Wendrow were ultimately dropped. Surprisingly, even with the evidence against the use of facilitated communication, it is still practiced (Lilienfeld, Marshall, et al., 2014). Thus, even when scientific evidence is presented, some practices are slow to die.

Science: An Approach and Method

Hopefully, you have noted the common thread in all of the aforementioned examples and events—a scientific approach. The scientific approach was the safeguard that prevented Mr. Wendrow from being charged falsely. This stance was what motivated Oskar Pfungst to go beyond a confirmation bias and test whether Clever Hans could actually demonstrate mathematical skills. Confirmation bias is the tendency for humans to seek evidence to confirm a preexisting belief. For example, von Osten was determined to teach Clever Hans and initially operated from a belief that Hans could perform mathematics and a number of other intelligent activities. Thus, all evidence following von Osten's hope had confirmed his preexisting belief. Had von Osten began with a question of whether Hans could even learn math, then the case of Clever Hans might have looked different.

Science as an approach is what led one of the authors to sift through empirical articles to make an informed decision about his son's surgery. This approach should not be new or foreign to you. The scientific approach has been regarded as a position that we all assume as early as infancy, as

Confirmation Bias

Tendency to only acknowledge information that confirms an existing belief

© pavla/Shutterstock.com

we approach the world with questions or concern and seek to test ourselves within our environment (Gopnick et al., 2001). For example, as a young child learning to walk and falling down several times, you began testing the concept of gravity. You did not formally use a method, but you were testing yourself within your environment. Another example might be all the questions you asked as a child. One of the author's sons typically asks why to any statement that is provided to him. He is curious and interested in the world. In other words, you naturally seem interested in the world, how it works, and seek to test things beyond how they initially appear. This approach can sometimes become peripheral as you habituate to phenomena, settle for what is initially presented, or dismiss information in order to confirm a bias.

Biases and habituation are what lead people to accept myths of abnormality. So, why might anyone do this? Less energy and time is exerted when relying on preexisting beliefs for understanding things. Movies, as the primary source of understanding abnormality, are a passive means to develop beliefs by which you may later draw from. Sometimes, it can seemingly serve people well to dismiss science as an approach for the use of myths. For example, a person who has heard of an old remedy for back pain, in which you place a bar of soap in your pocket, may be convinced to try it. Why not? A bar of soap may be a cheaper treatment than a number of other biological treatments. Thus, without even asking if this is effective, the person is convinced and tries it. Following using the soap, the person reports reduced back pain. This demonstrates two things: how someone might abandon psychological science for mental efficiency, and the placebo effect. The placebo effect is a change that occurs based on the expectation of an effect rather than the effect itself. When investigating the effectiveness of psychotherapy treatment, it is important to understand the effects of the treatment apart from the placebo effect. Much research and literature has attended to this difference in psychotherapy research (Lambert & Ogles, 2004).

Placebo Effect

A change that occurs based on the expectation of change

Along with psychotherapy research, it is also crucial to examine the effect of treatment apart from the spurious effects, or what we think to be effective. In an attempt to address this, Lilienfeld, Ritschel, and colleagues (2014) provided a taxonomy of 26 causes of spurious therapeutic effectiveness and ways to safeguard against these (Lilienfeld, Ritschel, et al., 2014). The placebo effect is one of these causes and the inclusion of measures of proposed mediators and measures of expectations are research safeguards (Lilienfeld, Ritschel, et al., 2014). Regression to the mean is another cause of spurious therapeutic effectiveness, in which patients often enter therapy when in an extreme situation and may return to their baseline without a regard to treatment (Lilienfeld, Ritschel, et al., 2014). Using pre- and post-test measures with high reliability may safeguard against this concern (Lilienfeld, Ritschel, et al., 2014).

Whether it is becoming complacent, going with the easiest path, or a human error, science operates in a manner to combat these issues and challenges myths. Science often seeks to dig deeper and fuels more questions. The scientist is usually the person, like Pfungst or Wegner, who appears to have questions and a certain level of doubt. The scientist is the one who thinks scientifically, which involves empiricism, rationalism, and skepticism (Schafersman, 2012). Empiricism consists of gathering evidence through observation and one's senses. Rationalism is the logical reasoning involved in understanding and making sense of evidence. Lastly, skepticism is the continuous questioning and reevaluation of evidence and beliefs.

Be cautious of the scientist that claims it is absolutely true, or strongly affirms some research claims as definitive, unchanging truisms, or frequently uses the word "proves." The scientist who approaches science with a healthy skepticism often has more questions and speaks in terms of *falsification* or *corroboration* rather than proof (Popper, 1999, p. 20). Karl Popper is a philosopher of science who affirms the stance of falsification. His approach is one of a few approaches to science.

Philosophies of Science. There are differing viewpoints on what constitutes a science (O'Donohue et al., 2007). O'Donohue and colleagues discussed these various philosophies of science, or images as they refer to them. Let's consider some of these philosophies before moving forward with the formal method of science.

As previously discussed, Karl Popper asserts that science is seeking falsification. Falsification means that your approach is to disconfirm or to find instances of a case being false. The idea is to find a theory false rather than seeking to prove any theory. One of the most common examples of this view is in thinking of swans. A statement such as "all swans are white" is a claim that can demonstrate the principle of falsification. If there were an instance of one green swan, or any other color, observed now or any time in the future, then the claim would be false. In other words, it only takes one non-white swan to be found to dismiss the claim. Thus, the approach of a scientist from this stance is to falsify claims rather than seeking to prove them. The goal is to corroborate your findings through trying to prove yourself wrong rather than trying to prove yourself right. In doing this, you protect yourself against biases and belief perseverance. Belief perseverance is the tendency to continue to hold a belief when presented with evidence that is contrary to your belief.

Science can also be viewed in terms of developmental changes or paradigmatic shifts (Kuhn, 1970; O'Donohue et al., 2007). Thomas Kuhn discusses science in terms of paradigms. A paradigm is a model that unifies a theory or scientific approach. Kuhn affirmed that science undergoes stages

Falsification

An approach to disconfirm findings rather than to prove true

Belief Perseverance

Tendency to continue to hold a belief when presented with evidence that is contrary to your belief

Paradigm

A unifying system or approach of science

of development. Science begins as an immature process where little or no agreement is defined and develops into an established approach. Then, when various anomalies or research studies cannot be accounted for by the established approach, then the paradigm shifts and a newer paradigm emerges. To illustrate this, think of how the Earth may have once been considered to be flat. How people operated in the world when holding this belief is different than when things have changed, and people have understood the Earth to not be flat. Upon newer evidence the paradigm shifts and we understand that the world is not flat.

Some authors have suggested that in science, anything goes (O'Donohue et al., 2007). Paul Feyerbend proposed that science is anarchistic. The approach of questioning and skepticism remains within this perspective. However, the image of science goes beyond just questioning what you know and extends to questioning the methods by which you seek to discover.

Science can also be viewed as persuasive (O'Donohue et al., 2007). This image of science suggests that scientists are operating to persuade themselves and then can persuade others. The use of a good research design or procedure that eliminates biases is a step to persuade yourself and others. The image is that a person has followed particular steps or procedures and thus any findings are more persuasive.

So, what is science? What makes psychology a science and does psychology uphold these images? O'Donohue and colleagues (2007) propose another image, in that psychologists have constructed their own images of science. O'Donohue and colleagues discuss three important figures (Freud, Skinner, and Rogers) who have had significant influence within clinical psychology and who have all demonstrated various images of science. They suggest that science involves more complexity than one specific image. However, they propose that science provides a foundation for clinical psychologists to effectively solve problems and approach questions about humans in a natural environment. Science provides "us with knowledge of [human] nature" (Kitcher, 2001, p. 9). Whether seeking to falsify claims or to persuade in answering questions or solving problems, clinical and counseling psychologists use the formal scientific method.

Scientific Method

The formal approach to solve problems

Scientific Method. The scientific method is the formal approach used for problem-solving and it helps you in myth busting. You probably use the scientific method more frequently, and less formally, than you realize. As you read through the formal processes of the scientific method, think about how you use these processes within your everyday life. The series of processes involved within the scientific method are: (1) generating a question or stating a problem, (2) formulating a hypothesis, (3) testing with an experiment, (4) collecting data, (5) analyzing data, and (6) drawing conclusions (See Figure 4.1).

Science and research often begins with some question or problem. You may have various questions that you want solved. Some questions may seem

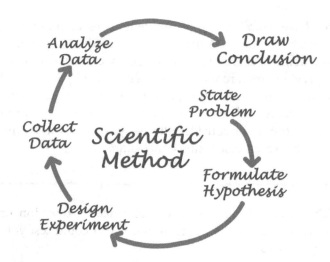

FIGURE 4.1   Processes of the Scientific Method
©arka38/Shutterstock.com

more innocuous than others. Maybe you want to know how to more effectively maximize your study behaviors, or you want to know how to effectively help someone who is struggling with depression. In either case, you have some problem that can also be phrased as a question.

In this process, you want to review what has already been asked and researched. There is rarely a need to test something that has already been well corroborated. Also, you want to determine if there is insufficient research in the area where you have stated a problem. One of the ways to achieve this goal is to conduct a literature review. A literature review is finding and reading various scholarly research articles on a specific topic. There are a number of databases that contain access to scholarly journal articles. In conducting a literature review, you will read research to determine what has been investigated with the given topic and what is missing. This process will provide you with answers to your initial problem, refine your research question, or do both.

Literature Review

Identifying and reading literature pertaining to a specific research topic

---

LET'S PRACTICE. Think of a research question or problem you would like to know more about. Write that problem down.

For example, a research question might be:

Do violent video games cause children to be more aggressive?

This is a research question that some people may have, especially if they are considering exposing a child to this media or games or even if they were exposed to violent media and games as a child.

Hypothesis

A prediction made about a testable phenomenon

Theory

A framework for understanding psychological phenomenon and processes

After you have established your problem or research question, then you will formulate a hypothesis. A hypothesis is a prediction you make in terms of a testable statement. It is a prediction made because it should be informed by theory, previous research, or inferences. A theory is a unifying framework for various claims and studies, often used to make predictions. The statement has to be testable so that you can corroborate your prediction and further build the theory or consider alternative theories, as Kuhn discussed. We will revisit this when discussing conclusions.

LET'S PRACTICE. Using your previous research question or problem, think about what you would expect to find if you could test your problem. Write your hypothesis.

Using the above question, a hypothesis could be developed for violent video game exposure and aggressive behavior. The hypothesis could be:

Violent video games increase aggressive behavior.

Operational Definitions

Specific statements of psychological variables that can be measured or manipulated

Construct

Conceptualization of a psychological phenomenon that is built by observations and research studies

Variables

Measures or manipulations

Dependent Variable

The behavior that is being measured

Following your hypothesis, then you will design your research experiment or study. In doing this it is vital to attend to the language you use. You will have to create operational definitions. Operational definitions are specific statements used for testing hypotheses. Think of the violent video game and aggressive behavior research question. What is aggression? The term is a bit vague and may lead to different thoughts about what constitutes aggression. Thus, aggression would be considered a psychological construct. A psychological construct is a broad conceptualization of a psychological phenomenon that is built by observations and research studies. Many people can probably conceptually think of various aggressive acts. For example, drop-kicking someone in the back of the head would be considered aggressive. Punching someone in the arm would qualify as an aggressive act. Also, yelling at someone could also fit the bill of aggression. Thus, when designing a study, it is imperative that you specifically define what you mean by your terms that you plan to test or manipulate.

The measures or manipulations are referred to as variables. There are two types of variables: dependent and independent variables. These terms sometimes can be confused with each other or incorrectly labeled. The dependent variable is what is being measured. Thinking about the aggression study, the dependent variable is aggression. Aggression is the dependent variable because you want to test what effect something has on this behavior being measured. To help you discern dependent variables, look for indicators of what is being measured or observed. In the above example, the question asks if aggressive behavior will be increased. To note an increase, this behavior must be measured or observed. Thus, the independent variable would be video games. An independent variable is a variable that is being manipulated. Therefore, you may want to manipulate exposure to video games: violent or non-violent. Then, you can compare the effect it has on the dependent variable, aggression. The hypothesis aforementioned was that violent video games would increase aggressive behavior. Thus, by manipulating exposure to a violent video game, you can compare aggressive behavior and determine if a significant difference exists.

Independent Variable

The condition or factor that is being manipulated or changed

LET'S PRACTICE with another study.

Say that you are interested in factors that influence people to go along with other group members, in that you are interested in conformity. After an exhaustive literature review and realizing that a number of social situations have varying numbers of choices for people, you decide you want to see how choice affects conformity. Thinking back to independent and dependent variables, can you identify each in this study?

Answers: Due to conformity being the variable that is being measured, it is the dependent variable. Due to you wanting to see the effects of choice, choice is the independent variable.

Thus, in designing an experiment it is crucial to determine the variables and the operational definitions. This step is important for you as the researcher to guide your research. Also, it is important for others who may want to know what you did exactly, how to understand your design, and to know the basis by which you are drawing your conclusions. Practice defining your variables based on your research question.

After establishing your variables within your design, you will plan your research procedures. Procedures are a specific plan for how the research will be conducted from the beginning to the very end. Your research procedures are written out explicitly and with as much specificity as possible. The idea is that whoever reads your procedures could run your study as if they were the researcher. Another way to think about the procedures section is to think about writing a how-to paper, such as how to make a peanut butter and jelly sandwich. If you write the procedure out of order, then you might be eating a jar of peanut butter instead of a pb and j sandwich.

After designing your research study, then you are almost ready to collect data. Prior to collecting data there is one more step that precedes data collection, which is seeking approval from the institutional review board or IRB. Institutional review boards are members of an institution that oversee research to ensure the safety and protection of human subjects. The task of the IRB is to determine that risks to the participants have been minimized. Many IRBs will ask that all researchers include some verification that they have completed a research ethics course for working with human subjects.

Once the IRB has approved the study then you may begin collecting data. Data collection is the process of following your research procedures and gathering data based on your design. Depending on your methods, data may be collected by the researcher, a research assistant, or collected through the participants' responses on forms or questionnaires. For example, a researcher measuring aggressive behavior, defined as the number of times a child punches a toy doll within a 10-minute interval, may collect the data by recording participants and subsequently counting frequencies of a behavior.

After you have collected your data then you are ready to analyze your data. This step is the final step that will assist you in determining if you are able to reject your hypothesis or fail to reject your hypothesis. Most researchers will transfer data into some software that has statistical functions. Though there is some software that is used more commonly than others, not all researchers use the same software. The statistical analyses conducted on the data will depend on the research question and design.

After you have analyzed your data, then you will interpret your findings and draw conclusions. Based on statistical analyses and your hypothesis, you will determine whether your predictions were observed or not. You may also note if there were any unanticipated results. In understanding your findings, you will consider the limitations of your research. In the words of research mentor Dr. Chris Hart, "There is no perfect research study." Thus, you need to consider the limitations of the study you conducted. This will assist you in the conclusions you draw and the implications of your current study. You will not want to draw conclusions based on analyses that were not conducted or make statements too broad for the study you conducted. For example, if you were to say that playing violent video games causes all people to be more aggressive when you only tested children, then this conclusion would be broader than the study you conducted.

Though no single study is perfect, each study conducted adds to the understanding of a psychological construct. A psychological construct unifies a related set of psychological process or phenomena. Remember that you are taking a construct, isolating a specific and measurable aspect of that construct, and making inferences that feed back into that construct (see Figure 4.2).

For example, if you wanted to study aggression, then aggression would be your construct. You may look at how violent video games affect aggressive behavior, namely punching a toy doll following exposure to the violent video game. This would be one study. Let's say that violent video games led to higher frequencies of punching a toy doll. Then, this study would add to what we know about aggression. Then, another study examines the effects of violent movies on aggressive behavior, such as the frequency of yelling at someone following the viewing of a violent show. This sequence of

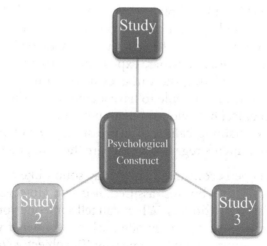

FIGURE 4.2   Psychological Constructs
Courtesy of Drew Curtis

conducting individual studies and drawing conclusions informs theory and helps us understand psychological constructs. This is the process of research.

Psychological Science Objectives

Psychological science helps us know things about ourselves and others and allows us to use that knowledge. The scientific approach and methods provide the basics for handling and gathering information. The reasons for employing a scientific approach and methods lead to broader objectives for psychological science. There are four main objectives of psychological science: describe, predict, explain, and control (Myers & Hansen, 2006).

The first objective involves describing human behavior. The scientific approach and method allows you to get a basic knowledge of a psychological construct (Myers & Hansen, 2006). For example, when you research depression you are able to develop a body of knowledge about the symptoms of depression. You can describe depression based on the symptoms that one may express. By describing depression, you will be more equipped to recognize it if someone is expressing symptoms of depression.

The second objective of psychological science is prediction. After recognizing and describing a psychological phenomenon, then you will be able to predict particular things related to that phenomenon that might occur in the future (Myers & Hansen, 2006). For example, if you know that most people who have major depressive disorder may have thoughts that reduce their motivation during an episode of depression, then you could predict that a person experiencing a depressive episode may avoid going to a therapy session or may not want to leave their house for a period of time. Prediction allows practitioners to work with clients and alter treatments based on what they might know about a disorder or human behavior.

The third object is for psychologists to explain human behavior. Through researching, understanding, and making predictions, psychologists are able to explain the psychological construct. The ability to explain allows others to reproduce the research. Further, explanation provides a greater depth of understanding by isolating the variables involved in the research. Thus, researchers and clinicians are able to have a commonly shared understanding of the psychological behavior or phenomenon (Myers & Hansen, 2006). For example, by explaining causes of depression, psychologists are able to provide similar treatments regardless of where they are practicing.

The last objective is control. Control may sound like a scary, *1984* big-brother type of objective, but rest assured, it is not. However, many people think psychologists try to do this. When you tell someone you are a psychologist or a psychology student, they often ask or wonder if you are analyzing them and will control them in some way. The objective of control is not intended for psychologists to play puppet-master with people, rather to assist others in controlling themselves and their environment. If you know all the variables of an environment that may lead (through prediction) to you feeling angry and becoming aggressive, then you can control your environment to avoid being aggressive. The objective of control differs from other objectives in that it extends beyond merely knowing about a phenomenon into acting upon that knowledge. Control is also why people seek out therapy, because they want to control their symptoms (Myers & Hansen, 2006). For example, people who have been diagnosed with major depressive disorder may want to go to a therapist so that they no longer experience depression, through controlling their thoughts and their environment.

Research Ethics and Designs

© Saverio blasi/Shutterstock.com

What are some of the ways that you think psychologists may conduct research with humans? What are some of the myths that you have heard or have come to believe about psychologists and studying abnormal human behavior? Do you think that psychologist go around shocking people? Have you ever signed up for a psychology study and suspiciously wondered if the researchers are tricking you about something?

Some of these conceptions or myths you have about psychological research may be based on some historical context. Historically, some psychological studies have been scrutinized based on ethics (e.g., Haney et al., 1973; Watson & Rayner, 1920). Other studies may have promoted ideas about psychological research and shock because of convincing participants that they delivered electric shock to other participants (Milgram, 1963). Whatever images or myths you may have about psychological research, you can rest assured that psychologists conduct research within the scope of ethical guidelines laid out by the American Psychological Association (2002, 2010). These ethical guidelines promote benefits and minimize harm to participants. Also, another ethical oversight for human participants, which was previously mentioned, is the IRB.

Psychologists conduct scientific research in a variety of ways. The types of research depend on the nature of what is being studied and situational demands or ethical considerations. The ideal research situation, often posed as a question in a research methods class is, "If you had unlimited resources, then what would you study and how?" With unlimited resources, time, and no situational constraints, a research study may look vastly different than typical studies conducted.

Experiments. Most psychology researchers will seek to conduct *experiments*. Experiments are valued due to the ability to isolate a variable and make a causal inference about human behavior. Essentially, by creating conditions where everything is similar except for the variable you want to test (the independent variable), you are able to compare its effect on what you are measuring (the dependent variable). By making causal inferences, you are able to meet the objectives of psychological science. Thus, using an experiment enables you to isolate a variable and attribute an effect to that variable, which allows you to control for that variable in future research or practice.

Experiments

Research studies that allow casual inferences to be made

In order to make sure conditions are as similar as possible, you need each group member to represent the general population equally. To do this, researchers will use *random selection*. Random selection of participants means that participants are chosen in an unbiased and randomized manner. Random selection will facilitate samples that are representative of the general population of interest. Doing so will allow researchers to generalize their findings. After you randomly select, *random assignment* is critical. Random assignment means that the researchers have used an unbiased method to place participants in each condition. This is done so that participants can be equally distributed in each condition. Random assignment will support comparisons that are being made by the measurements.

Random Selection

Choosing participants in an unbiased manner

Random Assignment

Using an unbiased method to place participants in each research condition

Let's reconsider the aggression and violent video game study. You want to see if the effects of violent video game exposure causes aggressive behavior. First you randomly select people to participate in your study. After random selection, you randomly assign people to one of two choice conditions: an

Experimental Condition

The research group that receives the manipulation or intervention of a variable

Control Condition

The research group that mimics the experimental condition but has no manipulation

experimental condition or a control condition. An experimental condition is the condition that contains the manipulation of the independent variable, which would be exposure to violent video games in this example. The control condition is the condition that mimics the experimental condition without the manipulation, which in this example would be a non-violent video game. In both conditions, all measures and procedures will be identical, with the exception of the nature of the video game. Thus, participants will all play video games but one group of participants will play a violent video game and the other group will play a non-violent video game (see Figure 4.3).

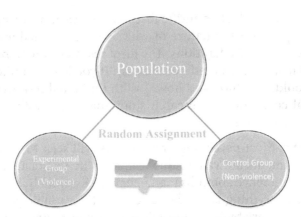

FIGURE 4.3   Experimental Design
Courtesy of Drew Curtis

In Figure 4.3 you see that random assignment of participants to each group creates similar groups with the only difference between the groups being the nature of the stimulus, violent video game or non-violent video game. Thus, when you measure aggressive behavior following the participants playing video games, you can then compare the amount of aggressive behavior between each condition. If there is a difference, then you may attribute the difference to the violence variable, as everything else remained the same and was tested on people who equally represented the population.

This is how experiments work. The idea is that by keeping everything the same except for the variable of interest, you can then draw a causal inference about the variable or generalize that the variable had some effect. Researchers use experiments to understand and treat mental disorders.

Much of psychotherapy research uses experiments to determine whether the treatments are empirically supported. The American Psychological Association Task Force on Promotion and Dissemination of Psychological Procedures (1995) published guidelines for empirically validated treatments. Empirically supported treatments (EST) are psychological treatments that have been "shown to be efficacious in controlled research with a delineated population" (Chambless & Hollon, 1998, p. 7). Efficacy refers to testing the effects of a treatment to a comparison condition when participants have been randomly assigned (Chambless & Hollon, 1998; Kendall et al., 2004). One of the early investigations of the efficacy of cognitive therapy for clients with depression compared cognitive therapy to pharmacotherapy (Rush et al., 1977). The study corroborated the use of cognitive therapy as an efficacious intervention for clients with depression.

Efficacy

The effects of a treatment compared to a comparison condition

Efficacy is different than the effectiveness of a treatment due to efficacy involving benefits of a treatment found from a single study. Effectiveness is the generalizability of a treatment and its use in multiple settings with a variety of practitioners and clients (Kendall et al., 2004). The idea for psychological treatments is that they would not only be efficacious but also effective and able to be used with a variety of clients in numerous settings.

Effectiveness

Generalizability of a treatment

Ideally, researchers will be able to conduct experiments to draw causal inferences. However, the reason that the ideal research question is ideal is because research does carry constraints. Some of the constraints are resources, time, and ethics. Due to these factors, other research designs may be used.

Correlational Studies. Is the use of social media and depression related? One research study explored how social comparison and the usage of time spent on Facebook were related to depressive symptoms (Steers et al., 2014). Steers and colleagues (2014) conducted two studies that found a relationship between social comparisons on Facebook and the amount of time using Facebook with depressive symptoms. Specifically, people who spent more time on Facebook and compared themselves to others had expressed more depressive symptoms.

This study highlights a correlational design. It was not an experiment due to not randomly assigning participants to use Facebook. Thus, causal inferences are unable to be made with the study. This is the biggest limitation of correlational studies. The inability to draw causal inferences leads people to only affirm the strength of a relationship between variables. Exercise caution when discussing the generalizations of correlational studies. A classic example of this would be that a strong positive correlation exists between the height of a person and their education. Height does not cause one to acquire education. However, they are related because often as one grows,

© PK Studio/Shutterstock.com

they learn more and become more educated. Thus, correlations do not equal causation. However, correlational designs provide useful information.

A correlational study is a research design that explores the relationships between two or more variables. Knowing the relationships between variables provides you with useful information. For example, the Steers and colleagues (2014) research offers quality information about relationships between social media usage and depressive symptoms. Knowing that greater use of Facebook and making social comparisons to others is related to greater depressive symptoms provides you with useful information. With this information you could reduce the amount of time spent on social media or alter the way in which you use social media in attempts to reduce depressive symptoms. For clinicians who are working with clients who are depressed, the clinician can assess the amount of time spent on social media and the social comparisons made for behavioral modifications or work with automatic thoughts.

As correlational designs investigate relationships, it is crucial to determine the strength and directionality of the relationship or what kind of relationship one variable has with another. Correlations may be positive or negative. A positive correlation means that as one variable increases so does the other. In contrast, a negative correlation means that as one variable increases, the other variable decreases. The correlation coefficient is a statistic that provides you with information about the strength of the relationship between the two variables. This coefficient can be computed on various statistical software programs. The correlation coefficient ranges between −1.0 to +1.0. The positive or negative sign indicates the relationship direction, positive or negative. As a correlation coefficient approaches one, then the relationship is deemed strong. Therefore, as a correlation coefficient approaches zero, this means that the correlation is weaker. Thus, a correlation coefficient of 0.87 would indicate a strong positive relationship between two variables.

Case Studies. A woman enters therapy and discusses her aunt who died. The aunt was made into a mummy so that she could be present at the family dinners. This is one case told by Jon Carlson which was published in a book with a number of other eminent therapists who shared their most unusual cases (Kottler & Carlson, 2003). These cases are examples of case studies.

Case studies have been a crucial part of the development of a variety of psychotherapy theories, research, training, and teaching. Case studies are often used to enhance learning about abnormal psychology (Oltmanns et al., 2012). In fact, graduate counseling and clinical psychology students will often be exposed to a number of different cases when learning a variety of skills. Some graduate psychopathology courses begin class with a case study activity, deemed a dose of Dr. House (Curtis et al., 2014). Students enter class and are presented with some details of a case in which they are asked to discuss potential diagnoses, differential diagnoses, and other questions or concerns they might have for the case.

Positive Correlation

A relationship between two variables in that as one variable increases so does the other

Negative Correlation

A relationship between two variables in that as one variable increases, then the other variable decreases

Correlation Coefficient

A statistic that provides you with information about the strength of the relationship between the two variables

Case Vignette

One of the cases presented on the first day of class looks similar to this:

A woman enters a psychologist's office, avoids eye contact, and speaks minimally, no more than five words. The client mostly shakes or nods her head to affirm or disconfirm questions that the therapist asks. The client seems noticeably more anxious when the therapist asks open-ended questions, exhibited by the client shaking and squeezing her hands together. The client indicated that she wanted the therapist to help her but did not offer much more than that.

Based on this case, practice writing some of your thoughts, potential diagnoses, differential diagnoses, and other questions or concerns they might have for the case.

© DedMityay/Shutterstock.com

One of the ways that you will gain conceptualization of the various disorders will be through case studies. Case studies can paint a picture for students to see what a disorder looks like. Through case studies, people can gain a greater understanding of a sample client and their struggles. Essentially, the imagination of what "crazy" looks like gets substituted with a genuine instance.

On the other hand, case studies may provide clinicians with a unique account of behaviors or a cluster of symptoms that has not been encountered previously or has yet to be fully understood, such as some of those cases described in Kottler and Carlson's (2003) text. Keep in mind that psychopathology deals with a small frequency, the lower end of the normative distribution. Thus, unique cases represent a very small percent of the population. Therefore, there may be more difficulty in understanding and treating some of these cases. This is especially true if you are seeking to research a group of people who exhibit the same aspects of psychopathology. By default, your population of a specific sample size of interest will be small. Detailing and disseminating unique cases allows practitioners and researchers to have some starting point in working with similar cases and in initiating other lines of research.

A number of notable and diverse psychological players have contributed through case studies (see Hersen, 2002). Some of these influential individuals include Sigmund Freud, Victor Frankl, Carl Rogers, and Aaron Beck. Much of psychoanalysis was developed through case studies, such as that of Anna O or Dora (Breuer & Freud, 1957; Freud, 1963). Case studies offer substantial benefits for clinical research and psychological theory. Davison and Lazarus (2007) discussed six features of how case studies contribute to research:

- ▶ A case study may cast doubt on a general theory.
- ▶ A case study may provide a valuable heuristic to subsequent and better controlled research.
- ▶ A case study can provide the opportunity to apply principles and notions in entirely new ways.
- ▶ A case study can, under certain circumstances, provide enough experimenter control over a phenomenon to furnish "scientifically acceptable" information.
- ▶ A case study may permit the investigation, although poorly controlled, of rare but important phenomena.
- ▶ A case study can put "meat" on "the theoretical skeleton."

Though case study methods offer clinicians robust information and even information that may challenge theoretical approaches, there are some limitations in its use. The primary limitation of the case study is that you are unable to draw causal inferences due to the lack of control. This is also important for generalizability. Depth of observation from one case or a few cases does not provide researchers with the authority to make large or broad conclusions to the general population.

The National Institute of Mental Health (NIMH) has put forth the Research Domain Criteria Initiative (RDoC). The initiative is designed to offer a framework for researchers to integrate multiple levels of analyses in understanding normal and abnormal human behavior (see Figure 4.4; NIMH, 2020). In understanding that psychopathology is dynamic (recall from Chapter 1) and that several factors contribute to its development (Diathesis-Stress Model), the RDoC is a framework that facilitates researchers to think about and contribute to understanding abnormal human behavior across those levels. Additionally, researchers can conduct studies drawing from various areas within their field or even across disciplines.

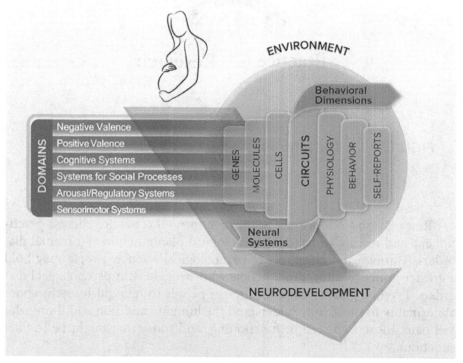

FIGURE 4.4   Research Domain Criteria Initiative (RDoC)
Courtesy of NIMH

Conclusion

Practitioners and researchers both play a key role in contributing to the development of research. There is often a gap between research and practice. Davison and Lazarus (2007) claimed, "Many regard the laboratory and the clinic as opposite ends of a continuum" (p. 149). Practitioners may be biased in favor of traditional psychotherapy methods or interventions at the expense of being helpful for clients. Practitioners may be viewed as bias-laden and anecdotal (Davison & Lazarus, 2007). Researchers may be partial to investigate issues that are popular or receive attention from granting bodies rather than attend to the needs of practitioners. Research may also be viewed as too "precise, controlled, and uncontaminated" (Davison & Lazarus, 2007, p. 149). However, it is essential that researchers and clinicians bridge the gap between research and practice to shape both. Practitioners can inform researchers about the issues that are important within practice or the areas that need more investigation. Researchers can contribute to practitioners as well through empirically validating treatments or adding to the knowledge base of psychopathology (see Figure 4.5).

Practice   Research

FIGURE 4.5   The Informative Role of Research and Practice
Courtesy of Drew Curtis

Research and science are ways to inform the public, clients, practitioners, and researchers about psychological phenomenon and mental disorders. Through the objectives of psychological science, people may hold a greater understanding about people who struggle with psychological disorders. Psychological science encourages people to relinquish myths about abnormality to more fully understand the human condition and those who feel pain, those impaired in functioning, and those that might be in fatal situations.

So, the next time you read headlines that state "research finds that eating chocolate promotes world peace" or some bold claim about research, then you should be more equipped to handle the claim rather than assume it is broadly established as true or that the research is bogus. You can ask questions such as for whom, how much chocolate, and world peace as operationally defined by what? Digging deeper into the research will provide you with these answers and reveal the limitations of the research. Also, you will become a better consumer of research. You do not necessarily need to be a researcher to understand the value of research. One of the greatest tools for busting myths is scientific inquiry, examination, and study. Understanding science and research should better equip you to handle myths, misconceptions, and to critically evaluate movies.

CHAPTER REVIEW

QUESTIONS

1. How did a horse contribute to psychological science? How is this related to facilitated communication?

2. What are the various images of science?

3. What is the scientific method and how does it assist people in daily living? How does it help clinical research and practice?

4. What are the objectives of psychological science?

5. What are some of the means by which science is conducted? What is the importance of case studies?

KEY TERMS

Skepticism

Empirical

Confirmation Bias

Placebo Effect

Falsification

Belief Perseverance

Paradigm

Scientific Method

Literature Review

Hypothesis

Theory

Operational Definitions

Construct

Variables

Dependent Variable

Independent Variable

Experiments

Random Selection

Random Assignment

Experimental Condition

Control Condition

Efficacy

Effectiveness

Positive Correlation

Negative Correlation

Correlation Coefficient

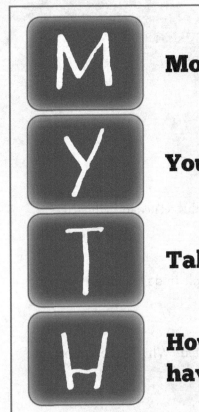

Movies

Your experience

Talk about the differences

How does this relate to what you have learned about abnormality?

CHAPTER FIVE

NEURODEVELOPMENTAL AND ELIMINATION DISORDERS

LEARNING OBJECTIVES

- ▶ Examine myths related to attention-deficit/hyperactivity disorder
- ▶ Identify diagnostic criteria of attention-deficit/hyperactivity disorder
- ▶ Discuss the 4 Fs of attention-deficit/hyperactivity disorder
- ▶ Differentiate gender and age factors related to attention-deficit/hyperactivity disorder
- ▶ Identify assessments for attention-deficit/hyperactivity disorder
- ▶ Explore a brief history of intellectual disability
- ▶ Discuss the DSM-5 criteria and 4 Fs of intellectual disability
- ▶ Examine the severity specifiers of intellectual disability
- ▶ Explore the etiology of intellectual disability
- ▶ Recognize myths and actual aspects of autism spectrum disorder
- ▶ Discuss the DSM-5 criteria and 4 Fs of autism spectrum disorder
- ▶ Explore the etiology of autism spectrum disorder
- ▶ Discuss elimination disorders
- ▶ Apply the diagnostic criteria of these disorders
- ▶ Examine treatments and theories of these disorders

CHAPTER OUTLINE

- ▶ ADHD: Pathologizing Children or a Real Problem?—MYTH
- ▶ DSM-5 Criteria for Attention-Deficit/Hyperactivity Disorder
- ▶ The 4 Fs of ADHD More Than "Oh Look, There's a Squirrel"
- ▶ ADHD: Gender and Age

- ▶ Assessments for ADHD
- ▶ Intellectual Disability: Humanity in Diminished Intellect
- ▶ The 4 Fs of Intellectual Disability
- ▶ The Etiology of Intellectual Disability
- ▶ Autism Spectrum Disorder—MYTH
- ▶ DSM-5 Criteria for Autism Spectrum Disorder
- ▶ The 4 Fs of Autism Spectrum Disorder
- ▶ Etiology of Autism Spectrum Disorder
- ▶ Elimination Disorders
- ▶ The 4 Fs of Elimination Disorders
- ▶ Theories and Treatments of Neurodevelopmental and Elimination Disorders
- ▶ ADHD
- ▶ Intellectual Disability
- ▶ Autism Spectrum Disorder
- ▶ Elimination Disorders

ADHD: Pathologizing Children or a Real Problem?

© one photo/Shutterstock.com

There are a wide array of opinions about Attention-Deficit/Hyperactivity Disorder (ADHD) and many of these beliefs may stem from myths we have developed about ADHD. Ideas you formed about ADHD may have come from movies, news, and your experiences. Some of these ideas may have elements of truth whereas others may not. Journal about your MYTHs related to ADHD. You can discuss movies that depict ADHD, how media portrays ADHD, and your own experiences or the experiences of others whom you know. Then, reflect on any differences and how these experiences and beliefs relate to what you have learned thus far about abnormality.

If you have seen the movie *Up* then you see an example of how films portray ADHD through a dog named Dug. In the movie, Dug is a talking dog who is easily distracted with squirrels. However, do people actually have ADHD?

One of the most popular myths about ADHD is that it is not real. The idea behind this myth is that psychologists, health professionals, teachers,

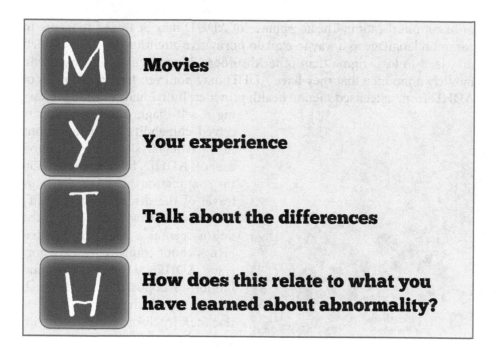

M Movies

Y Your experience

T Talk about the differences

H How does this relate to what you have learned about abnormality?

and parents have colluded in pathologizing children. The thought fueling the idea is that hyperactive kids are just kids being kids. There is no problem with kids being energetic and people should not pathologize them. This sentiment is certainly correct. First, kids are very energetic. If you want to feel the effects of age, then hang out with one or several children and you will quickly learn how you might not be as energetic as you thought. Even people who are very active and healthy can sometimes struggle to match the energy possessed by a child, or several children. Secondly, and more importantly, pathologizing a child for a normative aspect of development is problematic.

The idea of kids being energetic demonstrates only one aspect of ADHD, that is, hyperactivity. The other domain of ADHD involves attention or inattention. Losing focus or not maintaining complete, undivided attention is not a feature of ADHD. Rather, this is characteristic of being human. In reading this chapter you may have already temporarily lost focus and your mind drifted somewhere else, such as what has to get done tomorrow or what you need to finish for today. Maybe you looked at a text message or television show for a moment. This is human. Saying that one has a disorder based on the normative processes of attention would also be of grave consequence.

On the other side of pathologizing children, some people deem ADHD as one of the "cool" disorders. Recall in Chapter 3 how some disorders might be associated with more stigma than others. You may have said, or heard someone else say, something along the lines of, "Sorry, it is just my ADHD" when they are explaining away some normative lapse of attention in a task or in communication. The acceptance of ADHD may be linked to its use in common language as a way to explain normative attention processes, which may lead to less stigma than other disorders. Many, if not all, people who publicly announce that they have ADHD may not even have a diagnosis of ADHD from a licensed mental health provider. Individuals may be professing a self-diagnosis to lessen perceived culpability for their actions in a particular situation. Common use of ADHD in communication in conjunction with media portrayal of the disorder may solidify a more accepting attitude. Dug the dog is seen as a fun character that brings about comic relief. Dug portrays ADHD as entertaining and humorous opposed to movies such as *Identity*, which advance dissociative identity disorder as being grim and mortal.

The benefit of society's common self-proclamation of ADHD demonstrates that people have moved somewhat toward a more accepting attitude of ADHD and toward seeing the humanity in it. The detriment of this use is that it may downplay the severity of ADHD for those who actually feel pain from the disorder. In fact, many people who have ADHD do feel pain from the disorder and would like very much to control their behavior or focus on tasks. Many of these individuals do not wave an ADHD banner to gain sympathy or explain away responsibility. Thus, people who challenge ADHD as a real disorder may not have concern with people who actually suffer from ADHD but those who do not and claim that they do.

Self-Diagnosis

Tendency of a person to claim that they have a disorder when they do not

Another myth about ADHD can be found when someone claims to have Attention-Deficit Disorder (ADD) and ADHD. Self-diagnosis is when a person claims that they have a disorder or diagnosis without the diagnosis being provided by a health care professional. This perpetuates a myth that ADHD and ADD are two distinct disorders. These are not two separate disorders but rather a change in ADD to ADHD, to include hyperactivity in the name. The American Psychiatric Association (1987) made this change in the revised DSM-III.

To answer the question about ADHD and whether it is real or something made up for people to explain away bad behavior, let's consider the case of a young boy that we will refer to as Darin. While reading this case think about the 4 Fs. Following this case, you will read the DSM-5 criteria and the 4 Fs to see how ADHD may be different from normative attention and high energy.

Case Vignette

Darin is an 8-year-old child who attends public school. He began to have difficulties in school at the age of 6. He frequently gets in trouble at school for repetitively being out of his seat and constant verbal interruptions of lessons. He is out of his seat, on average, six times per lesson. Because of this behavior his teacher either speaks with him outside of class or sends him to the principal's office. His grades are poor and he is at risk for failing his grade level. Darin not only experiences problems at school, but also at home. At home he frequently cuts off his parents when they speak, fidgets with his hands, is unable to play quietly, has difficulty waiting to talk to his parents when his sister is talking, talks most of the day to himself or others, and is uncomfortable sitting still when watching shows that he enjoys. Darin deeply wishes that he could control his behavior and does not like that he gets in trouble or that his grades are suffering. Darin's parents and his teacher are greatly concerned for him.

DSM-5 CRITERIA FOR ATTENTION-DEFICIT/HYPERACTIVITY DISORDER

Diagnostic Criteria

A. A persistent pattern of inattention and/or hyperactivity-impulsivity that interferes with functioning or development, as characterized by (1) and/or (2):

1. **Inattention:** Six (or more) of the following symptoms have persisted for at least 6 months to a degree that is inconsistent with developmental level and that negatively impacts directly on social and academic/occupational activities:

    Note: The symptoms are not solely a manifestation of oppositional behavior, defiance, hostility, or failure to understand tasks or instructions. For older adolescents and adults (age 17 and older), at least five symptoms are required.

    a. Often fails to give close attention to details or makes careless mistakes in schoolwork, at work, or during other activities (e.g., overlooks or misses details, work is inaccurate).

    b. Often has difficulty sustaining attention in tasks or play activities (e.g., has difficulty remaining focused during lectures, conversations, or lengthy reading).

    c. Often does not seem to listen when spoken to directly (e.g., mind seems elsewhere, even in the absence of any obvious distraction).

    d. Often does not follow through on instructions and fails to finish schoolwork, chores, or duties in the workplace (e.g., starts tasks but quickly loses focus and is easily sidetracked).

    e. Often has difficulty organizing tasks and activities (e.g., difficulty managing sequential tasks; difficulty keeping materials and belongings in order; messy, disorganized work; has poor time management; fails to meet deadlines).

    f.   Often avoids, dislikes, or is reluctant to engage in tasks that require sustained mental effort (e.g., schoolwork or homework; for older adolescents and adults, preparing reports, completing forms, reviewing lengthy papers).

    g.   Often loses things necessary for tasks or activities (e.g., school materials, pencils, books, tools, wallets, keys, paperwork, eyeglasses, mobile telephones).

    h.   Is often easily distracted by extraneous stimuli (for older adolescents and adults, may include unrelated thoughts).

    i.   Is often forgetful in daily activities (e.g., doing chores, running errands; for older adolescents and adults, returning calls, paying bills, keeping appointments).

2. **Hyperactivity and impulsivity:** Six (or more) of the following symptoms have persisted for at least 6 months to a degree that is inconsistent with developmental level and that negatively impacts directly on social and academic/occupational activities:

Note: The symptoms are not solely a manifestation of oppositional behavior, defiance, hostility, or a failure to understand tasks or instructions. For older adolescents and adults (age 17 and older), at least five symptoms are required.

    a.   Often fidgets with or taps hands or feet or squirms in seat.

    b.   Often leaves seat in situations when remaining seated is expected (e.g., leaves his or her place in the classroom, in the office or other workplace, or in other situations that require remaining in place).

    c.   Often runs about or climbs in situations where it is inappropriate. (Note: In adolescents or adults, may be limited to feeling restless.)

    d.   Often unable to play or engage in leisure activities quietly.

    e.   Is often "on the go," acting as if "driven by a motor" (e.g., is unable to be, or uncomfortable being still for extended time, as in restaurants, meetings; may be experienced by others as being restless or difficult to keep up with).

    f.   Often talks excessively.

    g.   Often blurts out an answer before a question has been completed (e.g., completes people's sentences; cannot wait for turn in conversation).

    h.   Often has difficulty waiting his or her turn (e.g., while waiting in line).

    i.   Often interrupts or intrudes on others (e.g., butts into conversations, games, or activities; may start using other people's things without asking or receiving permission; for adolescents and adults, may intrude into or take over what others are doing).

B. Several inattentive or hyperactive-impulsive symptoms were present prior to age 12 years.

C. Several inattentive or hyperactive-impulsive symptoms are present in two or more settings (e.g., at home, school, or work; with friends or relatives; in other activities).

D. There is clear evidence that the symptoms interfere with, or reduce the quality of, social, academic, or occupational functioning.

E.   The symptoms do not occur exclusively during the course of schizophrenia or another psychotic disorder and are not better explained by another mental disorder (e.g., mood disorder, anxiety disorder, dissociative disorder, personality disorder, substance intoxication or withdrawal).

Specify whether:

314.01 (F90.2) Combined presentation: If both Criterion Al (inattention) and Criterion A2 (hyperactivity-impulsivity) are met for the past 6 months.

314.00 (F90.0) Predominantly inattentive presentation: If Criterion Al (inattention) is met but Criterion A2 (hyperactivity-impulsivity) is not met for the past 6 months. 314.01 (F90.1) Predominantly hyperactive/impulsive presentation: If Criterion A2 (hyperactivity-impulsivity) is met and Criterion Al (inattention) is not met for the past 6 months.

Specify if:

In partial remission: When full criteria were previously met, fewer than the full criteria have been met for the past 6 months, and the symptoms still result in impairment in social, academic, or occupational functioning.

Specify current severity:

Mild: Few, if any, symptoms in excess of those required to make the diagnosis are present, and symptoms result in no more than minor impairments in social or occupational functioning.

Moderate: Symptoms or functional impairment between "mild" and "severe" are present.

Severe: Many symptoms in excess of those required to make the diagnosis, or several symptoms that are particularly severe, are present, or the symptoms result in marked impairment in social or occupational functioning.

Reprinted with permission from the *Diagnostic and Statistical Manual of Mental Disorders,* Fifth Edition, (Copyright 2013). American Psychiatric Association.

The 4 Fs of ADHD: More Than "Oh Look, There's a Squirrel"

In addition to the DSM-5 criteria, you can determine if a disorder is a myth, or the real thing, by returning to the 4 Fs. How might the 4 Fs come into play with ADHD? The 4 Fs highlight how inattention and hyperactivity can be problematic and pathological, warranting a diagnosis of ADHD. Impaired functioning, frequency, feeling pain, and engaging in behaviors that could be fatal demonstrate that ADHD is not only real but is a disorder that negatively affects children and adults. Barkley, Cook, and colleagues (2002) claimed that overwhelming scientific evidence suggests ADHD does exist as a genuine disorder, which is recognized by major medical associations and government health agencies. Also, as you read through the 4 Fs, think of the case of Darin.

Frequency

One of the ways you may know that ADHD is not used to pathologize all children who are energetic, is by comparing them to their peers (Barkley, 2003). If few children are exhibiting hyperactivity for a lengthy time beyond that of other children their age, then you can easily see the ABCs of frequency.

A—Amount of Time: The DSM-5 specifies that in order to receive a diagnosis of Attention-Deficit/Hyperactivity Disorder, a person must have experienced symptoms in the inattention or hyperactivity and impulsivity domain for at least six months, and this period must be different from normal developmental functioning (American Psychiatric Association; APA, 2013). For the case of Darin you notice that his behavior and symptoms of hyperactivity have been occurring for the span of 2 years.

B—Behavior: The DSM-5 additionally specifies that a person must experience six or more of the inattention or hyperactivity and impulsivity during this 6-month period (APA, 2013). Further, the symptoms and behavior must be present in two or more settings. This requirement is very important to note. If symptoms are only present in one setting, then the symptoms may be a product of the context rather than a demonstration of a disorder. For example, displaying inattentive symptoms at school but in no other context could indicate academic issues and not ADHD. Contextual display of symptoms could indicate a variety of things including: a child may find class boring, lack of motivation, dislike a teacher, have problems with peers, or just not think that he or she is being academically challenged. For Darin, his hyperactivity behavior has been occurring an average of six times per lesson, exhibits six of the nine criteria, which have been present for 2 years. He also is showing symptoms in multiple settings.

Contextual Display

Symptoms are only present in a specific place or context

C—Curve: Approximately 5% of children and 2.5% of adults struggle with ADHD (APA, 2013). In the United States, Caucasian populations tend to have higher clinical identification rates compared to African American and Latino populations. Further, ADHD is identified in males more than females, a ratio of 2:1 in children and 1.6:1 in adults, respectively (APA, 2013). Darin's struggle with attention and hyperactivity occurs at a higher frequency than that of his peers, demonstrating a difference in normative frequency distribution.

The Good News: Many effective treatments exist for ADHD. Most people with ADHD will experience reduced hyperactivity symptoms into adolescence and adulthood (APA, 2013).

Function

Impaired functioning is one of the leading means by which ADHD is detected or becomes first noticed. One of the criteria of ADHD is that it impairs social, occupational, or academic functioning, and across multiple settings, including school, home, and with friends (APA, 2013). Impaired function also demonstrates how ADHD is much more than attempts to pathologize normal energetic behavior of children. For children, functioning is evident in school through academic performance, achievement, retention, and social relationships. For adults, impaired functioning might be evidenced in academic and occupational areas. Adults might struggle with performance, attendance, and even maintaining an occupation or retention in an academic program. Darin's grades suffering and his referral to an administrator demonstrates the impaired functioning of his behavior.

Feeling Pain

People who experience symptoms of ADHD often struggle or feel pain. People with ADHD report higher levels of psychological distress compared to those who have not been diagnosed (Barkley, Murphy, et al., 1996). For these individuals, it is not "cool" or an excuse, but a struggle, academically or occupationally. Some associated features could be agitation or mood lability (APA, 2013). It can be frustrating for an individual to work on a task at school and exert constant cognitive effort to draw focus and attention back to a task. The experience of ADHD can also lead to distress for parents (Anastopoulos et al., 1992). In the case example, Darin was feeling pain because he deeply desired to change and he did not like the consequences of his behavior.

Mood Lability
Changing of moods

Fatality

The hyperactivity symptoms are associated with numerous physical health concerns and even growth deficits (Barkley, 2003). Hyperactivity and impulsivity and inattention may lead to engaging in accident-prone behavior (Barkley, 2003). Some of these accidents may lead to head injuries, broken bones, and accidental poisonings (Barkley, 2003). Further, teens with ADHD had driven a car illegally, had their licensed revoked, and had multiple automobile accidents compared to those teens that were not diagnosed with ADHD (Barkley, Guevremont, et al., 1993). In fact, 40% of teens with ADHD had multiple car crashes compared to 5.6% of teens who were control subjects. Darin's behavior could be fatal if he were not attending while engaging in certain tasks, such as riding his bicycle on the streets.

ADHD: Gender and Age

Which of the following two pictures is more likely to get attention from the teacher of a classroom?

If you answered the boy, then you are probably right. This reflects the old saying that the squeaky wheel gets the grease. These two pictures tell the story of how ADHD may manifest differently for boys and girls. The prevalence rate of ADHD is higher for boys than girls with a ratio of 2:1 in children and 1.6:1 in adults (APA, 2013). It is important to note that females typically display predominantly inattentive symptoms. Boys who display hyperactivity and impulsivity symptoms of ADHD might receive more attention from teachers and administrators. Meanwhile, girls that display predominantly inattentive symptoms of ADHD may receive little attention or go unnoticed. For girls, this can be problematic because their inattention can affect academic functioning and ADHD remains undiagnosed, meaning no treatment. Therefore, girls with inattentive symptoms of ADHD may be viewed as poor students.

Traditionally, ADHD has been seen as a childhood developmental disorder, although adults may display symptoms of the disorder (APA, 2013; Fischer et al., 2002; McGough & Barkley, 2004). However, the onset of ADHD does not occur in adulthood. People do not develop ADHD as adults, the symptoms must have been present in childhood. Thus, for an adult to be diagnosed with ADHD, the onset must have occurred in childhood, must have been present before the age of 12, and persisted into adulthood (APA, 2013). This can be difficult to assess in some cases where there is not a documented history of ADHD in childhood. Further, due to unreliable accounts of memory, the DSM-5 indicates that ancillary information must be gathered to corroborate a diagnosis of ADHD for adults (APA, 2013). Ancillary information may include childhood school or medical records. Adult symptoms of ADHD may also look differently due to diminished hyperactivity symptoms (APA, 2013). Adults may still struggle with difficulties in planning, impulsivity, and inattention but the hyperactivity symptoms seem less evident (APA, 2013).

Ancillary Information

Additional documentation or records

Assessments for ADHD

Recall that accurate assessments lead to accurate diagnoses. There are numerous methods developed to assess and diagnose ADHD. One of the most utilized tools for clinicians has been the DSM. The focus of measuring the core symptoms of ADHD, in the literature on assessment, is yielded by the DSM (Pelham et al., 2005). The DSM is used in conjunction with a clinical interview to assess if clients meet diagnostic criteria.

Report forms are another means to discover people who have ADHD. The Behavior Assessment System for Children (BASC) was developed to assess behavioral problems or emotional disturbances in children (AGS, 2005; Doyle et al., 1997; Reynolds, & Kamphaus, 1994). The BASC also serves the purpose of differentiating between hyperactivity and inattention. Furthermore, the test contains multiple dimensions for measurement: parent rating scales (PRS), teacher rating scales (TRS), self-report of personality (SRP), structured developmental history, and the student observation system. The PRS contains items that measure behaviors in a home environment whereas the TRS contains items that measure behaviors in the school environment. Both the PRS and the TRS provide measures for the child's observable behavior; however, the SRP scale measures the child's thoughts and feelings. The overall psychometric properties of the BASC provides evidence of high consistency as a tool for assessing ADHD (alpha = .70 to .90).

Clinicians and researchers have also relied on continuous performance tasks (CPT) to assess ADHD. According to Chunzhen and colleagues (2002), CPT tests are widely used by researchers. There are various types of CPTs and they all seek to measure errors of omission and commission (Conners et al., 2003). These types of tests usually discriminate ADHD children by typically using inattention, hyperactivity, and impulsivity scales in measurement. These tests may present some series of visual (numbers or letters) and auditory stimuli, in which you are to respond only when hearing or seeing a specific stimulus and not when others are available. For example, you may be instructed to click on a computer mouse when hearing or seeing the number one and not click when seeing or hearing a number two. So, someone demonstrating hyperactivity would click when the number one was present and also when the number two was presented. Individuals demonstrating primarily inattentive symptoms would show a lack of responding when the number two appears (as instructed) and also when the number one appeared.

Along with behavioral rating scales and CPTs, there is research that supports the use of quantitative electroencephalograpic (QEEG) examinations of the prefrontal and frontal lobes to assess for ADHD (Monastra et al., 2001). Monastra and his colleagues found that QEEG was a highly reliable method that could differentiate patients with ADHD from nonclinical controls. This assessment offers clinicians and patients a laboratory test of ADHD.

Continuous Performance Tasks

A task that asks individuals to discriminate between pressing a button or inhibiting a response

Intellectual Disability: Humanity in Diminished Intellect

Do you dislike stupid people? If so, then you may not be alone. However, these negative attitudes may carry over into stigma of people with impaired intellectual performance. Let's consider a history of intelligence and figures who may have removed humanity from the equation. Some aspects of the history of intelligence have a grim tone.

Eugenics

Mate selection that involves selecting for good genes

In 1904, Sir Francis Galton proposed the advancement of an area he termed eugenics (Gillham, 2001). Eugenics roughly translated as "good genes." The idea behind eugenics was to actively use processes of mate selection to advance the human species through selecting desirable human traits. These traits could include intelligence. Thus, intelligent people might breed with other intelligent people and through active mate selection and natural selection, the human species might be more intelligent and advanced in other ways. Out of this scientific movement, politicians and governmental institutions took this idea and arguably corrupted it and misapplied it (Galton, 2005). Some of these political figures and organizations took the idea of eugenics and thought to move faster with it than any evolutionary process, which led to the Third Reich to actively exterminate groups of individuals and other political systems to impose sterilization, euthanasia, and infanticide policies, all in the name of eugenics (Galton, 2005). Therefore, a dislike of stupid people could lead one to take an idea such as eugenics and misapply it in ways that could be detrimental.

Some researchers have tried to use intelligence tests to demonstrate a lack of superiority between racial groups (Guthrie, 2004). Guthrie discussed several historical accounts of researchers using intelligence instruments to detect differences between White children and Black children, and inferring

Myths in Movies

I AM SAM

The movie *I Am Sam* depicts a compassionate man with an intellectual disability fighting for his daughter. While the movie tugs on emotions for the main character, consider how this film portrays intellectual disability and if it represents typical cases.

A scene from *I Am Sam*

© New Line Cinema/Photofest

that White individuals are superior to Black individuals. Many intelligence tests became corrupted based on these uses. Thus, psychometric credence of intelligence was also compromised due to its association with how people have used these instruments. Even when intelligence tests discern differences in intelligence, this does not warrant prejudicial attitudes or discriminatory behaviors toward those with lower IQ scores or intellectual disabilities. Many people with intellectual deficits may show immense compassion toward others. Diminished functioning in cognitive abilities does not closely approximate a lack of humanness.

In Chapter 3, you read about intelligence tests and how intelligence is assessed. When looking at intellectual disability (ID), it is imperative to assess an individual's intelligence. To meet criteria of an intellectual disability, the deficits in intellectual functioning need to be established through the use of intelligence tests (APA, 2013).

The 4 Fs of Intellectual Disability

Most individuals fall within a normative range of intelligence scores. Fewer have marked intellectual differences. These differences may lead to impaired functioning, feeling pain, and fatality. To consider frequency, look at the ABCs.

Frequency

A—Amount of Time: To be diagnosed with an ID, according to the DSM-5, an individual must experience impairment in everyday functioning (APA, 2013).

B—Behavior: Individuals evidencing an ID will have their intellectual functioning verified by intelligence testing (APA, 2013). Usually, individuals will have IQ scores that are two or more standard deviations below the mean. For IQ scores, this is approximately a score of 70 or lower.

C—Curve: The prevalence rate of ID occurs in about 1% of the population and .06% for severe ID (APA, 2013).

The Good News: Intellectual disabilities are generally nonprogressive (APA, 2013). Further, early assessment and diagnosis may lead to more support and treatment interventions for individuals and families.

Function

As indicated in severity and in frequency, deficits in cognitive domains lead to impairment in everyday functioning in multiple settings (APA, 2013). Individuals with an ID may have impaired functioning within academics. Academic settings may be one of the settings where intellectual deficits are

INTELLECTUAL DISABILITY SEVERITY

Mild	• Difficulties in academic skills • Difficulty in perceiving social interactions • Some support with complex tasks
Moderate	• Pre-academic skills develop slowly • Less complex language skills • Can care for basic personal needs; may need some teaching with these areas
Severe	• Limited conceptual skills, understanding written language, and numbers • Spoken words are limited • Support in all daily living activities
Profound	• Use physical objects rather than symbolic processes • Understands simple instructions • Dependent on others for most, if not all, aspects of living

*Based on DSM-5 Table (APA, 2013, p. 34–36)

first observed. A child who is not academically performing at a level comparable to his or her peers may be referred to a school psychologist for an evaluation. The school psychologist may evaluate the child and discover an ID. Depending on the severity of functioning, severe intellectual disabilities may be recognized by the age of 2 and mild severity may not be discernable until school age (APA, 2013).

Feeling Pain

One of the difficulties with people who have an ID has been in the perception of their inability to express pain or that they are unable to communicate their pain (Foley & McCutcheon, 2004). However, research has revealed that individuals with an ID can differentiate between pain and distress (Mckenzie et al., 2013). Difficulties in academics or daily living can lead a person with an ID to feel pain. It can be frustrating for an individual with ID who is failing courses or who needs assistance with hygiene. Further, many families who have children with an ID may become sad, angry, or confused when seeking resources for their child. Parents of children with Down syndrome may have more depressive symptoms compared to parents of children who had no disability (Scott et al., 1997).

Fatality

When people consider ID, they may not think of suicide. However, individuals with IDs may have suicidal ideation, attempts, and some complete suicide.

Individuals who have an ID are at a greater risk for suicide when they have a co-occurring disorder (APA, 2013). People with ID may act upon voicing suicidal ideation (Lunsky et al., 2012). Suicidal thoughts or attempts need to be taken seriously by all, even those with intellectual disabilities.

The Etiology of Intellectual Disability

Many intellectual disabilities are developed primarily through genetic and physiological factors (APA, 2013). One of the most common genetic disorders that results in an intellectual disability is Down syndrome (i.e., Trisomy 21). Down syndrome is a genetic syndrome in which a third chromosome is found on the 21st pair of chromosomes, in which it often is associated with some changes in physical characteristics and cognitive deficits. Fragile-X syndrome is one of the most common inherited causes of ID (Centers for Disease Control and Prevention; CDC, 2015b; Lubs et al., 2012). There are also a number of preventable causes of ID involving avoidance of teratogens. One of the most preventable causes of ID is Fetal Alcohol Syndrome (FAS). Increased frequency of consumption of alcohol may lead to increased risk of a child developing FAS.

Trisomy 21

A third chromosome is found on the 21st pair of chromosomes, often resulting in an intellectual disability

Fetal Alcohol Syndrome

Most preventable cause of an intellectual disability

Autism Spectrum Disorder

Autism has recently gained more attention. With attention, beliefs are developed. What are some of the beliefs you have about autism? How does it develop? Is it on the rise? What movies have you watched pertaining to autism? What experiences do you have with others who have autism?

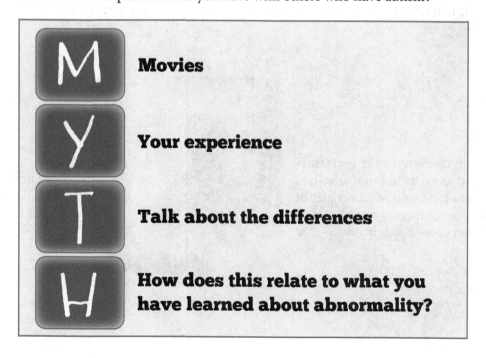

M **Movies**

Y **Your experience**

T **Talk about the differences**

H **How does this relate to what you have learned about abnormality?**

Myths in Movies

SHERLOCK

In the BBC Sherlock series, *The Hounds of Baskerville* episode, John Watson tells Detective Lestrade that Sherlock Holmes has Aspergers.

Asperger disorder was listed in the DSM-IV-TR and subsumed under Autism Spectrum Disorders in the DSM-5 (APA, 2013).

What do you think? How might Sherlock display these traits? How might Sherlock communicate myths about autism?

There are a number of myths about autism. Torres and colleagues (2020) conducted a study on myths of autism. They found that a majority of participants believed that people with autism have a dysfunction mirror neuron system. Additionally, they found that over half of participants believed that people with ASD have an above average IQ, have gifted levels of knowledge or talent, are unable to accept changes in their daily routine, and having a higher genetic risk means a child will develop autism. Another myth of autism is that it is on the rise and contagious. While not the majority, about 27% of

Myths in Movies

RAIN MAN

The movie *Rain Man* demonstrates a character named Raymond as an individual who has autism and is a savant. As you read on about autism reflect on how many people with autism may not have savant syndrome.

A scene from *Rain Man*

a college student and general public sample endorse this as definitely true or probably true (Torres et al., 2020). Years ago, it was learned that a mental health professional reported autism rates in a specific geographic area to be 20 times higher than the maximum prevalence rates of the DSM-IV-TR. This individual indicated that autism was on the rise. The introduction of awareness campaigns of autism, media attention toward vaccinations, and DSM changes (from DSM-IV-TR to DSM-5) may have contributed to beliefs about autism being on the rise or even contagious. The American Psychiatric Association (2013) suggested that it was unclear, and posited several reasons as to why the prevalence rates changed from the previous version to the DSM-5. Autism is not contagious and this belief of it being on the rise may have to do with better recognition of its symptoms and identifying other genetic contributions (Glicksman, 2012).

As you know that many myths develop from movies, think about the variety of movies that portray autism and the image that it impresses. Many movies and shows such as *Sherlock, Rain Man, Atypical, The Good Doctor, Temple Grandin,* and *Fly Away* attempt to paint the picture of autism. Some of these contain pieces of truth mixed with elements of exaggeration and emotional scenes. A number of movies and shows may depict people with autism as highly intelligent or as savants. For example, films like *Rain Man* and *Sherlock* show characters who have social deficits but excel in intellect or special abilities. However, according to the APA (2013), autism is often associated with intellectual impairment and even when there is an absence of an intellectual disability people have poor adult psychosocial functioning.

Regardless of the controversies about vaccinations and prevalence rates, autism reflects symptoms of social deficits and patterned behavior. In considering autism, think about one of the many things that you may take for granted, such as your ability to communicate. Reflect on how it is that you learned to communicate with others. Usually communication and social skill development involves a process of learned behaviors and discriminating nuances among numerous social-situational contexts. Think about eye contact. How did you learn about where to look when speaking with someone and how long you should look at them? Someone, such as a parent or care provider, may have told you that it is polite to make eye contact with someone when speaking with them. You may have also been coached to make eye contact when interviewing for a position. But how long do you look? Where do you look? The answer to these questions may have been social nuances that you learned over time and from interacting with people.

One of the things that you come to learn when making eye contact, is that looking someone in the eyes for an extended period of time can elicit awkward social exchanges. Usually, if you look someone in their eyes while not speaking for longer than 12 seconds then you and that person may feel awkward. Try it! Awkward extended eye contact has led to learning another rule about nonverbal communication, which is not to stare. So, somewhere between "make eye contact" and "do not stare" lies the optimal eye gaze social behavior.

The point is that you rarely, or never, have considered this behavior. Eye contact behavior is enacted almost effortlessly. However, this is not the case for someone with autism. Individuals with Autism Spectrum Disorder (ASD) have social deficits. Autism is different from intellectual disabilities because it is related to social and emotional functioning rather than intellectual functioning. However, many individuals with autism may also have an intellectual disability (APA, 2013). In Chapter 4 you were introduced to Aislinn, a girl with autism. Aislinn demonstrated a nonverbal aspect of autism, in which she was unable to communicate with her parents. When you review autism, think of Aislinn and consider another case, in which we will refer to this person as Amadeus.

DSM-5 CRITERIA FOR AUTISM SPECTRUM DISORDER

DIAGNOSTIC CRITERIA

A. Persistent deficits in social communication and social interaction across multiple contexts, as manifested by the following, currently or by history (examples are illustrative, not exhaustive; see text):

1. Deficits in social-emotional reciprocity, ranging, for example, from abnormal social approach and failure of normal back-and-forth conversation; to reduced sharing of interests, emotions, or affect; to failure to initiate or respond to social interactions.

2. Deficits in nonverbal communicative behaviors used for social interaction, ranging, for example, from poorly integrated verbal and nonverbal communication; to abnormalities in eye contact and body language or deficits in understanding and use of gestures; to a total lack of facial expressions and nonverbal communication.

3. Deficits in developing, maintaining, and understanding relationships, ranging, for example, from difficulties adjusting behavior to suit various social contexts; to difficulties in sharing imaginative play or in making friends; to absence of interest in peers.

    Specify current severity:

    Severity is based on social communication impairments and restricted, repetitive patterns of behavior.

B. Restricted, repetitive patterns of behavior, interests, or activities, as manifested by at least two of the following, currently or by history (examples are illustrative, not exhaustive):

1. Stereotyped or repetitive motor movements, use of objects, or speech (e.g., simple motor stereotypes, lining up toys or flipping objects, echolalia, idiosyncratic phrases).

2. Insistence on sameness, inflexible adherence to routines, or ritualized patterns of verbal or nonverbal behavior (e.g., extreme distress at small changes, difficulties with transitions, rigid thinking patterns, greeting rituals, need to take same route or eat same food every day).

3. Highly restricted, fixated interests that are abnormal in intensity or focus (e.g., strong attachment to or preoccupation with unusual objects, excessively circumscribed or perseverative interests).

4. Hyper- or hyporeactivity to sensory input or unusual interest in sensory aspects of the environment (e.g., apparent indifference to pain/temperature, adverse response to specific sounds or textures, excessive smelling or touching of objects, visual fascination with lights or movement).

Specify current severity:

Severity is based on social communication impairments and restricted, repetitive patterns of behavior.

C. Symptoms must be present in the early developmental period (but may not become fully manifest until social demands exceed limited capacities, or may be masked by learned strategies in later life).

D. Symptoms cause clinically significant impairment in social, occupational, or other important areas of current functioning.

E. These disturbances are not better explained by intellectual disability (intellectual developmental disorder) or global developmental delay. Intellectual disability and autism spectrum disorder frequently co-occur; to make comorbid diagnoses of autism spectrum disorder and intellectual disability, social communication should be below that expected for general developmental level.

Note: Individuals with a well-established DSM-IV diagnosis of autistic disorder, Asperger's disorder, or pervasive developmental disorder not otherwise specified should be given the diagnosis of autism spectrum disorder. Individuals who have marked deficits in social communication, but whose symptoms do not otherwise meet criteria for autism spectrum disorder, should be evaluated for social (pragmatic) communication disorder.

Specify if:

With or without accompanying intellectual impairment

With or without accompanying language impairment

Associated with a known medical or genetic condition or environmental factor (**Coding note:** Use additional code to identify the associated medical or genetic condition.) **Associated with another neurodevelopmental, mental, or behavioral disorder** (**Coding note:** Use additional code[s] to identify the associated neurodevelopmental, mental, or behavioral disorder[s].)

With catatonia (refer to the criteria for catatonia associated with another mental disorder, pp. 119–120, for definition) (**Coding note:** Use additional code 293.89 [F06.1] catatonia associated with autism spectrum disorder to indicate the presence of the co-morbid catatonia.)

Case Vignette

Amadeus was a high school student who had autism. He was referred to the principal after an incident where he was staring at girls and they reported him to their teacher. The teacher then referred Amadeus to the principal's office. Knowing that Amadeus had autism, he encouraged Amadeus to avoid eye contact with women. Then, Amadeus came back to the principal's office a few weeks later. This time he was referred for the same complaint, his abrupt avoidance of eye contact with women led to the women feeling uncomfortable.

The 4 Fs of Autism Spectrum Disorder

As noted, many people take their social communication skills for granted. Fewer people may have marked difficulties in communicating or understanding social cues. These social communication deficits and restricted patterns of behavior may lead to impaired functioning, feeling pain, and fatality. To consider frequency, look at the ABCs.

Frequency

A—Amount of Time: To be diagnosed with autism spectrum disorder the symptoms are persistent, pervasive, and sustained (APA, 2013).

B—Behavior: A person must experience symptoms of deficits in social communication and restricted, patterned behavior (APA, 2013). Deficits in social communication may involve not speaking with others to not encoding social cues from nonverbal behaviors. The repetitive patterned behavior may involve inflexible routines to fixated interests.

C—Curve: Autism occurs in about 1% of the population for adults and children (APA, 2013).

The Good News: Autism is not a degenerative disorder (APA, 2013). The absence of an intellectual disability comorbid with autism serves as a prognostic factor (APA, 2013). Further, autism can be recognized in the second year of life, which may lead to increased awareness, services, and treatment interventions. One semi-structured behavioral observation, the Autism Diagnostic Observation Schedule, Second Edition, assesses autism as early as 12 months (Lord et al., 2012). Further, having autism does not mean that someone is doomed to never be successful.

One of the most famous, and arguably successful, individuals with autism is Dr. Temple Grandin. Dr. Grandin's life has been documented through a film titled *Temple Grandin*. Dr. Grandin has become well-achieved in earning a PhD and teaching in animal science at Colorado State University (Grandin, 2016).

Dr. Temple Grandin and actress Claire Danes

© HBO/Photofest

Function

Given that a majority of life involves social interactions, you can easily deduce how autism may impair functioning. Autism occurs on a spectrum and functioning varies across the spectrum (APA, 2013). Many individuals with autism may have difficulties in academic and occupational situations. People with autism may face challenges in acquiring a job. Employment interviews often involve an exaggeration of positive characteristics (e.g., lying) about oneself. Individuals with autism are less likely than other normatively developing children to tell and maintain lies (Talwar et al., 2012). This is one aspect that can make it difficult to get a job. In fact, Dr. Temple Grandin suggested that in obtaining a job she never had a traditional interview (Grandin, 2016). Employers may not recognize that an individual has autism and may misattribute social deficits to some characteristics of a bad interviewee. Challenges can also occur at school through learning. A lack of social interactions or understanding social nuances may create difficult learning environments.

Think back to Amadeus. He had several encounters with others who did not understand his behavior and reported him to administrators. Amadeus's rigid rules for social behavior, from staring to abrupt aversion of his eyes, led to his behavior being misinterpreted and reported. Amadeus had difficulty with functioning in his academic-social environment.

Feeling Pain

Some individuals who have high-functioning autism may feel distress from wanting to engage others in social situations, but social communication deficits lead to challenges in doing so. In the case of Amadeus, he very much wanted to engage his peers and develop relationships. However, his rigid rules of eye contact behavior posed one of many challenges for him. Much like intellectual disability, lack of social communication skills may present care providers with difficulty in assessing a child's level of pain or distress.

Fatality

Individuals with ASD may be prone to risks where they are unable to speak or discuss things that have happened to them. One of the reasons that Mr. Wendrow's case gained so much popularity was the idea that he was sexually assaulting a child, his daughter Aislinn, who could not verbally substantiate or deny these claims. In other cases, children with ASD have had behavioral changes misattributed to their disorder instead of toxins that were ingested (Gharib et al., 2014).

Etiology of Autism Spectrum Disorder

With much of the awareness of autism came an interest in determining its cause. In looking for causes, vaccinations have been suggested to be a source contributing to the development of autism. This relationship is often referred due to ASDs generally being assessed during 12–24 months and numerous vaccinations occur within this time frame or shortly before. Thus, media, fears, and misunderstandings of science have perpetuated a myth about ASD, that vaccinations are the cause. To date, there is no current research that has corroborated such claims. Much of the research has indicated that there is lack of evidence to support the claims that autism is caused by or associated with vaccinations, even those containing thimerosal, which con-

Myths in Movies

VAXXED

The movie *Vaxxed* attempts to argue that vaccines cause autism. The film shows several scenes of parents of children with autism and attempts to connect emotional scenes with information indicating that autism will reach 50% of children (80% of boys) by year 2032. Based on scientific research and the information you have learned, what do you think?

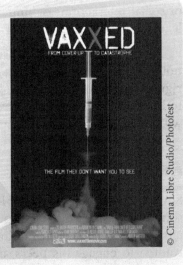

© Cinema Libre Studio/Photofest

tains mercury (Stehr-Green et al., 2003; Verstraeten et al., 2003). Even with this evidence about 25% of Americans still believe vaccinations cause autism (Gross, 2009). Due to this gap between public belief and lack of substantiated evidence, various health professionals have been encouraged to address this myth (Miller & Reynolds, 2009; White, 2014). The DSM-5 indicates that risk factors for ASD may include a variety of nonspecific environmental contributions and heritability (APA, 2013). The DSM-5 claimed that heritability estimates for ASD range from 37 to 90%.

Elimination Disorders

Elimination disorders, though not classified with neurodevelopmental disorders, are usually diagnosed in childhood and early adolescence. This group involves the elimination of feces or urine in places that are not deemed socially appropriate and occur beyond appropriate developmental markers. The two elimination disorders are enuresis and encopresis.

Enuresis involves urinating in a socially inappropriate place after the age of 5 years old. A film produced in 1976, *The Loneliest Runner,* shows a teen boy who struggles with wetting his bed. His mother tries to stop his behavior by placing his stained sheets out of the window. Due to a fear of friends seeing his sheets, he runs home quickly after school to remove them. Encopresis includes defecation in socially inappropriate places after the age of 4.

Enuresis

Urinating in non-socially appropriate places

Encopresis

Defecation in non-socially appropriate places

The 4 Fs of Elimination Disorders

Elimination disorders can be further evidenced as problematic by imposing the 4 Fs as criteria. In demonstrating frequency, you may notice that most U.S. children become toilet trained around the age of 3. Repetitive urination (amount of time) in places other than the toilet after the age of 5 and defecation in places other than the toilet by the age of 4 (behavior) occurs for minimal children (curve; 5 to 10% for enuresis at age 5; 1% for encopresis at age 5).

This behavior may impair a child's or adolescent's functioning. If a child is eliminating after age-appropriate stages, then the child may experience difficulties with social activities, self-esteem, and rejection (APA, 2013). Someone with elimination disorder may feel pain from social ostracism or humiliation resultant of peers and social groups who discover that a child or adolescent has eliminated in an inappropriate place. A person may subsequently avoid these social situations or places where shame or humiliation has occurred. Elimination disorders may also lead to increased incontinence and constipation in adulthood (APA, 2013). Feces can also dry out and the stool may need to be removed by a physician (Peterson et al., 2003).

Theories and Treatments of Neurodevelopmental and Elimination Disorders

Neurodevelopmental disorders are termed such due to their onset being related to early developmental stages. Thus, development and biology tend to typically hold more weight in understanding the etiology of many neurodevelopmental disorders. However, psychological and social factors still have a place in understanding these disorders, their onset, and course. Thus, keep in mind the diathesis-stress model from Chapter 2.

In conjunction with the diathesis-stress model, research informs practice of efficacious and effective treatments. There are numerous treatments for various neurodevelopmental disorders. The Society of Clinical Child and Adolescent Psychology dissemination task force collaborated with the Center for Children and Families at Florida International University and The Children's Trust to provide resources for parents and professionals regarding evidence-based treatments for neurodevelopmental treatments (Division 53 Task Forces, 2015).

ADHD

A former supervisor mentioned that if a child is struggling with ADHD, then you could give them a bottle of Mountain Dew to offset some of the symptoms. This method never seemed intuitive. How could giving a child, who is hyperactive, a bottle of caffeine be helpful?

Biological Treatments. Caffeine has been shown to have promising effects with improving attention deficits in rat models (Pandolfo et al., 2013). Psychostimulant medications "are prescribed for 600,000 to 1 million school children in the United States" (Fox et al., 2005, p. 367). The use of stimulants for treatment of ADHD has produced an issue of controversy among the scientific community. Some of the concerns of stimulant medication involve the time span of being on medication whereas other topics address the issue of the side effects produced.

Psychostimulant

Medications that increase sympathetic nervous system arousal

Lilienfeld (1994) reported that stimulants such as methylphenidate, dextroamphetamine, and pemoline were used in treating ADHD children in the 1930s, and since then the use of stimulants has drastically increased. The use of stimulants has shown, in laboratory measures, a decrease in hyperactivity, improved performance on cognitive tasks, and a decrease in disruptive behaviors (Dulcan, 1985). Some of the side effects that are recurrently reported include insomnia, anorexia, weight loss, irritability, and abdominal pain (Dulcan, 1985). Lilienfeld stated that approximately 20 to 30% of the ADHD children provide little to no clinical response to the use of stimulants. The other controversy involves the absence of evidence for stimulants regarding lasting improvement in symptoms (Fox et al., 2005). Researchers have claimed "the neuropsychological effects of Ritalin were eliminated when patients were tested without medication at 1 year follow-up" (Monastra, Monastra, & George, 2002, p. 245).

Psychological Treatments. Due to some parents' concerns with biological treatments, they have sought psychological treatments for their children with ADHD. Some of the more effective, empirically-based treatments for ADHD involve Behavior Therapy, and ineffective means include social skills training (Evans, Owens, & Bunford, 2014). Evans and colleagues reviewed literature published between 2007 and 2013 to establish empirically supported treatments for ADHD. They suggest the following empirically supported treatments work well:

- ▶ Behavioral parent training
- ▶ Behavioral classroom management
- ▶ Behavioral peer interventions
- ▶ Combined behavior management interventions
- ▶ Organization training

Multimodal Treatments. Another approach to treatment has been neurofeedback. It has been suggested that neurofeedback training is possibly efficacious (Evans et al., 2014). The process involves electrodes placed on the individual's head to measure electrical activity. Audio and visual feedback is then witnessed instantly by the individual. The individual is then able to alter the brainwave patterns. The design of neurofeedback permits individuals to train their brain waves. With neurofeedback training, a participant can control certain functions, appropriate for ADHD by altering brainwave activity (Fox et al., 2005). Neurofeedback is viewed as a viable alternative to psychostimulants for treatment of ADHD symptoms. One study compared the effectiveness of neurofeedback compared to stimulant medication in treating children with ADHD, and found success in reducing ADHD symptoms for both groups (i.e., neurofeedback, methylphenidate; Fuchs et al., 2003). The benefits derived from neurofeedback as a treatment alternative to psychostimulant medication are evidenced, but a limitation is its lengthy process (Fox et al., 2005).

Neurofeedback

Regulating brain waves through monitoring brain electrical activity

Due to many of the ADHD treatment plans providing evidence of limitations and the controversy over medication, an emergence of multimodal treatment programs began to surface during the 1970s and 1980s (Jacobvitz et al., 1990). Some multimodal treatments that have received attention are: (1) behavioral-psychosocial treatment and (2) the combination of behavioral-psychosocial treatment with stimulant medication (Root & Resnick, 2003). The behavioral-psychosocial treatment is typically preferred by parents and has strong empirical support for children with mild to moderate ADHD. The latter is considered when children exhibit more severe symptoms of ADHD and when a rapid response is desired.

Intellectual Disability

There are limited biological treatments for individuals with ID. However, recent research has investigated the use of a drug, donepezil, for adults with Down syndrome and found improvement in global functioning (Kishnani et al., 2009). Most individuals that have an ID will focus on services, academic accommodations, family education, societal awareness, and behavioral interventions. Children diagnosed with an ID may be placed in special education classes. For children with moderate to severe ID, behavioral interventions may be employed to enhance daily functioning.

Autism Spectrum Disorder

There are no cures for ASD. However, there are a number of treatments for various symptoms. These treatments primarily include biological and behavioral interventions.

Biological Treatments. The Centers for Disease Control (2015a) suggested that, "There are no medications that can cure ASD or treat the core symptoms." However, some medications have been investigated to work with the symptoms of the disorder. Aripiprazole, an atypical antipsychotic, has been suggested as an efficacious biological treatment to reduce irritability in ASD (Ghanizadeh et al., 2015). Newer research is looking at other medications to treat autism. One case study has investigated low dosage of anti-epileptic phenytoin to enhance social cognitive deficits (Bird, 2015). Recent findings have suggested that high-dose folinic acid improves verbal communication in children with ASD (Frye et al., 2018).

© Sergey Novikov/Shutterstock.com

Psychological/Behavioral Treatments. The two major guiding approaches for psychological and behavioral interventions of ASD are applied behavioral analysis (ABA) and developmental social-pragmatic (DSP; Ingersoll et al., 2005; Smith, 2011; Smith & Iadarola, 2015). An ABA intervention is implementing learning and behavioral principles for children in everyday living situations and classrooms. On the other hand, DSP involves others joining in to play established by a child with ASD. The most well-established empirically supported treatments for ASD include individual, comprehensive ABA and teacher-implemented, focused ABA + DSP (Smith & Iadarola, 2015).

Elimination Disorders

Most treatment plans for elimination disorders involve medication or behavioral principles. Some medications, such as duloxetine, treats stress incontinence (Waterfield, 2009). After ruling out any biological sources resulting in an elimination disorder, treatments will primarily involve behavioral principles. One of the most common behavioral approaches, referred to as the bell-and-pad method, involves placing a pad with a bell under a child while the child is sleeping (Vogel et al., 1996). The bell alarms when the child has released urine.

Conclusion

There are many myths about child-related disorders. Childhood disorders need to be considered seriously. Both extremes of either pathologizing or normalizing children may be detrimental. Over pathologizing normative behavior may lead to stigma and treatments that are not aligned with childhood experiences. Seeking a diagnostic label to lessen parental or teacher responsibility can be harmful to a child and compromise the integrity of actual childhood disorders. On the other hand, normalizing disorders may lead to no diagnosis and no treatment. Not treating a child who is suffering pain, having impaired functioning, or facing fatal consequences can be just as dangerous. Many childhood disorders are real. Discerning these differences can lead to a favorable prognosis.

Applied Behavioral Analysis

Implementing learning and behavioral principles in everyday living situations

Developmental Social-Pragmatic

A treatment for autism spectrum disorder where you join in play

CHAPTER REVIEW

QUESTIONS

1. How is ADHD different from children who are merely active? What are the differences for boys and girls who have ADHD?

2. What are some of the ways that intelligence has been used historically?

3. How are intellectual disabilities and autism different?

4. At what age can intellectual disabilities, ADHD, and autism first be assessed and diagnosed?

5. What are some of the treatments for intellectual disabilities, ADHD, and autism?

KEY TERMS

Self-Diagnosis

Contextual Display

Mood Lability

Ancillary Information

Continuous Performance Tasks

Eugenics

Trisomy 21

Fetal Alcohol Syndrome

Enuresis

Encopresis

Psychostimulant

Neurofeedback

Applied Behavioral Analysis

Developmental Social-Pragmatic

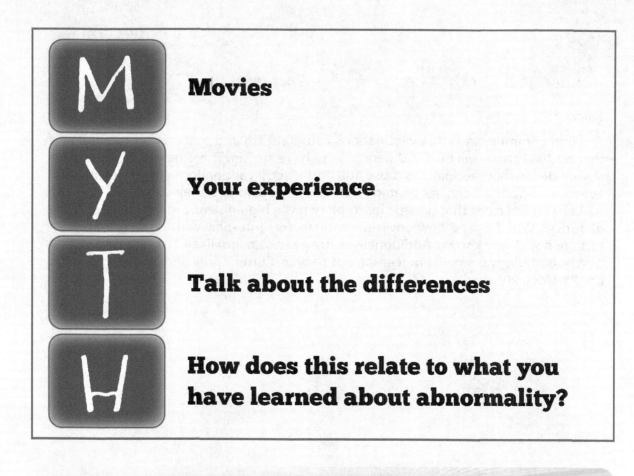

M Movies

Y Your experience

T Talk about the differences

H How does this relate to what you have learned about abnormality?

Myths in Movies Recap

I Am Sam

Like many movies that are looking at one specific situation, this one portrays an adult with ID in a unique legal context. This movie may show only challenges with an adult parent who has ID and not the struggles that children with ID face.

Sherlock and Rain Man

A number of movies and shows may depict people with autism as highly intelligent or as savants. *Rain Man* and *Sherlock* show characters who have social deficits but excel in intellect or special abilities. However, according to the APA (2013), autism is often associated with intellectual impairment and even when there is an absence of an intellectual disability people have poor adult psychosocial functioning.

Myths in Movies Recap

Vaxxed

The film communicates that vaccinations cause autism and that it is on the rise, and that by 2032 there will be 1 in 2 people who have autism. There has been no conclusive evidence that vaccinations cause autism. In fact, if vaccinations cause autism, then everyone who has been vaccinated should have autism and they clearly do not. The APA (2013) indicates that genetic heritability has a big influence in the development of autism. Whether and how environmental factors interplay with these genetic factors are not clearly known. Additionally, autism rates are not likely to become 1 in 2, as psychopathology is smaller percentage of people. Current prevalence rates of autism are 1% (APA, 2013).

CHAPTER SIX

SCHIZOPHRENIA SPECTRUM AND PSYCHOTIC DISORDERS

LEARNING OBJECTIVES

- ▶ Examine myths related to schizophrenia and psychotic disorders
- ▶ Discuss perspectives and experiences that reinforce these myths
- ▶ Become familiar with the history of psychotic disorders
- ▶ Discuss the 4 Fs of schizophrenia and psychotic disorders: frequency, function, fatality, and feelings of pain
- ▶ Identify diagnostic criteria of schizophrenia spectrum disorders
- ▶ Explore psychotic disorders other than schizophrenia
- ▶ Examine severity, course, and subtypes of schizophrenia disorders
- ▶ Discuss theories and treatments of schizophrenia and related disorders
- ▶ Differentiate biological and psychological theories and treatments of schizophrenia
- ▶ Explore the functions of medication treatments for schizophrenia and related disorders
- ▶ Discuss the limitations of treatments for schizophrenia spectrum and related disorders

CHAPTER OUTLINE

- ▶ MYTHs of Schizophrenia
- ▶ A Brief History of Psychotic Disorders
- ▶ The 4 Fs of the Schizophrenia Spectrum: The "Split-Mind" in Action
- ▶ Schizophrenia Course and Development
- ▶ DSM-5 Criteria for Schizophrenia
- ▶ Other Psychotic Disorders
- ▶ Theories and Treatments of Psychotic Disorders
- ▶ Biological and Environmental Theories of Psychotic Disorders

- ▶ Brain Structure and Function
- ▶ Neurotransmitters
- ▶ Biological Treatments of Schizophrenia Spectrum Disorders
- ▶ Psychological Treatments of Schizophrenia Disorders

MYTHs of Schizophrenia

Schizophrenia

In Greek, "schizo" means split and "phren" means mind; indicating a psychotic disorder wherein the mind splits from reality

Psychotic

Characterized by a break with the normal sensation and perception of reality, and typically experiencing hallucinations and delusions

Schizophrenia may be, at one and the same time, the most widely researched and most commonly misunderstood of all disorders. Myths about schizophrenia are abundant and some are quite wild, which should not surprise us, as the disorder itself is characterized by a wide variety of symptoms quite uncommon from most folks' daily experience. Before exploring some of these myths more closely, consider your ideas and impressions about schizophrenia or related psychotic disorders. Look at each of the categories below, which have likely influenced your perception in one way or another, and think about the impressions you have gathered from these various sources.

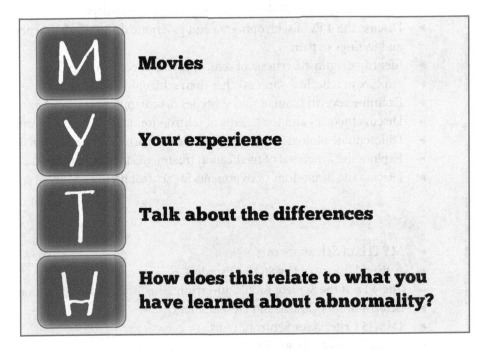

M Movies

Y Your experience

T Talk about the differences

H How does this relate to what you have learned about abnormality?

The preponderance of myths about schizophrenia make it difficult to know where to start. Among the more popular and commonly encountered myths is the idea that schizophrenia, which literally translated from the Greek means "split-mind," is the same as having multiple personalities, or what is known as dissociative identity disorder. While these disorders have been commonly confused in the past, especially by clinicians and researchers struggling to understand and accurately categorize disorders, we now know that the disorders are distinct, having their own symptoms and functional difficulties. Lindberg and Curtis (2018) reported that 70% of undergraduate psychology students in their sample (n = 178) endorsed (definitely or probably true) that schizophrenia is synonymous with dissociative identity disorder, and 55% believed that auditory hallucinations were probably the individual's other personalities.

Schizophrenia is often visually depicted in manner similar to dissociative identity disorder.

© Steve Allen/Shutterstock.com

Another interesting myth may have actually been perpetuated by classifications of the disorders. Specifically, some people tend to think of psychosis as categorical. In other words, individuals either have psychosis or they do not have it. As a means of changing the contemporary conceptualization of psychotic disorders, the DSM-5 has begun referring to a schizophrenia spectrum, rather than separate, categorical disorders. Placing schizophrenia and related disorders on a spectrum helps dispel the categorization myth, and appears more congruent with the reality seen by clinicians, that individuals can have a dash of delusion, a hint of hallucination, and a drop of disorganized thinking.

A Brief History of Psychotic Disorders

Despite the term's Greek roots, the word schizophrenia did not exist prior to the 20th century! Symptoms of schizophrenia and related disorders have been grouped together and cataloged in the annuls of history under a variety of other names, such as *dementia praecox* or premature dementia, adolescent insanity, hebephrenia, or simply madness. The term schizophrenia was not coined until Paul Eugen Bleuler first described the disorder as a splitting of the mind during a lecture in 1908 (Jablensky, 2010). How about this? Is it a myth or reality that the disorder of schizophrenia, as we know it today, did not exist prior to the 18th century? Reality: If you know the answer to this question, you should publish an article or book, because no one else seems to know definitively! A number of researchers have asked this question, and the origins of the collection of symptoms today that we call schizophrenia appear to be lost in the pages of history. Most researchers of the history of schizophrenia appear to agree that there is a dearth of historical records that depict symptoms clearly enough to come to a conclusion. Some researchers suggest that symptom profiles resembling schizophrenia can be found to demonstrate that the disorder did exist earlier in history, but that cases were rarer than they appear to have become since the 18th century (Jeste et al., 1985). Other researchers argue that despite some symptoms of psychosis being delineated in ancient times, the full range of schizophrenia symptoms as a collective diagnosis does not appear in ancient texts at all (Evans et al., 2003). Heinrichs (2003) suggested that attempting to establish the prevalence of schizophrenia prior to the 18th century was likely not feasible, and that the debate over how recently the disorder became common may not be able to be settled, though he points to some convincing records as early as the 14th century. As we come to know more about the etiology of the disorder, we may be able to draw conclusions regarding why schizophrenia appears to have become more prevalent since the 18th century; for example, conditions related to the industrial revolution or migration to life in cities.

Regardless of these debates, we know that by the middle of the 18th century, some researchers and clinicians were beginning to refer to the disorder as an early-life form of dementia (Jablensky, 2010). Perhaps the most well-known use of the term *dementia praecox,* was Emile Kraepelin's use to distinguish schizophrenia symptoms from symptoms of manic depression (bipolar disorder), and generally speaking to draw a strong distinction between psychotic disorders and mood disorders. This distinction is known today as the

Kraepelinian Dichotomy

Distinction made by Emile Kraepelin between psychotic disorders and mood disorders, especially bipolar disorder

Kraepelinian dichotomy. Kraepelin's research on schizophrenia was longitudinal, based on many years of work with schizophrenia patients, and he accurately collected a wealth of information on the disorder, including the recognition of catatonia, disordered thought, hallucinations and delusions, and emotional disturbances as belonging to the same disease, just with a variety of manifestations (Jablensky, 2010). In the days before antipsychotic medications to help control symptoms, it is no wonder that Kraepelin also concluded that the disorder was terminal and degenerative, as this likely reflected his experience of working with patients.

Interestingly, Bleuler, who coined the term schizophrenia in 1908 to replace the terminology of *dementia praecox*, did not come to the same conclusion. Rather than concluding that schizophrenia was necessarily terminal, he held that schizophrenia was a group of diseases, using the term "schizophrenias" and recognizing that some forms were more degenerative than others (Jablensky, 2010). Bleuler added further distinctions to those of Kraepelin, including the formation of subgroups of the disorder and a distinction between basic and accessory symptoms, which foreshadowed today's distinction between positive symptoms and negative symptoms; eventually, Kraepelin conceded that his formulation was perhaps incorrect (Jablensky, 2010). By 1952, with the American Psychiatric Association's publication of the first Diagnostic and Statistical Manual of Mental Disorders (DSM-I), many

Positive Symptoms

Symptoms of schizophrenia and related disorders in excess of normal human activities, for example, hallucinations

Negative Symptoms

Symptoms of schizophrenia and related disorders that are characterized by a deficiency or reduction in normal human activities, for example, reduced motivation

Emil Kraepelin

Source: Welcome Library, Library.

of the distinctions made by Bleuler and Kraepelin were solidified in the fields of psychiatry and psychology and are reflected in the original publication remaining somewhat similar throughout subsequent editions.

The 4 Fs of the Schizophrenia Spectrum: The "Split-Mind" in Action

Considering that schizophrenia and related disorders are characterized by such a wide range of symptoms, some of which can be severe and intense, teasing apart the "real" schizophrenia from the widespread myths becomes even more important, especially considering the level of dysfunction and suffering that some folks with this disorder experience. If you get confused by whether you are hearing a schizophrenia myth or reality, be sure to come back to the 4 Fs of schizophrenia to guide you, and to help you figure out the type and severity of schizophrenia or related disorder in question.

Frequency

A—Amount of Time: The amount of time that a person must experience symptoms for a diagnosis in the schizophrenia spectrum of disorders, varies widely and depends in large part on the disorder, as you can see from the list below (APA, 2013).

Brief Psychotic Disorder: Presence of symptoms for at least 1 day, but less than 1 month.

Delusional Disorder: Presence of at least one delusion for no less than 1 month.

Schizoaffective Disorder: Presence of delusions or hallucinations for at least 2 weeks without the co-occurrence of a major mood disorder episode. In addition, full criteria for a mood disorder episode must be met at times other than this 2-week period of delusions or hallucinations.

Schizophreniform Disorder: Presence of symptoms for at least 1 month, but less than 6 months.

Schizophrenia: Signs of continual symptoms for at least 6 months, during which the person must experience a 1-month period of symptoms meeting full criteria for the disorder.

Delusions

Strongly held beliefs, which are patently false, but held in spite of clear evidence of their inaccuracy

Hallucinations

Experiencing sensations in the absence of stimuli possible of causing the sensations

It is important to note that the criteria for these time periods reflect the disorders if left untreated or if treatment is not successful. If treatment begins prior to the period required for diagnosis, then the person may be diagnosed with a disorder without meeting the full-time requirement (APA, 2013). For example, imagine that a person has had signs of schizophrenia for 3 months, and after 3 weeks of meeting full criteria for the disorder, he or she begins taking antipsychotics. This patient may be diagnosed even if some symptoms

Positive Symptoms

- Delusions
- Hallucinations
- Disorganized thinking & speech
- Communication exaggerations & distortions
- Disorganized Behavior
- Catatonic Symptoms
- Agitation

Negative Symptoms

- Affective blunting
- Social & emotional withdrawal
- Passivity & reduced spontaneity
- Problems with abstract thinking
- Stereotypical thinking & speech
- Alogia: reduced speech output
- Avolition: reduced actions
- Anhedonia: reduced pleasure
- Impaired attention

FIGURE 6.1   Positive & Negative Symptoms of Schizophrenia
APA, 2013; Stahl, 2011, p. 251

subside prior to meeting the 1-month criteria.

B—Behavior: In terms of the frequency of behaviors related to schizophrenia spectrum disorders, for most of the above disorders, symptoms must be present for the majority of the time periods denoted above in section A, but which symptoms are present will vary from disorder to disorder, as will the level of dysfunction that the person may experience. As you may have figured by now, delusional disorder is characterized (almost exclusively) by delusions, whereas other schizophrenia spectrum disorders involve hallucinations, disorganized thinking or speech, and grossly abnormal or disorganized movement; for example, catatonia or repetitive motor movements (APA, 2013). In addition to the above symptoms, which are often referred to as positive symptoms, individuals across the schizophrenia spectrum may also experience negative symptoms characterized primarily by reduced emotional expression, reduced motivation and initiation of activities, referred to as avolition and frequently including alogia, anhedonia, and asociality, a reduced interest in social interactions.

C—Curve: Prevalence rates across the schizophrenia spectrum vary by disorder. All of these forms of psychoses are relatively rare within any given society, but some differences appear to exist between cultures. Additionally, men have been found to more frequently exhibit negative symptoms than women, and to more frequently have long-term varieties of the disorder characterized by worse overall outcomes (APA, 2013). Women, on the other hand, appear to more frequently suffer with briefer forms of the disorder, and also varieties of the disorder, which involve mood impairments; for example, schizoaffective disorder (APA, 2013). Overall, the prevalence rate of delusional disorder appears to be about 0.2%, whereas the rate of schizophrenia

Catatonia

Motor disorder characterized by disorganized behavior and/or the complete absence of movement

Avolition

Reduced or absent motivation to perform self-directed actions

Alogia

Reduction or absence of speech production

Anhedonia

Loss of pleasure in things once experienced as pleasurable

is estimated to be between 0.3 to 0.7%, and schizoaffective disorder is estimated to be 0.3% (APA, 2013). Among all occurrences of schizophrenia spectrum and related disorders, brief psychotic disorders occur most frequently, accounting for approximately 9% of individuals experiencing their first psychotic episode, and to be about two times more frequent among women than men (APA, 2013).

The Good News: Schizophrenia and related disorders are among the most widely researched disorders in the world, and treatments for schizophrenia spectrum disorders have continued to improve over the past 50 years. Persons diagnosed with the disorder are no longer considered to be beyond hope of improvement. Additionally, while the media may call attention to the worst cases of psychosis, many people only have brief cognitive disturbances, and then return to healthy functioning.

Function

Myth or Reality: Hallucinations in schizophrenia are primarily visual? Despite the manner in which Hollywood tends to portray schizophrenia, auditory hallucinations are actually more common in individuals suffering from schizophrenia. Waters et al. (2014) conducted a meta-analysis of studies related to visual hallucinations, reporting that 27% of individuals with schizophrenia experienced visual hallucinations across 29 previous studies, whereas 59% experienced auditory hallucinations. McCarthy-Jones et al. (2017) reported similar findings among participants from Ireland and Australia, with 63.9% and 79.8% experiencing auditory hallucinations, and 22.9% and 30.7% experiencing visual hallucinations, respectively. Interestingly, this study further reported that most patients only experienced one type of hallucination, though 30 to 37% of those with auditory hallucinations also experienced some visual hallucinations, whereas 83 to 97% of those with visual hallucinations also experienced auditory hallucinations (McCarthy-Jones et al., 2017).

With any discussion of hallucinations, it quickly becomes clear that the dysfunction related to schizophrenia can be severe, although consider also that many individuals with schizophrenia do not experience hallucinations at all. Due to the wide variety of ways that the disorder may present, the DSM-5 refers to it as a heterogeneous clinical syndrome (APA, 2013). Many people mistakenly believe that in order to have a diagnosis of schizophrenia, a person must experience hallucinations and delusions. In fact, this is another myth. The DSM-5 specifies that the only shared forms of dysfunction related to schizophrenia are problems with occupational and social difficulties (APA, 2013). In other words, the significance of distress related to schizophrenia is often serious enough to lead to difficulties with employment and in relationships, despite the variety of symptoms experienced. This variety can be understood clearly by the DSM-5 requirement that individuals diagnosed with schizophrenia must suffer from at least two of five

Myths in Movies

A BEAUTIFUL MIND and THE SOLOIST

Consider the movie, *A Beautiful Mind,* starring Russell Crowe as the mathematics genius John Nash. Despite the portrayal of Nash as suffering from visual and auditory hallucinations, his hullucinations were auditory, rather than visual. Of course, movies are a visual as well as an auditory artistic medium, but the frequent visual portrayal of hallucinations in the media has likely contributed to the myth that most hallucinations are are in fact visual. Think about how auditory hallucinations might work in conjunction with delusions to get a more clear idea of what life was life for John Nash. *The Soloist,* also based on a true story, more accurately portrays the auditory hallucinations of Nathaniel Ayers, a brilliant musician who goes from Juilliard to homelessness as a result of schizophrenia.

© Universal Pictures/Photofest

Another myth that may have inadvertently been promoted by the telling of John Nash's story, unlike the story of Nathaniel Ayers, is the idea that individuals with schizophrenia are frequently able to exert control over their psychotic symptoms. We will explore this myth further in our next segment of *Myths in Movies.*

© DreamWorks/Photofest

symptoms, including hallucinations, delusions, disorganized thinking or speech, disorganized behavior or catatonia, and negative symptoms. In addition to this requirement, one of the symptoms must be either hallucinations, delusions, or disorganized speech. Consider the possible combinations of symptoms that a clinician might experience or write down a few possible combinations of symptoms.

Hopefully, you are beginning to grasp a much clearer experiential picture of the functional difficulties related to schizophrenia. An important question you may have asked yourself by this point is, "What happens to people who have schizophrenia?" It is a commonly held myth that everyone with schizophrenia will end up homeless, or the reverse is sometimes held that virtually all homeless people have schizophrenia or a related severe mental illness. Though broad generalizations are often somewhat inaccurate, those involving homelessness and schizophrenia are founded upon a bit of truth, as experiencing schizophrenia does increase one's risk of periods of homelessness. Folsom & Jeste (2002) conducted a review of the literature, finding across the 10 most rigorous studies that between 4 to 16% of homeless individuals had schizophrenia, despite some earlier claims between 45 to 50%. While these findings suggest much lower rates than previously believed, an average rate of 11% of homelessness related to schizophrenia reported by Folsom and Jeste (2002), suggests a profound need for programs to assist those with this debilitating disorder.

Fatality

Do folks with schizophrenia have higher mortality rates? Research has suggested not only that the mortality rate for individuals with schizophrenia is higher, but that it is double the rate found in the general population, and increasing. Hoang et al. (2011) investigated the mortality rate of schizophrenia patients after discharge from a hospital setting, and discovered that the rate has climbed from 1.6 times that of the general population in 1999, to 2.2 times higher in 2006. They reported that rates of death by unnatural causes were greater than the general population, suggesting that individuals with schizophrenia are at a substantial risk of death due to accidents and injuries, but also that the rate of death by natural causes appeared to be increasing more rapidly, suggesting that poor self-care, access to medical care, and other functional impairments are also likely contributing to worse physiological health (Hoang et al., 2011). In line with these findings, the primary causes of death for individuals with schizophrenia appear to be related to suicide, cancer, and cardiovascular disease, some of which may be exacerbated by the increased use of tobacco, drugs, and alcohol among schizophrenia patients (APA, 2013; Bushe et al., 2010). The suicide risks for these individuals is high after onset of the disorder and across the lifespan, with increased risks for those experiencing command hallucinations. Approximately 20% of individuals with schizophrenia attempt suicide, and 5 to 6% of schizophrenia patients complete suicide (APA, 2013).

Another common myth is the idea that all people who have schizophrenia are always dangerous. This myth is important to dispel due to the potential for increased stigmatization of individuals with the disorder. First, it is important to recognize that younger males with schizophrenia and those who have a history of impulsivity, substance abuse, and past violence appear to be more prone to aggression (APA, 2013). Additionally, a subset of individuals with schizophrenia and related disorders, especially individuals who experience paranoid delusions and violent command hallucinations, are more likely to be a danger to others than most individuals with schizophrenia; however, this group represents only a small portion of individuals with the disorder. Interestingly, Lindberg and Curtis (2018) discovered that 55% of undergraduate students in their sample (n = 178) believed that individuals

Case Vignette

Claude is a 22-year-old college student. One day his mom tells him that he needs to go register for classes for the next semester, so he gets online later in the day to find that registration is not yet open. When Claude tells his mother this news the following day, she does not recall their earlier conversation, and he becomes worried that she may be messing with him to make him feel crazy. He begins to consider all the reasons that she is wrong, and diligently starts looking for evidence. Claude finds a call logged on his phone from around the time the conversation took place, and his roommates confirmed that they heard him talking to someone in his bedroom about class schedules, and he even finds a course catalog with classes and dates circled, and notes he took during the discussion. Is his mother doing this vindictively? If not, why is she having memory problems? He wonders if he needs to try and find a good doctor to help her.

This scenario is meant to illustrate the subtlety and confusion that oftentimes occurs for people with schizophrenia, some of whom seem to be more aware that there is a problem, while others are more entirely convinced by their delusions and hallucinations. Both situations can be seriously distressing.

with schizophrenia are more likely to be a danger to other people than they are to themselves. Regardless of the fact that most people with schizophrenia are not a danger to others, the majority of us would likely still not feel comfortable leaving our children alone with a person experiencing active psychosis, even if the person is not experiencing hallucinations or delusions of a violent or suspicious nature. The difficulty with this myth is that the content and course of psychotic episodes are unreliable, and with violence being one possibility, even if only present within a small subset of schizophrenia patients, people unfamiliar with the disorder are likely to guard against the worst-case scenario. In reality, individuals with schizophrenia, the majority of whom are not violent, are more frequently the victims of violence compared to the general population (APA, 2013).

Feeling Pain

Pain may come in many forms for those with schizophrenia and related disorders. Consider the distress of being vaguely aware that what you're experiencing is not quite right, but being able to do little to stop it. Consider, on the other hand, being totally convinced that your mother and father want to poison your food or get you kicked out of school. Individuals with more awareness may be more capable of purposefully choosing to seek help, though

Myths in Movies

DONNIE DARKO AND SUCKER PUNCH

Fictitious cult flicks such as *Donnie Darko* and *Sucker Punch* tend to overemphasize violence, confuse imagination and psychosis, and accordingly make it appear that individuals may have more control over their symptoms than is actually the case. As we have discussed, individuals on the schizophrenia spectrum are not inherently a threat to others, and most individuals with the disorder have little or no control over their hallucinations and delusions. *Sucker Punch* gets the award for cliche' here; however, with the quintessential portrayal of patients in an asylum. These patients are being taught to use imagination/hallucination to escape their problems, and in a similar way, Donnie Darko's hallucinations and delusions provide key insights that lead him to solve

Scenes from *Donnie Darko* (above) and *Sucker Punch* (below)

a crisis facing his town. When confronted with these portrayals, it is important to reemphasize that most individuals on the schizophrenia spectrum are neither aware, nor capable, of controlling their symptoms.

this awareness can also wax and wane. Be that as it may, self-awareness and awareness of symptom severity appears to be diminished for the majority of individuals with schizophrenia, who often struggle to understand their deficits in attention, memory, and other areas of cognitive function (Medalia & Lim, 2004; Pinkham et al., 2018; Poletti et al., 2012).

Another area of distress that sometimes gets overshadowed by emphasis on delusions and hallucinations involves the confusion of disorganized thinking and speech that often characterizes schizophrenia. In the above example, Claude seems to be thinking somewhat clearly, especially by looking for evidence that a conversation occurred, but upon consideration, any of these events could have taken place in the context of a delusion or could have been co-opted from other conversations or memories to support the delusion. Here we see a lack of insight, coupled with the experience of irrelevant material as meaningful. Therapists will often report that some of their most powerful experiences of working with individuals on the schizophrenia spectrum have involved disorganized thinking used to support delusions.

Disorganized thinking and speech have often been described as loosely connected, tangential, and incoherent, sometimes referred to as "word salad" (APA, 2013). Look at Figure 6.2. Responses 2–4 demonstrate milder disorganized thinking, less tangential, with more coherence and connection. Responses 5–8 demonstrate more severe disorganized thinking, with more loosely connected ideas and almost complete incoherence (word salad). As you can imagine, this can be difficult for therapists, even with milder disorganized thinking because it can be more difficult to recognize, and more meaning can be inferred from the statements.

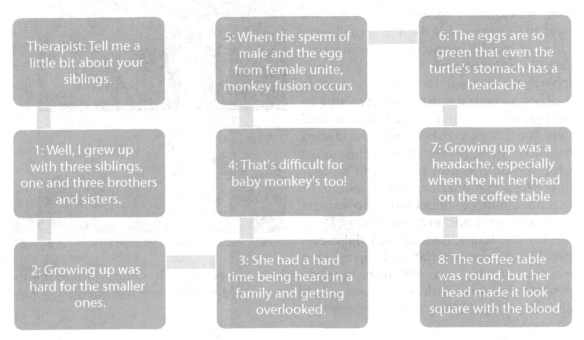

FIGURE 6.2   **An Example of Disorganized Thinking and Speech**
Courtesy of Leslie Kelley

Schizophrenia Course and Development

Why do you think that some of the early schizophrenia theorists considered schizophrenia a form of dementia? At least part of the answer to this question lies in the course and development of the disorder. Among the strangest and most disturbing aspects of the schizophrenia spectrum disorders is the fact that onset for psychosis typically does not occur until late adolescence or early adulthood, before which the person can appear to be doing completely fine. Another interesting fact is that onset typically differs between males and females, with males typically experiencing their first psychotic episode in their early to mid-20s, and females in their late 20s (APA, 2013). The typical range for onset is between late adolescence and mid-30s, and though cases do occur with earlier and later onset, they are rare and many questions remain in regard to the similarities and differences of these various forms of the disorder. For example, late-onset schizophrenia, after the age of 40, appears to be more common among women, and is predominated by psychotic features with fewer affective and social functioning problems (APA, 2013).

In regard to onset, schizophrenia appears much like forms of dementia. An individual can appear to be doing fine at work or in school, even excelling in academics or their career, and then begin to experience onset with little or no warning after which he or she may then struggle, for the remainder of their life in some cases, just to return to a semblance of their prior functioning. Researchers do not yet know why outcomes are better for some individuals than they are for others, but around 20% of people diagnosed with schizophrenia appear to have a favorable outcome, and a small portion of these folks have been reported to experience complete recovery (APA, 2013).

DSM-5 CRITERIA FOR SCHIZOPHRENIA

DIAGNOSTIC CRITERA

A.   Two (or more) of the following, each present for a significant portion of time during a 1-month period (or less if successfully treated). At least one of these must be (1), (2), or (3):

1.   Delusions.

2.   Hallucinations.

3.   Disorganized speech (e.g., frequent derailment or incoherence).

4.   Grossly disorganized or catatonic behavior.

5.   Negative symptoms (i.e., diminished emotional expression or avolition).

B.   For a significant portion of the time since the onset of the disturbance, level of functioning in one or more major areas, such as work, interpersonal relations, or self-care, is markedly below the level achieved prior to the onset (or when the onset is in childhood or adolescence, there is failure to achieve expected level of interpersonal, academic, or occupational functioning).

C.   Continuous signs of the disturbance persist for at least 6 months. This 6-month period must include at least 1 month of symptoms (or less if successfully treated) that meet Criterion A (i.e., active-phase symptoms) and may include periods of prodromal or residual symptoms. During these prodromal or residual periods, the signs of the disturbance may be manifested by only negative symptoms or by two or more symptoms listed in Criterion A present in an attenuated form (e.g., odd beliefs, unusual perceptual experiences).

D.   Schizoaffective disorder and depressive or bipolar disorder with psychotic features have been ruled out because either (1) no major depressive or manic episodes have occurred concurrently with the active-phase symptoms, or (2) if mood episodes have occurred during active-phase symptoms, they have been present for a minority of the total duration of the active and residual periods of the illness.

E. The disturbance is not attributable to the physiological effects of a substance (e.g., a drug of abuse, a medication) or another medical condition.

F. If there is a history of autism spectrum disorder or a communication disorder of childhood onset, the additional diagnosis of schizophrenia is made only if prominent delusions or hallucinations, in addition to the other required symptoms of schizophrenia, are also present for at least 1 month (or less if successfully treated).

Specify if:

The following course specifiers are only to be used after a 1-year duration of the disorder and if they are not in contradiction to the diagnostic course criteria.

First episode, currently in acute episode: First manifestation of the disorder meeting the defining diagnostic symptom and time criteria. An *acute episode* is a time period in which the symptom criteria are fulfilled.

First episode, currently a partial remission: *Partial remission* is a period of time during which an improvement after a previous episode is maintained and in which the defining criteria of the disorder are only partially fulfilled.

First episode, currently in full remission: *Full remission* is a period of time after a previous episode during which no disorder-specific symptoms are present.

Multiple episodes, currently in acute episode: Multiple episodes may be determined after a minimum of two episodes (i.e., after a first episode, a remission and a minimum of one relapse).

Multiple episodes, currently in partial remission

Multiple episodes, currently in full remission

Continuous: Symptoms fulfilling the diagnostic symptom criteria of the disorder are remaining for the majority of the illness course, with subthreshold symptom periods being very brief relative to the overall course.

Unspecified

Specify if:

With catatonia (refer to the criteria for catatonia associated with another mental disorder, pp. 119–120, for definition).

Coding note: Use additional code 293.89 (F06.1) catatonia associated with schizophrenia to indicate the presence of the comorbid catatonia.

Specify current severity:

Severity is rated by a quantitative assessment of the primary symptoms of psychosis, including delusions, hallucinations, disorganized speech, abnormal psychomotor behavior, and negative symptoms. Each of these symptoms may be rated for its current severity (most severe in the last 7 days) on a 5-point scale ranging from 0 (not present) to 4 (present and severe). (See Clinician-Rated Dimensions of Psychosis Symptom Severity in the chapter "Assessment Measures.")

Note: Diagnosis of schizophrenia can be made without using this severity specifier.

Other Psychotic Disorders

Previously, in this chapter, we have discussed the duration of various schizophrenia spectrum disorders. Let's turn now to a discussion of the diagnostic criteria for the disorders other than schizophrenia.

Did you know that the DSM-5 has now pathologized jealousy? Perhaps funnier still is that even in our suffocating climate against stereotyping, the DSM-5 proclaims that the jealous type of delusional disorder is "probably more common in males than females," without further explanation (APA, 2013, p. 92). As disappointing as this lack of clarity may be, it is found in several areas of the manual, and points toward the reality that many disorders involve excesses or deficiencies of normal human experience. A proficient psychologist or researcher knows where to draw the line between normal and abnormal. In other words, there is a difference between jealously, which all of us experience at some point, and the jealous subtype of delusional disorder. Thinking in terms of the 4 Fs can help you determine where to draw this line.

Including the jealous subtype, Delusional Disorder can be classified into a total of seven subtypes: jealous, erotomanic, grandiose, persecutory, somatic, mixed, and unspecified. See Table 6.1 for a further explanation and example for each subtype. Delusional Disorder is considered to be on the less severe end of the schizophrenia spectrum, and generally causes less severe global functioning decline, though declines can be severe if delusions intensify in the absence of other symptoms (APA, 2013). Hallucinations and mood disturbance may also be experienced as part of delusional disorder, but cannot be a prominent part of the clinical picture, and hallucinations are generally related closely to the theme of a delusion. If symptoms other than delusions become more serious, a different diagnosis on the schizophrenia spectrum is more likely to be accurate.

© Rasulov/Shutterstock.com

A grandiose delusion, perhaps!

Brief Psychotic Disorder, another disorder on the less severe end of the schizophrenia spectrum, is characterized by at least one of the following symptoms: delusions, hallucinations, disorganized speech and/or thinking, or disorganized and/or catatonic behavior. Brief Psychotic Disorder differs from more severe forms of schizophrenia, however, both in terms of the brevity of symptoms, lasting less than 1 month, and in the presence of fewer symptoms. Prognosis for those with Brief Psychotic Disorders tends to be good, despite the high rates of relapse, and social and occupational functioning are generally far less compromised than with more severe forms of psychosis (APA, 2013).

TABLE 6.1   Delusional Subtypes

Erotomanic	• Delusions centered around another person being in love with oneself • Example: The belief that the grocery store clerk is madly in love with you. She's always so kind to you, after all!
Grandiose	• Delusions involving oneself as being especially important or talented • Example: The belief that you are the president or invented something important! So, you came up with the idea of toothpaste, did you!
Jealous	• Delusions centered around one's partner being unfaithful • Example: The belief that your husband or wife is having an affair. I was with you the entire afternoon, how could I have seen another man!
Persecutory	• Delusions related to someone cheating, conspiring against, or otherwise persecuting oneself • Example: The belief that the CIA is after you. My phones are tapped!!! When I took it apart, I found this strange piece inside of it!
Somatic	• Delusions involving a physiological function or sensation • Example: The belief that a small physical pain is a much larger problem. I know that pain in my stomach must be cancer, or at least a tumor of some kind!
Mixed	• Subtype used when no one type of delusion is predominant • Example: Any combination of the above. I know you're in love with me, so why are you with that other man, especially when I'm a billionaire!
Unspecified	• Subtype used when no central theme of the delusions can be determined • Example: Delusions of reference (i.e., falsely believing things to refer to oneself). Why are those people at the park always talking about me?

APA, 2013

Perhaps one of the least understood and discussed disorders on the schizophrenia spectrum, Schizophreniform Disorder, is characterized by the same symptom profile as schizophrenia, albeit with a shorter period of dysfunction, less than 6 months. Prognosis is mixed for those with the disorder, and better outcomes are more likely if the patient is confused or perplexed by the onset of symptoms, has had better social and occupational functioning prior to the onset of symptoms, has not experienced flat or blunted affect, and/or if any significant psychotic symptoms begin within 4 weeks of other changes in behavior (APA, 2013). The prevalence of Schizophreniform

Disorder is believed to be comparable to schizophrenia, with one third of individuals originally diagnosed with the disorder recovering within 6 months, and receiving no other diagnosis. The other two thirds experience a further decline in functioning, and therefore receive a more severe psychotic diagnosis (APA, 2013).

Another schizophrenia spectrum disorder, which is easily confused with certain mood disorders, even among clinicians, is Schizoaffective Disorder. Schizoaffective Disorder can be considered schizophrenia plus a mood disorder, and accordingly to receive this diagnosis a person must meet criteria for either a manic or depressive episode, while concurrently meeting the basic symptom criteria (Criterion A) for a diagnosis of schizophrenia. In addition to this, delusions or hallucinations must be present for at least 2 weeks without a mood episode, though individuals must meet the criteria for mood episodes for the majority of the duration of the illness (APA, 2013). Schizoaffective Disorders are often clinically confused with severe depressive or bipolar disorders with psychotic features. While there is significant overlap, it may be helpful to think of Schizoaffective Disorder as schizophrenia plus a mood disorder and to think of severe mood disorders with psychotic features as mood disorder plus psychotic features. That is, full criteria cannot be met for schizophrenia or else you're looking at Schizoaffective Disorder. Though Schizoaffective Disorder is less prevalent than schizophrenia, the suicide risk is comparable, at approximately 5% completing suicide (APA, 2013). Individuals with Schizoaffective Disorder, however, are not required to meet the criteria of social and occupational impairment as with schizophrenia, and individuals with the disorder vary widely in terms of dysfunction and outcome (APA, 2013).

Schizotypal (Personality) Disorder, within the last several editions of the DSM, has been understood and listed with personality disorders, but is understood to fall within the schizophrenia spectrum, and has even been listed with other schizophrenia disorders as schizotypal disorder in the last two versions of the International Classification of Diseases (ICD-9 & ICD-10). Schizotypal Personality Disorder is characterized by persistent symptoms, which are less severe than many other schizophrenia spectrum disorders, for example, paranoid or referential ideation, without paranoid or referential delusions. As with other personality disorders, Schizotypal Disorder is pervasive, with a fairly stable course, and few individuals go on to develop symptoms consistent with more severe psychotic disorders. Schizotypal Personality Disorder will be further discussed with other personality disorders in Chapter 16.

For all of the disorders on the schizophrenia spectrum, with the exception of Schizotypal Personality Disorder, severity of symptoms is important, recognizing that any given psychotic disorder may be experienced with lesser or greater severity. The DSM-5 has clinicians rate the severity of symptoms

TABLE 6.2 **Symptoms of Catatonia**

Stupor	• Absence of psychomotor activity or reaction to stimuli in environment
Catalepsy	• Passively accepting a body posture held against gravity
Waxy Flexibility	• Having a consistently slight resistence when being positioned by an examiner
Mutism	• Little or no verbal responses without the presence of aphasia
Negativism	• Not responding or being opposed to instructions or other stimuli
Posturing	• Actively and spontaneously maintaining a posture against gravity
Mannerism	• Odd caricatures of typical actions
Stereotypy	• Frequently repeating movements with not clear direction or goal
Agitation	• Agitation in the absense of stimuli capable of causing agitation
Grimacing	• Facial expressions of discomfort, often in the absence of stimuli
Echolalia	• Repeating the speech of another person
Echopraxia	• Repeating the movements of another person

APA, 2013

on a five-point scale, based on the most severe symptoms over the past 7 days, with zero indicating that a symptom was not present at all, and four representing that the symptom was both present and severe (APA, 2013).

Another important category of specification is catatonia, which often accompanies disorders on the schizophrenia spectrum, but can also occur along with many other disorders (APA, 2013). Catatonia can present in a large variety of manners, and individuals need only meet three out of 12 possible symptoms. See Table 6.2 for a description of the different symptoms of catatonia. The DSM-5 specifies that catatonia is generally diagnosed in an inpatient setting, estimating that approximately 35% of individuals with schizophrenia experience catatonia, and that the majority of catatonia cases are related to mood disorders (APA, 2013).

Theories and Treatments of Psychotic Disorders

One of the most insidious myths related to schizo-phrenia is the idea that the disorder is untreatable or that someone with this diagnosis is beyond hope. While schizophrenia and related psychotic disorders can often take a degenerative course, this is not the case for everyone. Most researchers and clinicians agree that the combination of biological and psychological treatments is most likely to bring about the best possible functioning for those on the schizophrenia spectrum, and most clinicians will

The myth that schizophrenia is always degenerative may impact how we conceptualize treatment.

refuse to work with individuals experiencing active psychosis if they are not taking medications. Imagine that someone is delusional and speaking in a confused manner, to what degree is talk therapy likely to be helpful to the person?

Biological and Environmental Theories of Psychotic Disorders

When discussing biological theories of schizophrenia and related disorders, we must think back to the diathesis-stress model and the dynamic interac-tion of biology and environment. While a wealth of research has implicated genes, brain abnormalities, neurotransmitters, and experiential components, many routes to the disorder may exist, with varying degrees of influence from each of these components. As Murphy (2010) puts it, "Schizophrenia is currently best understood as an illness whose symptoms are related to brain abnormalities that are the final common pathway from a multitude of etiol-ogies, due to the assorted interaction of specific genetic and environmental factors" (p. 203).

Genetic Factors

Biological theories strongly emphasizing genetics, are more likely to con-sider schizophrenia to be a "heritable brain illness" (Sekar et al., 2016, p. 177). Some genetic theories of schizophrenia rely on evidence from family and twin studies. These studies have demonstrated that having a 50% genetic similarity (one parent, a fraternal twin, or another sibling) to someone with schizophrenia increases the risk of developing the disorder to 10 to 14%, whereas having a 100% genetic similarity (identical twin) or if both par-ents had schizophrenia, then the risk increases dramatically to 40 to 50%

(Gottesman, 1991; Murphy, 2010). These genetic risks remain comparable, even when a child is adopted and raised in a home apart from biological relatives with the disorder. While family studies provide strong evidence for the involvement of genetic factors, it is also important to note that not everyone with an identical twin or two parents with schizophrenia develops the disorder. In two thirds of cases the affected person has no relative with the disorder, suggesting environmental causes are likely also at work in the development of the disorder (Murphy, 2010). Epigenetic studies have pointed to a similarity in genetic expression among identical twins who both have schizophrenia, and a dissimilarity between sets of identical twins wherein only one has the disorder (Petronis et al., 2003). Despite identical twins sharing the same DNA sequence, Petronis and colleagues suggested that the affected identical twin of a pair discordant for schizophrenia may be more epigenetically similar in some ways to other individuals with schizophrenia than to his or her own identical twin.

Epigenetics

The study of genetic changes due to external or environmental factors

A host of specific genes have been potentially implicated in the etiology of schizophrenia, including neregulin-1, dysbinding, the 5-HT2A receptor gene, catechol-O-methyltransferase, and the G72 protein gene, many of which are linked to neurodevelopment, including neurotransmitter function and brain structure (Mäki et al., 2005; Murphy, 2010). Be this as it may, many of the largest genome-wide studies have failed to find a genetic marker strongly related to the disorder (Murphy, 2010). The patterns of inheritance of genes which predispose individuals to schizophrenia is highly complex, likely involving many genes, with linkages between psychotic disorders, personality disorders, mood disorders, autoimmune disorders, and other disorders (Murphy, 2010). For example, one large-scale study from Sweden calculated the genetic correlation between schizophrenia and bipolar disorder to be 0.6, and other researchers are looking closely at common susceptibility genes that may be activated in different manners, leading to one disorder versus another (Bjarkam et al., 2009; Lichtenstein et al., 2009).

One promising theory receiving recent support has been referred to as the Immune System Dysfunction Theory, and involves the Major Histocompatibility Complex (MHC), which plays an important role in immunity during brain development, and has been recognized by some researchers as having the strongest genetic relationship to schizophrenia (Debnath et al., 2013; Sekar et al., 2016). Particularly, varying C4 gene alleles within the MHC may be implicated in decreased synapse development in key areas of the brain related to development of schizophrenia symptoms (Sekar et al., 2016). Exactly how the genetic template of those predisposed to schizophrenia become activated in some and not in others, especially in the cases of one identical twin and not the other, is quite a mystery. Hess et al. (2019) have suggested that a polygenic resilience score, attempting to account for a wide array of genetic variants associated with resilience to the development of schizophrenia, may help unravel the sources of their differential genetic etiology. Additionally, however, researchers have suggested that prenatal, perinatal, and a host of other environmental risk factors may help explain some aspects of the mystery.

Environmental Factors

A wide array of environmental factors have been explored as potentially contributing to the development of schizophrenia. Be clear that this is not an understatement! These studies have explored prenatal exposure to infection and other maternal nutrition and health issues, season of birth, age of one's father, a variety of perinatal health complications, breastfeeding, a variety of infections during childhood, urban living, migration, childhood trauma and other stressors, cannabis and substance abuse, exposure to toxins, head injuries, and the list goes on (Murphy, 2010). Researchers have posited a "two-hit" hypothesis, suggesting that being exposed to one of these factors during developmental periods may prime a person for schizophrenia, and additional exposures may then lead more directly to the expression of symptoms (Murphy, 2010).

Environmental factors, including maternal illness, may increase risk.

© mathom/Shutterstock.com

Interestingly, some of these environmental factors are likely linked. For example, some research has found that individuals with schizophrenia are more likely to be born between winter and spring, with frequencies 5 to 8% higher, and it is during this time that individuals are more likely to have infections such as the flu, which has been found to double a person's risk of schizophrenia if their mother has the influenza virus during the second trimester (Mäki et al., 2005). Three categories of prenatal and birth complications have been linked to increased risk of the development of schizophrenia, including pregnancy complications (e.g., pre-eclampsia, iron deficient anemia, diabetes, low folic acid levels), abnormal fetal development (e.g., smaller head circumference, congenital malformation, and reduced birth weight), and delivery complications (e.g., loss of oxygen, uterine atony, emergency deliveries), all of which likely predispose an individual to schizophrenia or similar disorders (Cannon et al., 2002; Mäki et al., 2005; Murphy, 2010). Certain psychosocial factors during pregnancy have also been found to be more common in those with schizophrenia, many of which appear to be related to maternal stress, including loss of one's husband during pregnancy, exposure to war and disasters during pregnancy, and even experiencing an unwanted pregnancy (Mäki et al., 2005).

Other significant psychosocial factors likewise increase the risk of schizophrenia by impacting prenatal development, including maternal use of tobacco and alcohol, the latter of which can lead to other serious complications, such as fetal alcohol syndrome, and even fetal death. Breastfeeding has been demonstrated as a potential protective factor, with individuals breastfed for less than 2 weeks at an increased risk for schizophrenia (Murphy, 2010). Childhood risk factors for the development of the disorder include middle ear infections and central nervous system infections such as meningitis. These infections may lead to damage to key portions of the central nervous system related to schizophrenia symptoms during important developmental periods; for example, middle ear infections were highly correlated with the later development of auditory hallucinations, possibly related to damage to portions of the temporal lobe or auditory cortex (Murphy, 2010).

Some of the psychosocial factors that are believed to be connected to the development of schizophrenia are still much more questionable and need further investigation; for example, urban living and socioeconomic status. While higher rates of schizophrenia are found in people raised in urban areas and belonging to lower socioeconomic classes, the manner in which these factors are related to the development of the disorder remain unclear; for example, impoverished nutrition or environment, exposure to toxins, and so on (Murphy, 2010). Migration, on the other hand, has a much more strongly established history of being related to schizophrenia, which may suggest social isolation and discrimination as mediating factors (Mäki et al., 2005; Murphy, 2010). Interestingly, some research has suggested that individuals living in developing countries tend to experience a better course and outcome, compared to those in developed countries (Jablensky, 2000). Perhaps one of the most frequently discussed factors that has been researched in relation to schizophrenia is childhood adversity and trauma. Interestingly, though some research has shown a clear connection between the disorder and childhood adversity, it remains unclear if some stressors (e.g., childhood abuse and neglect) are more significant than others (e.g., migration, bullying, or parental separation; Murphy, 2010).

Can smoking marijuana make you psychotic? While this does not happen for most people, it is not uncommon, and speaks to the importance of considering the role that drugs of abuse may play in the development of schizophrenia and related disorders. As with most disorders, in order to receive a diagnosis of schizophrenia, a person's symptoms cannot merely be caused by the use of a drug. The use of marijuana and other drugs can lead to a form of psychosis called drug-induced psychosis which in some cases can be the first sign of the development of a more severe psychotic disorder. At least one study has demonstrated that a large portion (44.5%) of individuals first diagnosed with cannabis-induced psychosis were later diagnosed with a schizophrenia-related disorder (Arendt et al., 2005). Drugs of abuse sometimes seem to function as a catalyst or "second hit" that

© Cristina Conti/Shutterstock.com

Drug use, even marijuana, can increase paranoia and trigger a psychotic episode.

leads to a psychotic episode and the development of a longer-term disorder on the spectrum. Other drugs of abuse, such as methamphetamines, ecstasy, cocaine, angel dust, and abuse of solvents, demonstrate similar outcomes. Similarly, those exposed to certain toxins in the environments may also be at an increased risk. Perrin et al. (2007) found a relative risk 3.4 times greater of developing schizophrenia among children of dry cleaners, which was believed to be linked to a specific chemical used in the dry-cleaning process.

A picture may be forming in your mind related to these risks, of increased stress as a child ages, and this would not be an inaccurate picture. In some cases, at least, it appears that individuals who develop schizophrenia may be exposed to stress beginning in the womb, and then on other occasions throughout the life span. Studies indicate that individuals with schizophrenia can experience both hyper- and hypofunction within the hypothalamic-pituitary-adrenal (HPA) axis, a brain system that regulates stress (Bradley & Dinan, 2010). Environmental stressors and poor HPA axis function, coupled with genetic risk factors, may culminate in poor brain development and neurotransmitter function.

Brain Structure and Function

Widespread abnormalities in brain structure have been found among individuals with schizophrenia, which has led to the idea that schizophrenia is a disease that quite literally destroys the brain. But is this real or a myth? Some research has suggested that untreated schizophrenia leads to the deterioration of many brain structures, although other researchers have suggested that causes other than schizophrenia may be involved in the brain abnormalities found post-morbid in schizophrenia patients. Regardless of causation, brain structure abnormalities appear to be at work in both the development and outcomes of schizophrenia.

Although onset of schizophrenia symptoms during childhood is rare, some indicators of later onset have been discovered, including delayed motor and speech milestones, solitary play, adjustment difficulties, including friendships and scholastic performance, certain intellectual impairments, and some minor abnormalities in parts of the body that share an origin in early growth with important brain regions (Murphy, 2010). Many of these early indicators provide evidence for brain differences beginning early in life, an etiology suggested by the neurodevelopmental theory of schizophrenia. Much of the research, however, finds only a small increase in ventricle size and a small reduction in hippocampus and overall brain volume, suggesting that the bulk of brain deterioration may be occurring after the onset of the first psychotic episode (Murphy, 2010).

After onset of the disorder, more dramatic brain changes become evident, including, but not limited to, volume reductions in gray matter

Neurodevelopmental Theory

Theory of schizophrenia as arising from abnormal development of certain areas of the brain

in a wide array of brain areas, such as the temporal and prefrontal lobes (Karlsgodt et al., 2010). The hippocampus, involved with episodic memory and learning, appears to be another of the most heavily impacted area, likely leading to some of the emotional and cognitive deficits related to schizophrenia (Prossin et al., 2010). Another brain structure related to the limbic system that research has demonstrated experiences similar reductions is the thalamus, which is likely related to executive functioning and sensory/perceptual deficits (Cronenwett & Csernansky, 2010). The prefrontal cortex also appears to suffer volume reductions, and in conjuction with the deficits in the thalamus and hippocampus, related emotion regulation and executive functioning problems appear (Prossin et al., 2010).

Additional structural deficits have been consistently demonstrated in schizophrenia patients. For example, changes related to deficits in occipital lobe function are believed to be related to difficulties recognizing the emotional expressions of faces, as well as other perceptual difficulties such as object recognition (Javitt & Coyle, 2004). Within the temporal lobe, which primarily functions as our auditory processing system, some rather interesting differences have been discovered, in addition to overall volume reductions. During auditory hallucinations, researchers have discovered that there is activation of the right hemisphere which correlates to word processing areas (e.g., Broca's area) in the left hemisphere (Sommer et al., 2008). Additionally, activation of parts of the left temporal lobe to actual emotion-laden language may suggest more rational or factual processing of emotional language, which typically involves more right hemisphere activation (Prossin et al., 2010).

While most areas of the brain in schizophrenia are characterized by decreased activity, related to many of the negative symptoms of the disorder, in structures of the basal ganglia an increase in activity and a corresponding volumetric enlargement have been observed, related to many of the positive symptoms of the disorder (Mamah et al., 2007). For example, within the basal ganglia, increased activity in the substantia nigra and increased activity between the substantia nigra and the striatum were understood to be related to more positive psychotic features (Yoon et al., 2013). Interestingly, most of the brain's dopamine is produced in the basal ganglia, so the discoveries of excessive activity and enlargement of the basal ganglia dovetail with some dopamine theories of schizophrenia mentioned below.

Ventricles

Fluid-filled cavities within the interior sections of the brain

Although you may not be aware of it, we all have cavities in our brain. Not the kind that you get filled at the dentist office, though on occasion teeth have been found in some peoples' brain. Not a myth! The ventricles are two empty spaces, or cavities, within our brain. In individuals with schizophrenia, the ventricles are consistently enlarged. As cellular death occurs in other areas of the brain, leading to decreased volumes, the ventricles continue to enlarge.

THE BRAIN IN SCHIZOPHRENIA

MANY BRAIN REGIONS and systems operate abnormally in schizophrenia, including those highlighted below. Imbalances in the neurotransmitter dopamine were once thought to be the prime cause of schizophrenia. But new findings suggest that impoverished signaling by the more pervasive neurotransmitter glutamate—or, more specifically, by one of glutamate's key targets on neurons (the NMDA receptor)—better explains the wide range of symptoms in this disorder.

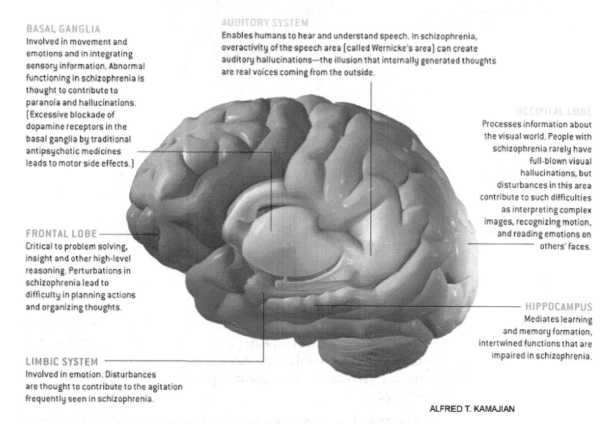

BASAL GANGLIA
Involved in movement and emotions and in integrating sensory information. Abnormal functioning in schizophrenia is thought to contribute to paranoia and hallucinations. (Excessive blockade of dopamine receptors in the basal ganglia by traditional antipsychotic medicines leads to motor side effects.)

AUDITORY SYSTEM
Enables humans to hear and understand speech. In schizophrenia, overactivity of the speech area (called Wernicke's area) can create auditory hallucinations—the illusion that internally generated thoughts are real voices coming from the outside.

OCCIPITAL LOBE
Processes information about the visual world. People with schizophrenia rarely have full-blown visual hallucinations, but disturbances in this area contribute to such difficulties as interpreting complex images, recognizing motion, and reading emotions on others' faces.

FRONTAL LOBE
Critical to problem solving, insight and other high-level reasoning. Perturbations in schizophrenia lead to difficulty in planning actions and organizing thoughts.

HIPPOCAMPUS
Mediates learning and memory formation, intertwined functions that are impaired in schizophrenia.

LIMBIC SYSTEM
Involved in emotion. Disturbances are thought to contribute to the agitation frequently seen in schizophrenia.

ALFRED T. KAMAJIAN

Neurotransmitters

Both decreases and increases in neurotransmitter activity can lead to mental health problems, and several neurotransmitter hypotheses have been enumerated to explain the development of schizophrenia. The oldest and most widely accepted of these is the dopamine hypothesis of schizophrenia, but there are similar hypotheses related to glutamate and serotonin. For example, glutamate is an excitatory neurotransmitter which acts as a "master switch" for many other neurons in the brain. Deficiencies and excess in

Dopamine Hypothesis
Original neurotransmitter hypothesis of schizophrenia, suggesting that the disorder is due to excessive dopamine in specific brain regions

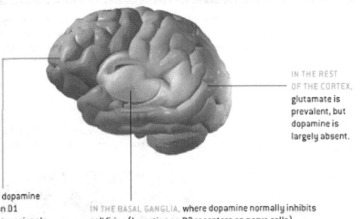

DIFFERENT NEUROTRANSMITTERS, SAME RESULTS

SOME SCIENTISTS have proposed that too much dopamine leads to symptoms emanating from the basal ganglia and that too little dopamine leads to symptoms associated with the frontal cortex. Insufficient glutamate signaling could produce those same symptoms, however.

IN THE REST OF THE CORTEX, glutamate is prevalent, but dopamine is largely absent.

IN THE FRONTAL CORTEX, where dopamine promotes cell firing (by acting on D1 receptors), glutamate's stimulatory signals amplify those of dopamine; hence, a shortage of glutamate would decrease neural activity, just as if too little dopamine were present.

IN THE BASAL GANGLIA, where dopamine normally inhibits cell firing (by acting on D2 receptors on nerve cells), glutamate's stimulatory signals oppose those of dopamine; hence, a shortage of glutamate would increase inhibition, just as if too much dopamine were present.

ALFRED T. KAMAJIAN

glutaminergic systems may thereby be at the root of lower or higher levels of dopamine (Stahl, 2011). The dopamine hypothesis suggested that the development of schizophrenia and related disorders was due to the excess of dopamine in several areas of the brain, especially limbic areas and parts of the frontal lobe.

As these hypotheses have continued to develop, researchers have begun looking toward the many interactions of the neurotransmitters throughout many different pathways in the brain. The integrated dopamine hypothesis of schizophrenia proposes that most of the symptoms of schizophrenia can be explained by hyperactivity or hypoactivity within some of the dopamine pathways in the brain. Hyperactivity in the mesolimbic pathway, which delivers dopamine to a portion of the striatum called the nucleus accumbens, is likely responsible for many of the positive symptoms of the disorder, such as delusions and hallucinations (Stahl, 2011). Lower levels of dopamine in the mesocortical pathway to various areas of the frontal lobe is likely related to more of the negative, cognitive, and affective symptoms of schizophrenia (Stahl, 2011).

Integrated Dopamine Hypothesis

A more refined hypothesis of schizophrenia development involving the differential activity of dopamine in different areas of the brain

Biological Treatments of Schizophrenia Spectrum Disorders

Myth or Reality: When it comes to schizophrenia, the treatment is worse than the disorder itself? This is often stated in regard to the many side effects of antipsychotic medications, but the reality of this statement depends largely on the severity of one's symptoms. Unfortunately, individuals with the disorder, especially those who have more severe variations of the disorder, are often not thinking clearly enough to make the decision to go off their medications. Most individuals with a diagnosis on the schizophrenia spectrum will experience benefits to medication usage that outweighs the potentially negative consequences. One area in which we must accept some ambiguity on this point, however, is the potential impact of long-term antipsychotic use on the brain. Some studies have suggested that the long-term use of some antipsychotic medications may increase brain degeneration, and potentially lower life expectancy (Weinmann et al., 2009). Regardless of how we answer this question, everyone agrees that antipsychotic medications are quite powerful, and many of these medications bind to a variety of receptors in the brain, potentially causing a host of side effects. On the other hand, prior to the development of antipsychotic medications in the 1950s, individuals with the disorder were often simply locked up and restrained to keep them from hurting themselves or others. Early treatments, such as insulin coma therapy and electroconvulsive therapy (ECT) were either found to be too dangerous, or ineffective (Valenstein, 2010). Some research suggests that modern ECT methods in conjunction with antipsychotic

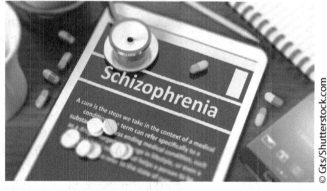

medications may enhance the function of the thalamus compared to antipsychotic medications alone, which may enhance some sensory deficits related to schizophrenia (Wang et al., 2020). Regardless, for many schizophrenia patients, antipsychotic medications offer the only possible solution for retaining some semblance of their life before the onset of the disorder.

Antipsychotics are generally divided into two categories: conventional ("typical") and atypical. Early antipsychotic medications were discovered haphazardly, when a drug belonging to the class of antihistamines was found to help with psychotic symptoms (Stahl, 2011). Conventional antipsychotics are effective by means of controlling dopamine receptors, and include Thorazine and Haldol (haloperidol), to name a few. Atypical antipsychotics generally act on both dopamine and serotonin receptors, and include Zyprexa, Seroquel, Geodon, Abilify, and Risperidol among others (Stahl,

Tardive Dyskinesia

A common side effect of conventional antipsychotic medications characterized by involuntary movements of the face and other parts of the body

2011). The earlier conventional antipsychotics tended to carry a much greater risk of side effects, including tardive dyskinesia, a movement disorder characterized by involuntary movements, as one of their primary areas of activation involves motor areas within the brain. Another drawback to the conventional antipsychotics is that they generally only help with the positive symptoms of the disorder, whereas some of the newer atypical antipsychotics can also aid in treating some of the negative symptoms.

Psychological Treatments of Schizophrenia Spectrum Disorders

Psychological treatments for individuals with schizophrenia must take into account the severity of the disorder, as well as the patient's current status. Particularly, therapy with clients suffering from more severe variations of the disorder is likely to place emphasis on life skills and disease management, rather than to attempt a discovery of groundbreaking insights from deep within the unconscious. The Society of Clinical Psychology (Division 12) of the American Psychological Association has recognized seven therapeutic modalities as having strong research support in the treatment of schizophrenia and related disorders, and another three modalities are recognized as having modest research support (Klonsky, 2013).

Understandably, with an eye to teaching life skills and disease management, many of these research modalities have a strong emphasis in Cognitive-Behavioral Therapy (CBT) principles. CBT is understood to have strong support for working with clients with schizophrenia, utilizing behavioral experiments and reality testing, self-monitoring, cognitive restructuring, and emphasizing the normalization of psychotic experiences, as much as is realistic, and less confrontational ways of relating to the client (Rector & Beck, 2001). Similarly, Social Skills Training (strong support), Social Learning/ Token Economy Programs (strong support), Cognitive Remediation (strong support), Acceptance and Commitment Therapy (modest support), and Cognitive Adaptation Training (modest support), all heavily involve cognitive and/or behavioral therapy strategies aimed at helping individuals to work around or compensate for cognitive and motivational losses they have experienced because of the disorder (Klonsky, 2013). Bechi et al. (2019) reported that schizophrenia patients treated with Cognitive Remediation combined with Theory of Mind training were found to maintain positive sociocognitive and functional outcomes at a 3-year follow-up, recommending this combination of treatment as it helps improve social well-being, a critical area of concern.

Other psychotherapy modalities address social aspects of life more directly. The creation of a supportive and stable environment is another key component shared by many of the research-based treatments listed by division 12 for the treatment of schizophrenia. Assertive Community Treatment (strong support), Family Psychoeducation (strong support), Supported Employment (strong support), and several of the modalities already listed above place a direct emphasis on working with families and communities of individuals with schizophrenia to set up networks of professionals, peers, and family so that these clients have ongoing support available to them at all times (Klonsky, 2013). Many early models of schizophrenia treatment relied heavily on Psychodynamic techniques that have more recently fallen out of favor for a variety of reasons, often coming down to the difficulty to study these techniques empirically. Some problems have also been noted, such as deep interpretation of psychotic content, but many psychodynamic approaches have specifically relied on familial and social support to help the patient function to the best of their ability (Alanen, 2018).

Last of all, many of these therapy modalities utilize a disease management or compensation approach. For example, Illness Management and Recovery (modest support) emphasizes the combination of psychoeducation, medication management using CBT schedules, relapse prevention planning, social skills training, and coping skills training to aid the individual in having a supportive environment, and tolerating difficult experiences related to the symptoms and life changes related to their illness (Klonsky, 2013). With an emphasis on life skills, the development of a supportive environment, and skills to manage disease symptoms, individuals with schizophrenia are far more likely to experience better long-term outcomes.

Conclusion

Hopefully, you have begun to recognize the serious complexities of the schizophrenia spectrum disorders. Though only a small portion of the population will experience a disorder on this spectrum, they are often chronic and seriously debilitating. Regardless, they need not be considered a death-sentence. Many of the experiences of individuals with schizophrenia are not far removed from some of our own everyday experiences. Who among us has not thought we heard or saw something, only to turn around and nothing is there? Or strongly believed something to be the case that turned out to be wrong? Keep this in mind. And if you know or meet someone who falls somewhere along this spectrum, consider that the disordered thinking, hallucinations, or delusions he or she may be experiencing are simply a sign of their need for preferential recognition of their dignity as a human person. Think of the 4 Fs of the schizophrenia spectrum, and maybe consider your similarities, as well as your differences.

CHAPTER REVIEW

QUESTIONS

1. How does schizophrenia differ from other psychotic disorders on the schizophrenia spectrum? What subtypes and severity levels are used to differentiate these disorders? Why are these distinctions important?

2. What are some of the ways that schizophrenia and other psychotic disorders impact people differently based on specific characteristics? Male and female? Life experiences? Where one lives? Age of onset?

3. How have conceptualizations of schizophrenia changed over the course of history?

4. What is the conceptual difference between the positive and negative symptoms of schizophrenia? What are the positive symptoms? What are the negative symptoms? Describe the symptoms, including different variations of specific symptoms.

5. What are some of the theories and treatments for schizophrenia and related disorders? What neurotransmitters have been implicated in these disorders? Which medications are used to target which neurotransmitters? In what circumstances are medications necessary for psychotherapy to be effective?

KEY TERMS

Schizophrenia

Psychotic

Kraepelinian Dichotomy

Positive Symptoms

Negative Symptoms

Delusions

Hallucinations

Catatonia

Avolition

Alogia

Anhedonia

Epigenetics

Neurodevelopmental Theory

Ventricles

Dopamine Hypothesis

Integrated Dopamine Hypothesis

Tardive Dyskinesia

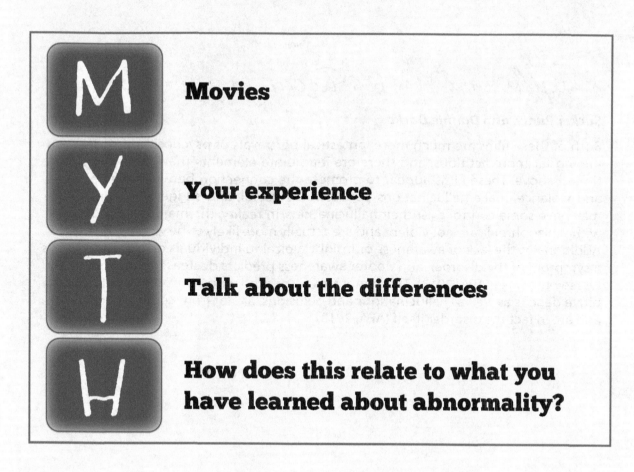

M Movies

Y Your experience

T Talk about the differences

H How does this relate to what you have learned about abnormality?

Myths in Movies Recap

A Beautiful Mind and The Soloist

While both of these movies demonstrate incredibly talented men with hopes and dreams for their lives that are radically altered by the development of schizophrenia, *The Soloist* more accurately demonstrates the primacy of auditory, over visual, hallucinations. In reality, both of these men experienced primarily auditory hallucinations, the most common type of hallucinations experienced by individuals on the schizophrenia spectrum (McCarthy-Jones et al., 2017; Waters et al., 2014).

Myths in Movies Recap

Sucker Punch and Donnie Darko

Both of these films are much more fantastical portrayals of psychosis, purposely containing far more fictitious, and therefore inaccurate elements than the movies mentioned above. These films appear to promote the connection between mental illness and violence, make hallucinations appear to be useful, and suggest that individuals may have some control over their hallucinations. In reality, the majority of individuals with schizophrenia are not violent and are actually more likely to be victims (APA, 2013). Additionally, the lack of awareness or insight typical to individuals on this spectrum is a symptom of the disorder, and poorer awareness predicts decreased functioning and worse outcomes (APA, 2013). The symptoms associated with schizophrenia, both cognitive deficits as well as hallucinations and delusions, are far from coping mechanisms, and are in fact the disorder itself (APA, 2013).

CHAPTER SEVEN

DEPRESSIVE AND BIPOLAR DISORDERS

LEARNING OBJECTIVES

- ▶ Examine myths related to depression and bipolar disorder
- ▶ Discuss experiences that reinforce these myths
- ▶ Overview the history of depressive and bipolar diagnoses
- ▶ Discuss the 4 Fs of depression and bipolar disorders: frequency, function, fatality, and feelings of pain
- ▶ Identify diagnostic criteria of mood disorders
- ▶ Apply the diagnostic criteria of these disorders
- ▶ Examine depressive diagnoses other than major depression
- ▶ Explore severity, course, and subtypes of mood disorders
- ▶ Examine disorders related to bipolar disorder
- ▶ Discuss theories and treatments of mood disorders
- ▶ Differentiate biological and psychological theories and treatments of mood disorders
- ▶ Identify neurotransmitter and hormone theories of mood disorders
- ▶ Explore the functions of medication treatments for mood disorders
- ▶ Explore other biological treatments for depression
- ▶ Discuss the limitations of a medication only approach
- ▶ Examine combined treatments for mood disorders

CHAPTER OUTLINE

- ▶ Depressive Disorders: Thinking About "Feeling Blue"—MYTH
- ▶ A Very Brief History of Depression
- ▶ The 4 Fs of Depression: Would the "Real" Depression Please Stand Up?
- ▶ Other Depressive Disorders

© sirtravelalot/Shutterstock.com

Depressive Disorders: Thinking About "Feeling Blue"

Just as depression is one of the most common mental illnesses with which people struggle, myths about depression likewise abound, and some of these myths have seriously skewed popular opinion about the disorder. The term depression, from the Latin **deprimere**, literally meaning to press down, carries the idea of a great weight holding one down. But how does this differ from typical sadness, which everyone experiences? Take some time to consider your experiences and ideas about depression or feeling blue. Consider not only experiences you have had, but also others who you may have witnessed going through a difficult time. Think about each aspect of the MYTHs of depression.

Deprimere

Latin, literally meaning "to press down"

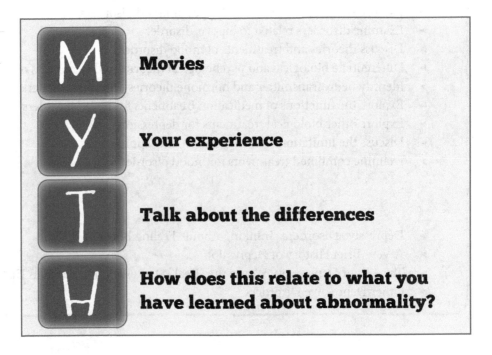

M — **Movies**

Y — **Your experience**

T — **Talk about the differences**

H — **How does this relate to what you have learned about abnormality?**

One of the most popular myths about depression, which you've likely encountered, is the idea that people with depression are just sad, and do not actually have a disorder. Gieselman & Curtis (2018) conducted a study with undergraduate students, discovering that 38.7% believed that individuals with Major Depressive Disorder (MDD) were a danger to others, 58.8% endorsed the idea that medications for depression were addictive, and 22.1% believed that depression was used as an excuse to get out of everyday life. You may have heard someone say, "Oh, she just feels down because . . ." or "He'll snap out of it soon." In fact, sometimes people do not even believe that depression is a real mental illness. These folks may say something like, "Just get over it" or "Just go do something and you'll feel better." While everyone feels sad from time to time over different life events, far fewer people (think: frequency) actually suffer from clinical depression. And while some may try to dismiss the seriousness of this mental disorder, people who have experienced episodes of depression know otherwise, and therapists who have worked with severely depressed clients, can attest that depression is a serious mental health condition.

To illustrate this point, it may be helpful to visualize depression as a person moving through a thick fog or sludge. A psychological term that seems to capture this image is the term lassitude, which refers to the sluggishness, lethargy, and lifelessness individuals struggling with depression often experience. The term lassitude is often used with a related term, malaise (mal-ease), indicating a discomfort or despondency without an identified cause. Current diagnostic language would use the terms psychomotor retardation and agitation, along with other related symptoms to describe lassitude-malaise.

© Creative Photo Corner/Shutterstock.com

Lassitude

Lacking energy, feeling weak, weary, and lethargic

Malaise

Discomfort, uneasiness, and feeling sick or in pain

Another frequently abused myth about depression, one which finds its roots in the annuls of psychiatry, is the belief that depression is merely a biological problem, a chemical imbalance, endogenous depression, or due to humorous fluids. Throughout the history of depression and related diagnoses, theorists have argued to greater or lesser degrees that depression is primarily a biological problem necessitating a biological treatment. Yet, throwing an antidepressant alone at a depressed individual rarely brings about the resolution the client hopes to achieve. As we have previously discussed, it is important to keep in mind that depression, just like most other mental disorders, is dynamic, and involves biological, psychological, social, and spiritual elements to greater or lesser degrees. To complicate the matter further, in some cases depressive symptoms appear to be more directly related to neurochemicals, whereas in other cases the same symptoms appear to be more closely related to psychological or social problems. In many severe cases of depression, antidepressants seem to be necessary, but rarely are they sufficient to correct the underlying problems at the root of the depression. In many cases, on the other hand, psychotherapy alone appears to be sufficient to bring about a long-term remission of depressive symptoms. Now let's take a look back at some of the movements and counter-movements in the history of depression which brought us to such a strong emphasis on a biological fix, before diving into current trends for understanding and treating depression.

Case Vignette

The following case study illustrates the tension between fatigue and discomfort typical of major depression. Without prodding, Georg would never get out of bed. When he would eventually get up, he would literally walk slowly wherever he went. Therapy sessions were often a trial in patience, as he would even think and talk slowly throughout the session. Emotionally, he was likewise caught in the sludge, feeling hopeless about any prospect of future activity, and constantly thinking about ending his life. While Georg clearly struggled with severe depression, individuals with milder cases often experience many of the same symptoms.

Georg perfectly illustrates the problem of medicating a depression, without making the behavioral, social, and cognitive changes needed for long-term recovery. After 20 years of trial and error on every imaginable cocktail of antidepressants, anxiolytics, and antipsychotics, his depression was no better than when he started treatment. A proponent of a strict biological approach might correctly point out that Georg had also been through 20 years of a wide variety of psychotherapy, which also had failed to relieve his depression; however, he was still struggling with the developmental roots of his depression after all this time.

Georg had not therapeutically addressed thoughts and feelings of worthlessness, hopelessness, and helplessness; likewise he had not addressed several impasses in significant personal relationships. Georg had somehow managed to avoid making the psychological, social, and behavioral changes that likely would have led to long-term improvement, instead relying on a purely biological remedy that had kept him barely able to function for the past two decades. As a result, he never developed the belief that his life could change, and without this belief, he remained stuck in a quasi-functional behavioral pattern for many years. As a therapist, what might you do to help Georg break out of a 20-year pattern of depressive dysfunction?

A Very Brief History of Depression

You probably would never guess that the term depression has only come into popular use within the past 50 years, at the same time that the diagnosis of depression also became more popular. This intertwined history of the common use and diagnostic use of the word depression further complicates myths surrounding the disorder. Horowitz (2010) points out that "before the 1970s, depression was usually considered a relatively rare condition involving feelings of intense meaningless and worthlessness often accompanied by vegetative and psychotic symptoms and preoccupations with death and dying" (p. 113). Prior to the 1970s, clients who reported general mental health difficulties related to problems of everyday life were understood to be suffering from anxiety rather than depression (Horowitz, 2010). An emphasis on greater empirical specificity regarding the categorization of mental illnesses, coupled with a renewed interest in biological perspectives of abnormality, changed the manner in which common mental health issues were conceptualized and diagnosed.

This emphasis on a biological explanation of abnormality was nothing new. Remember the Greek physician, Hippocrates, who we met in Chapter 1? You should recall that he taught mental health problems were caused by a chemical imbalance related to four fluids, or "humors," in the body. Melancholia was understood to be a result of an excess of black bile. In fact, the word melancholy literally means "black bile" in Greek. According to Hippocrates, this excess of black bile was the cause of many of the symptoms typically characteristic of the modern diagnosis of depression. And while we may look askance at him for thinking that depression is caused by too much black bile in the spleen, in humility we should also wonder in amazement at his ability to correctly recognize many of the symptoms of depression over 2,500 years ago. For example, Hippocrates recognized that melancholia was characterized by long-lasting despondencies and fears, difficulties with sleeping and eating, and restlessness, to name a few. Equally amazing, Hippocrates' conception of melancholia persisted and dominated educated discourse about what we now call depression for nearly 2,000 years.

To illustrate the significance of Hippocrates' contribution to the history of depression, one has only to look to authors such as the Greek philosopher Aristotle, who recognized a difference between a melancholic character type and a sickness arising from excessive black bile, which could manifest in a more sluggish, depressed manner, or in a more excited, manic manner, depending on the temperature of the bile (Pies, 2007). Likewise,

Melancholy

Greek, literally meaning "black bile" and referring to a feeling of sadness and despondency, often involving bodily symptoms without a clear cause

Hippocrates

© Everett Historical/Shutterstock.com

Galen, a Greek physician, spread the idea of the four humors throughout the Roman Empire in the second century AD, and Avicenna, who's *Cannon of Medicine* expanded the idea of the humors throughout the Arabic world and into Europe in the 11th century A.D.

Medieval Christian theologians went beyond the biological perspective of the humors, and emphasized spiritual elements of depression, portraying symptoms related to depression in terms of a struggle between vice and virtue. St. Thomas Aquinas, a 13th-century Dominican friar, described the phenomenon of depression in terms of an internal pain or sorrow, distinguishing between many different elements of what we today call depression (Loughlin, 2005). For example, Thomas distinguished between *misericordia*, understood as sorrow or pity for the plight of another person, and *aggravation*, understood as being weighed down by the sorrow one is experiencing (Loughlin, 2005). Interestingly, Thomas also understood *anxietas*, or anxiety, as a form of sorrow wherein a person feels weighed

Aristotle

down by a situation from which they cannot break free. Thomas posits as the most profound form of sorrow or depression, *acedia*, commonly translated as sloth, which he describes in terms of a loss of joy in life, social isolation, and the slowing down of one's physical movement and speech, even to the point of paralysis (Loughlin, 2005).

The Latin term *deprimere* appears to have come into usage in relation to a decline in mood as early as the 14th century; however, the concept of melancholy remained primary for scholars studying the phenomenon up until the 19th century. As discussed in previous chapters, several scholars in the 19th century were beginning to develop and revise classification

St. Thomas Aquinas

Phillipe Pinel

systems for a variety of health problems, including mental disorders. Phillipe Pinel (1745–1826) and Emil Kraepelin (1856–1926) were both proponents of the biological perspective who emphasized the classification of mental disorders.

Pinel, a French physician, continued to conceive of depression in terms of melancholy, but drew clear distinctions between mania, and a variety of melancholic moods, as well as recognizing that some patients went through periods of mania mixed with melancholy. Recall that Pinel also championed more humane treatment for those in asylums, and attempted psychotherapy with patients almost a century before Freud. Kraepelin further distinguished several of the mental health categories devised by Pinel, and generally gets most of the credit for Pinel's classifications. Kraepelin is generally credited with drawing a strong distinction between manic depression and schizophrenia, but also recognized as a different phenomenon, what we today call personality disorders. For the current discussion on depression, Kraepelin's most important contribution is likely the collection of the symptoms related to all forms of depressive diagnoses under the general heading of manic-depressive insanity, which he originally understood as an endogenous mood disorder, as opposed to a psychotic disorder (Goldstein & Anthony, 1988). By the eighth edition of his handbook on psychiatry, Kraepelin (1921) eventually distinguished between endogenous (melancholic) depression, described as having a biologically foundation, and exogenous (neurotic) depression, described as having a psychogenic foundation.

The contrast between Freudianism and biological perspectives by the 1920s led to strongly divided camps attributing depression to nurture or nature, respectively (Goldstein & Anthony, 1988). Lewis (1938) attempted to unify these perspectives by emphasizing a range of depressive expressions from mild to severe, which could occur temporarily or in a more chronic manner. With the rise of the DSM in the early 1950s, the mental health community began to see more diagnostic uniformity within the field of psychiatry, though many changes have occurred in the language and conceptualization of depression and many other disorders since the days of the original DSM. The DSM-I and DSM-II placed emphasis on depression as capable of occurring due to psychogenic and/or biological causes. Depressive reaction was labeled as neurotic, while manic-depression and psychotic depression were

Endogenous

Rooted in an internal origin or cause, often understood to be biological

Exogenous

Rooted in an external origin or cause, often understood to be rooted in experiential stressors (e.g., developmental or social)

Neurotic

(As in DSM I and II)—A milder form of mental illness characterized by less severe loss of touch with reality than psychosis, and often understood to be rooted in environmental stressors

Psychotic

(As in DSM I and II)—A more severe form of mental illness characterized by a more profound loss of touch with reality, characterized by hallucinations and delusions, and understood as originating in biology

labeled as psychotic. The DSM-I and DSM-II also emphasized the possibility of chronic depressive symptoms rooted in personality, labeled Cyclothymic Personality (Goldstein & Anthony, 1988). While only slight changes in depression terminology occurred between DSM-I and DSM-II, the DSM-III radically changed the conceptualization of depressive disorders, categorizing them under a single heading of Affective Disorders, and emphasizing Lewis's and other theorists' distinctions regarding the severity and longevity of the symptoms. DSM-III also appeared to place more emphasis on the biological etiology of depressive disorders, and took the diagnosis of depression out of the category of personality disorders. Again, it is important to reiterate that how one understands a disorder changes the manner in which it will be conceptualized, explained, and treated. By the time the DSM-III was published, Freudianism and experiential-based explanations of depression had fallen out of favor among many psychiatrists, and a division had grown up further differentiating the fields of psychology from psychiatry.

Myths in Movies

MELANCHOLIA and ENTANGLEMENT

Though it may be difficult to imagine, Hollywood has even portrayed depression in fantastical ways. Consider the movie *Melancholia,* which depicts a bride with profound depression symbolized in many various ways including a cataclysmic collision of two worlds (Wedding & Niemiec, 2014). In another scene, she is being swept down a river, with only her wedding dress holding her back, and in yet another scene, she appears so lifeless that she is unable to even move her body into a bath. The movie *Entanglement* also takes on the dynamic of love and depression, with a recently divorced young man who is recovering from a suicide attempt and falls in love with a woman who was almost his adopted sister. Does the fantastical nature of these movies glamorize the disorder in unrealistic ways? Can you imagine a depression so severe that it is even difficult to move?

A scene from *Melancholia*

© Magnolia Pictures/Photofest

© AF archive/Alamy Stock Photo

DSM-5 CRITERIA FOR MAJOR DEPRESSIVE DISORDER

DIAGNOSTIC CRITERIA

A. Five (or more) of the following symptoms have been present during the same 2-week period and represent a change from previous functioning; at least one of the symptoms is either (1) depressed mood or (2) loss of interest or pleasure.

    Note: Do not include symptoms that are clearly attributable to another medical condition.

    1. Depressed mood most of the day, nearly every day, as indicated by either subjective report (e.g., feels sad, empty, hopeless) or observation made by others (e.g., appears tearful). (**Note:** In children and adolescents, can be irritable mood.)

    2. Markedly diminished interest or pleasure in all, or almost all, activities most of the day, nearly every day (as indicated by either subjective account or observation).

    3. Significant weight loss when not dieting or weight gain (e.g., a change of more than 5% of body weight in a month), or decrease or increase in appetite nearly every day.

        (**Note:** In children, consider failure to make expected weight gain.)

    4. Insomnia or hypersomnia nearly every day.

    5. Psychomotor agitation or retardation nearly every day (observable by others, not merely subjective feelings of restlessness or being slowed down).

    6. Fatigue or loss of energy nearly every day.

    7. Feelings of worthlessness or excessive or inappropriate guilt (which may be delusional) nearly every day (not merely self-reproach or guilt about being sick).

    8. Diminished ability to think or concentrate, or indecisiveness, nearly every day (either by subjective account or as observed by others).

    9. Recurrent thoughts of death (not just fear of dying), recurrent suicidal ideation without a specific plan, or a suicide attempt or a specific plan for committing suicide.

B. The symptoms cause clinically significant distress or impairment in social, occupational, or other important areas of functioning.

C. The episode is not attributable to the physiological effects of a substance or to another medical condition.

Note: Criteria A–C represent a major depressive episode.

Note: Responses to a significant loss (e.g., bereavement, financial ruin, losses from a natural disaster, a serious medical illness or disability) may include the feelings of intense sadness, rumination about the loss, insomnia, poor appetite, and weight loss noted in Criterion A, which may resemble a depressive episode. Although such symptoms may be understandable or considered appropriate to the loss, the presence of a major depressive episode in addition to the normal response to a significant loss should also be carefully considered. This decision inevitably requires the exercise of clinical judgment based on the individual's history and the cultural norms for the expression of distress in the context of loss.[1]

D. The occurrence of the major depressive episode is not better explained by schizoaffective disorder, schizophrenia, schizophreniform disorder, delusional disorder, or other specified and unspecified schizophrenia spectrum and other psychotic disorders.

E.   There has never been a manic episode or a hypomanic episode.

Note: This exclusion does not apply if all of the manic-like or hypomanic-like episodes are substance-induced or are attributable to the physiological effects of another medical condition.

[1]In distinguishing grief from a major depressive episode (MDE), it is useful to consider that in grief the predominant affect is feelings of emptiness and loss, while in MDE it is persistent depressed mood and the inability to anticipate happiness or pleasure. The dysphoria in grief is likely to decrease in intensity over days to weeks and occurs in waves, the so-called pangs of grief. These waves tend to be associated with thoughts or reminders of the deceased. The depressed mood of MDE is more persistent and not tied to specific thoughts or preoccupations. The pain of grief may be accompanied by positive emotions and humor that are uncharacteristic of the pervasive unhappiness and misery characteristic of MDE. The thought content associated with grief generally features a preoccupation with thoughts and memories of the deceased, rather than the self-critical or pessimistic ruminations seen in MDE.

In grief, self-esteem is generally preserved, whereas in MDE feelings of worthlessness and self-loathing are common. If self-derogatory ideation is present in grief, it typically involves perceived failings vis-à-vis the deceased (e.g., not visiting frequently enough, not telling the deceased how much he or she was loved). If a bereaved individual thinks about death and dying, such thoughts are generally focused on the deceased and possibly about "joining" the deceased, whereas in MDE such thoughts are focused on ending one's own life because of feeling worthless, undeserving of life, or unable to cope with the pain of depression.

Coding and Recording Procedures

The diagnostic code for major depressive disorder is based on whether this is a single or recurrent episode, current severity, presence of psychotic features, and remission status. Current severity and psychotic features are only indicated if full criteria are currently met for a major depressive episode. Remission specifiers are only indicated if the full criteria are not currently met for a major depressive episode.

Reprinted with permission from the *Diagnostic and Statistical Manual of Mental Disorders,* Fifth Edition, (Copyright 2013). American Psychiatric Association.

DEPRESSIVE DISORDER SEVERITY/COURSE

Mild	• Only symptoms required to make the diagnosis are present, or only a few others; symptom distress is manageable; only minor impairment
Moderate	• The intensity and number of symptoms and functional problems are between mild and severe
Severe	• Number of symptoms far in excess of those required for diagnosis; symptoms cause intense distress, unmanageability, & dysfunction
Remission	• Full: At least 2 months with no sigificant symptoms of a depressive/manic episode • Partial: Symptoms present w/o full criteria met, or remission less than 2 months

APA, 2013

The 4 Fs of Depression: Would the "Real" Depression Please Stand Up?

With such a dynamic and changing history related to the phenomenon of depression, teasing apart the "real" depression from the myths becomes even more complicated. When it becomes difficult to know whether you are looking at a depression myth, or the real thing, you can always return to the 4 Fs of major depression to guide you in determining the type and severity of depression you are encountering.

Frequency

A—Amount of Time: The DSM-5 specifies that in order to receive a diagnosis of major depression, a person must have experienced depressive symptoms for at least 2 weeks, and this period must be different from prior functioning (APA, 2013).

B—Behavior: The DSM-5 additionally specifies that a person must experience symptoms nearly every day, for the majority of the day, during this 2-week period of depression.

C—Curve: Within a 12-month period in the U.S., approximately 7% of individuals will struggle with depression, though young adults (age 18–29 years) more frequently suffer from depression than older adults, and are three times more likely to experience depression than those 60 years and older (APA, 2013). Likewise, females tend to be diagnosed with depression between 1.5 to 3 times more frequently than males (APA, 2013).

© fizkes/Shutterstock.com

The Good News: Many effective treatments exist for depression, and approximately two out of five depressed individuals will begin to recover by 3 months after onset of a depressive episode; four out of five will begin recovery by 1 year after onset (APA, 2013).

Function

Although sadness or depressed mood is the most well-known functional impairment of major depression, in reality, depressive disorders are characterized by a host of other functional difficulties. To receive the diagnosis of depression, a person must experience depressed mood or anhedonia, loss of pleasure or interest in activities that were previously experienced as enjoyable. Including one or both of these symptoms, a person must experience a

Anhedonia

Literally from the Greek—"absence of pleasure"—inability to experience pleasure, even in the presence of pleasurable stimuli

total of five symptoms from the diagnostic criteria. Additional symptoms include increased or decreased appetite/weight, increased or decreased sleep, increased or decreased psychomotor activity, fatigue, worthlessness or guilt, difficulty thinking or concentrating, and recurrent thoughts of death, suicidal ideation, or suicide attempts (APA, 2013). As you can surmise from considering these symptoms, a person suffering from depression is weighed down internally and this weight is manifested in a variety of ways. For some, it may be experienced in a more bodily way, with functional difficulties related to eating, sleeping, or fatigue. For others, it may be experienced in a cognitive manner, with thoughts of worthlessness and guilt, thoughts of death or suicide, or thinking and concentration problems. And still for others, the functional difficulties may be experienced in a more social or behavioral manner, with difficulties related to less contact with social support, due to losing interest in participating in life, increased suicidal contemplation or attempts, or just feeling like they have nothing to offer. For many people who suffer from depression, their experience is a combination of these symptoms, although it is important to note that this is not always the case, which means that depression can look quite different from person to person. This lengthy list of functional problems can seem overwhelming, so it may be helpful for you to create an acronym or to categorize the symptoms in some way in order to help you remember these symptoms. Here's one acronym to get you started!

Sad / Depressed Mood
Anhedonia / Loss of Interest
Death / Suicide

Sleep
Appetite
Psychomotor Problems

Fatigue
cOncentration / Thinking Problems
Guilt / Worthlessness

Feeling Pain

As you can piece together from what has already been mentioned, folks who struggle with depression experience significant pain and distress. Experientially, we have described this as a sludge, and feeling weighed down, as if by internal forces. In terms of symptoms, however, this sluggishness is only one of many pains that a depressed individual may experience. Recall from the previous section on the history of depression that in many ways the diagnosis of depression has become a catch-all for a variety of commonly experienced problems. This is evident when considering the specific symptoms mentioned in the DSM-5. According to the DSM-5, depression has been linked with daily feelings of sadness, hopelessness, emptiness, and at times, especially in children, this may present as irritable mood or separation anxiety (APA, 2013). Additionally, the DSM-5 discusses the loss of pleasure (anhedonia), restlessness or psychomotor retardation, daily experiences of worthlessness or guilt, despondency, and hopelessness to the point of recurrent thoughts of suicide and death. In the DSM-5, we also find associated features including brooding, worry over physical health, complaints of bodily pains, phobias, anxiety, and rumination (APA, 2013). Additionally, it is important to consider that a wide range of cultural diversity has also been found in studies regarding depression, with prevalence rates seven times higher in some cultures than others (APA, 2013). We should expect individuals who have been previously given a diagnosis of depression to have experienced a wide range of symptoms and experiences. This being said, recall also that to receive a diagnosis of depression a person must have experienced either depressed mood or anhedonia. These two symptoms should be understood as the core markers for distress in persons with depression.

Suicide

The term suicide is a conjunction of two Latin words, *sui-*, which means 'related to onself,' and *-cidium*, which means 'to kill.' Hence, homicide, is the killing of a *homo-*, which means 'man,' as in another person.

Fatality

Depressed individuals struggle with thoughts of suicide and death, and are at a significant risk for attempted and completed suicide. As with depression, myths of suicide abound. In an unpublished manuscript with a community sample, Kelley et al. (2020) found that 77.6% believed that youth (age 10–24) are at a higher risk of suicide than individuals over age 65, 67.1% endorsed that most failed suicide attempts lead to additional attempts, 49.5% believed that most failed attempts lead to suicide completion, and 45.9% thought that women were less likely to attempt suicide than men. While females are at an increased risk for attempted suicide, males complete suicide more frequently. Some research has suggested that women are more likely to ruminate than men, which was found to be associated with higher rates depression, perhaps a key mechanism in higher suicide attempt rates among women (Johnson & Whisman, 2013; Nolen-Hoeksema et al., 2008). Men, on the other hand, have been found to have higher suicide completion rates than women, perhaps due to the use of more lethal means of suicide or the seriousness of intent, and older men appear to be particularly at risk (Canetto, 2015; Freeman et al., 2017). Further, depression has been associated with a sixfold increase in the risk for a suicide attempt, and suicide accounts for the majority of the association between high mortality and depression (Nock et al., 2008). Suicide, however, is not the only cause of death related to depression. Individuals who feel extremely hopeless, helpless, and worthless may even suffer to the point of becoming completely incapable of taking care of themselves, neglecting hygiene and nutritional needs, remaining in bed most of the day, or even experiencing catatonia. For example, persons suffering from depression who are admitted to a nursing home have been found to be at an increased risk of death within the first year (APA, 2013).

Myths in Movies

13 REASONS WHY and THE VIRGIN SUICIDES

The portrayal of suicide by the media frequently meets with backlash, as the public becomes concerned that glamorizing suicide may increase the likelihood the people will make attempts. The TV show *13 Reasons Why* had a similar backlash, as many people thought that it portrayed suicide as a viable solution to life's problems. The National Association of School Psychologists (2017) even issued a recommendation that vulnerable youth avoid the show, highlighting that school counselors and parents are portrayed as inadequate and unaware. A popular saying refers to suicide as a permanent solution to a temporary problem. This may be an adept analysis when considering the problems faced by the main characters in *13 Reasons Why*, as well as the movie *The Virgin Suicides*, wherein suicide becomes the solution for five daughters in response to their mother's overbearing parenting. Whether it's high school troubles or even parents' strict rules, a few years later these problems will frequently have faded into the past. Considering the severity of the topic, how much responsibility does the media have for the way in which they portray suicide? Is it primarily the responsibility of parents and the public to guard themselves and their children against potentially dangerous media?

A scene from *13 Reasons Why*
© Netflix/Photofest

A scene from *The Virgin Suicides*
© Paramount Classics/Photofest

Other Depressive Disorders

The DSM-5 enumerates several other depressive disorders with a range of depressive symptoms. Did you know that the DSM-5 now has a diagnosis for moody kids? Disruptive Mood Dysregulation Disorder is characterized by a chronic and severe irritability lasting for at least 12 months during which the person did not experience 3 months without symptoms. This diagnosis is only for children and adolescents, and should only be given to clients between the ages of 6 and 18, with onset prior to age 10. Though it might seem like clinicians will now be giving this diagnosis to every kid out there, since they all get moody, it's important to consider that the irritability described by this disorder is profound and persistent. The DSM-5 reports that between 2 to 5% of children and adolescents probably will experience this disorder in a 6-month to 2-year period (APA, 2013).

Persistent Depressive Disorder (PDD), which was previously called Dysthymic Disorder, can be thought of as long-term depression, which is less severe than major depression. Persistent Depressive Disorder is characterized by depressed mood that lasts almost all day long, more often than not, for at least 2 years (1 year for children and adolescents). The person cannot

Dysthymic Disorder
Chronic form of depression, which is less severe than major depression

DSM-5 recognizes a depressive disorder reserved only for children.

© vladm/Shutterstock.com

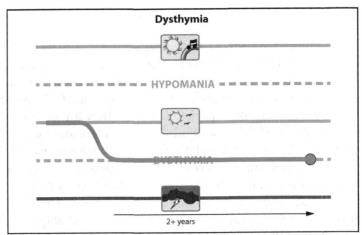

experience a 2-month period without symptoms during this 2-year period, and diagnosis requires the presence of two other depressive symptoms, in addition to depressed mood. Many of the additional symptoms of persistent depression are less severe than major depression, and may include poor appetite or overeating, insomnia or hypersomnia, fatigue or decreased energy, low self-esteem, decision-making or concentration problems, and feelings of hopelessness (APA, 2013). A diagnosis of persistent depressive disorder may also include many of the specifiers of major depression.

Did you know that the DSM-5 finally pathologized PMS? While some may perceive the APA's inclusion of Premenstrual Dysphoric Disorder in this way, women who suffer from this disorder experience serious mood problems in conjunction with their menstrual cycle. The APA (2013) estimated between 1.8 to 5.8% of U.S. women suffer from the disorder, which is characterized by mood disturbance; for example, lability, dysphoria, anxiety, or irritability, which begins 1 week before menses and remits within a week after menses begins. Symptoms must be present in most cycles for the past year, and diagnosis requires the presence of five symptoms, including marked affective lability, irritability, depressed mood, or anxiety, as well as decreased interest in activities, concentration problems, lethargy, appetite changes, hypersomnia or insomnia, feeling overwhelmed, or physical symptoms (e.g., tenderness of breasts, other pains, bloating or weight gain; APA, 2013).

Labile

Characterized by instability of mood, mood shifts (e.g., abrupt sadness, and hypersensitivity)

Dysphoria

A state of uneasiness or discomfort and sadness, often understood technically as a mix of anxious and depressive states

The DSM-5 recognizes a variety of additional depressive disorders under the category of other specified depressive disorders, including recurrent brief depression, short-duration depressive episode, and depressive episode with insufficient symptoms (APA, 2013). All other depressive disorders, not meeting full criteria for one of these diagnoses, but causing significant impairment and distress, would fall under the category of unspecified depressive disorder.

DEPRESSIVE AND BIPOLAR DISORDER SUBTYPES

Anxious Distress	• Client experiences at least 2 significant anxiety symptoms
Mixed Features	• Marked by presence of at least 3 hypomanic / manic symptoms without full criteria for mania
Melancholic Features	• Loss of pleasure or reactivity to pleasurable stimuli and at least three other symptoms, indicating client is nearly incapable of feeling pleasure
Atypical Features	• Marked by mood reactivity (improvement) to some stimuli, as well as two additional symptoms, (e.g., increased appetite, hypersomnia, rejection sensitivity, etc.)
Psychotic Features	• Mood congruent or mood-incongruent psychotic features (e.g., hallucinations and/or delusions) are present
Catatonia	• Presence of three or more catatonic features (e.g., no psychomotor activity, cataplexy, mutism, echolalia, echopraxia, posturing, stereotypy, etc.)
Peripartum Onset	• Onset of bipolar or major depressive episode begins during pregnancy or within four weeks after delivery
Seasonal Pattern	• Depressive, hypomanic, or manic episodes occur in relation to a particular time of year, for at least two years, and abate or change polarity as the seasons change
Rapid Cycling	• Bipolar I & II only: At least four depressive, hypomanic, or manic episodes occur and remit or change polarity within a 1-year period, meeting full criteria for each episode

APA, 2013

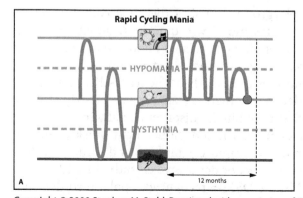

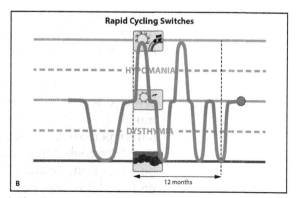

Bipolar Disorders: From Low to High

While depressive disorders are characterized by ongoing low or depressed mood, bipolar disorders, as you can probably work out from the name, are characterized by mood that changes between high and euthymic (normal) or low. Manic behavior is the characteristic feature of these disorders, though a popular understanding of mania has been lacking, confused with terminology like "maniac." Take a moment to consider MYTHs of Bipolar disorder that you have encountered.

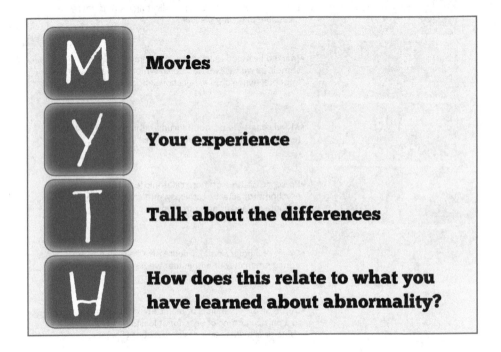

M — **Movies**

Y — **Your experience**

T — **Talk about the differences**

H — **How does this relate to what you have learned about abnormality?**

The 4 Fs of Bipolar Disorders: Mood Swing Anyone?

How about a whole mood playground? One of the most common myths of bipolar disorder is that people's mood will quickly swing at any given moment from euthymic to sad or angry. A related myth is that these mood swings will happen with great frequency in a short period of time. While these myths are based to some degree in truth, as the irritability and lability involved with bipolar disorder may sometimes appear like quickly-shifting mood, the defining characteristics of bipolar disorder actually involve much longer periods of manic or depressed mood, rather than quickly shifting mood. Even what clinicians refer to as rapid-cycling bipolar disorder, involves only four or more manic, hypomanic, or depressive episodes in a 12-month period. Unlike previous DSMs, the DSM-5 recognizes bipolar disorders as a bridge between schizophrenia/psychotic disorders and depressive disorders, as similarities exist between bipolar disorders and both of these other classes of disorders, not only in symptomology, but as you may recall from Chapter 6, also in regard to social and genetic factors (APA, 2013).

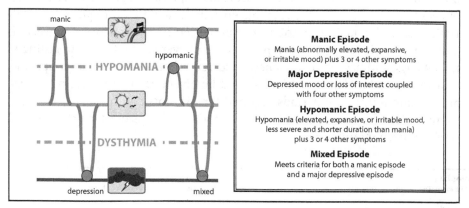

Manic Episode
Mania (abnormally elevated, expansive, or irritable mood) plus 3 or 4 other symptoms

Major Depressive Episode
Depressed mood or loss of interest coupled with four other symptoms

Hypomanic Episode
Hypomania (elevated, expansive, or irritable mood, less severe and shorter duration than mania) plus 3 or 4 other symptoms

Mixed Episode
Meets criteria for both a manic episode and a major depressive episode

Myths in Movies

MANIAC

What do you think of when you hear the word maniac? Most of us probably think of someone with a large bloody knife running around in the middle of the night killing people. If you take a look at movies with maniac in the title, you will discover exactly this. The 2018 TV miniseries with this title—*Maniac*, took a somewhat new spin on the old repertoire and follows a man with schizophrenia and a woman with addictive, borderline and manic characteristics. Their rela-

A scene from *Maniac*

© Netflix/Photofest

tionship ensues through a (seriously unethical) psychiatric drug trial, which paints a wonderfully horrific and dystopian portrait of psychiatric science in the process. At one point the female character even exclaims that she's not crazy, she's goal-oriented! Is the mania of bipolar disorder really behind classic maniac behavior? Does mania actually share characteristics with the other disorders in *Maniac*?

Frequency

Mania

Elevated or irritable mood, characterized by a range of specific symptoms related to euphoria, grandiosity, and increased energy

Hypomania

A less severe form of mania, which is characterized by the same basic symptoms

A—Amount of Time: To be diagnosed with a bipolar I disorder, according to the DSM-5, an individual must experience a full manic episode, characterized as lasting at least 1 week, representing a marked change from previous behavior, and not requiring a previous depressive episode (APA, 2013). However, if the intensity of the manic episode is such that it requires hospitalization, an individual need not have experienced symptoms for a full week. If a person experiences manic symptoms of less severity, hypomania, lasting at least 4 days, and has also experienced a current or previous depressive episode, a diagnosis of bipolar II disorder should be given. Though 4 days or 1 week are the minimum time periods required for diagnostic purposes, please keep in mind that without treatment of some kind, manic episodes may last several weeks or even months.

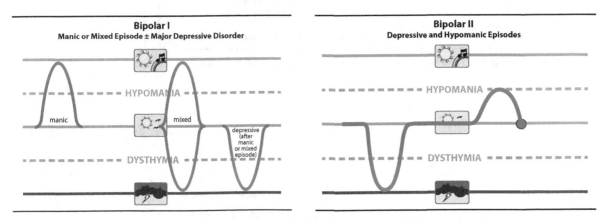

B—Behavior: Similar to depression, the DSM-5 specifies that a person must experience symptoms of mania or hypomania nearly every day, for the majority of the day, during this 4-day or 1-week period.

C—Curve: The 12-month prevalence in the United States for bipolar I disorder is estimated at 0.6%, and it appears to be less common in low-income countries (0.7%) compared to high-income countries (1.4%) (APA, 2013). Bipolar II disorder appears to have a similar frequency in the United States, with a 12-month prevalence of 0.8%. All bipolar disorders are estimated to have a prevalence rate of 1.8%, with an increased prevalence (2.7%) in adolescents (APA, 2013). The male-to-female ratio for bipolar I disorder appears to be roughly equal, 1.1:1, respectively, and the APA (2013) reports that findings are unclear regarding gender differences related to bipolar II disorder. Interestingly, popular myth, with its emphasis on PMS and mood swings, would have us believe that bipolar disorders are more common in women, despite the prevailing science, which has yet to support the myth!

The Good News: While fewer treatments exist for bipolar disorder than depression, several effective psychological and biological treatments do exist, which can help remit or decrease the intensity of manic and depressive periods, keeping a person more even-keel and off the affective rollercoaster.

Function

Like depression, bipolar disorder is characterized by a number of serious psychological and mood impairments. Though elevated or irritable mood is the most well-known functional impairment and is required for diagnosis of bipolar disorder, in reality, people who suffer from a bipolar disorder experience many other functional difficulties. Other symptoms include the pursuit of goals, which often carry the potential for harmful consequences, or else lead to the neglect of other important duties. Persons struggling with bipolar disorder also often experience ideational problems, including flights of ideas or racing thoughts, distractibility, as well as thoughts of grandiosity, or even hallucinations and/or delusions. The DSM-5 points out that approximately 30% of individuals with bipolar disorder experience severe impairment regarding their occupational functioning, and that these impairments frequently lag behind symptom recovery, likely resulting in lower socioeconomic status among individuals with the disorder (APA, 2013). As you can expect, a person experiencing a manic episode may put much time and energy into work or a relationship, leading to a great deal of success in some areas of life. However, as the person's mood begins to further increase or decline, these successes often turn out to be short-lived. An on-going insistence that activities must be performed in terms of the goals held to be most crucial may push others further away, or if the person becomes euthymic or depressed and no longer has the energy for an activity that they previously had, others may become disheartened with the person.

"Chapter 3," and "Chapter 9" from *Marbles: Mania, Depression, Michelangelo, and Me: A Graphic Memoir* by Ellen Forney, copyright © 2012 by Ellen Forney. Used by permission of Gotham Books, an imprint of Penguin Publishing Group, a division of Penguin Random House LLC. All rights reserved.

In case you enjoyed the last acronym, here's one for bipolar symptoms!

Decreased Sleep

Elevated or Irritable Mood

Agitation (psychomotor without a goal) or Increased Goal-directed Activity

Distractibility

FLight of Ideas or Racing Thoughts

Increased or Pressured Speech

Painful Consequences Related to Behavior

Self-esteem Inflation or Grandiosity

Myths in Movies
LADY DYNAMITE

Lady Dynamite is loosely based on the life of comedian Maria Bamford, who is portrayed as attempting to manage bipolar disorder after being released from a psychiatric hospital. While the show portrays the many relationship difficulties with which she struggles, as a comedy it sometimes makes light of more serious symptoms of bipolar disorder. Also, the experiences of Bamford, such as being in a commercial for sexy ramen noodles or having shirts with her image donated to an African children's army, are clearly more unique than most individuals with bipolar disorder.

© Netflix/Photofest

A scene from *Lady Dynamite*

Feeling Pain

For those of you who have never experienced mania or depression, it may be difficult to enter into just how painful bipolar disorder can be for those who experience it. Figure 7.1 depicts the vast differences in mood that individuals with bipolar disorder can experience. Particularly after a drop in elevated mood, energy, or thoughts and feelings of grandiosity, imagine what this "coming down," so to speak, must be like for individuals. At times, this slide can be from a full manic state into a depressed state, literally changing

FIGURE 7.1   **Depiction of Bipolar States**

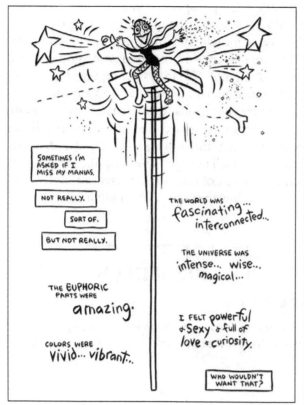
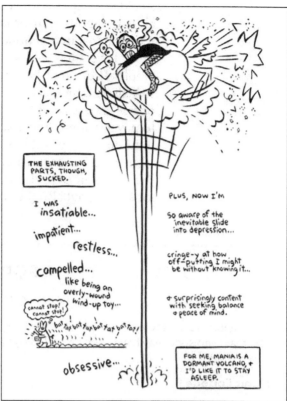

one's perspective on oneself and the world from confidence, motivation, and everything being possible, into hopeless, helpless, and worthless, at the same time as the person may be starting to realize the impact of their behaviors on their own life and the lives of their loved ones. As the DSM-5 points out, gambling, and antisocial behaviors such as physically threatening or assaulting others, and suicidality, can lead a person experiencing mania to serious financial and legal troubles, or even to involuntary hospitalization (APA, 2013).

Fatality

Along with anorexia nervosa, bipolar disorders are among the most deadly psychological disorders. Though depression is often associated with suicide, and rightly so, bipolar disorder, in fact, increases the risk of a suicide attempt sevenfold, compared to the sixfold risk related to depression (Nock et al., 2008). As many as 25% of all completed suicides are believed to be related to bipolar disorder, and the disorder is estimated to increase a person's risk of completed suicide 15 times, compared to the population at large (APA,

2013). Bipolar I and bipolar II disorders are associated with similar rates of suicide attempts; however, suicide attempts appear more lethal in individuals with bipolar II disorder (APA, 2013). Merikangas and colleagues (2011) reported that internationally, 25% of individuals suffering from bipolar I disorder have attempted suicide, whereas 20% of individuals diagnosed with bipolar II disorder have made an attempt. Regardless of bipolar type, individuals with the disorder are at significant risk for suicide, and any indication of self-harm should be taken extremely serious. Clinicians are often taught to pay attention to increased energy in depressed clients, as this may be an indicator of a possible suicide attempt. Individuals with bipolar disorder often experience increased energy, as well as regret over impulsive behaviors during manic periods, which may lead not only to an increased motivation for suicide, but also the energy to follow through with an attempt.

DSM-5 CRITERIA FOR BIPOLAR DISORDERS

DIAGNOSTIC CRITERIA

For a diagnosis of bipolar 1 disorder, it is necessary to meet the following criteria for a manic episode. The manic episode may have been preceded by and may be followed by hypomanic or major depressive episodes.

Manic Episode

A. A distinct period of abnormally and persistently elevated, expansive, or irritable mood and abnormally and persistently increased goal-directed activity or energy, lasting at least 1 week and present most of the day, nearly every day (or any duration if hospitalization is necessary).

B. During the period of mood disturbance and increased energy or activity, three (or more) of the following symptoms (four if the mood is only irritable) are present to a significant degree and represent a noticeable change from usual behavior:

1. Inflated self-esteem or grandiosity.

2. Decreased need for sleep (e.g., feels rested after only 3 hours of sleep).

3. More talkative than usual or pressure to keep talking.

4. Flight of ideas or subjective experience that thoughts are racing.

5. Distractibility (i.e., attention too easily drawn to unimportant or irrelevant external stimuli), as reported or observed.

6. Increase in goal-directed activity (either socially, at work or school, or sexually) or psychomotor agitation (i.e., purposeless non-goal-directed activity).

7. Excessive involvement in activities that have a high potential for painful consequences (e.g., engaging in unrestrained buying sprees, sexual indiscretions, or foolish business investments).

C. The mood disturbance is sufficiently severe to cause marked impairment in social or occupational functioning or to necessitate hospitalization to prevent harm to self or others, or there are psychotic features.

D. The episode is not attributable to the physiological effects of a substance (e.g., a drug of abuse, a medication, other treatment) or to another medical condition.

Note: A full manic episode that emerges during antidepressant treatment (e.g., medication, electroconvulsive therapy) but persists at a fully syndromal level beyond the physiological effect of that treatment is sufficient evidence for a manic episode and, therefore, a bipolar 1 diagnosis.

Note: Criteria A–D constitute a manic episode. At least one lifetime manic episode is required for the diagnosis of bipolar 1 disorder.

Hypomanic Episode

A. A distinct period of abnormally and persistently elevated, expansive, or irritable mood and abnormally and persistently increased activity or energy, lasting at least 4 consecutive days and present most of the day, nearly every day.

B. During the period of mood disturbance and increased energy and activity, three (or more) of the following symptoms (four if the mood is only irritable) have persisted, represent a noticeable change from usual behavior, and have been present to a significant degree:

   1. Inflated self-esteem or grandiosity.
   2. Decreased need for sleep (e.g., feels rested after only 3 hours of sleep).
   3. More talkative than usual or pressure to keep talking.
   4. Flight of ideas or subjective experience that thoughts are racing.
   5. Distractibility (i.e., attention too easily drawn to unimportant or irrelevant external stimuli), as reported or observed.
   6. Increase in goal-directed activity (either socially, at work or school, or sexually) or psychomotor agitation.
   7. Excessive involvement in activities that have a high potential for painful consequences (e.g., engaging in unrestrained buying sprees, sexual indiscretions, or foolish business investments).

C. The episode is associated with an unequivocal change in functioning that is uncharacteristic of the individual when not symptomatic.

D. The disturbance in mood and the change in functioning are observable by others.

E. The episode is not severe enough to cause marked impairment in social or occupational functioning or to necessitate hospitalization. If there are psychotic features, the episode is, by definition, manic.

F. The episode is not attributable to the physiological effects of a substance (e.g., a drug of abuse, a medication, other treatment).

Note: A full hypomanic episode that emerges during antidepressant treatment (e.g., medication, electroconvulsive therapy) but persists at a fully syndromal level beyond the physiological effect of that treatment is sufficient evidence for a hypomanic episode diagnosis. However, caution is indicated so that one or two symptoms (particularly increased irritability, edginess, or agitation following antidepressant use) are not taken as sufficient for diagnosis of a hypomanic episode, nor necessarily indicative of a bipolar diathesis.

Note: Criteria A–F constitute a hypomanic episode. Hypomanic episodes are common in bipolar 1 disorder but are not required for the diagnosis of bipolar 1 disorder.

Major Depressive Episode

A. Five (or more) of the following symptoms have been present during the same 2-week period and represent a change from previous functioning; at least one of the symptoms is either (1) depressed mood or (2) loss of interest or pleasure.

Note: Do not include symptoms that are clearly attributable to another medical condition.

1. Depressed mood most of the day, nearly every day, as indicated by either subjective report (e.g., feels sad, empty, or hopeless) or observation made by others (e.g., appears tearful). (**Note:** In children and adolescents, can be irritable mood.)

2. Markedly diminished interest or pleasure in all, or almost all, activities most of the day, nearly every day (as indicated by either subjective account or observation).

3. Significant weight loss when not dieting or weight gain (e.g., a change of more than 5% of body weight in a month), or decrease or increase in appetite nearly every day. (**Note:** In children, consider failure to make expected weight gain.)

4. Insomnia or hypersomnia nearly every day.

5. Psychomotor agitation or retardation nearly every day (observable by others; not merely subjective feelings of restlessness or being slowed down).

6. Fatigue or loss of energy nearly every day.

7. Feelings of worthlessness or excessive or inappropriate guilt (which may be delusional) nearly every day (not merely self-reproach or guilt about being sick).

8. Diminished ability to think or concentrate, or indecisiveness, nearly every day (either by subjective account or as observed by others).

9. Recurrent thoughts of death (not just fear of dying), recurrent suicidal ideation without a specific plan, or a suicide attempt or a specific plan for committing suicide.

B. The symptoms cause clinically significant distress or impairment in social, occupational, or other important areas of functioning.

C. The episode is not attributable to the physiological effects of a substance or another medical condition.

Note: Criteria A–C constitute a major depressive episode. Major depressive episodes are common in bipolar 1 disorder but are not required for the diagnosis of bipolar 1 disorder.

Note: Responses to a significant loss (e.g., bereavement, financial ruin, losses from a natural disaster, a serious medical illness or disability) may include the feelings of intense sadness, rumination about the loss, insomnia, poor appetite, and weight loss noted in Criterion A, which may resemble a depressive episode. Although such symptoms may be understandable or considered appropriate to the loss, the presence of a major depressive episode in addition to the normal response to a significant loss should also be carefully considered. This decision inevitably requires the exercise of clinical judgment based on the individual's history and the cultural norms for the expression of distress in the context of loss.

Bipolar 1 Disorder

A. Criteria have been met for at least one manic episode (Criteria A–D under "Manic Episode" above).

B. The occurrence of the manic and major depressive episode(s) is not better explained by schizoaffective disorder, schizophrenia, schizophreniform disorder, delusional disorder, or other specified or unspecified schizophrenia spectrum and other psychotic disorder.

Coding and Recording Procedures

The diagnostic code for bipolar I disorder is based on type of current or most recent episode and its status with respect to current severity, presence of psychotic features, and remission status. Current severity and psychotic features are only indicated if full criteria are currently met for a manic or major depressive episode. Remission specifiers are only indicated if the full criteria are not currently met for a manic, hypomanic, or major depressive episode.

In recording the name of a diagnosis, terms should be listed in the following order: bipolar I disorder, type of current or most recent episode, severity/psychotic/remission specifiers, followed by as many specifiers without codes as apply to the current or most recent episode.

Reprinted with permission from the *Diagnostic and Statistical Manual of Mental Disorders,* Fifth Edition, (Copyright 2013). American Psychiatric Association.

BIPOLAR I DISORDER SEVERITY/COURSE

Mild	• Only symptoms required to make the diagnosis are present, or only a few others; symptom distress is manageable; only minor impairment
Moderate	• The intensity and number of symptoms and functional problems are between mild and severe
Severe	• Number of symptoms far in excess of those required for diagnosis; symptoms cause intense distress, unmanageability, & dysfunction
Remission	• Full: At least 2 months with no sigificant symptoms of a depressive/manic episode • Partial: Symptoms present w/o full criteria met, or remission less than 2 months

APA, 2013

Other Bipolar and Related Disorders

Like its immediate predecessor, the DSM-5 recognizes two primary bipolar disorders, despite a wide variation that exists in regard to the manner in which manic and depressive features may be intermingled in a person's actual life.

Many additional variations on bipolar and related disorders are discussed in the DSM-5 and elsewhere. Cyclothymic Disorder is characterized by a chronic cycling between hypomanic symptoms and depression over an extended period of at least 2 years, or 1 year in children. Hypomanic symptoms must not meet criteria for a bipolar II diagnosis, and symptoms must be present for at least half of the time during this 2-year period. This period is generally characterized by multiple episodes of depression and hypomanic symptoms, and must be persistent; that is, cannot have a 2-month period

Cyclothymia Disorder

Disorder characterized by long-term cycling between depressive and hypomanic symptoms; less severe hypomanic symptoms than bipolar II.

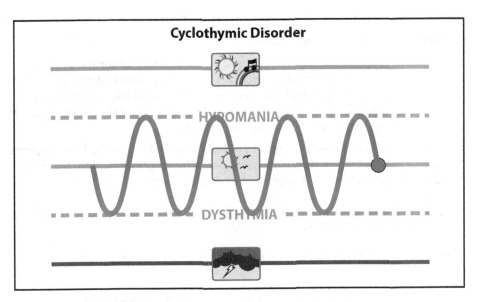

without symptoms. The DSM-5 suggests a prevalence rate between 3 to 5%, and a 15 to 50% risk that individuals with cyclothymic disorder will develop bipolar I or bipolar II disorders (APA, 2013).

Stahl (2011) discussed 10 different bipolar disorders existing on a bipolar spectrum, some of which were previously listed as not otherwise specified in the DSM-IV-TR. The DSM-5 recognized four variations of specified bipolar and related disorders including short-duration (2–3 days) or insufficient symptom hypomanic episodes with major depressive episodes, hypomanic episode with no previous major depressive episodes, and short-duration cyclothymia (less than 2 years; APA, 2013). Many of the other various bipolar and related disorders enumerated by Stahl and others would be coded as unspecified in the DSM-5.

Theories and Treatments of Mood Disorders

Over the history of psychology and psychotherapy, many theories have been developed exploring the phenomenon, function, and etiology of depression from different perspectives. **Quick Reminder:** As you read about and consider the theories of depression discussed below, keep in mind our discussion of the dynamic aspect of psychopathology from Chapters 1 and 2. How we think about a disorder informs how we choose to treat the disorder, and though symptoms may appear the same, etiology may differ from person to person! Many theories of depression focus on one or two of the dynamic dimensions of depression, neglecting other areas of functioning. As previously discussed, taking a biological perspective may lead a clinician to neglect cultural, relational, and individual aspects of a person's depression.

Likewise, theorists have sometimes emphasized culture, relationships, thought, actions, or feelings, to the neglect of other important elements of depression. As one example of a more dynamic way of thinking about depression, recall also our discussion of the diathesis-stress model of psychopathology from Chapter 2. Understanding that depression may be the result of a genetic or biological predisposition paired with an experiential or environmental stressor may help you to identify some of the limitations of these theories and their corresponding treatments.

Psychological Theories and Treatments of Mood Disorders

Over a century of psychotherapy research has led to the conclusion that many psychological treatments for depression are more or less equally effective. In the 1980s, the National Institute of Mental Health began comparing treatments and concluded that both Interpersonal Therapy (IPT) and Cognitive-Behavior Therapy (CBT) were just as effective as medication in the treatment of depression (Elkin et al., 1989; Shea et al., 1992). A wide variety of psychological treatments have been developed since this time, such that by the beginning of 2016, Division 12 of the American Psychological Association (the Society for Clinical Psychology) had identified 13 research-based psychological treatments for depression (Strunk, 2013). To complicate matters, seven of these therapeutic systems have been labeled as having modest research support, while six have been labeled as having strong research support, and some evidence also suggests that factors common to several of these treatments, as well as characteristics unique to clients and therapists, may also play a role in determining the effectiveness of depression treatment (Strunk, 2013). As Abramson and colleagues (1989) pointed out, clinicians have "long suggested that depression is not a single disorder but rather a group of disorders heterogeneous with respect to symptoms, cause, course, therapy, and prevention" (p. 359).

For bipolar disorders, APA Division 12 reported only three research-supported treatments for the manic episodes of bipolar disorders, with psychoeducation and systemic care receiving the accolade of "Strong Research Support," and cognitive therapy receiving the accolade of "Modest Research Support" (Johnson & Fulford, 2013). Systemic care is a form of treatment which involves the creation of a treatment routine in which patients have frequent and ongoing access to a system of care, including group therapy, appointments with psychiatrists and nurses, and supervision by an entire outpatient team specializing in the care of bipolar disorder (Johnson & Fulford, 2013). Cognitive Therapy for bipolar disorder will be discussed below. Division 12 adds the note that medications are the recommended first line of treatment for bipolar disorders, and many psychotherapists will testify to the difficulty of treating clients during an unmedicated manic period (Johnson & Fulford, 2013).

Psychodynamic/Interpersonal Theory and Treatment of Depression. Early psychodynamic conceptualizations of depression implicated, as Freud did with most mental health problems, childhood development and early relationships. Psychodynamic approaches have developed a wide variety of explanations for the development of depression; however, what these theories generally share in common is an emphasis on relationships and the internalization of a negative experience of the self. This negative experience of the self has been described in many different ways, including anger directed inward, loss of an important relational object, and overdevelopment of the super-ego, to name a few (Goldstein & Anthony, 1988).

The different descriptions of this negative experience of the self should be understood to be related to the manner in which the depressive symptoms are understood to develop. For example, theories of anger turned inward were generally understood to have a foundation in experiences of loss or rejection, leading to the perception of the self as unworthy, whereas theories of an overdeveloped super-ego were generally understood to be rooted in overbearing, authoritarian parenting. As Goldstein and Anthony (1988) explained, "In depression, there is the tendency to turn aggression against the self . . . the superego is often characterized by an especially rigid and punitive conscience, and a very lofty and unattainable ego ideal" (p. 182). Resolving this unconscious conflict is achieved by exploring beliefs, expectations, and life events in order to gain an awareness of the development of the unhealthy ego formation.

Mania, on the other hand, was understood in relation to ego defenses fighting against depressive loss and internalized anger. In mania, according to psychodynamic theories, a person utilizes denial and holds tightly to an idealized view of the self and the world, exaggerating "good" objects that the person longs for, in an effort to defend against the potential for losing them (Klein, 1994). The Interpersonal Psychotherapy (IPT) approach conceptualizes depression in relation to four main problem areas: grief, interpersonal (role) disputes, role transitions, and interpersonal deficits or sensitivity (Robertson et al., 2008). Notice that these four problem areas still revolve around relationships and negative experiences of the self, which often leads IPT to be grouped with psychodynamic theories, despite its differential origin.

An interesting piece of research by Green and colleagues (2012) may provide some evidence for Freud's suggestion of a link between guilt (overdeveloped super-ego) and self-blame (turning anger inward) with depression. Green and colleagues utilized fMRI to demonstrate that persons who had struggled with depression were more likely to show activation of brain regions associated with feelings of guilt or self-blame. Additionally, we should not forget that Freud was a psychiatrist, a medical doctor, and taught, in fact, that some cases of depression had a biological etiology, rather than a psychological etiology. In some ways, this distinction, made by Freud and some of his early modern predecessors, anticipated the diathesis-stress model and other complex contemporary perspectives on depression.

It should be noted, as you will likely perceive from reading the following sections, that psychodynamic conceptualizations of depression (and other disorders) have greatly impacted many of the other theories of depression, whether directly, as is the case with the IPT, cognitive, and experiential theories, or because of a rejection of Freudian conceptualizations, as is the case with behavioral theories of depression.

Cognitive Theory Depression. As previously discussed in Chapter 3, individuals suffering from depression have been found to make internal attributions of their failures, and external attributions of their successes, which is the exact opposite from what is typically found in persons with good mental health. This is just one way of conceiving the problematic thinking involved with depression, but imagine what may happen if a person spends weeks, months, or even years making these kinds of attributions.

A. T. Beck and colleagues (1979) proposed that manifestations of depression could be conceptualized as a cognitive triad described as the interaction of negative cognitions or interpretations about the self, the world, and the future. In essence, A. T. Beck theorized that depressed persons will be troubled by thoughts of their own worthlessness, thoughts that the world cannot offer sufficient help for them (helplessness), and thoughts about the hopelessness of their future. The person is overwhelmed by these negative interpretations, and can think of no way out of their current state. They are mentally trapped in a thick fog. In addition to this cognitive triad, A. T. Beck and colleagues proposed that these thoughts may become solidified on a deeper level of functioning as core beliefs, which will in turn direct future thinking, feeling, and behavior.

Core Beliefs

Cognitive Therapy concept describing the deepest set of values and beliefs held by a person

J. S. Beck's cognitive triad of depression is another way to help us distinguish a depression myth from the real thing. If you were a cognitive

FIGURE 7.2   Cognitive Triad of Depression

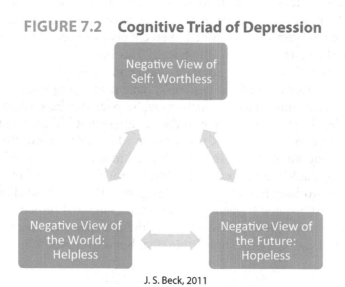

J. S. Beck, 2011

therapist, where would you intervene first on the triad in order to attempt to create psychological change? Why would you choose that part of the triad? Write down some reasons.

Behavioral Theory of Depression. Early behavioral theories of psychology advanced as more scientific alternatives to Freudian theories focused primarily on the manner in which individuals responded to the stimuli in their environment, and the manner in which they were rewarded or reinforced to develop specific patterns of behavior. Martell and colleagues (2010), proponents of a system of psychotherapy called Behavioral Activation, described that depressed individuals will often avoid unrewarding, unpleasant situations as a means to cope with their depressed mood, but this attempt to cope can then backfire, leading to a pattern reinforcing their depression. This pattern is characterized by ruminative thinking, inactivity, and isolation, which then becomes a vicious depression cycle leading back to a further dearth of rewarding experiences. Additionally, Martell and colleagues further hypothesized that in response to negative events, depressed individuals will often remain passive or stick to familiar patterns of behavior, thereby limiting their repertoire of behaviors, and decreasing the likelihood of positively reinforcing experiences.

Cognitive Behavioral Therapy. Whatever its mechanisms, it is clear that CBT is highly effective for some individuals with depression. Further, publications and research on cognitive behavioral approaches to therapy have burgeoned over the past 50 years, such that a myth has developed around CBT being the most effective form of treatment for depression. While the truth is that other approaches have been demonstrated as equally effective, it should be noted that CBT does have the most robust research base for depression compared to all other contemporary psychotherapy systems.

A functional analysis of a client's behaviors allows therapists to help determine what situations may provoke an increase in depressed mood, establishing the where, when, and how of one's depression. After situations or events related to depression are established, then clients can begin to challenge dysfunctional thoughts through reality testing. This involves questioning whether one's automatic thoughts are accurate, and confirming or disconfirming this with evidence from one's life. For example, remember Georg from earlier in the chapter, he would often have automatic thoughts related to his own helplessness; for example, "I will never be able to do anything right!" With reality testing, Georg was able to vocalize many situations in which this was not the case, and these automatic thoughts can then be changed to something more like, "I can make healthy choices that improve my life!" For a clear idea of how automatic thoughts are working in a client's life, therapists will often have clients keep a thought record, logging triggering events, their emotional response, and automatic thoughts. This record is reviewed by the therapist as a means to aid the client in challenging dysfunctional thinking, but also serves to help the client

FIGURE 7.3   Automatic Thoughts and Depression

J. S. Beck, 2011

become more aware of their problematic thinking. Here's an example of what Georg's thought records might often look like:

Automatic Thought Record			
As situations arise that seem significant to you, please briefly write down what happened, your emotional response to the event, and any automatic thoughts that you may have in relation to the event.			
Date	**Situation**	**Affect**	**Thoughts**
Jan. 10	Left work early	Tired, anxious, unhappy	I'm terrible at this job. Eventually, my boss will find out.
Jan. 11	Stayed in bed all day	Sad, lethargic	I will never accomplish anything. My life is over.
Jan. 13	Haven't gotten out of bed in 2 days; holding medication bottle in hand thinking of suicide	Worthless and numb	I should go ahead and end this pain. No one cares.
Jan. 14	Phone call from mom; spoke harshly to her	Guilty, sad	I shouldn't have spoken to her like that. I'm a bad son.

Last of all, therapists aid clients in recognizing and changing their deeper intermediate and core beliefs at the root of their depressed mood. These core beliefs are organized into the three categories previously mentioned:

fundamentally unlovable (referred to as hopeless above), fundamentally helpless, and as fundamentally worthless (J. S. Beck, 2011). As clients become more aware of their core beliefs, and how they are impacting their thoughts and behaviors, they can begin to retrieve or create a more functional and healthy set of core beliefs. See Figure 7.4 for a visual example of this relationship between thoughts and core beliefs. Changing core beliefs is accomplished by continually eliciting positive data disconfirming dysfunctional core beliefs, and by asking clients to examine their experiences through a healthier construal of events, allowing them to begin recognizing positive aspects of life on their own (J. S. Beck, 2011). Eventually, through ongoing systematic work, depressive core beliefs are modified, leading to more functional automatic thinking, and a newer and stronger sense of oneself as valuable and competent to face the difficulties of life.

FIGURE 7.4   Information-Processing Model of Depression

This diagram shows the manner in which negative information is processed, leading to an affirmation of an inaccurate core belief, while positive information goes unnoticed, is discounted, or is transformed into something negative (J. S. Beck, 2011).

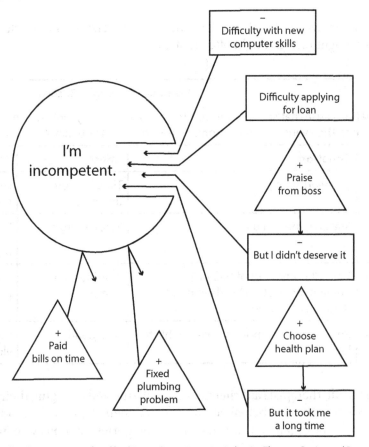

Cognitive Behavioral Therapy is also helpful in the treatment of bipolar disorder, and researchers have relied heavily on techniques drawn from CBT for depression in the construction of models aimed at treating mania. Specifically, CBT for bipolar disorder places additional emphasis on activity scheduling and mood monitoring, so that fluctuations and shifts in mood can become more clearly understood, thereby allowing for early intervention for manic and depressive episodes (Lam et al., 1999).

Process-Experiential/Emotion-Focused Theories and Treatments. Watson et al., (2003), proponents of emotion-focused therapy [EFT], conducted a study with clients diagnosed with Major Depressive Disorder comparing CBT and EFT, concluding that clients showed equal improvement in levels of depression, self-esteem, distress, and lower levels of reactive and suppressive coping strategies. However, EFT, more than CBT, demonstrated a profound decrease in client self-reports of interpersonal problems (Watson et al., 2003). In 2015, Harris and colleagues posited that of all the therapies for depression on the APA Division 12 list utilizing experiential components, two hypotheses of depression could be identified: maladaptive emotions and experiential avoidance. The EFT approach makes a distinction between primary and secondary emotions, as well as adaptive and maladaptive emotions. The experiential hypothesis of depression revolving around maladaptive emotions posits that secondary or maladaptive emotions can, at times, cover up more primary, adaptive emotions, keeping a person stuck in a maladaptive way of responding to their environment. On the other hand, the experiential hypothesis revolving around experiential avoidance posits that depression may be caused by the avoidance of memories and experiences associated with painful life events, leading again to a person's emotional responses becoming limited or blocked.

"The only way out is through" (Pascual-Leone & Greenberg, 2007, p. 875). This EFT motto helps explain the general process utilized by EFT to treat depression. Rather than turning away from painful experiences and memories, EFT emphasizes emotional coaching to work with a person's strengths and to promote emotional awareness, confront painful emotions, and experience events through a new emotional lens. A variety of therapeutic interventions are utilized to accomplish this, but perhaps the most interesting and well-known are the empty-chair dialogue and two-chair dialogue techniques discussed in Chapter 2. After the development of an empathic relationship, exploring sources of depression, and direct emphasis on blocked emotion and body sensations, EFT therapists will often utilize empty-chair and two-chair dialogues to further deepen recollections of memories, helping to further unblock emotions and create a new experience of past experiences at the root of depression (Elliot et al., 2004). As Elliot et al. pointed out, the center of the EFT "approach to depression is accessing core emotional experiences and memories to bring them into awareness, label them, reflect on them, and develop alternative ways of responding, thus making sense of experience in new ways" (p. 294).

Biological Theories and Treatments of Mood Disorders

A vast array of biological differences have been linked with depression, including genetic factors, neurotransmitter and endocrine functioning, and factors related to deficits in the function and structure of specific brain regions. Some of the difficulties with these theories resides in the close interconnection of various systems of the brain, as well as individual differences in brain functioning for individuals with mood disorders. This should not be overly surprising, however, as we have seen in discussing the history of depression, a distinction has long been made between more biological types of depression, and those of a more psychological type. In this regard, some research suggests that depression that begins in childhood may be more strongly rooted in genetics than depression starting later in life (Levenson, 2010). First-degree relatives of people with major depression appear to have a two to four times greater risk of the disorder, with approximately 40% heritability (i.e., individuals contracting depression whose parents had the disorder; APA, 2013). With bipolar disorders, the risk appears even higher, with a risk 10 times higher for folks with a family history of the disorder. Unfortunately, it is difficult to differentiate how much of the etiology of these disorders are related to genetics versus behaviors and coping mechanisms learned environmentally.

A number of different brain regions appear to be implicated in mood disorders. Brain images of depressed individuals seem to indicate reduced activity and brain volume in the hippocampus and several regions of the prefrontal cortex, which may help explain motivational issues and cognitive/decision-making difficulties (Stahl, 2011). On the other hand, some research has demonstrated increased activity and enlargement of the amygdala, which may be related to emotional dysfunctioning and rumination over negative memories (Saveanu & Nemeroff, 2012; Stahl, 2011). Similar patterns of brain activity are found in manic individuals, but with activity frequently in the opposite direction than depression (e.g., hyperactivity in prefrontal cortex areas; Stahl, 2011). Dysfunction in the hippocampus may be related to bipolar disorder, but has not been as clearly implicated in the symptoms of the disorder as increased activity in the amygdala and striatum, which appear to be related to emotion and reward processing difficulties (Cerullo et al., 2009; Man et al., 2019; Rich et al., 2007). Additionally, increased activity in the orbital frontal cortex has been demonstrated and may help explain difficulties individuals with bipolar disorder experience with impulse control (Stahl, 2011).

Neurotransmitters and Hormones. Three specific **monoamine** neurotransmitters, **norepinephrine**, **dopamine**, and **serotonin** have been understood to be associated with the development of mood disorders. These neurotransmitters are highly interrelated, forming what some researchers refer to as the **trimonoaminergic neurotransmitter system** (Stahl, 2011). As one example, norepinephrine binding to presynaptic receptors can block the release of serotonin, whereas norepinephrine binding to receptors on the cell body can increase the release of serotonin. In addition, serotonin can also have regulatory effects on both norepinephrine and dopamine. Further exploration and understanding of these interactions is needed to understand the dynamic nature of neurotransmitters, but some research implicates the serotonin transporter gene, linking neurotransmitter malfunctioning to potential genetic heritability (Saveanu & Nemeroff, 2012).

Classic monoamine hypotheses of depression were related to decreased production of one of these neurotransmitters, leading to a deficiency of one or more monoamines, which was believed to cause depression. Hyperactivity of these neurotransmitters are hypothesized to be responsible for mania in bipolar disorder, with emphasis placed on the role of dopamine in the limbic system, which may be related to an increased desire for stimulation, risk taking, and grandiosity (Stahl, 2011). As theories have become more dynamic, postsynaptic receptors have also been implicated. The monoamine receptor hypothesis posits that depression may be caused by an increase in the number and sensitivity of monoamine receptors on post-synaptic neurons (Stahl, 2011). To complicate matters further, enzymes in the presynaptic neuron or in the synapse can also break down or produce these neurotransmitters, thereby impacting the amount of available neurotransmitters in the synapse.

Hormones within the neuroendocrine system also appear to be related to the symptoms of mood disorders. The hypothalamic-pituitary-adrenal (HPA) axis is a highly interconnected endocrine system that links many areas of the brain including the amygdala, involved with emotions, the hippocampus, involved with memory, and the prefrontal cortex, involved with decision-making and other executive functions. Many of these functions are impaired during the episodes of a mood disorder, and are likely related in some way to poor hormone functioning in the HPA axis. Regarding individuals with depressive symptoms, the HPA axis may be overproducing the hormones cortisol and corticotropin-releasing hormone (CRH), which are related to chronic stress and difficulty returning to a calm state after a stressful event (Saveanu & Nemeroff, 2012). Long-term cortisol exposure may lead to neuronal death in brain regions associated with the HPA axis, and may be responsible for decreased brain volume in the hippocampus and other regions, as well as potentially changing the processing of monoamine

Monoamine Hypothesis

Classic neurotransmitter hypothesis of depression stating that a dysfunction in monoamine production is responsible for depression

Monoamine Receptor Hypothesis

An updated version of the monoamine hypothesis, implicating monoamine receptors, rather than monoamine production

neurotransmitters in the brain (Southwick et al., 2005). This hypothesis may well help explain the high occurrence of depressed individuals also reporting high levels of anxiety, sometime referred to as dysphoria.

Dysphoria

A state of uneasiness or discomfort and sadness, often understood technically as a mix of anxious and depressive states

Medication Treatments for Mood Disorders. As you might imagine, for virtually every biological theory related to depression and bipolar disorders, a medication or procedure has been developed to target the relevant dysfunction. In addition, several drugs that were created to treat other problems, such as seizures and psychotic episodes, have also been found helpful in the treatment of mood disorders. Let's make a few distinctions prior to looking at a few of the specific medications. First, when discussing medications for mood disorders, the distinction between antidepressants and mood stabilizers is the first major distinction. In general practice, as you can probably surmise from the broad titles of these drugs, antidepressants are used primarily in the treatment of depression, and mood stabilizers are used primarily in the treatment of bipolar and related disorders. Second, considering specifically antidepressants used in psychiatric practice, a distinction is generally made between first-line and second-line monotherapies, with second-line treatments carrying a greater burden of side effects (Stahl, 2011). Second-line treatments include many of the older antidepressants, for some of which alternatives have been found, which target the intended neurotransmitters, without the byproduct of impacting additional neurotransmitters that cause unintended side effects. Last of all, considering bipolar disorder, various types of medications have been used in attempts to quell the highs of mania and prevent depressive bottoms. These include medications ranging from the classic mood stabilizer, Lithium, as well as anticonvulsants, atypical antipsychotics, and several additional medications to treat additional symptoms (e.g., antidepressants for a depressive episode or a benzodiazepine or gabapentine for anxiety or agitation). Though controversial due to the potential for abuse, the FDA approved the restricted use of Ketamine for treatment-resistant depression (TRD) in 2019. Serafini et al. (2014) conducted a systematic review of Ketamine for TRD, reporting that it worked rapidly with a decrease in symptoms of depression within hours.

Medications for Depression. An important consideration of medication treatments for mood disorders is the mechanism of action. The mechanism of action for some medications, such as Lithium, remain unclear, in that we really do not know for sure how it works! Other medications, such as SSRIs, have been specifically designed to target specific receptors, enzymes, or the reuptake process. First-line depression medications include serotonin selective reuptake inhibitors (SSRI), norepinephrine and dopamine reuptake inhibitors (NDRI), and serotonin norepinephrine reuptake inhibitors (SNRI). The phrase reuptake inhibitor describes the mechanism of action of these medications, all of which work by blocking the reuptake of specific neurotransmitters back into the pre-synaptic neuron, thereby leading to an increased amount of the neurotransmitter available in the synapse and increasing the likelihood of absorption by post-synaptic neurons. The increased availability of the neurotransmitters over time is hypothesized to lead to downregulation (fewer receptors) and desensitization (less sensitive receptors) in the post-synaptic neuron, such that less of the neurotransmitter is needed to activate the neurons. This downregulation and desensitization may account for the reason that positive effects of antidepressants often do not occur for several weeks after monoamine treatment begins (Stahl, 2011).

Second-line depression medications include medications with a variety of neurological actions, and generally include alpha-2 antagonists also known as serotonin and norepinephrine disinhibitors (SNDI), selective norepinephrine reuptake inhibitors (NRI), tricyclic antidepressants, serotonin antagonist/reuptake inhibitors (SARI), and monoamine oxidase inhibitors (MAOI). NRIs function in a similar manner to the other reuptake inhibitors discussed in the previous paragraph, whereas SNDIs block presynaptic alpha-2 receptors, disinhibiting signals to shut down serotonin and norepinephrine production, thereby leading to increased amounts of these neurotransmitters in the synapse (Stahl, 2011). SARIs appear to function by blocking both presynaptic reuptake and specific postsynaptic serotonin receptors. MAOIs are classic antidepressants which function by destroying monoamine oxidase (MAO), an enzyme that metabolizes serotonin, dopamine, and norepinephrine.

You have likely seen warnings about MAO inhibiting medications, as this mechanism of action has been found to have potentially harmful side effects when paired with certain food or other medications. Certain wines, tap beers, cheeses, and other foods are high in tyramine, a chemical which increases norepinephrine production. The pairing of increased production without the MAO enzyme to destroy excess norepinephrine, has been found to lead to a rise in blood pressure and even more severe hypertensive crises, causing a brain hemorrhage and death (Stahl, 2011). Interestingly, a "cheese myth" has arisen around this reaction leading people to believe that all cheeses must be avoided when taking MAOIs; however, the truth is that only cheeses with high levels of tyramine will cause an increase in blood pressure.

The last class of antidepressants we will discuss here is another group of classic antidepressants known as tricyclic antidepressants. Tricyclics were originally developed to treat psychosis in schizophrenia, but were not found to be effective, and the medication line was almost abandoned (Stahl, 2011). Tricyclic antidepressants have a host of different mechanisms of action, generally involving the blockage of reuptake and postsynaptic receptors. Unfortunately, tricyclics generally impacts a large array of additional receptors and sodium channels, leading to a variety of severe side effects such as a drop in blood pressure, blurred vision, cardiac problems, seizures, and coma (Stahl, 2011). They also carry a serious risk of overdose, often leading to death, with the use of only three to four times what may be prescribed daily (Nolen-Hoeksema, 2014). As you can see from these descriptions, a wide array of antidepressant functioning is possible, which is why extremely close monitoring of antidepressant use is warranted with many of these medications. With this vast array of functions, it should not surprise us that the same medication can cause differential outcomes in different clients.

Medications for Bipolar Disorders. Lithium, which has been used in the treatment of bipolar disorder for over 50 years, is an ion that brings about a range of changes impacting not only neurotransmitters, but also enzymes, proteins, and gene expression, to name a few (Stahl, 2011). Although we are unsure what exactly makes it work, lithium has long been considered effective in helping persons struggling with bipolar disorder, especially during manic periods, and is often a fallback when newer bipolar medications are not working for a particular patient. Anticonvulsants, originally developed to treat seizures, have been found to vary in their effectiveness for the treatment of bipolar disorder, likely due to a wide variety in the mechanisms of action by which they work, some of which are not yet understood (Stahl, 2011). One of the main mechanisms by which anticonvulsants may decrease mania is the moderation of sodium channels, reducing sodium influx into neurons, thereby impacting glutamate and/or GABA production, two neurotransmitters that have been implicated with mania (Stahl, 2011).

Atypical antipsychotics, originally developed to treat symptoms of schizophrenia, may also be effective in the treatment of bipolar disorder, even when bipolar symptoms are not accompanied by psychosis. Some atypical antipsychotics have been found useful for maintenance of symptoms related to mood disorder, as they have been shown to reduce the likelihood of recurring manic or depressive episodes (Stahl, 2011). Atypical antipsychotics may work differently in the treatment of psychotic and nonpsychotic mania, on the one hand, by reducing dopamine activity related to psychosis, and on the other hand, reducing glutamate activity related to mania (Stahl, 2011). However, further research is needed to determine exactly how these medications are working. Medication treatments for bipolar disorder are often augmented with other medications, in order to treat additional symptoms not controlled by the bipolar medications; for example, depressive or anxiety symptoms. For example, the use of antidepressants during a depressive episode of bipolar disorder is sometimes warranted, but should generally be undertaken with much caution, as antidepressants may carry the potential to swing an individual back into a manic period.

Other Physiological Treatments for Mood Disorders. In case you are not into drugs and would prefer electricity and convulsions, magnets, or surgery, a variety of other physiological treatments have been developed to directly impact the functioning of various brain regions as a means to treat depression. Electroconvulsive therapy (ECT), although highly controversial, has been touted as effective by some clinicians, despite conflicting evidence; for example, relapse rates for depression after receiving ECT have been up to 85% (Fink, 2001). ECT utilizes an electrical current, which is passed through one or both hemispheres of the brain, initiating a seizure in the brain. Neuroimaging after ECT has demonstrated decreased activity in some brain regions believed to be related to improvements in depression symptoms; however, the exact mechanisms by which ECT may work are unknown, and in addition, cognitive and memory deficits, potentially long-term, have also frequently occurred (Henry et al., 2001; Sackeim et al., 2007).

Some newer physiological treatments include repetitive transcranial magnetic stimulation (rTMS), vagus nerve stimulation (VNS), and deep brain stimulation. As the names imply, all three of these methods are oriented toward stimulation of the brain; however, each works in a slightly different manner. Treatment with rTMS involves repeated extra-cranial exposure to high-intensity magnetic pulses to induce activity in the prefrontal cortex and the amygdala (Stahl, 2011). This treatment does not require surgery, but the effectiveness of the procedure remains unclear (Slotema et al., 2010). Vagus nerve stimulation and deep brain stimulation both require surgery to implant a pulse generator in the chest wall and electrodes at various locations of

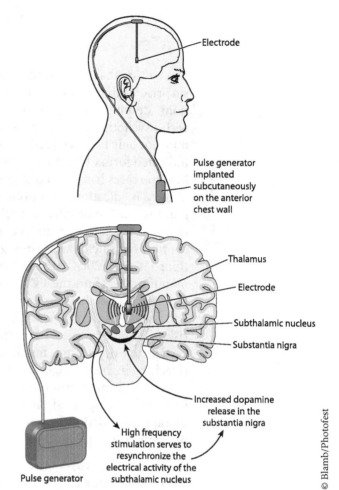

Deep Brain Stimulation

© Blamb/Photofest

the nervous system (Stahl, 2011). Electrodes for VNS are attached to, and increase the function of, the vagus nerve, which is upstream from the brainstem and many other brain regions, including the hypothalamus and the amygdala (Slotema et al., 2010; Stahl, 2011). Deep brain stimulation requires that an electrode be implanted directly into an area of the brain; for example, cerebral cortex or thalamus, which some researchers understand to be functioning as one part of a systemic brain dysfunction at the root of depression (Mayberg et al., 2005; McIntyre et al., 2004). It is vital to note that some of these more intrusive methods of treating depression, like some of the drug treatments for depression, do not have a robust and consistent research base and should be considered highly experimental (Stahl, 2011).

Combined Treatments and the Limitations of a Medication-Only Approach

In a culture that often wants a quick fix for everything, perhaps it should not surprise us that mood disorders are often treated with nothing but medications, despite a wealth of research suggesting that combining medications with psychotherapy produces the best results. A medication-only approach may not only be less effective, on occasion, medications may not even be the indicated form of treatment. In fact, prescribing antidepressant medications in some cases has led to disastrous consequences, likely due to streamlining of these medications for public use, and drug manufacturer's desire to maintain the illusion of safety for all potential customers. Between 2002–2004, a number of reports began to come out of teens and young adults who were committing suicide while being on Paxil and related antidepressant medications (Waters, 2004). These reports for some time went unheeded by drug manufacturers and the FDA. Eventually, research began to exonerate these families' claims that their children's symptoms, especially suicidal thoughts and attempts, were due to the drugs. Research has demonstrated that the risk of suicide increases for children and young adults who are prescribed certain antidepressant medications, and this risk has been related more closely to higher dosages of these drugs (Hammad et al., 2006; Miller et al., 2014). While medications may help on the molecular level, they cannot help to directly change dysfunctional thoughts, feelings, and behaviors. Psychotherapy is needed to help these clients develop new core beliefs, values, and perceptions of their lives and the situations they encounter.

Combining psychotherapy with medication has often demonstrated a host of benefits for individuals with clinical depression and other mood disorders. At times, clients may be so depressed or manic that medications are needed to help them open up to the treatment process, while alternatively, psychotherapy can help clients become aware of potential benefits of medications or to overcome biases against medications (Beitman & Saveanu, 2005). Some research suggests that combining psychotherapy and medications may be more beneficial for individuals with more severe, chronic forms of depression, and that psychotherapy alone is likely enough in mild or moderate cases that are less chronic (de Maat et al., 2007). Similarly for bipolar disorders, the combination of medications with psychotherapy appears to be more efficacious than medication alone (Otto et al., 2006). These findings may especially make sense in light of long-held distinctions between more biologically rooted forms of mood disorders that tend to be more severe and chronic, and other forms of mood disorders, more clearly rooted in experience or life events.

"Just Get Over It!"

As you have hopefully surmised, people with depression cannot always break free of the emotional grip of depression and "just get over it." And though depressive and manic episodes can sometimes remit without treatment, if one does not learn to change the underlying thoughts, feelings, and behaviors, and in certain circumstances treat the physiology as well, then individuals are likely to relapse into these disordered states. Until a person's core beliefs and day-to-day patterns of life have changed, they are likely to remain chronically depressed, scared, and even suicidal in some cases. With properly regulated medications and the recognition of maladaptive cognitive, emotional, and behavioral patterns, clients are likely to become more psychologically stable, and to begin healing broken relationships. Though this is not always the outcome in severe cases, proper psychiatric and psychological management can serve as an important catalyst for these changes!

Mood disorders are complex phenomena, requiring complex treatment! This is true whether we view these disorders through a biological or psychological lens, or even in a more complex, interactionary manner. When you hear the reductionist viewpoints, reducing this complexity to simplistic explanations, whether they are rooted in biological myth, psychological myth, or even popular myth, be sure to challenge them, and to remember the complexity of what you have studied! Most importantly, be sure to challenge the myths suggesting that depression is not real, whether from the movies you watch or from family and friends. Remember, defending against these myths, in essence, is defending the many hurting individuals that encounter them!

CHAPTER REVIEW

QUESTIONS

1. How does major depressive disorder differ from bipolar disorder? What are some of the differences between bipolar I, bipolar II, and other mania-related disorders? What subtypes and severity levels are used to differentiate these disorders? Why are these distinctions important?

2. Describe some of the major conceptualizations of depression that have been posited over the course of the history. Who are some of the key theorists that discussed depressive symptoms over the course of history? How have diagnostic criteria in the DSM changed over the course of time?

3. What is the relationship between suicide and depression? Suicide and bipolar disorder? What signs might indicate an increased potential for a suicide attempt?

4. What are some of the theories and treatments for depressive and bipolar disorders? What neurotransmitters are likely to be involved, and which medications should be used for the various disorders? In what circumstances might medications and psychotherapy be more or less helpful in the treatment of these disorders?

KEY TERMS

Deprimere

Lassitude

Malaise

Melancholy

Endogenous

Exogenous

Neurotic

Psychotic

Anhedonia

Suicide

Dysthymia

Labile

Dysphoria

Mania

Hypomania

Cyclothymia

Core Beliefs

Monoamine Hypothesis

Monoamine Receptor Hypothesis

Dyphoria

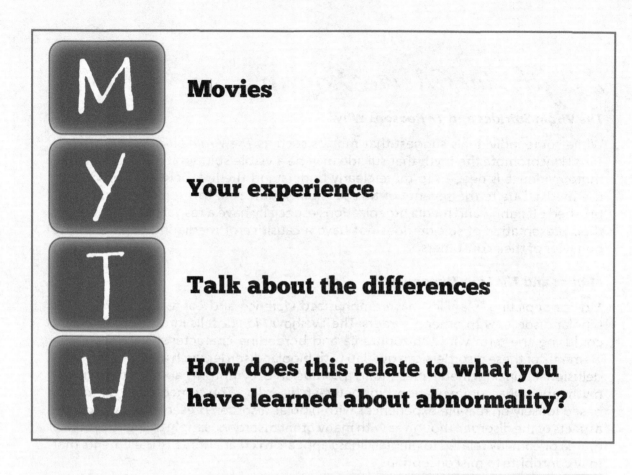

M Movies

Y Your experience

T Talk about the differences

H How does this relate to what you have learned about abnormality?

Myths in Movies Recap

Melancholia and Entanglement

Melancholia is a visually stunning movie; however, the artistically stimulating images in the movie do set the symptoms of depression in stark contrast to the manner in which they are generally experienced as drab and lifeless. *Entanglement,* though less artistically elaborate, similarly places a depressed character in an unrealistic situation, often with cartoonish experiences. Both of these films appear to glamorize depression in different, but fantastical ways. That being said, while a depression so severe that one lacks even the motivation or ability to move may seem overly dramatized, the DSM-5 does recognize a subtype of depressive and bipolar disorders characterized by catatonic symptoms, one of which entails the complete absence of psychomotor activity (APA, 2013).

Myths in Movies Recap

The Virgin Suicides and 13 Reasons Why

While some individuals suggest that movies such as *The Virgin Suicides* and *13 Reasons Why* promote the myth that suicide may be a viable solution to life's difficulties, more evidence is needed to more clearly understand the link between suicide and the media. Due to the severity of this possibility, however, this topic should not be brushed off lightly, and media organizations especially have a responsibility to ensure their presentation of suicide does not have a causitive or mediating impact on the behavior of their consumers.

Maniac and The Lady Dynamite

Movies depicting "maniacs" have emphasized violence and confused the mania of bipolar disorder with other disorders. The TV show *Maniac* falls into this problem by confusing the term with schizophrenia and borderline characteristics. While some elements of these disorders can overlap with bipolar disorder, such as impulsivity and delusional thinking, media presenting a confusion of symptoms appears to promote myths about inaccurate relationships between disorders. The comedy *Lady Dynamite*, based loosely on real-life experiences with bipolar disorder, presents many accurate aspects of the disorder, though as with many other disorders, simply trying to produce drama or comedy related to mental illness appears to create unrealistic elements that may contribute to misconceptions.

CHAPTER EIGHT

ANXIETY DISORDERS, OBSESSIVE-COMPULSIVE DISORDERS, AND RELATED DISORDERS

LEARNING OBJECTIVES

- ▶ Examine myths related to anxiety disorders and OCD and related disorders
- ▶ Identify normative anxiety
- ▶ Discuss diagnostic criteria of anxiety disorders and OCD and related disorders
- ▶ Recognize the 4 Fs for anxiety disorders and OCD and related disorders
- ▶ Differentiate components of anxiety
- ▶ Apply diagnostic criteria of anxiety disorders and OCD and related disorders with case studies
- ▶ Distinguish between anxiety disorders and OCD and related disorders
- ▶ Examine treatments and theories of these disorders

CHAPTER OUTLINE

- ▶ Anxiety: Benefit or Burden?—MYTH
- ▶ The Anxiety Quadripartite: Physiological, Emotional, Cognitive, and Behavioral Components
- ▶ The 4 Fs of Anxiety Disorders: Think About Everything That Could Go Wrong
- ▶ Panic Disorder
- ▶ Agoraphobia
- ▶ Specific Phobia Disorder
- ▶ Social Anxiety Disorder
- ▶ Generalized Anxiety Disorder
- ▶ Obsessive-Compulsive and Related Disorders—MYTH
- ▶ Obsessive-Compulsive Disorder
- ▶ Trichotillomania and Excoriation Disorder

- ▶ Body Dysmorphic Disorder
- ▶ Hoarding Disorder
- ▶ The 4 Fs of Obsessive-Compulsive and Related Disorders
- ▶ Theories and Treatments of Anxiety Disorders and Obsessive-Compulsive and Related Disorders

Anxiety: Benefit or Burden?

"There are indeed (who might say Nay) gloomy & hypochondriac minds, inhabitants of diseased bodies, disgusted with the present, & despairing of the future; always counting that the worst will happen, because it may happen. To these I say how much pain have cost us the evils which have never happened!"

—Thomas Jefferson (1816)

What do you worry about? Is that worry or anxiety helpful? What are your thoughts about anxiety? As in other chapters, a preliminary discussion of myths and ideas are reflected on and written down. Write down your MYTHs related to anxiety. You can discuss movies that depict anxiety, how it's portrayed in media, and your own experiences or the experiences of others whom you know. Then, reflect on any differences and how these experiences and beliefs related to what you have learned thus far about abnormality. Is anxiety abnormal?

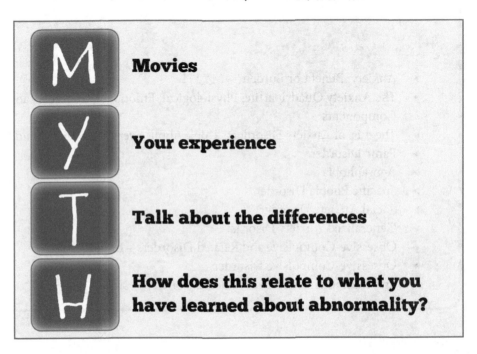

M **Movies**

Y **Your experience**

T **Talk about the differences**

H **How does this relate to what you have learned about abnormality?**

Myths in Movies

40 YEAR OLD VIRGIN

The *40 Year Old Virgin* is a film that attempts to portray social anxiety disorder in a comedic fashion. The main character, Andy, has concerns with engaging in romantic relationships. However, Andy appears to have no concerns with interacting with his friends or others. Do you think that most people with social anxiety disorders only struggle with romantic relationships? How might this film promote myths? What tone does this film set related to social anxiety disorders, humorous?

Steve Carell in *40 Year Old Virgin*

© Universal Pictures/Photofest

There are a number of movies that depict various forms of anxiety and anxiety disorders. The *40 Year Old Virgin* is a comedy that supposedly portrays features of social phobia, *Copycat* is a thriller movie that tells a story of a psychologist with agoraphobia, and *Panic Room* centers on a woman who appears to suffer from claustrophobia (Wedding & Niemiec, 2014). In thinking about these movies and others, what are the thoughts you hold about anxiety and anxiety disorders? What aspects of these movies might be inaccurate, exaggerated, or altered for entertainment?

One of the most popular myths about anxiety revolves around the idea that less is good and none is best. Experiencing stress, worry, and anxiety can be a normative response. In fact, some stress or sympathetic nervous system arousal can be good for you. Let's consider the Yerkes and Dodson (1908) model to analyze normative levels of anxiety and worry. The Yerkes and Dodson results suggested that the relationship between anxiety and performance is best explained by an inverted U-shaped curve (see Figure 8.1).

This figure is based on the Yerkes-Dodson's principle that performance

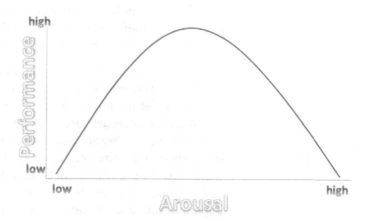

FIGURE 8.1   Inverted U-Curve of Performance and Arousal

Courtesy of Drew Curtis. Data based on Yerkes, R. M., & Dodson, J. D. (1908). The relation of strength of stimulus to rapidity of habit-formation. *Journal of Comparative Neurology & Psychology, 18*(5), 459. doi:10.1002/cne.920180503

is optimal with a moderate level of arousal. To illustrate this concept, reflect on a few examples. First, let's look at driving. Think back to when you first began learning how to drive a car. You were probably a bit nervous, right? There were many things to pay attention to, such as applying the gas, looking at the mirrors, staying in the lanes, and oh, not hitting any other cars. All of this was probably done with someone in the car who was evaluating every move or constantly correcting every decision you made. This was slightly anxiety provoking. Thinking back to that time when you first learned how to drive, you were probably not the expert driver you are now. You probably made more poor decisions based on the heightened level of nervousness. This anxiety best estimates high levels of arousal. Now, jump forward in time. You have been driving awhile and grown accustomed to all the nuances of gas, brakes, and car watching. Do you remember a time where maybe you were so comfortable driving that you ran a red light, missed a stop sign, forgot moments of your drive, or even got in a wreck? This best illustrates low levels of arousal. When you have too much or too little arousal your driving performance is likely to be poor.

What about playing a musical instrument, singing, theatre, or public speaking? The same concept applies here. The first time you performed in front of a crowd, you may have been so nervous that you missed some notes, forgot lines, or fumbled through a piece. High levels of arousal do not do well for your performance in these situations. On the other hand, low levels of arousal can decrease performance. If you have ever had a professor who has been jaded and has repetitively taught the same material year after year, then you have experienced firsthand how not caring can decrease performance.

Lastly, you see this model evidenced with test taking. When you have been highly nervous about performing on a test, you probably did not do so well. You may have forgotten information or misread some of the items. Back to the other side of the inverted-u, when you have shown up for a test without caring to be there or making any grade, your grade generally suffers.

Stress, nervousness, worry, and anxiety are not necessarily a bad thing. This is why you may procrastinate on schoolwork. If you do not care much about completing homework (low level of arousal), then it may not get completed until it becomes more important and urgent (higher levels of arousal). Thus, stating you want no anxiety can be outside of normative. Having no sympathetic nervous system arousal would mean you are dead. However, what most people with anxiety disorders struggle with is heightened arousal or too much sympathetic nervous system arousal. This anxiety can cause impaired functioning and feeling pain. Most individuals with anxiety disorders might think that they want to rid their anxiety because it seems like it is more than they can handle.

Another myth revolves around the idea of anxiety and depression being the same disorder. This idea stems from the notion that both are the same because the biological treatment is the same for both disorders. Lilienfeld

(1994) addresses this concern in his book *Seeing Both Sides*. Lilienfeld selected two articles that argue for and against depression and anxiety being separate and distinct disorders and constructs. Anxiety disorders are distinct from depression in that there is anticipation of future events going awry. Hamilton (1988) argued that anxiety and depression are separate entities and Dobson (1985) argued that they are more alike.

Anxiety and depression may sometimes be viewed as similar disorders because the biological treatment is generally similar. Antidepressant medication is typically prescribed for both disorders. Thus, if how you understand psychopathology informs treatment, then you may presume that treatment is a reflection of its conceptualization. However, this is not a completely accurate train of thought. Similarities in treatment do not necessarily mean that the construct or disorder is the same. Remember that psychopathology is dynamic and because similarities are found at a molecular level does not mean other levels overlap. In fact, one of the major differences between anxiety and depression can be found at the individual level. As you read in the previous chapter, depression involves a lack of meaning in one's life and beliefs of worthlessness, helplessness, and hopelessness (Beck, 2011). An individual with depression often believes he or she is helpless or has learned helplessness. Essentially, the thinking is that the future does not matter and may not be able to be changed, so there is no need to try. In contrast, the beliefs people hold who have anxiety disorders is that they can control the future and it is worth changing, which often leads to anticipation of numerous outcomes, causing anxiety. Thus, with these illustrations depression and anxiety can be viewed as very distinct, and even opposite, regarding a person's beliefs of control and helplessness.

The Anxiety Quadripartite: Physiological, Emotional, Cognitive, and Behavioral Components

As you examine the various anxiety disorders, you will notice the following quadripartite components involved: physiological, emotional, cognitive, and behavioral. The Yerkes-Dodson (1908) model depicts high levels of the sympathetic nervous system related to anxiety. Many of the physiological or somatic displays of anxiety are those of increased sympathetic nervous system arousal. Bodily processes associated with increased sympathetic nervous system arousal are:

Increased heart rate
Increased perspiration
Increased respiration
Pupil dilation
Muscle tension

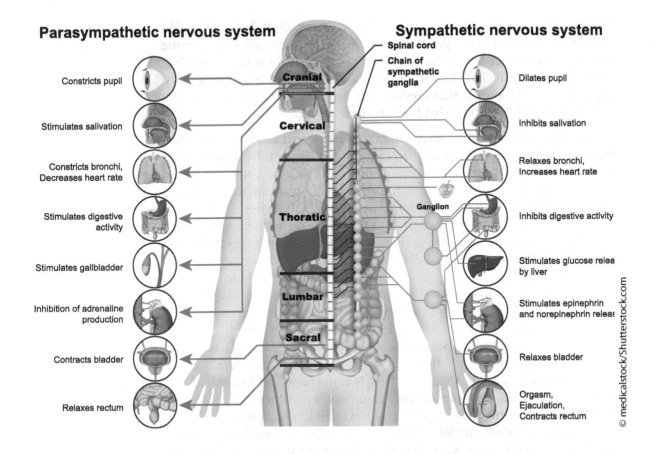

Parasympathetic nervous system | Sympathetic nervous system

Constricts pupil — Dilates pupil

Stimulates salivation — Inhibits salivation

Constricts bronchi, Decreases heart rate — Relaxes bronchi, Increases heart rate

Stimulates digestive activity — Inhibits digestive activity

Stimulates gallbladder — Stimulates glucose relea by liver

Inhibition of adrenaline production — Stimulates epinephrin and norepinephrin releas

Contracts bladder — Relaxes bladder

Relaxes rectum — Orgasm, Ejaculation, Contracts rectum

Spinal cord, Chain of sympathetic ganglia, Cranial, Cervical, Thoratic, Ganglion, Lumbar, Sacral

© medicalstock/Shutterstock.com

Fear

Adaptive emotional response to threat

Emotionally, anxiety is similar to fear. Fear is related to anxiety but is also distinct (APA, 2013). The DSM-5 differentiates the two by stating that fear is an emotional reaction and anxiety involves anticipation (APA, 2013). Hence, fear is the adaptive emotional response to threat, and anxiety involves cognitive mechanisms of thinking about potential threats. As you think about threats, think about the difference between fear and anxiety in responses. How might you categorize an exam in relation to fear and anxiety?

One of the unique attributes of human beings is the ability to project into the future. You are able to plan for your day, your week, and even your year. Your ability for foresight allows you to make plans and achieve many goals. However, this same ability is what is linked to the anxiety that people experience. In thinking about the future, people tend to make negative cognitive appraisals of situations. A cognitive appraisal is how you interpret a situation or the meaning you assign to a situation. Many times, when experiencing anxiety, you may think of all the things that could potentially go wrong. Many of the things that we think could go wrong never actually occur, much like the Thomas Jefferson quote introducing this chapter. Rarely, you might

Cognitive Appraisal

The way in which you interpret a situation

think of all the potentially positive outcomes. In fact, think about the times when you anticipated some task such as taking an exam. You may have pondered all the questions that may be on a test and how to avoid failing. You may have thought how you would do your best and if you do not get the outcome you want, then entertain other options. You probably do not think about how you will be successful and what it will mean to make a passing or stellar grade.

Many stimuli and situations do not directly threaten you but the thoughts you have associated with the stimuli are what affect you. For example, when you think about an exam, do you think about how it might jump up and bite you on your leg, causing a mortal wound or do you think about how failing an exam could lead to a series of negative events? You may think, "If I fail this exam, then I will fail this class, get kicked out of school, never get a job, never make money, become rejected by my family and friends, and be destined to live on the streets scrounging for food and water." Exams, homework, papers, and deadlines do not directly pose a threat but cause anxiety because they usually all involve some negative thought stemming from a cognitive appraisal that may reflect a belief about the self, world, or future (i.e., Beck, 2011). For instance, your thought may be, "If I fail this exam, then I am a failure." The fear is not the test but what a person's performance on the test might mean about the person or who they are to become.

Think to a time when you first spoke publicly in front of many people. If you recall feeling nervous, where did you want to be? You probably wanted to be anywhere but there. Behaviorally, when we experience anxiety we want to typically engage in escape or avoidance behavior. We want to escape situations in which we anticipate threat, such as encountering a scary bear. We sometimes think of sympathetic nervous system arousal in terms of a fight-or-flight response. When we experience sympathetic nervous system arousal we may have adrenaline to fight a threat or flee a situation. The latter is viewed as escape behavior. Escape behavior often serves as negative reinforcement, which leads to future avoidance. When you feel anxiety about speaking in front of others, it might seem easier to just leave. Leaving would allow you to escape the perceived or anticipated threat (i.e., the crowd or their evaluations of you). Once you escape, then your arousal diminishes and you may perceive the threat to be removed. This reinforces avoidance behavior. In the future, you may want to avoid speaking in public.

© LightField Studios/Shutterstock.com

As you explore the various anxiety disorders consider how each of these quadripartite components are present and contribute to the development or maintenance of these disorders. Also, think about how each of these components interact together to explain anxiety responses in humans. Consider how these components may lead to the 4 Fs.

The 4 Fs of Anxiety Disorders: Think About Everything That Could Go Wrong

The 4 Fs provide criteria to help distinguish between normative levels of anxiety, nervousness, and worry compared to what might be deemed pathological. The 4 Fs highlight how intense fear, heightened sympathetic nervous system arousal, catastrophic thinking, and escape and avoidance behaviors can lead to diagnoses of anxiety disorders. Anxiety disorders may lead to impaired functioning, altered frequency in behaviors, feeling pain, and engaging in behaviors that could be fatal with a variety of stimuli. Anxiety disorders may be resultant of specific people or things, perceptions of one's body, and a general worry about everything or nothing. Let's consider the 4 Fs for various anxiety disorders before looking at diagnostic criteria for each.

Frequency

In sum, anxiety disorders are more prevalent than most disorders. A 12-month prevalence of all anxiety disorders is about 18% (Kessler et al., 2005). The 12-month prevalence estimates from the DSM-5 for all anxiety disorders range from 21.5 to 26.5% (APA, 2013; see Table 8.1). Unpacking the ABCs of frequency will be a way to distinguish normative anxiety from that which may be more pathological.

A—Amount of Time: The DSM-5 specifies anxiety disorders differ from normative fear based on its persistence (APA, 2013). To meet diagnostic criteria for a generalized anxiety disorder, specific phobia, social phobia, agoraphobia, and separation anxiety disorder in adults, the symptoms last for 6 months or more (APA, 2013). The duration is 1 month or more for panic disorder, selective mutism, and separation anxiety disorder in children (APA, 2013).

B—Behavior: Anxiety disorders also differ from normative fear due to the excessiveness of the fear, or it being present often and in many situations. People with anxiety disorders may surrender much of their time to thinking about potential negative outcomes that will never happen, much like the Thomas Jefferson quote at the beginning of this chapter. Also, distinct from fear, anxiety may lead people to avoid one or several situations due to the fear of a situation or object related to a situation. Individuals may constantly ruminate over objects or situations that are associated with fear or anxiety.

Ruminate

To think on something for extended periods of time

TABLE 8.1   **Prevalence Rates for Anxiety Disorders**

Anxiety Disorder	Prevalence Rate (12 months)
Generalized Anxiety Disorder	0.9% in adolescents; 2.9% in adults (U.S.)
Panic Disorder	2–3%
Agoraphobia	1.7%
Specific Phobia	7–9%
Social Phobia	7%
Selective Mutism	.03–1%
Separation Anxiety Disorder	0.9–1.9%

*Based on DSM-5 Table (APA, 2013, pp. 34–36)

For example, many people might be afraid to speak in public. However, this fear of speaking in public may not lead to dropping out of school, quitting a job, or constantly thinking about how someone may ask you, at any moment, to make an announcement in front of others.

C—Curve: Anxiety disorders are also identified in females more than males, a ratio of 2:1 (APA, 2013). Research has suggested that the reason women experience symptoms of anxiety disorders is because women tend to engage in rumination more than men (Johnson & Whisman, 2013; Nolen-Hoeksema, 2000). Though all anxiety disorders combined have a relatively high prevalence rate, 18 to 26.5% (APA, 2013; Kessler et al., 2005), it still falls below one standard deviation of the normative distribution. Further, the prevalence for each of the anxiety disorders is much smaller in percentage. See Table 8.1 for prevalence rates for each anxiety disorder (APA, 2013).

The Good News: Many effective treatments exist for anxiety disorders. Division 12 of the American Psychological Association (2013; the Society for Clinical Psychology) has identified research-based psychological treatments for various anxiety disorders.

Function

Anxiety disorders impair various aspects of functioning, including social, occupational, and physical (APA, 2013). Anxiety disorder presentations may lead to high economic costs and individuals frequently visiting the hospital or medical facilities (APA, 2013). One of the reasons that people may go to the hospital is that they experience the physiological symptoms and may interpret these symptoms as a heart attack or another physiological condition.

When you are anticipating many things that could go wrong, then you are typically not focused on current tasks. Time committed to worry may prevent productivity of other tasks or duties. For example, if you constantly fret about a job performance evaluation and potential outcomes, then you may not dedicate much time to work or the time you do spend working may not be worthwhile.

The escape and avoidance behavior may lead people to frequently leave occupational or educational settings and avoid them subsequently. Leaving work or school and missing many days may lead to getting fired from a job, decreased pay, quitting school, or failing coursework. Generalized anxiety disorder is responsible for 110 million disability days in the United States of America (APA, 2013). Further, avoiding social situations due to anxiety may lead to impairment in social functioning. Social relationships may become strained or dissipate over time with avoiding interactions. Intimacy and sexual performance can decrease due to high levels of anxiety.

Anxiety disorders can also lead to impaired physical functioning. People who experience high arousal for extended periods of time may become exhausted, fatigued, irritable, and weak. Further, sleeping, concentration, or engaging in physical activity can become challenging (APA, 2013).

Feeling Pain

People experiencing high levels of anxiety can be in pain. Individuals generally want to be anywhere other than when they are experiencing anxiety because of the pain felt in those situations. Individuals experiencing panic attacks may think that they are having a heart attack, suffering some physical ailment, or even dying. Individuals with anxiety disorders do not like the feeling, which is the reason that many who seek treatment want no more anxiety. The chronic experience of anxiety may lead to the continued feelings of pain in bodily fatigue and sleeplessness (APA, 2013).

Fatality

Many anxiety disorders may place individuals in harmful situations. For example, having a specific phobia of spiders could compromise driving if a spider is found to be in the car when driving. A person with this specific phobia might swerve their car and even get in a wreck to avoid the spider. Escape and avoidance behaviors can pose a threat to many individuals given the situational context. Further, many of the various anxiety disorders increase the risk of suicide attempts (APA, 2013). Individuals who have been diagnosed with a specific phobia are more likely (60%) to attempt suicide (APA, 2013).

Panic Disorder

Your heart is pounding, your body is trembling, you feel intense pain in your arm and chest, you are sweating, and you are light-headed. What might you think is going on? How about having a heart attack? Individuals who experience the symptoms of panic attacks (some of those described) may think that they are having a heart attack. Thinking that you are having a heart attack is a calming thought, right? Usually the thought of a heart attack will increase sympathetic nervous system arousal and contribute to the panic attack.

© DimaBerlin/Shutterstock.com

Panic Attack

A variety of somatic symptoms associated with sympathetic arousal within a 10-minute period

Somatic

Aspects of a person's body or physiology

A number of people might have panic attacks in various situations. The 12-month prevalence rate for experiencing panic attacks is approximately 11% in the United States (APA, 2013). Panic attacks involve a relatively quick (though it may not seem that way to the individual in the moment) period of intense fear and somatic complaints (APA, 2013). Somatic symptoms are those that affect a person's body or physiological processes. When the 4 Fs become present with those panic attacks, then it may be a panic disorder.

The things that contribute to a panic disorder being strengthened are the somatic symptoms, cognitive appraisal, and learning principles. To remember these things, you may think of ACE.

> **A**ttend to your bodily processes
> **C**ognitive appraisal
> **E**scape the situation

Attention to your bodily processes, namely sympathetic nervous system arousal, has the potential to become scary and influence you to leave your current situation. When you notice that your heart is racing, you may then think a number of thoughts. People that experience panic disorder may have thoughts of an inability to control their body, or thoughts that something bad is going to happened to them. These types of thoughts may elicit fear. Then, a person may want to run away or escape their current context. When people do leave, then the escape/avoidance behavior is reinforced. Consider the case on the following page.

In this example, Beatrice experienced a panic attack, seemingly in response to an argument over finances. Then, Beatrice began to attend to her heart racing and pain in her chest. Beatrice perceived her somatic symptoms as a heart attack and became very fearful of dying. Lastly, Beatrice escaped the argument by going to the hospital. Unfortunately, a hospital visit, in this situation, served as negative reinforcement. Perceiving panic attacks in the future may lead Beatrice to claim that she is having a heart attack.

Many clients who seek therapy for panic attacks or panic disorder may have previously gone to a hospital, clinic, or some health care facility prior to a therapist's office. In some ways, this is detrimental to clients due to it potentially reinforcing the belief that the bodily sensations are the result of a heart attack or some physiological illness, leading to several medical visits and financial costs. However, given the option of error, it is probably more advantageous for clients (and therapists) to erroneously see a physician when having panic attacks versus having a heart attack in a therapist's office.

To examine the criteria for panic disorder, review the DSM-5 criteria. The DSM-5 reveals how the various somatic symptoms along with the persistent worry about panic attack consequences, and impaired functioning qualify for a panic disorder.

Agoraphobia

Agoraphobia

Fear or worry of having panic attacks in several different places

The roots of agoraphobia are found from a psychiatrist named Carl Westphal, who labeled the disorder as "die agoraphobie" (Westphal & Schumacher, 1988). The word agoraphobia comes from Greek words "agora" and "phobia." In Greece there are open speaking places where the ancient Greek philosophers and others would speak to individuals, called the agora. Phobia is roughly translated to an intense fear. Thus, agoraphobia can be roughly translated as an intense fear of open places. This translation explains agoraphobia in some aspects but also contributes to some myths and misconceptions. It is often believed that agoraphobia means fear of open places, which results in an individual staying inside their house or residence at all times. Agoraphobia is not a fear or phobia of open places; rather, the fear is having panic attacks in several places.

Case Vignette

Beatrice is a 38-year-old married woman with two children. She generally oversees her family finances. Sometimes the finances are low and it is difficult to cover some bills. Recently, her husband discovered that a bill was unable to be paid, which led to an argument between Beatrice and her husband. When her husband was asking her questions related to the finances, Beatrice began to feel her heart racing and pain in her chest. She immediately told her husband that she thought she was having a heart attack and that she was going to die. Her husband immediately called 911 and an ambulance was dispatched. The paramedics took Beatrice to the hospital. After assessments at the hospital, Beatrice was informed that she did not have a heart attack but may be experiencing stress and anxiety.

DSM-5 CRITERIA FOR PANIC DISORDER

DIAGNOSTIC CRITERIA

A. Recurrent unexpected panic attacks. A panic attack is an abrupt surge of intense fear or intense discomfort that reaches a peak within minutes, and during which time four (or more) of the following symptoms occur:

Note: The abrupt surge can occur from a calm state or an anxious state.

1. Palpitations, pounding heart, or accelerated heart rate.
2. Sweating.
3. Trembling or shaking.
4. Sensations of shortness of breath or smothering.
5. Feelings of choking.
6. Chest pain or discomfort.
7. Nausea or abdominal distress.
8. Feeling dizzy, unsteady, light-headed, or faint.
9. Chills or heat sensations.
10. Paresthesias (numbness or tingling sensations).
11. Derealization (feelings of unreality) or depersonalization (being detached from one self).
12. Fear of losing control or "going crazy."
13. Fear of dying.

Note: Culture-specific symptoms (e.g., tinnitus, neck soreness, headache, uncontrollable screaming or crying) may be seen. Such symptoms should not count as one of the four required symptoms.

B. At least one of the attacks has been followed by 1 month (or more) of one or both of the following:

1. Persistent concern or worry about additional panic attacks or their consequence (e.g., losing control, having a heart attack, "going crazy").

2. A significant maladaptive change in behavior related to the attacks (e.g., behavior designed to avoid having panic attacks, such as avoidance of exercise or unfamiliar situations).

C. The disturbance is not attributable to the physiological effects of a substance (e.g., a drug of abuse, a medication) or another medical condition (e.g., hyperthyroidism, cardiopulmonary disorders).

D. The disturbance is not better explained by another mental disorder (e.g., the panic attacks do not occur only in response to feared social situations, as in social anxiety disorder, in response to circumscribed phobic objects or situations, as in specific phobia; in response to obsessions, as in obsessive-compulsive disorder; in response to reminders of traumatic events, as in posttraumatic stress disorder; or in response to separation from attachment figures, as in separation anxiety disorder).

Think of panic disorder and panic attacks. Say that you are going to your local grocery store (or all-in-one big corporate shopping center) and you have a panic attack while shopping. Immediately, you leave the store. Then, you avoid going back to that store because of the fear of having a panic attack there. At a theatre, you have a panic attack and leave the show. Then you avoid going back to the theatre to watch movies. At the library you have a panic attack, which results in escape and avoidance behavior as well. On a plane you had a panic attack. It was very difficult for you to leave the plane, which intensified your panic and fears. Once you landed, you vowed to never fly again. Now, there are several places and situations that you avoid. You do not avoid them because you are fearful of the grocery store, movies, planes, and library. The worry is that you will have a panic attack in those places, which is why you avoid them. This is the picture of agoraphobia. How have movies or personal experiences affected your ideas about agoraphobia? To help challenge inaccurate beliefs and faulty portrayals of agoraphobia, consider how the 4 Fs and the DSM criteria relate to this conceptualization.

Specific Phobia Disorder

Are you afraid of lions, tigers, and bears? Oh my. What are you afraid of? When you think about it, what immediately elicits fear and accelerates your heart? Are you afraid of spiders, mice, roaches, snakes, blood, needles, clowns, sharks, heights, or flying?

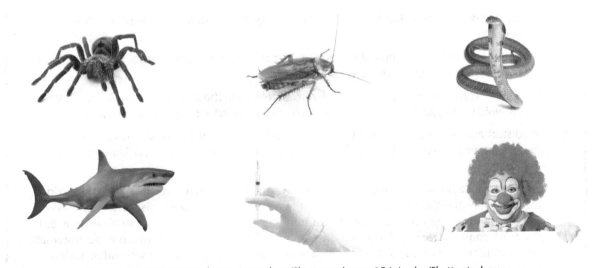

©Susan Schmitz/Shutterstock.com; ©anat chant/Shutterstock.com; ©Eric Isselee/Shutterstock.com; ©Catmando/Shutterstock.com; ©AlexandrBognat/Shutterstock.com; ©Alexander Raths/Shutterstock.com

There are numerous myths about specific phobias. One myth that gets perpetuated is the belief that a phobia is any fear about a specific object or situation. Having a fear about any of the above does not mean that you necessarily have a phobia. Fear and phobia are often used interchangeably in language, which contributes to the belief that an intense fear is also a phobia.

There are a number of people that claim to have unique phobias, some of which may be fears but others may actually be phobias. Some people have claimed a variety of specific phobias. Even specific phobias from movies such as *E.T.* have been reported (Quintero, 2016). When investigating the difference between fears and phobias, it is crucial to recall the 4Fs and the DSM-5. The DSM-5 includes specifiers for phobic stimuli (APA, 2013):

- ▶ Animal
- ▶ Natural Environment
- ▶ Blood-Injection-Injury
- ▶ Situational
- ▶ Other

Myths in Movies

ARACHNOPHOBIA (LEFT), FEAR FACTOR (RIGHT)

Movies and shows may perpetuate myths about specific phobias too. There are various movies and shows that attempt to do this. The movie *Arachnophobia* and *Harry Potter Chamber of Secrets* speak to the fears people have of spiders. Stephen King's book and movie, *It*, plays on the fear of clowns. An older television show titled *Fear Factor* would ask individuals to put themselves into fear-inducing situations, such as lying in tanks of roaches, snakes, and so on.

© Buena Vista/Photofest

© Universal Orlando/Photofest

Phobia

A marked fear occurring at a high frequency that impairs functioning, leads to feeling pain, and may be fatal

A phobia definitely involves a fear of a specific object or situation but also causes impaired functioning, is marked higher in frequency than other normative fears, leads to feeling pain, and can be fatal.

A person with a specific phobia might swerve their car and even get in a wreck to avoid a spider. Escape and avoidance behaviors can pose a threat to many individuals given the situational context and the specific object related to the phobia. For example, having a phobia of needles can be detrimental if you avoid seeking health care services because of the association with syringes. To help you distinguish between a fear and a phobia, look at the DSM-5 criteria and the 4 Fs.

Social Anxiety Disorder

© marcovarro/Shutterstock.com

You approach the podium and gaze out at the sea of blurry faces. You look down to gain some composure. As you clear your throat and take a breath, you look back up and feel your heart pounding, hands sweating, and legs shaking. You do everything you can to muster the energy to just make the words form from your mouth. This public speaking situation is similar to how many people who fear public speaking might feel. How do you feel about public speaking? Does thinking about giving a speech in front of your peers lead to sympathetic nervous system arousal?

Sometimes, speaking in front of others or interacting with people you have never met before can be much more frightening than snakes, spiders, and needles. Public speaking is one of the most frequently reported fear-inducing social situations (Wittchen & Fehm, 2003). In fact, one study that asked 815 students to rank order their fears corroborated that speaking publicly in front of a group has been ranked as more fearful than the fear of death (Dwyer & Davidson, 2012). Table 8.2 reflects Dwyer and Davidson's findings about common fears.

Though the fear of public speaking and social anxiety disorder share the common fear of negative evaluation by others, there are differences. The same consideration of differentiating between a fear and specific phobia applies for social phobia. There is a difference between normative fears of speaking publicly and social anxiety disorder. Much like a specific phobia, social anxiety disorder involves a specific threat or target, humans. Further,

TABLE 8.2   Common Fears

Common Fears	2010 Findings					1973 Bruskin Associate's Findings		
	Ranking[a]	n	%	% Men[b]	% Women[c]	Ranking[d]	n	%
Speaking before a group	1	503	61.7	57.2	65.9	1	1,032	40.6
Financial problems	2	447	54.8	52.1	58.0	4	559	22.0
Death	3	352	43.2	40.1	46.8	7	476	18.7
Loneliness	4	312	38.3	35.3	40.3	9	346	13.6
Heights	5	307	37.7	36.1	39.1	2	814	32.0
Insects & bugs	6	294	33.4	33.8	42.2	3	562	22.1
Deep water	7	222	27.2	19.5	34.8	5	547	21.5
Darkness	8	172	21.1	11.5	30.0	12	201	7.9
Sickness	9	154	18.9	17.9	20.4	6	478	18.8
Flying	10	68	8.3	4.8	11.3	8	465	18.3
Elevators	11	66	8.0	4.5	10.8	13	193	7.6
Driving/riding car	12	34	4.2	3.2	5.0	11	224	8.8
Dogs	13	25	3.1	1.6	4.3	10	285	11.2
Escalators	14	22	2.7	1.0	4.1	14	122	4.8

[a]n = 815.
[b]n = 374.
[c]n = 417.
[d]n = 2,543.

"Is Public Speaking Really More Feared than Death?" by K. K. Dwyer & M. M. Davidson in *Communication Research Reports* (2012), 29(2): p. 104. Published by Taylor & Francis Ltd., reprinted by permission of the publisher Taylor & Francis Ltd, http://www.tandfonline.com.

social anxiety disorder involves much more than merely a fear of speaking in front of others. People with social anxiety disorder often have an intense fear of others in social situations or being negatively evaluated by people (APA, 2013). Further, the fear leads to avoiding social situations, causes distress, and impairs functioning (APA, 2013). Social anxiety disorder mostly begins (75% of cases) between the ages of 8 and 15 years of age (APA, 2013). The disorder may develop from a history of shyness and from a stressful or embarrassing social situation (e.g., children bullying or making fun of you; APA, 2013). Consider the following case to help you conceptualize the disorder and to help differentiate between public speaking.

Case Vignette

Clara was a 28-year-old single female who entered therapy with her head down, avoiding eye contact. She spoke few words and mostly answered questions by nonverbally shaking or nodding her head. Clara indicated that she wanted therapy to help her interact with people and establish relationships. She indicated that she did not know how to have relationships and that she was not good at them. She also said that she was fearful to speak to people. Clara worked from home and was not forced to interact with others. She ordered most of her goods from the internet. She went out once a month to grocery stores and did so at early morning or late at night times to avoid being around others. Clara stated that sometimes she will go without eating if she thinks that she has to face people in stores to purchase food. She stated that when she thinks about interacting with people she is afraid, her body shakes, she thinks people will laugh at her, which is why she has chosen to stay away from people as much as she can. Clara indicated that she remembers wanting to become invisible from everyone after an incident in her earlier education years. She stated that in 6th grade some other girls in gym class had pulled down her gym shorts and undergarments during class. She stated that other boys and girls saw her exposed and she became immediately embarrassed and attempted to run away. She stated that she fell down while running and then felt more embarrassed because everyone in the gym was laughing at her and no one helped her up. She stated she vaguely remembers leaving the gym and never wanting to interact with people again after she left.

Generalization

Learning based on one situation has become associated with many situations

The case of Clara demonstrates how marked fear of people and negative social evaluation may lead someone to escape and avoid situations involving people. For Clara, her fear from her peers negatively evaluating her generalized and persisted into adulthood. Generalized means that the learning based on one situation has become associated with many situations or applied beyond the one situation. For Clara, she wanted to avoid people in every social context after the embarrassing event in junior high gym class. You may see how the 4 Fs are present for the case as Clara feels pain from not interacting with others, has impaired functioning, and is potential fatal if she ceases eating due to not buying food for fear of interacting with others. You may also look to DSM-5 for the specific criteria.

Generalized Anxiety Disorder

Conceptually think of generalized anxiety disorder (GAD) as worrying about everything and nothing. The idea behind the name "generalized" is that the anxiety has no specific object or target or that numerous objects and targets lead to anxious thoughts and marked fear. The lack of a specific target or situation is how GAD is distinct from panic disorder, specific phobia, and social anxiety disorders. Individuals with GAD may become anxious about a range of things including employment, tests, performance evaluation, social situations, health, daily living, washing the dishes, brushing teeth, and so on. There is not a typical theme related to the anxiety such as that found with social phobia, where the fear is based on evaluations of others. GAD is also distinct from agoraphobia because the fear is of multiple things or situations rather than a fear of having a panic attack in multiple situations.

People who have GAD may report feeling nervous throughout their entire lives with varying levels of intensity at different times (APA, 2013). The onset of GAD is around the age of 30 and occurs in females more so than males, with 55 to 60% females in clinical settings (APA, 2013). Due to the anxiety carrying numerous targets or no specific target, the 4 Fs may vary based on the individual client. However, the frequency of worry is often much higher than normative worry, the functioning is impaired (depending on the context), and can be fatal depending on the situation. The DSM-5 contains the specific criteria of GAD.

Obsessive-Compulsive and Related Disorders

There are numerous movies, shows, and media that portray obsessive-compulsive disorder (OCD).

Write out some MYTHs related to OCD. You can discuss movies, how it's portrayed in media, and your own experiences or the experiences of others whom you know. Then, reflect on any differences and how these experiences and beliefs relate to what you have learned thus far about abnormality.

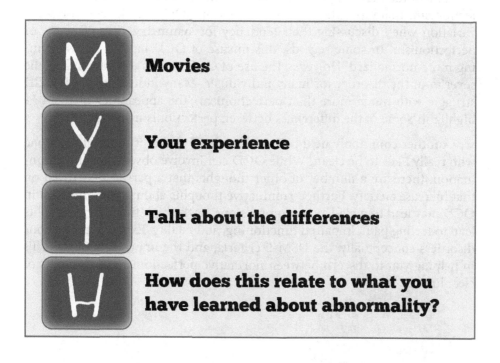

M Movies

Y Your experience

T Talk about the differences

H How does this relate to what you have learned about abnormality?

Myths in Movies

MATCHSTICK MEN

Movies and shows such as *As Good As It Gets*, *Matchstick Men*, and *Monk* depict OCD. As you think about films or experiences, note how this has shaped your beliefs about OCD.

A scene from *Matchstick Men*

Traditionally, as found in the DSM-IV-TR, OCD fell under the anxiety disorders (APA, 2000). The reason for this is because anxiety is a component of OCD. The DSM-5 suggests that OCD and anxiety disorders have a close relationship (APA, 2013). In the DSM-5, OCD and other disorders are under the category titled obsessive-compulsive and related disorders (APA, 2013). One of the reasons for this change is because OCD and related disorders, though involving anxiety, contain additional components and diagnostic validators that led to them being grouped together (APA, 2013).

One of the major myths held about OCD is that it is just a form of perfectionism. Many people may say "it's just my OCD tendencies" or some variation when discussing their tendency for symmetry, completeness, or perfectionism. In some regards, this misuse of OCD has led to it becoming more normalized. However, the use of OCD in this way downplays the severity of the disorder for many individuals. Many individuals with OCD struggle with much more than perfectionism. The appearance of the 4 Fs highlights some of the differences between perfectionism and OCD.

Another commonly held belief about OCD is that it is about someone who really likes to be clean. While OCD can involve obsessions of contamination, there are a number of other thoughts that a person may dwell on that increase anxiety. Further, ruminative thoughts about contamination in OCD may lead to maladaptive compulsions, or the high frequency thoughts lead to feeling pain, impaired functioning, and fatality. Examine the various disorders conceptually, the DSM-5 criteria, and the imposition of the 4 Fs in helping you to discern between normative perfectionism or thoughts of cleanliness.

Obsessive-Compulsive Disorder

Many people may check that they locked their car door more than once. If you have an electronic locking system that sounds an alarm or beeps, then you probably might press the remote lock button several times. The beeping sound of your car operates as a conditioning principle of learning. Hearing the beep reassures you that no one would ever be able to break into your car. Hearing the beep several times feels really good, like extra safety, in that you know your car is locked, which means it is completely safe from anything, right? Does it sound absurd? Yet, many of us will lock our car doors or house doors several times or check a few times to see if it is locked. Why? You may perform these acts because that is what you did last time and when you returned to your car or house everything was safe and not broken into or burglarized (i.e., classical and operant conditioning at work).

The tendency to check your doors or even wash your hands more than once is something that many people can connect to. This is not "crazy" behavior. Thus, when you examine OCD, you will see that individuals who suffer share some commonalities with you. Their thoughts may not be more irrational than yours and their learned behaviors are more related than you might think. The imposition of the 4 Fs help you understand how these behaviors may be pathological.

There are two major components found in OCD, obsessions and compulsions. Obsessions are essentially recurrent and persistent thoughts that increase anxiety (APA, 2013). These thoughts can involve a number of different themes including contamination, symmetry, order, aggression, sexual, religious, and harm (APA, 2013). Compulsions are the recurrent behaviors that a person feels motivated to perform in response to obsessions to reduce anxiety (APA, 2013). These behaviors can be vast and may relate directly to the various obsessions. Some of these behaviors could include handwashing, checking locks or other features of safety, or counting.

Obsessions

Recurrent and persistent thoughts that increase anxiety

Compulsions

Recurrent behaviors that a person feels motivated to perform in response to obsessions to reduce anxiety

Contamination obsessions with handwashing compulsions is the most salient image for people when they think of OCD. Some of this may be due to portrayal within movies such as *As Good As It Gets* or even the recognition of the disorder with famous individuals, such as David Beckham and Dr. Elizabeth McIngvale. Less attention is usually given to other obsessions and compulsions. Some individuals may suffer with obsessions of harm and behaviors related to safety. Consider the following case to help you think about OCD.

© A and N photography/Shutterstock.com

Case Vignette

Judith is a 39-year-old woman who entered therapy stating that she struggled with arriving to work on time. She indicated that she often locks her door five times before leaving her apartment. After leaving her apartment she constantly worries that maybe she forgot to completely turn the key the last time she locked her door and worries that maybe someone will break into her apartment. Sometimes she returns back to her apartment after having driven to work, which causes her to be late. She also says that when she parks her car in a parking lot she will park her car furthest from any other car. After getting out of her car, she uses a tape measure to measure the distance her car is from each parking lane. She stated that her car has to be equidistant on each side or she will move her car until this goal is achieved. Judith stated that she checks her parking to be sure that her car will not be damaged or hit by another automobile. She stated that she also feels compelled to lock her car door 10 times. While Judith is working she states that she has a hard time focusing because she worries about her car being damaged, her apartment being broken into, and her purse being stolen. She states that she carries her purse on her body at all times and will zip it and unzip it 10 times, at various times throughout the day, to ensure that all of her belongings are there. Judith reported that she has always locked her door several times beginning when she was 15 years old.

As you read the diagnostic criteria and subsequently examine the 4 Fs, think about how Judith may meet criteria for OCD. Also, think about the humanity of Judith and how conceptually her behaviors may have resulted through learning principles.

DSM-5 CRITERIA FOR OBSESSIVE-COMPULSIVE DISORDER

DIAGNOSTIC CRITERIA

A. Presence of obsessions, compulsions, or both:

Obsessions are defined by (1) and (2):

1. Recurrent and persistent thoughts, urges, or images that are experienced, at some time during the disturbance, as intrusive and unwanted, and that in most individuals cause marked anxiety or distress.

2. The individual attempts to ignore or suppress such thoughts, urges, or images, or to neutralize them with some other thought or action (i.e., by performing a compulsion).

Compulsions are defined by (1) and (2):

1. Repetitive behaviors (e.g., handwashing, ordering, checking) or mental acts (e.g., praying, counting, repeating words silently) that the individual feels driven to perform in response to an obsession or according to rules that must be applied rigidly.

2. The behaviors or mental acts are aimed at preventing or reducing anxiety or distress, or preventing some dreaded event or situation; however, these behaviors or mental acts are not connected in a realistic way with what they are designed to neutralize or prevent, or are clearly excessive.

Note: Young children may not be able to articulate the aims of these behaviors or mental acts.

B. The obsessions or compulsions are time-consuming (e.g., take more than 1 hour per day) or cause clinically significant distress or impairment in social, occupational, or other important areas of functioning.

C. The obsessive-compulsive symptoms are not attributable to the physiological effects of a substance (e.g., a drug of abuse, a medication) or another medical condition.

D. The disturbance is not better explained by the symptoms of another mental disorder (e.g., excessive worries, as in generalized anxiety disorder; preoccupation with appearance, as in body dysmorphic disorder; difficulty discarding or parting with possessions, as in hoarding disorder: hairpulling, as in trichotillomania [hairpulling disorder]; skin picking, as in excoriation [skin picking] disorder; stereotypies, as in stereotypic movement disorder; ritualized eating behavior, as in eating disorders; preoccupation with substances or gambling, as in substance-related and addictive disorders; preoccupation with having an illness, as in illness anxiety disorder; sexual urges or fantasies, as in paraphilic disorders; impulses, as in disruptive, impulse-control, and conduct disorders; guilty ruminations, as in major depressive disorder; thought insertion or delusional preoccupations, as in schizophrenia spectrum and other psychotic disorders; or repetitive patterns of behavior, as in autism spectrum disorder).

Specify if:

With good or fair insight: The individual recognizes that obsessive-compulsive disorder beliefs are definitely or probably not true or that they may or may not be true.

With poor insight: The individual thinks obsessive-compulsive disorder beliefs are probably true.

With absent insight/delusional beliefs: The individual is completely convinced that obsessive-compulsive disorder beliefs are true.

Specify if:

Tic-related: The individual has a current or past history of a tic disorder.

Trichotillomania and Excoriation Disorder

What are your reactions to the picture?

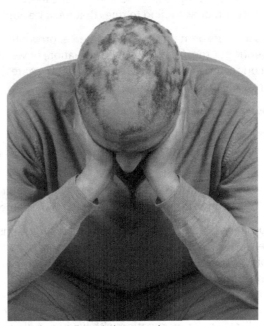

© Fresnel/Shutterstock.com

Trichotillomania

Hairpulling disorder where individuals recurrently pull out their hair from any area of their body

Shame

Emotional response from thinking you are a bad person

Guilt

Emotional response from remorse for an action

Many people have reactions of surprise, shock, and disgust when noticing the hair loss resultant of trichotillomania. Trichotillomania (TTM) is a hairpulling disorder where individuals recurrently pull out their hair from any area of their body. The phrase of "I'm so stressed I could pull out my hair" is common vernacular for many people who experience stress. However, many people are unaware of this hairpulling disorder or have even ever heard of the name.

Your reactions to the picture above will play a crucial role in understanding, awareness, and contribution to helping individuals with trichotillomania. Your immediate, visceral, social responses are what you need to be aware of and possibly change when confronted with a plethora of mental health issues, specifically TTM. On a daily basis, people with trichotillomania encounter people's reactions of surprise and disgust. Being exposed to these reactions of others may induce shame and feelings of guilt. Shame is an emotional response that someone feels when they think they are a bad person and guilt arises from when someone experiences remorse for their actions.

Etiology and Features. In the DSM-IV-TR, TTM was listed under impulse-control disorders and has been moved under OCD and related disorders in the DSM-5. One of the reasons TTM was under impulse control is due to the habitual hairpulling behaviors. However, the maladaptive behavioral coping of hairpulling for relief in response to stress or anxiety fit clinically under OCD and related disorders. Normative hairpulling may be seen in people as early as infancy but usually resolves by early development (APA, 2013). People may twirl or play with their hair and see some hair loss in various places such as beds, showers, in brushes, or at their laptops. Playing with one's hair and subsequent hair loss may be normative. Females are more likely than males to be affected with trichotillomania by a 10:1 ratio (APA, 2013). Some of the reasons are based on it either reflecting a true gender ration or being the result of gender-based social norms (APA, 2013).

The disorder may develop due to a variety of diathesis-stress factors. The DSM-5 indicates that a typical onset occurs with puberty and genetic vulnerability plays a role (APA, 2013). In some instances, core beliefs, ineffective affective expression, interpersonal factors, and learning may increase the appearance of, or maintain trichotillomania. For example, a child who engages in normative hair twirling behavior may receive a negative comment from her mother, such as "stop pulling your hair or you will look ugly," which may bring awareness of hairpulling behavior, develop beliefs of being unlovable, induce stress, and elicit feelings of shame or guilt.

For the development and maintenance of TTM, there are often three components. You can remember these components by the three A's of TTM.

Arousal—high or low

Affect—shame or guilt

A sense of relief, pleasure, or gratification

An individual may have high or low levels of arousal. Preceding hairpulling behaviors, individuals may be exposed to stress, experience anxiety, or experience boredom (APA, 2013). Secondly, a person develops a habit in response to the stress (i.e., pulling hair). People have vast responses to stress or boredom. Some people eat tubs of ice cream, others go running, and some people have a glass or several of wine. For TTM, hairpulling forms as a response to stress and boredom. Secondly, people with TTM may experience affect preceding or occurring with hairpulling (APA, 2013). Individuals with TTM may experience shame or guilt. They may experience shame from identifying as a bad person who pulls their hair or guilty for their hairpulling actions. These feelings can become worsened when other people express disgust and surprise in response to seeing a person with hair loss or bald patches resulting from TTM. Lastly, people with TTM get a sense of relief, pleasure, or gratification from pulling their hair (APA, 2103). Feeling relief or pleasure from the stress and affect reinforces the hairpulling behavior and urges.

Hairpulling behaviors may have varying levels or conscious awareness (APA, 2013). Hence, people with TTM may be engaged in automatic thinking and controlled thinking when pulling their hair. Automatic thinking is

Automatic Thinking
Unintentional and seemingly minimal effort thinking

Controlled Thinking
Intentional and effortful thinking

unintentional and seemingly minimal effort thinking. Controlled thinking is intentional and effortful thinking. A person may twirl or play with their hair without much awareness, as an automatic thinking process. Then, this individual becomes aware of hairpulling behavior through seeing his or her hair or having someone else comment on their hairpulling, which often result in shame feelings. Boredom or the stress response may lead a person to pull more. The controlled thoughts of hairpulling may become automatic and hairpulling as a stress response may be maintained.

Excoriation. Excoriation operates on the same mechanisms as TTM. Excoriation is a skin-picking disorder that involves individuals picking at their skin or scabs. The habitual picking at a scab or skin may have varying levels of awareness and also involve the three A's previously mentioned. Individuals may pick in high or low levels of arousal, experience affect, and get a sense of relief from picking. Individuals may search for specific types of scabs to pull and may play with skin and put it in their mouth after it has been pulled (APA, 2013). Excoriation may develop after a dermatological condition (APA, 2013).

When the hairpulling or skin picking is evident beyond early childhood, meets diagnostic criteria and you see the 4 Fs, then TTM or excoriation should be considered. Further, the hair loss from TTM and skin picking is not directly a result of a medical condition (e.g., alopecia instead of TTM).

Excoriation

A skin-picking disorder that involves individuals picking at their skin or scabs

Body Dysmorphic Disorder

Myths in Movies

CYRANO DE BERGERAC and ROXANNE

Cyrano de Bergerac is an intelligent, gifted poet, musician, and French nobleman in Rostand's 1897 play, *Cyrano de Bergerac* (Rostand & Bair, 1972). Cyrano de Bergerac was in love with a beautiful and intelligent woman named Roxanne. The only problem was Cyrano de Bergerac's nose. He had much doubt to profess his love to Roxanne because he thought she would never love a man with such a large and ugly nose. Therefore, he recruited another person by the name of Christian, to vicariously win over Roxanne's love. The same plot was later developed into a film titled, *Roxanne*.

© United Artist/Photofest

© Columbia Pictures/Photofest

While not formally diagnosing Cyrano de Bergerac, he seemed to have a preoccupation with his nose which led to him not professing his love for someone he deeply cared about. Body dysmorphic disorder involves a preoccupation and concern with a part (or parts) of your body. Many people may have preoccupations with various body characteristics. Consider the following statements and if you have ever said or thought them.

"My nose is so monstrous, it is all that people see when they look at me."

"My [insert body part] are/is too big."

"Everyone will notice this mark on my face."

"One of my _____ is so much bigger than the other."

The difference between these statements and body dysmorphic disorder are the specific DSM-5 criteria and the 4 Fs. After reviewing the 4 Fs, think about Cyrano de Bergerac or Charlie from Roxanne to decide what you think about his nose.

How about the classic Disney film, *Snow White,* and the obsession with the mirror on the wall? People who suffer from body dysmorphic disorder may ruminate about specific features of their body (or nonexistent features) by constantly checking in the mirror (Veale & Riley, 2001). Individuals may experience distress and impairment in their functioning. Body dysmorphic disorder is not the same thing as anorexia nervosa, which will be discussed in a later chapter, as anorexia nervosa is specific to fear of weight gain. One of the controversies around body dysmorphic disorder includes seeking out cosmetic surgery for the perceived problem area. Some researchers have found that 3 to 8% of patients seeking cosmetic surgery may have body dysmorphic disorder. Recommendations have been made for physicians to screen people seeking cosmetic surgery for body dysmorphic disorder and make appropriate referrals for assessment or treatment with mental health professionals (Crerand & Sarwer, 2010).

Hoarding Disorder

Hoarding has gained much attention through television shows like *Hoarders, Hoarding: Buried Alive,* or movies like *Clutter.* These types of shows are entertaining for people because they enjoy watching the face of "crazy" from a distance, or to feel more normal through social comparison. However, like many symptoms of psychological disorders, it may be closer than we think. For example, what would

© Phil McDonald/Shutterstock.com

you feel or do if you lost your most prized possession (such as a wedding ring, family heirloom, or any other sentimental gift)? The anxiety you may feel would not be that different from someone who experiences features of hoarding. In fact, while you may see their possessions as trash, one could say the same thing about your sentimental treasure. Hoarding disorder was first listed in the DSM-5 under OCD and related disorders due to the features of rumination about possessions and anxiety from getting rid of items (APA, 2013). People with hoarding disorder may collect and have difficulty parting with a variety of objects from trash to animals. The accumulation of possessions may impair functioning, cause pain when discarding the objects, and be fatal to a person's health by poor and unsanitary living conditions. Keep in mind that merely accumulating many items is not sufficient to warrant a diagnosis. When you watch shows like *Hoarders* or are worried that you or someone you know may have hoarding disorder, then remember to examine the DSM-5 diagnostic criteria and the 4 Fs. Also, remember the humanity and shared experiences with someone who suffers from this disorder.

Hoarding

Collecting and having difficulty parting with a variety of objects

The 4 Fs of Obsessive-Compulsive and Related Disorders

Many people may feel anxiety from certain thoughts. Some people even engage in behaviors that reduce that anxiety. However, fewer people ruminate on thoughts that impair functioning or lead to maladaptive behaviors. These differences may lead to impaired functioning, feeling pain, and fatality. To consider frequency, look at the ABCs.

Frequency

A—Amount of Time: To be diagnosed with an OCD and other related disorders, time is a key feature. For OCD, thoughts and compulsive behaviors usually occur more than 1 hour per day (APA, 2013). For other related disorders it may be recurrent maladaptive behaviors (APA, 2013).

B—Behavior: Individuals evidencing an OCD have recurring thoughts and behaviors that impair functioning, lead to feeling pain, or fatality. With the related disorders, intrusive and persistent thoughts or recurrent behaviors are evident that lead to impaired functioning, increased anxiety, feeling pain, and fatality.

C—Curve: The prevalence rate of OCD occurs in about 1.2% of the population (APA, 2013). Body dysmorphic disorder prevalence rates are about 2.4% of the population (APA, 2013). Hoarding prevalence rates are 2 to 6% in the United States and Europe (APA, 2013). Trichotillomania has a prevalence rate of 1 to 2% and excoriation is about 1.4% (APA, 2013).

The Good News: Many of these disorders can have a good prognosis with treatment interventions. As with anxiety and other disorders, Division 12 of the American Psychological Association (the Society for Clinical Psychology) has identified a few research-based psychological treatments for OCD (Division 12 of the American Psychological Association, 2013).

Function

When you are constantly thinking a thought or perseverating on an image, then it may become difficult to get out of your house, go to work, make it to class, or meet with friends. The presence of OCD symptoms may lead to greatly impaired social and occupational functioning (APA, 2013). Think back to the case of Judith, who missed work. Some people who attend work or class may not be productive because the entire time they are there they are fighting an obsession. In some cases of OCD, individuals may leave their home due to fears of contamination. Your functioning is impaired when you are unable to access rooms in your house due to hoarding items. Fear of feeling ashamed due to people at work or school laughing at you because you are missing eyelashes or because you have bald patches on your head may cause someone to avoid going to those places.

Feeling Pain

Many people with OCD feel marked pain and anxiety from their intrusive thoughts. People with TTM and excoriation disorder may feel shame and distress from their behaviors and from others' reactions. People who have body dysmorphic disorder may continually think about a perceived physical defect and desire to rid the defect. The inability to rid the perceived body problem may lead to feeling intense pain. Further, people who have hoarding disorder may feel anxious from losing objects or if another person claims to remove those objects.

Fatality

About 50% of individuals with OCD have suicidal ideation and 25% attempt suicide (APA, 2013). In some cases, people with contamination-focused OCD may develop skin lesions due to excessive washing of their hands (APA, 2013). Consistent skin lesions might even lead to infection. Individuals with TTM may have various medical and dental consequences from biting their hair or swallowing their hair (trichophagia; APA, 2013). Individuals with excoriation disorder may also have medical concerns from tissue damage and infection (APA, 2013).

Theories and Treatments of Anxiety Disorders and Obsessive-Compulsive and Related Disorders

A typical social response to people who may be experiencing anxiety is to tell them "just calm down" or "relax." If you have been told to calm down then you have a first account of the reason this is ineffective. This is problematic because many people want to calm down and do not want to feel the effects of anxiety. They have likely even tried to calm down and feel more anxious that they are unable to control their racing heart. Thankfully, your heart beats without conscious control, due to the autonomic nervous system. However, when people experiencing anxiety try to control their anxiety or bodily symptoms, then the perceived lack of control may have counterproductive effects. When you think about anxiety disorders, OCD, and related disorders, think about how thoughts, behaviors, and biology contribute.

Remember Little Albert? In Chapter 2 you read about John Watson's research based on conditioned emotional responses (Watson & Rayner, 1920). Conditioned emotional responses are synonymous with fear. Many fears and much of anxiety involve learned behaviors and cognitive appraisals. Some of your fears or moments that contributed to anxiety can be remembered, whereas others may have occurred prior to the consolidation of semantic memory and may be more difficult to recall.

Obsessive-compulsive and related disorders involve a bit more than anxiety disorders in the development and maintenance of the disorder. Hence, some treatments may involve components that address the habitual stress response of compulsions, hairpulling, or skin picking. Along with learning and cognitive principles, it is always important to consider other aspects of biology or components of the diathesis-stress model.

© Shay Yacobinski/Shutterstock.com

Biological Treatments

It is important to consider biological treatments for anxiety due to a higher proportion of visits to family practitioners or internal medicine physicians compared to mental health professionals (Harman et al., 2006). Biologically, medications that may be prescribed to treat anxiety disorders are antidepressants or anxiolytics. As discussed at the beginning of this chapter, one of the reasons people may have difficulty distinguishing between anxiety and depression is due to being prescribed similar treatments, namely antidepressants. Antidepressants typically work on systems of dopamine, serotonin, and norepinephrine. Also, antidepressants are typically prescribed for OCD and related disorders.

Anxiolytics

Medications that are central nervous system depressants and influencing GABA

Anxiolytics are aimed at reducing anxiety as a central nervous system depressant and influencing GABA. Barbiturates, benzodiazepines, and ethanol are anxiolytics. One of the more commonly prescribed anxiolytics for anxiety disorders is Alprazolam (Xanax). Xanax may be fast acting, however, due to potential for addiction and abuse, people may be reluctant to take Xanax. Recently, literature has discussed that drug development for antidepressants and anxiolytics have stalled and has suggested looking at biological models beyond neurotransmitter models (Schatzberg, 2015).

Psychological Treatments

As previously mentioned in the good news section, Division 12 of the American Psychological Association has identified research-based psychological treatments for various anxiety disorders (see APA Presidential Task Force on Evidence-Based Practice, 2006). Table 8.3 displays various psychological treatments for differing anxiety disorders and OCD (Division 12 of the American Psychological Association, 2013; Hajcak 2013; Klonsky et al., 2013; Teachman, 2013). Along with these evidenced-based practices, cognitive behavioral therapy has been shown to be an effective means for treating body dysmorphic disorder (Veale et al., 1996).

Reactive

Dealing with anxiety in the moment

Proactive

Techniques that address beliefs related to anxiety, which lead to long-term change and reduction of anxiety symptoms

Some of these treatments share some overlap with regards to the use of some techniques. Many of these psychological treatments are aimed at working with an individual's thoughts, behaviors, and emotions. Some of the techniques involve two components to therapy, being reactive and proactive.

TABLE 8.3   Empirically Supported Psychological Treatments for Anxiety Disorders and OCD

Psychological Treatment	GAD	Panic Disorder	Specific Phobia	Social Anxiety Disorder	Mixed Anxiety	OCD
Cognitive Behavioral Therapy	Strong	Strong		Strong		Strong
Applied Relaxation		Modest				
Psychoanalytic		Modest/ Controversial				
Exposure			Strong			
Exposure and Response Prevention						Strong
Acceptance and Commitment Therapy					Modest	Modest

*Table based on information from Division 12 of the American Psychological Association (2013).

© fizkes/Shutterstock.com

Reactive means are those that deal with anxiety in the moment. Breathing techniques, muscle relaxation techniques, and fast acting medications serve as effective means that help reduce anxiety in the moment.

Proactive techniques are those that address the thoughts, beliefs, and develop behavioral and emotional strategies that assist with preventing anxiety or managing it before it occurs. Individuals who have anxiety disorders, OCD, or related disorders may hold beliefs related to control. Individuals may want to control their anxiety and do so in maladaptive ways with some of these disorders. For Cognitive Behavioral Therapy, individuals challenge and consider changing beliefs of helplessness or control. Developing accurate thoughts that you are able to change some things and have no control over others will reduce anxiety, feelings of fear, and escape or compulsive behaviors. Acceptance and Commitment Therapy (Hayes, Follette, et al., 2004; Hayes, Wilson et al., 1996) works a similar way, in which individuals will acknowledge their thoughts, emotions, and behaviors and not try to fight them but, in the words of the Beatles, "let it be." Behaviorally, individuals may relearn newer behavioral responses, instead of escape, hairpulling, or other compulsions. Exposure and response prevention exposes people to stimuli that causes stress, boredom, or anxiety and then individuals seek to perform other behaviors. These behaviors are different from escape/avoidance, hairpulling, skin picking, or handwashing. In doing this, individuals learn to extinguish associations with the anxiety-producing stimuli and modify behavioral responses to reduce its frequency or develop newer behaviors.

Conclusion

Anxiety has become highly prevalent in the United States and a growing number of individuals have anxiety disorders. Individuals perceive a number of things to be threatening. Further, many myths have developed based on what people say anxiety is, how it is portrayed in films, and how people try to socially respond. Think about expressing empathy next time someone expresses they are feeling anxious rather than telling them to relax or calm down. Remember that anxiety, OCD, and related disorders are diagnostic if DSM-5 criteria are met, and if the 4 Fs are considered, there are a number of treatments available for these individuals.

CHAPTER REVIEW

QUESTIONS

1. Is low level of arousal or worry best? What does the Yerkes-Dodson model of arousal suggest?

2. What are the four components involved in anxiety (quadripartite)?

3. How is panic disorder different from generalized anxiety? How is it different from a specific phobia and social phobia?

4. Does agoraphobia mean people are afraid to go into open places?

5. What are obsessions? Compulsions? How do these two typically present within OCD?

6. What is trichotillomania and excoriation? How are these similar to OCD?

KEY TERMS

Fear

Cognitive Appraisal

Ruminate

Panic Attack

Somatic

Agoraphobia

Phobia

Generalization

Obsessions

Compulsions

Trichotillomania

Shame

Guilt

Automatic Thinking

Controlled Thinking

Excoriation

Hoarding

Anxiolytics

Reactive

Proactive

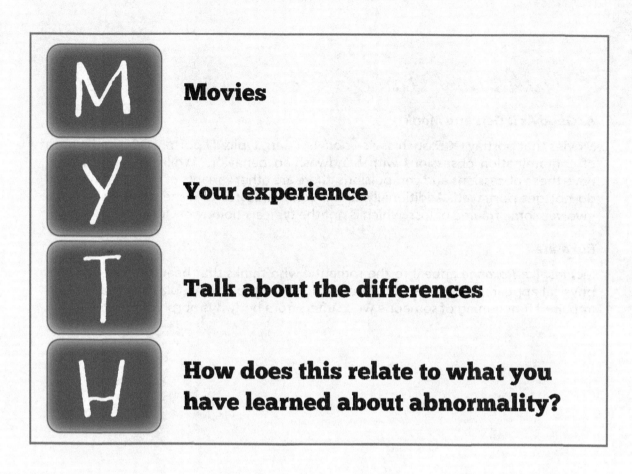

M   **Movies**

Y   **Your experience**

T   **Talk about the differences**

H   **How does this relate to what you have learned about abnormality?**

Myths in Movies Recap

Arachnophobia and _Fear Factor_

Many movies or shows that display phobias typically seek to create a sympathetic nervous system arousal from viewers, who watch with unease at a safe distance. However, giant spiders do not exist as they do in *Harry Potter* and millions of spiders do not overtake a house as seen in *Arachnophobia*. While *Fear Factor* could be a useful way to engage in flooding, most people do not seek to flood themselves with stimuli that brings intense fear.

Myths in Movies Recap

As Good As It Gets and *Monk*

Movies that portray OCD, such as *As Good As It Gets*, typically portray OCD in the form of contamination obsessions with handwashing behaviors. While people certainly have these obsessions and compulsions, there are other variants of OCD that typically do not get portrayed. Additionally, *Monk* communicates that the etiology for OCD involves some trauma or loss, which is not the typical etiology of OCD.

Roxanne

Movies like *Roxanne* appeal to the romantic who thinks that beauty is deeper than physical appearance. Movies like *Roxanne* do not completely display the distress and impaired functioning of someone who suffers from body dysmorphic disorder.

CHAPTER NINE

TRAUMA AND DISSOCIATIVE DISORDERS

LEARNING OBJECTIVES

- ► Examine myths related to trauma and dissociative disorders
- ► Discuss media, perspectives, and experiences that contribute to these myths
- ► Identify types of trauma
- ► Discuss the 4 Fs of schizophrenia and psychotic disorders: frequency, function, fatality, and feelings of pain
- ► Explore how individuals respond to trauma
- ► Differentiate between resilience and psychopathology resulting from trauma
- ► Examine the 4 Fs of trauma and dissociative disorders
- ► Discuss disorders that develop from trauma
- ► Distinguish dissociative identity disorder from other disorders
- ► Identify the diagnostic criteria of post-traumatic stress disorder and dissociative disorder theories and treatments of schizophrenia and related disorders
- ► Consider media's influence on trauma and dissociative disorders
- ► Discuss theories and treatments of trauma and dissociative disorders

CHAPTER OUTLINE

- ► Trauma: When Bad Things Happen—MYTHs
- ► The 4 Fs of Trauma-Related Disorders
- ► Post-Traumatic Stress Disorder
- ► Other Trauma-Related Disorders
- ► Dissociative Disorders—MYTHs
- ► The 4 Fs of Dissociative Disorders

Trauma: When Bad Things Happen

Recently, the coronavirus has swept across the world , resulting in death for a number of people. On October 1, 2017, a mass gun shooting occurred in Las Vegas that resulted in the deaths of 58 people and over 400 people

© Songquan Deng/Shutterstock.com

being injured. You may recall on September 11, 2001, in the United States an event occurred involving planes crashing into the World Trade Center and Pentagon. This event was traumatic for a large number of people across the nation. Horrible, unspeakable, and stressful events may occur for people throughout their lives. These events may be labeled as a **psychological trauma**. Psychological trauma involves a threat, intense fear, helplessness, and loss of control (Andreasen, 1985; Herman, 1997). Look at each of the MYTH categories below, which have likely influ-

Psychological Trauma

Events that pose a threat and involve intense fear

enced your thinking or understanding of trauma, and journal about the impressions you have gathered from these various sources.

Trauma has recently become a hot topic. Over the years there has been an influx of movies and news articles that discuss or depict trauma. Research from Schroeder, Curtis, and Kelley (2019) found a significant difference in films produced with PTSD content after 2001, in which there were twice as many films on average. A study that looked at *New York Times* coverage of PTSD found that the "number of articles published annually increased from two in 1980 to 70 in 2014" (Purtle et al., 2016, p. 633). With this increase in films and news, two things emerge: more awareness and misinformation. More coverage usually indicates a growing awareness, which can be good for the public to understand how trauma may affect people and how some people may suffer from symptoms of trauma-related disorders. On the other hand, more films, media, and attention can lead to a growth of misinformation and perpetuation of myths.

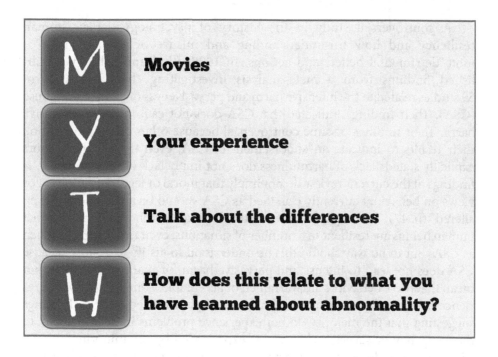

M Movies

Y Your experience

T Talk about the differences

H How does this relate to what you have learned about abnormality?

Myths in Movies

© Summit Entertainment/Photofest

THE HURT LOCKER and BORN ON THE FOURTH OF JULY

There are a number of movies that portray trauma and Posttraumatic Stress Disorder (PTSD), including *The Hurt Locker* and *Born on the Fourth of July* (Wedding & Niemiec, 2014). What are your thoughts about how these movies convey how trauma affects people? How might films such as these shape thoughts about PTSD and related disorders?

A scene from *Hurt Locker*

A common myth about trauma is that experiencing trauma means an inescapable direct path to psychopathology. Movies often convey the myth that some single traumatic event leads to the development of psychopathology (Hyler, 1988; Wedding & Niemiec, 2014). This is not necessarily the case. Recall the Diathesis-Stress model of psychopathology. While trauma can lead to psychopathology, not all traumatic or stressful situations will lead to a disorder. In fact, most individuals who experience trauma and stressful situations have the mechanisms for resiliency. Resilience is the ability to overcome stress or return to functioning briefly after enduring a trauma.

Resilience

Ability to overcome stress or return to functioning briefly after enduring a trauma

A controversial study in the history of psychology depicts human resiliency and how misunderstanding and misuse of science can promote detrimental beliefs and actions. In 1998, Rind and colleagues published findings from a meta-analysis investigating the effect sizes of 59 studies related to the intensive harm and pervasiveness of child sexual abuse (CSA). Their findings indicated that CSA does not cause intense, pervasive harm. Their findings became controversial because other organizations took their results to indicate an endorsement of CSA, even though the authors explicitly stated "lack of harmfulness does not imply lack of wrongfulness . . . findings of the current review do not imply that moral or legal definitions of or views on behaviors currently classified as CSA should be abandoned or even altered" (p. 47). The implications from the findings corroborated the idea that human beings are resilient in a number of situations, even traumatic ones such as CSA. But in no way should this be understood to justify CSA. Just because CSA does not lead to intense and pervasive harm for many people, does not mean that these behaviors are warranted or acceptable. Some people will experience behavioral and mental health issues directly related to CSA. Findings suggesting that the majority do not experience problems in no way speak to the frequency or severity of problems experienced by the minority who do. We, and others, do not believe that CSA is acceptable behavior and it may lead to psychopathology (APA, 2013; Herman, 1997). In fact, CSA is one of the traumatic events explicitly listed that meets the diagnostic criteria for PTSD (APA, 2013). In some cases people are not resilient, for one reason or another, and those individuals may develop psychopathology. In this chapter, we will explore cases where traumatic events were not encountered with resiliency, but with maladaptive coping.

Another myth held about trauma and psychopathology is that war is the sole cause. While war-related trauma can certainly contribute to the onset of disorders such as PTSD, there are a number of types of trauma that may result in psychopathology. Further, not all trauma may lead to psychopathology.

Types of Trauma. Briere and Scott (2006) stated that trauma is the event and not the response. There are a number of events that are types of trauma identified by Briere and Scott:

- Natural disasters
- Mass interpersonal violence
- Large-scale transportation accidents
- House or other domestic fires
- Motor vehicle accidents
- Rape and sexual assault
- Stranger physical assault
- Partner batter
- Torture
- War

- Child abuse
- Emergency worker exposure to trauma

The DSM-5 states that traumatic events include those that are directly experienced and witnessed events (APA, 2103). The DSM-5 lists those identified by Briere and Scott (2006) and includes the following (APA, 2013):

- Threatened physical assault
- Threatened sexual assault
- Being kidnapped
- Being taken hostage
- Incarceration as a prisoner of war
- Human-made disasters
- Sudden, catastrophic medical events

The DSM-5 also includes the following as witnessed events that are traumatic (APA, 2013):

- Observing threatened injury
- Unnatural death
- Physical or sexual abuse of another person due to violent assault
- Domestic violence
- Accident
- War or disaster
- Medical catastrophe in one's child

At the beginning of the chapter you read about the terrorist attacks occurring on September 11th. This would be an example of a mass interpersonal violence trauma. Though the event was traumatic, many people were resilient and many came together, in cohesion, as a nation exhibiting patriotism. Once again, take caution in concluding that resilience justifies the means. By no means is terror or other trauma endorsed. For others, the event led to responses that impaired functioning, led to feeling pain, and other behaviors.

Mass Interpersonal Violence Trauma

Events that threaten or bring fear to a large number of people

In September 2005 a massive hurricane, Katrina, hit the Gulf Coast causing many people to evacuate and left some stranded to die. A month later another hurricane, Rita, led to those who evacuated to Houston, Texas, having sought refuge in Houston. These hurricanes are examples of natural disaster traumas. Once again, many people were resilient in

© Gregory Pelt/Shutterstock.com

© Monkey Business Images/Shutterstock.com

Reproductive-Related Trauma

Trauma from miscarriages, stillbirths, and neonatal deaths

Perinatal Loss

Death of a child occurring during perinatal development

Stillbirth

Death of a child at 20 weeks gestation or later

their evacuations and were subsequently able to rebuild their lost homes. However, not everyone who faced these traumas were resilient.

Another type of trauma, that is often not discussed, is reproductive-related trauma (Born et al., 2006; Jaffe & Diamond, 2011). Reproductive-related trauma involves traumas such as miscarriages, stillbirths, and neonatal deaths. A perinatal loss can be devastating and detrimental to emotional, psychological, and physical well-being (Bright, 1991; Cacciatore, 2010). Stillbirths occur more frequently than people might be aware, in approximately one in 110 births (Cacciatore, Schnelby, & Frøen, 2009; Silver, 2007). A stillbirth is the death of a child occurring at 20 weeks gestation or later (American Congress of Obstetricians and Gynecologists, 2016). One of the factors that complicated reproductive trauma was that until 1970s stillbirths were managed as a "rugby pass" and were viewed as something to disregard and mothers rarely had opportunities to see, hold, or take pictures of their children (Cacciatore, Rådestad, Frøen, 2008, p. 313).

Trauma or Not? Controversy on Abortion. Abortion is often a topic that is heated and controversial. Much of the discussion about abortion pertains to issues of life and women's rights regarding pregnancy. So, what about abortion and trauma? Can abortion be a reproductive-related trauma? What do you think? The controversy of abortion even finds itself in research and practice related to the relationship between abortion and mental health issues, with some researchers asserting that abortion experiences are traumatic, and others claiming that problematic responses are more directly related to preexisting mental health conditions or one's cognitive stance toward abortion. Major and colleagues (2009) concluded that current evidence does not suggest that abortion, *per se*, results in mental health problems, emphasizing however the importance of taking into account the great variability in women's experience of abortion and preexisting or co-occurring factors. Melba Vasquez (2012), previous president of the American Psychological Association, pointed out that the American Psychological Association task force on abortion and mental health's (TFMHA) findings, which suggested that "no credible evidence that a single elective abortion of an unwanted pregnancy in and of itself causes mental health problems for adult women" were "hotly contested," and caused a great deal of controversy in the field of psychology (p. 343). In response to the findings of the task force, Coleman (2011) conducted

©a katz/Shutterstock.com

a meta-analysis and quantitative synthesis of abortion research published between 1995 and 2009, demonstrating a significant increase in mental health problems among women who have experienced induced abortion. Coleman (2011) reported an "81% increased risk for mental health problems" compared to pregnancies carried to full-term, "and nearly 10% of the incidence of mental health problems was shown to be attributable to abortion." (p. 180). Coleman and colleagues (2009) utilizing the National Comorbidity Survey (NCS), suggested links between abortion and mental health prob-

© Art Babych/Shutterstock.com

lems, including major depression, panic attacks, panic disorder, bipolar disorder, substance use, and post-traumatic stress disorder. With such discrepancies among researchers' claims the issue seems far from resolved.

The Trauma Response. What leads to one person developing psychopathology over another? How can one person be uplifted and relocated from their home due to a natural disaster and not develop any residual psychopathological symptoms and yet another person responds differently? First, consider the normative response of a person to extreme stress or trauma. When people are presented with danger or threat, then they typically experience sympathetic nervous system arousal, much like that discussed regarding anxiety. Sympathetic nervous system arousal stems from perceiving stimuli as a threat and prepares an individual for action. The individual may use the arousal for defending against the threat by overcoming the stimulus or by fleeing. For trauma-related disorders the ability to oppose a stimulus or escape is not likely, which may lead to thoughts of helplessness (Herman, 1997).

The responses to trauma may vary and individuals may experience anxiety, anhedonia, externalizing anger, or dissociative symptoms (APA, 2013). Dissociation is a disturbance in the integration of memory and awareness (APA, 2013). Recall that the Diathesis-Stress model accounts for how people develop disorders, including trauma-related disorders. There are person-specific variables and environmental variables. Briere and Scott (2006) claimed that there are three variables related to the development of post-traumatic symptoms: individual variables, the stressor, and the social response.

Dissociation

Disturbance in the integration of memory and awareness

Individual, or victim, variables include genetic predispositions, previous exposure to trauma, dysfunctional nervous system, age, gender, race, socioeconomic status, less functional coping mechanisms, previous history of trauma, and previous history of a mental disorder (see Briere & Scott, 2006). Stressor characteristics involve intentional acts of violence, life threat, physical injury, duration of combat exposure in war, witnessing death, loss of a loved one due to trauma, unpredictability and uncontrollability, and sexual victimization (see Briere & Scott, 2006). Social support for trauma is one of the most powerful factors for reducing the likelihood of psychopathological symptoms and ameliorating the pain resulting from trauma (Briere & Scott, 2006). However, a lack of social support or even social stigma and prejudice following a trauma may increase the likelihood of post-traumatic symptoms (Briere & Scott, 2006).

The 4 Fs of Trauma-Related Disorders

Given that many people may endure traumatic events and live through stressful situations, how might some show different responses than others? Remember that responses may vary based on the Diathesis-Stress model and may look differently based on the four Fs. Therefore, when trauma develops into psychopathology, you may want to ask if the 4 Fs are present and examine the DSM-5 diagnostic criteria.

Frequency

A—Amount of Time: The amount of time that a person must experience symptoms may vary depending on the disorder. The symptoms for reactive attachment disorder may be present for several years (APA, 2013). Symptoms of disinhibited social engagement disorder may be present from the age of 2 through adolescence years (APA, 2013). For PTSD, individuals experience symptoms for at least 1 month and those symptoms may persist throughout life (APA, 2013). Presence of symptoms for acute stress disorder occur 3 days to 1 month following the trauma (APA, 2013). Symptoms of adjustment disorder occur within 3 months of onset of the stressors (APA, 2013).

B—Behavior: Exposure to a threat involves several behavioral responses, ranging from anxiety-based reactions to dissociative responses. For anxiety-based behaviors, recall the quadripartite components of sympathetic nervous system, emotions of fear, thoughts of helplessness, and escape and avoidance behaviors. Individuals who experience these anxiety-based responses or dissociative responses to trauma well after the trauma and when in non-threatening environments may feel pain and impaired functioning in these contexts. For PTSD, individuals may experience recurrent thoughts or images of the traumatic event (APA, 2013). Dissociative responses could include flashbacks to the traumatic event (APA, 2013). The thoughts and anxiety may lead to the individual leaving the situation in which those images are associated and subsequently avoiding those situations (APA, 2013).

C—Curve: Previously mentioned, many people may face trauma and stressful situations throughout their lives. In the face of these traumas and stressful situations a great deal of people triumph and show resiliency. However, a smaller percentage of individuals may not and may feel pain, experience impairment in functioning, and may be at a greater risk for harm or suicide.

The lifetime prevalence rate of PTSD is 8.7% and a 12-month prevalence rate of 3.5% (APA, 2013). The rates of PTSD are higher for trauma related to rape, survivors, military combat, and survivors of government internment and genocide (APA, 2013). For acute stress disorder, it is identified in less than 20% of cases, whereas adjustment disorder ranges from 5 to 20% (APA, 2013). Reactive attachment disorder and disinhibited social engagement disorder prevalence rates are unknown (APA, 2013).

The Good News: There is growing attention to the awareness and treatment of trauma-related disorders, specifically PTSD. This awareness has led to increased efforts for prevention, social support, and for resources for treatment. The American Psychological Association (2015) has even put forth Guidelines on Trauma Competencies for Education and Training.

Function

Trauma-related disorders affect functioning due to the anxiety-based and dissociative symptoms. Remembering a traumatic event while removed from the event may heighten anxiety in a non-threatening situation. The ruminative thoughts of the traumatic event and subsequent anxiety may be distracting or lead to the person wanting to escape the situation. The DSM-5 indicates that PTSD is associated with impaired functioning in social, occupational, interpersonal, developmental, physical, and educational settings (APA, 2013). For example, an individual who has suffered combat-related PTSD experiences a trigger that leads to flashbacks of the traumatic event while in class. The individual feels heightened levels of anxiety and leaves class. The person subsequently avoids attending class and his academic performance and grades suffer. This is one way that trauma-related disorders may be seen to affect functioning. The trauma is relived or remembered in safe or innocuous contexts, which leads to escaping or avoiding these environments based on the new associations with the trauma.

Feeling Pain

People who have a trauma-related disorder experience pain frequently. When the traumatic event is relived or remembered, then all the pain associated with those memories is re-experienced. A DSM-5 criterion for PTSD is that intense psychological distress is present when exposed to cues of the traumatic event (APA, 2013). Thus, the painful moment that was escaped and intentionally avoided is relived in a variety of contexts. One of the reasons that individuals may have dissociative episodes is to avoid the painful memories. The avoidance of painful memories is also a criterion of PTSD (APA, 2013). Further, individuals with PTSD may experience a range of negative emotions (APA, 2013).

Fatality

A trauma can change the meaning of your life (Briere & Scott, 2006). The change in meaning and experience and re-experience of intense pain may lead to suicidal ideation or attempts. Traumatic events may increase the risk of suicide (APA, 2013). The presence of PTSD may lead to increased suicidal ideation and attempts (APA, 2013). There are complexities intertwined in ascertaining which types of trauma may increase the risk of suicide attempts, with media portrayals of Vietnam veterans' deaths having occurred more frequently with suicide than war (see Herman, 1997). However, suicide risk appears to be increased from combat-related trauma (Pollock et al., 1990).

Post-Traumatic Stress Disorder

Many people are resilient to trauma. However, some people are not as resilient and develop the symptoms of PTSD. These individuals relive and re-experience trauma. The re-experiencing of the trauma in non-threatening situations is what leads to the 4 Fs. Assuming you do not have PTSD and feel comfortable doing so, think about a time when you experienced some extreme stressor or trauma. Maybe you were in a car accident or maybe experienced a natural disaster. Now think about if this memory were to pop up in a number of situations, from work to social interactions. Also, assume that this memory causes intense pain. You can see how it might be difficult to focus, pay attention to your job, or engage socially while thinking of the memory. This in conjunction with the DSM-5 criteria is what warrants a diagnosis. In thinking of the 4 Fs and the DSM-5 criteria, consider the following case.

Case Vignette

Leah was pregnant with her very first child. She and her husband were overjoyed with expectations of her daughter's birth. They had baby gifts and dedicated time to get the nursery in order. They often spent much of their time thinking about what life would be like after the birth of their daughter. Twenty-six weeks into her pregnancy, Leah had noticed that her daughter was not kicking as much as she had been. She and her husband decided to visit the hospital for a check-up to make sure everything was alright. When the sonographer had checked on the baby, there were no sounds, no sounds of a baby's heart beating. The couple soon learned that their daughter had died and would need to be delivered soon, or stillborn. This experience was traumatic for the couple. A couple of months after losing her daughter, Leah returned to school. At school, she could barely focus on lectures and constantly thought about her missing child. One day in class, another classmate brought her newborn. The infant's cries triggered the memory of Leah's experience with her stillborn baby and thoughts of never being able to hear her child cry. Leah felt high levels of anxiety and pain and immediately left the classroom. After leaving class, Leah had no desire to return to that class and had considered dropping out of school. Leah frequently had nightmares, in which there was some variation of her daughter's death. Leah also thought that she could not continue to work, so she quit her job. These thoughts, nightmares, and desire to avoid school and work had continued for 4 months. Leah even wondered occasionally if she should take her own life so that she could end her pain and join her daughter.

The case of Leah reveals how the 4 Fs and DSM-5 criteria could be used to diagnose Leah as having PTSD. Leah was exposed to a traumatic incident of death and relived the experience in non-threatening situations. The memories were pervasive and intrusive and affected her functioning. She was frequently distressed by the thoughts and avoided situations that became associated with the thoughts or in which the trauma was triggered. Lastly, Leah indicated suicidal ideation in response to the trauma.

DSM-5 CRITERIA FOR POST-TRAUMATIC STRESS DISORDER

DIAGNOSTIC CRITERIA

Note: The following criteria apply to adults, adolescents, and children older than 6 years. For children 6 years and younger, see corresponding criteria below.

A. Exposure to actual or threatened death, serious injury, or sexual violence in one (or more) of the following ways:

1. Directly experiencing the traumatic event(s).

2. Witnessing, in person, the event(s) as it occurred to others.

3. Learning that the traumatic event(s) occurred to a close family member or close friend. In cases of actual or threatened death of a family member or friend, the event(s) must have been violent or accidental.

4. Experiencing repeated or extreme exposure to aversive details of the traumatic event(s) (e.g., first responders collecting human remains; police officers repeatedly exposed to details of child abuse).

   Note: Criterion A4 does not apply to exposure through electronic media, television, movies, or pictures, unless this exposure is work-related.

B. Presence of one (or more) of the following intrusion symptoms associated with the traumatic event(s), beginning after the traumatic event(s) occurred:

   1. Recurrent, involuntary, and intrusive distressing memories of the traumatic event(s).

      Note: In children older than 6 years, repetitive play may occur in which themes or aspects of the traumatic event(s) are expressed.

   2. Recurrent distressing dreams in which the content and/or affect of the dream are related to the traumatic event(s).

      Note: In children, there may be frightening dreams without recognizable content.

   3. Dissociative reactions (e.g., flashbacks) in which the individual feels or acts as if the traumatic event(s) were recurring. (Such reactions may occur on a continuum, with the most extreme expression being a complete loss of awareness of present surroundings.)

      Note: In children, trauma-specific reenactment may occur in play.

   4. Intense or prolonged psychological distress at exposure to internal or external cues that symbolize or resemble an aspect of the traumatic event(s).

   5. Marked physiological reactions to internal or external cues that symbolize or resemble an aspect of the traumatic event(s).

C. Persistent avoidance of stimuli associated with the traumatic event(s), beginning after the traumatic event(s) occurred, as evidenced by one or both of the following:

   1. Avoidance of or efforts to avoid distressing memories, thoughts, or feelings about or closely associated with the traumatic event(s).

   2. Avoidance of or efforts to avoid external reminders (people, places, conversations, activities, objects, situations) that arouse distressing memories, thoughts, or feelings about or closely associated with the traumatic event(s).

D. Negative alterations in cognitions and mood associated with the traumatic event(s), beginning or worsening after the traumatic event(s) occurred, as evidenced by two (or more) of the following:

   1. Inability to remember an important aspect of the traumatic event(s) (typically due to dissociative amnesia and not to other factors such as head injury, alcohol, or drugs).

   2. Persistent and exaggerated negative beliefs or expectations about oneself, others, or the world (e.g., "I am bad," "No one can be trusted," "The world is completely dangerous," "My whole nervous system is permanently ruined").

   3. Persistent, distorted cognitions about the cause or consequences of the traumatic event(s) that lead the individual to blame himself/herself or others.

4. Persistent negative emotional state (e.g., fear, horror, anger, guilt, or shame).

5. Markedly diminished interest or participation in significant activities.

6. Feelings of detachment or estrangement from others.

7. Persistent inability to experience positive emotions (e.g., inability to experience happiness, satisfaction, or loving feelings).

E. Marked alterations in arousal and reactivity associated with the traumatic event(s), beginning or worsening after the traumatic event(s) occurred, as evidenced by two (or more) of the following:

1. Irritable behavior and angry outbursts (with little or no provocation) typically expressed as verbal or physical aggression toward people or objects.

2. Reckless or self-destructive behavior.

3. Hypervigilance.

4. Exaggerated startle response.

5. Problems with concentration.

6. Sleep disturbance (e.g., difficulty falling or staying asleep or restless sleep).

F. Duration of the disturbance (Criteria B, C, D, and E) is more than 1 month.

G. The disturbance causes clinically significant distress or impairment in social, occupational, or other important areas of functioning.

H. The disturbance is not attributable to the physiological effects of a substance (e.g., medication, alcohol) or another medical condition.

Specify whether:

With dissociative symptoms: The individual's symptoms meet the criteria for post-traumatic stress disorder, and in addition, in response to the stressor, the individual experiences persistent or recurrent symptoms of either of the following:

1. **Depersonalization:** Persistent or recurrent experiences of feeling detached from, and as if one were an outside observer of, one's mental processes or body (e.g., feeling as though one were in a dream; feeling a sense of unreality of self or body or of time moving slowly).

2. **Derealization:** Persistent or recurrent experiences of unreality of surroundings (e.g., the world around the individual is experienced as unreal, dreamlike, distant, or distorted).

Note: To use this subtype, the dissociative symptoms must not be attributable to the physiological effects of a substance (e.g., blackouts, behavior during alcohol intoxication) or another medical condition (e.g., complex partial seizures).

Specify if:

With delayed expression: If the full diagnostic criteria are not met until at least 6 months after the event (although the onset and expression of some symptoms may be immediate).

Post-Traumatic Stress Disorder for Children 6 Years and Younger

A. In children 6 years and younger, exposure to actual or threatened death, serious injury, or sexual violence in one (or more) of the following ways:

1. Directly experiencing the traumatic event(s).

2. Witnessing, in person, the event(s) as it occurred to others, especially primary caregivers.

   Note: Witnessing does not include events that are witnessed only in electronic media, television, movies, or pictures.

3. Learning that the traumatic event(s) occurred to a parent or caregiving figure.

B. Presence of one (or more) of the following intrusion symptoms associated with the traumatic event(s), beginning after the traumatic event(s) occurred:

1. Recurrent, involuntary, and intrusive distressing memories of the traumatic event(s).

   Note: Spontaneous and intrusive memories may not necessarily appear distressing and may be expressed as play reenactment.

2. Recurrent distressing dreams in which the content and/or affect of the dream are related to the traumatic event(s).

   Note: It may not be possible to ascertain that the frightening content is related to the traumatic event.

3. Dissociative reactions (e.g., flashbacks) in which the child feels or acts as if the traumatic event(s) were recurring. (Such reactions may occur on a continuum, with the most extreme expression being a complete loss of awareness of present surroundings.) Such trauma-specific reenactment may occur in play.

4. Intense or prolonged psychological distress at exposure to internal or external cues that symbolize or resemble an aspect of the traumatic event(s).

5. Marked physiological reactions to reminders of the traumatic event(s).

C. One (or more) of the following symptoms, representing either persistent avoidance of stimuli associated with the traumatic event(s) or negative alterations in cognitions and mood associated with the traumatic event(s), must be present, beginning after the event(s) or worsening after the event(s):

Persistent Avoidance of Stimuli

1. Avoidance of or efforts to avoid activities, places, or physical reminders that arouse recollections of the traumatic event(s).

2. Avoidance of or efforts to avoid people, conversations, or interpersonal situations that arouse recollections of the traumatic event(s).

Negative Alterations in Cognitions

3. Substantially increased frequency of negative emotional states (e.g., fear, guilt, sadness, shame, confusion).

4. Markedly diminished interest or participation in significant activities, including constriction of play.

5. Socially withdrawn behavior.

6. Persistent reduction in expression of positive emotions.

D. Alterations in arousal and reactivity associated with the traumatic event(s), beginning or worsening after the traumatic event(s) occurred, as evidenced by two (or more) of the following:

1. Irritable behavior and angry outbursts (with little or no provocation) typically expressed as verbal or physical aggression toward people or objects (including extreme temper tantrums).

2. Hypervigilance.

3. Exaggerated startle response.

4. Problems with concentration.

5. Sleep disturbance (e.g., difficulty falling or staying asleep or restless sleep).

E. The duration of the disturbance is more than 1 month.

F. The disturbance causes clinically significant distress or impairment in relationships with parents, siblings, peers, or other caregivers or with school behavior.

G. The disturbance is not attributable to the physiological effects of a substance (e.g., medication or alcohol) or another medical condition.

Specify whether:

With dissociative symptoms: The individual's symptoms meet the criteria for post-traumatic stress disorder, and the individual experiences persistent or recurrent symptoms of either of the following:

1. **Depersonalization:** Persistent or recurrent experiences of feeling detached from, and as if one were an outside observer of, one's mental processes or body (e.g., feeling as though one were in a dream; feeling a sense of unreality of self or body or of time moving slowly).

2. **Derealization:** Persistent or recurrent experiences of unreality of surroundings (e.g., the world around the individual is experienced as unreal, dreamlike, distant, or distorted).

Note: To use this subtype, the dissociative symptoms must not be attributable to the physiological effects of a substance (e.g., blackouts) or another medical condition (e.g., complex partial seizures).

Specify if:

With delayed expression: If the full diagnostic criteria are not met until at least 6 months after the event (although the onset and expression of some symptoms may be immediate).

Other Trauma-Related Disorders

Some of the other trauma-related disorders carry a number of similar features of PTSD. However, the symptoms, severity, and duration are discrepant. Acute stress disorder consists of a number of the symptoms found with PTSD and may be diagnosed after 3 days of a trauma (APA, 2013). However, the duration is less than 1 month. Acute stress disorder may progress into PTSD and symptoms occurring beyond 1 month will need the consideration of PTSD (APA, 2013). Adjustment disorder is considered when individuals are having difficulty in adjusting to extreme stressors or death within 3 months (APA, 2013). These symptoms are in response to a specific stressor but do not carry the other components of PTSD or acute stress disorder (e.g., avoidance of stimuli, nightmares; APA, 2013).

Dissociative Disorders

Dissociative Identity Disorder

A psychological disorder involving the presence of two or more personality states and usually in response to early childhood trauma

People usually have many questions and thoughts about dissociative disorders. Along with these questions and thoughts, beliefs are formed in which some beliefs are less accurate than others. Further, dissociative disorders are a class of disorders that usually gain much attention because of it being a disorder that appears to be more strongly associated with "crazy." Some dissociative disorders, such as **dissociative identity disorder** (DID; commonly thought of as multiple personality disorders) are even portrayed as disorders that cause people to murder (in movies such as *Identity*).

Myths in Movies

THREE FACES OF EVE, DR. JEKYLL AND MR. HYDE, SPLIT, AND FIGHT CLUB

Due to the intrigue with watching or reading about "crazy" from afar, there have been a number of books and films that depict dissociative disorders, specifically DID. Along with *Identity*, other movies and stories include *Split*, *United States of Tara*, *Dr. Jekyll and Mr. Hyde*, *Three Faces of Eve*, *Sybil*, and *Fight Club*. So, what are

© Twentieth Century Fox Film Corporation/Photofest   © Everett Historical/Shutterstock.com

© Universal Pictures/Photofest   © Twentieth Century Fox/Photofest

some of the movies you have seen, how have they influenced your beliefs of dissociative disorders, and what thoughts do you have about disorders such as DID?

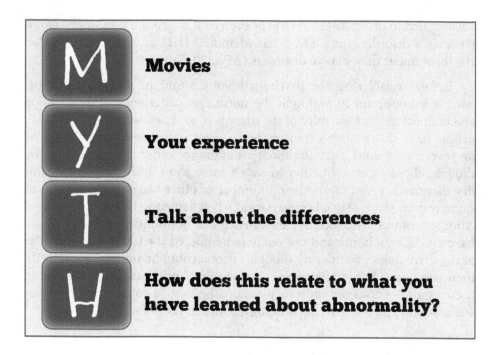

Years ago, a specific shirt was very popular that read something to the effect of, "I used to have schizophrenia but we are all okay now." What are your thoughts about this shirt? This shirt and others similar probably contributed to one of the most commonly inaccurate beliefs about two disorders, schizophrenia and DID. The phrase communicates a misunderstanding of the two disorders due to schizophrenia not consisting of an individual having multiple personalities. Schizophrenia, as discussed, is referred to as split-brain, which may have been confusing to the creator of the shirt. Split-brain means a splitting off from reality but not a splitting into multiple personalities. The shirts may have read more accurately had they stated, "I used to have dissociative identity disorder but we are all okay now."

Movies are likely to be another source of misinformation related to this misunderstanding between schizophrenia and DID (Hyler, 1988). In fact, Hyler noted "Hollywood's" frequent perpetuation of the lay misconception that schizophrenia involves a "split personality," and he referenced the film *Psycho* (pp. 197–198). Even recent movies, such as *Split,* may contribute to this misunderstanding by its title associated with the portrayal of dissociative identity disorder.

Some dissociative disorders have been criticized as not being distinct. Namely, dissociative identity disorder has historically been argued as one of these disorders that emits controversy regarding it's distinctiveness (Lilienfeld, 1994; Lilienfeld & Arkowitz, 2011). Lilienfeld presented two articles that argue opposing sides of DID being distinct. While some people have argued to distinctness of DID or even challenged the notion of its existence as a disorder, the DSM-5 has identified DID as a distinct disorder, classified under dissociative disorders (APA, 2013).

Before considering the psychopathology found in dissociative disorders, it is important to highlight the normative experience of dissociation and connect to the humanity of the disorders, as they are not "crazy." Many people have dissociative experiences. In reading this, you probably have, on several occasions, thought about a number of other things. Maybe you thought about dinner, whether to watch some show and what show, laundry that needs to get cleaned, or a number of other tasks. You might occasionally even leave a social conversation when someone is talking with you. Another common dissociative experience can be found in driving. If you have ever driven home and not really remembered the last 5 or 10 minutes of the drive due to wandering thoughts (not alcohol or substance induced), then you might have experienced dissociation. Your wavering attention in these examples does not indicate psychopathology. In considering how dissociation may lead to psychopathology, consider the 4 Fs.

The 4 Fs of Dissociative Disorders

Dissociation seems to be a protective factor. It helps to mentally remove you from a situation you are currently facing. If that situation is traumatic, then dissociation appears to be a very effective means to help you escape the painful situation. However, the dissociative response can become problematic when you look at the dissociative response from the lens of the 4 Fs and the DSM-5 diagnostic criteria.

Frequency

A—Amount of Time: Time varies for a variety of dissociative disorders. The variation in how long the disorder may be present and how frequently it affects individuals. For example, DID often is a result of early childhood trauma and may develop in childhood or adulthood and persist throughout one's life (APA, 2013). For DID, there are recurrent lapses in recalling daily activities (APA, 2013). Depersonalization/derealization disorder is persistent (APA, 2013). The persistence of many of these dissociative disorders depends on a variety of diathesis-stress factors such as the nature of the trauma and the person variables.

B—Behavior: As previously mentioned, dissociative episodes may be normative for people. Some research has indicated that dissociation can categorically fall into either non-pathological or pathological dissociation (Waller et al., 1996). Further, dissociation can be part of religious cultural experiences

(Holmes et al., 2005). However, when dissociative experiences are chronic, frequent, and impair functioning, then these experiences may reveal psychopathology (APA, 2013; Waller et al., 1996).

C—Curve: Many people are resilient to trauma. A smaller percentage of the population may develop symptoms of PTSD. An even smaller percentage of people may develop symptoms of DID. Many people face trauma and stress but few may experience dissociation that leads to impairment in functioning, feeling pain, and increasing the risk for suicide. The 12-month prevalence rate of DID is 1.5%, with 1.6% for males and 1.4% for females (APA, 2013). Dissociative amnesia 12-month prevalence rates has been 1.8% (APA, 2013). The lifetime prevalence rates for depersonalization/derealization disorder are about 2% with the 12-month rates unavailable (APA, 2013).

The Good News: There are treatment facilities that are specifically designed to work with individuals who have endured intense trauma leading to a dissociative disorder. Further, there are specific guidelines for treating individuals with dissociative identity disorder (International Society for the Study of Trauma and Dissociation [ISSTD], 2011). Treatment has been shown to greatly improved personal and occupational functioning (APA, 2013).

Function

The DSM-5 indicates that dissociative symptoms may affect various areas of daily living and functioning and the severity may vary with each case (APA, 2013). Of these areas, memory dysfunction is found to occur with DID (Dorahy, 2001). Social, educational, and occupational functioning may be impaired due to dissociative symptoms occurring while at work, school, or in various relational contexts. Individuals may have a trauma triggered in a non-threatening situation, which may lead to dissociative symptoms. Dissociative symptoms resulting in difficulty with recall or the emergence of other personality states can be personally problematic for functioning in the aforementioned areas. Further, individuals with DID may be stigmatized due to the presence of additional personalities, possibly leading to being fired from a job, having to quit, and potentially a strain on relationships.

Feeling Pain

The pain experienced with dissociative disorders may come from re-experiencing any earlier trauma, frustrations with dissociative symptoms, and the stigma from others. If individuals with dissociative disorders are in intimate relationships, then these relationships may be strained as well (MacIntosh, 2013). Dissociative identity disorder is also comorbid with a variety of other disorders, which may lead to experiencing pain (APA, 2013).

Complex Trauma

An event, several events, or repeated exposure to events that contribute to multiple psychological responses

Fatality

Suicide risk for people with dissociative disorders is high. More than 70% of individuals with DID, outpatients, have attempted suicide with multiple attempts (APA, 2013). Suicide attempts may be what leads individuals with dissociative disorders seeking inpatient treatment.

Dissociative Identity Disorder: Who Is the Real Client?

© Stepan Kapl/Shutterstock.com

The appearance of DID symptoms usually emerges as a result of some trauma (APA, 2013). Some authors have regarded DID as a response to complex trauma or as a variation of complex PTSD (Loewenstein, 2005). Dissociation from one's identity or from a sense of self has been reported by individuals who experienced severe early childhood trauma (Briere & Scott, 2006).

One of the reasons that DID is fascinating for many people is that the disorder is characterized by the presence of two or more personality states (also informally referred to as multiple personality disorder). This disorder has also brought controversy in which individuals have expressed that it is a genuine disorder, while others have skeptically questioned its validity as being nothing more than a sociocultural phenomenon (Reinders et al., 2012).

Myths in Movies

SYBIL

This controversy can even be evidenced in the book *Sybil* which subsequently became a film (Schreiber, 1973; Woodward et al., 2006). The story of Sybil details an account of a client who experienced early childhood abuse from her mother, which resulted in DID. In the book *Sybil Exposed*, the author argues how the book, *Sybil*, was created to generate income rather than the account of the real client, Shirley Mason, depicting symptoms of DID (Nathan, 2011).

Look into these accounts and use what you know about abnormal psychology to decide whether the case may be based on a true client with DID or whether it was all fabricated to gain book sales.

© NBC/Photofest

A scene from *Sybil*

There is also much debate as to the nature of the alters (see Merckelbach et al., 2002). Alter is a term that is used to refer to the separate personality states. Merckelbach and colleagues stated that some authors have viewed alters as distinct persons while others claim that alters are not people or even personalities. Some cases have been documented involving a patient with DID having 169 alters (Merckelbach et al., 2002). Research has indicated that DID is not a result of fantasy proneness (Reinders et al., 2012) and it is currently listed as a disorder in the DSM-5 (APA, 2013). The DSM-5 refers to alters as distinct personality states (APA, 2013). Many people are fascinated with the alters in DID and intrigue usually pulls attention toward a desire to understand how someone can be multiple people. You may think of personality states as symptoms of DID and remember that they are not distinct people. The ISSTD (2011) stated that "the DID patient is a single person who experiences himself or herself as having separate alternate identities" (p. 120). Lilienfeld and Arkowitz (2011) even suggested that a better approach is to help patients understand their pain not created from multiple personalities but related to one personality that is experiencing distress. One way to conceptualize this is that for PTSD, individuals may want to escape the trauma or dissociate, whereas for DID personality states emerge to allow the person to escape and cope with the trauma. For the specific criteria of DID, please refer to the DSM-5.

Alters

Term used to refer to personality states

DSM-5 CRITERIA FOR DISSOCIATIVE IDENTITY DISORDER

DIAGNOSTIC CRITERIA

A. Disruption of identity characterized by two or more distinct personality states, which may be described in some cultures as an experience of possession. The disruption in identity involves marked discontinuity in sense of self and sense of agency, accompanied by related alterations in affect, behavior, consciousness, memory, perception, cognition, and/or sensory-motor functioning. These signs and symptoms may be observed by others or reported by the individual.

B. Recurrent gaps in the recall of everyday events, important personal information, and/or traumatic events that are inconsistent with ordinary forgetting.

C. The symptoms cause clinically significant distress or impairment in social, occupational, or other important areas of functioning.

D. The disturbance is not a normal part of a broadly accepted cultural or religious practice.

   Note: In children, the symptoms are not better explained by imaginary playmates or other fantasy play.

E. The symptoms are not attributable to the physiological effects of a substance (e.g., blackouts or chaotic behavior during alcohol intoxication) or another medical condition (e.g., complex partial seizures).

Reprinted with permission from the *Diagnostic and Statistical Manual of Mental Disorders,* Fifth Edition, (Copyright 2013). American Psychiatric Association.

Other Dissociative Disorders

© Realstock/Shutterstock.com

Other dissociative disorders include dissociative amnesia and depersonalization/derealization disorder. These disorders encompass the same symptoms of dissociation, usually resulting from some trauma. Dissociative amnesia involves difficulty in recall autobiographical information not related to forgetting (APA, 2013). In some instances dissociative amnesia may include fleeing one's home and wandering, which is referred to as dissociative fugue.

Dissociative Fugue

Dissociative amnesia occurring with fleeing from a residence or wandering

Depersonalization

Experiences of being outside of your body

Derealization

Experiences of detachment from surroundings

Depersonalization/derealization disorder involves the persistent experiences of depersonalization or derealization (APA, 2013). Depersonalization is having experiences of being outside of your body or an unreal sense of self (APA, 2103). Derealization is a detachment from surroundings (APA, 2013). Individuals who experience this disorder may look into a mirror and not recognize themselves or have an experience of being outside of their body and watching themselves do some task that seems mechanical. It is important to note that these experiences do not involve a lack of understanding reality or psychotic features (APA, 2013). Individuals who do not recognize themselves in the mirror know that they are seeing themselves and do not believe there is someone else there (i.e., a hallucination). For the specific criteria of DID, please refer to the DSM-5.

Theories and Treatments of Trauma and Dissociative Disorders

When considering working with clients who have PTSD, trauma-related disorder, or dissociative disorder, it is strongly encouraged that health care providers have specific training and education related to these issues. Trauma work offers specific complexities and issues that are not present with other disorders. Surprisingly, a number of training programs do not include trauma classes within their programs and there is a great need for trauma training (Courtois & Gold, 2009). Treating trauma may take many more psychotherapy sessions than typical. Briere and Scott (2006) stated that there are some broad components of working with trauma, which transcend any specific theoretical orientation. These include (Briere & Scott, 2006):

- ► Supportive environment
- ► Psychoeducation about trauma

> ► Stress management and reduction
> ► Cognitive strategies that address core beliefs, intermediate beliefs, and negative automatic thoughts
> ► Constructing a narrative of the trauma
> ► Exposure to memories
> ► Using the therapy relationship for processing interpersonal issues
> ► Increase awareness and self-acceptance

Another concern found in working with trauma is how the trauma may affect the therapist. Sometimes when a client discusses details of a trauma they faced, that trauma has the potential to be traumatic for a therapist (Pearlman & Saakvitne, 1995). McCann and Pearlman (1990) named this phenomenon vicarious trauma, or trauma resulting from the exposure to another person's trauma. Vicarious trauma has the capacity to negatively affect trauma therapists, especially if those therapists have a history of trauma (Pearlman & Mac Ian, 1995).

Vicarious Trauma

Trauma resulting from the exposure to another person's trauma

Biological Theories and Treatment of Trauma and Dissociative Disorders

The biological mechanisms that underpin trauma are complex and involve multiple systems (Briere & Scott, 2006). Due to research implicating various systems, the current state of medications for trauma disorders involve a range of possible medications (Briere & Scott, 2006). The hypothalamic-pituitary adrenal axis and adrenergic system is involved in trauma responses and an imbalance of the system results in PTSD (see Briere & Scott, 2006; Raison & Miller, 2003). The neuroscience perspectives of dissociative symptoms indicate glutamate playing a role (Loewenstein, 2005). Further, serotonin and noradrenergic systems have been suggested to be involved in some dissociative symptoms, such as flashbacks (Loewenstein, 2005).

A variety of medications may be used with different patients who have PTSD and acute stress disorder. Some of these medications include antidepressants (SSRIs; SNRIs; MAOIs; Tricyclics), benzodiazepines, mood stabilizers, nonselective beta-adrenergic blocking agents (e.g., Propranolol), alpha 2-adrenergic agonists (e.g., Clonidine), and antipsychotics (Briere & Scott, 2006). For the treatment of people with DID, it has been suggested that psychopharmacologic interventions "are primarily adjunctive and empirical in nature" and the "majority of problems . . . in DID are most efficaciously addressed psychotherapeutically, hypnotherapeutically, or both" (Loewenstein, 2005, p. 668). Thus, the medications prescribed may range based on the specific symptoms that the client presents with in addition to dissociative symptoms (Loewenstein, 2005). Some of these medications include antidepressants, mood stabilizers, and benzodiazepines, depending on the additional presentation of other psychological symptoms (Loewenstein, 2005).

Psychological Theories and Treatment of Trauma and Dissociative Disorders

Exposure

Attending to a memory or stimulus in attempts to extinguish the negatively reinforcing escape/avoidance behavior

Some aspects of psychological treatment for trauma may be somewhat counterintuitive. Rather than assist a client in avoiding painful memories related to trauma, a therapist invites a client to re-experience the painful memories through a technique called exposure. Exposure therapy consists of exposing a client to memory of the traumatic event in attempts to extinguish the negatively reinforcing escape/avoidance behavior. Recall that trauma responses from trauma-related disorders involve intense pain and individuals want to avoid the pain. The memories that elicit the pain are then associated in newer, non-threatening situations, which lead to escape and avoidance responses. Individuals seek to avoid the painful memories and escape situations where those memories emerge. Thus, exposure therapy provides clients with the opportunity to be exposed to the memory without the escape or avoidance response, leading to new learning and processing of the memory. The same exposure techniques used in phobias and anxiety disorders are often used in treating clients with trauma disorders, specifically PTSD. Exposure therapy is one of the strongly supported treatments for PTSD (see Table 9.1)

Psychological treatments for trauma-related disorders involve all the aforementioned broad components suggested by Briere and Scott (2006). A protective factor for dealing with trauma is a supportive environment from therapist and other relationships (Briere & Scott, 2006). This is true for dealing with a number of traumas, including perinatal death (Cacciatore, 2010; Cacciatore, Rådestad, & Frøen, 2008). As far as empirically supported treatments, the Society of Clinical Psychology (Division 12, 2013) of the American Psychological Association lists various treatments and corresponding research support status. Table 9.1 displays various psychological treatments

TABLE 9.1   Empirically Supported Psychological Treatments for PTSD

Psychological Treatment	PTSD
Prolonged Exposure	Strong
Present-Centered Therapy	Strong
Cognitive Processing Therapy	Strong
Seeking Safety (PTSD with Substance Use Disorder)	Strong
Stress Inoculation Therapy	Modest
Eye Movement Desensitization and Reprocessing	Strong/Controversial
Psychological Debriefing	No Research Support/Potentially Harmful

*Table based on information from Division 12 of the American Psychological Association (2013).

for PTSD (Division 12 of the American Psychological Association, 2013; Hajcak & Starr, 2013).

Regarding DID, the ISSTD Treatment Guidelines for Dissociative Identity Disorder in Adults discusses a developmental model in which children who were exposed to trauma before the age of 5 do not develop a sense of self (ISSTD, 2011). The treatment of dissociative disorders there have been myths and controversy related to treatment being harmful (Brand, Loewenstein, & Spiegel, 2014). Brand and colleagues identified and discussed some of the myths regarding the treatment of DID. They suggested that complex trauma beginning in early childhood needs careful attention to a number of different symptoms. The authors reviewed literature and research to discern if treatment of DID is harmful. Among the literature reviewed, the authors discussed the ISSTD's Treatment Guidelines for Dissociative Identity Disorder in Adults for treating DID by implementing a tri-phasic, multi-modal approach (Brand et al., 2014; ISSTD, 2011). Brand and colleagues suggested that the current evidence in favor of phasic treatment for DID improves symptoms and functioning, and harm may come from not providing clients with treatment. Further, the authors suggested that there is a dire need for more empirical support from random clinical trials for treatment with DID.

Conclusion

You are now more equipped to conceptually think about trauma and publicly dispel myths related to psychopathology from trauma. You now know that schizophrenia is not the same thing as having multiple personalities. So, if you see someone sporting one of those shirts as mentioned earlier in the chapter, see that as an opportunity for your sociopolitical responsibility to help educate the public (Blashfield & Burgess, 2007). Remember that not all trauma leads to psychopathology and a number of people are resilient to trauma. However, there are a number of individuals who suffer from trauma and it greatly affects their lives and functioning. Think of the 4 Fs and DSM-5 criteria before considering if trauma responses are pathological. There are treatments to improve symptoms of trauma-related disorders, though the treatment may involve confronting the trauma. Not seeking treatment might be more harmful.

CHAPTER REVIEW

QUESTIONS

1. Are all psychological disorders the result of a single traumatic event? Does all trauma lead to the development of a disorder?

2. What are various types of traumatic events? What are the reasons that some people develop a disorder over others?

3. Does PTSD result from only those who have been in war?

4. How is schizophrenia different from dissociative identity disorder? What are reasons that people often think they are the same disorder?

5. What are some of the controversies with dissociative identity disorder?

KEY TERMS

Psychological Trauma

Resilience

Mass Interpersonal Violence Trauma

Reproductive-Related Trauma

Perinatal Loss

Stillbirth

Dissociation

Dissociative Identity Disorder

Complex Trauma

Alters

Dissociative Fugue

Depersonalization

Derealization

Vicarious Trauma

Exposure

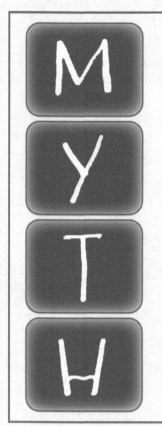

M   Movies

Y   Your experience

T   Talk about the differences

H   How does this relate to what you have learned about abnormality?

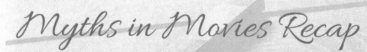

Myths in Movies Recap

The Hurt Locker

Schroeder et al. (2019) found a significant difference in films produced with PTSD content after 2001. Movies increased from one a year to two per year on average. Many movies that depict PTSD often show combat-related trauma. Around 51% of news coverage of PTSD has focused on military populations (Purtle et al., 2016). While war and combat-related trauma can lead people to experience PTSD, there are a number of other psychological traumas that can result in PTSD. Thus, people may think of PTSD as solely related to military trauma or combat trauma as the representative case.

Three Faces of Eve, Dr. Jekyll and Mr. Hyde, Split, Fight Club, and Sybil

Dissociative identity disorder is often portrayed in films with numerous misconceptions. A number of movies that show DID consist of the main character engaged in violent acts or killing others. The sad reality is that people who experience DID are often more likely to commit suicide, with over 70% having multiple suicide attempts (APA, 2013).

SOMATIC SYMPTOM AND RELATED DISORDERS

> ▶ Biological Theories and Treatment of Somatic Symptom and Related Disorders
> ▶ Psychological Theories and Treatment of Somatic Symptom and Related Disorders

It Is All in Your Head: Somatic Symptom and Related Disorders

Psychosomatic

Physical symptoms expressed due to a psychological cause

Ricky Bobby, from the film *Talladega Nights*, had a father who abandoned him during childhood. He fortuitously replaced a Nascar driver in a race, which ended poorly for Ricky. After he crashed, he was in a health care facility complaining of being paralyzed. Two of his friends show up and tell him that he is not paralyzed and that it is all "in his head." Ricky soon learns that his paralysis was psychosomatic after he stabs himself in the leg, discovering his leg is fully functioning and capable of feeling much pain. Psychosomatic means that the physical symptoms are resulting from an underlying psychological cause.

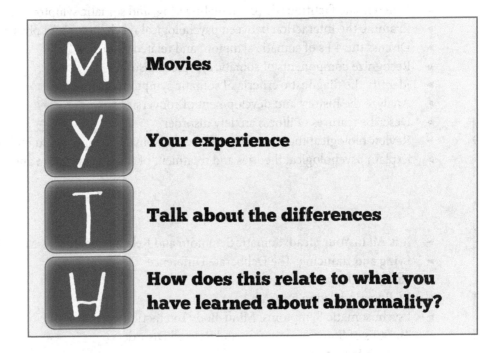

M Movies

Y Your experience

T Talk about the differences

H How does this relate to what you have learned about abnormality?

While *Talladega Nights* and other films provide entertainment, they may promote some misconceptions about disorders. Media and films may often exaggerate everyday life or symptoms of a disorder for entertainment's sake. Further, some films may add to the existing myths about somatic symptom disorders. One phrase from *Talladega Nights* that is found in popular culture

Myths in Movies

TALLADEGA NIGHTS

There are various movies that depict aspects of somatic symptom and related disorders. Along with *Talladega Nights*, some other films that contain characters portrayed as having somatic symptom disorders include *My Girl, Bandits*, and *Safe* (see Wedding & Niemiec, 2014). When

A scene from *Talladega Nights*

thinking about somatic symptom disorders and related disorders some thoughts affect our understanding of these disorders, such as whether psychological symptoms have an effect on physical symptoms and whether physical symptoms lead to psychological distress. What beliefs do you have about somatic symptom disorders and how did these beliefs develop?

is, "It is all in your head." This commonplace phrase emphasizes a central theme found among psychosomatic symptoms. Psychosomatic symptoms are physical complaints related to an underlying psychological cause. The phrase "It's all in your head" is a commonplace statement used when there is no apparent organic cause for physical complaints or symptoms. In the case of Ricky Bobby, the psychosomatic symptom was leg paralysis due to the stressor of crashing his car. To look at this further, consider the following case.

Case Vignette

Lili suddenly seemed to lose all functioning in her right arm. Her arm was paralyzed and no matter how hard she tried to move it, she could not. She became terrified and decided to go to the emergency room at the local hospital. After she was assessed, the physician told Lili that there was no physiological reason for her arm to be immobile. The physician told Lili that it appeared as if her arm was fine and fully capable of movement.

What do you think of Lili? Is it all in her head? Do you think people, such as the case of Lili, lie about symptoms or do you think she might have some concern? The case of Lili provides a conceptual example of somatic symptom and related disorders.

Now put yourself in Lili's shoes. What would it be like if you lost functioning in your arm or experienced some general pain and subsequently went to a physician to get it assessed and diagnosed? However, when you arrive you are told that your complaints are not congruent with a physiological cause. How would you respond to this? Maybe you would seek a second opinion. The next doctor (and possibly the next three depending on how many you seek) tells you the same thing. Now, what do you think? Maybe you start to think you are "crazy." This is an experience that is sometimes close to home for those with somatic symptom or related disorders.

A myth with these disorders is that people do not actually have anything wrong with them but rather they are making it up. People with somatic symptom disorder, conversion disorder, or illness anxiety disorder do not intentionally produce these symptoms. The symptoms are manifested from underlying psychological causes or stressors. However, some people may feign symptoms. When people lie about their symptoms or induce symptoms, this may be referred to as either factitious disorder or malingering.

Lying and Inducing: The Deliberate Difference

©Pixel-Shot/Shutterstock.com

When you are sick or ill what do others do? Do people take care of you? When people are sick, they often get attention from friends, family, coworkers, and loved ones. Loved ones may ask if you need anything, offer to make you soup, try to make you more at ease, or provide any variety of caretaking behaviors. If others do not do any of this, then you may need to reconsider your friends and loved ones.

The attention gained from sickness may reinforce illness feigning or inducing behaviors, which in turn may lead to factitious disorder. Factitious disorder and malingering involve people intentionally feigning or inducing symptoms for some gain, whether the incentive is external or internal. It is not surprising, given that people lie, some people telling many more lies than others (DePaulo & Bell, 1996; DePaulo & Kashy, 1998; Kashy & DePaulo, 1996; Serota & Levine, 2015; Serota et al., 2010; Vrij, 2000), that some people may lie about their symptoms in order to assume a sick role or to some external gain (e.g., money, mitigate a legal sentence).

Factitious Disorder

A literary character by the name of Baron Munchausen has been best credited for his fantastical tales and adventures, which include rocks into a bear's mouth, riding a cannonball, and tying his horse to a stump to later find it hanging in a steeple (Raspe, 2006). These fantastical stories have made an impact on modern film and can be viewed in the Terry Gilliam (1988) movie titled *The Adventures of Baron Munchausen*. Baron not only had an influence in film but also on a physician named Richard Asher, in which he coined the term Munchausen's Syndrome, which is synonymous with factitious disorder (Asher, 1951; Turner & Reid, 2002).

The Adventures of Baron Munchausen

© Columbia/Photofest

Munchausen's Syndrome

The original name of what is now referred to as factitious disorder

Factitious Disorder

Intentionally feigning or inducing symptoms to assume a sick role

Factitious disorder involves feigning or inducing symptoms or injury to present as sick or ill, without being motivated by an external incentive (APA, 2013). Factitious disorder is different from somatic symptom and related disorders due to the intentionality (Ferrara et al., 2013). The motivation for feigning or inducing symptoms is to assume the sick role (Ferrara et al., 2013). Many people may get sick and will receive care from others (e.g., physicians, nurses, family, and friends). The care received from others results in attention given to the individual who is sick. Thus, attention is reinforcing in feigning symptoms or assuming a sick role (see Figure 10.1).

FIGURE 10.1   Attention as a Reinforcer

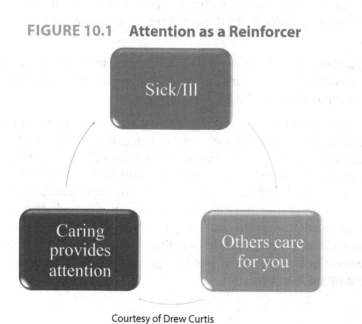

Sick/Ill

Caring provides attention

Others care for you

Courtesy of Drew Curtis

Myths in Movies

GREY'S ANATOMY

Factitious disorder has been portrayed within some shows. An episode of *Grey's Anatomy* titled, "Deny, Deny, Deny" depicts a character with factitious disorder. A woman by the name of Kalpana Vera earned her doctorate and travels to various places. Unbeknownst to the medical staff, Kalpana intentionally induces ventricular arrhythmia, which results in medical care. The medical staff stop discussions and immediately care for Kalpana when she becomes sick, reinforcing her

A scene from *Grey's Anatomy*

sickness inducing by providing her with attention. The medical staff eventually discover that Kalpana has been inducing ventricular arrhythmia and confront her with this evidence. How might this film portray factitious disorder? What might the accuracies and inaccuracies be?

Most people do not feign or induce sickness to receive attention. The DSM-5 states that the prevalence rates for factitious disorder are unknown but estimates about 1% of individuals may meet diagnostic criteria (APA, 2013). When people intentionally make themselves sick for the sake of attention, it can be fatal and impair many aspects of functioning. Hospital visits alone can be very costly. Further, if a person is ingesting chemicals or bacteria, then they could be putting themselves at a great risk for serious injury or death.

Factitious is not fictitious. While there certainly are examples of factitious disorder found in film and on television, factitious disorder is real and some people induce or lie about symptoms.

Some cases of factitious disorder have involved exaggerations of physical symptoms, lying about history, and self-injurious behavior to seek medical attention (Hagglund, 2009). Hagglund discusses the case of 30-year-old Kim who reported a variety of somatic complaints including vomiting, dizziness, anorexia, rectal bleeding, sprained limbs, 16 tooth extractions, and many more. Factitious disorder can even be found with pediatric cases. Uzuner et al. (2013) discuss a 10-year-old girl who was admitted for complaints of hemoptysis and hematuria. It was discovered that the blood coming from the patient's mouth was not due to a general medical condition but by the patient biting her cheek.

Due to factitious disorder involving feigning or inducing symptoms, it is often first seen by physicians and nurses. The presentation of factitious disorder symptoms typically fall into four categories (Thompson, 2003):

- ► Abdominal
- ► Bleeding
- ► Neurological
- ► Miscellaneous (including pyrexia, dermatological, endocrine, and other)

Factitious Disorder Imposed on Another (by Proxy). People may also lie about others' symptoms or intentionally making someone else sick. Typically, factitious disorder imposed on another (or by proxy) may be a parent or guardian making their child sick with the intent to gain attention.

Once again, factitious is not fictitious. Though films portray sides of factitious disorder imposed on another, this disorder is real and may have detrimental consequences. One controversial case of factitious disorder imposed on another was in the media in the 1990s. Jennifer Bush was an 8-year-old child who had undergone over 40 surgeries (Candiotti, 1999). In 1996, she

Factitious Disorder Imposed on Another

Intentionally lying about others' symptoms or intentionally making someone else sick not for external incentives

---

Myths in Movies

THE SIXTH SENSE and THE ACT

The movie *The Sixth Sense* shows a scene depicting factitious disorder imposed on another. A father learns about his daughter's death by watching a video recording of his wife secretly keeping his daughter sick by mixing cleaning agents into her soup and meals. This behavior eventually killed his daughter. How might this film portray factitious disorder imposed on another? What might the accuracies and inaccuracies be?

A scene from *The Sixth Sense*

©Buena Vista/Photofest

© Album / Alamy Stock Photo

The Act is a television series, produced by Hulu, which is based on the life of Gypsy Rose Blanchard and her mother, Dee Dee. *The Act* and HBO film, *Mommy Dead and Dearest*, were designed to portray aspects of factitious disorder imposed on another through Dee Dee and her death by the hand of her daughter, Gypsy. How might these films portray accuracies and inaccuracies related to factitious disorder imposed on another?

was removed from her parents' home and placed in foster care, where she was reported to have been living a normal life without surgeries or hospitalization (Candiotti, 1999). In 1999, a Florida jury found Jennifer's mother, Kathy Bush, guilty for aggravated child abuse and fraud for making her daughter sick and having her go through the numerous surgeries (Candiotti, 1999). The case has recently had new evidence that brings controversy. Nineteen years later Jennifer Bush released a written statement that her mother never abused her and the lawyer of Kathy Bush, Robert Buschel, stated that he thinks the diagnosis was flawed (McMahon, 2015).

On January 22, 2014, a 5-year-old child, Garnett, was declared brain dead from sodium poisoning (McCoy, 2015). His mother, Lacey Spears, was convicted of second-degree murder on March 2, 2015, due to sodium poisoning through his stomach tube (Higgins, 2015; McCoy, 2015). Lacey Spears had documented her and her son's life on a blog titled "Garnett's Journey." In the blog, she stated that they struggled with health concerns and losing her husband and Garnett's father. The acting state Supreme Court Justice Robert Neary stated that a person does not have to be a psychologist to realize [Lacey Spears] suffers from a mental illness, Munchausen's by proxy (Higgins, 2015).

These are a few cases that made it to the media. Unfortunately, it is not clear how many people may suffer from factitious disorder imposed on another due to not all cases being detected or leading to criminal behavior. Some people may induce sickness in their children and it may never be detected. This is one of the reasons that some discuss the use of video recordings in hospitals (Morrison, 1999). In some cases of factitious disorder imposed on another, mothers and fathers have suffocated or harmed their children (Boros et al., 1995). Recordings may assist law enforcement and courts with evidence for making arrests and convictions related to harming victims. Videos may also assist psychologists by providing evidence that corroborates a diagnosis of factitious disorder imposed on another.

Malingering: Lying for Gain

Malingering

Intentionally feigning or inducing symptoms for external incentives

Self-Oriented Lies

Lying for personal gain

Have you ever played as if you were sick in order to get out of work, school, or some other function? Were you successful? Do people make up complaints to get things or to get out of situations, such as calling in to work saying you are sick when you are not sick? Some people may lie by faking symptoms in order to receive some external incentive, which is known as malingering (APA, 2013). Malingering is distinct from factitious disorder in that individuals are lying about symptoms for an external incentive rather than to assume a sick role. Lying for personal gain is referred to as self-oriented lies (DePaulo et al., 1996).

External incentives can be in the form of obtaining rewards or avoiding aversive consequences. Clients and patients may be motivated to lie about symptoms for various types of external incentives including avoiding military duty, getting out of work, getting financial compensation, evading or mitigating criminal prosecution, and seeking drugs (APA, 2013). Research has documented that individuals in the military have been diagnosed as malingering, though the occurrence is a small percentage (Lande & Williams, 2013). Malingering can also be seen in people who fake symptoms of pain in order to obtain prescriptions (Jung & Reidenberg, 2007). In these cases, physicians may face criminal consequences if a patient's deception leads to the physician prescribing a controlled substance (Jung & Reidenberg, 2007).

© Brian A Jackson/Shutterstock.com

The DSM-5 states that malingering should be suspected if there is the presence of any of the following (APA, 2013):

1. Medicolegal situations
2. Inconsistencies of observations and a person's stated stress
3. Minimal cooperation or compliance with treatment
4. A diagnosis of antisocial personality disorder

Medicolegal

Situations involving forensic evaluations or legal contexts

There are several clinical assessments that may be used to aid in detecting whether a client is malingering (Rogers & Bender, 2018). Some assessments, such as the Minnesota Multiphasic Personality Inventory-II (Butcher et al., 2001) contain various scales that indicate if a client may be attempting to lie, respond in a socially desirable manner, or fake psychopathology (Greene, 2000). This assessment has been shown to detect malingering with a high level of accuracy (Bianchini et al., 2008). Another assessment, The Millon Clinical Multiphasic Inventory-III (Millon et al., 2009), also has scales that indicate if clients are responding in a manner that indicates social desirability, omission of information, or exaggeration of negative aspects (Groth-Marnat, 2009). High scores on these particular scales may provide a clinician with information regarding the validity of interpreting the test and can inform the clinician about particular behaviors related to malingering.

© Production Perig/Shutterstock.com

Psychosomatic Symptoms: Mind-Body Interaction

If people are not lying or inducing symptoms, how then might a psychological mechanism account for a physiological expression of pain or loss in functioning? Simply think about stress. Have you ever experienced stress? Assuming the answer is yes, then when stressed have you ever felt the effects of stress anywhere in your body? Maybe you have headaches, neck aches, back pains, or other pains from stress. Voilà! A psychological mechanism (i.e., stress) has caused physiological symptoms or complaints (e.g., back pain). If you ever felt the physiological effects of stress, you probably have not said that it is all in your head, or all in someone else's head. You seem to accept and understand that stress can lead to physiological responses. Stress is not the only psychological mechanism that may result in physiological expression. Consider the following case.

Case Vignette

Ludwig, a 38-year-old man, had recently lost his wife, Johanna, in a tragic car accident. A few months later, Ludwig was attending a family function, thinking that he would need some social support during this intense time of grief. As he was at the function, he began to have intense pains in his chest. His eyes were tearing and he was speechless except saying "my chest." One of his family members rushed to him quickly to discern if he was having a heart attack.

Ludwig was not having a heart attack but was grief-struck. A thought of his wife and her indefinite absence triggered an intense sadness for Ludwig. The sadness was expressed somatically through chest pains. Even psychological mechanisms such as grief can be expressed somatically. Thus, there is an interplay of psychological and physiological processes that may precipitate somatic symptoms. To determine when those symptoms become problematic, it is important to refer to the 4 Fs and the DSM-5.

The 4 Fs of Somatic Symptom and Related Disorders

Merely experiencing a headache from stress or chest pains from grief does not constitute psychopathology. The 4 Fs provide criteria that reveal how somatic expression of underlying psychological causes may affect functioning, feeling pain, and fatality.

Frequency

A—Amount of Time: The amount of time that a person experiences various somatic complaints is generally present for at least 6 months (APA, 2013). For somatic symptom disorder, symptoms are present more than 6 months (APA, 2013). Illness anxiety disorder involves a preoccupation with an illness for at least 6 months (APA, 2013). The amount of time that symptoms are present for conversion disorder may vary, in that an acute episode involves symptoms present for less than 6 months and a persistent specifier includes the presence of symptoms for longer than 6 months (APA, 2013).

B—Behavior: Somatic symptom disorder, illness anxiety disorder, and conversion disorder involve a higher frequency of thoughts, feelings, or behaviors related to somatic symptoms, health, or bodily processes and functioning (APA, 2013). Because of the preoccupation with health and somatic symptoms, individuals may frequently visit primary care physicians or hospitals. Persistent thoughts related to somatic symptoms may also lead people to search various internet sites for illnesses, diseases, and problems related to symptoms.

C—Curve: Many people may have some concern about their health. It is often beneficial for people to think about their health. You may think about wellness check-ups or behaviors to contribute to a healthier lifestyle. A smaller percentage of people may ruminate on their somatic complaints leading to impairment in functioning, feelings of pain, or fatality. The prevalence rates of somatic symptom disorder is not known but is expected to be between 1% and 19%, approximately 5 to 7% for the adult population, due to some of the changes from the DSM-IV-TR to the DSM-5 (APA, 2013). The DSM-5 removed somatization disorder (previously less than 1% prevalence rates) and undifferentiated somatization disorder (prevalence rate of 19%; APA, 2013). Further, the removal of hypochondriasis in the DSM-5 has led to the inclusion of approximately 75% of individuals previously having this diagnosis to be subsumed under somatic symptom disorder (APA, 2013). While most cases of hypochondriasis have been subsumed under somatic symptom disorder, a small percentage of cases may be more appropriately labeled as illness anxiety disorder (APA, 2013). Thus, the DSM-5 has based prevalence rates of illness anxiety disorder on former estimates of hypochondriasis, with 1- to 2-year prevalence of health anxiety ranging from 1.3 to 10% (APA, 2013). Further, the 6-month to 1-year prevalence for ambulatory medical populations is between 3 to 5% (APA, 2013). The prevalence rates of conversion disorder are unknown but found in approximately 5% of referrals to neurology clinics (APA, 2013). The DSM-5 estimates persistent conversion symptoms to be 2–5 per 100,000 per year (APA, 2013).

The Good News: There has been much attention toward reworking the classification system to better account for and understand these classes of disorders. The DSM-5 indicates that it is not appropriate to make a diagnosis due to a medical cause not being evident and removing the emphasis of a lack of medical explanation assists in validating patients and clients who do experience physical symptoms (APA, 2013).

Function

Constant worry about a person's health may negatively affect relationships and lead to missing work, school, or other areas of functioning (APA, 2013). People who are focused on somatic symptoms and health-related concerns may also frequently visit health care facilities. It can be financially costly to frequently visit primary care, urgent care, or emergency care facilities. Further, somatic symptom disorder is associated with impairment in health status (APA, 2013). More specifically, conversion disorder is directly related to impaired function, in which symptoms alter motor or sensory functioning (APA, 2013).

Feeling Pain

People who have various somatic symptoms disorders frequently and persistently feel pain related to the somatic symptoms. Some somatic symptoms might be experienced as physical pain. A specifier of somatic symptoms disorder is with predominant pain, which was previously classified as pain disorder (APA, 2013). Other somatic symptoms or loss of functioning might elicit psychological pain related to the worry and anxiety of the symptoms. Individuals may often think about the somatic complaints and would like them to not be present. Frustration might occur when the somatic symptoms do not quickly or easily resolve. The distress is what usually influences visits to health care facilities. Further, it can be demeaning for people if they are not believed as experiencing real symptoms or when they are perceived as "crazy."

Fatality

Due to the association of somatic symptom disorder with depressive disorders, there is an increased risk of suicide (APA, 2013). A study conducted in Germany which assessed 142 patients who met diagnostic criteria for a somatoform disorder reported that 23.9% of patients had active suicidal ideation in the past 6 months and 17.6% had attempted suicide (Wiborg et al., 2013). The researchers tested two models and reported that comorbid symptoms of depression and dysfunctional illness perceptions were independently associated with suicidal ideation (Wiborg et al., 2013).

Somatic Symptom Disorder

Somatic symptom disorder involves feeling pain (emotional or physical) related to somatic symptoms and excessive thoughts about those symptoms, which impairs a person's daily functioning (APA, 2013). These symptoms are not intentionally produced as seen with factitious disorder or malingering. The symptoms experienced may be specific or nonspecific and can represent normative sensations (APA, 2013). However, somatic symptom disorder may be associated with another medical condition. The key feature of the disorder is that an individual ruminates and is bothered extensively by the somatic symptoms.

© antoniodiaz/Shutterstock.com

Somatoform disorder in the DSM-IV was replaced by somatic symptom disorder in the DSM-5 to reduce overlap in classifications and categories and to reduce ambiguity and confusion for clinicians (APA, 2013). As previously mentioned, a larger percentage of individuals who were previously diagnosed with hypochondriasis would now fall under the somatic symptom disorder (APA, 2013). For the diagnostic criteria, refer to the DSM-5 (APA, 2013).

Somatoform Disorder

A psychological disorder listed in the DSM-IV and replaced by somatic symptom disorder in the DSM-5

Conversion Disorder: Historically Hysteria

Anna O., whose real name was Bertha Pappenheim, was a 21-year-old female patient who had symptoms of paralysis, losing sensations in limbs on the right side of her body and at times had difficulty speaking (Breuer & Freud, 1957; Kaplan, 2004). Anna O. was a patient of Dr. Josef Breuer, in which he diagnosed her as having hysteria (Breuer & Freud, 1957). Hysteria, derived from Greek, meaning womb, was first noted as a mental disorder by Hippocrates who viewed this disorder as only affecting women (Thorne & Henley, 2001). Hippocrates believed that the "wandering uterus" caused a variety of somatic symptoms and its treatment involved marriage and pregnancy to aid in the uterus returning to its original position (Thorne & Henley, 2001).

Hysteria

A mental disorder identified by Hippocrates, which later was refined and understood to be conversion disorder

This disorder gained attention and controversy. Maines (1998) discussed some of the controversy of hysteria being a diagnosis for women and pathologizing normative experiences. Maines also discussed some of the controversial history of Western medicine and how it treated hysteria by genital massage to orgasm from a midwife or physician. In the later 1800s, a physician, George Taylor, patented a powered vibrating massage apparatus intended to use for female disorders, though others, such as Mortimer Granville, were opposed to using these devices to treat hysteria (Maines, 1998). In 2011, a film titled *Hysteria* was released to portray aspects of this history.

Freud and Breuer re-conceptualized hysteria. This was primarily brought out through Breuer's discussion of Anna O.'s treatment, the talking cure (Kaplan, 2004). This led Freud to conceptualize hysteria as a disorder due to underlying psychological causes, namely trauma (Kaplan, 2004). Subsequently, Freud and Breuer wrote about their cases and developed underpinnings of psychoanalysis (Breuer & Freud, 1957; Kaplan, 2004). Freud (1963) further advanced understanding of hysteria through another famous case, known as Dora. Freud discussed the associations between Dora's somatic complaints with psychological and interpersonal concerns. Hysteria was later deemed conversion disorder, found in the DSM-III, due to the psychological mechanisms being converted into somatic complaints (APA, 1980; Breuer & Freud, 1957).

Conversion Disorder

Loss of functioning not explained by other disorders or conditions

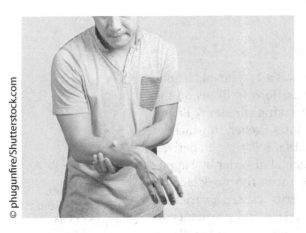

Conversion disorder primarily involves a loss of functioning that is not better explained by another medical or mental disorder and causes distress and impairment in various areas of life (APA, 2013). Conversion disorder may involve paralysis, abnormal motor movement, swallowing symptoms, speech impairment, non-epileptic seizures, sensory loss or sensory symptoms, or a mix of somatic symptoms (APA, 2013). These symptoms or loss of functioning must be incompatible with a neurological disease (APA, 2013). The suggested etiology of conversion disorder is stress or trauma, though it is not a requirement to make a diagnosis (APA, 2013).

Illness Anxiety Disorder

Illness anxiety disorder consists of individuals who are constantly concerned and anxious with having or getting a serious illness, which leads to excessive health-related behaviors (APA, 2013). As previously noted, individuals formerly diagnosed with hypochondriasis would either be subsumed under somatic symptom disorder (majority) or illness anxiety disorder (minority of cases; APA, 2013). The preoccupation with being sick or acquiring a disease may lead to either frequently visiting health care providers or avoiding doctors and hospitals (APA, 2013). Illness anxiety disorder may have an onset of early to middle adulthood due to stress or a benign threat to a person's health (APA, 2013).

Myths in Movies

STONEHEARST ASYLUM

The movie *Stonehearst Asylum* opens with a scene of a professor who is teaching a class about symptoms of hysteria in a female patient, Lady Eliza Graves. Lady Graves is brought into a classroom in a wheelchair, slouched over. The professor states that he has drugged the patient with heroin and discusses how there are many trigger points for hysteria in a female that may include her breasts, inner thighs, and ovaries. The professor then grabs Lady Graves, close to her ovaries, and she then tenses her muscles and passes out.

A scene from *Stonehearst Asylum*

© Millennium Entertainment/Photofest.com

What are your thoughts of the movie's portrayal of hysteria? The movie may be attempting to portray a historical view of hysteria. You may find it relieving to know that current treatments of conversion disorder do not involve therapists grabbing clients' ovaries or sedating them with heroin.

Biological Theories and Treatment of Somatic Symptom and Related Disorders

Some literature has suggested that pharmacotherapy is an effective, financially effective, and simple treatment for somatic symptom and related disorders (Somashekar et al., 2013). These authors have argued that comorbidity of anxiety and depressive disorders may contribute to somatic symptoms persisting (Somashekar et al., 2013). Somashekar and colleagues stated that the evidence indicates five groups of drugs to be an effective means for treating somatic symptom disorders:

- ► Tricyclic antidepressants
- ► SSRIs
- ► SNRI
- ► Atypical antipsychotics
- ► Herbal medications (e.g., St. John's Wort)

Somashekar and colleagues (2013) claimed that there is no known studies that have evaluated the effectiveness of psychopharmacology for conversion disorders. However, there have been case study reports of using antidepressants and benzodiazepines for treating symptoms of conversion disorder in a female patient (Oulis et al., 2009).

Psychological Theories and Treatment of Somatic Symptom and Related Disorders

Historically, psychological treatments that were used with somatic symptoms appeared to range with talk therapy as being noted to have some success, and documented with its use for hysteria (Breuer & Freud, 1957). Somatic disorders usually involve a preoccupation with health or bodily functioning and commonly presenting after the presence of environmental stress or trauma (APA, 2013). Thus, one successful psychological approach to treating somatic symptom disorders has been the use of Cognitive Behavioral Therapy (CBT; Woolfolk & Allen, 2012).

Treating somatic symptom disorders from a CBT approach involves identifying and restructuring dysfunctional beliefs and thinking, behavioral activation, problem-solving, and relaxation training (Woolfolk & Allen, 2012). Studies using randomized control trials on CBT for somatization have revealed significantly greater improvement in somatic complaints compared to standard medical care and lasting effects in changing inaccurate beliefs (Speckens et al., 1995; Woolfolk & Allen, 2012). Efficacy of CBT on full somatization disorder has been shown to have long-term improvements in symptoms, functioning, and health care utilization (Allen et al., 2006; Woolfolk & Allen, 2012). Due to some changes in categorical descriptions from DSM changes, from hypochondriasis to somatic symptom disorder and illness anxiety disorder (APA, 2013), there is a dearth of empirical studies directly addressing these categories. However, a variety of CBT techniques have been empirically supported in treating somatic disorders that were categorically listed in the DSM-IV-TR (see Woolfolk & Allen, 2012).

Conclusion

Hopefully, you now reconsider telling someone that it is all in their head when they complain of somatic symptoms or pain. There are several disorders where people may experience actual somatic complaints and ruminate on those somatic features. Telling people that it is all in their head may be invalidating and influence them to think they are misunderstood, isolated, or question their own symptoms. However, there are cases where people may fake these symptoms to assume a sick role or for some external incentive. While there may be particular contexts where lying may be more likely, people are generally not good at detecting deception (Bond & DePaulo, 2006).

CHAPTER REVIEW

QUESTIONS

1. Are people who complain of symptoms in which there is no physical cause merely lying?

2. What is a reason that people might intentionally make themselves sick? What about making someone else sick?

3. How is factitious disorder different from malingering? How are both different from somatic symptom disorder?

4. How can psychological factors lead to physical pain or somatic complaints?

5. How was hysteria historically viewed and how has this changed to reflect disorders within the DSM-5?

KEY TERMS

Psychosomatic

Munchausen's Syndrome

Factitious Disorder

Factitious Disorder Imposed on Another

Malingering

Self-Oriented Lies

Medicolegal

Somatoform Disorder

Hysteria

Conversion Disorder

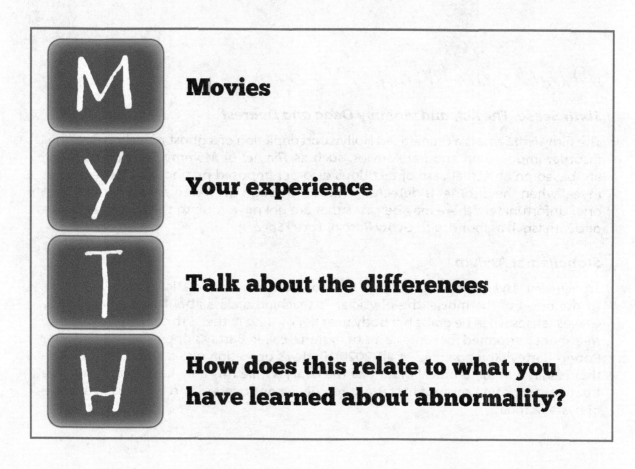

M   **Movies**

Y   **Your experience**

T   **Talk about the differences**

H   **How does this relate to what you have learned about abnormality?**

Myths in Movies Recap

Talladega Nights

Movies such as *Talladega Nights* may put forth the image of somatic symptom disorders or conversion disorders as comedic. Additionally, the movie may perpetuate the notion that someone is faking their symptoms or making them up.

Grey's Anatomy

Grey's Anatomy has a fairly large following and while this episode shows some features of factitious disorder, it may promote some false images as well. The character, Kalpana, appears to be highly educated and calculated with ways to induce sickness. Not all individuals who display symptoms of factitious disorder may be as meticulous and calculated. One of the dangers of factitious disorder is that people may induce sickness that leads to more detrimental effects on their health or even resulting in death.

Myths in Movies Recap

Sixth Sense, The Act, and Mommy Dead and Dearest

The film *Sixth Sense* is a dramatized Hollywood depiction of a ghost revealing factitious disorder imposed on another. Movies, such as *The Act* or *Mommy Dead and Dearest*, are based on an actual case of factitious disorder imposed on another. These movies reveal when the disorder is detected, which is through the death or murder of someone. Unfortunately, there may be cases that are unknown due to the lack of evidence or death (such as found with *Gypsy Rose* or *Lacey Spears*).

Stonehearst Asylum

Stonehearst Asylum sets a grim dark tone of violence and isolation many years ago. At the onset of the movie, the physician is teaching a class about hysteria and Lady Graves tenses when he grabs her body near her ovaries. In the 19th century, there was a treatment performed for some cases of hysteria, called Battey's operation, named after Robert Battey (Komagamine et al., 2020). Battey's operation was a surgical procedure that resulted in the removal of part of the ovary. While this may have been used as a treatment for some cases of hysteria, it has been controversial and is not used in cases of hysteria today.

CHAPTER ELEVEN

EATING DISORDERS

LEARNING OBJECTIVES

- ► Examine myths related to eating disorders
- ► Review the history of eating disorders
- ► Recognize the factors that contribute to the development of eating disorders
- ► Discuss the 4 Fs of eating disorders
- ► Explain characteristics of anorexia nervosa
- ► Identify the diagnostic criteria of anorexia nervosa
- ► Explain characteristics of bulimia nervosa
- ► Identify the diagnostic criteria of bulimia nervosa
- ► Discuss treatment for eating disorders

CHAPTER OUTLINE

- ► Food Everywhere: Beliefs About Food and Eating Behaviors—MYTHs
- ► The History and Influences of Eating Disorders
- ► The 4 Fs of Eating Disorders
- ► Anorexia Nervosa
- ► DSM-5 Criteria for Anorexia Nervosa
- ► Bulimia Nervosa
- ► DSM-5 Criteria for Bulimia Nervosa
- ► Other Feeding and Eating Disorders
- ► Treatment for Eating Disorders

Food Everywhere: Beliefs About Food and Eating Behaviors

"eating, from birth on, is always closely intermingled with interpersonal and emotional experiences, and its physiological and psychological aspects cannot be strictly differentiated"

—Hilde Bruch (1973, p. 3).

Eating behavior and eating disorders bring up a number of thoughts and beliefs. With the saliency and availability of food within the United States of America, there are a number of people who hold numerous beliefs about what people should eat and not eat, how they should eat, what foods lead to poor health, and diets that affect psychological functioning. With the saliency of food and food choices in the United States, there has been an influx of television shows that are focused on eating, food, and weight. For example, there are a wide array of shows about cooking and cooking competitions, such as *MasterChef, Hell's Kitchen,* and *Cupcake Wars.* There has also been the emer-

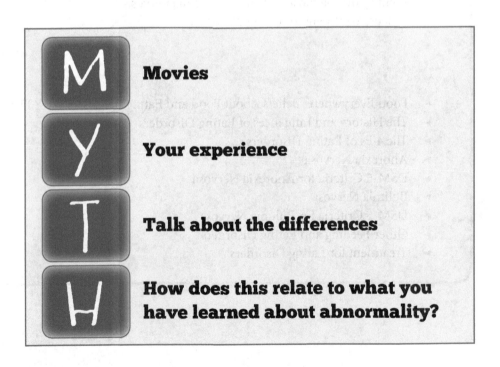

M Movies

Y Your experience

T Talk about the differences

H How does this relate to what you have learned about abnormality?

gence and popularity of food documentaries such as *Super Size Me, Food, Inc.,* and *Fat, Sick & Nearly Dead.* There are films and shows that portray obesity and weight loss, such as *The Biggest Loser, Shallow Hal,* and *The Nutty Professor.* Some films even portray eating disorders, such as *Hunger Point, For the Love of Nancy,* and *Sharing the Secret.* When thinking about eating disorders what beliefs do you have and how did these beliefs develop? How does this shape your thoughts about eating disorders?

There are several myths about eating disorders. Many myths might be perpetuated by films, experience, and unclear lines between science and pseudoscience (Lilienfeld, 2012). One of the most commonly held inaccurate, beliefs is that people with eating disorders do not eat. While there may be restricting behaviors, meaning that people may restrict the amount that they eat or the caloric intake, people with eating disorders do eat. The characteristics of eating disorders involve eating behaviors that have a high frequency of impaired function, lead to feeling pain, affect health, and may be fatal (i.e., the 4 Fs.).

Another mistakenly held belief is that people with eating disorders are extremely thin. While some eating disorders involve criteria that lead to low body weight, there are a number of eating disorders that do not. For example, individuals who suffer with bulimia nervosa, do not have a low body weight. People with eating disorders may change eating behaviors that affect their health but not necessarily their weight.

Bulimia Nervosa

An eating disorder that involves episodes of binge-eating and compensatory behaviors

Another myth about eating disorders is that only women are affected. While prevalence rates are much higher for women than for men, eating disorders can be found to affect men (APA, 2013). Some literature suggests that men with eating disorders may be underdiagnosed and discuss stigma and issues that may complicate treatment (Strother et al., 2012).

Obesity is not considered a mental disorder by APA (2013). The APA stated that it is not included due to various factors (i.e., genetic, physiological, behavioral, and environmental) that are different for each person. However, the APA does state that obesity is associated with a number of mental disorders. Further, obesity, though not recognized as a mental disorder, does not imply that it is not a health concern.

The History and Influences of Eating Disorders

Various accounts of fasting, self-starvation, and diminished food consumption with differing motivations have been documented throughout history (see Bemporad, 1996). However, a number of these accounts do not necessarily point to eating disorders. People who fast for religious or spiritual reasons may do so for different motivations than what is found underly-

Anorexia Nervosa

An eating disorder involving a fear of being fat and low body weight

ing specific eating disorders, namely anorexia nervosa. A physician by the name of Louis-Victor Marce was the first to publish a formal account of anorexia, identifying women with the disorder to have a conviction about not eating (Bemporad, 1996; Silverman, 1989). The first formal attempts to understand, differentiate, and term anorexia from other disorders, such as hysteria and fasting behaviors, was done so through two physicians, Lasègue and Gull (Bemporad, 1996; Gull, 1874). The formal attempts of categorization and differentiation led to identifying mechanisms that contribute to etiology of eating disorders; recall the Diathesis-Stress Model.

Biological Contributions. Eating disorders involve eating behavior, which has a direct effect on a person's body. The position of the Academy for Eating Disorders (AED) is that "anorexia nervosa and bulimia nervosa, along with their variants, are biologically based, serious mental illnesses" (Klump et al., 2009, p. 97). Klump and colleagues discussed how eating disorders have a heritability that is similar to other disorders, estimating 50 to 83% accounted for by genetic influence.

Poor nutrition and starvation affect brain function, as "it uses 20% caloric intake" (Treasure et al., 2010, p. 585). This may be dire, given that eating disorders have a typical onset during a critical stage in development (Treasure et al., 2010). Biological influences of eating disorders have also been corroborated within animal models (Klump et al., 2009).

Social and Cultural Contributions. Social and cultural influences are closely intertwined. Cultures that promote and reinforce values of thinness are associated with environmental factors that play a role in the development of some eating disorders (APA, 2013). As mentioned at the beginning of this text, there are countless films, shows, and media that expose people to messages about food, eating, and weight. While anorexia occurs cross-culturally, it is most prevalent in higher income, post-industrialized countries, such as the United States (APA, 2013).

One of the reasons may be due to the abundance of access of food. In the United States, and some other higher income, post-industrialized countries, people can gain easy access to food. You can probably take minimal effort to gain food right now if you wanted. Maybe you could walk to a vending machine, take a 5-minute drive to a convenience store or fast-food restaurant, or even have it delivered to your door. Food in many post-industrialized countries is easily accessible and available. Not only is food readily available in some of these countries, you can have food prepared any way you want it. Another reason that there may be cultural differences in eating disorders, along with access to food, may be due to the emphasis on food. Due to food access, many people can more easily discriminate between what food they choose to eat. This may lead to discussions of dietary choices, restrictions, and preferences. With easy access to a variety of food sources, people are able to pick and choose what they want to eat or not eat. Individuals in poorer countries, with less access or abundance of food are less able to discriminate. The decision you make may be between eating and not eating as opposed to deciding if you want your pizza to have thin crust or deep dish.

Outside of emphasis on food and food access, many people express beliefs and thoughts about weight that may contribute to cultural influences. What do you say to others who have lost weight or what do others say to you when you have lost weight? The phrase most commonly heard or said is that "You look good." This is often accompanied with additional questions that offer praise for the weight loss, such as, "What is your secret?" or "What did you do to lose weight?" in attempts to offer sentiments of envy and applause for someone's weight loss success. Essentially, when you or others make these statements or inquire with praise, the weight loss is reinforced. People, collectively, reinforce weight loss and associated looking good and beauty with thin. The message you convey is that looking good means being thin or losing weight. How many times do people say "You look good" or ask, "What is your secret?" when someone gains weight? These phrases are probably unheard of within the United States, unless the weight gain is in muscle tone. Rarely do people say that fat accumulation is good. Thus, thinness equals good and fat equals bad.

Not only are these messages expressed explicitly among people but also conveyed in films and popular magazines. A film series, titled *Killing Us Softly 4: Advertising's Image of Women*, reviews advertising in print and television and how advertising perpetuates beliefs about women, including thinness (Jhally & Kilbourne, 2010). Jean Kilbourne discussed how advertising promotes thinness through making fun of celebrities who gain weight, historical sex symbols are considered fat by modern standards, and increasing thinness of models and the use of Photoshop to make them appear more thin (Jhally & Kilbourne, 2010). In addition to these claims, Kilbourne claimed that advertising trivializes eating disorders. A study published in 2011, investigated the additional seven categorical assertions, includ-

© Photographee.eu/Shutterstock.com

ing the trivialization of eating disorders displayed in magazines (Coonley & Ramsey, 2011). The researchers did not observe any categories of mocking eating disorders among advertising (Coonley & Ramsey, 2011). With that, film, magazines, and media are not free from influence. One study recruited

© Iulian Valentin/Shutterstock.com

366 adolescents and 70 college undergraduates to measure exposure to television, rate thin-ideal and fat-characters, and measured eating disorder symptoms (Harrison, 2000). The results revealed that exposure to fat-characters significantly predicted symptoms of bulimia and exposure to thin-ideal magazines significantly predicted anorexia symptoms (Harrison, 2000). A meta-analysis of 25 studies investigated the effect sizes of mass media images on body image, finding that body image was significantly more negative after viewing thin media images compared to average size models, plus size models, or inanimate objects (Groesz et al., 2002).

The influence of media, film, and magazines is apparent. This coupled with messages that you convey to others may perpetuate beliefs that thin is good and fat is bad. When these messages are communicated via social, cultural, and environmental channels, then it may be easy to see the influence leading to the development of eating disorders with some individuals. Much like many other disorders, the risk for an eating disorder is multifaceted and may consist of other contributing factors, such as preexisting anxiety disorders or obsessional thoughts in childhood, and genetic factors (APA, 2013). Further, not all who are exposed to media and cultural influences develop eating disorders.

Psychological Contributions. Along with societal and cultural influences, two psychological mechanisms emerge that differentiate eating behaviors and eating disorders: control and self-perception. People with anorexia nervosa may seek to control their weight through restricting food intake or purging (APA, 2013). Individuals may control their body weight through monitoring and regulating caloric intake, in which food and caloric intake is a means for control (Abbate-Daga et al., 2013). The need to control your own thoughts is a metacognitive variable that research has identified among people with anorexia nervosa (McDermott & Rushford, 2011; Olstad et al., 2015). People with bulimia nervosa experience a lack of control over eating during binge episodes and exerting control when trying to prevent weight gain through purging or fasting behaviors (APA, 2013). Control is also a factor in binge eating, in which a lack of self-control beliefs are associated with increased binge eating (Reese et al., 2016).

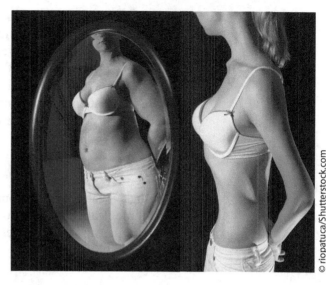

© riopatuca/Shutterstock.com

Purging

Restricting food intake or removing calories

The other mechanism involves self-perception and distorted thinking of body size. Bruch (1973) discussed a disturbance in size awareness involved in anorexia. Bruch talked about a patient who, when looking in the mirror, could not see how thin she was even though she knew she was thin through feeling her bones. Individuals diagnosed with anorexia nervosa typically overestimate their body size (Farrell et al., 2005). In their review of research in body size estimation, Farrell and colleagues identified three methods for assessing body size estimation, which include:

▶ Analogue scales (adjusting light or body calipers to display body width)

▶ Image marking (drawing your body on a piece of paper mounted on a wall)

▶ Optical distortion (using a photograph of a person which can be altered in width through an adjustable lens; involves asking a person to adjust a lens to their accurate size)

Essentially, these various techniques involve participants making some adjustment to estimate their body size based on their beliefs or perceptions. These research techniques used in various studies have found evidence corroborating that patients with eating disorders overestimate their body size, not due to a sensory deficit (Farrell et al., 2005). Overestimation of body size has been suggested to possibly be a symptom related to eating disorders (Farrell et al., 2005).

These psychological influences may also accompany other factors that affect the development and maintenance of eating disorders. Along with self-perceptions, people with eating disorders may deny the dangers of their eating behaviors (APA, 2013). Also, guilt and shame may be experienced through messages expressed by family members and friends. To help derive a more complete picture of how cultural and psychological influences relate to eating disorders, it is imperative to consider the four Fs.

The 4 Fs of Eating Disorders

Skipping a meal, changing your diet, or even fasting does not indicate a psychopathological eating disorder. The 4 Fs provide criteria that reveal how various types and frequencies of eating behaviors may affect functioning, feeling pain, and fatality.

Frequency

A—Amount of Time: The amount of time that a person engages in particular eating behavior may vary. For anorexia nervosa, the behavior is persistent (APA, 2013). Depending on the specifier, restricting or binge-eating/purging, these behaviors are present for at least 3 months (APA, 2013). Bulimia nervosa involves recurrent episodes of binging and recurrent compensatory behaviors at least once per week, in a discrete time period, for 3 months (APA, 2013). Similarly, binge-eating disorder consists of recurrent episodes of binge eating once per week, in a discrete time period, for 3 months (APA, 2013). Avoidant/restrictive food intake disorder involves persistently not meeting nutritional needs (APA, 2013). Rumination disorder and pica involve repeated and persistent behaviors occurring for at least 1 month (APA, 2013).

B—Behavior: Anorexia nervosa consists of a higher frequency of behaviors that lead to significant weight loss or low body weight (APA, 2013). These behaviors may involve restricting caloric intake through dieting or fasting (APA, 2013). Likewise, these behaviors are evidenced with avoidant/restrictive food intake disorder (APA, 2103). However, for anorexia, there may also be a significantly low body weight due to purging behaviors, such as vomiting, or using laxatives (APA, 2013). Present in bulimia nervosa and binge-eating disorder are high frequency eating behaviors in a short or discrete time period, referred to as binge eating (APA, 2013). However, individuals with bulimia nervosa will frequently demonstrate compensatory behaviors to prevent weight gain (e.g., vomiting, laxatives; APA, 2013). Rumination disorder involves repeated regurgitation of food, such as chewing and spitting out food, and it is not due to a medical condition (APA, 2013). Pica includes eating nonnutritive, nonfood materials (APA, 2013).

Binge Eating

High frequency eating behaviors in a short or discrete time period

Pica

Eating nonnutritive, nonfood materials

C—**Curve:** A major marker of anorexia nervosa is that body weight is significantly lower than that of most people and what is expected for a person's body mass index (BMI; APA, 2013). Anorexia nervosa is more frequently prevalent in females than males, with a 10:1 ratio, and a 12-month prevalence rate for females is 0.4% (APA, 2013). The same 10:1 female-to-male ratio is seen with bulimia nervosa and 12-month prevalence rates for females is 1 to 1.5% (APA, 2013). The 12-month prevalence rates for binge-eating disorder are about 1.6% for females and 0.8% for males (APA, 2013). Prevalence for rumination disorder and pica are unclear and inconclusive though the DSM-5 suggests that they both are more commonly seen with intellectual disability (APA, 2013). Though prevalence rates for rumination disorder are unclear, some researchers have found that regurgitation behaviors (i.e., chewing and spitting) have been found to occur within 24.5% of a sample of people with eating disorders (Song et al., 2015).

The Good News: There is much attention from various organizations that is directed toward eating disorder research, treatment, education and awareness, and prevention. One of these organizations is the Academy for Eating Disorders. The AED promotes research, hosts conferences, and serves as a source for public education (AED, 2016; http://www.aedweb.org/index.php).

Function

Eating behaviors and thoughts about food and self-perceptions may significantly impair functioning within people's lives. Hilde Bruch (1973) stated that eating function may be misused to mask problems of living. The functioning of people with anorexia nervosa and bulimia may range in impairment depending on the individual (APA, 2013). Although a number of people with eating disorders may appear to function well with a variety of activities, a number of individuals may become socially isolated, failing in academics, or neglecting career and job responsibilities (APA, 2013; Klump et al., 2009). Further, there is some evidence that patients with anorexia nervosa have impaired sexual functioning (Gonidakis et al., 2015).

Feeling Pain

There appears to be a paradox regarding feeling pain with eating disorders, in which values on thinness may reinforce some eating disorder symptoms that are simultaneously praised by others in some contexts and pain for the person in other contexts. Consider the case of Fanny.

Case Vignette

Fanny is a 13-year-old female and the oldest of three children. She is 4'10" and weighs 80 lbs, with a BMI of 16.7 kg/m². She had developed restricting type eating disorder, anorexia nervosa. She counted calories and avoided high-calorie meals. She would often eat oat cereal, about a 1-inch full sandwich bag, throughout the morning and midday. For dinner she would eat spinach salads with mustard. When Fanny began losing weight her friends told her how great she looked and she highly enjoyed the attention. Her friends' comments motivated her to lose more weight. She then began exercising more routinely. She would run frequently and attempted to run for longer intervals. She lost 8 lbs, weighing 72 lbs, with a BMI of 15 kg/m². Her friends stopped commenting on her weight when they realized she became consumed with her weight loss. Fanny wondered why they stopped commenting. She became greatly upset and thought maybe she was not losing enough weight. She was terrified of gaining weight. Fanny thought that she might need to exercise more frequently.

In the case of Fanny, she initially receives praise for caloric- and food-restriction behaviors that lead to weight loss. The praise, in behavioral terms, serves as positive reinforcement for engaging in weight loss behaviors. However, when friends stop providing praise, then Fanny becomes more fearful of gaining weight and experiences distress. Thus, some aspects of eating disorders may not lead a person to experience pain and distress, whereas some other components elicit more pain. Individuals with anorexia nervosa and bulimia nervosa indicate low quality of life and other relational distress (see Klump et al., 2009).

Some of the symptoms of eating disorders may also lead to physical pain. With anorexia nervosa, individuals may experience pain associated with restricted intake of food or purging behaviors. People who restrict food may experience exhaustion, fatigue, and hunger. Constipation, abdominal pain, or cold intolerance may be present in anorexia nervosa (APA, 2013). People who engage in binge-eating behaviors may experience physical pain from overeating.

Fatality

"I just want to be thin. If it takes dying to get there, so be it. At least I'll get there."

—Alisa Williams (*Thin,* 2006)

Eating disorders are not fairy tales, and many do not have a happy ending. Unfortunately, a number of clients and patients who struggle with eating disorders may die or complete suicide (APA, 2013). Death and suicide risks are increased in people with anorexia nervosa and bulimia nervosa, in which suicide rates are 12 per 100,000 per year for anorexia nervosa (APA, 2013).

Along with increased risk for death and suicide, there are numerous other risks for people with eating disorders. Some risks associated with anorexia nervosa include sinus bradycardia, low bone mineral density, electrolyte disturbances, hypercholesterolemia, leukopenia, and other health concerns (APA, 2013). Risks associated with bulimia nervosa include nutritional deficiencies, electrolyte disturbances, esophageal tears, gastric rupture, and cardiac arrhythmias (APA, 2013). Both anorexia nervosa and bulimia nervosa increase the likelihood of amenorrhea, menstrual irregularity, or delayed menarche (APA, 2013). Amenorrhea is the lack of menstruation. Menarche is the first menstruation.

Amenorrhea
Lack of menstruation

Menarche
First menstruation

Anorexia Nervosa

When you see this woman, what is your social response? In other words, if she told you she was fat, what would you say?

© Den Rise/Shutterstock.com

Would you tell her "no way, you are not fat" or some version of this? Would thoughts of "Are you serious?", "You need to gain weight," or some other thoughts related to surprise or shock come to mind? The importance of knowing your social response may be helpful in understanding people who suffer with anorexia nervosa. If you tell someone with anorexia nervosa that she or he is not fat, then they may not believe you and subsequently dismiss your opinion. Remember that body perception may lead someone to believe they are larger than they are and they also are fearful of becoming fat. Thus, your social response is small granule compared to the pre-existing, crystallized belief. For example, think about gravity. If someone holds an object in the air and then releases it, what would you expect to happen? You would expect it to fall down. The concept of gravity is crystallized strongly within you over years of experience. If the object did not fall, then what would you think? You still probably would not renounce gravity but rather some unknown magician trick playing with the concept of gravity and perception. Hence, you would probably dismiss the one case of the object not falling. Much like this example, the beliefs held by people with anorexia may be deeply held that offering one piece of evidence contrary to a belief, such as saying you are not fat, may be easily dismissed. The beliefs of not being thin, not being thin enough, and fear of being fat may be deeply held and reinforced from society and media over time. Thus, individuals may persistently not recognize the seriousness of their low body weight (APA, 2013).

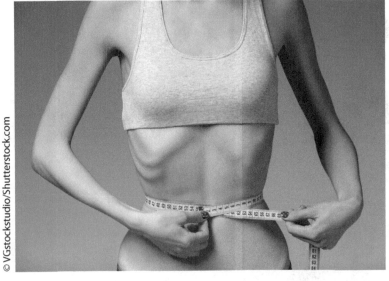

© VGstockstudio/Shutterstock.com

Anorexia nervosa consists of much more than not eating. The cultural and psychological mechanisms influencing eating disorders along with the 4 Fs paint the picture of how eating behaviors and particular beliefs may lead to a disorder. One of the defining characteristics of anorexia nervosa is that individuals have significantly low body weight or less than minimally normal (APA, 2013). Beliefs of not being thin enough and fear of being fat may influence eating behaviors that lead to being significantly underweight. Think back to the case of Fanny. She was underweight with her BMI of 16.7 kg/m^2, then she continued to lose weight leading to being more severely underweight. The DSM-5 provides severity specifiers for anorexia nervosa (see diagnostic criteria below; APA, 2013). Fanny had moderate severity of anorexia nervosa and then as she continued to lose weight, her severity fell on the border of severe and extreme.

DSM-5 CRITERIA FOR ANOREXIA NERVOSA

DIAGNOSTIC CRITERIA

A. Restriction of energy intake relative to requirements, leading to a significantly low body weight in the context of age, sex, developmental trajectory, and physical health. *Significantly low weight* is defined as a weight that is less than minimally normal, or, for children and adolescents, less than that minimally expected.

B. Intense fear of gaining weight or of becoming fat, or persistent behavior that interferes with weight gain, even though at a significantly low weight.

C. Disturbance in the way in which one's body weight or shape is experienced, undue influence of body weight or shape on self-evaluation, or persistent lack of recognition of the seriousness of the current low body weight.

Coding note: The ICD-9-CM code for anorexia nervosa is **307.1,** which is assigned regardless of the subtype. The ICD-10-CM code depends on the subtype (see below).

Specify whether:

(F50.01) Restricting type: During the last 3 months, the individual has not engaged in recurrent episodes of binge eating or purging behavior (i.e., self-induced vomiting or the misuse of laxatives, diuretics, or enemas). This subtype describes presentations in which weight loss is accomplished primarily through dieting, fasting, and/or excessive exercise.

(F50.02) Binge-eating/purging type: During the last 3 months, the individual has engaged in recurrent episodes of binge eating or purging behavior (i.e., self-induced vomiting or the misuse of laxatives, diuretics, or enemas).

Specify if:

In partial remission: After full criteria for anorexia nervosa were previously met, Criterion A (low body weight) has not been met for a sustained period, but either Criterion B (intense fear of gaining weight or becoming fat or behavior that interferes with weight gain) or Criterion C (disturbances in self-perception of weight and shape) is still met.

In full remission: After full criteria for anorexia nervosa were previously met, none of the criteria have been met for a sustained period of time.

Specify current severity:

The minimum level of severity is based, for adults, on current body mass index (BMI) (see below) or, for children and adolescents, on BMI percentile. The ranges below are derived from World Health Organization categories for thinness in adults; for children and adolescents, corresponding BMI percentiles should be used. The level of severity may be increased to reflect clinical symptoms, the degree of functional disability, and the need for supervision.

Mild: BMI $\geq$ 17 kg/m^2

Moderate: BMI 16–16.99 kg/m^2

Severe: BMI 15–15.99 kg/m^2

Extreme: BMI < 15 kg/m^2

Myths in Movies

THIN

The documentary film *Thin* portrays several patients, who suffer from eating disorders, at an inpatient treatment facility. The documentary was created to shed light on the struggles of recovery and issues faced by people with eating disorders. Three of the four individuals that the film focused on were diagnosed with anorexia nervosa. Shelly, Polly, and Brittany were the main women filmed, who all had anorexia nervosa. How do you think this film might shape perceptions of eating disorders?

An actor from *Thin*

Thin provides a glimpse into severe eating disorders that occur within an inpatient setting. Themes of food aversion, body image, and control are evidenced in watching the film. Some scenes in the film showed that patients saw some food as aversive or with disinterest. One scene depicts a person who has an aversion to a nutritional drink supplement. If you listen to the individuals throughout the film you will hear mention of control, in that many of the individuals discuss being in control when restricting food and losing weight. The women also discuss desires to be thin and fears of gaining weight. The women also shared that they had previous suicide attempts or suicide ideation. For the complete diagnostic criteria, refer to the DSM-5. As you look over the diagnostic criteria, think about the 4 Fs and how these related to the case of Fanny.

Myths in Movies

TO THE BONE

A scene from *To the Bone*

To the Bone is a film that is themed around eating disorders, specifically focusing on a young woman, Collins, who has anorexia nervosa. Collins struggles with anorexia nervosa, a will to live, and family problems. Through the film she checks into a group residential treatment facility with some unconventional methods. Toward the end of the movie, the main character's mother treats her as a baby and feeds her with a bottle, as a means of overcoming some past interpersonal rift. Lastly, the movie ends with imagery that leads to an epiphany, seemingly to treat the character. So, how might this film depict anorexia?

Bulimia Nervosa

Think of Thanksgiving. If you celebrate Thanksgiving, what do you typically do? What is the first word that comes to mind? Food, right? Many people associate Thanksgiving with food. It seems to have become more of a holiday of feasting. People prepare a plethora of favorite dishes including turkey, stuffing, potatoes (and sweet potatoes), rolls, green bean casserole, and the pies. After your meal, or maybe even before your meal, you consume a slice of pie or many slices of several pies. You may have pecan pie, pumpkin pie, buttermilk pie, coconut crème pie, and apple pie. Many people may eat much more on Thanksgiving than a typical day. You may eat so much that you are stuffed and even have to loosen your belt, unbutton your jeans, or even change into your expandable

pants or pajamas. This example of eating behavior best illustrates a binge episode. Following the big Thanksgiving feast, some people may rethink their eating behaviors and even say, "I shouldn't have had that second (or third) piece of pie." In fact, people may feel guilty about the large quantity of food and calories consumed. This is one of the reasons that running events, such as turkey trots, are hosted the day after Thanksgiving.

So, what does this have to do with bulimia nervosa? Does this mean that you have an eating disorder? No! Remember that the 4 Fs help you check behaviors to determine if they are pathological. The reference to Thanksgiving eating behaviors, or other contexts where you may binge eat, such as buffets, is simply to help you connect with and understand some components of bulimia nervosa. People who have bulimia nervosa are not "crazy" and not too distant from behaviors and thoughts you may have experienced (i.e., Thanksgiving eating).

When you think about a Thanksgiving dinner or going to a buffet you may deviate from a normal diet and feel a lack of control, in that you are going to eat whatever you want. You may preemptively give yourself permission to not regulate how much you eat and eat as much as you want or more. People who experience symptoms of bulimia nervosa will have a sense of lack of control when binge eating (APA, 2013). If people in your life, magazines, social media, and film convey messages of how you are to look and eat, then you are implicitly being told you need to control your weight and eating. Thus, a binge episode directly defies these messages and a person may feel a lack of control. However, the binge-eating behavior is not usually a public display. The binge eating may be done in secrecy or privacy.

In revisiting the documentary film discussed previously, titled *Thin*, one of the women filmed, Alisa, discussed how a pediatrician had told her mother that her mother needed to control her weight at the age of 7. The message stuck with Alisa as she was subsequently put on a diet. Alisa discussed one of her binges, in which she drove to several fast-food restaurants and a grocery store to purchase a variety of food. She later brought the food home and engaged in a binge episode, eating much of the food until she was physically hurting. Following the binge, she reported vomiting and then binging again until all the food was gone.

The guilt or remorse following a large Thanksgiving dinner may influence subsequent behaviors, such as working out harder the next day or running a 5k. Some people may even run prior to Thanksgiving, anticipating a large meal. The guilt or remorse you feel that influences your behaviors is similar to bulimia nervosa. Binge eating is followed by recurrent compensatory behaviors that prevent weight gain (APA, 2013). Some of these purging behaviors involve self-induced vomiting, using diuretics, laxatives, and excessive exercise (APA, 2013).

The difference between Thanksgiving eating behaviors and bulimia nervosa involves the 4 Fs and the DSM-5 diagnostic criteria. Thanksgiving eating rituals occur once per year; individuals with bulimia nervosa have recurrent binge episodes and compensatory behaviors once a week for at least 3 months (APA, 2013).

DSM-5 CRITERIA FOR BULIMIA NERVOSA

DIAGNOSTIC CRITERIA

A. Recurrent episodes of binge eating. An episode of binge eating is characterized by both of the following:

1. Eating, in a discrete period of time (e.g., within any 2-hour period), an amount of food that is definitely larger than what most individuals would eat in a similar period of time under similar circumstances.

2. A sense of lack of control over eating during the episode (e.g., a feeling that one cannot stop eating or control what or how much one is eating).

B.   Recurrent inappropriate compensatory behaviors in order to prevent weight gain, such as self-induced vomiting; misuse of laxatives, diuretics, or other medications; fasting; or excessive exercise.

C.   The binge eating and inappropriate compensatory behaviors both occur, on average, at least once a week for 3 months.

D.   Self-evaluation is unduly influenced by body shape and weight.

E.   The disturbance does not occur exclusively during episodes of anorexia nervosa.

Specify if:

In partial remission: After full criteria for bulimia nervosa were previously met, some, but not all, of the criteria have been met for a sustained period of time.

In full remission: After full criteria for bulimia nervosa were previously met, none of the criteria have been met for a sustained period of time.

Specify current severity:

The minimum level of severity is based on the frequency of inappropriate compensatory behaviors (see below). The level of severity may be increased to reflect other symptoms and the degree of functional disability.

Mild: An average of 1–3 episodes of inappropriate compensatory behaviors per week.

Moderate: An average of 4–7 episodes of inappropriate compensatory behaviors per week.

Severe: An average of 8–13 episodes of inappropriate compensatory behaviors per week.

Extreme: An average of 14 or more episodes of inappropriate compensatory behaviors per week.

Reprinted with permission from the *Diagnostic and Statistical Manual of Mental Disorders*, Fifth Edition, (Copyright 2013). American Psychiatric Association.

Other Feeding and Eating Disorders

Eating ice tastes really good when it is paired with colorful sugary liquids. Usually, snow cones are a nice summer treat. Did you know that eating ice, without sugar or in the form of a snow cone may be a form of psychopathology? Poulakou-Rebelakou and colleagues (2015) suggested that Byzantine emperor Theophilus is the first case of pagophagia, eating snow and ice, which is considered a form of pica. Pica involves eating nonnutritive food and may begin at any stage across the life span with childhood onset being the most common stage of onset (APA, 2013). Pica may involve eating numerous nonnutritive substances, such as dirt, soap, coffee grounds, glue, paper, and toothpaste (Mills, 2007). Pica can be present in some cases of pregnancy (APA, 2013; Mills, 2007). Remember, that merely ingesting nonnutritive substances does not qualify you for having a disorder. You may

Pagophagia

Eating snow and ice

© Aleph Studio/Shutterstock.com

Rumination

Spitting out,
re-chewing, or
re-swallowing food

have tried to eat soap once when you were a toddler or you ate some glue in grade school. These behaviors do not mean you have pica. The persistence in eating nonnutritive food, inappropriate for the developmental level, at a frequency higher than socially normative and causing some pain or fatality may lead to disorder. Sometimes pica and rumination disorder are found to occur with individuals who have an intellectual disability (APA, 2013).

Rumination disorder involves repetitively regurgitating food over a period of at least 1 month (APA, 2013). Sometimes, these behaviors are found among other eating disorders. In the film *Thin*, Brittany discussed how she and her mother engaged in what they called chew-and-spit. She stated that they would buy candy, chew it, and spit it out to avoid the calories. She stated that at the time she did this with her mother, she thought it was a fun activity. Rumination may involve spitting out food, but may also include re-chewing or re-swallowing food (APA, 2013).

Avoidant/restrictive food intake disorder consists of disinterest in food or avoiding food. The disorder may lead to weight loss, lack of nutrition, needing nutritional supplements, or interfering with social functioning (APA, 2013). The symptoms do not occur during the course of anorexia nervosa or bulimia nervosa (APA, 2013). The onset of avoidant/restrictive food intake disorder is usually in infancy or early childhood (APA, 2013). If the symptoms occur in infancy, then it may affect sleep and difficulty consoling a child (APA, 2013).

Binge-eating disorder involves recurrent episodes of binge eating and these behaviors are not associated with compensatory behaviors found in bulimia nervosa (APA, 2013). Binge-eating disorder usually occurs in people who range in weight from normative to overweight and those who are obese (APA, 2013). Though binge-eating disorder may occur in obese individuals, most obese individuals do not engage in recurrent binge eating (APA, 2013).

Treatment for Eating Disorders

One particular individual who had an eating disorder for 20 years, Jenni Schaefer, and her therapist, Thom Rutledge, wrote about their treatment in their book titled *Life Without Ed* (Schaefer & Rutledge, 2004). They drew the analogy of Jenni's eating disorder as a distinct person, Ed (for eating disorder), and her treatment was one of involving a relational divorce from her relationship with her eating disorder, Ed. Jenni reported a successful treatment that she and her therapist hoped to pass along to many others who suffer from eating disorders.

Treatment for eating disorders has brought controversy and challenge. Banker and Klump (2010) discussed literature suggesting the clinical psychology has neglected science in the practice of treating eating disorders. Thus, Banker and Klump reviewed the science-practice gap and suggested that to remedy the gap there are strategies and action plans developed by the AED (www.aedweb.org). Among these strategies, Banker and Klump suggested joining research-practice networks, accessing treatment research, utilizing case studies in practice for research, and incorporating research and treatment outcome into practice.

With the movement to bridge the science-research gap in eating disorders, the "three-legged stool" of evidence-based practice has been suggested (Peterson et al., 2016; Spring, 2007). The three legs refer to best available "research, clinical expertise, and patients" values and preferences (Peterson et al., 2016; Spring, 2007).

Biological Treatment of Eating Disorders

Due to eating disorders involving eating behavior and nutritional deficits, a number of biological treatments are aimed at restoring nutritional balance. It has been suggested that treatment for anorexia nervosa involves two stages: weight restoration and psychotherapy (Garner & Bemis, 1985). Many pathophysiological effects can be ameliorated through improving nutrition (Treasure et al., 2010). Low BMI and diminished nutritional levels should be treated slowly with orally administered food supplements that contain multivitamins and multiminerals and refeeding procedures suggested by the guidelines from the United Kingdom's National Institute for Health and Clinical Excellence (NICE, 2006; Treasure et al., 2010).

Some biological treatments have been used and assessed for eating disorders. Pharmacological treatments have included various antidepressants, antipsychotics, zinc, drugs for osteoporosis/osteopenia, anticonvulsants, appetited suppressors, and obesity drugs (see Treasure et al., 2010). For anorexia nervosa, "no strong evidence lends support to drug treatment either in acute or maintenance phases of the illness" (Treasure et al., 2010, p. 588). Concerning bulimia nervosa and binge-eating disorder there is evidence that pharmacotherapy with antidepressants is strong for the former and moderate for the latter (Treasure et al., 2010). However, tricyclics or fluoxetine combined with cognitive behavioral therapy (CBT) does not significantly add to the effects of CBT. Anticonvulsants and obesity drugs reveal moderate effectiveness for treating binge-eating disorder (Treasure et al., 2010).

Psychological Treatment of Eating Disorders

Various psychological treatments for eating disorders exist. Division 12 of the American Psychological Association has identified research-based psychological treatments for eating disorders and obesity (see APA Presidential Task Force on Evidence-Based Practice, 2006). Table 11.1 displays various psychological treatments from Division 12 (APA Presidential Task Force on Evidence-Based Practice, 2006; Chambless et al., 1998; Loeb, 2013). Even though obesity is not a disorder, Division 12 has included research for individuals who seek treatment with obesity.

Empirically supported treatments are only good if they are implemented. Some of the difficulties that emerge from the research-practice gap with eating disorders (Banker & Klump, 2010) are that only a small minority use or draw from empirically validated treatment (Haas & Clopton, 2003; Tobin et al., 2007). Haas and Clopton found that only 16.9% definitely used empirically supported treatments for eating disorders. Cognitive behavioral therapy seeks to behaviorally work with clients' eating behaviors and identify and challenge dysfunctional thinking related to worth, body image, weight, and control.

TABLE 11.1   2015 EST Status: Empirically Supported Psychological Treatments for Eating Disorders and Obesity

Psychological Treatment	Anorexia Nervosa	Bulimia Nervosa	Binge-Eating Disorder	Obesity and Pediatric Overweight
Cognitive Behavioral Therapy	Modest research support for post-hospitalization relapse prevention/ Controversial for acute weight gain	Strong	Strong	
Family-Based Treatment	Strong	Modest		
Interpersonal Psychotherapy		Strong	Strong	
Healthy-Weight Program		Controversial		
Behavioral Weight Loss Treatment				Strong

*Table based on information from APA Presidential Task Force on Evidence-Based Practice (2006).

Conclusion

Now you are more equipped to challenge myths about eating disorders and maybe even connect with the humanity in eating disorders. People with eating disorders do eat, they are not all thin, and men are affected as well as women. You are also more aware of how your social responses related to weight and body image of someone with anorexia nervosa may be dismissed or discredited due to pervasive and fixed beliefs. Although eating disorders may have numerous detrimental consequences, there are a number of successful empirically supported treatments. It is important that therapists use these treatments and clients who have an eating disorder seek these treatments out.

CHAPTER REVIEW

QUESTIONS

1. What influences the development of eating disorders? How do cultural influences play a role?

2. What are some research methods that have been used to look at body image and body perception?

3. What are some risks (fatal) for eating disorders?

4. How is anorexia nervosa different from bulimia nervosa?

5. What might telling someone with anorexia nervosa "you are not fat" do?

6. What is eating nonnutritive food referred to as?

KEY TERMS

Bulimia Nervosa

Anorexia Nervosa

Purging

Binge Eating

Pica

Amenorrhea

Menarche

Pagophagia

Rumination

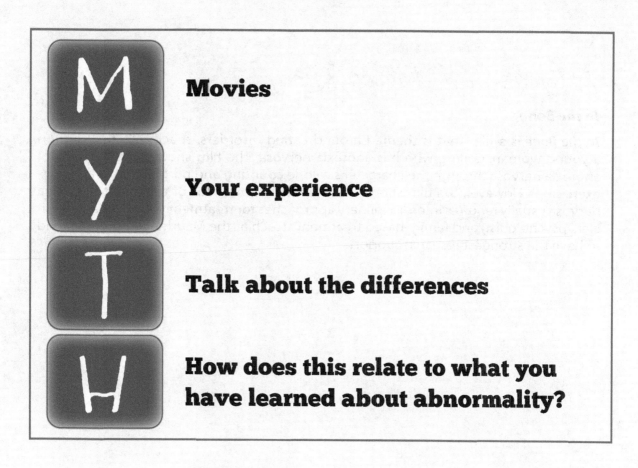

Movies

Your experience

Talk about the differences

How does this relate to what you have learned about abnormality?

Myths in Movies Recap

Thin

Overall, the film *Thin* does a great job portraying many aspects of eating disorders. The documentary also shows the interdisciplinary nature of inpatient treatment. However, it does not capture all severities of eating disorders. *Thin* primarily focuses on inpatient treatment, while many people with eating disorders may present with less severe symptoms or may not be admitted into inpatient facilities. The film also did not capture aspects of fatality. Polly completed suicide approximately 2 years after the film (Nelson, 2008). Lastly, the film may promote a belief that psychiatric hospitals or impatient settings are not helpful (Wedding & Niemiec, 2014).

Myths in Movies Recap

To the Bone

To the Bone is a film that is themed around eating disorders, specifically focusing on a young woman, Collins, who has anorexia nervosa. The film shows some aspects of anorexia nervosa through the character's calorie counting and purging behaviors (e.g., exercising). However, the film shows unconventional methods of treatment. Anorexia nervosa usually requires interdisciplinary approaches for treatment (i.e., dietitian, physician, psychologist) and family-based treatments (such as the Maudsley Approach) tend to have the strongest research support.

CHAPTER TWELVE

SLEEP DISORDERS

▶ Narcolepsy
▶ Other Sleep-Wake Disorders
▶ Treatment for Sleep Disorders

The Value of Sleep

"I will sleep when I'm dead" is a common phrase people say. How many times have you ever said or heard someone say this? This phrase communicates a value that you hold about sleep. The value is, simply, that sleep is unimportant. You need sleep to live and function in day-to-day living. In fact, several studies discovered that total sleep deprivation in rats led to death within 11 to 32 days (Everson et al., 1989; Rechtschaffen et al., 1989).

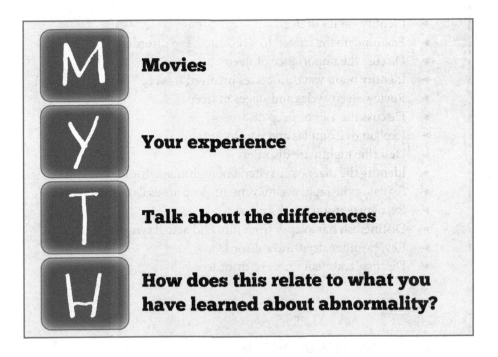

Sleep is a basic physiological need, along with food, water, and oxygen (Maslow, 1943). There are accounts of people, such as Mahatma Gandhi, fasting for 21 days and others fasting for up to 40 days (International Business Times, 2012; Lieberson, 2004). Thus, in some cases you can survive longer without food than without sleep. You can definitely live longer without achievement than without sleep (Maslow, 1943). Either way, you probably have never said nor heard someone say "I will eat when I die" or "I will work harder when I die."

© pathdoc/Shutterstock.com

The phrase "I will sleep when I am dead" communicates a value about sleep, that it is unimportant. You spend one fifth to one third of your life sleeping though it does not get the same attention as other activities. You are sure to plan and discuss several meals you eat throughout the day and you might sacrifice sleep to achieve work or educational goals. Thus, sleep is important but often undervalued. Some cities even pride themselves on productivity over sleep. New York City is sometimes referred to as the city that never sleeps. Even when you acknowledge the importance of sleep your behaviors may indicate otherwise. You may say "I think sleep is important" or "I want to sleep, right now," yet you may rarely sleep or get the full restful sleep you need.

Myths in Movies

NIGHTMARE ON ELM STREET

Along with your values of sleep, you may develop various beliefs about sleep and sleep disorders. Some of these beliefs may be influenced by films. The classic horror film, *Nightmare on Elm Street*, depicts the dangers of falling asleep and nightmares becoming fatal realities. *Come Back to Me* is another thriller-killer movie that associates night terrors with someone who kills and rapes people only to revive them. *Inception* is a film that portrays dream states and various levels of consciousness. Other sleep themed or portrayed movies include: *Insomnia, Lost in Translation*, and *The Machinist* (Wedding, Boyd, & Niemiec, 2005). When thinking about sleep disorders think about the movies and other sources of influence that have shaped your thoughts about sleep and sleep disorders.

© New Line Cinema/Photofest

Numerous beliefs and myths are found when discussing sleeping behaviors and sleep disorders. Some of the numerous myths identified in literature include (Ancoli-Israel, 1997; Breus, 2016; Lilienfeld et al., 2010; National Sleep Foundation, 2016):

▶ Watching movies on your television, computer, tablets, or phones in your bed will help you relax and fall asleep
▶ "Counting sheep" helps you fall asleep
▶ Having a glass of wine or a scotch helps you sleep
▶ Dreams only last a few seconds
▶ Drinking caffeine during the day does not affect you at night
▶ You can learn new information while sleeping
▶ Many people do not ever dream
▶ Dreaming about death leads to actual death
▶ Your brain "rests" during sleep
▶ Awaking someone who is sleepwalking is dangerous
▶ Older adults need less sleep

Some of these myths will be addressed in this chapter. However, there are many sources that contain a variety of myths about sleep and sleep disorders. For a more comprehensive list of myths about sleep disorders, look at these sources. Lilienfeld and colleagues' (2010) *50 Great Myths of Popular Psychology: Shattering Widespread Misconceptions about Human Behavior* provides many more examples of myths of sleep and consciousness. The National Sleep Foundation (2016) also lists several myths and facts about sleep and sleep disorders.

Sleep: Importance and Cycles

"Early to bed and early to rise makes a man healthy, wealthy, and wise"

—Benjamin Franklin

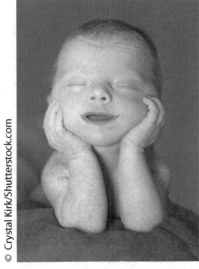

© Crystal Kirk/Shutterstock.com

Many people also state that they want to sleep like a baby. It is unclear why you may want to wake up every 1½–3 hours throughout the night. A better phrase may be to "sleep like a husband" because they seem to sleep right through the newborns who wake up crying every few hours. Maybe the emphasis is not on the intervals a baby sleeps but the overall duration, as babies sleep about 16 hours per day (Ferber, 2006). Or maybe adults mean that they want to sleep in fetal position. Regardless of your sleeping position, sleep is important and its deprivation may lead to death (Everson et al., 1989; Rechtschaffen, Bergmann, et al., 1989). Further, sleep is universal and different patterns of sleep

TABLE 12.1   Recommended Hours of Sleep Throughout the Stages of Life

Stage	Hours of Sleep
Newborns (0–3 months)	14–17
Infants (4–11 months)	12–15
Toddlers (1–2 years)	11–14
Preschoolers (3–5 years)	10–13
School-Aged Children (6–13 years)	9–11
Teenagers (14–17 years)	8–10
Young Adults (18–25 years)	7–9
Adults (26–64 years)	7–9
Older Adults (65 years or more)	7–8

*Table based on information from Hirshkowitz, Whiton, and colleagues (2015).

© Twin Design/Shutterstock.com

occur for humans across the life span (Hirshkowitz, Moore, & Minhoto, 1997).

Table 12.1 displays the sleep that people, at different developmental stages, typically get in a day. Infants will sleep twice as much as adults (Hirshkowitz, Moore, & Minhoto, 1997), though it may not always feel like it. Regarding older adults, one myth that is pervasive is that they need less sleep (Ancoli-Israel, 1997). Ancoli-Israel suggested that older adults do not necessarily need less sleep but that the ability for restorative sleep decreases with age. The overall sleep time decreases throughout the life span and various sleep stages change (Hirshkowitz, Moore, & Minhoto, 1997).

Various assumptions and speculations have been made about the nature and function of sleep but the reasons for sleeping, the causes of sleep, and purpose remain not completely understood (Ferber, 2006). We do know that it is vital for life (Hirshkowitz, Moore, & Minhoto, 1997). Though much is still to be learned about the science of sleep, there have been several theories proposed (Hirshkowitz, Moore, & Minhoto, 1997). The three major theories of sleep are the adaptive theory, energy conservation theory, and restorative theory of sleep (see Hirshkowitz, Moore, & Minhoto, 1997; Zepelin & Rechtschaffen, 1974). These theories posit that sleep is adaptive for survival and differs between species, metabolic rates are related to sleep duration, and sleep restores functioning (respectively; Hirshkowitz, Moore, & Minhoto, 1997).

Brain Waves. Another myth about sleep is that you are unconscious or that your brain shuts down during sleep. Sleep is an active process even though there is behavioral inactivity (Hirshkowitz, Moore, & Minhoto, 1997). Things are happening during sleep. Though you may be in a lower level of consciousness, you are not unconscious. For example, do you use an alarm clock? If an alarm clock wakes you up (even if it is temporarily for you to hit snooze several more times), then this reveals that you are conscious enough to wake when hearing this sound. If you were unconscious, then an alarm would do nothing. Our brain emits various waves depending on the stage of wakefulness or sleep (see Figure 12.1).

Brain waves are measured by electroencephalography (EEG). Activity of EEG is displayed in wave frequency and wave amplitude (Hirshkowitz, Moore, & Minhoto, 1997). Wave frequency is the number of

Electroencephalography

A measurement of brain electrical activity through the use of electrodes

Wave Frequency

The number of times the wave appears in a given point in time

Wave Amplitude

The height of the wave

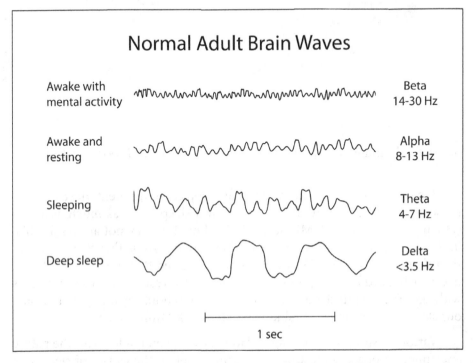

FIGURE 12. 1   Wake-Sleep Adult Brain Waves
© Alila Medical Media/Shutterstock.com

times the wave appears in a given point in time and the wave amplitude is the height of the wave (Hirshkowitz, Moore, & Minhoto, 1997). Beta waves are associated with typical, daily wakeful activity. In the figure above, you can see that beta waves have a higher frequency and lesser amplitude. When you are resting and awake you may be experiencing alpha waves. Alpha rhythm is the EEG activity associated with resting wakefulness. Alpha waves are experienced when you are awake and your eyes are closed. Imagine reclining in a chair after a long day and closing your eyes. This relaxed feeling is the alpha rhythm, the best! Delta waves are usually associated with deep sleep. These waves have greater amplitude and lower frequency.

Alpha Rhythm

EEG activity associated with resting wakefulness

A myth about sleep that was listed in the beginning of this chapter was that you can learn new information while you are sleeping (Lilienfeld et al., 2010). Though your brain is active during sleep, various brain waves relate to the levels of consciousness and sleep. One of the most common ways that people attempt to do this is through playing audio of information while sleeping (Lilienfeld et al., 2010). However, Lilienfeld and colleagues discussed confounds in research that led to this belief, in that the audio may have wakened participants in research and discussed how controlled studies do not yield results of sleep-assisted learning. Thus, being more alert and aware allows for the retention of information and learning.

Sleep Cycle. In 1962 a geologist by the name of Michel Siffre decided to live underground in Midnight Cave, Texas (Foer & Siffre, 2008). He stayed there in isolation, with no clock, calendar, or sun for 2 months with the goal of exploring natural human rhythms (Foer & Siffre, 2008). Siffre discovered numerous findings related to dreaming and sleep and how it affected humans. One specific finding was that longer days led to shorter reaction times during subsequent wakeful cycles (Foer & Siffre, 2008). Siffre's experiments also tapped into aspects of circadian rhythms. Circadian rhythm is a biological bodily cycle that approaches geophysical cycles of day and night (Campbell, 1997). Siffre found that sleep/wake cycles were about 24 hours and 30 minutes (Foer & Siffre, 2008).

Circadian Rhythms

Biological bodily cycle

A polysomnograph is a complete picture of a person's sleep record during a main sleep period by using EEG, eye movement, and chin muscle measurements (Hirshkowitz, Moore, & Minhoto, 1997). Standards for recording and classifying sleep stages can be found in Rechtschaffen and Kales's (1968) manual titled *A Manual of Standardized Terminology, Techniques and Scoring System for Sleep Stages of Human Subjects* (see Hirshkowitz, Moore, & Minhoto, 1997). Sleep cycles ebb and flow between stages of deep sleep and rapid eye movement sleep (see Figure 12.2).

Polysomnograph

A complete picture of a person's sleep record during a main sleep period

Rapid eye movement (REM) sleep involves saccadic eye movements and a loss of voluntary muscle tone and movement (Hirshkowitz, Moore, & Minhoto, 1997). Dreaming is also associated with REM sleep (Aserinsky & Kleitman, 1953). Delta waves are the slow wave sleep usually found within stages three and four of the sleep cycle (Hirshkowitz, Moore, & Minhoto, 1997). A working knowledge of sleep waves and sleep cycles is imperative to

Rapid Eye Movement

A sleep stage involving saccadic eye movements

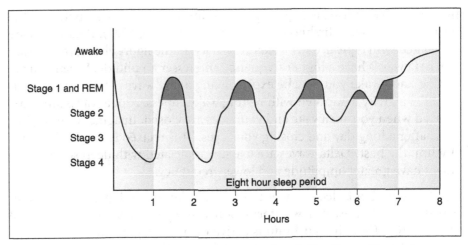

FIGURE 12.2 Sleep Cycles for an Eight-Hour Period
© Blamb/Shutterstock.com

understand sleep disorders and how sleep may affect function, feeling pain, and fatality. Assessing a person's sleep habits are highly important. Sleep may affect a person's functioning or a disorder that may affect a person's sleep.

The 4 Fs of Sleep Disorders

While falling asleep during a lecture may certainly cause pain (usually for the professor and not the student), this is not pathological. Pulling an all-nighter, having nightmares, and waking up at night do not necessarily indi-

© wavebreakmedia/Shutterstock.com

cate that you have a sleep disorder. The 4 Fs provide criteria that reveal how various types and frequencies of sleeping behaviors may affect functioning, feeling pain, and fatality.

Frequency

A—Amount of Time: The amount of time by which sleeping behavior is affected matters. Insomnia disorder, hypersomnolence disorder, also known as excessive sleepiness, and narcolepsy symptoms occur for at least 3 nights per week and for at least 3 months (APA, 2013). If an individual displays cataplexy with narcolepsy, then it must be present at least a few times per month (APA, 2013). Non-rapid eye movement sleep arousal disorders involve repeated episodes of sleepwalking or sleep terrors lasting a few minutes usually but can last up to an hour (APA, 2013). The amount of time that nightmare disorders occur is specified as either acute (1 month or less), subacute (more than 1 month and less than 6 months), and persistent (6 months or greater; APA, 2013).

B—Behavior: Insomnia involves a low frequency or quality of sleep (APA, 2013). Insomnia also consists of often having difficulties going to sleep or frequently waking up throughout the night (APA, 2013). Hypersomnolence disorder is a high frequency of sleepiness occurring after sleeping for a full cycle (APA, 2013). Narcolepsy involves high frequency of sleeping, napping, or wanting to sleep throughout the day (APA, 2013). Non-rapid eye movement sleep arousal disorders involve repeated episodes of sleepwalking or sleep terrors lasting a few minutes usually but can last up to an hour (APA, 2013). Non-rapid eye movement sleep arousal disorder involves repeated or frequent incomplete awakening from sleep, in the form of sleepwalking or sleep terrors (APA, 2013). The frequency of nightmares is specified by a severity indicator of mild (less than one per week on average), moderate (one or more a week but not nightly), and severe (nightly episodes; APA, 2013).

C—Curve: Approximately 100% of people sleep. Dr. Richard Ferber (2006), a director of the Center for Pediatric Sleep Disorders at the Children's Hospital in Boston, stated from early on, most children have the ability to sleep well. A smaller percentage of people develop sleeping disorders. Insomnia involves a low frequency or quality of sleep (APA, 2013). Insomnia also consists of often having difficulties going to sleep or frequently waking up throughout the night (APA, 2013). Hypersomnolence disorder is a high frequency of sleepiness occurring after sleeping for a full cycle (APA, 2013). Narcolepsy involves high frequency of sleeping, napping, or wanting to sleep throughout the day (APA, 2013). Non-rapid eye movement sleep arousal disorders involve repeated episodes of sleepwalking or sleep terrors lasting a few minutes usually but can last up to an hour (APA, 2013). Non-rapid eye movement sleep arousal disorders are common, with 10 to 30% of children sleepwalking once, 2 to 3% sleepwalking often, and 1 to 7% of

Hypersomnolence Disorder

Excessive sleepiness after getting a main sleep period of at least seven hours

adults sleepwalking (APA, 2013). However, sleepwalking disorder prevalence rate occurs in 1 to 5% (APA, 2013). Prevalence rates for sleep terrors are not known (APA, 2013). However, sleep terror episodes occur in 36.9% for 18-month-old children, 19.7% for 30-month-old children, and 2.2% in adults (APA, 2013). Approximately 1.3 to 3.9% of parents report that their children have nightmares often or always (APA, 2013). The prevalence for adults who have nightmares monthly is 6% and frequent nightmares occur in 1 to 2% of adults (APA, 2013).

The Good News: Many organizations realize the impact of sleep on daily living and have responded by providing resources to help people better understand sleep and increase healthy sleeping behaviors. The American Psychological Association's Division of Health Psychology (Division 38) along with editors Pressman and Orr (1997) published a comprehensive work, titled *Understanding sleep: The evaluation and treatment of sleep disorders*. This book is aimed to advance understanding and practice related to sleep and health. Other organizations, such as the the National Center on Sleep Disorders Research, function to promote research, training, technology transfer, and coordination of efforts related to sleep disorders (http://www.nhlbi.nih.gov/about/org/ncsdr/).

Function

If you have ever had a long, sleepless night, then you are well aware of the impact it can have on your functioning. Disrupting sleep cycles or not getting enough quality sleep can affect multiple areas of your life. As previously mentioned, you need sleep to function. Sleep disorders may affect areas of interpersonal, occupational, social, and educational functioning (APA, 2013).

Did you know that a lack of sleep can impair functioning similarly to that of alcohol? One study recruited 39 subjects to compare responses on several cognitive performance measures between conditions of alcohol and sleep deprivation (Williamson & Feyer, 2000). All subjects underwent both conditions, alcohol consumption and sleep deprivation, with the order assigned being counterbalanced, meaning that one group consumed alcohol first and the other group was sleep-deprived first (Williamson & Feyer, 2000). The measures included Mackworth clock, simple reaction time, tracking, dual task, symbol digit test, spatial memory search, memory and search test, and grammatical reasoning (Williamson & Feyer, 2000). The researchers found that performance when people were deprived of sleep for 16.91 to 18.55 hours was the same or worse compared to performance when blood alcohol concentration (BAC) was 0.05% (Williamson & Feyer, 2000). Also, performance at 17.74 and 19.65 hours of wakefulness was similar to that when BAC was 0.1% (Williamson & Feyer, 2000).

The similarities between alcohol and sleep deprivation are noteworthy due to the unbalanced attention with less consideration to the effects of sleep deprivation. There is much attention to the effects of drinking on driving, with good reason. Driving with a BAC that ranges between those in the Williamson and Feyer (2000) study is usually considered illegal in many states. While the effects of alcohol on driving are grave, there appears to be less awareness of the effects of sleep deprivation on driving. An estimated 4% of drivers have reported falling asleep while driving within the last month of being asked (Wheaton et al., 2014). Even drowsy driving may impair functioning and lead to automobile accidents. Tefft and the AAA Foundation for Traffic Safety (2014) analyzed data of 21,292 crashes in the United States from 2009–2013. Results indicated that 6% of all crashes involved a driver who was drowsy. Some sleep disorders, such as obstructive sleep apnea hypopnea have a sevenfold higher risk of automobile crashes (APA, 2013). Thus, sleep deprivation appears to have dire effects on driving, similar to that of drinking and driving. Due to these effects, eight states have laws regarding driver fatigue and 19 states require that police officers receive training over risks related to driver fatigue (Clemmitt, 2010).

Sleep deprivation can also affect other areas of cognitive functioning. Ross (1965) reported a case of a 17-year-old male who had been sleep-deprived for 264 hours (11 days). Some of what the patient had experienced included irritability, visual misperceptions, temporal disorientation, cognitive disorganization, a brief delusional episode, and difficulty speaking (Ross, 1965). After 264 hours the patient slept for almost 15 hours and was healthy afterward (Ross, 1965).

There are numerous other effects on functioning that result from sleep disorders. A number of sleep disorders, including insomnia disorder, hypersomnolence, and nightmare disorder can lead to irritability, decreased attention span, memory deficits, and impaired concentration (APA, 2013). Chronic symptoms of insomnia may lead to myocardial infarction, hypertension, major depression, and missing work or not functioning productively (APA, 2013). Individuals with narcolepsy often have impaired functioning with driving and working (APA, 2013).

Feeling Pain

People who have poor quality of sleep or low quantity do not typically like the effects and may desire more restful sleep. People who suffer from chronic symptoms of insomnia, obstructive sleep apnea hypopnea, and restless legs syndrome may have a reduced quality of life (APA, 2013). Individuals with narcolepsy may struggle with social relationships due to controlling emotions to prevent episodes of cataplexy (APA, 2013). Individuals with non-rapid eye movement sleep arousal disorders may feel embarrassed and socially isolated (APA, 2013). Nightmare disorders and non-rapid eye movement sleep arousal disorders may lead to parents or others feeling pain and distress (APA, 2013).

Fatality

A lack of sleep can lead to death. As mentioned at the beginning of this chapter, sleep deprivation in rats led to death (Everson et al., 1989; Rechtschaffen, Bergmann, et al., 1989). Hirshkowitz, Moore, & Minhoto (1997) claimed "many sleep disorders are life threatening, either directly or indirectly" (p. 29). Men and women who reported usually sleeping significantly more or less than 7–8 hours per night had increased mortality rates (Kripke et al., 1979; Hirshkowitz, Moore, & Minhoto, 1997). Insufficient sleep can also lead to a variety of accident-prone behaviors, which may be fatal. Revisiting the Tefft and AAA Foundation for Traffic Safety (2014) study, 21% of all fatal crashes involved a driver who was drowsy. Sleep disorders and unhealthy sleep behaviors may increase the risk for suicide (Bernert & Joiner, 2007). Some research has even found that insufficient sleep may lead to increased suicidality among adolescents (Lee et al., 2012).

Sleep Disorders: Dyssomnias and Parasomnias

Dyssomnias

The change in quality or quantity of sleep

Parasomnias

Behaviors that occur during sleep or affect sleep

Sleep disorders were originally classified in the late 19th century and classifications continued to develop and were refined (see Rothenberg, 1997). From these early classifications emerged the terms dyssomnia and insomnia (Rothenberg, 1997). Dyssomnias are "alterations in the quality, amount, or timing of sleep" (Rothenberg, 1997, p. 61). Parasomnias are "behavioral and physiological events occurring during sleep or sleep-wake transitions" (Rothenberg, 1997, p. 61). The DSM-5 uses the similar perspective of parasomnias and includes, under this category, non-rapid eye movement sleep arousal disorders and rapid eye movement sleep disorders (APA, 2013). However, the DSM-5 adopted a newer approach to classification of sleep disorders referred to as either lumping or splitting depending on the disorder (APA, 2013). Thus, the DSM-5 lists 10 sleep disorders under the category of sleep-wake disorders (APA, 2013).

Nightmare Disorder

One of the authors had a terrifying nightmare as a child, in which Freddy Krueger (pictured at the beginning of the chapter) was on Mario star power, chasing the author. This is probably the result of a childhood with video games and watching horror films. Thankfully, the nightmare did not cause psychological trauma or persist and become a disorder.

Nightmares typically occur during REM sleep and occur more commonly in the second half of a main sleep period (APA, 2013). Nightmares are similar to dreams with the distinction that they usually contain a stimulus that induces fear or negative emotion (APA, 2013). Think of the example above; Freddy Krueger is a very scary stimulus. If you add the invincibility of star power, then you have a very horrifying stimulus. The nightmares themselves typically end when you wake but your body

remains in arousal and in a fearful or negatively emotional state (APA, 2013). Remember that nightmares alone do not equate to a disorder. Remember the 4 Fs and the DSM-5 diagnostic criteria (APA, 2013). Let's consider the case of Antonio.

Case Vignette

Antonio is a 17-year-old who has reported struggling with schoolwork and feeling tired throughout the day. He says that he often has a difficult time sleeping well through the night because of a recurrent nightmare. He has been having the same nightmare about three to four times per week. In his nightmare he is searching through a house looking for people to rescue. He then turns around to see a man looking at him through the window with a shotgun pointed at Antonio. In the nightmare Antonio then begins to run for his life with the man chasing him for a long time. At the end of his nightmare, the man catches up to Antonio after he falls down. When Antonio turns around, on the ground, Antonio looks up to see the gun pointed at his face. Antonio then wakes up scared. He stated that he wakes up very alert and scared and has a difficult time going back to sleep. He stated that when he wakes up frightened he will often go watch television for several hours to distract him from the nightmare.

As you think of Antonio, think of the 4 Fs. How might Antonio's nightmare affect areas in his life differently from individuals who have an occasional nightmare with no impaired functioning? Also, as you review the DSM-5 diagnostic criteria (APA, 2013), think about the case of Antonio and how he may meet diagnostic criteria.

Non-Rapid Eye Movement Sleep Arousal Disorders

Sleep Terrors

Episodes of arousal that occur within non-REM sleep

Now imagine seeing someone who is asleep and running around as if they were being chased by Freddy Krueger. This is an example of someone who may be experiencing sleep terrors found in non-rapid eye movement disorders. Sleep terrors are episodes of arousal that occur usually within the first third of a main sleep period and last up to 10 minutes (APA, 2013). Sleep terrors are distinct from nightmares for a number of reasons, primarily occurring during the non-REM sleep (APA, 2013). Due to this, individuals are usually difficult to awaken and when they do wake, they may not have a recollection of their dream or behavior (APA, 2013).

Sleepwalking

Walking and movement that occurs during non-REM sleep

Non-rapid eye movement disorders may also be accompanied with sleepwalking (APA, 2013). Sleepwalking is, as the name implies, unresponsive walking that occurs during non-REM sleep. There are various films that portray the perils of sleepwalking, such as *Step Brothers* and *Sleepwalk with Me*. These movies depict sleepwalking as humorous with destructive consequences. Sometimes, the image that people may have in mind when they think about sleepwalking is a zombie. The image usually involves a person walking with their arms reached straight out in front of them. This is

© Ljupco Smokovski/Shutterstock.com

a common misconception. Many adults who sleepwalk may have their eyes open and engage in various tasks such as eating and moving furniture (Gunn & Gunn, 2006). One of the myths noted at the beginning of this chapter involved the dangers of waking someone when they are sleeping (see Lilienfeld et al., 2010). Sleepwalking may pose risk for harm and dangers for people during sleepwalking episodes (Gunn & Gunn, 2006; Lilienfeld et al., 2010). However, waking a person from sleepwalking does not put them in any danger (Lilienfeld et al., 2010). In fact, due to the dangers that may occur in sleepwalking episodes, waking someone from sleepwalking might save their life or be more advantageous (Boyd, 2007).

DSM-5 CRITERIA FOR INSOMNIA DISORDER

DIAGNOTIC CRITERIA

A.   A predominant complaint of dissatisfaction with sleep quantity or quality, associated with one (or more) of the following symptoms:

   1.   Difficulty initiating sleep. (In children, this may manifest as difficulty initiating sleep without caregiver intervention.)

   2.   Difficulty maintaining sleep, characterized by frequent awakenings or problems returning to sleep after awakenings. (In children, this may manifest as difficulty returning to sleep without caregiver intervention.)

   3.   Early-morning awakening with inability to return to sleep.

B. The sleep disturbance causes clinically significant distress or impairment in social, occupational, educational, academic, behavioral, or other important areas of functioning.

C. The sleep difficulty occurs at least 3 nights per week.

D. The sleep difficulty is present for at least 3 months.

E. The sleep difficulty occurs despite adequate opportunity for sleep.

F. The insomnia is not better explained by and does not occur exclusively during the course of another sleep-wake disorder (e.g., narcolepsy, a breathing-related sleep disorder, a circadian rhythm sleep-wake disorder, a parasomnia).

G. The insomnia is not attributable to the physiological effects of a substance (e.g., a drug of abuse, a medication).

H. Coexisting mental disorders and medical conditions do not adequately explain the predominant complaint of insomnia.

Specify if:

> **With non-sleep disorder mental comorbidity,** including substance use disorders
>
> **With other medical comorbidity**
>
> **With other sleep disorder**

Coding note: The code 780.52 (G47.00) applies to all three specifiers. Code also the relevant associated mental disorder, medical condition, or other sleep disorder immediately after the code for insomnia disorder in order to indicate the association.

Specify if:

> **Episodic:** Symptoms last at least 1 month but less than 3 months.
>
> **Persistent:** Symptoms last 3 months or longer.
>
> **Recurrent:** Two (or more) episodes within the space of 1 year.

Note: Acute and short-term insomnia (i.e., symptoms lasting less than 3 months but otherwise meeting all criteria with regard to frequency, intensity, distress, and/or impairment) should be coded as an other specified insomnia disorder.

Reprinted with permission from the *Diagnostic and Statistical Manual of Mental Disorders,* Fifth Edition, (Copyright 2013). American Psychiatric Association.

Insomnia Disorder

The band Green Day, in their song "Brainstew," discussed difficulties with going to sleep and how counting sheep was not an effective means. The song alludes to the effects of sleep deprivation. There are numerous sources that influence our understanding of disorders such as insomnia. One of the most commonly held beliefs about insomnia disorder is that people with this sleep disorder never sleep, similar to the belief that people with anorexia never eat. This is a distortion of the disorder.

People with insomnia disorder do sleep but the quality or quantity may be low (APA, 2013). The dissatisfaction with quantity or quality of sleep may be related to difficulties going to sleep, remaining asleep, or waking up early in the morning and being unable to go back to sleep (APA, 2013). The lack of quantity or quality, occurring at least three nights each week for at least 3 months, leads to impairment in functioning and causes distress (APA, 2013). Sleep quality is usually reported as poor or nonrestorative (Morin, 1993). It is the dissatisfaction with sleep or complaint that leads to meeting diagnostic criteria (APA, 2013; Morin, 1993). Regarding gender differences, insomnia occurs more frequently among women than men and the onset for women is typically related to birthing a child or menopause (APA, 2013).

Narcolepsy

A commonly held belief and misconception about narcolepsy is that people spend most of their time sleeping (National Institute of Neurological Disorders and Stroke; NINDS, 2016). The NINDS, of the National Institute of Health, addresses this common belief and suggests that people with narcolepsy do not spend greater time sleeping during 24-hour cycles compared to normal sleepers. Some commonly held beliefs and misconceptions about narcolepsy may arise from popular movies and films.

Myths in Movies
MOULIN ROUGE

The movie *Moulin Rouge!* portrays narcolepsy by an Argentinian character who frequently passes out and stays asleep while others are dancing and singing around him. In one scene he is referred to as an unconscious Argentinian who falls through the roof.

A scene from *Moulin Rouge*

© 20th Century Fox/Photofest

Another film that shows an interpretation of narcolepsy is *Deuce Bigalow: Male Gigolo.* The woman named Carol in the movie states that she has narcolepsy. When she introduces herself to Deuce she falls asleep and falls backward onto the floor. In another scene, Carol falls asleep while she is throwing a bowling ball, not letting go of the ball and falling on the bowling lane. How might movies such as these promote myths about narcolepsy?

Cataplexy involves a brief and sudden loss of muscle tone with maintained consciousness, meaning that you are still awake and aware (APA, 2013). Episodes of cataplexy are one of three criteria that must be present for a diagnosis of narcolepsy (APA, 2013). Thus, cataplexy is not a requirement for narcolepsy and individuals may have narcolepsy and not have cataplexy (APA, 2013). Let's consider Wolfgang.

Cataplexy

Brief and sudden loss of muscle tone with maintained consciousness

Case Vignette

Wolfgang is a 22-year-old male who entered counseling because he has been having difficulties with academics and his job. He stated that he has been failing classes and struggles to concentrate during classes and at work. He often takes naps during classes, even the ones that he highly enjoys. Wolfgang feels exhausted throughout much of the day and occasionally has brief episodes that consist of him losing control of his muscles. He stated that he is concerned for his academics and is worried that he may fall asleep on his drive to school and work. Wolfgang reported that he is in his car driving for an average of 3 hours and 30 minutes daily.

The case of Wolfgang demonstrates how an individual with narcolepsy with episodes of cataplexy may have high frequency of feeling a need for sleep, impaired functioning, feeling pain from the symptoms, and at a risk for fatality. Wolfgang's concerns are his academic performance and concern of automobile accidents due to the symptoms of narcolepsy.

Other Sleep-Wake Disorders

We presented four out of the 10 sleep-wake disorders that are listed in the DSM-5 list of 10 sleep disorders (APA, 2013). Some of the other sleep-wake disorders include hypersomnolence disorder, breathing-related sleep disorders (i.e., obstructive sleep apnea hypopnea, central sleep apnea, and sleep-related hypoventilation), circadian rhythm sleep-wake disorders, rapid eye movement sleep behavior disorder, restless legs syndrome, and substance/medication-induced sleep disorder (APA, 2013). These other disorders range in symptoms from difficulties with apneas, which are the cessation of airflow, to painful or discomforting feelings in a person's legs (i.e., restless legs syndrome; APA, 2013). These symptoms essentially affect functioning in daily living, occur at greater frequencies compared to others, lead to feeling pain, and may be fatal.

Apneas

Cessation of airflow during sleep

Treatment for Sleep Disorders

© OneO2/Shutterstock.com

One of the commonly heard, thought, or discussed sleep prescriptions is counting sheep (Lilienfeld et al., 2010). Lilienfeld and colleagues stated that this is a myth and counting sheep does not help people with insomnia fall asleep. There is some research that suggests imagery distraction (such as imagining an interesting and relaxing situation) techniques sustained for 2 minutes yielded shorter sleep onset time and less distress compared to people who were instructed to complete their bedtime routine as they normally do (Harvey & Payne, 2002). Along with techniques such as these, there are various treatments for the differing sleep disorders (Pressman & Orr, 1997; Stahl, 2011).

Biological Treatment of Sleep Disorders

Roehrs and Roth (1997) stated that "virtually every drug that crosses the blood-brain barrier can affect sleep" (p. 339). This includes the commonly

© August_0802/Shutterstock.com

used social drugs, such as caffeine and alcohol (Roehrs & Roth, 1997). Some people may use alcohol as a means to treat sleep problems or sleep disorders by drinking a glass of wine or some other alcohol drink (i.e., nightcap). Alcohol seems to have some paradoxical effects on sleep. While drinking alcohol may lead to falling asleep faster and initially improving sleep, it may lead to sleep disturbances, such as suppressing REM sleep (Roehrs & Roth, 2001). Suppressing REM sleep by alcohol consumption may lead to you feeling tired the day after you ingested alcohol. Alcohol can be a pharmacological impediment to some sleep disorders, such as sleep apnea, by making them worse (Saskin, 1997). However, small amounts of alcohol may be beneficial in people with insomnia (Roehrs & Roth, 2001). Individuals with a history of alcoholism or drug abuse are discouraged from using alcohol and some other drugs (Roehrs & Roth, 1997).

Depending on the sleep disorder, the nature of the biological treatment may vary. Sleep apneas are often associated with patients who are overweight and, thus, weight loss is a goal for treatment (Saskin, 1997). In other cases, sleep apnea may be treated with techniques such as dental devices, surgery, and nasal machines (Saskin, 1997).

For drug treatments of insomnia and narcolepsy, refer to Stahl's (2011) *Stahl's essential psychopharmacology*. Further, the *Journal of Psychosocial*

Nursing & Mental Health Services (2010) provides a drug chart of FDA-approved drugs to treat sleep disorders. The "Clip & Save: Drug Chart" (2010) includes the following drugs for insomnia:

- ▶ Doxepin (Silenor)
- ▶ Estazolam (Prosom)
- ▶ Eszopiclone (Lunesta)
- ▶ Flurazepam (Dalmane)
- ▶ Quazepan (Doral)
- ▶ Ramelteon (Rozerem)
- ▶ Temazepam (Restoril)
- ▶ Triazaolam (Halcion)
- ▶ Zaleplon (Sonata)
- ▶ Zolpidem tartrate (Ambien, Ambien-CR; Edluar; Zolpimist)

For narcolepsy the "Clip & Save: Drug Chart" (2010) includes the following:

- ▶ Dextro-amphetamine (Dexedrine)
- ▶ Mixed amphetamine salts (Adderall)
- ▶ Methylphenidate (Metadate ER; Ritalin)
- ▶ Modafinil (Provigil, Alertec, Modiodal)
- ▶ Sodium oxybate (Xyrem)

Clip & Save: Drug Chart. FDA-Approved Drugs to Treat Sleep Disorders. (2010). *Journal of Psychosocial Nursing & Mental Health Services, 48*(10), pp. 7–8. doi:10.3928/02793695-20100903-02

Stahl, S. M. (2011). *Stahl's essential psychopharmacology: Neuroscientific basis and practical applications* (3rd ed.). Cambridge UP.

These drug treatments involve a qualified medical professional to assess, diagnose, and treat the various sleeping disorders. Some of these medications may work with various aspects of sleep. For example, Stahl (2011) provides a list of various hypnotic drugs for sleep onset and sleep maintenance or for slow-wave sleep. Stahl also lists adjunctive treatments, such as the use of melatonin.

Psychological Treatment of Sleep Disorders

There are various psychological treatments for sleep disorders. Depending on the nature of the sleep disorder, one specific treatment may work better than others. Division 12 of the American Psychological Association has identified research-based psychological treatments for insomnia disorder (see APA Presidential Task Force on Evidence-Based Practice, 2006). Table 12.2 displays various psychological treatments from Division 12 for insomnia (APA Presidential Task Force on Evidence-Based Practice, 2006; Ritterband & Clerkin, 2013).

TABLE 12.2 Empirically Supported Psychological Treatments for Insomnia

Psychological Treatment	Insomnia
Cognitive Behavioral Therapy	Strong
Sleep Restriction Therapy	Strong
Stimulus Control Therapy	Strong
Relaxation Training	Strong
Paradoxical Intention	Strong
Electromyograph (EMG) Biofeedback	Modest

*Table based on information from APA Presidential Task Force on Evidence-Based Practice (2006)

Paradoxical Intention

Telling yourself to stay awake when you go to bed as a means to relax

Cognitive behavioral therapy works with clients' beliefs that contribute to sleep disturbances, dysfunctional beliefs about sleep, and learned sleep behaviors (Bootzin & Rider, 1997). One of the techniques used is referred to as paradoxical intention. Paradoxical intention is a prescription offered to clients to go to bed and try to stay awake (Bootzin & Rider, 1997). The technique helps with sleep onset due to changing the thought of "I must go to sleep," thereby reducing worry or anxiety related to sleep, and leading to clients falling asleep much faster.

One of the authors made a dire parental mistake of telling his son that due to the family waking up early for camping the next day, he informed his son to go to sleep quickly. His son did fall asleep shortly afterward. The mistake was soon noticed around 1:00 a.m. when his son ran into his bedroom asking, "Is it time to go camping?" His son did this a couple more times, at 3:00 a.m. and 4:20 a.m. The mistake was realized the next tiresome morning when heading to the campgrounds. The anticipation of camping and waking up early had contributed to thoughts that influenced behavior upon wakefulness. Also, the excitement probably contributed to less restorative sleep for the child.

Think about the times you may have struggled with going to sleep. How about the night before Christmas, a birthday, a job interview, the first day of class, or an important exam? Much like the camping trip, these are examples of events that may have led to you having difficulty going to sleep or remaining asleep due to excitement, anticipation, worry, stress, or anxiety. You may have tried to force sleep by stating, "It's a big day tomorrow, I better sleep, now!" These thoughts may lead to anxiety, excitement, or general arousal.

The more you experience sympathetic arousal the less likely it may be for you to sleep, which may lead to subsequent thoughts of "It has been 30 minutes and I still can't sleep," or "What am I doing still awake?" These thoughts help you sleep, right? No, usually this perpetuates the sleepless cycle.

Forcing sleep can be a detriment for sleeping. As previously mentioned, paradoxical intention or imagery distraction may be useful (Bootzin & Rider, 1997; Harvey & Payne, 2002). Another technique is referred to as thought stopping (Bootzin & Rider, 1997). Thought stopping, as you might intuit, involves a person saying "stop!" when he or she is having repetitive thoughts, which is deemed to have some effectiveness because it interrupts the thought cycle (Bootzin & Rider, 1997).

Thought Stopping

Telling yourself "stop!" when having repetitive thoughts prior to sleep

Along with these treatments, psychoeducation about sleep and sleep hygiene is seen at least as an adjunctive to treatment (Stahl, 2011) or even "a core component of all treatments for insomnia" (Bootzin & Rider, 1997, p. 316). Sleep hygiene consists of behaviors that promote high-quality sleep and daytime alertness (Bootzin & Rider, 1997). Some of these behaviors include (Bootzin & Rider, 1997):

- ▶ Associate bed with sleep and few activities
- ▶ Do not spend too much time in your bed
- ▶ Exercise and be active during the day
- ▶ Strive for a daily bedtime schedule
- ▶ Avoid routine use of caffeine, nicotine, and alcohol
- ▶ Avoid exercise or emotionally arousing situations before bedtime
- ▶ Have a comfortable bed
- ▶ Have a good sleep environment (not distracting environment)

Conclusion

If you have made it thus far without going to sleep, then congratulations to you! Sometimes the best sleep aid may be cozying up with a textbook. It is undeniable that sleep is vital and often underemphasized or undervalued. All people sleep but not all get good, restful sleep all the time. Sleeping patterns, quality, and quantity may affect psychological functioning and overall health. There are numerous factors that contribute to the problems with sleep. Some problems may lead to sleep disorders. If you are concerned about having a sleep disorder, there are various effective treatments available, depending on the nature of the sleep disorder. Whether you may have a sleep disorder or not, many people are encouraged to become educated about sleep stages and cycles as well as good sleep hygiene.

CHAPTER REVIEW

QUESTIONS

1. How important is sleep for functioning? How does sleep deprivation affect people?

2. How does the amount of sleep needed change throughout the life span?

3. How is sleep usually measured?

4. What are the differences between dyssomnias and parasomnias?

5. How might drugs affect sleep?

KEY TERMS

Electroencephalography

Wave Frequency

Wave Amplitude

Alpha Rhythm

Circadian Rhythms

Polysomnograph

Rapid Eye Movement

Hypersomnolence Disorder

Dyssomnias

Parasomnias

Sleep Terrors

Sleepwalking

Cataplexy

Apneas

Paradoxical Intention

Thought Stopping

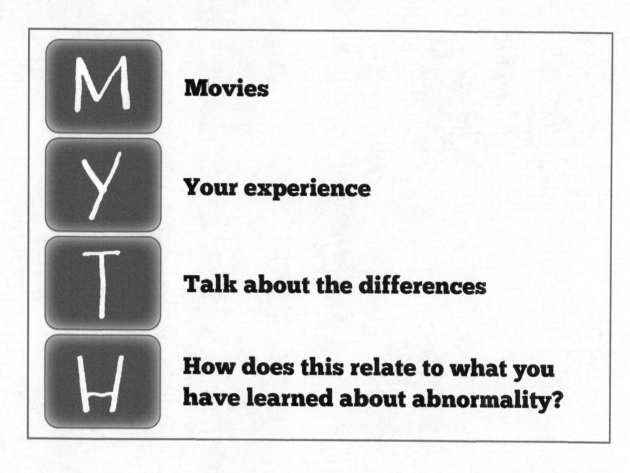

M	Movies
Y	Your experience
T	Talk about the differences
H	How does this relate to what you have learned about abnormality?

Myths in Movies Recap

Nightmare on Elm Street

Many movies that are themed around sleep or sleeping disorders are often dark, horrors, or contain violence and suspense. While nightmares can often be intensely scary and sometimes result in death in the dream, that does not lead to a death in waking. Unfortunately, creating fear associations with sleep can make going to sleep even more difficult.

Moulin Rouge

Movies that depict narcolepsy often show it in a comedic fashion, as someone who falls asleep mid-sentence or standing up. These movies displaying someone falling over asleep is an exaggeration of cataplexy and one that people often find humorous. The risks and fatal components are rarely revealed.

CHAPTER THIRTEEN

SEX AND GENDER DISORDERS

MYTHs of Sexual Disorders

Sexual dysfunctions and other sexual disorders may be among the most difficult disorders to discuss, particularly with clients, as they often involve highly private matters, not to mention the abundant stereotypes that surround virtually all things "sexual." Myths about sex and sexuality intermingle and overlap with these stereotypes, and many people go on believing some of the myths for long periods of time, especially because people may feel too embarrassed to discuss sexual issues. Before we look more closely at these disorders, take some time to think about your own understanding and experience regarding sexual dysfunction and related disorders. Look at the categories that follow and consider which have likely influenced your thinking in some way, considering the impressions you have from these various sources.

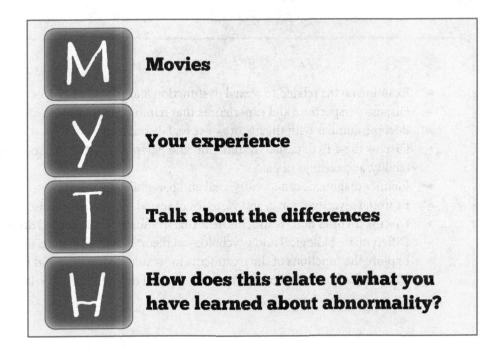

M Movies

Y Your experience

T Talk about the differences

H How does this relate to what you have learned about abnormality?

Perhaps among the most commonly held myths about sexual disorders is the idea that they simply do not exist. In this same vein, some individuals may approach disorders, especially those involving sexuality, simply in terms of normal variations of sexual development or preference, rather than characterize them as disordered. Clinical experience working with individuals suffering from sexual disorders will clearly alleviate any disbelief in these myths. A look at the last several versions of the DSM demonstrates how beliefs about sexual disorders are also in flux within the professional community, especially regarding how to draw lines between normal and disordered sexuality. More and more emphasis appears to be placed on the distress caused by specific behaviors, rather than the manner in which persons self-identify or the specific behaviors in which they participate. An

Myths in Movies

SEX, LIES, AND VIDEOTAPES

Consider Soderbergh's (1989) highly acclaimed film *Sex, Lies, and Videotape*, which integrates sexual problems such as infidelity in relationships with behaviors that may be labeled disordered, such as impotence or voyeuristic disorder. Many of the relationships in this film are characterized by the lack of communication and stereotypes about sexuality

© MGM-UA/Photofest

A scene from *Sex, Lies, and Videotapes*

and sexual disorders. Are sexual disorders actually related this closely to problems with infidelity, relationship struggles, and divorce?

---

example of the flux of diagnostic criteria related to psychopathology and sexuality is the inclusion of homosexuality in early versions (DSM-III) of the DSM, which was removed in 1973. Ego-dystonic homosexuality was especially focused upon in the DSM, prior to its complete removal, as individuals distressed by their same-sex attractions were still understood to need treatment. In 2009, the American Psychological Association's Task Force on Appropriate Therapeutic Responses to Sexual Orientation stated that therapeutic efforts to change sexual orientation did not have a sufficient research base to justify their use, further suggesting that attempts to change sexual orientation may be harmful to clients. In a similar way, some of the diagnoses related to sexual disorders are still being debated, and diagnoses could potentially change as new versions of the DSM are created.

In this chapter, we will focus on three categories of disorders related to sex and gender: Sexual Dysfunctions, Gender Dysphoria, and Paraphilic Disorders. According to the DSM-5, sexual dysfunctions typically involve prominent disturbance in an individual's sexual function, including problems with sexual responsiveness and sexual pleasure (American Psychiatric Association [APA], 2013). These disorders include erectile dysfunction, delayed ejaculation, premature ejaculation, male hypoactive sexual desire disorder, female sexual interest/arousal disorder, genito-pelvic pain/penetration disorder (APA, 2013). These disorders should be understood as distinct, although an individual may simultaneously experience more than one. Gender Dysphoria, on the other hand, is a distinct disorder that was labeled Gender Identity Disorder in previous

Ego-Dystonic

A person's thoughts, actions, feelings, or impulses being in conflict with their core beliefs, personality, and/or self-image

Sexual Dysfunctions

A class of disorders related to problems with sexual desire, response, or pleasure across any point of the sexual response cycle

Gender Dysphoria

Distress in relation to incongruence between a person's sex (assigned gender) and expressed or experienced gender

Paraphilic Disorders

A class of disorders characterized by sexual attraction or interest in activities, persons, or things that are not typically or inherently sexually arousing for most people

versions of the DSM. Gender Dysphoria is characterized by an incongruence between one's birth gender and one's experienced or expressed gender (APA, 2013). Last of all, Paraphilic Disorders are a class of disorders characterized by sexual attraction or interest in activities, objects, or persons (e.g., children, corpses, amputees) other than typical, consensual genital stimulation or foreplay with a mature human partner (APA, 2013).

The 4 Fs of Sexual Dysfunctions: The Ups and Downs of Sex

As sexual dysfunctions represent a large class of behaviors and disturbances, it can be difficult to identify what is common to all. In this section, we will therefore discuss frequencies specific to each disorder, followed by the broad Fs consistent between many of the disorders falling into the category of sexual dysfunctions.

Frequency

Despite sexual dysfunctions involving a large class of disorders, diagnostic criteria for the disorders involve surprising similarities in regard to the frequencies of the disorders. The frequencies also help clue us into the reality of these disorders, clarifying how debilitating they can be, how much distress they can cause, and the clarity that sexual disorders are not just myths.

A—Amount of Time: In order to be diagnosed with any of the sexual dysfunction disorders, a person must experience persistent symptoms for no less than 6 months (APA, 2013). However, some individuals may have had symptoms since their first sexual experience, in which case their dysfunction would be specified as lifelong.

B—Behavior: For the majority of sexual dysfunction disorders identified by the DSM-5, individuals must experience symptoms related to the specific dysfunction during 75 to 100% of their sexual experiences (APA, 2013). The two exceptions to this frequency are genito-pelvic pain/penetration disorder, which appears to be generalized to all situations, and male hypoactive sexual desire disorder, the judgment of which is made by the clinician based on a variety of factors, such as age and life context (APA, 2013).

C—Curve: Prevalence rates for various sexual dysfunction disorders vary more widely than diagnostic criteria related to frequencies of behavior and length of symptoms. Below is a list of the various sexual dysfunctions identified in the DSM-5, and the prevalence rated of these disorders.

Delayed Ejaculation: The prevalence of delayed ejaculation is not well-established, but the DSM-5 estimates that less than 1% of men will report difficulties reaching climax that persist six months or longer (APA, 2013).

Erectile Dysfunction: Prevalence rates for erectile dysfunction vary by age, with 2% of men younger than 40–50 years experiencing persistent symptoms, and 40 to 50% of men older than age 60–70 experiencing symptoms (APA, 2013).

Female Orgasmic Disorder: The DSM-5 specifies that between 10% to 42% of women experience persistent symptoms related to achieving orgasm, and that these rates vary widely based on age and culture, though many women do not report distress despite difficulties achieving orgasm (APA, 2013). However, around 10% of women are reported as not achieving orgasm over the course of their lifetime (APA, 2013).

Female Sexual Interest/Arousal Disorder: This disorder, as described by the DSM-5, lacks sufficient evidence to determine prevalence rates. Research on this disorder as described in previous versions of the DSM as female sexual arousal disorder have returned a wide range of results, suggesting prevalence from 6 to 21% (Simons & Carey, 2001). A more recent large-scale study found 9.1% of women met criteria for the disorder, although 55.8% reported a lack of interest or arousal lasting 6 months or more (Mitchell et al., 2015).

Genito-Pelvic Pain/Penetration Disorder: The DSM-IV-TR dignoses of vaginismus and dyspareunia were combined and replaced by genito-pelvic pain/penetration disorder in the DSM-5 (Binik, 2010). The DSM-5 estimates that approximately 15% of women report frequent pain during sexual penetration, although prevalence rates of women diagnosed with this disorder are unknown (APA, 2013).

Vaginismus

Diagnosis in previous versions of the DSM characterized by emphasis on vaginal spasms or contractions upon attempted penetration as the defining feature

Dyspareunia

Diagnosis in previous versions of the DSM characterized by emphasis on vaginal pain during intercourse as the defining feature

Male Hypoactive Sexual Desire Disorder: According to the APA (2013), prevalence rates for male hypoactive sexual desire disorder vary widely by age, country of origin, and assessment method. Approximately 6% of men between the ages of 18–24 are estimated to experience low sexual desire, whereas the rate is 41% among men age 66–74 years; however, only 1.8% of men between the ages of 18–44 are believed to experience symptoms for 6 months or longer (APA, 2013).

Premature (Early) Ejaculation: Prevalence rates for ejaculating quickly during intercourse likely vary by age, with higher prevalence rates among older men (APA, 2013). The DSM-5 redefined this disorder, lowering the swiftness of ejaculation to approximately 1 minute of penetration, which is estimated to have lowered the prevalence rates to 1 to 3% overall (APA, 2013).

SPECIFIERS OF SEXUAL DYSFUNCTION DISORDERS

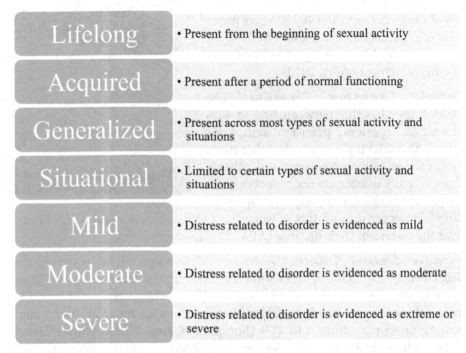

Lifelong	• Present from the beginning of sexual activity
Acquired	• Present after a period of normal functioning
Generalized	• Present across most types of sexual activity and situations
Situational	• Limited to certain types of sexual activity and situations
Mild	• Distress related to disorder is evidenced as mild
Moderate	• Distress related to disorder is evidenced as moderate
Severe	• Distress related to disorder is evidenced as extreme or severe

The specifiers Generalized and Situational are not used for Genito-Pelvic Pain/Penitration Disorder.

APA, 2013

Function

As you've probably already put together by the names of the various sexual dysfunctions, a wide range of functional difficulties are present in this category. The DSM-5 specifies that these disorders share a common general dysfunction in that persons with these disorders experience difficulty with regard to sexual response and/or sexual pleasure (APA, 2013). Disorders primarily related to problems with sexual response include delayed ejaculation, premature ejaculation, erectile disorder, female orgasmic disorder. Disorders primarily related to difficulties with sexual pleasure include male hypoactive sexual desire disorder. Female sexual interest/arousal disorder and genito-pelvic pain/penetration disorder involve difficulties with both response and pleasure.

Men experiencing delayed ejaculation may struggle simply with a delay in ejaculation, or may experience infrequent or even a total absence of ejaculation. As mentioned above, men struggling with premature ejaculation, as defined by the DSM-5, will typically experience orgasm within 1 minute of penetration, although individuals may also receive this diagnosis if they ejaculate quickly prior to penetration (APA, 2013). Erectile disorder is

Myths in Movies

MY HUSBAND WON'T FIT

The Netflix show *My Husband Won't Fit* tells the story of a newly married woman who is struggling with Genito-pelvic pain/penetration disorder, with an emphasis on penetration, as you probably figured out form the title. Though the show brings up some of the romantic and relation difficulties typical of the disorder, it deviates from the typical symptoms by having the protagonist have sex with other men without vaginal constriction or pain. For most women with this disorder, the norm is avoidance of sexual situations and vaginal penetration, which has been described as similar to phobic responses (APA, 2013).

© Tetiana Peliustka/Shutterstock.com

characterized by significant difficulty acquiring or maintaining an erection, or by difficulties maintaining sufficient penile rigidity during sexual activity. Female orgasmic disorder, which is similar to delayed ejaculation for men, is characterized by a delay or absence of orgasm, or by a decrease in the strength of orgasm.

Female sexual interest/arousal disorder, which is perhaps the most diagnostically complex of the sexual dysfunctions, is characterized by at least three symptoms, potentially including decreased or absent interest in sex, decreased or absent sexual thoughts or fantasies, decreased or absent initiation of or response to sexual activity, decreased or absent pleasure or excitement during sex, reduced or absent arousal to sexual cues, and/or reduced or absent sensations during sexual activity (APA, 2013). Genito-pelvic pain/penetration disorder is also a fairly complex disorder, involving both expectations and emotional responses to sex, as well as physical reactions and sensations. For this diagnosis, a woman must experience difficulties with vaginal penetration, pain in the vaginal or pelvic areas during penetration or attempted penetration, significant fear or anxiety prior to or during penetration, or the constriction of certain pelvic muscles during penetration or attempted penetration (APA, 2013). Male hypoactive sexual desire disorder is primarily characterized by a decrease or absence in thoughts, fantasies, and desires of a sexual nature.

Johnson and Masters

If you are familiar with Masters and Johnson's (1970) sexual response cycle, you'll likely have noticed that some of these dysfunctions involve difficulties with the desire phase, whereas other disorders involve other phases, including arousal, plateau, orgasm, and resolution, and that each disorder involves these phases in different ways. Some disorders, such as female sexual interest/arousal disorder may involve several different phases of the response cycle. Additionally, the broad distinction between response and pleasure in the DSM-5 can be considered a simplified manner of understanding these phases.

Fatality

Although contrary to popular opinion among young men, no one has died as a direct result of the inability to have an orgasm or become aroused. That being the case, some research suggests that sexual dysfunction can sometimes lead to relational difficulties, depression, and anxiety, which in some cases may increase overall stress and the likelihood of suicidality (Brotto et al., 2016; Dell'Osso et al., 2009). Difficulties with mood and anxiety appear to be commonly associated with a variety of sexual dysfunction disorders, which likely act together in a vicious cycle to reinforce one another. To exacerbate this problem, medications used to treat other psychiatric disorders can sometimes decrease sexual desire or arousal. Individuals experiencing mania, on the other hand, are more likely to experience an increase in sexual arousal, frequently leading to sexual behavior they may later regret, thereby increasing distress and the risk of suicide. Personality traits may additionally be associated with certain sexual dysfunctions. For example, younger men with neurotic personality traits and men older than age 40 with submissive personality traits may be at an added risk of erectile problems (APA, 2013). Additionally, environmental factors, such as the experience of relational violence, gender expectations, religious and sexual norms learned during development, and certain medical conditions, such as thyroid problems, may predispose certain men and women to experience various sexual dysfunctions (APA, 2013; Nobre & Pinto-Gouveia, 2006). While studies have not discovered a direct link between increased mortality and sexual dysfunction, they have demonstrated a link with many other issues, which are linked with increased mortality.

Feeling Pain

As you can imagine, individuals experiencing sexual dysfunctions can experience significant pain; in some of these disorders physically, but emotionally and psychologically in most of the disorders. The manner in which distress is manifested regarding sexual function is likely impacted significantly by cultural norms and expectations regarding sex. In the United States, men experiencing sexual or erectile dysfunctions are often characterized as less masculine, and experience corresponding distress. In other countries, different expectation may mediate distress. For example, in certain Polynesian cultures, the lack of an erection simply implies that a man is not currently wanting to have sex, and in certain African cultures, vaginal dryness is preferred for sexual intercourse (Brown et al., 1993; Mannino, 1999). Ongoing sexual dysfunction for both men and women is likely to increase relationship stress, and vice versa (McCarthy & Thestrup, 2008; Rosen et al., 2016). In many cases, sex may become a source of tension, frustration, and argument, rather than a source of bonding and bringing partners into increased intimacy. A recent study discovered that not only do men with sexual dysfunctions report lower levels of relationship happiness and sexual satisfaction, but their female partners also report decreased levels of relationship happiness and sexual satisfaction (Rosen et al., 2016). In addition to relationship difficulties, attitude and self-image problems are also clearly related to the distress experienced by individuals with sexual dysfunctions. Inaccurate perceptions related to performance anxiety, or even cultural expectations, likely play a role in many problems with sexual desire, arousal, and response (Barlow, 1986; Masters & Johnson, 1970).

The 4 Fs of Gender Dysphoria Disorder

Gender Dysphoria, referred to as Gender Identity Disorder in previous editions of the DSM, is commonly understood to be a disorder characterized by an incongruence between a person's sex and gender. It can be difficult to discuss due to strong opinions regarding the disorder, not to mention a plethora of popular myths that have surrounded the disorder. Some individuals and researchers would say that being transsexual, which is a common name used to denote an identity characterized by an incongruence between sex and gender, is not actually disordered, pointing out that the distress experienced by individuals with this condition is related to the dysphoria they experience, often caused by a lack of acceptance

© Svetlanamiku/Shutterstock.com

Intersex

Also referred to as disorders of sexual development, intersex conditions are characterized by a biological mixing of male and female sexual organs

Transgender

A condition characterized by enduring or temporary identification with a gender incongruent with one's assigned gender/sex

Transsexual

A condition characterized by enduring or temporary social/public identification with a gender incongruent with one's assigned gender/sex, which may or may not involve attempts to biologically change one's sexual characteristics

from society (Lev, 2004). Other individuals and researchers hold that the experience of being transgender is itself distressing, evidence that the condition is actually a mental disorder, and that the distress individuals experience is caused primarily by the identification with the gender incongruent with their sex (McHugh, 2004).

Another example of confusion is the sheer number of different ways that people use language about gender and sexual issues related to gender dysphoria. The DSM-5 attempts to give some basic definitions to help alleviate this problem. Many people are not fully aware of the distinction between intersex conditions and gender dysphoria. Intersex conditions are characterized by ambiguous biological indicators related to sex; for example, the biological development of both male and female internal and/or external genitalia. Gender dysphoria, on the other hand, may be experienced in conjunction with or in the absence of an intersex condition, according to the DSM-5, though the development of the disorder among those with an intersex condition can vary widely compared to those without (APA, 2013). The previous version of the DSM, the DSM-IV-TR, did not allow for the diagnosis of gender identity disorder in conjunction with an intersex condition, instead describing the disorders as more distinct phenomenon (APA, 2000). Another important distinction to clarify: Transgender refers to a broad spectrum of individuals who identify in some way with a gender different from their sex, whereas transsexual refers to an individual who has sought or gone through a transition from male to female or vice versa, which sometimes involves taking hormones of the opposite sex or sex reassignment surgery (APA, 2013).

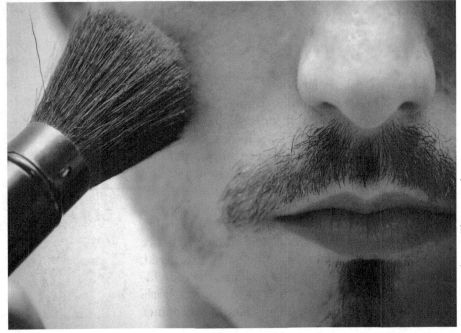

© Marco Brockmann/Shutterstock.com

Myths in Movies

THE ROCKY HORROR PICTURE SHOW and TRANSAMERICA

Like all things sexual, Hollywood seems to have an ever-growing fascination with all things transgender. Just consider the cult classic *The Rocky Horror Picture Show*, the comedy *Transamerica*, or the popular TV show *Transparent*. Despite the media's glamorizing and popularizing of transgender issues, the struggles and trials of persons experiencing gender dysphoria are not often displayed for all the world to see. For example, consider the often invisible voices of individuals who have undergone surgery to change their genitalia, but later regret the decision. How can the media more accurately portray the distress often felt by individuals with gender incongruence?

© Twentieth Century Fox Film Corp./Photofest

A scene from *The Rocky Horror Picture Show*

© The Weinstein Company/Photofest

A scene from *Transamerica*

Frequency

A—Amount of Time: Gender dysphoria may be diagnosed in children or in adolescents/adults, and involves different age-appropriate diagnostic criteria for each group. In terms of time, both age groups must experience symptoms related to incongruence between their experienced/expressed gender and assigned gender for no less than 6 months (APA, 2013).

B—Behavior: Individuals diagnosed with gender dysphoria will insistently experience symptoms related to gender incongruence which persist over the course of the 6-month period of time required for diagnosis. Gender dysphoria in both children and adolescents/adults, according to the DSM-5, must be accompanied by significant distress in social functioning, including relationships with peers, occupational functioning, school functioning, and other areas of functioning (APA, 2013).

Assigned Gender

A person's sex/gender as designated prenatally by chromosomes and hormones, and recognized in utero or at birth, and therefore sometimes used synonymously with the term natal gender

C—**Curve:** Despite greater exposure of transgender issues in the media, the prevalence of gender dysphoria is quite low. The DSM-5 estimates that for adults born as males, the prevalence ranges from 0.005 to 0.014%, whereas for adults born as females, the prevalence ranges from 0.002 to 0.003% (APA, 2013). In children, the ratio of referrals for the diagnosis ranged from two to 4.5 males for every female (APA, 2013). Generally, more males experience gender dysphoria than females, though in a few countries (e.g., Japan and Poland) females appear to more frequently experience the disorder (APA, 2013).

Function

One important myth concerns those who are socially labeled as "tomboys" or "girly-boys" having gender dysphoria. In fact, the DSM-5 explicitly states that the diagnosis does not simply describe gender role nonconformity in behavior, and rather requires distress (APA, 2013). In order for children to be diagnosed with gender dysphoria, they must meet a somewhat more stringent criteria marked by at least six of the eight gender-incongruence symptoms designated by the DSM-5. Adolescents and adults, on the other hand, need only experience two symptoms to receive diagnosis. Because children express distress differently than adults, the functional difficulties related to gender incongruence look quite different between the two groups.

To receive a diagnosis, children must experience the strong desire for, or be insistent that they are, a gender different from their assigned gender (APA, 2013). Children must experience five additional functional problems, including a strong preference for cross-dressing, a strong preference for play or fantasy in the role of the other gender, a strong preference for play with activities, toys, or games associated with the other gender, a strong preference for friends of the other gender, a strong rejection of toys or play associated with their assigned gender, strongly disliking one's own sexual anatomy, and/or a strong desire for the sex characteristics of the other gender (APA, 2013). In adolescents and adults, possible symptoms include a significant incongruence between sex characteristics and experienced or expressed gender, a strong desire to be rid of or stop the development of sex characteristics, a strong desire for the sex characteristics of the other gender, to become the other gender, to be treated like the other gender, and/or a strong conviction that one has the typical experience (e.g., feelings and reactions) of the other gender (APA, 2013). These symptoms may cause social and other functional problems, including school refusal related to teasing, failing to develop peer relationships, the preoccupation with being the other sex may interfere with the activities of daily living, individuals with the disorder may experience difficulties in romantic and sexual relationships, an aversion to others seeing or touching their sexual organs, occupational and school performance issues, and experiences of discrimination and stigmatization (APA, 2013).

Fatality

Myth or Reality: Suicide risks are equivalent to the general population after individuals with gender dysphoria obtain sex reassignment surgery or opposite-sex hormones. Contrary to what is often heard in popular media, the DSM-5 specifies that the risk of suicide may persist after surgery or hormones (APA, 2013). A long-term study from Sweden concluded that individuals who had reassignment surgery were almost 20 times more likely to commit suicide than peers of the same age and birth sex (Dhejne et al., 2011). Additionally, transsexual individuals in this study were found to have higher mortality rates in general, higher rates of suicide attempts, and were more likely to be in inpatient psychiatric care (Dhejne et al., 2011). Individuals with gender dysphoria appear more likely to experience a host of other mental health issues, including depression and anxiety. Additionally, persons with gender dysphoria are also at a far higher risk of suicide attempts and completions than the general population, not

only after transition, but before sex reassignment as well. One multinational European study demonstrated 70% of individuals seeking sex reassignment surgery at clinics in four countries had a comorbid disorder, mood and anxiety disorders were most common, and 30% were at risk of suicide (Heylens et al., 2014). In addition to this, 15% of these participants met diagnostic criteria for a personality disorder, far higher than the rate among the general population (Heylens et al., 2014). Other comorbid disorders include substance abuse disorders, disruptive and impulse-control disorders, transvestic disorder, body dysmorphic disorder, psychotic disorders, and autism spectrum disorders, especially in children referred for gender dysphoria (APA, 2013; Heylens et al., 2014).

Feeling Pain

Individuals with gender dysphoria appear to vary in terms of the pain and distress they experience related to their gender incongruence. Some individuals appear to experience intrusive and obsessive thoughts and desires about being the opposite gender and obtaining hormones or sex reassignment, while others appear less distressed and may not even wish to seek to change their sex characteristics. Some evidence suggests that those who have more severe symptoms in childhood are more likely to experience symptoms persisting into adolescence and adulthood; however, in natal males with gender dysphoria in childhood, studies have found that symptoms persist in only 2.2 to 30%, and in natal females only 12 to 50% (APA, 2013). In the majority of childhood cases, individuals become comfortable with their sex assigned at birth, and often these children go on to identify as lesbian or gay (APA, 2013).

Some evidence suggests that distress related to gender incongruity may be reduced or mitigated in environments that support a child's desire to live as the other gender or in adults who are able to receive hormones or sex reassignment surgery (APA, 2013). Regardless, a significant number of transgender persons experience intense anguish over the mismatch of their experienced gender and their natal gender, thereby meeting criteria for a formal diagnosis of gender dysphoria. Lev (2004) suggested that it "is rare for someone struggling with gender incongruence not to experience some psychological symptomology, e.g., insomnia, isolation, dysthymia, anxiety, weight loss or gain, and work or school difficulties" (p. 10).

DSM-5 CRITERIA FOR GENDER DYSPHORIA DISORDER

DIAGNOSTIC CRITERIA

Gender Dysphoria in Children

A. A marked incongruence between one's experienced/expressed gender and assigned gender, of at least 6 months' duration, as manifested by at least six of the following (one of which must be Criterion A1):

1. A strong desire to be of the other gender or an insistence that one is the other gender (or some alternative gender different from one's assigned gender).

2. In boys (assigned gender), a strong preference for cross-dressing or simulating female attire; or in girls (assigned gender), a strong preference for wearing only typical masculine clothing and a strong resistance to the wearing of typical feminine clothing.

3. A strong preference for cross-gender roles in make-believe play or fantasy play.

4. A strong preference for the toys, games, or activities stereotypically used or engaged in by the other gender.

5. A strong preference for playmates of the other gender.

6. In boys (assigned gender), a strong rejection of typically masculine toys, games, and activities and a strong avoidance of rough-and-tumble play; or in girls (assigned gender), a strong rejection of typically feminine toys, games, and activities.

7. A strong dislike of one's sexual anatomy.

8. A strong desire for the primary and/or secondary sex characteristics that match one's experienced gender.

B. The condition is associated with clinically significant distress or impairment in social, school, or other important areas of functioning.

Specify if:

With a disorder of sex development (e.g., a congenital adrenogenital disorder such as 255.2 [E25.0] congenital adrenal hyperplasia or 259.50 [E34.50] androgen insensitivity syndrome).

Coding note: Code the disorder of sex development as well as gender dysphoria.

Gender Dysphoria in Adolescents and Adults

A. A marked incongruence between one's experienced/expressed gender and assigned gender, or at least 6 months' duration, as manifested by at least two of the following:

1. A marked incongruence between one's experienced/expressed gender and primary and/or secondary sex characteristics (or in young adolescents, the anticipated secondary sex characteristics).

2. A strong desire to be rid of one's primary and/or secondary sex characteristics because of a marked incongruence with one's experienced/expressed gender (or in young adolescents, a desire to prevent the development of the anticipated secondary sex characteristics).

3. A strong desire for the primary and/or secondary sex characteristics of the other gender.

4. A strong desire to be of the other gender (or some alternative gender different from one's assigned gender).

5. A strong desire to be treated as the other gender (or some alternative gender different from one's assigned gender).

6. A strong conviction that one has the typical feelings and reactions of the other gender (or some alternative gender different from one's assigned gender).

The condition is associated with clinically significant distress or impairment in social, occupational, or other important areas of functioning.

Specify if:

With a disorder of sex development (e.g., a congenital adrenogenital disorder such as 255.2 [E25.0) congenital adrenal hyperplasia or 259.50 [E34.50] androgen insensitivity syndrome).

Coding note: Code the disorder of sex development as well as gender dysphoria.

Specify if:

Post-transition: The individual has transitioned to full-time living in the desired gender (with or without legalization of gender change) and has undergone (or is preparing to have) at least one cross-sex medical procedure or treatment regimen—namely, regular cross-sex hormone treatment or gender reassignment surgery confirming the desired gender (e.g., penectomy, vaginoplasty in a natal male; mastectomy or phalloplasty in a natal female).

The 4 Fs of Paraphilic Disorders: For the Love of . . .

Paraphilia

Characterized by sexual attraction or interest in activities, persons, or things that are not typically or inherently sexually arousing for most people

Paraphilic disorders, similar to sexual dysfunctions, represent a wide variety of behaviors and disturbances, such that it can be difficult to identify commonalities between the disorders. The name of the disorder gives us a clue. Paraphilia, rooted in Greek, literally means a (-philia) love that is (para-) abnormal or beyond/outside the norm. Paraphilic disorders all share an intensity of sexual interest and arousal toward objects, actions, or persons that typically are not sexually stimulating for most people. A shift between the DSM-IV-TR and the DSM-5 was the recognition of paraphilic disorders as different from paraphilias. Whereas paraphilias were understood to be disordered in the DSM-IV-TR, the DSM-5 specifies that paraphilias only become a diagnosable condition, or paraphilic disorders, when they involve distress, typically because of harm to self or others (APA, 2013). In this section, we will explore the broad Fs consistent between most of the disorders related to paraphilias.

Frequency

Similar to sexual dysfunctions, diagnostic criteria for paraphilic disorders are surprisingly similar in regard to the frequencies describing the disorders. While the frequencies can help clue us into the reality of these behaviors as disorders, the functional impairments related to paraphilic disorders provide even greater clarity that the pathologies related to sexual attachment to things of a non-sexual nature are not just myths.

A—Amount of Time: In order to be diagnosed with any of the paraphilic disorders, a person must experience a recurrent and intense sexual arousal, specific to the disorder in question, for no less than 6 months (APA, 2013). Some of these disorders, such as pedophilia, can sometimes quickly lead individuals to jail or another restricted environment such as an inpatient setting, in which case he or she may not have the opportunity to act on their desires for a period of 6 months. A key specifier for most of these disorders is the designation describing whether or not the person is in a controlled environment.

B—Behavior: All paraphilic disorders are understood to involve sexual arousal to typically non-sexual things, actions, or people, which is described as recurrent and intense (APA, 2013). Within the 6-month period required for diagnosis, symptoms must be present on an ongoing basis, and not just periodically. An additional specifier for most of the paraphilic disorders, designating the requirements for a person to be in full remission, helps describe how insidious and difficult to break these disorders can be. In

Myths in Movies

At no other time in history has a culture displayed atypical loves as explicitly as the popular media in our own day and age. Consider movies like *Crash, 8mm, Eyes Wide Shut,* or *50 Shades of Grey,* which mingle sex with everything from car crashes and handicaps to secret societies and pain. While most of these movies glamorize paraphilias, some of them do tackle the boundary issues, distress, and related sexual issues that often accompany paraphilias. As our society consumes more and more of this content, does it come to be normalized in the minds of the people, despite the relative infrequency of these behaviors amongst the general population?

A scene from *8mm*

© Fine Line Features/Photofest

A scene from *Crash*

© Columbia Pictures/Photofest

A scene from *Eyes Wide Shut*

© Warner Brothers/Photofest

order to be considered in full remission for all of the paraphilic disorders except pedophilic disorder, an individual must experience no distress and/or acted on paraphilic urges for a minimum of 5 years (APA, 2013). The DSM-5 specifies that pedophilia appears to be a life-long condition, though the course and behaviors related to pedophilic disorder may change over time (APA, 2013).

Voyeurism

C—Curve: Prevalence rates for different paraphilic disorders vary to some degree. Below paraphilic disorders identified in the DSM-5 are described separately, along with estimated prevalence rates for each disorder.

Voyeuristic Disorder: Voyeuristic disorder is characterized by sexual arousal from watching others in a sexual manner (e.g., naked, having sex, or disrobing) who are unaware they are being watched. The prevalence of voyeuristic disorder in the population is considered unknown, but the DSM-5 estimates that the highest possible prevalence for men is around 12%, and for women is around 4% (APA, 2013).

Exhibitionistic Disorder: Exhibitionistic disorder is characterized by intense sexual arousal from exposing one's genitalia to someone who is not expecting it. Like the prevalence of voyeuristic disorder, the prevalence of exhibitionistic disorder in the population is unknown. The DSM-5 estimates that the highest possible prevalence for men is around 2 to 4%, and is considered much lower, but not estimated, for women (APA, 2013).

Exhibitionism

Frotteuristic Disorder: Frotteuristic disorder is characterized by intense sexual arousal from rubbing against or touching someone who has not consented to this behavior. The DSM-5 estimates that between 10 to 14% of adult men experience this disorder, and estimates for women are not established (APA, 2013).

Frotteurism

Sexual Masochism Disorder: Masochistic disorder is characterized by sexual arousal from being physically or psychologically hurt by others, often involving bondage, being beaten, and/or being spoken to or yelled at harshly. Again, the DSM-5 describes the disorder as lacking sufficient evidence to determine prevalence rates, but cites an Australian study reporting prevalence of 2.2% among men and 1.3% among women for participation in sadistic or masochistic sexual behaviors (APA, 2013).

Sexual Sadism Disorder: Sexual sadism disorder is characterized by intense sexual arousal related to the psychological or physical pain of another person. Prevalence rates are estimated to vary widely between 2 to 30%, with higher rates among those who have carried out homicides that were sexually motivated, but less than 10% among sex offenders that were civilly committed (APA, 2013). Chan and Beauregard (2015) found higher rates of disordered personality traits and participation in a wide range of paraphilic behaviors in sex offenders who committed homicide compared to those sex offenders who had not committed homicide.

© rangizz/Shutterstock.com

© photomak/Shutterstock.com

© Antonio Guillem/Shutterstock.com

© Bildagentur Zoonar GmbH/Shutterstock.com

TABLE 13.1   **Paraphilic Disorders**

DSM-5 Paraphilic Disorders	DSM-IV-TR Paraphilias	Description
Voyeuristic Disorder	**Voyeurism**	Sexual arousal from observing an unsuspecting person who is dressing, naked, or having sex
Exhibitionistic Disorder	**Exhibitionism**	Sexual arousal from being watched by others during sex or exposing one's genitalia to an unsuspecting person
Frotteuristic Disorder	**Frotteurism**	Sexual arousal from touching or rubbing against someone who does not give consent
Pedophilic Disorder	**Pedophilia**	Sexual arousal and preference to children who are prepubescent
Sexual Masochism Disorder	**Sexual Masochism**	Sexual arousal from being beaten, humiliated, bound, or otherwise made to suffer
Sexual Sadism Disorder	**Sexual Sadism**	Sexual arousal from inflicting pain, suffering, or humiliation on another person
Fetishistic Disorder	**Fetishism**	Sexual arousal from inanimate objects or non-sexual body parts
Transvestic Disorder	**Transvestic Fetishism**	Sexual arousal from dressing in clothing typical of the opposite sex

APA, 2000; 2013; McManus et al., 2013

Pedophilic Disorder: Pedophilic disorder is characterized by intense sexual arousal to fantasies, sexual urges, and behaviors with children who are prepubescent, considered approximately age 13 or younger (APA, 2013). The highest estimated prevalence for pedophilic disorder among men is considered to be 3 to 5%, with too little known about women to establish a prevalence (APA, 2013).

Transvestic Disorder: Transvestic disorder is characterized by intense sexual arousal to dressing in clothes typically associated with the other gender. The DSM-5 specifies that the prevalence for this disorder is unknown, adding that less than 3% of males report having been sexually aroused by cross-dressing (APA, 2013). A Swedish study found approximately 2.8% of men and 0.4% of women had at least one arousing cross-dressing experience, and a strong correlation in these individuals to positive attitudes toward other paraphilic behaviors (Långström & Zucker, 2005).

Transvestism

© Discovod/Shutterstock.com

Podophilia

Telephone Scatologia

Fetishistic Disorder: Fetishistic disorder involves intense sexual arousal with nonliving objects or specific body parts that are non-genital; for example, an elbow or leg. Prevalence rates are unknown for this disorder. Some research suggests higher prevalence for fetishes involving certain body parts and objects related to these body parts, especially legs and feet, than to any other objects, behaviors, or body parts (Scorolli et al., 2007).

Other Specified Pedophilic Disorders: Examples of diagnoses falling into the category of Other Specified Paraphilic Disorder include intense sexual arousal involving urine (urophilia), enemas (klismaphilia), excrement (coprophilia), uninvited sexual phone calls (telephone scatologia), animals (zoophilia), or dead bodies (necrophilia), among others (APA, 2013).

Though little research has been done with many of these disorders, a recent case study on zoophilia presented a comprehensive treatment plan, leading to a successful outcome, as the young man in the case study "stopped having sex with cows" (Singg, 2017, p. 1).

The Good News: A wide array of biological and psychological treatments have been developed to treat various sexual and paraphilic disorders, with a great deal of success in some cases. Though these disorders can be severe and long-lasting, most individuals who seek help are able to accomplish a more functional and less distressing level of sexual activity.

Function

For the majority of paraphilic disorders, the second key criteria requires either an impairment in function or increased distress, either for oneself or another person. Specifically, for most of these disorders, individuals frequently have acted on their sexual urges with someone who has not consented; for example, touching someone, watching someone undress, or causing someone else pain during sex. These behaviors can often lead to severe functional problems, especially when a person violates another person's boundaries, including the loss of employment, the loss of significant and romantic relationships, registration as a sex offender, and even imprisonment. Certain disorders do not include criteria related to acting on sexual impulses with nonconsenting persons, for one reason or another. For example, in masochistic disorder a person receives punishment, rather than giving it, and so cannot act on urges with a nonconsenting person, and pedophilic disorder by definition involves prepubescent children, who are unable to give consent. Some disorders involve objects or other things, which cannot give consent; for example, certain fetishes, cross-dressing, corpses, or animals, whereas other disorders are more directly related to the violation of others; for example, obscene phone calls. Even disorders that do not have criteria related to a violation of nonconsenting person do include criteria specifying that one's behaviors, urges, or fantasies cause distress leading to similar functional difficulties in interpersonal, social, and occupational areas of functioning (APA, 2013).

Certain paraphilic disorders are characterized by additional functional problems that typically, but not always, accompany the disorder. Exhibitionistic disorder is often characterized by attraction to exposing oneself to specific groups of people; for example, prepubescent children, mature individuals, or both (APA, 2013). Sexual masochistic disorder sometimes involves choking or the restriction of air, known as asphyxiophilia. Transvestic disorder may also involve other fetishes, as well as sexual arousal by men to ideas or fantasies of oneself as female, known as autogynephilia (APA, 2013). Pedophilic disorder can be manifested in an array of ways, involving types that are exclusive to children or not, types involving same-sex or opposite-sex attractions, or both, and some pedophilia appears to be limited to incest (APA, 2013).

Asphyxiophilia

Characterized by sexual attraction or interest in restricting the oxygen intake of oneself or one's sexual partner, sometimes referred to as erotic or autoerotic asphyxiation

One controversy that involves individuals with pedophilic disorder is the assertion that they are more likely to have homosexual, rather than heterosexual attraction, though others suggest that this is a myth. While acts of pedophilia are more often committed against girls than boys, some research suggests that male sex offenders are only twice as likely to target girls, and that proportionally, those who are sexually aroused by prepubescent children are more frequently found among individuals with a homosexual development than those with a heterosexual development (Bickley & Beech, 2001; Freund et al., 1984; Freund & Watson, 1992). Some studies suggest that as many as 30 to 40% of pedophilic acts may be perpetrated by gay men, whereas other studies have found rates as low as 0 to 3.1%, a rate which would suggest a proportional similarity

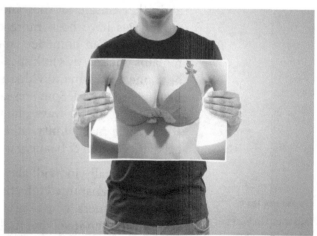

Autogynephilia

Characterized by sexual attraction or interest to ideas or fantasies of oneself as female

Myths in Movies

THE SILENCE OF THE LAMBS

In the film *The Silence of the Lambs*, the serial killer was represented as having a transvestic disorder (Demme et al., 1991). But is this link between paraphilic disorders and murder a myth, or is there evidence to support it?

© Orion Pictures Corporation/Photofest

between homosexual and heterosexual men (Bickley & Beech, 2001; Freund et al., 1984; Jenny et al., 1994). Regardless of the popular myths that have arisen about this topic, the research appears to be inconclusive in this controversial area.

Fatality

While paraphilic disorders typically do not lead directly to death, some can lead directly to a person's death; for example, masochistic asphyxiation and other unsafe fetishes and sexual practices. As previously mentioned, paraphilias have been more commonly found among sex offenders who have committed homicide, and although the exact link between these two remains unclear, this link speaks to the severity at which these disorders may be connected to an individual's maladjustment to their social world (Chan & Beauregard, 2015). Some research suggests that men who kill in particularly vicious and brutal ways often experienced childhood abuse, have doubts about their masculinity, and are more likely to participate in paraphilic behaviors (Chan & Beauregard, 2015; Megargee, 2006).

Additionally, individuals with paraphilic disorders are at an increased risk of sexually transmitted infections, especially if their sexual behavior includes multiple partners. Hypersexuality, a condition involving increased sexual drive, and often involving multiple partners, was proposed by Kafka (2010) for inclusion in the DSM-5, citing a long history of specifiers related to excessive sex drive in previous DSMs and other pathology coding systems. The International Classifications of Diseases continues to have several categories

Hypersexuality

Engaging in excessive sexual behavior, sometimes used synonymously with the phrase sex addition

of sexual dysfunction related to hypersexuality, but using the DSM-5 system, this problem is generally understood as an impulse-control disorder or another specified sexual dysfunction. Several categories of paraphilic disorders, such as sadistic and masochistic disorders, are commonly confused with hypersexuality, which can lead to similar problems. Freud (1920/1990) hypothesized that excessive interest in sexuality was related to *thanatos*, or a death wish, rather than *eros*, or the life instinct. Some evidence appears to support this connection, as individuals in an inpatient setting who met criteria for a paraphilic disorder had been hospitalized for psychiatric reasons more frequently, and were more likely to have attempted suicide (Marsh et al., 2010). Studies have also found that individuals with paraphilic disorders were more likely to report being a victim of childhood sexual abuse (APA, 2013; Marsh et al., 2010). Though an exact relationship between abuse and paraphilias is unknown, this may suggest that some paraphilic behaviors may be rooted in significant distress and attempts to relive and/or work out distress related to abuse.

Myths in Movies

BREAKING THE WAVES

© October Films/Photofest

No one is surprised to hear yet another mention of the link between sex and the movies. For decades, Hollywood has been perfecting the art of filming sex and things of a sexual nature. Much of what we see in the movies involves hypersexuality, and is often much more intense and out-of-the-box than most of us experience on a regular basis. This may not be the case for individuals with hypersexuality and paraphilic disorders. The movie *Breaking the Waves* depicts the impact a man's hypersexuality and voyeurism has on his wife (von Trier & Asmussen, 1996). After an accident leaving him paralyzed and unable to have sex, the man asks his wife to have sex with other men and come back to tell him about it. But do accounts like this really happen? Consider the story of Richard in the following Case Vignette, and the impact of his sexual addiction on his wife.

Case Vignette

Richard was a 44-year-old married man with three grown children. He was seeking treatment for sexual addiction after his wife discovered that he had multiple recent sexual relationships with other women, in addition to many previous affairs over the course of their 23-year marriage. Despite her discovery of his infidelity, and despite being a highly successful lawyer herself, and despite in no way needing his financial assistance, he had no concern that she would leave him because she "loved him so desperately." He reported that he was in love with her as well, but that he did not always find her as attractive or arousing as many of the other women he was seeing on the side. Approximately 4 years prior to seeking treatment, he had expressed to his wife concerns regarding his lack of arousal to her, after which she began working out more regularly and had her breasts enlarged. He reported that this helped increase his arousal for a short while, but he continued to need more and different stimulation, including watching women perform sexual acts with other men in-person, and performing sexual acts with different women in front of other people.

Over time Richard found himself increasingly aroused to these sexual activities, and eventually asked his wife if she would participate. In spite of her initial protests, she agreed to join him and have sex with another man while he watched, and to watch him have sex with the other man's wife. He reported higher levels of arousal than ever to the new sexual stimuli of watching his wife have sex with another man, and told his wife afterward, "You never looked more beautiful to me than you did tonight!" After a few additional group sexual encounters, Richard's wife decided that she did not want to participate in these behaviors anymore, and refused. Richard became increasingly troubled by her refusal, as he did not want to stop these behaviors. His wife became adamant that he stop and told him she considered it cheating for him to continue. He promised to quit, but quickly fell back into the behavior and began lying to his wife about it. As time passed, Richard's wife began to express regret and frustration that she let her husband convince her to participate in his sexual addiction, and experienced difficulty having sex with Richard, as she was always thinking about him watching her during the group sexual encounters. She noticed that Richard would often inconspicuously show up anytime she was changing clothes, and she began feeling uncomfortable allowing him to see her naked. Additionally, neighbors began to complain that Richard seemed to be hanging out around their bedroom windows and looking over their fences more and more frequently. The distress that his sexual problems appeared to cause for his wife and their relationship was palpable. Richard clearly met criteria for a diagnosis of hypersexuality or impulse-control disorder, in relation to his ongoing sexual activity with other women and groups. What do you think? Does Richard additionally meet criteria for a paraphilic disorder? If so, just one?

Feeling Pain

Regardless of how closely related to prior abuse an individual's paraphilic disorder may be, it is clear that these disorders themselves carry a high potential from causing pain and discord in a person's life. The DSM-5 suggests a host of risk factors for the development of a paraphilic disorder, including not only sexual abuse, but also emotional abuse, alcohol or substance misuse, hypersexuality or sexual preoccupation, and even neurodevelopmental concerns in utero for pedophilic disorder (APA, 2013). Also, individuals are at a higher risk of paraphilic disorders, including pedophilia, frotteuristic disorder, and exhibitionistic disorder, if they have antisocial personality disorder/traits or conduct disorder in childhood, which is quite understandable as these disorders are all rooted in the objectification and violation of other people (APA, 2013).

Just as these other conditions are frequent among persons with paraphilic disorders, so also do they struggle with the related emotional, psychological, and physical distress. Individuals with paraphilic disorders have been found to frequently suffer from mood disorders and anxiety disorders, including social phobia, as well as impulsivity related to sex, such as compulsive masturbation, hypersexuality, pornography dependence, obsessive-compulsive disorders, and ADHD in childhood (Bradford, 1999; Kafka & Prentky, 1994; Kafka & Prentky, 1998). Individuals with hypersexuality often need treatment as a means of reducing their shame and guilt, though treatment-seeking and increased distress may be more likely initiated as a result of the consequences of failing to control sexual impulses, and in the case of paraphilic disorders, social or legal consequences (Gilliland et al., 2011).

Theories and Treatments of Sexual Disorders

A wide variety of theories regarding the development of sexual disorders, and the treatment or resolution of such disorders, have been proposed over the past several decades. Treatments are quite different for sexual dysfunctions, gender dysphoria, and paraphilic disorders, though all have been approached from both biological and psychological perspectives. Individuals seeking treatments for one of these disorders are also likely to be differentially motivated to seek treatment. For example, individuals with sexual dysfunctions may be more likely to experience relationship distress as a result of poor sexual functioning, whereas individuals with gender dysphoria may be more likely to seek treatment related to self-related identity issues, and those with paraphilic disorders may seek treatment as a result of problematic behaviors. Treatments are similarly related to the stressors unique to each disorder.

Psychological Theories and Treatments of Sexual Disorders

Many of the psychological perspectives on sexual disorders have been rooted in behavioral and psychodynamic theories, although a host of other theories have proposed adaptations in the way to treat the various sexual disorders. Individuals with these disorders, as previously explored, have a wide variety of distress, and accordingly some are more likely to be resolved with psychotherapy alone, whereas others may require conjunctive treatment with biological treatments, and still others, such as pedophilia, are considered a life-long phenomenon for which treatment, whether biological or psychological, is simply understood to aid in adjustment, rather than to resolve the condition.

Sexual Dysfunctions. Sexual dysfunctions may be treated with couples' therapy, such as sensate focus therapy, various types of sex therapy, and behavioral therapies. As we have discussed throughout this book, how one conceives of the problem will determine how one treats it. Perhaps as importantly, with sexual dysfunctions, how the problem arises matters. For example, if one's sexual dysfunction is rooted in other mental health conditions, such as depression, then treating the other disorder is sometimes enough to resolve the sexual dysfunction. Some individuals may have received a poor formation in regard to sexuality or experienced trauma, for which therapies such as psychodynamic or experiential therapies that can aid the person in resolving their fear, shame, or other maladaptive responses to sex may be more helpful. Sensate focus therapy may be helpful in overcoming some of the issues related to poor formation about sex, and is understood to be effective by means of training clients to focus on sensual feelings, beginning with non-genital stimulation, and to communicate and guide each other to perform sexually satisfying activities, all the while deemphasizing orgasm (Seftel et al., 2004; Masters & Johnson, 1970). Deemphasizing orgasm is common among several treatments for sexual dysfunction, as the pressure to climax or to climax at the right time is often a focus causing considerable anxiety for individuals with these dysfunctions. For women who experience a genito-pelvic pain/penetration disorder, especially those who experience problems with a tensing or tightening of vaginal muscles and corresponding difficulties with penetration, behavioral exercises may be helpful. These exercises pair relaxation with penetration, gradually increasing the dilation

© Phovoir/Shutterstock.com

of the penetrative object, with the goal of eventually being able to guide her partner in penetration without anxiety or vaginal tightening.

Gender Dysphoria. As previously discussed, theories and treatments for gender dysphoria are highly controversial. Psychosocial theories related to gender dysphoria generally posit that socialization by parents may contribute to the development of the disorder, and some research supports that parents of boys with the disorder were less likely to socialize them in typically masculine ways (Green, 1985). Among the earliest theories of gender development, Freud (1905/2011) suggested that all people are born mentally bi-sexual (not meaning bi-sexually attracted) and are therefore able to develop in more masculine or more feminine ways, which occurs through identification with their parents during the phallic stage of development. Individuals who have a poor identification with the same-sex parent, along with other possible developmental issues, were therefore understood to be more likely to develop same-sex attractions. The desire for affection from the same-sex or opposite-sex parent, which is never given by the parent, is hypothesized by some researchers in this line of thinking to lead to an attraction and/or obsession leading to an attraction to the same-sex and/or identification with the opposite sex (Lev, 2004). Psychodynamic therapy in this tradition therefore focused on healing these broken relationships, and was understood to lead the client to be more comfortable with his or her natal gender.

© LuckyImages/Shutterstock.com

Individuals and psychological organizations disagreed with these gender theories, and developed alternative ways of focusing on treatment. Today, several mental health organizations are beginning to focus on affirming identity and orientation from a person's perspective rather than examining and treating psychopathology related to symptoms of sexual and gender-based disorders or developmental issues in childhood. The American Psychological Association (2015) developed guidelines for working with transgender and gender nonconforming (TGNC) persons, "to assist psychologists in the provision of culturally competent, developmentally appropriate, and trans-affirmative psychological practice . . . that is respectful, aware, and supportive of the identities and life experiences of TGNC people" (pp. 832–833). These approaches are understood to help individuals with gender dysphoria become more comfortable with their nonconforming gender expression by providing them a safe and supportive environment for exploring issues related to their sexuality.

Paraphilic Disorders. Behavioral theories are perhaps the most well-known approaches to understanding and treating paraphilic disorders. Classic behavioral theories suggest that paraphilias develop through conditioning, with the object of paraphilic attraction being paired with sexual arousal early in development. For example, a child who is choked while being sexually stimulated may repeatedly imagine or repeat this behavior while masturbating, thereby reinforcing the association of choking or other painful behaviors with sexual arousal. As an adolescent, this may lead to further sexual experiences connecting pain and arousal, further solidifying the paraphilia. Social learning theories have added to these behavioral perspectives, by suggesting that individuals who have behaviors such as corporal punishment or aggression modeled to them, may be more likely to generalize these behaviors to sexual activity. This can play out in a manner of ways; for example, an individual who is harmed in a particular way by a parent may transpose this into a sexual context and do the same to a sexual partner, or as in pedophilia, an abused individual may be afraid to be with an adult, and thereby seek out children, who seem safer (Seto, 2009).

Aversion Therapy

A form of behavioral therapy pairing an aversive stimuli with a behavior the client wishes to change, in order to extinguish a previously conditioned pleasurable response

Behavioral treatment focuses on breaking the association of pleasure or arousal and the paraphilic object. Aversion therapy is a behavioral approach used to break or "extinguish" the connection between paraphilic objects and arousal by pairing an aversive stimuli to a paraphilic object, often while conversely attempting to reduce any existing anxieties or fears about more typical, age-appropriate sexual contact. As you're probably already thinking, this approach can be highly controversial, as it involves the administration of painful aversive stimuli, a practice not commonly undertaken in therapies treating other conditions. Cognitive-based treatments for paraphilic disorders are frequently coupled with behavioral treatments to help address obsessive thinking and to guide clients in developing a plan for managing social relationships without resorting to paraphilic behaviors. Some research suggests that cognitive and behavioral treatments of this type may be more effective in treating paraphilias that do not involve predatory behaviors (Darcangelo, 2008).

Biological Theories and Treatments of Sexual Disorders

As with many other mental disorders, biological theories and treatments abound, and vary widely depending on which sexual disorder one is experiencing. Researchers of sexual dysfunctions have developed medication and mechanical approaches to aiding individuals with these dysfunctions. Medical professionals working with individuals struggling with gender dysphoria have traditionally relied on opposite-sex hormone regimens and surgically changing individuals genitalia in attempts to treat this disorder. For paraphilic disorders, biological treatments have ranged from medications to surgical castration. Castration has generally been reserved to cases involving individuals who have committed, and are at risk of repeating, serious sexual crimes, and who consent to the procedure.

Sexual Dysfunctions. There's probably no one left on the planet that hasn't heard of Viagra! Viagra and similar drugs are the treatments most commonly associated with sexual dysfunctions, likely because erectile dysfunction has received the most media attention. Addressing the cause of the dysfunction is extremely important in the treatment of these disorders, as for example, it makes little sense to put someone on a medication when the problem's primary cause may be psychological. The same is true on the purely biological level. Sexual dysfunctions may be caused by a medication taken for another medical concern, or even substance abuse, in which case the most appropriate approach will be to change the medication or cease substance use, rather than throw another medication in the mix. Unfortunately, this happens all too often, especially in the treatment of erectile dysfunction. Additional approaches have been developed to help men achieve an erection, including vacuum pumps, saline pumps, and prosthetic devices creating a permanent erection, though these methods do not aid in psychological, or in some cases even physiological, arousal (Delizonna et al., 2001).

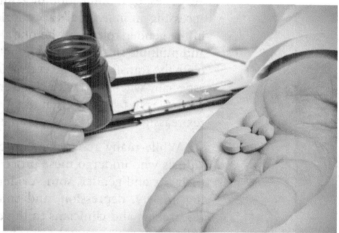

© nito/Shutterstock.com

In addition to erectile dysfunction medications for men, similar medications have been developed for women to assist in vaginal lubrication and stimulation, though results have been inconsistent with these medications, possibly due to arousal in women being related more to emotional and psychological conditions than physiological (Althof & Needle, 2013; Basson & Gilks, 2018; Montgomery, 2008). Certain classes of antidepressants are known to cause sexual dysfunctions, including medications targeting serotonin (SSRIs). Switching these medications can lead to the resolution of the sexual dysfunction. Additionally, testosterone has been used to treat dysfunctions involving low sexual arousal or desire in both men and women. These treatments run the risk of potential masculinizing effects such as vocal changes and hair growth when used by women, as well as potential harm to a fetus if the woman becomes pregnant (Shifren et al., 2000). Pacik & Geletta (2017) have proposed a promising mixed-methods treatment for vaginismus, which entails the use of botox and bupivacaine to reduce pain, combined with slowly increasing dilation of the vagina with light sedation and a dilator that remains in the vagina, anxiety/pain and dilation logs, and ongoing support through office visits and other contact. Approximately 71% of women in their study were able to achieve intercourse without pain by around 5 weeks (Pacik & Geletta, 2017).

Gender Dysphoria. Theories of the development of gender dysphoria have suggested etiologies related to prenatal neurological exposure to opposite-sex hormones or the lack of congruent sex hormones, although researchers remain consistent that we are still uncertain of the exact mechanisms leading to the disorder (Baba et al., 2007; Hines et al., 2003; Zucker & Wood, 2011). In line with theories suggesting hormonal causes, some researchers suggest that children or adolescents with this disorder may benefit from treatment with hormone blockers, which can delay puberty. Others suggest the use of opposite-sex hormones during puberty to promote the development of secondary sexual characteristics of the other sex, though this is considered more radical by many medical professionals as it can lead to permanent sterilization. Some researchers also promote surgical modification of one's sexual characteristics as a means of treating the disorder. Surgeries for modification of genitals generally involve a lengthy process of accessing an individual's appropriateness for the surgeries, including living in the gender-role opposite one's sex for a period of time prior to surgery, and multiple surgeries in conjunction with opposite-sex hormones to complete the transition (Byne et al., 2012). These methods can be controversial, especially when used with children. Lilienfeld (1995) edited a book on controversies in psychology, among which was the question of whether or not sex reassignment surgery was an effective treatment for the disorder.

While many researchers agree that evidence does suggest that individuals who undergo these procedures feel more of an alignment between their sex and gender, some evidence suggests that overall distress, including anxiety, depression, and suicidality does not change, leading some researchers and clinicians to the conclusion that these procedures may be colluding with a mental disorder by increasing mistaken self-perceptions, rather than treating it (Meyer & Reter, 1979). McHugh (2004), previously a psychiatrist-in-chief at Johns Hopkins University Hospital, has likened these procedures to medical abuse, especially as some of the procedures used with children and young adults are irreversible and may sterilize a person for life. Some suggest that this is particularly concerning in light of the high numbers of children who eventually choose to live as their natal gender.

On the other hand, some evidence suggests that positive outcomes of surgically changing genitalia are possible (Klein & Gorzalka, 2009; Murad et al., 2010). The DSM-5 diagnosis of the disorder calls for clinicians to specify whether or not an individual is post-transition, living as the gender that is experienced or expressed, has received a course of cross-sex hormones, or has had a cross-sex medical procedure (APA, 2013). Regardless of whether one may believe that the pain transgender individuals experience is due primarily to the lack of social acceptance, distress over gender incongruence, or a combination of both, it is clear that individuals with gender dysphoria are at a high risk of suicide and comorbid disorders, and the mental health community has much work to do in terms of helping to protect them from these risks.

Paraphilic Disorders. Medications used to treat paraphilic disorders have generally targeted the hypersexuality that are often involved with the disorders. The monoamine hypothesis for the development of paraphilias suggests that these disorders may be related to monoamine dysfunction. As discussed in previous chapters, monoamines are a group of neurotransmitters including dopamine, serotonin, and norepinephrine. These neurotransmitters are known to play a significant role in human sexual function (Kafka, 2003). As discussed above, SSRIs are known to decrease sexual functioning, and this side effect has proven effective in the treatment of some cases of paraphilias, and may work primarily by the reduction of hypersexuality (Greenberg et al., 1996).

Additionally, surgical castration has been used in some extreme cases involving sexual offenders, and as expected works by means of the reduction of testosterone production, though this method is no longer commonly practiced (Seto, 2009). This practice is considered unethical by some researchers, amounting to cruel and unusual punishment. The use of medications that can virtually eliminate one's sex drive, sometimes referred to as chemical castration, is more commonly utilized with sex offenders as well as sex addicts. Drugs that can function as antiandrogens, such as Depo Provera, which was developed as a hormonal contraception for women, have been found to lower testosterone levels and reduce paraphilic sexual desires (Guay, 2009; Money, 1981). Other medications, such as Naltrexone, which is commonly used to reduce addictive cravings for substances, are also being used in the treatment of paraphilic disorders and hypersexuality to reduce sexual craving and impulsivity without the severity of chemical castration (Berner & Briken, 2007; Firoz et al., 2014).

Monoamine Hypothesis

The hypothesis that dysfunctions among a group of neurotransmitters called monoamines, including dopamine, serotonin, and norepinephrine, may be responsible for paraphilic behaviors

Naltrexone

A drug commonly used for substance addictions to reduce cravings

Conclusion

As the authors of this textbook, we strongly believe that regardless of what anyone may conceive to be normal or disordered human sexual behavior, each and every person in this world is equal in human dignity and value, regardless of whether they struggle with this or that disorder, or no disorder at all! An intense amount of stigma and distress surrounds those who struggle with the sexual disorders we have described in this book, and our culture needs to place a certain priority on those who suffer, whether it be from a sexual disorder or some other health concern. Some of these disorders carry with them the possibility of extreme distress and high mortality rates, suggesting that we are still doing far too little to meet the needs of individuals struggling with these disorders. Sexual disorders are also often associated with relationship problems and isolation, likely fueling the fires of distress and dysfunction. Our hope is that rather than seeing these hurting persons as "others," through greater awareness we can reach out to those who are lonely and marginalized, treating all people with the dignity and respect they deserve.

CHAPTER REVIEW

QUESTIONS

1. What are the differences between sexual dysfunctions, gender dysphoria, and paraphilic disorders? Are there any overlapping symptoms between these disorders?

2. How do the sexual dysfunctions related to males differ from the sexual dysfunctions related to females? Are there differences between males and females in regard to gender dysphoria and paraphilic disorders?

3. Describe some of the conceptual changes from the DSM-IV-TR to the DSM-5 in regard to gender dysphoria and paraphilic disorders. Why were these changes deemed to be important? What are the differences between intersex, transgender, and transsexual conditions?

4. What are some of the theories for the development of the various sex and gender disorders? How are they treated? What are some of the concerns and controversies regarding some of these treatments?

KEY TERMS

Ego-Dystonic

Sexual Dysfunctions

Gender Dysphoria

Paraphilic Disorders

Vaginismus

Dyspareunia

Intersex

Transgender

Transsexual

Assigned Gender

Paraphilia

Asphyxiophilia

Autogynephilia

Hypersexuality

Aversion Therapy

Monoamine Hypothesis

Naltrexone

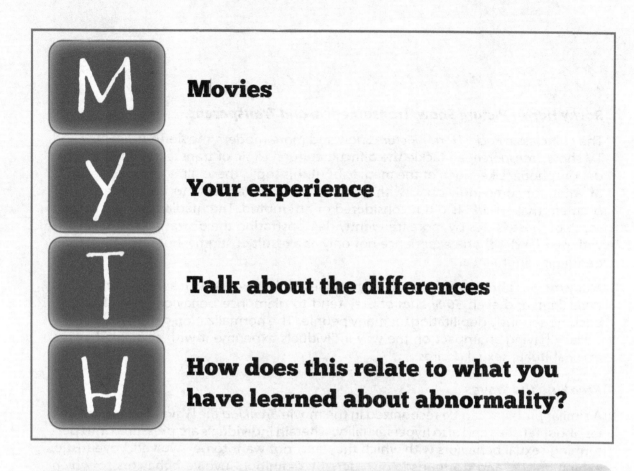

M Movies

Y Your experience

T Talk about the differences

H How does this relate to what you have learned about abnormality?

Myths in Movies Recap

Sex, Lies, and Videotapes

Sex, Lies, and Videotapes portrays adults in tumultuous relationships, and suggests a connection between sexual disorders, infidelity, and divorce. Though exaggerated in the film, the DSM-5 does suggest that problems with relationship satisfaction, fertility, and decreased self-esteem increases the likelihood of infidelity and divorce. In regard to the videotape aspect of this film, a major factor that has been related to sexual dysfunction is increasing use of pornography, which in turn has been found closely linked with divorce (de Alarcón et al., 2019; Doran & Price, 2014).

My Husband Won't Fit

My Husband Won't Fit implies that the main female character in the show cannot have sex with her husband due to genito-pelvic pain/penetration disorder, but can have sex with other men. This disorder is characterized as pervasive in the DSM-5, the only sexual dysfunction disorder which does not include a specifier for generalized or situational types.

Myths in Movies Recap

Rocky Horror Picture Show, Transamerica, and Transparent

The cult classic *Rocky Horror Picture Show* and more modern movie *Transamerica* and TV show *Transparent* all tackle the difficult cultural topic of transsexualism and gender dysphoria. Like much of the media about this topic, these films make a spectacle of what, for some individuals with gender dysphoria, appears to be such a serious problem that suicide is often considered or attempted. The media can help correct some of these issues by more frequently demonstrating the distress that individuals with gender dysphoria experience not only as a result of stigma, but also about their gender incongruence.

Many movies about atypical and fetishistic sexual behaviors such as *Crash, 8mm, Eyes Wide Shut,* and even *50 Shades of Grey* tend to glamorize behaviors that often can become seriously debilitating for many people. The normalization of these behaviors is likely having an impact on the way individuals experiment with sexual behaviors and habituate sexual desires.

Breaking the Waves

A similar problem can be recognized in the movie *Breaking the Waves* and other movies about fetishes and also hypersexuality, wherein individuals are pressured into performing sexual behaviors with which they may not want to be involved. Voyeuristic, exhibitionistic, and frotteuristic disorders by definition involve behaviors to which others have not consented (APA, 2013). And research has demonstrated that increased porn use is connected with more frequent requests for pornographic behaviors, as well as decreased sexual desire and performance with partners (sexual dysfunction), and increased desire for sexual novelty (de Alarcón et al., 2019).

The Silence of the Lambs

The Silence of the Lambs explores the classic Freudian connection of sex and violence, suggesting a link between paraphilic disorders and violence or murder, and while the vast majority of individuals who are struggling with paraphilic disorders are far from violent, research has demonstrated that individuals who have committed violent crimes and homocides more frequently participated in paraphilic behaviors than the general population (Chan & Beauregard, 2015; Megargee, 2006).

CHAPTER FOURTEEN

SUBSTANCE-RELATED, IMPULSE-CONTROL, AND CONDUCT DISORDERS

LEARNING OBJECTIVES

- ▶ Examine myths related to substance-related and impulse-control disorders
- ▶ Discuss media portrayals and experiences that contribute to these myths
- ▶ Explore differences between substance-related disorders
- ▶ Explore differences between impulse-control disorders
- ▶ Analyze the 4 Fs of substance-related and impulse-control disorders
- ▶ Recognize elements of substance-related and impulse-control disorders
- ▶ Examine the interaction between psychological and physical symptoms
- ▶ Identify the diagnostic criteria common to substance-related disorders
- ▶ Analyze the differences in diagnostic criteria of substance-related disorders
- ▶ Describe diagnostic features of impulse-control disorder
- ▶ Explain psychological theories and treatment of substance and impulse-control disorders
- ▶ Review biological theories and treatment of substance and impulse-control disorders

CHAPTER OUTLINE

- ▶ MYTHs of Substance-Related Disorders
- ▶ The 4 Fs of Addictive Disorders: Up, Down, and Out-of-this-World
- ▶ Specific Substance-Related and Addictive Disorders: A Variety of Addictions
- ▶ Theories and Treatments of Substance-Related and Addictive Disorders
- ▶ MYTHs of Disruptive, Impulse-Control, and Conduct Disorders
- ▶ Disruptive, Impulse-Control, and Conduct Disorders: Stop Right There!!!
- ▶ Treatments of Disruptive, Impulse-Control, and Conduct Disorders

MYTHs of Substance-Related Disorders

What do you think of when you hear the words "drug addict" come out of someone's mouth? Likely, your thoughts have a negative connotation, though if you've had exposure to individuals with substance-related disorders, then you may have a more empathetic response, being aware of the horrors and tragedies that often accompany these disorders. As the saying goes with rock stars, addicts can burn out or fade away, and both can be accompanied by a great deal of misery. Many of us have had first- or secondhand experiences of tragedies caused by addiction, and you have likely seen a host of movies that have left you with a plethora of ideas about drugs and addiction. Spend some time considering the thoughts and beliefs you tend to hold regarding this disorder.

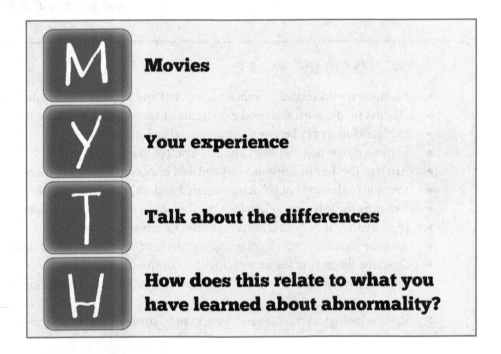

M   **Movies**

Y   **Your experience**

T   **Talk about the differences**

H   **How does this relate to what you have learned about abnormality?**

Although some people seem capable of remaining marginally functional while excessively using alcohol or drugs, individuals who have a substance-related disorder, by diagnostic definition, are experiencing serious dysfunction and distress. These impairments often impact most areas of their lives, including social functioning and job performance. Though individuals can have severe substance-related reactions with just a single use, there appear to be some real and significant differences between addicts and those who do not become addicted. Consider the following examples to demonstrate these points:

Case Vignettes

Frederic was a 24-year-old single man, who had recently begun experimenting with alcohol and marijuana. He had only drank a few times, but he enjoyed it thoroughly. When the opportunity to smoke marijuana became available, he was eager to try it. He reported that he did not recall the details of what happened after he smoked the marijuana, but did recall his friends telling him that there was no one outside the house talking, after which he became worried that they were lying to him and might try to rob him. By the next day, he found himself in the psychiatric wing of a general hospital, diagnosed with substance-induced psychosis. When he was released to outpatient care after being discharged, he was still slightly paranoid and reported faintly hearing things he could not explain. Do you think Frederic ever returned to a pre-psychotic state of consciousness? He had not yet developed an addiction, but could he?

Barbara was a 32-year-old married woman, who had struggled with alcohol use since she was age 15. She vividly and joyfully recalled the moment she became an alcoholic, which she believed was at her first drink. She described the experience as a wonderful escape from the chaotic and abusive household where she grew up. She said that she felt it was the first time in her life that she was really relaxed and comfortable. She described this experience by saying, "At that moment, it was like I finally knew who I was. I finally found my identity." Can addiction be so powerful that it can function as an identity?

While many of us may find it hard to relate to these experiences, individuals struggling with addiction have experienced or know others who have experienced many similar phenomena. Those with family members addicted to substances often fear the death of their loved one, but addicts who are struggling to break free from their addiction often fear the slow fade-away just as much. Consider this description of the experience of addiction, "Yeah, I'm afraid to die, but you know what I'm really afraid of the most, staying alive and addicted for decades, for the rest of my life." Addiction can steal one's very life, but it can also steal the joy of living out of life.

Myths in Movies
PULP FICTION and THE BIG LEBOWSKI

Hollywood has spent a great deal of time glamorizing drug use and addiction, however, the drama of addiction has not been lost on Hollywood. Just consider the dichotomy between movies like *Pulp Fiction* and *Leaving Las Vegas*. In the one, serious drug abusers are portrayed as gangsters who are almost invincible, whereas in the other, the glory days of alcohol addiction have faded into ruin, and the main character is slowly killing himself with his drug of choice. See Wedding, Boyd, and Niemiec (2005) for many additional movies that seem to fall into one of these categories.

A scene from *Pulp Fiction*

A scene from *The Big Lebowski*

With certain addictions, the slow fade-away can be hard to notice. Consider films like *The Big Lebowski*, wherein the main character, an unemployed, aging marijuana user, appears to have little clue as to how he should navigate life. But is this a myth or has Hollywood gotten it right this time?

The 4 Fs of Addictive Disorders: Up, Down, and Out-of-this-World

Perhaps the simplest way to think about the effects of drugs on the body is the distinction between uppers and downers. And while this distinction is an appropriate description of most drugs, certain drugs, such as hallucinogens, have a primary impact on a person's perception of the world, rather than speeding them up or slowing them down. When considering the substance-related disorders discussed in this chapter, it will be helpful to keep in mind the specific type of impact each drug has on its user. Below we will look at the 4 Fs common to most of the addictive disorders, after which we will explore the specific substance-related disorders in more detail.

Frequency

A—Amount of Time: In order to be diagnosed with a substance-related disorder, an individual must experience two symptoms related to a specific substance within a 1-year period. Most of the diagnostic criteria is virtually the same from one substance to another, as we will see below. Additionally, an individual can simultaneously be diagnosed with multiple addictions, as long as they meet two-symptom criteria for each of the substances within the last year. The only exception to the two criteria in 12 months rule, among addictive disorders, is gambling disorder, which requires four symptoms specific to gambling within a 1-year period (American Psychiatric Association [APA], 2013).

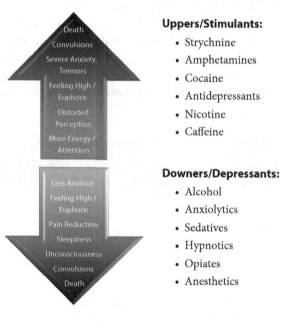

Uppers/Stimulants:

- Strychnine
- Amphetamines
- Cocaine
- Antidepressants
- Nicotine
- Caffeine

Downers/Depressants:

- Alcohol
- Anxiolytics
- Sedatives
- Hypnotics
- Opiates
- Anesthetics

FIGURE 14.1   **Stimulants and Depressants**
Courtesy of Leslie Kelley

B—Behavior: Individuals with addiction issues often spend a great deal of time using or obtaining substances, and as the drug problem worsens, they may begin to do nothing except seeking drugs and figuring out ways to pay for their drug habit. As mentioned above, two symptoms are needed for a person to be diagnosed with a disorder, including taking drugs in larger amounts or for longer periods of time than intended, a desire and/or unsuccessful attempts to quit using, and excessive time spent obtaining substances, often resulting in negative social or relationship problems (APA, 2013). Do addicts have cravings and urges

Tolerance

A state in which one's body becomes habituated and less responsive to a drug, thereby requiring higher doses to achieve similar effects

Withdrawal

A state in which one's body becomes habituated to a drug, such that in the absence of the drug, negative physiological and/or psychological symptoms occur

to use for the rest of their lives? While craving substances is common among addicts, some individuals seem to experience stronger cravings than others, and some individuals report that they have no cravings. Interestingly, some people who have been in remission for many years or decades say they still have cravings for their drug of choice, while cravings completely cease at some point in recovery for others. In addition to cravings and urges, individuals may experience tolerance or withdrawal, may continue to use even when it can be dangerous, and drug use is often continued in spite of previous physiological, social, and psychological problems related to using (APA, 2013). Individuals with substance-related disorders may give up trying to fulfill obligations to work, family, or friends, and reduce activities with others or even quit their job, in order to devote more time to using substances.

C—Curve: While lots of people drink alcohol and many even experiment with illegal drugs, far fewer are diagnosable. Prevalence rates for different substances vary widely, and in many ways. For example, younger adults (age 18–29) tend to have a higher prevalence of alcohol use (16.2%) within the last year than other age groups (APA, 2013). Actually, a popular saying among drug counselors is that if you get clients to their 27th birthday, their chances of surviving and breaking the addiction increase substantially. Statistically, this may be evidenced by prevalence rates dropping in middle age for many substance use disorders. Additionally, for most classes of drugs, men tend to more frequently be abusers than women. See Figures 14.2 and 14.3 for more info of age prevalence rates.

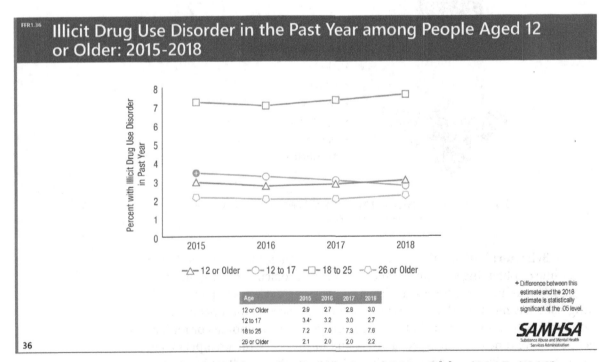

Age	2015	2016	2017	2018
12 or Older	2.9	2.7	2.8	3.0
12 to 17	3.4+	3.2	3.0	2.7
18 to 25	7.2	7.0	7.3	7.8
26 or Older	2.1	2.0	2.0	2.2

FIGURE 14.2   Substance Abuse by People Aged 12 or Older (2015–2018)
https://www.samhsa.gov/data/sites/default/files/cbhsq-reports/NSDUHffrBriefingSlides2018_w-final-cover.pdf

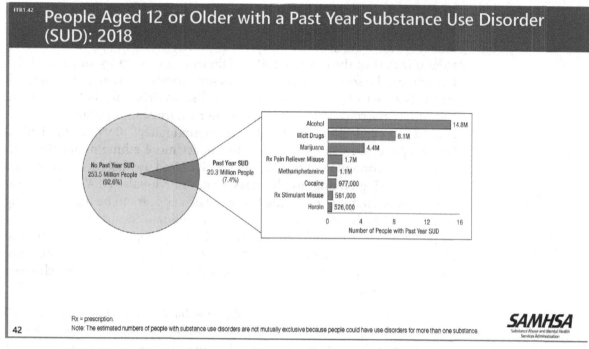

FIGURE 14.3   Prevalence of Specific Substance Use Disorders (2018)
https://www.samhsa.gov/data/sites/default/files/cbhsq-reports/NSDUHffrBriefingSlides2018_w-final-cover.pdf

By far, alcohol is the most widely abused substance. Approximately 4.6% of adolescents and 8.5% of adults (age 18 and up) struggle with an alcohol use disorder, though among adults 12.4% of males abuse alcohol, whereas only 4.9% of females abuse alcohol (APA, 2013). Cannabis use disorder has been found to have a 12-month prevalence of 1.5% for adults, and interestingly, 3.4% for adolescents age 12–17 (APA, 2013). The yearly prevalence rates of other drugs are significantly less than both alcohol and cannabis disorders. For example, inhalant disorder appears to affect about 0.4% of adolescents and 0.02% of adults; opiate use disorder seems to impact about 0.37% of adults; sedative-, hypnotic-, and anxiolytic- use disorder affects approximately 0.3% of adolescents and 0.2% of adults; stimulant use disorders affect approximately 0.2% of both adolescents and adults, with higher rates of adolescent girls than boys, and equal gender rates among adults (APA, 2013). Prevalence rates for hallucinogen use disorder varies by the type of hallucinogen used, with approximately 2.5% of individuals reported to have ever used PCP, with higher rates among older individuals, whereas a 12-month prevalence around 0.5% for adolescents and 0.1% for adults have been found for other hallucinogens such as MDMA, LSD, and Mescaline (APA, 2013). Interestingly, adolescent girls appear to be using other hallucinogens at a higher rate than boys, though the same is not true for hallucinogens belonging to the PCP class. Last of all, gambling disorder impacts approximately 0.2 to 0.3% within the past year, with slightly higher (0.4 to 1.0%) prevalence rates over the lifetime (APA, 2013).

PCP

Phencyclidine, commonly referred to as "angel dust," was developed as an anesthetic in the 1950s; causes hallucinogenic and dissociative symptoms

MDMA

Methylenedioxy-methamphetamine, commonly referred to as "ecstasy," is a hallucinogenic drug, causing euphoria and many other effects

LSD

Lysergic acid diethylamide, commonly referred to as "acid," is a highly potent hallucinogenic drug

Part of the difficulty of determining prevalence rates for substance and addictive disorders is the fact that prevalence depends to some degree on what's available and where, which likely varies widely from city to city, and even from one part of the city to another. Likewise, a wide range of cultural differences can be seen in prevalence rates for various disorders. Do you think that it is a myth that Eastern Europeans like to drink alcohol, as they are commonly portrayed? Interestingly, Eastern Europeans appear to have the highest rate of alcohol use disorders at approximately 10.9%. In the United States, opioid use disorder appears to impact more ethnic minorities with lower socioeconomic status (SES), although opioid use disorder also appears to be increasing among middle-class white individuals (APA, 2013). Conjointly, amphetamine use in the United States appears to be highest among white individuals, with around 66% of individuals admitted primarily for amphetamine use being White, followed by Hispanic individuals at around 21% (APA, 2013). Inhalant use, on the other hand, appears to be more common among certain individuals with lower SES, such as homeless children involved in gangs (APA, 2013).

The Good News: Treatments for addiction have been around for nearly 100 years, even before the advent of Alcoholics Anonymous in the 1930s. Though individuals with substance disorder often tend to isolate themselves as their addictions progress, many recovery groups exist for almost any kind of imaginable addiction, and persons with addictions and their families do not need to be alone. Additionally, a host of biological and psychological treatments have been developed to help increase motivation to quit substance use, and to reinforce a healthy, drug-free lifestyle.

Function

Continual abuse of substances often leads to severe dysfunction in many areas of life. Individuals who have substance use and addictive disorders often struggle to fulfill their work, home, and school obligations, experience persistent and increasing discord in social and interpersonal relationships, and often give up healthy recreational activities substituting them with using behaviors (APA, 2013). As an addiction progresses, individuals spend more and more time thinking about and obtaining substances, which is often coupled with more frequent deceit within their relationships, as they attempt to create a story to cover up the amount of time spent obtaining and using substances. Additionally, substance use and addictive disorders can be extremely expensive, leading to financial ruin in many cases. These individuals often spend increasing amounts of money on substances, but may face even greater financial difficulties in terms of the lack of income from missing work or being unemployed, as well as the costs of legal fees related to criminal charges for illegal drugs or crimes committed to fund their addictions.

Feeling Pain

Stories of the loss and pain related to addiction and "hitting rock bottom," can be difficult to hear. So often people label addictive disorders as "crazy" because individuals that do not struggle with addictive impulses find it hard to understand how someone can experience so much pain and dysfunction without changing their behavior. Physiologically, the pain from taking large quantities of drugs, as well as the pain related to withdrawal, can be extreme and even fatal with certain drugs. Symptoms of withdrawal can include nausea and vomiting, tremors, seizures, appetite and sleep difficulties, abdominal pain, and fever and chills, to name a few (APA, 2013). Individuals who are intoxicated are often involved in accidents, which can lead to serious pain and health complications, and can begin a vicious circle, compounding their addiction problems, as doctors will prescribe commonly abused pain relievers to help them cope with the pain from an accident. In turn, the person may then come to abuse these medications, leading them back to their drug or addiction of choice. The psychological and emotional impact is no less severe, as in the course of one **binge**, over a single night or a week, an individual can find themselves having lost their job, their marriage, and incarcerated with serious criminal charges. The case below illustrates the pain related to substance-use disorder:

© maradon 333/Shutterstock.com

Binge

A period of time in which a person indulges excessively in a behavioral or substance addiction

Case Vignette

Joseph liked to party with his friends when he was young and experimented with many illegal and prescription drugs, often combining them in various ways. As he aged, he participated less and less in this lifestyle, but would drink alcohol several days per week and occasionally would hang out with old friends and take illegal drugs. Joseph had been married for about 2 years, and had an 8-year-old daughter from a previous relationship. He was continually trying to reduce his alcohol and illegal drug consumption, but would often use one or both substances when he was stressed. Over the course of a few days, work and family life had become increasingly stressful, and he had been in an ongoing argument with his daughter's mother about custody issues over the summer. To blow off some steam, he went to a friend's house one night and began drinking and was given a few Xanax by his friend to help him calm down. When he woke up the next morning, he was extremely hungover and could not recall exactly what happened before he blacked out in the early hours of the morning. He did recall that he needed to drive his daughter to school and realized he could get there right on time if he hurried. He took a small glass of vodka with him to help get rid of his headache, and hurried back to his house. Imagine the possible ways that this scenario could end, and the pain that these addictive behaviors could entail.

Myths in Movies

TRAFFIC

Individuals with certain substance-related disorders, for example, heroin, methamphetamines, and cocaine, are also at an increased risk of death due to a higher likelihood of relying on drug dealing, theft, prostitution, and other dangerous criminal activities, as a means of funding their addictions (APA,

A scene from *Traffic*

2013). If you have seen the movie *Traffic*, you likely remember the scene in which a young lady pays her drug dealer with her body, discovering heroin in the process (Soderbergh, 2000). Take a minute to consider how the addictive pull of drugs can be this strong. While we often like to avoid considering these types of events, it is important to note how we draw the line between myth and reality when it comes to addiction, as events like this happen frequently, and we can sometimes think of them as myths to create a comfortable distance from this stark reality.

Fatality

As you can imagine from the case of Joseph, substance use disorders can be extremely fatal for patients or for others around them. Individuals with substance use disorders are at an increased risk for both suicide and violence toward others (APA, 2013). The DSM-5 reported estimates that 20% of ICU admissions are alcohol-related, and that alcohol accounts for 55% of fatal driving accidents (APA, 2013). Some studies have found that substance-related disorders are the most common disorder related to suicides, with various studies reporting that

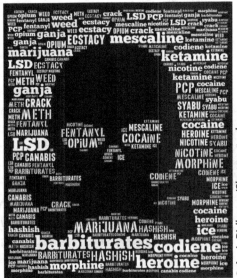

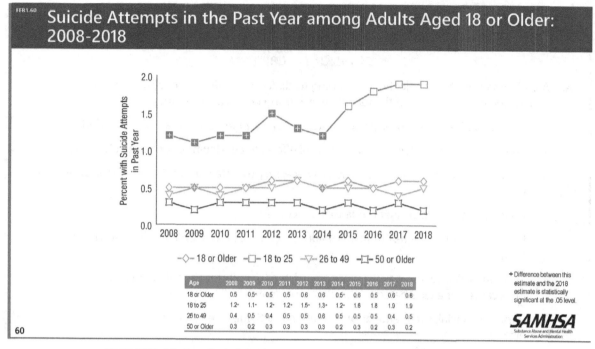

FIGURE 14.4   Suicide Attempts From 2008–2018 by Age
https://www.samhsa.gov/data/sites/default/files/cbhsq-reports/NSDUHffrBriefingSlides2018_w-final-cover.pdf

between 19 to 63% of individuals who completed suicide were suffering from a substance use disorder (Schneider, 2009). And while older adults tend to be at a higher risk of suicide in general, young adults (18–25) appear to be at a higher risk of suicide attempts than older adults (Substance Abuse and Mental Health Services Administration [SAMHSA], 2018). Individuals with certain substance-related disorders (for example, opioid use disorder), are at a higher risk of suicide related to deliberate or accidental overdose, which may be compounded due to an increased likelihood of depression during withdrawal related to the use of opiates (APA, 2013). A common clinical scenario includes a seriously depressed individual in recovery from opiates who returns to opiate use and dies as a result of using the same amount of heroin as they used prior to detoxification. Withdrawal from certain drugs can also lead to severe health complications (e.g., seizure and coma) and even death. Severe complications are more common in relation to certain substance-use disorders, such as opioid withdrawal, alcohol withdrawal, and withdrawal from certain sedative, hypnotic, or anxiolytic drugs. More specifically, death appears to occur more frequently as a result of withdrawal from substances such as alcohol and benzodiazepines, compared to prescription opioids and heroin.

Detoxification

A process in which a person is coming off of a drug, often with the help of mental health and medical professionals; elimination of toxins from one's body

DSM-5 ALCOHOL USE DISORDER DIAGNOSTIC CRITERIA

DIAGNOSTIC CRITERIA

A. A problematic pattern of alcohol use leading to clinically significant impairment or distress, as manifested by at least two of the following, occurring within a 12-month period:

1. Alcohol is often taken in larger amounts or over a longer period than was intended.

2. There is a persistent desire or unsuccessful efforts to cut down or control alcohol use.

3. A great deal of time is spent in activities necessary to obtain alcohol, use alcohol, or recover from its effects.

4. Craving, or a strong desire or urge to use alcohol.

5. Recurrent alcohol use resulting in a failure to fulfill major role obligations at work, school, or home.

6. Continued alcohol use despite having persistent or recurrent social or interpersonal problems caused or exacerbated by the effects of alcohol.

7. Important social, occupational, or recreational activities are given up or reduced because of alcohol use.

8. Recurrent alcohol use in situations in which it is physically hazardous.

9. Alcohol use is continued despite knowledge of having a persistent or recurrent physical or psychological problem that is likely to have been caused or exacerbated by alcohol.

10. Tolerance, as defined by either of the following:

    a. A need for markedly increased amounts of alcohol to achieve intoxication or desired effect.

    b. A markedly diminished effect with continued use of the same amount of alcohol.

11. Withdrawal, as manifested by either of the following:

    a. The characteristic withdrawal syndrome for alcohol (refer to Criteria A and B of the criteria set for alcohol withdrawal, pp. 499–500).

    b. Alcohol (or a closely related substance, such as a benzodiazepine) is taken to relieve or avoid withdrawal symptoms.

Specify if:

In early remission: After full criteria for alcohol use disorder were previously met, none of the criteria for alcohol use disorder have been met for at least 3 months but for less than 12 months (with the exception that Criterion A4, "Craving, or a strong desire or urge to use alcohol" may be met).

In sustained remission: After full criteria for alcohol use disorder were previously met, none of the criteria for alcohol use disorder have been met at any time during a period of 12 months or longer (with the exception that Criterion A4, "Craving, or a strong desire or urge to use alcohol" may be met).

Specify if:

In a controlled environment: This additional specifier is used if the individual is in an environment where access to alcohol is restricted.

Code based on current severity: Note for ICD-10-CM codes: If an alcohol intoxication, alcohol withdrawal, or another alcohol-induced mental disorder is also present, do not use the codes below for alcohol use disorder. Instead, the comorbid alcohol use disorder is indicated in the fourth character of the alcohol-induced disorder code (see the coding note for alcohol intoxication, alcohol withdrawal, or a specific alcohol-induced mental disorder). For example, if there is comorbid alcohol intoxication and alcohol use disorder, only the alcohol intoxication code is given, with the fourth character indicating whether the comorbid alcohol use disorder is mild, moderate, or severe: F10.129 for mild alcohol use disorder with alcohol intoxication or F10.229 for a moderate or severe alcohol use disorder with alcohol intoxication.

Specify current severity:

305:00 (F10.10) Mild: Presence of 2–3 symptoms.

303.90 (F10.20) Moderate: Presence of 4–5 symptoms.

303.90 (F10.20) Severe: Presence of 6 or more symptoms.

Specific Substance-Related and Addictive Disorders: A Variety of Addictions

While substance-related disorders share many common elements, there are also many complications unique to each disorder. Take a glance at the diagnostic criteria for alcohol use disorder. The first 10 criteria are the same for each substance-related disorder, and only criteria 11 differs because some classes of drugs are not associated with withdrawal symptoms. For all substance-related disorders, the DSM-5 also includes specifiers for remission, controlled environment, and severity. See Table 14.1 for a description of specifiers. Certain disorders involve additional specifiers, which will be discussed below. As you may expect, the specific effects of intoxication differ greatly from one drug to another, and interestingly withdrawal symptoms also differ widely, related to the differing physiological effects of specific drugs.

Alcohol-Related Disorders. A commonly held myth about alcohol is that it is a stimulant. Actually, alcohol has a depressant effect on the body, but because it lowers one's inhibitions and often leads people to do "wild" and "crazy" things they otherwise never do, people often confuse it for a stimulant.

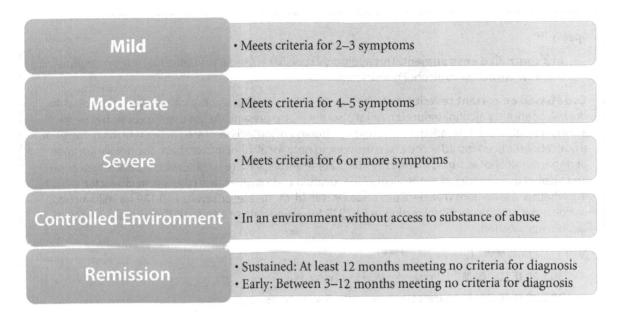

Mild	• Meets criteria for 2–3 symptoms
Moderate	• Meets criteria for 4–5 symptoms
Severe	• Meets criteria for 6 or more symptoms
Controlled Environment	• In an environment without access to substance of abuse
Remission	• Sustained: At least 12 months meeting no criteria for diagnosis • Early: Between 3–12 months meeting no criteria for diagnosis

TABLE 14.1   Specifiers for Substance-Related and Addictive Disorders
APA, 2013

Nystagmus

Involuntary movements of the eyes, which may occur horizontally and vertically

Alcohol intoxication often involves one or more changes in functioning including impaired judgment, mood lability, speech deficits, a lack of coordination, difficulty walking straight, uncontrolled eye movements known as nystagmus, attention and memory impairments, aggressive or inappropriate sexual behavior, and possibly even stupor or coma (APA, 2013). Withdrawal from persistent, heavy alcohol use can be fatal and includes at least two of the following symptoms beginning within a few hours or even days after a person quits drinking alcohol: hyperactivity of the body (e.g., sweating or increased pulse), nausea or vomiting, insomnia, visual, tactile, or auditory illusions or hallucinations, psychomotor agitation, hand tremors, anxiety, and/or seizures (APA, 2013). Alcohol withdrawal has been described as occurring in three stages, the last of which is characterized by delirium tremens, commonly referred to as DTs, which can involve severe hallucinations and delusions, and can be fatal (Brick, 2008). Withdrawal is more likely to occur in persons over age 30, and symptoms generally increase with age, and may involve death related to extreme fever (hyperthermia) and vascular issues (APA, 2013). Long-term heavy alcohol use can also lead to many severe health complications, including various cancers, cirrhosis, dementia, depression, gout, and pancreatitis, among other conditions.

Delirium Tremens

A withdrawal condition causing delusions and hallucinations, body tremors, sweating, and disorientation, which is typical in cases of long-term, heavy alcohol abuse

Cannabis-Related Disorders. A commonly held idea, especially among marijuana users, is the perspective that marijuana use is far safer than alcohol consumption, especially as it relates to functioning; for example, operating a car. But is this a myth? While there are reports of a decrease in drunk-driving related accidents and deaths in Colorado since the legalization of marijuana, a 2015 report on the impact of marijuana legalization in the state revealed that 41% of DUIs in 2014 involved marijuana only and 77% involved marijuana used in conjunction with another substance; the report also revealed that fatal car accidents related to marijuana use nearly doubled to account for almost 20% of all fatal car accidents (Wong & Clarke, 2015).

Cannabis intoxication is characterized by uncoordinated motor functioning, anxiety and sometimes paranoia, impaired decision-making, euphoria, the feeling that time is moving more slowly, social withdrawal, and physiological symptoms such as dry mouth, reddening of the eyes, increased appetite, and increased heart rate (APA, 2013). Withdrawal from persistent and heavy cannabis use can be characterized by aggression or irritability; feeling nervous, anxious or restless; impaired sleep, including dream disturbances, depressed mood, appetite loss, and physiological symptoms such as tremors, abdominal pain, fever, or headache (APA, 2013). Most individuals will not experience many of these symptoms, but similar to withdrawal from other drugs, withdrawal from marijuana is a warranted diagnosis if a person is experiencing at least three of these symptoms. So much for the myth that a person cannot get addicted to marijuana!

Hallucinogen-Related Disorders. Hallucinogen intoxication can involve a wide range of physiological and perceptual disturbances, varying to some degree based on the type of hallucinogen used. Symptoms of PCP intoxication include belligerence and a tendency to assault, impulsiveness, psychomotor agitation, impaired decision-making, and physical symptoms that may include increased heart rate, nystagmus, diminished pain response, ataxia, unclear speech articulation, muscle rigidity, seizures or coma, or sensitivity to certain sounds (APA, 2013). Other hallucinogens can include many of these symptoms, but are primarily characterized by ideas of reference, concerns about "losing your mind," paranoia, intensifications of perception, synesthesia, illusions, hallucinations, derealization, depersonalization, and dilation of the pupils (APA, 2013). While hallucinogens are generally not understood to have withdrawal symptoms, *per se*, some individuals will experience a condition called Hallucinogen Persisting Perception Disorder, which is characterized by ongoing perceptual disturbances continuing past the period of intoxication (APA, 2013). This condition is not well-researched, but may last anywhere from weeks or months, and in some patients can even last for years (APA, 2013).

Opiate-Related Disorders. Individuals who suffer from opiate-related disorders may be addicted to a wide array of opiates, and may have come by their addiction in many ways. One common way that individuals become addicted to heroin is by beginning with prescription opiates, either recreationally or prescribed for pain, which they begin using at higher amounts. It is very expensive to buy these drugs illegally, and so drug dealers often will guide their customers to a much more cost-effective option, heroin. Opiates, especially at high doses, have a sort of double effect, characterized initially by intense euphoria, which is later followed by apathy, psychomotor agitation

Ataxia

Loss of control over one's voluntary body movements

Ideas of Reference

Ideas, which can become delusional, in which a person believes that events refer personally to oneself

Synesthesia

The experience of a certain sensation caused by stimuli acting on a different sensation (e.g., seeing something causes one to have a tactile response)

Dysphoria

A state of uneasiness or discomfort and sadness, often understood technically as a mix of anxious and depressive states

Piloerection

Physiological reaction of one's hairs stand erect, sometimes caused by drug use

or retardation, impaired decision-making, pupil constriction, drowsiness or coma, speech deficits, attention and memory problems, and dysphoria (APA, 2013). Many individuals report that they begin by chasing their "first high," and eventually continue just to stave off severe and painful withdrawal symptoms. These symptoms include nausea or vomiting, diarrhea, aching muscles, increased fluid in the eye ducts or nasal cavity, pupil dilation, piloerection, sweating, yawning, fever, insomnia, or dysphoric mood (APA, 2013).

Because individuals experiencing opiate addictions often progress to intravenous use of the drug, opiate use is associated with extremely high risk of contracting an infectious disease, such as HIV or hepatitis C, from sharing dirty needles. The DSM-5 reported findings suggesting that as many as 90% of individuals who inject opiates may have hepatitis C (APA, 2103). Serious skin infections are also a common problem, especially after individuals are no longer able to use their veins to "shoot-up." While opiate intoxication can be fatal, opiate withdrawal is typically not fatal, though it can be painful. A common story in rehabs involves individuals enduring a painful withdrawal from heroin in jail, while on the other hand, those withdrawing from alcohol are often taken to a detox facility instead. And while heroin tends to get most of the press, the rate of prescription painkiller abuse has risen far more in the last few decades than the rate of heroin abuse, especially among women. Conjointly, the rate of prescription painkiller overdose and death has risen along with increased sales, and both death from overdose and sales tripled from 1999–2010 (Center for Disease Control [CDC], 2013).

Myths in Movies

REQUIEM FOR A DREAM

The movie *Requiem for a Dream* also portrays some of the serious consequences of drug use. When the heroin dries up in their city, the protagonist of the movie directs his girlfriend to a place she can prostitute for heroin, and then goes on an expedition to find more of the drug, only to wake up in the hospital with his arm amputated due to an infection (Aronofsky, 2000). Do movies such as this glorify or over-dramatize heroin use? Can movies make someone more or less interested in using heroin?

A scene from *Requiem for a Dream*

© Artisan Entertainment /Photofest

Sedative-, Hypnotic-, or Anxiolytic-Related Disorders. Intoxication within this class of drugs results in a depressant effect on the body, and therefore includes the same basic symptoms as alcohol intoxication, such as impaired judgment, mood lability, speech deficits, a lack of coordination, difficulty walking straight, nystagmus, attention and memory impairments, aggressive or inappropriate sexual behavior, and possibly even stupor or coma (APA, 2013). Likewise, sedative-, hypnotic-, or anxiolytic-withdrawal includes the same symptoms as alcohol withdrawal, except for an increased likelihood of seizures (APA, 2013). This class of drugs includes popular anxiety medications such as valium, klonopin, and Xanax, and common sleep medications, such as Ambien. Despite being commonly prescribed by medical doctors, many of these drugs are highly addiction-forming, and long-term usage can lead to serious health problems.

Stimulant-Related Disorders. Stimulant intoxication can be characterized by euphoria or a lack of affect, hypervigilance and anxiety, differences in socializing, interpersonal sensitivity, anger, impaired decision-making, and physiological changes such as increases or decreases in blood pressure and heart rate, dilation of the pupils, perspiration or chills, nausea or vomiting, weight loss, psychomotor changes and bodily weakness or pain (APA, 2013). Additional complications can involve confusion, seizure, dyskinesia, dystonia, and/or comas, although the exact intoxication symptoms vary by the type of stimulant used. Stimulant-related disorders are specified by the type of stimulant being used, into categories including amphetamine-type substances, cocaine, and other (APA, 2013). Stimulant withdrawal is characterized by dysphoric mood, as well as fatigue, excessive sleep or insomnia, increased appetite, vivid dreams that are often unpleasant, and increases or decreases in psychomotor activity (APA, 2013). After excessive usage of stimulants, especially at high doses, an individual may "crash," becoming depressed and despondent, fatigued for several days, and may even become suicidal (APA, 2013).

Dyskinesia

A state of deficient control over one's body movements

Dystonia

A state of abnormal muscle spasm and body posture

Other Substance-Related Disorders. Many additional substances can be used in a disordered manner, not all of which fit clearly into the categories of the DSM-5. It almost seems that every few months or years a new drug of abuse becomes popular, synthesizing drugs that typically are not used together, distilling active elements of certain drugs to make them stronger, or even the use of common household goods as a means to achieve a high. With the serious effects of some of the drugs mentioned above, it can be easy to dismiss more commonly used substances, such as tobacco and caffeine. Can these cause the serious problems similar to those listed previously, or is this a myth? Although the DSM-5 does not include a diagnosis for caffeine use disorder, it does include diagnoses for caffeine intoxication and withdrawal, both of which can be severe, sometimes leading to permanent heart problems requiring medication, or even to social and occupational difficulties. You may recall the story of Josh Hamilton, who played baseball for the Texas Rangers, and his struggles with alcoholism. During a sober period in 2012, he missed several games related to visual problems, which were later reported to be caused by excessive caffeine consumption. Could this be considered a relapse into addiction?

While the DSM-5 does not specify a caffeine use disorder, it does recognize caffeine intoxication and withdrawal as disorders. It also recognizes tobacco use disorder, characterized by the same 10 diagnostic criteria as other substance use disorders, as well as criteria for tobacco withdrawal. While it may be hard to imagine smoking cigarettes to be causing serious disturbances and distress in one's life, consider the difficulty some tobacco users have quitting, even after being diagnosed with cancer or emphysema in some cases, directly related to their smoking. Ongoing smoking under conditions such as these are likely to cause discord in their relationships or even isolation to hide their tobacco use.

The DSM-5 additionally includes diagnostic criteria for inhalant use disorder, which is characterized by the inhalation of toxic gases to bring about a psychoactive response, and which are designated by the type of gas abused; for example, nitrous oxide use disorder (APA, 2013). Adolescents are more likely to abuse these gases, and typically do not persist in their use into adulthood, though in some cases, these individuals can die as a direct result of "sudden sniffing death" as some of the chemicals used can be deadly with excess exposure (APA, 2013). Chemicals commonly used to achieve inhalant intoxication include gasoline, lighter fluid, glues, paint products, and polishes. Inhalation of butane, propane, and other volatile hydrocarbons can be fatal, even on first use, possibly due to their wide array of impact on the functioning of the heart, brain, lungs, and digestive systems (APA, 2013).

Gambling Disorder. Perhaps the oddest disorder included by the DSM-5 within the category of substance-related and addictive disorders is gambling disorder, which is characterized by increased desire to gamble in an attempt to achieve previous or increasing levels of excitement, often involving potential loss of ever increasing quantities of money (APA, 2013). Similar to substance use, individuals with gambling disorder have difficulty quitting, and may become irritable or restless when they try, experiencing increased preoccupation by thoughts and memories of gambling (APA, 2013). A person with this disorder gambles to escape stress, chases after their losses, lies to conceal their addiction to gambling, and may often rely on others for funds to continue gambling or to relieve financial difficulties, after spending their own money gambling (APA, 2103). As you can imagine, these behaviors can create increasing amounts of discord and tension significantly damaging relationships, and leading to the loss of friends, career opportunities, and even relationships (APA, 2013).

Gambling disorder can be an episodic or persistent problem, and like substance use disorders, it can be mild, moderate, or severe, depending on the number of symptoms a person is experiencing. Approximately 0.2 to 0.3% of individuals will develop a gambling disorder within a 12-month period, with higher rates among men than women (APA, 2013). If a person with gambling disorder is able to live for 3 months without meeting any symptom criteria, they are considered to be in early remission, which is considered to be sustained remission at 12 months. In the DSM-IV-TR, gambling disorder was referred to as pathological gambling and categorized as an impulse-control disorder (APA, 2000). The change in the DSM-5 to include it as a behavioral addictive disorder along with substance-related disorders comes in response especially to neurological research suggesting that gambling activates the reward pathways in the brain in a manner similar to drugs and alcohol (Holden, 2010). Additionally, gambling seems to have similar outcomes related to distress, functioning problems, and relationship discord, as is found in cases of substance abuse.

Theories and Treatments of Substance-Related and Addictive Disorders

Biological, psychological, and sociocultural factors have all been suggested contributors to the development of addictive disorders. Genetic studies have found a significant link between family members for various addictions. Children whose parents struggle with alcohol addiction have a three to four times higher risk of developing alcohol use disorder, even when raised by an adoptive parent without the disorder (APA, 2013). Additionally, some research suggests a common genetic basis predisposing individuals not only to alcohol use, but also the use of other substances and even conduct problems (APA, 2013). The reward pathway in the brain is activated by means of dopamine and related neurotransmitters when we experience pleasure. Virtually all psychoactive drugs of abuse encourage excess dopamine in the reward pathway, which is responsible for the euphoria or "high" that an individual experiences from drugs. Chronically using drugs of abuse increases the number of dopamine receptors in the reward pathways, such that when the drugs, and therefore the dopamine, are not present in the system, a person can experience intense cravings for their drug(s), anhedonia, and even depressed mood. Excess dopamine receptors, with too little dopamine to fill them, leads to less activation of these neurons, and higher levels of dopamine are then required to activate them. The number of receptors are understood to decrease with an extended period of sobriety, but this can be a slow recovery process, during which the person must learn to tolerate the negative symptoms associated with quitting, without turning to another addictive behavior.

Psychological and sociological theories have suggested a wide variety of explanations for why individuals develop addictions. Social learning theories posit that exposure to and modeling of addictive behaviors may account for the development of these disorders, which may be evidenced by lower rates of substance-related disorders in societies that do not accept or have more restrictions regarding alcohol use (Sher et al., 2005). The expectations that are set within the culture seem to matter greatly, in terms of the development of addictions, especially as evidence suggests that the earlier a person begins using drugs and alcohol, the more likely they are to continue using (see Figure 14.5).

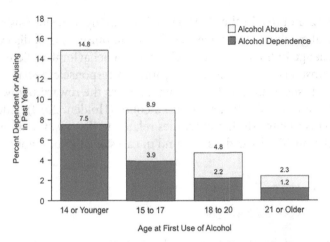

FIGURE 14.5   Alcohol Use Based on Age of First Use
http://www.samhsa.gov/data/sites/default/files/
NSDUHresultsPDFWHTML2013/Web/NSDUHresults2013.pdf

Other theories focus on the higher incidence of addictions in individuals who are high in personality traits related to pleasure or excitement-seeking, on the one hand, versus those who may be using substances as a means of self-medicating in response to pain or trauma. These approaches need not be opposed, as one can seek pleasure to medicate pain, though some individuals may also lean more in one way than the other. Some evidence suggests a strong relationship between stress and substance abuse, but the relationship is quite complex. Chronic alcohol use appears to disrupt the function of the HPA axis, leading to increased difficulties responding to stress, and an increased likelihood to use alcohol and other substances to cope (Sher, 2007). Interestingly, researchers are also theorizing that these same HPA axis dysfunctions, initiated earlier in life due to chronic stress or the lack of nurturing, may be responsible for the development of substance-related and addictive disorders in the first place, as individuals with poor stress tolerance often turn to addictive processes as a means to cope (Sher, 2007).

As we have frequently discussed, how we understand that a problem developed will inform our treatment, and perhaps more importantly in this case, how the addiction developed should guide us in treating individuals with these disorders. A wide range of treatment options are available for individuals with addictions. See Figures 14.6 and 14.7 for information on where individuals with substance-use

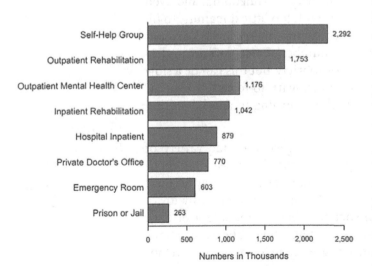

FIGURE 14.6   Where Treatment Was Received
http://www.samhsa.gov/data/sites/default/files/
NSDUHresultsPDFWHTML2013/Web/NSDUHresults2013.pdf

disorders seek treatment, and reasons they do not seek treatment, even when it is warranted.

While the APA Society of Clinical Psychology (Div. 12) does not recognize anonymous groups as research-supported treatments, a psychologist or counselor cannot work for very long among those in recovery, without gathering strong clinical experience to suggest the efficacy of these programs. It does not take long, in the world of psychotherapy, to meet someone whose life was radically changed and their addiction ceased through their participation in Alcoholics Anonymous (AA) and similar groups. As the saying goes, "It works if you work it . . ." Regard-

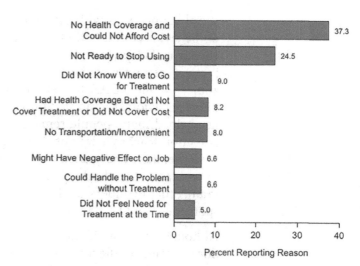

FIGURE 14.7 Reasons for Not Receiving Treatment
http://www.samhsa.gov/data/sites/default/files/NSDUHresultsPDFWHTML2013/Web/NSDUHresults2013.pdf

less, some common criticisms of anonymous groups remain, including the inability of the group to change maladaptive cognitive processes, and the insistence upon the disease model of addiction, including a strong emphasis on the recognition of oneself as an addict for life. The AA model may primarily work by providing a supportive environment, accountability, and

Myths in Movies

FIGHT CLUB

© Twentieth Century Fox/Photofest

Do recovery groups really exist for every kind of addiction? It would seem that this myth may almost be reality. Run a web search on "list of anonymous groups" to check it out. And while most of these individuals are likely not hopping around from group to group or hanging out in an underground *Fight Club*, like in the movie, there does exist a group devoted to more addictive issues than most of us can imagine, including some devoted to emotions such as anger. To name a few, there are anonymous groups for alcoholics (of course), gamblers, codependents, debtors, underearners, bloggers, clutterers, kleptomaniacs and shoplifters, sex addicts, those with unwanted same-sex attraction, and food addicts. But are these peer-led recovery groups really effective?

social connections with others in recovery. While the model focuses both on behavior cessation and cognitive change, its primary function is not to change maladaptive cognitions, and according to some perspectives, it may increase certain maladaptive cognitions, for example, "I will always be an addict." While the AA model cannot offer the services of a well-trained cognitive behavioral therapist, it provides a way of thinking about addiction that has helped many people remain in long-term recovery. The AA model of addiction teaches a way of thinking about addiction that is held by long-term members and passed on to new members. When new members come in with addictive thinking, sometimes called "stinkin' thinkin'" in the program, other members can help them to recognize cognitive errors and blind spots they would otherwise overlook.

Although Division 12 does not recognize the efficacy of these groups, it does recognize effective psychotherapy treatments for several substance disorders. Among approaches that have the strongest research support, Motivational Interviewing (MI), Motivational Enhancement Therapy plus Cognitive Behavior Therapy, and more direct behavioral approaches like Prize-Based Contingency Management, appear to be most effective. Motivational approaches focus on increasing an individual's motivation to change problematic addictive processes, by evoking the use of clients' resources, strengths, and potential (Najavits et al., 2013). The prize-based behavioral approaches function, as we have discussed elsewhere, by setting up a system of rewards to reinforce healthy behaviors, but include the use of urine testing to verify patients are "clean," which in turn increases the likelihood of their winning prizes (Najavits et al., 2013).

Medications have also been developed to treat addictive processes, which can work by reducing cravings, causing a nauseous or emetic response, or simply helping reduce withdrawal effects. See Table 14.2 for a list of these medications and their function. Evidence also suggests the clinical effectiveness of Medication-Assisted Treatment (MAT), which combines some of these psychotherapy approaches with medications, to increase the likelihood of recovery (SAMHSA, 2015).

Medication	Function
Methadone (Dolophine)	• Used for opioid disorders • Delays withdrawal & reduces craving
Buprenorphine (Suboxone)	• Used for opiod disorders • Delays withdrawal & reduces cravings
Naltrexone (Vivitrol)	• Used for opiod, alcohol, & other disorders • Blocks euphoria & sedative effects of drugs
Disulfiram (Antabuse)	• Used for alcohol disorders • Emetic and nauseous response to alcohol
Acamprosate (Campral)	• Used for alcohol disorders • Reduces craving without stoping withdrawal

TABLE 14.2   Medications to Treat Substance-Related Disorders

SAMHSA, 2015

MYTHS of Disruptive, Impulse-Control, and Conduct Disorders

Individuals with impulse-control disorders often feel that they find themselves in the middle of impulsive situations before they even realize what has happened. In this regard, many of us can relate to situations that have gotten out of hand, and then coming to a point where we recognize the ridiculousness of the situation, we change our behaviors. Do individuals with impulse-control disorders not have the capacity to change course when they come to this realization, or is this a myth? In many cases, learning to control behaviors can be taught, however, developing an awareness and concern for the rights and dignity of others may be more difficult. Take some time to reflect on your thoughts and experiences of impulsivity and related conduct disorders.

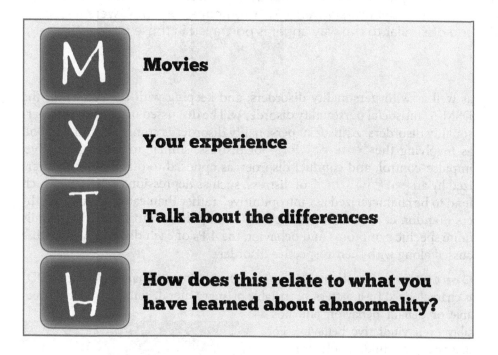

M — **Movies**

Y — **Your experience**

T — **Talk about the differences**

H — **How does this relate to what you have learned about abnormality?**

Disruptive, Impulse-Control, and Conduct Disorders: Stop Right There!!!

Disruptive, impulse-control, and conduct disorders are characterized by struggles related to the violation of others, such as stealing, destruction of property, vindictiveness, or even harm to persons and/or animals. This group of disorders includes six disorders: Oppositional Defiant Disorder, Intermittent Explosive Disorder, Conduct Disorder, Pyromania, and Kleptomania. Antisocial Personality Disorder is listed by the DSM-5 under this group of disorders,

Myths in Movies

ADAM SANDLER

© RoidRanger/Shutterstock.com

Adam Sandler seems to really enjoy playing roles about angry men! Consider *Anger Management, Punch Drunk Love*, and *The Waterboy*, among others. Sandler plays the role of an angry, explosive man in each of these movies. But can a person really become a football star by tapping into intense anger about people making fun of his mom? While it may not go back to mom in all cases, the fast-paced change of behavior demonstrated by Sandler in these movies is no myth. Consider times when you or someone you know were angry. How was it similar and dissimilar to the way anger is portrayed in these movies?

Externalizing Disorders

Disorders characterized by a focus oriented toward the external world as a means of reducing one's psychological and emotional distress

Internalizing Disorders

Disorders characterized by a focus oriented toward the self or characteristics about oneself as a means of reducing one's psychological and emotional distress

as well as with personality disorders, and keeping with the pattern of the DSM-5, antisocial personality disorder will be discussed more fully with personality disorders. Antisocial personality disorder is commonly understood as involving the "externalizing" of distress, similar to other disruptive, impulse-control, and conduct disorder, as opposed to diagnoses characterized by an "internalizing" of distress, such as depression or anxiety, which tend to be characterized as "intropunitive," rather than causing harm to others (Tandon et al., 2009). As each of the impulse-control disorders entails quite specific symptoms and behavior, the 4 Fs of each disorder will be discussed along with their respective disorder.

Oppositional Defiant Disorder. Oppositional defiant disorder (ODD) is characterized by a pattern of irritable or angry mood, coupled with disagreeable or defiant behavior, and possibly even vindictive behavior. For diagnosis, a child, adolescent, or adult must experience a pattern of at least four symptoms for at least 6 months, and must have an oppositional interaction with at least one person who is not a sibling (APA, 2013). Apparently, someone working on the DSM-5 realized that fighting with your brothers and sisters is quite normal indeed! That being the case, the initial recognition of these disorders often comes

© Brian A Jackson/Shutterstock.com

within close relationships in the household or school, as parents and caregivers begin to notice an intensification of these problems, not seen in other siblings or students. Diagnosable symptoms related to the disorder include losing one's temper, annoyance, frequent anger or resentfulness, argumentativeness with others, including authority figures, refusal to comply with rules and/or requests from authority, purposeful annoyance of others, displacement of blame for their own mistakes, and being spiteful or vindictive at least twice in a 6-month period (APA, 2013). A person may experience this disorder in mild, moderate, or severe forms, depending on whether he or she is oppositional in one, two, or more settings, respectively (APA, 2013). The pervasiveness of the disorder is the determinant for severity. For example, a 10-year-old boy who meets criteria for the disorder, but the behavior is only happening at home, is considered to have a mild case, whereas if it is happening at home, school, and when playing with friends, the case would be considered severe.

The DSM-5 specifies that approximately 3.3% of individuals will experience ODD, and in children the prevalence tends more toward boys than girls, 1.4 to 1 (APA, 2013). ODD is difficult not only for the individual struggling with the disorder, but also everyone within their social network. Functionally, individuals with ODD are likely to encounter significant problems within many or all of their important relationships, which can result in lasting problems in virtually all areas of functioning, including employment, education, and their familial and romantic lives (APA, 2013). Imagine the pain of continually arguing with everyone in your life, and the impact that this may have on the development of a child, especially as these symptoms tend to increase at certain important developmental times, such as preschool and adolescence (APA, 2013). Additionally, ODD is often the first sign of more severe problems that are likely to develop over time, and many children diagnosed with ODD go on to develop conduct disorder

© OSTILL is Franck Camhi/Shutterstock.com

(Biederman et al., 1996). There also appears to be a strong overlap with ADHD, as ODD is found to be much higher among a sample of children who already have a diagnosis of ADHD (APA, 2013). Children with ODD have also been found to be much more likely to have experienced prior physical or sexual abuse and other traumas, as well as harsh and neglectful parenting (APA, 2013; Ford et al., 2000). While the symptomology of ODD does not inherently imply increased likelihood of death, it does increase one's likelihood of encountering aggression or violence from others. Additionally, the subset of individuals with ODD whose symptoms progress to conduct disorder, may also be an increased risk of death related to the criminal nature of their activity, or at a higher risk of suicide later in life, due to poor emotional and social adjustment (Riley et al., 2016).

Intermittent Explosive Disorder. Intermittent explosive disorder (IED) occurs in approximately 2.7% of individuals in the United States, and tends to be

more prevalent in persons below the age of 35–40, and boys and men more frequently than girls and women, though some studies have demonstrated no gender differences (APA, 2013). IED is characterized by impulsive aggressive acts an individual has difficulty controlling. For diagnostic purposes, these acts must be either verbally aggressive or behaviorally aggressive, and the individual must be at least 6 years old. If symptoms consist primarily of verbal aggression and/or physical aggression that does not cause property damage or physical injury to a person or animal, these behaviors must occur an average of twice per week for at least 3 months to warrant diagnosis (APA, 2013). If an individual's behavioral aggression has crossed the line into property damage or physical harm, they must have had at least three of these incidents within a 1-year period to warrant diagnosis (APA, 2013). Remember, these acts must be impulsive, and not premeditated. If the conclusion is drawn that an action has been premeditated, a different diagnosis, potentially conduct disorder or a personality disorder, would better explain the clinical picture. Additionally, the magnitude of these reactions must be significantly disproportionate to the stressor provoking the response, and these behaviors lead to significant distress or social, financial, and/or legal consequences (APA, 2013).

Similar to ODD, IED may be related to childhood abuse and neglect and/ or modeling of aggressive behaviors, and first-degree relatives of someone with IED are at an increased risk of developing the disorder (APA, 2013). Adults with IED have been found in some studies to have higher rates of childhood maltreatment than individuals with no psychiatric diagnosis and also individuals with psychiatric diagnoses without comorbid IED (Fanning

et al., 2014). While the intense physiological arousal of anger related to this disorder is not inherently fatal, the impulsive behaviors associated with this reaction can be. In fact, the combination of aggression and impulsivity, may be particularly dangerous, both for individuals with IED and those around them (Gvion & Apter, 2011). Studies have indicated high rates of suicide attempts (12.5%), and also self-harm (16%) among individuals with IED (McCloskey et al., 2008). Individuals with certain personality disorders and comorbid IED have been found to be at a significantly increased risk of self-harm and suicidal attempts compared to those with personality disorders alone (Fanning et al., 2014; Jenkins et al., 2015). Many other disorders can be comorbid with IED, such as bipolar disorder, substance use, anxiety and depressive disorders, and conduct and personality disorders, and in turn IED can increase the likelihood of death, which is already high among many of these disorders (APA, 2013).

Conduct Disorder. Of all the disorders that belong to this class of disorders, conduct disorder may be the most insidious and debilitating. Individuals with conduct disorder repeat a pattern of disregarding the rights of others or breaking serious age-appropriate social norms (APA, 2013). For diagnosis, an individual must meet at least three of the 15 criteria for the disorder within the last 12 months, at least one of which must have occurred in the last 6 months (APA, 2013). These criteria include behaviors belonging to four classes: (1) Aggression toward people or animals, such as fights, intimidation, use of a weapon, cruelty to people or animals, confrontations involving theft, and forced sexual activity; (2) Property destruction, such as by setting fires or other means; (3) Theft or deceit, such as breaking and entering, lying for gain, or theft without confrontation; (4) Major rule violations, staying out at night below age 13, running away overnight or for a longer period of time, or truancy (APA, 2013). With this many potential criteria, conduct disorder may take many forms. See Table 14.3 for subtypes and specifiers related to this diagnosis.

© Luis Louro/Shutterstock.com

Onset	• Childhood-Onset: symptoms prior to age 10 • Adolescent-Onset: symptoms after age 10 • Unspecified Onset: insufficient information to determine time of onset
Limited Prosocial Emotions	• Lack of remorse: violates rules w/ no guilt • Lack of empathy: no concern for others • Performance: no concern about performance • Affect deficit: limited expression of affect
Severity	• Mild: barely meets critera; minor symptoms • Moderate: intermediate number & severity of symptoms • Severe: severe symptoms (e.g., rape, cruelty)

TABLE 14.3   Specifiers for Conduct Disorder
APA, 2013

© Elnur/Shutterstock.com

Approximately 4% of individuals will experience conduct disorder, and those for whom onset occurs in childhood, tend to experience more severe symptoms (APA, 2013). Prevalence is higher for males than females, and in cases with childhood-onset, individuals are typically males who are frequently physically aggressive toward others, have troubled relationships with peers, and likely may have already experienced oppositional defiant disorder (APA, 2013). Onset of conduct disorder is rare after age 16, and in most cases symptoms remit by adulthood; adults can be diagnosed with conduct disorder, but it is rare, and adults with these symptoms likely meet criteria for a related personality disorder, for example, antisocial or borderline personality disorder (APA, 2013). As with IED and ODD, persons struggling with conduct disorder are more likely to have been abused, neglected, or treated harshly in early childhood, and parental criminality and rejection may also have been modeled to the individual (APA, 2013). Interestingly, behaviors in males and females tends to be different, with males being more likely to participate in vandalism, stealing, physical aggression or assaults, and discipline issues at school, while females are more likely to use substances, run away, be truant at school, lie, and be involved in prostitution (APA, 2013). Individuals experiencing conduct disorder are not only at a serious risk of harming others, but they are also at an increased risk of harm to self, either through the results of their criminal activity or due to suicidality. Some research suggests those with conduct disorder are at a significantly higher risk of suicide, possibly related directly to aggression and irritability, and "familial transmission of aggressive and suicidal behaviors" may be related (APA, 2013; Gvion & Apter, 2011, p. 96).

© cunaplus/Shutterstock.com

Kleptomania. Kleptomania is characterized by repeated inability to resist urges to steal objects that are not needed, an increasing tension prior to the act, and obtaining pleasure or relief from the theft, which is not done for monetary gain, out of vengeance, anger, or for some alternative reason (APA, 2013). Kleptomania does not require a specific amount of time for diagnosis, as it involves a specific behavior, and therefore only requires a repetition of this behavior, which tends not to be premeditated. Approximately 0.3 to 0.6% of individuals meet criteria for the disorder, which is three times more common in females than in males (APA, 2013). Individuals with kleptomania may be at an increased risk of other compulsive behaviors, substance abuse, anxiety and mood disorders, and personality disorder, and first-degree relatives have been found to have increased rates of obsessive-compulsive disorder (APA, 2013). Due to the criminal nature of stealing, individuals with kleptomania are likely to experience legal issue, although due to the distress related to these behaviors, they may also experience functional difficulties in familial and other relationships, and at work. This distress may be severe for individuals with the disorder. Odlaug and colleagues (2012) conducted a study on individuals with kleptomania, finding that 24.3% had attempted suicide, and that most attempts were related to distress over an incidence of theft. Interestingly, this study also revealed high comorbidity with bipolar disorder, and high rates of being arrested, and the authors suggested that being caught for stealing may be a high-risk period for suicide for individuals with kleptomania (Odlaug et al., 2012).

Pyromania. Pyromania, as a diagnostic category, has been around since at least 1833, and was discussed by Kraepelin, Freud, and was even in the original DSM (Burton et al., 2012). According to the DSM-5, it is characterized by repeated, purposeful setting of fires, a tense affective arousal prior to the act, an attraction or fascination with things related to fire, and obtaining pleasure or relief from setting fire, which is not done for monetary or political gain, or for some alternative reason (APA, 2013). Like kleptomania, pyromania also does not require a specific amount of time for diagnosis, but only a repetition of problematic fire-setting behavior. Pyromania is believed to be quite rare, and is more com-

mon among men. Prevalence rates for the disorder are unknown, but the lifetime prevalence for the fire-setting component of pyromania is approximately 1.13%, however, even among a group of individuals in legal trouble for repeatedly setting fires, only 1 to 3.3% have been found to meet criteria for the disorder (APA, 2013; Ritchey & Huff, 1999). Due to the dangerousness and criminality of fire-setting, individuals with the disorder are at an increased risk of injury or death, as well as legal issues, including assault or homicide, as other's may be injured or killed by their behaviors (APA, 2013).

Many comorbidities are common with pyromania and fire-setting in general, including bipolar disorders, schizophrenia, antisocial personality disorder, and substance abuse (APA, 2013; Ritchey & Huff, 1999). Individuals with pyromania may act impulsively, although by diagnostic definition, they must also set fires in a prearranged, premeditated manner on some occasions (APA, 2013). As many as 90% of individuals with pyromania have been suggested to experience serious distress in relation to starting fires, and as many as 33% have been reported to contemplate suicide in order to control their fire-setting behaviors (Burton et al., 2012). More research is needed to understand the lethality of the disorder, as well as the relationship of pyromania to other disorders. This research is difficult as pyromania occurs in such a small portion of the population; however, based on current research, pyromania should be considered highly dangerous for individuals with the disorder and for those around them.

Treatments of Disruptive, Impulse-Control, and Conduct Disorders

Treatment of oppositional-defiant and conduct disorders with medications has not been well-established. Since many individuals with these disorders have other comorbid disorders, medications targeting the comorbid disorder are sometimes used, which have been found in some cases to help with conduct disorder symptoms. For example, atypical antipsychotics and stimulant-based ADHD medications have been somewhat effective in reducing aggression, serotonin-selective reuptake inhibitors (SSRIs) have shown some promise reducing irritability and agitation, and certain mood stabilizers (e.g., lithium and anticonvulsants) have also been found to reduce aggressive symptoms (Chang & Simeonova, 2004; Emslie et al., 2004; Pappadopulos et al., 2006;). Some researchers posit that a serotonin imbalance may be involved with intermittent explosive disorder (IED), suggesting treatment with current SSRIs is beneficial, but imperfect, in the treatment of the disorder (Coccaro et al., 2015). Like IED, ODD, and conduct disorder, biological treatments for pyromania and kleptomania have also not been clearly established. Piquet-Pessôa and Fontenelle (2016) have suggested that opioid-antagonists, such as naltrexone, may be useful in the treatment of kleptomania, by reducing urges to steal. Proposed treatments for pyromania have included antidepressants, antiepileptics, atypical antipsychotics, lithium, and anti-androgen medications (Burton et al., 2012).

Psychological treatments for disruptive, impulse-control, and conduct disorders can be particularly complicated by the presence of another comorbid condition, and treatments have not been clearly demonstrated for the treatment of multiple co-occurring disorders (Grant et al., 2005). Treatments for oppositional-defiant disorder (ODD) and conduct disorder, especially when occurring in children, have often focused on the family to address change on a more global level, though research has also suggested that group treatments for youth with conduct disorders may impede progress and even exacerbate issues (Kazdin, 1997). Cognitive Problem-Solving Skills Training may be helpful in the treatment of ODD and conduct disorders as they aid individuals in recognizing maladaptive cognitions and skill deficits related to their conduct problems (Kazdin, 1997). Family-oriented treatments, such as Parent Management Training, Functional Family Therapy, and Multisystemic Therapy, may be helpful in changing maladaptive familial patterns exacerbating conduct problems, as well as helping to train family members how to better respond when crises arise (Kazdin, 1997).

Psychotherapeutic interventions for pyromania, kleptomania, and IED also have not been clearly established. Although kleptomania was historically treated with psychoanalytic interventions, establishing a symbolic meaning for stealing, which was then restructured. Some researchers have suggested that this approach is not beneficial, especially in contrast to results obtained through treatment with medications (Durst et al., 2001). Alternatively, cognitive behavioral therapies may be more successful by utilizing aversion therapy and systematic desensitization to decrease urges related to stealing and increase alternative rewarding behaviors (Durst et al., 2001). Similarly, some research has suggested that cognitive behavioral treatments may also be effective for the treatment of pyromania and IED. Cognitive behavioral approaches can help individuals with these disorders to recognize triggers, change maladaptive cognitive patterns surrounding the disorders, and develop new patterns of behavior to halt fire-setting and aggressive behaviors (Burton, McNeil, & Binder, 2012; McCloskey et al., 2008).

Systematic Desensitization

Psychotherapeutic intervention used in cognitive behavioral therapies to increase an individual's tolerance of arousing situations by exposing an individual to increasingly arousing stimuli while inducing relaxation

Conclusion

Substance-related, impulse-control, and conduct disorders all often involve a violation of rules, people, property, and/or animals, and as such, they frequently lead to highly distressing and dysfunctional situations. Family members of those affected by these disorders frequently feel that they can do nothing to help, and often must distance themselves for the sake of safety. The result is that individuals with these disorders, who are already highly distressed, no longer have the support they need to make the changes necessary to improve their functioning. Some of these individuals end up homeless, in prison, prostituting, and selling drugs as a result of this all-too-common course of events. Many sources of support remain for both the families and the patients, and it is incumbent upon our society to do what we can to help these individuals find the support they need.

CHAPTER REVIEW

QUESTIONS

1. How do various substances of abuse differentially impact a person? Which substances are considered stimulants and which are considered depressants? Hallucinogens? How are the diagnostic criteria similar and different for various substance-related disorders? What is the primary mechanism through which addiction forms for most of these disorders?

2. How do the substance-related disorders vary by age and gender? What are the key differences between tolerance and withdrawal? How are they related? What are the specifiers for substance-related disorders? What are some treatments for these disorders? Which treatments are most used and most effective?

3. Describe the different disruptive, impulse-control, and conduct disorders. How are these disorders similar and different? How are these disorders related to other disorders, such as certain personality disorders? What are some of the specifiers for these disorders?

4. Consider the 4 Fs of impulse-control and conduct disorders. What are some of the dangers associated with each of the disorders? How are harm to self and others, depression, relationship problems, and other concerns related to these disorders?

5. What are some of the theories for the development of these disorders? Which treatments have been found effective for each of the disorders? Why might the treatments for these various disorders be effective?

KEY TERMS

Tolerance

Withdrawal

PCP

MDMA

LSD

Binge

Detoxification

Nystagmus

Delirium Tremens

Ataxia

Ideas of Reference

Synesthesia

Dysphoria

Piloerection

Dyskinesia

Dystonia

Externalizing Disorders

Internalizing Disorders

Systematic Desensitization

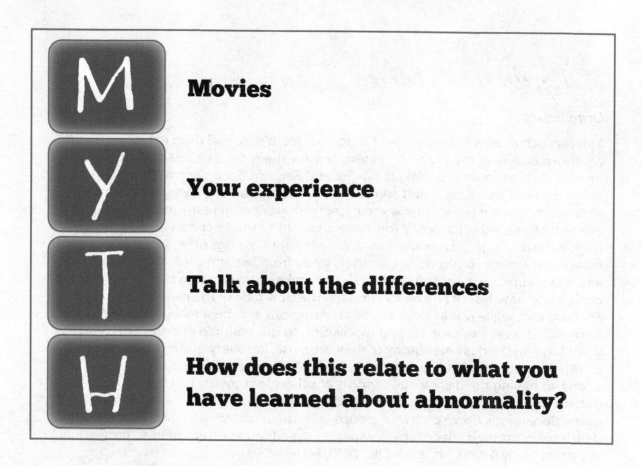

M Movies

Y Your experience

T Talk about the differences

H How does this relate to what you have learned about abnormality?

Myths in Movies Recap

Drug Issues

Movies such as *Pulp Fiction,* while at times can illuminate real drug issues such as the overdose of one of the main characters, but for the most part are dramatized. Even movies such as *Leaving Las Vegas, Traffic,* and *Requiem for a Dream,* though emphasizing more of the distress and sorrows of addiction, can at times glamorize the use of substances. One aspect that is accurately represented in many movies about drug use and abuse is the tendency for those involved to utilize criminal activity, such as theft, drug dealing, and prostitution, in order to obtain drugs (APA, 2013). While these movies may invite some and scare others away from initiating substance use behaviors, other films, such as *The Big Lebowski* can make drug use seem more like a lifestyle choice, and have less of an aversive impact. The slow fade of the main character in *The Big Lebowski,* while not as dramatic of an issue, can also be a reality that individuals using substances can face, lacking motivation to get their life in order and reach for goals beyond the daily monotony of their drug use. Recovery groups such as Alcoholic's Anonymous, as portrayed in *Fight Club* may be particularly helpful in these situations, as having the daily social support of others in recovery can be the crucial key to help some people break free from addictive behaviors. While some mental health professionals look down on these groups, it is important to recognize that some evidence supports their effectiveness, especially as adjunctive treatment to professional therapies (Kelly & Yeterian, 2015; Lile, 2003; Miller, 2003).

Adam Sandler

Adam Sandler wonderfully plays the role of an angry man in many different movies, *Anger Management, Punch Drunk Love, The Waterboy,* to name a few. His tendency to fly into a rage at the drop of a hat is indeed characteristic of some impulse-control and conduct disorders, though of course his peculiar comic approach to anger is quite different from similar real-life situations. Regardless, many of these disorders are characterized by outbursts and the inability to control behaviors (APA, 2013).

CHAPTER FIFTEEN

NEUROCOGNITIVE DISORDERS

MYTHs of Neurocognitive Disorders

Neurocognitive Disorders (NCDs) involve a variety of cognitive declines, perhaps the most popularly discussed cause of which is Alzheimer's disease. A common myth of neurocognitive disorders, and of memory in general, is the idea that memory is a singular human ability and when it declines, all areas of memory functioning decline together. In reality, the general concept of memory is comprised of many subtypes, differentially affected as various parts of the brain are impacted by NCDs. Depending on which brain structures are compromised, a wide variety of symptoms and symptom combinations can arise. For example, in some neurocognitive disorders, episodic memory can decline, while procedural memory remains intact. Another common myth involves the idea that memory deficits are the only symptom of neurocognitive disorders, though in reality, diagnosis of a neurocognitive disorder also requires a deficit in at least one other area of cognition, and memory deficits are not consistent across all NCDs. Take some time to review your thoughts and experiences with regard to these and other MYTHs of neurocognitive disorders.

Episodic Memory

Memory related to the events or episodes of our life

Procedural Memory

Memory related to the activities and habits that we learn

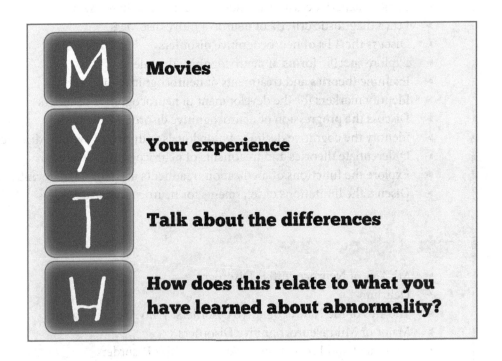

M **Movies**

Y **Your experience**

T **Talk about the differences**

H **How does this relate to what you have learned about abnormality?**

Delirium

Delirium is characterized by a significant disturbance of awareness and attention, such that an individual is less oriented to their surroundings, and struggling to maintain and shift their focus on events (American Psychiatric Association [APA], 2013). For a diagnosis of delirium, these symptoms must be markedly different from previous cognitive functioning, must develop quickly within a few days or hours, and may fluctuate throughout the day (APA, 2013). Additional cognitive disturbances are common in delirium, including language problems, perceptual and visuospatial deficits, and deficits with memory or orientation, and at least one additional cognitive disturbance is required for diagnosis (APA, 2013). Delirium may be induced by substance intoxication or withdrawal, prescribed medications, another medical condition such as a stroke, or as a result of multiple etiologies (APA, 2013). Prevalence rates for delirium in the general population are estimated as low as 1 to 2%, but this prevalence increased dramatically with age, such that 60% of nursing home residents experience delirium, and 83% of all individuals suffer from it during the final stages of life (APA, 2013). Many of us have an "Ole Grandpa Joe," who just can't seem to pay attention and may have even begun having memory problems. In some cases, what "Ole Grandpa Joe" may be experiencing is actually delirium. Delirium can be acute, lasting only a few days or hours, or persistent, lasting several weeks or months, and individuals can experience either psychomotor hyperactivity with labile mood and irritability, or psychomotor hypoactivity, feeling so sluggish and lethargic that they are almost in a stupor (APA, 2013). Psychomotor activity may even be mixed, with episodes of both hyper- and hypoactivity.

© michael sheehan/Shutterstock.com

In addition, delirium may also include emotional difficulties (e.g., fear, apathy, depressive or euphoric states, or irritability), as well as agitation at night or a reversing of one's sleep cycle (APA, 2013). One of the main differences between delirium and major or mild neurocognitive disorders, is that delirium generally remits, leading back to full functioning, though in some cases it may lead to progressive declines resulting in seizure, coma, and even death, and some evidence suggests that as many as 40% of diagnosed cases of delirium lead to death within 12 months (APA, 2013). Risk factors for worse delirium outcomes include being relatively inactive or immobile, repeated falls, delirium severity, having premorbid depression or another NCD, and use of illegal drugs and certain medications (APA, 2013; Jackson et al., 2016).

DSM-5 CRITERIA FOR MAJOR OR MILD NEUROCOGNITIVE DISORDERS

DIAGNOSTIC CRITERIA

Major or Mild Neurocognitive Disorder Due to Alzheimer's Disease

A. The criteria are met for major or mild neurocognitive disorder.

B. There is insidious onset and gradual progression of impairment in one or more cognitive domains (for major neurocognitive disorder, at least two domains must be impaired).

C. Criteria are met for either probable or possible Alzheimer's disease as follows:

For major neurocognitive disorder:

Probable Alzheimer's disease is diagnosed if either of the following is present; otherwise, **possible Alzheimer's disease** should be diagnosed.

1. Evidence of a causative Alzheimer's disease genetic mutation from family history or genetic testing.

2. All three of the following are present:

    a. Clear evidence of decline in memory and learning and at least one other cognitive domain (based on detailed history or serial neuropsychological testing).

    b. Steadily progressive, gradual decline in cognition, without extended plateaus.

    c. No evidence of mixed etiology (i.e., absence of other neurodegenerative or cerebrovascular disease, or another neurological, mental, or systemic disease or condition likely contributing to cognitive decline).

For mild neurocognitive disorder:

Probable Alzheimer's disease is diagnosed if there is evidence of a causative Alzheimer's disease genetic mutation from either genetic testing or family history.

Possible Alzheimer's disease is diagnosed if there is no evidence of a causative Alzheimer's disease genetic mutation from either genetic testing or family history, and all three of the following are present:

1. Clear evidence of decline in memory and learning.

2. Steadily progressive, gradual decline in cognition, without extended plateaus.

3. No evidence of mixed etiology (i.e., absence of other neurodegenerative or cerebrovascular disease, or another neurological or systemic disease or condition likely contributing to cognitive decline).

D. The disturbance is not better explained by cerebrovascular disease, another neurodegenerative disease, the effects of a substance, or another mental, neurological, or systemic disorder.

Coding note: For probable major neurocognitive disorder due to Alzheimer's disease, with behavioral disturbance, code first **331.0 (G30.9)** Alzheimer's disease, followed by **294.11 (F02.81)** major neurocognitive disorder due to Alzheimer's disease. For probable neurocognitive disorder due to

Alzheimer's disease, without behavioral disturbance, code first **331.0 (G30.9)** Alzheimer's disease, followed by **294.10 (F02.80)** major neurocognitive disorder due to Alzheimer's disease, without behavioral disturbance.

For possible major neurocognitive disorder due to Alzheimer's disease, code **331.9 (G31.9)** possible major neurocognitive disorder due to Alzheimer's disease. (**Note:** Do *not* use the additional code for Alzheimer's disease. Behavioral disturbance cannot be coded but should still be indicated in writing.)

For mild neurocognitive disorder due to Alzheimer's disease, code **331.83 (G31.84)**. (**Note:** Do *not* use the additional code for Alzheimer's disease. Behavioral disturbance cannot be coded but should still be indicated in writing.)

Reprinted with permission from the *Diagnostic and Statistical Manual of Mental Disorders,* Fifth Edition, (Copyright 2013). American Psychiatric Association.

The 4 Fs of the Neurocognitive Disorders: Who Are You Again?

Neurocognitive disorders (NCDs) are unique in a few important ways. While many disorders involve cognitive deficits, only disorders involving cognitive deficits as their primary features are considered NCDs, and these cognitive deficits are acquired later in life, unlike most other disorders with significant cognitive impairments, which begin prior to adulthood (APA, 2013). Also, while the etiologies of many other disorders are often shrouded in mystery, the etiologies of NCDs are often able to be discovered (APA, 2013). We will begin by exploring the 4 Fs common to the NCDs, followed by a discussion of the characteristics specific to NCDs.

Frequency

   A—Amount of Time: As a class of disorders, subtypes of NCDs vary in terms of the time in which functional, cognitive, and behavioral declines occur, and certain declines are specific to certain subtypes (APA, 2013). Diagnosis is generally based on which symptoms are present and the discovery of a cause or markers for certain disorders. For example, NCDs, such as those due to Parkinson's, stroke, traumatic brain injury (TBI), and some others, have a cause that can be detected physiologically, and discovering these markers is an essential part of accurate diagnosis (APA, 2013). NCDs caused by a specific event, such as stroke or TBI have an onset beginning with the event, and are only diagnosed if cognitive deficits remain after the initial stroke or trauma symptoms, such as inflammation or swelling, subside (APA, 2013). NCDs caused by neurodegenerative diseases, such as in Alzheimer's and frontotemporal dementia, have a slow

Traumatic Brain Injury

Brain injury due to hitting one's head or to a sudden, violent jarring of one's head, leading to the movement of the brain inside the skull resulting in brain injury

© Photographee.eu/Shutterstock.com

and subtle onset and can progress gradually over a long period of time (APA, 2013). NCDs with onset during adolescence or childhood can be particularly difficult to determine due to the impact of these disorders on development, which in some cases result in additional deficits, such as an intellectual disability (APA, 2013).

B—Behavior: While the behaviors characteristic of some subtypes of NCDs vary considerably from others, all share the same basic diagnostic criteria, categorized as either major or mild, depending on the severity of the symptoms. Individuals with NCDs experience significant or modest cognitive decline, and are diagnosed accordingly as having either a major or mild NCD. Impairments common to an NCD diagnosis include problems with at least some of the following six domains: Complex Attention, Executive Function, Learning and Memory, Language, Perceptual-Motor Abilities, and Social Cognition (APA, 2013). See Table 15.1 for a description of each of these categories.

C—Curve: The prevalence of NCDs varies by age and subtype, but generally increases significantly after the age of 60, and major NCDs are estimated to occur in 1 to 2% of individuals at 65 years old and increase to as many as 30% of individuals at 85 years old (APA, 2013). Mild NCDs may occur in as many as 10% of individuals at 65 years old, and as many as 25% at 85 years old (APA, 2013). Women are more likely to have certain subtypes of NCDs, likely due to women living longer than men. Women tend to be older at onset, and have more co-occurring disorders or diseases (APA, 2013; Gatz, 2007).

Complex Attention

Ability to maintain attention to specific events, despite competing stimuli

Executive Function

Ability to think through, plan, and make important decisions

The Good News: A plethora of research is being conducted. We are likely to see significant advances in our knowledge of NCDs, and hopefully also in our ability to detect NCDs earlier, to prevent the progression of these disorders, and to reverse neuronal damage that has already occurred.

Function

© Fresnel/Shutterstock.com

The diagnostic criteria of NCDs specifies that cognitive and behavioral deficits are significant enough to cause problems with occupational and social functioning, as well as interfere with the activities of daily living, such as household chores or taking medications correctly (Ganguli et al., 2011). In addition to these objective functional issues, diagnosis requires that the individual or someone who knows the individual closely has concerns that the patient has experienced a significant cognitive decline, and preferably that these concerns be backed up with neuropsychological testing (APA, 2013; Ganguli et al., 2011). In milder forms of NCDs, individuals can be more aware of their functional difficulties, causing additional distress; however, with major forms, functional problems may become so severe that individuals have trouble with dressing, bathing, and eating, and in some cases may appear altogether unaware of there being a problem.

TABLE 15.1   **Neurocognitive Domains**

Cognitive Domain	Examples of Symptoms
Complex Attention	Difficulty maintaining prolonged attention
	Time delays and errors on common tasks
	Problems attending to one stimuli in the midst of others
	Difficulty attending to multiple stimuli simultaneously
Executive Function	Problems with decision-making and task preparation
	Deficits in working memory impacting task performance
	Problems finishing complex tasks and/or novel tasks
	Difficulty turning attention from one activity to another and multitasking
Learning & Memory	Repetitions in speech and behavior
	Difficulty retaining current or recent information
	Memory difficulties persist even with cues
	In major NCD, deficits with the meaning of words, past events of one's life, and implicit/procedural memory
Language	Searches for words and has difficulty expressing oneself
	Difficulty understanding what is said to oneself
	Repetition of one's own or others' words and phrases
	Errors with language fluency and naming objects
Perceptual-Motor Abilities	Difficulty performing previously known tasks
	Difficulty moving or traveling in low-light conditions
	Increasingly challenged with directions, especially in novel or unknown places
	Lost in tasks and need for more effort with spatial tasks
Social Cognition	Has considerable difficulty recognizing and responding to the emotions of others
	Behaves in a socially unacceptable manner
	Maintains focus on topic other than topic of conversation
	Decrease in empathy and considering others' mental state

APA, 2013

© IAKOBCHUK VIACHESLAV/Shutterstock.com

Feeling Pain

Many NCDs are progressive and, therefore, the functioning of the individual will decline to the point that they can no longer work, socialize with others, or even recognize their closest friends and family. The caregivers of individuals with NCDs, especially major forms of the disorder, often experience a great deal of stress caring for their loved one, which in some cases can even lead to conflict and abuse from the caregiver (Llanque et al., 2016). The loved ones of individuals with NCD, themselves, are often experiencing grief over the loss of their relationship to the person, which may go unrecognized by friends and relatives, especially since the patient is still alive. In addition to *The Notebook*, other movies, such as *On Golden Pond*, have taken on this theme of loss in dementia, and while caregivers may wait in hope to regain moments of their lost relationship, the reality of daily caregiving often keeps the caregiver rooted in the reality of the progressive nature of most of these disorders (Wedding & Niemiec, 2014). Imagine losing your relationship with the person you're closest to, without losing the person. A number of behavioral disturbances can happen as a result of NCDs, including psychotic symptoms such as hallucinations and delusions, though episodes of psychosis in NCD generally are not characterized by disorganized behavior or speech (APA, 2013). Psychosis is common in several NCDs, as well as other potentially problematic behaviors, such as hyperphagia, wandering, hoarding, sleep disturbances, and mood problems, such as depression, anxiety, agitation, frustration, confusion, and apathy (APA, 2013).

Hyperphagia

Disordered behavior characterized by overeating, often to the point of harming oneself

Fatality

© alphaspirit/Shutterstock.com

As many NCDs are caused by degenerative diseases, fatality is often a certain result, though death can occur in many different manners. Accidents are a common cause of death among individuals with NCDs, who are six to seven times more likely to die as the result of an accident (Crump et al., 2013). Some individuals with NCDs wander into traffic or other unsafe situations leading to death. Others may take the wrong medications, or have a fall as a result of declining sensorium, or try to drive their car long after they are no longer capable. Many individuals with NCDs die of other causes, such as cardiovascular disease or cancer, though a recent study found that individuals with NCDs most frequently die of the disorder itself or cardiovascular disease (van de Vorst et al., 2016).

Major or Mild Neurocognitive Disorders

Major NCDs were referred to as dementia prior to the DSM-5, which specifies that the term dementia is also frequently used in some of the specific subtypes, for example, Lewy Body Dementia (APA, 2013). One significant myth regarding NCDs is that the symptoms are really just the result of aging, such that everyone who gets old enough would eventually get "senile." A caricature of this myth, may be the frequent use of the term "old-timers disease," when discussing Alzheimer's. The line between normal and abnormal can become particularly difficult in cases of mild NCDs. Many mild forms remain undiagnosed as it can be difficult to differentiate mild deficits from the process of typical aging (APA, 2013). Family members, and even clinicians, may just write off symptoms as caused by aging. Be that as it may, the research into these disorders appears to put this myth to rest, as evidence

Dementia

Literally meaning out of (*de-*) one's mind (*-mentis*), this term was used as a diagnostic label prior to the DSM-5

Myths in Movies

DEMENTIA 13

What comes to mind when you think of the word dementia? How about the word demented?

© AF archive/Alamy Stock Photo

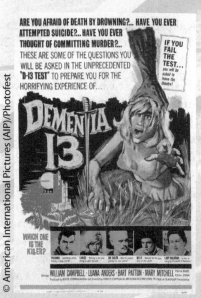

ARE YOU AFRAID OF DEATH BY DROWNING?... HAVE YOU EVER ATTEMPTED SUICIDE?... HAVE YOU EVER THOUGHT OF COMMITTING MURDER?...
THESE ARE SOME OF THE QUESTIONS YOU WILL BE ASKED IN THE UNPRECEDENTED "D-13 TEST" TO PREPARE YOU FOR THE HORRIFYING EXPERIENCE OF...

IF YOU FAIL THE TEST...

© American International Pictures (AIP)/Photofest

While these words likely brought to mind very different images for you, movies have not always made a clear distinction, depicting dementia as horror and violence. The trailer for Francis Ford Coppola's 1963 classic film *Dementia 13* even juxtaposes these words with the title: The Damned—The Dead—The Demented—*Dementia 13*. The 2017 remake of this film follows a similar storyline of murder and violence, and though individuals with dementia are clearly not murderous villains, is there any truth to the increased likelihood of violence among people suffering from these disorders?

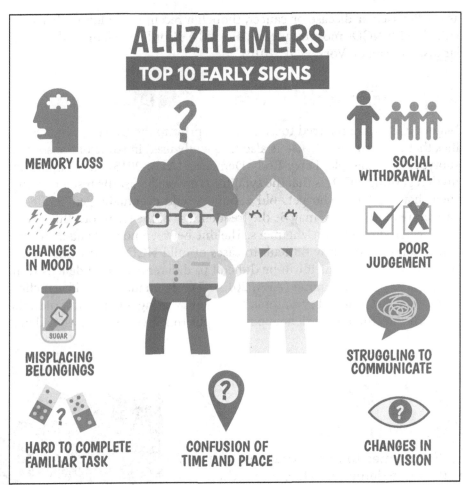

© Falara/Shutterstock.com

Amnestic

Characterized by
amnesia: loss of
memories, often
interrelated memories
are forgotten together
as a group

Aphasic

Characterized by
aphasia: an impairment
of language production
or fluency

Myoclonus

Uncontrollable
twitching or jerking of
various muscle groups
caused by muscular
contractions

seems to point to dysfunctional neurological processes as the source of most NCDs. Why these processes almost never begin to occur before age 60, however, remains somewhat of a mystery.

Alzheimer's Disease. NCD due to Alzheimer's disease is characterized by a slow onset and gradual progression, and impairment in at least two of the six cognitive domains of NCDs (APA, 2013). The initial decline of individuals with NCD due to Alzheimer's is usually in terms of mild executive functioning, learning, and memory impairments, referred to as amnestic, but they may also present as an aphasic variant, and these mild states are followed by a progression to more profound deficits in social cognition, perceptual motor problems, and linguistic issues (APA, 2013). Consistent with these functional impairments, NCD due to Alzheimer's disease is a cortical NCD related to deficits in the cortex of the brain, rather than the subcortical areas. As the disease becomes more severe, individuals are more likely to experience myoclonus, psychotic features, irritability, being combative, wandering, dysphagia, incontinence, difficulties walking in their typical manner, and seizures (APA, 2013). Diagnosis is considered

Myths in Movies

THE NOTEBOOK

If you've seen the movie *The Notebook*, or read the book by Nicolas Sparks (1996) on which it is based, you may have found it hard to forget scenes where Allie, who is in an assisted living facility, forgets her husband Noah, or when she comments to a nurse that she would like to hear someone play piano, to which the nurse replies that Allie should play. Sitting down at the piano, she discovers that she can play beautifully by memory (Wedding & Niemiec, 2014). Can NCDs actually affect memory in a wide variety of ways? Does the decline of memory tend to be similar to the manner it appears in *The Notebook*? Can individuals really have episodes of recalling memories that they had previously forgotten?

A scene from *The Notebook*

© New Line/Photofest

"probable" if genetic tests or family history demonstrates evidence of the genetic mutations commonly associated with Alzheimer's, and "possible" if symptoms are consistent, but no such evidence exists (APA, 2013). Census estimates suggest that around 7% of the Alzheimer's population are age 65–74, 53% are age 75–84, and 40% are age 85 and up, and women more frequently than men suffer from the disease (APA, 2013; Gatz, Reynolds, et al., 2006). NCD due to Alzheimer's appears to be uncommon prior to age 60 (APA, 2013).

Recently, a debate has arisen among Alzheimer's researchers about whether or not Alzheimer's disease even exists. And while researchers on both sides agree that the declines collected under the umbrella of "Alzheimer's disease" are real, they disagree about whether or not the construct of "Alzheimer's disease" is sufficient for explaining the disorder (Whitehouse & George, 2015). After all, constructs have been wrong before, and memory loss associated with aging has been blamed on moral degeneracy, bad blood, witchcraft, and the migration of vital energy away from the brain (Whitehouse & George, 2015).

Today, bad genes and other related physiological phenomena are often posited as the cause of Alzheimer's disease, and for good reasons, as some twin studies have demonstrated heritability rates as high as 58 to 79% (Gatz, Reynolds, et al., 2006). Additionally, the cognitive deficits of Alzheimer's disease and other NCDs have generally been understood to be connected to insufficient levels of the neurotransmitter acetylcholine, though medications targeting the neurotransmitter have had mixed results (Martorana et al., 2010). Many researchers believe that Alzheimer's disease is largely related to an increase in β-amyloid plaques and neurofibrillary tangles, as these are commonly found in the brains of individuals with Alzheimer's, although research has also failed to demonstrate a linear correlation (Iacono et al., 2014). Plaques and tangles can lead to cellular death in the amygdala, hippocampus, and cortical areas, and result in enlargement of the ventricles. The brain areas destroyed by Alzheimer's disease are strongly associated with memory, personality, affect, and decision-making. These plaques and tangles are made of different types of proteins. Plaques are composed of the protein β-amyloid and form outside of the cell body disrupting signals from one cell to another, whereas tangles are made of a protein called tau, and form within the cell body disrupting the activity of the cell itself. Several gene studies on twins have also implicated the apolipoprotein E4 (ApoE4) gene, which has been associated with earlier onset, increased levels of β-amyloid, increased frequency of comorbid disorders, and the acceleration of decline in Alzheimer's (Iacono et al., 2014; Iacono et al., 2016). Interestingly, another ApoE gene

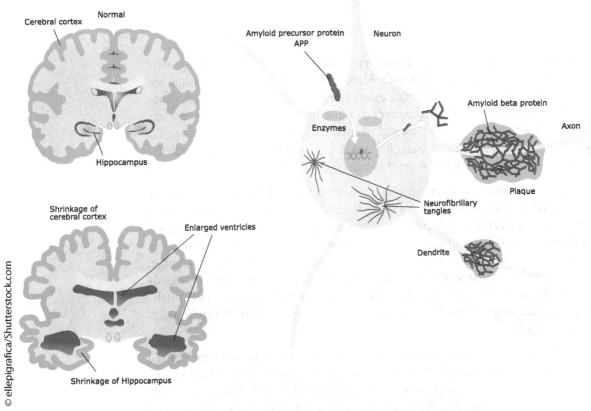

The Effect of Plaques and Tangles in the Brain

variant, ApoE2, is being investigated for possible protective features against the development of Alzheimer's, and has been associated with reduced levels of β-amyloid and other proteins associated with NCDs (Iacono et al., 2016).

Some researchers suggest that these neurological and genetic findings may not be connected with Alzheimer's as strongly as many believe. Whitehouse and George (2015) put it this way:

> …people without cognitive impairment can have plaques and tangles, and persons with "clinical" Alzheimer's can have an absence of such features. Even people with familial Alzheimer's disease who carry rare autosomal dominant mutations demonstrate different brain biologies and clinical presentations…scientists in the field acknowledge that we know so little about the true nature of plaques and tangles and their related proteins. Yet the fact that these "pathological hallmarks" clearly don't correlate with dementia does not stop us from making massive investments in trying to cure the disease (¶ 2).

Whitehouse and George (2015) further argue that our strong emphasis on these biological components have turned us away from other potentially beneficial avenues of investigation. Regardless of how one categorizes these

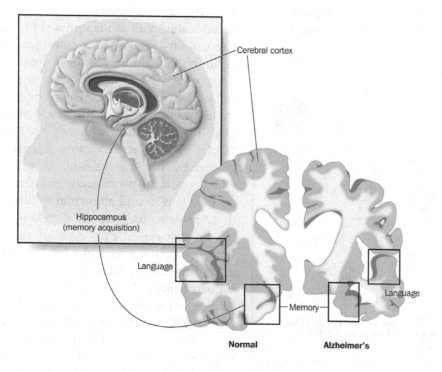

© Juan Gaertner/Shutterstock.com

Functional Areas of the Brain Affected by Alzheimer's Disease

disorders, Alzheimer's is a seriously debilitating disease, and diagnosis still relies on discovery of physiological markers for the disorder. On average, individuals with Alzheimer's die within 10 years of onset, though in some research, averages have been found between 4–20 years from diagnosis to death (APA, 2013; Iacono et al., 2016). Though myths arise from time to time that an Alzheimer's preventative or cure has been found, at this time, these remain myths.

Frontotemporal Neurocognitive Disorder. Like Alzheimer's disease, Frontotemporal NCD begins slowly and progresses gradually, but typically involve the retention of perceptual motor skills, and learning and memory (APA, 2013). This disorder can present in a behavioral manner, involving personality changes due to disinhibition, apathy, loss of empathy/sympathy, changes in diet or hyperorality, and/or repetitious, compulsive, or stereotyped behavior (APA, 2013). Frontotemporal NCD can also present in a linguistic manner, characterized by declines in language such as difficulties with finding or comprehending words, naming objects, speech production, and/or grammar (APA, 2013). Frontotemporal NCDs account for approximately 5% of all NCD cases, and onset is typically earlier than other NCDs, occurring as early as young adulthood, yet most commonly in one's 50s (APA, 2013). Between 20 to 25% of cases occur after age 65, and decline is more rapid than with Alzheimer's with individuals dying within 6–11 years after symptom onset or 3–4 years post initial diagnosis (APA, 2013).

Prion Disease. Ever heard of mad cow disease? Mad cow disease is a variant of prion diseases, and cross-species transmission is possible (APA, 2013). In humans, these diseases include fatal familial insomnia (FFI) and Creutzfeldt-Jakob disease, among others, although the familial forms of the disorder are rare. NCD due to prion disease can occur from adolescence to the latest stages of life, and some forms appears to peak in individuals in their 60's (APA, 2013). NCD due to prion disease is caused by the transmission of prions, which refers to proteinaceous infection particle (PrP^c), and abnormal folding of these proteins leads to the development of the disease-causing type of prions (PrP^{Sc}). These diseases involve insidious onset and can quickly progress to the status of major NCD within 6 months, leading to impairments in cognition and motor skills, such as myoclonus, ataxia, dystonia, chorea, and in the case of FFI, severe insomnia leading eventually to death (APA, 2013).

Hyperorality

Excessively sticking things, especially non-edible items, in one's mouth

Dystonia

Disorder causing involuntary muscular contractions and reduced motor speed

Chorea

Disorder causing involuntary jerking and motor movements

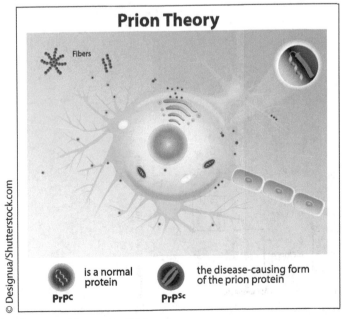

Prion Theory

Fibers

PrP^c — is a normal protein

PrP^{Sc} — the disease-causing form of the prion protein

© Designua/Shutterstock.com

Neuronal Impact of Prions

Parkinson's Disease. Parkinson's disease is characterized by the presence of Lewy Body proteins in the brainstem, leading to poor dopamine transmission, and in some cases these abnormal proteins can migrate to the striatum and other basal ganglia areas, leading to NCD due to Parkinson's (NCDP) disease. Due to the impact on the basal ganglia and related areas of the brain, NCDP is understood to be primarily a subcortical neurocognitive disorder, despite the fact that cortical areas may also be affected in some cases. Michael J. Fox and Pope John Paul II are among the famous people diagnosed with Parkinson's disease.

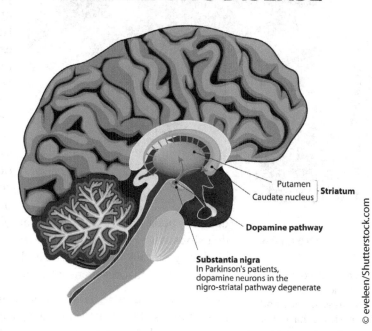

PARKINSON'S DISEASE

Putamen
Caudate nucleus — **Striatum**

Dopamine pathway

Substantia nigra
In Parkinson's patients, dopamine neurons in the nigro-striatal pathway degenerate

© eveleen/Shutterstock.com

PARKINSON'S DISEASE

WHAT IS PARKINSON'S DISEASE?	PARKINSON'S DISEASE SYMPTOMS
BRAIN	MEMORY LOSS, DEMENTIA
NEURON CELL	ANXIETY, DEPRESSION
	HALLUCINATIONS
NEURON CELL	SLOW BLINKING
	NO FACIAL EXPRESSION
TERMINAL BRANCH	DROOLING
	DIFFICULTY SWALLOWING
TERMINAL BRANCH	SHAKING, TREMORS
DOPAMINE	LOSS OF SMALL OR FINE HAND MOVEMENTS
DOPAMINE	PROBLEM WITH BALANCE OR WALKING
	STOOPED POSTURE
WEAK SIGNAL	ACHES AND PAINS
	CONSTIPATION

© Designua/Shutterstock.com

© giulio napolitano/Shutterstock.com

REM Sleep Behavior Disorder

Sleep disorder characterized by aggressive vocal and physical behaviors, in which a person acts out a current dream

In the case of John Paul II, the disease progressed slowly, leading to speech and motor problems, as well as difficulties with memory, and likely caused or exacerbated symptoms eventually leading to his death (Brown, 2008). NCDP is characterized by insidious onset and slow progression and the individual must have an onset of Parkinson's symptoms (e.g., tremors and motor skill deficits) prior to the development of the NCD, which leads to more severe cognitive symptoms, including memory loss, learning and comprehension deficits, personality changes, apathy and depression, hallucinations and delusions, and REM sleep behavior disorder (APA, 2013). Onset of Parkinson's generally occurs in the early 60's, and approximately 75% of individuals with Parkinson's eventually meet criteria for a major NCD (APA, 2013).

Lewy Body Dementia. In contrast to Parkinson's disease, NCD with Lewy Bodies (NCDLB) is characterized by the presence of Lewy body proteins primarily in the cerebral cortex (APA, 2013). NCDLB involves fluctuating cognitive deficits in executive functioning and attention, ongoing visual and other sensory hallucinations, REM sleep behavior disorder, and may involve features of Parkinson's disease, so long as cognitive deficits occur prior to Parkinson's features (APA, 2013). Additional features of NCDLB include loss of consciousness, frequent falls, delusions, urinary incontinence and other autonomic problems, and depression (APA, 2013). Individuals with NCDLB often experience premorbid delirium, and cases of NCDLB can be easily confused with delirium due to the fluctuation of cognition (APA, 2013). Approximately 0.1 to 5% of elderly individuals are believed to suffer from NCDLB, and women are over five times more likely to have the disorder than men, though this may be due to onset typically occurring in one's mid-70's, but as early as one's 50's (APA, 2013).

Apraxia

Full loss of the ability to complete purposeful, voluntary actions

Huntington's Disease. NCD due to Huntington's disease (NCDH) involves slow onset and progression, and is estimated to be quite rare, caused by hereditary transmission of an abnormal huntingtin gene leading to the destruction of neurons in the cerebral cortices and basal ganglia, and enlargement of the ventricles (APA, 2013). The symptoms of NCDH varies between individuals, but typically begins with mild mood or anxiety issues and may involve behavioral disinhibition, leading to more severe problems such as significant depression or apathy, impairments in cognition speed and insight, apraxia and choric movements, ataxia and posture problems, and serious problems with speech production, to the point wherein the person may become non-ambulatory and unable to eat or swallow (APA, 2013).

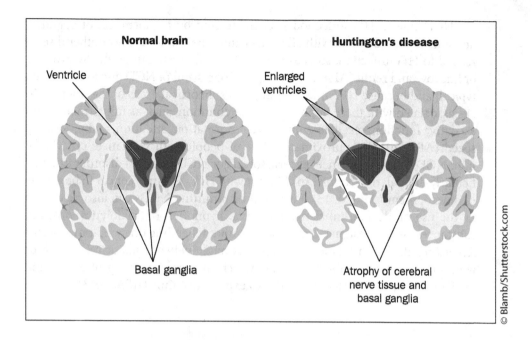

© Blamb/Shutterstock.com

Other Neurocognitive Disorders. NCDs can be the result of many additional causes, and additional diagnoses include Vascular NCD, NCD due to Traumatic Brain Injury (TBI), NCD due to HIV infection, and Substance/Medication-Induced NCD (APA, 2013). Though these subtypes of NCDs share the overarching diagnostic criteria of NCDs, a considerable amount of differences are evidenced. The etiologies of these NCDs are evident, related to a cerebrovascular event, such as a stroke, in the case of Vascular NCD, to head trauma in the case of NCD due to TBI, to the use of substances or medications, or to complications related to HIV infection. Vascular NCDs are the second most common type of NCDs, and can happen abruptly at any stage in life, although it is less common before a person is 65 years old (APA, 2013). As the name suggests, Vascular NCDs are caused by successive small strokes, and occur more frequently in individuals who have high blood pressure. Cognitive declines depend on which portions of the brain are impacted, and declines in functioning increase as cerebral vascular accidents (e.g., strokes) occur (APA, 2013). Vascular NCDs are estimated to occur in 16% of people over age 80, resulting in partial improvement for some and progressive decline for others however, the disorder leads to death for most individuals in approximately 2–3 years (APA, 2013).

NCD due to TBI result in a variety of different cognitive dysfunctions, related to what portions of the brain are injured. TBI events are generally associated post-trauma with losing consciousness, amnesia, confusion or disorientation, and/or another neurological indicator, such as anosmia, seizures, or hemiparesis (APA, 2013). Approximately 2% of individuals are estimated to have TBI-related disabilities, and behavioral symptoms tend to be worst shortly after the traumatic event, followed by significant or complete recovery, unless the initial TBI was severe (APA, 2013).

Anosmia

The loss of one's sense of smell

Hemiparesis

Weakness in one's entire side of the body, in TBI, typically the side opposite from the brain injury

NCD due to HIV infection is characterized by impairments of cognitive domains in an individual with HIV that cannot be explained by another disease related to HIV infection, such as meningitis, and either can gradually progress or improve and remit (APA, 2013). Rapid progression of NCD due to HIV is not typical, and because HIV infection impacts subcortical areas of the brain, deficits associated with these brain regions are common, such as impairments with executive function, recall, learning novel information, attention, and processing speed (APA, 2013). Approximately 25% of people with HIV meet criteria for mild NCD, whereas 5% meet criteria for major NCD, and this disorder can particularly difficult to recognize in children with HIV, as it may appear to be a delay in development (APA, 2013). Persistent or remitting NCDs can also be caused by the use of alcohol, inhalants, sedatives, hypnotics, or anxiolytics, or other substances, and is designated as major or mild depending on symptom severity. Regarding alcohol, a further distinction is made between major NCD with or without amnestic-confabulatory type, which involves forgetting of events and the fabrication of distorted memories to explain lost time (APA, 2013).

Treatment and Prevention of Neurocognitive Disorders

While medications to cure or prevent NCDs have not yet been discovered, some medications have been developed that slow the progression of these disorders and help with related symptoms. Cholinesterase inhibitors, such as Razadyne (galantamine) and Reminyl (donepezil), help aid in the transfer of acetylcholine between neuronal synapses, leading to a reduction of some cognitive symptoms of NCDs (Martorana et al., 2010). Namenda (memantine), on the other hand, increases the availability of glutamate in the neuronal synapses, and is believed to help improve learning and memory

deficits related to NCDs (Martorana et al., 2010). These drugs may work by providing excess neurotransmitters in areas potentially blocked by abnormal proteins, such as β-amyloid plaques and/or by keeping neurotransmitters available for cells compromised by interior proteins, such as tangles, thereby allowing for more activation of the neurons, which in some cases may keep these cells alive longer. Additional medications, such as antipsychotics, antidepressants, and anxiolytics, may be helpful in the treatment of symptoms of some NCDs, as well as in individuals with NCD who have other comorbid disorders.

Many clinicians believe that psychotherapeutic treatments only offer little assistance to individuals with NCDs and their families, though behavioral treatments have been demonstrated to offer assistance with behavioral disinhibition and related dysfunctions. Some research suggests that individuals with NCDs can demonstrate improvements with certain behavioral and psychological issues, such as activities of daily living, arguments with caregivers, wandering, and depression, through psychotherapeutic work with individuals and their families (Brodaty & Arasaratnam, 2012). Additionally, psychotherapy and education-based programs appear effective in assisting caregivers of individuals with NCDs by reducing their own distress and by learning to respond better to behavioral problems common with these disorders (Brodaty & Arasaratnam, 2012; Kurz et al., 2010). Interestingly, some research has suggested that education and/or increased intellectual activity may be a preventative factor, as individuals with higher educational attainment have been found to be at a reduced risk for developing NCDs (Carpenter et al., 2011; Gatz, Mortimer, et al., 2007; Sharp & Gatz, 2011). In the well-known nun studies, researchers tracked the development of NCDs, discovering that those with higher intellectual abilities were more capable of retaining their abilities, even when the physiological signs (plaques and tangles) of Alzheimer's were present, and in some cases sisters would have little intellectual decline despite advanced physiological symptoms (Snowdon et al., 2003; Tyas et al., 2007). Perhaps this will encourage us all to try and form good intellectual "habits."

Conclusion

Disorders occurring in the stages of later life are often quite concerning, as individuals are often more fragile and less capable of recovery as they age. A great deal of research on NCDs continues to be underway, and funding for research for these disorders is often plentiful. The simple thought of "losing one's mind" or losing one's "relationship" with a loved one while he or she is still alive, is disturbing and should not be sugar-coated. Most NCDs are severe, debilitating disorders that none of us want to be involved with in any way. We can place some hope in science, looking forward to a day when we will find preventions or treatments, but it is perhaps more important to place our hope in the triumph of the human family, and our responsibility to care for those most in need.

CHAPTER REVIEW

QUESTIONS

1. What are some of the key differences between neurocognitive disorders? What is delirium and how is it related to neurocognitive disorders? How does one determine whether a neurocognitive disorder should be considered major or mild?

2. How do neurocognitive disorders vary by age and gender? What might explain some of these differences?

3. What are the six cognitive domains recognized by the DSM-5? Which symptoms of neurocognitive disorders fall into each cognitive domain?

4. What are some of the theories for the development of the various neurocognitive disorders? In what ways do the theories overlap? What makes them different? How are treatment and prevention efforts progressing? What factors seem to help deter the impact of these disorders?

KEY TERMS

Episodic Memory

Procedural Memory

Traumatic Brain Injury

Complex Attention

Executive Function

Hyperphagia

Dementia

Amnestic

Aphasic

Myoclonus

Hyperorality

Dystonia

Chorea

REM Sleep Behavior Disorder

Apraxia

Anosmia

Hemiparesis

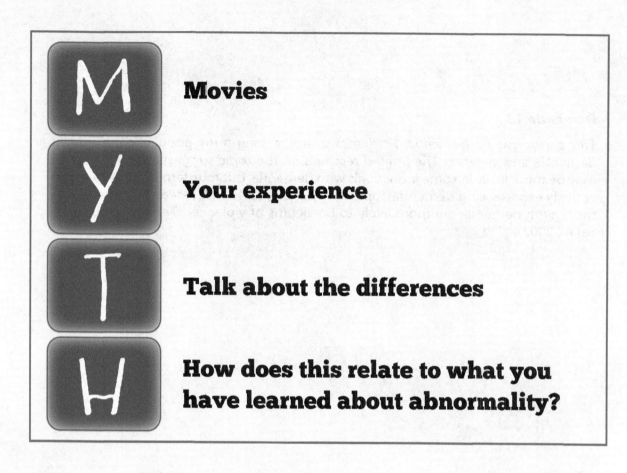

M Movies

Y Your experience

T Talk about the differences

H How does this relate to what you have learned about abnormality?

Myths in Movies Recap

The Notebook

While *The Notebook* is a sweet, romantic comedy that accurately depicts the difference between declines in episodic memory without corresponding declines in procedural memory, the movie does seem to become fantasy toward the end when Allie recovers her memory just before death. Though this type of paradoxical or terminal lucidity, as it has been called, is not the typical experience with NCD declines, it does occur and researchers are beginning to explore the ramifications for our current understanding of the relationship between brain structure and cognitive function (Mashour et al., 2019 ; Nahm et al., 2012).

Myths in Movies Recap

Dementia 13

The classic movie *Dementia 13* demonstrates a long-term popular confusion of dementia and violence. The limited research on the topic suggests that aggression may be more likely in some individuals with dementia, but murderous behavior while actively experiencing dementia appears to be rare, and some research suggests that those with dementia are more likely to be victims of violence (Cipriana et al., 2015; Salari, 2007).

PERSONALITY DISORDERS

MYTHs of Personality Disorders

Theories of personality disorders have a long history of conflict and turmoil, and are among the least agreed upon diagnoses in the field of psychotherapy. Myths and movies about personality disorders likewise portray extreme symptoms in a variety of perplexing ways. Skinner (1957) suggested that personality disorders, and the concept of personality itself, were virtually a fiction to explain certain behaviors, whereas some psychodynamic theorists have considered personality to be what "one *is* rather than what one *has*," and disorders of personality are therefore simply exaggerations of what is typically human (Psychodynamic Diagnostic Manual [PDM], 2006, p. 17). Popular media has not deemed it important to come to the aid of psychology in this regard, and in fact, has likely added to the confusion surrounding these disorders. Take a few minutes to explore your beliefs and experiences with MYTHs of personality disorders.

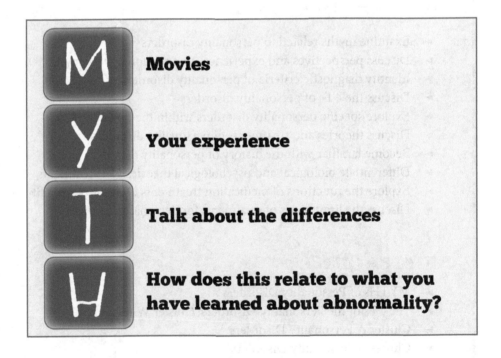

M Movies

Y Your experience

T Talk about the differences

H How does this relate to what you have learned about abnormality?

Regardless of the linguistic debate among theorists about the nature of personality, the phenomenon of personality disorders are unmistakable when encountered in a clinical setting. A debate does, however, remain in regard to whether or not personality disorders are dimensional along a continuum, or categorical, as our diagnostic criteria seems to suggest (Fowler et al., 2007; Hopwood et al., 2018). The significance of this debate lies in

Myths in Movies

AMERICAN PSYCHO, TAXI DRIVER, BASIC INSTINCT and SEVEN PSYCHOPATHS

Consider the movies *American Psycho*, *Taxi Driver*, and *Basic Instinct*. Although the characters in these movies all portrayed individuals with symptoms of different personality disorders, they were all depicted as violent (Wedding & Niemiec, 2014). The movie *Seven Psychopaths*, on the other hand seems to promote the exact opposite premise, that one disorder (Antisocial Personality Disorder) can appear in a wide variety of ways. Do individuals with different personality disorders really share the same basic instincts, uh, um, symptoms?

Scene from *Basic Instinct*

Scene from *American Psycho*

Scene from *Seven Psychopaths*

Scene from *Taxi Driver*

whether we conceptualize all of the personality disorders as one disorder with many manifestations, or as distinct disorders. The experience of many clinicians even seems to be varied, with some clients clearly manifesting symptoms specific to only one personality disorder, while other clients seem to possess characteristics belonging to several different personality disorders. So while there may be some validity to the myth that some of these disorders overlap, the idea that most individuals with a personality disorder are prone to violence is quite inaccurate. Though individuals suffering from certain personality disorders appear to be more prone to violence than the general population, the majority of individuals with personality disorders do not seem prone to commit acts of violence.

DSM-5 CRITERIA FOR GENERAL PERSONALITY DISORDER

DIAGNOSTIC CRITERIA

A. An enduring pattern of inner experience and behavior that deviates markedly from the expectations of the individual's culture. This pattern is manifested in two (or more) of the following areas:

1. Cognition (i.e., ways of perceiving and interpreting self, other people, and events).

2. Affectivity (i.e., the range, intensity, lability, and appropriateness of emotional response).

3. Interpersonal functioning.

4. Impulse control.

B. The enduring pattern is inflexible and pervasive across a broad range of personal and social situations.

C. The enduring pattern leads to clinically significant distress or impairment in social, occupational, or other important areas of functioning.

D. The pattern is stable and of long duration, and its onset can be traced back at least to adolescence or early adulthood.

E. The enduring pattern is not better explained as a manifestation or consequence of another mental disorder.

F. The enduring pattern is not attributable to the physiological effects of a substance (e.g., a drug of abuse, a medication) or another medical condition (e.g., head trauma).

Reprinted with permission from the *Diagnostic and Statistical Manual of Mental Disorders,* Fifth Edition, (Copyright 2013). American Psychiatric Association.

The 4 Fs of the Personality Disorders: Cluster What?

Personality disorders are generally understood to share a deeper foundation in an individual's personality, which may be a contributing factor to the overlap of symptoms among several different personality disorders. Though the DSM-5 retains the categorical approach of previous DSMs, recognizing 10 personality disorders, belonging to three clusters, like its immediate predecessor, it also recognizes the value of considering these disorders from a dimensional perspective (American Psychiatric Association [APA], 2013). Along these lines, the diagnostic criteria of general personality disorder represent what is common to all of the personality disorders. Among these commonalities, regardless of whether one takes a categorical or dimensional approach, is the recognition that personality disorders are all rooted in an individual's personality, understood as the enduring patterns of thinking, feeling, and behaving characteristic of a person (APA, 2013). When these enduring patterns vary significantly from what is typical in one's culture in a way that leads to significant distress, this is considered a personality disorder. The three clusters of personality disorders are as follows: Cluster A includes paranoid, schizoid, and schizotypal personality disorders; Cluster B includes antisocial, borderline, histrionic, and narcissistic personality disorder; Cluster C includes avoidant, dependent, and obsessive-compulsive disorders (APA, 2013; Fowler et al., 2007). Before discussing these specific, categorical personality disorders recognized by the DSM-5, we will explore the 4 Fs common to all of these disorders.

Frequency

A—Amount of Time: Personality disorders are conceptually different from most other disorder due to their being founded upon personality. Because of this, personality disorders are understood to be ever present across a range of situations, rather than occurring for a specific, limited amount of time. The DSM-5 simply specifies that personality disorders must be long enduring and stable as far back as at least early adulthood or adolescence (APA, 2013). In order to be diagnosed prior to the age of 18, however, a person must have experienced symptoms for at least 1 year, though this is quite rare and the manifestation of the disorder typically changes as the individual continues to develop (APA, 2013). Antisocial personality disorder is the one exception to this, as it cannot be diagnosed prior to the age of 18, before which adolescents with these symptoms are typically diagnosed with conduct disorder.

B—Behavior: Individuals with personality disorders may exhibit a wide range of behaviors, varying to greater or lesser degrees across the various personality disorders. Behaviors specific to each disorder are discussed below. For General Personality Disorder, the DSM-5 specifies that individuals must have deficits in at least two out of four areas of functioning, including cognitive, affective, interpersonal, or impulse control deficits (APA, 2013). Though these symptoms are characteristic of all personality disorders, looking at the specific disorders one finds that the possible combinations of these deficits can appear in a wide array of manifestations, with more emphasis on cognitive and emotive deficits or interpersonal and cognitive deficits, or all of the above.

C—Curve: While we all have interesting and quirky personality characteristics, whether they be a penchant for being solitary, or the craving of excitement and adventure, or just the need to do things in a very specific order each time we do them, individuals with truly disordered personality characteristics experience more extreme personality traits, which are far less common. The DSM-5 estimates a prevalence rate of approximately 9.1% for all personality disorders, with prevalence rates of approximately 5.7% for Cluster A disorders, 1.5% for Cluster B disorders, and 6.0% for Cluster C disorders (APA, 2013). Please note that the overall estimates include individuals with multiple comorbid personality disorders from different clusters, such that it may not be the case that 9.1% of the population has a personality disorder. On the other hand, some estimates have suggested as much as 15% of U.S. adults may have a personality disorder

Cluster A Disorders

A cluster of personality disorders similar to schizophrenia and related disorders, which are characterized by odd and eccentric behaviors and personality features

Cluster B Disorders

A cluster of personality disorders similar to impulse-control and conduct disorders, which are characterized by emotional instability and dramatic, impulsive behaviors and personality features

Cluster C Disorders

A cluster of personality disorders similar to anxiety and obsessive-compulsive disorders, which are characterized by anxious and fear-based behaviors and personality features

(APA, 2013). Additionally, some gender-related differences have been evidenced, with males more frequently diagnosed with antisocial personality disorder, and women more frequently diagnosed with dependent, histrionic, and borderline personality disorders (APA, 2013). Some researchers suggest that these differences are less rooted in gender than in social expectations about gender, but the DSM-5 posits that these differences are probably rooted in real differences between men and women (APA, 2013).

The Good News: Although an attitude of hopelessness is still sometimes prevalent among clinicians that work with individuals diagnosed with personality disorders, several treatment options have been developed for working with even the most severely dysfunctional types of personality disorders. Some of these treatments have demonstrated promising results, offering individuals with these disorders more hope for the future than many researchers and clinicians once thought to be possible. Beliefs about life-long, unremitting, and unmanageable personality disorders are beginning to change, and the DSM-5 even notes that some personality disorders can remit or become less evident as a person ages, though this does not appear to be true for all personality disorders (APA, 2013). This being the case, one should not confuse the reality that personality disorders are pervasive and often particularly difficult to treat with the mistaken belief that they are untreatable (Fowler et al., 2007).

Function

Functional difficulties related to personality disorders can be quite different from disorder to disorder, though generally, deficits in cognition, affect, interpersonal relationships, and impulse control can all independently lead to problems functioning at work, school, and in other social situations. Imagine having multiple domains of dysfunction, and experiencing them pervasively in almost all situations. The cognitive deficits related to these disorders can often lead to poor decision-making, difficulties with communication, and difficulties seeking help when needed. The affective deficits vary from the almost complete absence of emotion in some disorders, to elevated and even highly disproportionate emotion in other disorders. These deficits can lead to interpersonal and occupational difficulties, such as isolation or dramatically important, but shallow, relationships. Impulse control issues often lead to legal problems, relationship troubles, and even health-related concerns due to dangerous behaviors such as substance abuse or sexual risk-taking behaviors. Dysfunction can sometimes depend on the fit between the person, the disorder with which they struggle, and the specific situations of their

The pervasiveness of personality disorders can lead to conflict from many different domains within a person's life.

© ArtFamily/Shutterstock.com

life. For example, an individual with schizoid personality disorder is likely to better maintain occupational functioning if their job does not require social interaction (APA, 2013).

Feeling Pain

Individuals with personality disorders can often be highly distressed, and this is particularly characteristic of some personality disorders, whereas in others, the distress may be more related to confusion or the lack of affect. Similar to substance abuse disorders, individuals with personality disorders often are labeled as "crazy" because they elicit intense or eccentric, dysfunctional behavior coupled with great

Personality disorders sufficiently vary with some characterized by absent emotion and others involving intense emotion.

© ArtFamily/Shutterstock.com

difficulty changing this behavior. Individuals with personality disorders also frequently experience a host of comorbid disorders, including substance abuse disorders, mood disorders, anxiety and phobic disorders, obsessive-compulsive disorders, and are more likely to have experienced childhood physical and sexual abuse, early loss of a parent, and hostile environments with some disorders (APA, 2013). Consider the mixture of deficits found in the maestro described in the following case study.

Case Vignette

Johannes was in rehab again. He had been living with his mother recently and didn't think that his drug use had gotten so out of control this time. Maybe his mother just didn't want him around for awhile, and so she sent him away on purpose to catch a break. His drug use surely wasn't the problem, but here he was anyway. The people at rehab did not seem trustworthy to him, though his buddy Franz, who he met a few days ago, was turning out to be the best friend he ever had. He'd been sticking close to Franz since he got in the place, and felt comfortable with Franz most of the time, but occasionally he felt angry with Franz because he was paying so much attention to other patients. His therapist seemed okay some of the time, but he didn't know why she kept wanting to know more about his music career, he had already told her that he had recorded a multi-platinum album and was a millionaire. He planned to continue making records when he got out of rehab. He had his own recording studio and could make a new album every few months. Eventually, Johannes got pretty pissed off with Franz, who began asking him the names of his albums and inquiring more about the music.

He had answered all of the questions perfectly, so why was Franz acting like he was lying? Johannes frequently thought about how he hated being "called a liar." He decided to show Franz how serious he was about his music, so he got a sharp pin and cut the name of his band into his arm. He also decided to tell Franz that if he wouldn't believe him, then Johannes would have no other choice than to hang himself with his shoelaces in the closet of his room. After this, Franz began distancing himself, and Johannes felt abandoned yet again. This always seemed to happen to him.

In this case study, Johannes exhibits symptoms belonging to several personality disorders, which makes it particularly difficult to determine an appropriate diagnosis. This can often be the case for individuals with these disorders, as they may cope with their distress by turning to substances, as well as by trying to find solace in individuals they may not know as well as they perceive. At times, the grandiosity of bipolar disorder can also look very similar to the unstable self-image that is common among certain disorders. If you were a clinician, what diagnosis (or diagnoses) would you give Johannes?

Fatality

Some evidence suggests that having a personality disorder will significantly decrease a person's life expectancy. Fok and colleagues (2012) conducted a large-scale study in the UK on personality disorders and life expectancy, reporting that women with personality disorders had an 18.7-year reduction in their life span compared to the general population, while men with personality disorders had a 17.7-year reduction. Some of the suggested reasons for decreased life expectancy including heavy substance abuse, long-term use of psychotropic medication, inadequate health care, and increased cardiovascular problems have been linked with certain personality disorders (Fok et al., 2012). In addition to this, suicide risks are particularly high with certain personality disorders. For example, approximately 8 to 10% of individuals with borderline personality disorder complete suicide, and individuals with antisocial personality disorder are more likely to die as a result of suicide, homicide, or accidents (APA, 2013). Björkenstam and colleagues (2015) reported significantly increased mortality rates in all personality clusters, as high as have been found in individuals with anorexia, with significantly increased mortality and suicide rates for individuals with Cluster B personality disorders.

Cluster A Personality Disorders

Individuals with Cluster A disorders often experience many of the symptoms of those with schizophrenia and related disorders, including paranoia, confusion, odd ideas and beliefs, and blunted or inappropriate affect (APA, 2013). In line with these symptoms, this cluster is often referred to as odd/eccentric (Fowler et al., 2007). In terms of symptomology, schizotypal personality disorder is understood to have a closer relationship to schizophrenia than schizoid personality disorder. And while paranoid personality disorder is understood to be even less closely related to schizophrenia, all three disorders can be antecedent diagnoses for schizophrenia and related disorders. Let's look more closely at each of these disorders independently.

Paranoid Personality Disorder. Prevalence rates between 2.3 to 4.4% have been suggested for paranoid personality disorder (PDP), which is characterized by pervasive suspicion and distrust of the intentions of others, often believed to be malicious (APA, 2013). Individuals with PDP unreasonably suspect others of intending them harm, are preoccupied with friends and acquaintances being untrustworthy, and are therefore reluctant to put confidence in other people, misunderstanding remarks as implying threats or being degrading, and often holding grudges (APA, 2013). Additionally, these individuals often have a sense that their reputation is being attacked, and perhaps most specifically, often are suspicious and accuse their spouse of infidelity (APA, 2013). During particularly stressful times, a person with PDP may have a brief psychotic episode, which in turn may lead to a diagnosis of schizophrenia or a related disorder (APA, 2013). Other comorbid disorders include major depression, obsessive-compulsive disorder, agoraphobia, and substance-related disorders, as well as other comorbid personality disorders, most often other Cluster A disorders, narcissistic, avoidant, and borderline personality disorders (APA, 2013). Unfortunately, PDP has received far too little attention in the field of psychopathology research, especially in light of the frequency and pervasiveness of the disorder (Fowler et al.; 2007).

Schizoid Personality Disorder. The term "schizoid" was first used by Bleuler (1924) to indicate an inclination away from the external world and into one's internal world. Today, schizoid personality disorder is characterized, in much the same way, by a disconnection from relationships and socialization, as well as a limited range of affective expression (APA, 2013). Prevalence rates for schizoid personality disorder are estimated between 3.1 to 4.9%, according to the DSM-5 (APA, 2013). Specific diagnostic criteria for this disorder includes a lack of desire for or enjoyment of intimate relationships, continually choosing activities wherein they are alone, little interest in

sexual contact with others, little or no pleasure in activities, few, if any, intimate relationships other than close relatives, indifference to criticism or praise, and/or flat, detached affect (APA, 2013). This emotional coldness may particularly be evident when an individual is provoked in a manner that typically leads to anger, but instead has difficulty with the expression of anger and therefore appears to be emotionless (APA, 2013). Schizoid personality disorder tends to be more severe and more frequent in men than in women, and often occurs as an antecedent to schizophrenia or related disorders, or comorbid with major depression, other Cluster A symptoms, and avoidant personality disorder (APA, 2013). Schizoid personality features represent a middle ground between paranoid and schizo- typal personality features, often with more difficulty relating directly to others than is seen in individuals with paranoid personality disorder, yet typically with- out the cognitive and perceptual distortions often characteristic of schizotypal personality disorder.

Schizotypal Personality Disorder. Schizotypal personality disorder is characterized by a lack of comfort in relationships, and especially by significant social anxiety, which familiarity is unable to remit, cognitive and perceptual distortions distinct from delusions and hallucinations found in schizophrenia (particularly in terms of being less severe), and suspicious, paranoid, or bizarre thinking and preoccupations (APA, 2013). The disorder is also characterized by eccentric/odd appearance or behavior, often demonstrated in superstitious beliefs, and odd manners of speech and behavior (APA, 2013). Prevalence rates for the disorder are suggested to be approximately 3.9 to 4.6%, with lower

Myths in Movies

CHARLIE AND THE CHOCOLATE FACTORY

The movie *Charlie and the Chocolate Factory* portrays Willy Wonka, the owner of an extrav- agant chocolate factory. Wonka initiates a contest for five recipients of golden tickets to enter his sensational chocolate factory, which is operated by Oompa-Loompas. Willy Wonka leads the five winners through his unreal chocolate factory with intent to find an heir to his factory.

Johnny Depp as Willy Wonka

© USA Films/Photofest

Johnny Depp's portrayal of Willy Wonka in the 2005 remake of *Charlie and the Chocolate Factory* has been described as "one of the best depictions of schizotypal personalities captured on film" (Wedding, Boyd, & Niemiec, 2005, p. 252). Wonka's isolation and proclivity toward unconventional and unusual manners of accomplishing tasks fits well with the characteristics of schizotypal personality disorder. Be this as it may, presenting the disorder in the context of an elaborate fantasy world can serve to hide the distress typical of schizotypal personality disorder.

prevalence rates in clinical populations, likely due to the infrequency of seeking help as a result of fear, suspicion, or paranoia about the motives of others (APA, 2013). These individuals often experience restricted or inappropriate affect, participate in magical thinking and rituals, have beliefs that they have special powers to influence events, and/or have ideas of reference. Some of these characteristics are depicted in *Taxi Driver*, wherein the character Travis Bickle, played by Robert De Niro, is a loner who understands himself to have a special role in a political election and becomes a vigilante to this end (Wedding & Niemiec, 2014). Though this film does a good job drawing out symptoms related to ideas of reference and paranoia, De Niro's character does appear to have an interest in people, unlike classic cases of schizotypal personality disorder, and as previously mentioned, the movie also suffers from the portrayal of individuals with this disorder as being violent. Like other Cluster A disorders, schizotypal personality disorder symptoms and diagnosis often occurs prior to onset of a diagnosis of schizophrenia, and at times the boundaries between schizotypal personality disorder can be difficult to differentiate with schizophrenia and related disorders, as well as severe mood disorders with psychotic features and autism spectrum disorders (APA, 2013; Bollini & Walker, 2007). The DSM-5 suggests that 30 to 50% of individuals with this disorder may have comorbid major depression, and schizotypal personality disorder often occurs along with other Cluster A disorders, avoidant, and borderline personality disorders (APA 2013).

Cluster B Personality Disorders

Cluster B personality disorders have been characterized as dramatic, emotional, and erratic, and are typically characterized as conceptually similar to impulse-control and conduct disorders (APA, 2013; Fowler et al., 2007). This similarity extends even to the intensity of distress experienced by individuals with Cluster B disorders, especially in terms of unreasonable, impulsive, emotion-based behaviors that are particularly risky or dangerous.

Antisocial Personality Disorder. Whether because of the severity of behaviors related to the disorder, or the ease with which it can be dramatized, perhaps no other disorder has grabbed the attention of the media and the public quite like antisocial personality disorder (Patrick, 2007). By definition, a diagnosis of antisocial personality disorder requires the violation of the rights of others, and though the results are not always as spectacular and horrific as one might see on the big screen, in truth, they sometimes are quite horrific. A look at the diagnostic criteria for the disorder helps explain this horror, as individuals with antisocial personality disorder repeatedly commit crimes, fail to abide by laws and social norms, are typically deceitful, even to the point of using aliases or cons for their own pleasure or profit, and frequently act on impulse to get what they want (APA, 2013). In addition, these individuals are frequently aggressive and may repeatedly assault others, are irresponsible in regard to meeting their obligations, have almost no regard for the safety of themselves or others, and perhaps most frightening, have no remorse for the harm they have caused others (APA, 2013).

Prevalence rates for this disorder are estimated between 0.2 to 3.3%, although more than 70% of individuals with antisocial personality disorder are estimated to be men (APA, 2013). Philippe Pinel (1801/1962) characterized individuals that had this disorder as being dominated by fury, as if they only experienced deficits in their affective faculties. Similar to narcissistic personality disorder, individuals with antisocial personality disorder have

Myths in Movies

AMERICAN PSYCHO, SILENCE OF THE LAMBS, and DEXTER

Consider the films *American Psycho* or *The Silence of the Lambs*, two examples wherein the blatant disregard for the rights and welfare of others reaches spectacular extremes (Wedding & Niemiec, 2014). The popular TV series *Dexter* provides another interesting example, and with a main character who is portrayed as a "lovable serial killer," this series wonderfully demonstrates the media's penchant for myth-making (DePaulo, 2010, para. 1). How well do these movies portray the features of antisocial personality disorder? Do you think Dexter accurately represents a typical case of antisocial personality disorder or psychopathy? If Dexter were your close friend, would you have the same thoughts about him compared to a character distanced by film? Are most individuals with antisocial personality disorder systematic serial killers?

Scene from *Dexter*

© Showtime/Photofest

Scene from *Silence of the Lambs*

© Anton_Ivanov/Shutterstock.com

been characterized as having a mask of sanity, to be intelligent, and even charming (Cleckley, 1941). In addition to this, Cleckley (1976) provided a description of their sex life as being impersonal and trivial, and of individuals with the disorder as being pathologically egocentric. Cleckley's characterization of the disorder almost seems like a trailer for the movie *American Psycho*, which depicts these behaviors with a clarity that can provoke the cautious feeling clinicians often develop after working for some time with individuals with Cluster B disorders. Some research suggests that over 80% of individuals with the disorder also have comorbid substance abuse problems, both of which are considered externalizing disorders (Patrick, 2007). The DSM-5 suggests that depressive and anxiety disorders, somatic disorders, gambling and impulse-control disorders, and other Cluster B disorders are more common in individuals with Antisocial Personality Disorder, and a person is at a much higher risk of developing antisocial personality disorder if they were diagnosed with conduct disorder prior to age 10 (APA, 2013).

Borderline Personality Disorder. Have you ever wondered what the term borderline means? What are the borders that this disorder falls between? Oddly, if you ask five different clinicians, you may get five different answers. Early conceptualizations of the disorder characterized borderline as being situated between neurosis and psychosis, or in other words having some of the cognitive disorganization of psychosis, mixed with the emotional and impulsivity deficits characteristic of neurotic patients (Bradley et al., 2007; Kernberg, 1967). After working with individuals suffering from BPD, psychotic disorders, and histrionic personality disorder, one begins to recognize the borders more clearly, though there is frequently overlapping symptoms, as described with other personality disorders. Working with patients who have BPD, clinicians often recognize that they are generally easier to communicate with than patients who have psychosis; however, communication is typically more difficult than with patients experiencing histrionic features, despite similar emotional instabilities.

Borderline personality disorder (BPD) is perhaps second only to antisocial personality disorder in the portrayal of spectacle and tragedy capturing the fascination of popular media. As portrayed in many Hollywood scenes, BPD is characterized primarily by the feeling of being abandoned, whether real or imagined, coupled with attempts to avoid this abandonment, and also by intense and tumultuous relationships typically fluctuating between idealization and depreciation of others (APA, 2013). This feature of the

Instability of emotion and self-image are characteristic of BPD.

disorder can keep a clinician on their toes, as one session you may be the greatest therapist who ever lived, and in the next session, the worst of the 46 therapists with whom the patient has worked. Additionally, BPD is characterized by an unstable sense of one's identity, impulsivity that is damaging (e.g., sex, substance abuse, money), recurrent behaviors or threats that are self-injurious or suicidal, reactivity of mood causing affective instability, chronically feeling empty, intense or inappropriate anger, and paranoid thinking or significant dissociation (APA, 2013).

While the features of BPD can be severe, especially considering the increased risk of suicide, some longitudinal research has demonstrated remission rates as high as 69% after 6 years (Bradley et al., 2007; Zanarini et al., 2003). As with other personality disorders, BPD shares comorbidity with substance-related disorders, bulimia, PTSD, ADHD, bipolar disorder, depressive disorders, and other personality disorders (APA, 2013). Individuals with BPD comorbid with substance abuse disorders and depressive disorders appear to be at an increased risk for suicidal behavior (Bradley et al., 2007).

Myths in Movies

BASIC INSTINCT, FATAL ATTRACTION, and GIRL, INTERRUPTED

Hollywood has depicted borderline personality disorder in movies like *Basic Instinct* and *Fatal Attraction*, which portray more extreme, externalized borderline characteristics, and *Girl, Interrupted*, which takes on a more internalized approach (Wedding, Boyd, & Niemiec, 2005). Interestingly, all of the characters in these films are also women. But are there really more externalized and internalized cases of BPD? Are only women diagnosed with borderline personality disorder?

Scene from *Fatal Attraction*

© Paramount Pictures/Photofest

Scene from *Girl, Interrupted*

© Sony Pictures Entertainment/Photofest

DSM-5 CRITERIA FOR BORDERLINE PERSONALITY DISORDER

DIAGNOSTIC CRITERIA

A pervasive pattern of instability of interpersonal relationships, self-image, and affects, and marked impulsivity, beginning by early adulthood and present in a variety of contexts, as indicated by five (or more) of the following:

1. Frantic efforts to avoid real or imagined abandonment. (Note: Do not include suicidal or self-mutilating behavior covered in Criterion 5.)

2. A pattern of unstable and intense interpersonal relationships characterized by alternating between extremes of idealization and devaluation.

3. Identity disturbance: markedly and persistently unstable self-image or sense of self.

4. Impulsivity in at least two areas that are potentially self-damaging (e.g., spending, sex, substance abuse, reckless driving, binge eating). Note: Do not include suicidal or self-mutilating behavior covered in Criterion 5.)

5. Recurrent suicidal behavior, gestures, or threats, or self-mutilating behavior.

6. Affective instability due to a marked reactivity of mood (e.g., intense episodic dysphoria, irritability, or anxiety usually lasting a few hours and only rarely more than a few days).

7. Chronic feelings of emptiness.

8. Inappropriate, intense anger or difficulty controlling anger (e.g., frequent displays of temper, constant anger, recurrent physical fights).

9. Transient, stress-related paranoid ideation or severe dissociative symptoms.

Reprinted with permission from the *Diagnostic and Statistical Manual of Mental Disorders,* Fifth Edition, (Copyright 2013). American Psychiatric Association.

Histrionic Personality Disorder. While histrionic personality disorder (HPD) retains the last linguistic vestiges of the classic psychological theories of hysteria, the disorder is characterized primarily by the inappropriate emotional instability and attention seeking of classic hysteria cases, rather than the physiological symptoms now classified as conversion disorder, previously discussed in Chapter 10 (APA, 2013). Despite this distinction made in the past several DSMs, it is important to note that these individuals often do still have a tendency to express somatic complaints (APA, 2013). According to the DSM-5, a person with HPD will often primarily demonstrate a strong desire for attention, becoming uncomfortable when he or she is not the center of attention, and to this end, the person may exhibit seductive sexual behavior, shallow and shifting emotional expressions, and utilize their physical appearance to gain attention (APA, 2013). When you are in a social situation with a person who has HPD, these behaviors

Myths in Movies

AMERICAN BEAUTY

Consider the role of the mother in *American Beauty*, played by Annette Bening, who demonstrates histrionic features by her constant search for attention and gratification, often saying and doing whatever pleases her (Wedding & Niemiec, 2014). Is this a realistic portrayal of the disorder? How do you think people tend to respond to the continual demands for attention and gratification typically the case with histrionic personality disorder?

© Dreamworks/Photofest

Scene from *American Beauty*

are frequently easy to recognize, and the intensity of these behaviors can even be off-putting to others, though they usually succeed in reinforcing the person's craving for attention. In addition to these behaviors, an individual with HPD frequently uses a highly emotional and dramatic manner of speech (APA, 2013). Persons with HPD often perceive a deeper level of intimacy in relationships than is accurate, often leading to disappointment and conflict in relationships. On the other hand, these individuals are also highly suggestible, and submit often to another's requests to participate in risky behaviors (e.g., sexual or substance use behaviors), as a means to leaving an impression or obtaining attention (APA, 2013). Though they may submit to the requests of others in some situations, it should be noted that individuals with HPD also crave immediate gratification, and will often become irritated when gratification is delayed (APA, 2013).

Those with HPD are similar to those with narcissistic traits in their desire for attention, but individuals with HPD are often willing to appear as weak or needy, rather than superior, in order to acquire this attention (APA, 2013). Disorders comorbid with HPD include other Cluster B personality disorders, dependent personality disorder, major depression, and conversion or other somatic disorders (APA, 2013). Prevalence rates are estimated around 1.84 to 3%, and while some research suggests that women are more likely to be diagnosed with HPD than men, the degree to which this may be the case is unclear (APA, 2013; Blagov et al., 2007). The personality features of HPD lend themselves to a host of functional problems, including difficulties in relationships due to alienating friends through one's attention seeking, occupational, and educational problems due to difficulties following through with activities after beginning them, especially without attention or gratification, and though suicide rates for the disorder are unknown, individuals with HPD commonly express suicidal gestures and behaviors for attention from friends and caregivers (APA, 2013).

Narcissistic Personality Disorder. The concept of narcissism is quite common, a hallmark of contemporary U.S. culture, and some researchers suggest that narcissistic traits are becoming more frequent, especially among younger people (Levy et al., 2007). When you think of narcissism, what comes to mind? You likely think of people who are arrogant and full of themselves, right? And while this is not exactly a myth, it is important to consider the personality features beneath this façade, characterized as a "weak ego" by some psychodynamic theorists. These theorists conceived of the grandiosity characteristic of narcissism as a means of defending against feelings of insignificance (Levy et al., 2007). While we all know someone who is particularly full of himself or herself, diagnostic criteria requires that this grandiosity of one's importance and exaggerated achievements be coupled with other features, such as a preoccupation with fantasies of endless beauty, success, power, or ideal love, a firm belief that he or she is unique or special and should only associate with people and places of a high status, or the need for excessive admiration (APA, 2013). In addition to these features, other criteria include a sense of entitlement, exploitation of others, lacking empathy or being unwilling to recognize other people's feelings, envy of others or the belief that others are envious of him or her, and frequent conceited or arrogant attitudes and behaviors (APA, 2013).

Is the grandiosity of narcissism an attempt to protect oneself from a weak, undervalued self developed in childhood?

Community samples have demonstrated prevalence rates as high as 6.2% for individuals with narcissistic personality disorder (NPD), although the actual rates may be quite lower (APA, 2013). Similar to HPD, these individuals often alienate friends and acquaintances by their egotistical behavior, though as their self-esteem is almost always fragile, they are unable to tolerate any remarks or suggestions of their own imperfections, further causing divide in their relationships (APA, 2013). Similarly, this dynamic of grandiosity with underlying fragility can lead to difficulties in work, school, and other social settings. This fragility can also be recognized especially by the increased risk of suicide among people with NPD. Apter and colleagues (1993) researched the diagnoses of a group of men who committed suicide, finding over 20% had been diagnosed with NPD. Particularly concerning, in this regard, is the infrequency with which individuals with NPD seek help or therapy, as it is perceived to demonstrate a sign of weakness or imperfection.

Cluster C Personality Disorders

Cluster C personality disorders share a great deal in common with various anxiety disorders, and are exemplified by anxious or fearful personality features (APA, 2013; Fowler et al., 2007). Cluster C disorders, however, vary in terms of the object of fear, as well as how one attempts to alleviate this anxiety. Individuals with avoidant personality disorder attempt to reduce anxiety by avoiding social interactions. Those with dependent personality disorder attempt to reduce anxiety by clinging tightly to others. And persons with obsessive-compulsive personality disorders attempt to reduce anxiety by exhibiting more control over their behaviors or environment.

Avoidant Personality Disorder. Prevalence rates for avoidant personality disorder have been estimated to be 2.4%, and similar to narcissistic and related personality disorders, this disorder is characterized by feeling inadequate and being highly sensitive to negative evaluations (APA, 2013). In contrast to schizoid personality disorder, individuals with avoidant personality disorder would like connections with others but isolate themselves out of fear and thoughts of inadequacy. In contrast to individuals with narcissistic traits, individuals with avoidant personality disorder attempt to steer clear of any situation in which disapproval may occur, rather than exhibit grandiosity to obtain approval. These individuals tend to avoid working in jobs that require high levels of interpersonal contact to circumvent criticism or rejection, do not interact with others without an assurance of being liked, and fail to engage fully in relationships to avoid ridicule or shame (APA, 2013). In contrast to the preoccupations with success and power found in narcissism, people with avoidant personality traits are preoccupied with concerns of rejection or criticism, especially in social settings, and in new social settings are inhibited due to feeling like they are not good enough (APA, 2013). In terms of self-perception, these individuals view themselves to be inept, unappealing, and inferior, and are therefore typically reluctant to try new activities or to take interpersonal risks (APA, 2013).

Individuals with Avoidant Personality Disorder often long for connection but avoid others due to feelings of inadequacy.

All this being said, some researchers question whether avoidant personality disorder even exists, instead likening it to an extreme and generalized form of social anxiety disorder (Herbert, 2007). Regardless of how one categorizes the disorder, researchers agree that these individuals experience severe distress. Individuals with avoidant personality disorder are often isolated, despite deep desires for acceptance and affectionate relationships, and research suggests that they tend to be at an increased risk for comorbid depression, anxiety, and bipolar disorders, as well as Cluster A and borderline personality disorders (APA, 2013). Contrary to what one might expect, avoidant and dependent personality disorders are overlapping and often co-occurring diagnoses (Herbert, 2007). Though individuals with avoidant personality disorder may generally attempt to avoid others who might reject them, when they find an individual with whom they feel comfortable, they are likely to cling tightly to this relationship due to concerns that it might end (APA, 2013).

Dependent Personality Disorder. Imagine feeling so insecure that you could not function without the input of another person and you are close to understanding dependent personality disorder (DPD). The DSM-5 indicates that approximately 0.49 to 0.6% are estimated to struggle with DPD, though other researchers have found prevalence rates around 8% for men, and significantly higher for women, at 11% (Bornstein, 2007). The characteristics of DPD consist of serious difficulty making decisions without significant reassurance and advice from others, coupled with the need for others to take responsibility for significant areas of one's life, and difficulty initiating or completing tasks without ongoing input (APA, 2013). Underlying these difficulties with behavior is a profound deficit in self-confidence in one's abilities and decisions, rather than motivational issues, and this lack of self-confidence leads the person to desperately seek relationships for support and care after a significant relationship ends (APA, 2013). When persons with DPD do have another person to cling to, they will often avoid difficulties with conflict and disagreement, fearing that the other might not give support or approval, generally going to great lengths to obtain this support, even if this entails volunteering

Individuals with Dependent Personality Disorder tend to cling to others due to feelings of inadequacy, looking for affirmation and even help making simple decisions.

for unpleasant activities (APA, 2013). People with DPD will often make extraordinary self-sacrifices leading to relationship imbalances, and will even tolerate psychological, physical, and sexual abuse in order to maintain the relationship (APA, 2013). Additionally, individuals with DPD often feel especially helpless and uncomfortable when they are alone, due to fears that they are incapable of taking care of themselves, even becoming inappropriately preoccupied with the fear of being left alone (APA, 2013).

Dependent Personality Disorder is often found to be comorbid with borderline, histrionic, and avoidant personality disorders, as well as depressive and anxiety disorders (APA, 2013). Similar to narcissism, individuals with DPD are also characterized as having a "weak ego," frequently considering criticism or disagreement as evidence for their worthlessness, though because of the vast difference in the means of protecting against this "weak ego" the disorders are less likely to co-occur (APA, 2013; Bornstein, 2007). Some research suggests that individuals with DPD are at a higher risk of suicide than individuals with other Cluster C disorders, and data from a small Norwegian sample found that 35% of the individuals with DPD had attempted suicide, though more research is needed to confirm the strength of this link (Chioqueta & Stiles, 2004). A larger-scale study on individuals with depressive disorders found similar results for those with comorbid DPD, as they were 4.43 times more likely to attempt suicide than depressed individuals without comorbid DPD (Bolton et al., 2010).

Obsessive-Compulsive Personality Disorder. Obsessive-compulsive personality disorder (OCPD) is characterized by a preoccupation with control over many areas of life (e.g., organization, making lists or schedules, focus on details) to such an extreme that the significance of an activity is overshadowed by these attempts to control (APA, 2013). Though the name is similar to obsessive compulsive disorder (OCD) and some of the symptoms appear to share features, OCPD is not OCD. The DSM-5 suggests that approximately 2.1 to 7.9% of people have OCPD, making it one of the most frequent personality disorders in the general population, and it is believed to occur about two times more in men than in women (APA, 2013). In addition to this focus on controlling many areas of life, people with OCPD tend to have personality features that are perfectionistic, overly conscientious, or scrupulous, which often interferes with their ability to complete tasks (APA, 2013). Individuals with OCPD also tend to be excessively consumed with their occupation to such a degree that they are unable to participate in leisure activities, and are typically rigid and inflexible in terms of how they go about tasks and in regard to moral and ethical matters (APA, 2013). OCPD tends to be characterized by difficulty discarding old or worthless possessions, even those objects that have no sentimental worth, as well as significant difficulty delegating tasks and working with others due to concerns about how these tasks will be accomplished (APA, 2013). A pervasive stubborn and rigid attitude is generally exhibited by these individuals, and they frequently will spend as little money as possible, miserly hoarding it for future calamities (APA, 2013).

© fizkes/Shutterstock.com

Is there only one correct way to dry off after taking a shower? How about starting your car in the morning and driving to work?

Individuals with OCPD have been described by some theorists and clinicians as exhibiting excessive rigidity in order to control internal feelings of defiance and rebellion that they deem to be dangerous, becoming caught in a vicious cycle of internal rebellion and external submission and control (Bartz, Kaplan, & Hollander, 2007). Interpersonal and functional difficulties related to OCPD can be severe, as other individuals may become frustrated with the excessive rigidity and time delays associated with OCPD, work or educational activities may suffer due to their inability to finish projects, and virtually any activity can become delayed or incomplete while the individual with OCPD waits for assurance that a task will be completed perfectly (APA, 2013). Individuals with anxiety disorders, phobias, and obsessive-compulsive disorder (OCD) have an increased risk of developing OCPD, and individuals with OCPD may also be at an increased risk of comorbidity with mood disorders and eating disorders (APA, 2013).

Subtypes of Other Personality Disorders

In addition to the above personality disorders, the DSM-5 recognizes that personality changes can be due to another medical condition, or an individual can be given a diagnosis of "unspecified" or "other specified" personality disorder if they are experiencing significant distress, impairment, and dysfunction, but do not meet criteria for one of the specific personality disorders (APA, 2013). Think back to Chapter 2 and how this might be similar to personality changes of Phineas Gage due to a tamping rod. Table 16.1 further explains the DSM-5 specifiers for subtypes of "other specified" personality disorders. The diagnosis of "unspecified" personality disorders typically indicates a situation in which a clinician has insufficient information to determine a more specific diagnosis (APA, 2013).

TABLE 16.1   Subtypes of "Other Specified" Personality Disorders

Label Type	• Subtype characterized by affective instability and quickly changing emotionality
Disinhibited Type	• Subtype characterized by difficulty with impulse control, especially regarding sexual behavior
Aggressive Type	• Subtype characterized by aggressive behavior
Apethetic Type	• Subtype characterized by indifference or apathy
Paranoid Type	• Subtype characterized by paranoia and suspicion
Other Type	• Subtype characterized by features other than those listed above
Combined Type	• Subtype charaterized by features belonging to more than one of the subtypes above

APA, 2013

Theories and Treatments of Personality Disorders

At the outset of this section, it should be noted that people have been theorizing about disordered personality since ancient times, and while we know far more than we did even 100 years ago, we know far less than we need to know, and there are substantial gaps in the research. Similar to other disorders, such as schizophrenia and bipolar disorders, the etiology of personality disorders is likely highly complex and dynamic, potentially involving physiological, environmental, developmental, and other psychological elements. Even among researchers, a great deal of disagreement exists regarding the relationship of personality disorders and other disorders, and whether or not personality disorders deserve their own diagnostic category, not to mention how best to treat the various disordered personality characteristics. With this in mind, we present merely a brief sketch of the theories and treatments related to personality disorders.

Biological Theories and Treatments of Personality Disorders

Some evidence suggests a potential genetic link between all three Cluster A personality disorders and relatives with schizophrenia and related disorders, though the research is unclear regarding the degree to which this link may be environmental or developmental, rather than genetic. Twin, adoptive, and family studies do support a genetic link for schizotypal personality disorder and schizophrenia, but concordance rates are low enough that environmental factors likely also play a significant role (Bollini & Walker, 2007). Brain imaging studies on individuals with schizotypal personality disorder have also found similar structural (e.g., enlarged ventricles), functional (e.g., dopamine metabolism rates), and HPA axis brain abnormalities as have been found in schizophrenia, and in some cases these abnormalities are more severe than found with schizophrenia patients (Bollini & Walker, 2007). Medications found to be helpful in the treatment of schizophrenia have also been used to treat individuals with Cluster A disorders. Specifically, atypical antipsychotic medications, such as Risperdal, Abilify, and Seroquel, have been used to treat Cluster A disorders, and some research has demonstrated a reduction in both positive and negative symptoms with the use of some atypical antipsychotics (Bollini & Walker, 2007).

Likewise, a genetic link for Cluster B disorders has received some research support, suggesting an increased risk for individuals with first-degree relatives who have one of these disorders. Antisocial personality disorder is more common among first-degree relatives with the disorder, with a stronger link between relatives of females who have the disorder than for relatives of males with the disorder, and adoption studies likewise suggest a possible genetic link (APA, 2013). Similarly, borderline personality disorder occurs approximately five times more frequently in persons with a biological relative with the disorder (APA, 2013). Research on histrionic and narcissistic personality disorders have discovered similar genetic links, though some researchers suggest that results have been inflated, and instead that research is insufficient to consider Cluster B disorders highly heritable (Blagov et al., 2007; Levy et al., 2007). A wide range of psychotropic medications have been used to treat individuals with Cluster B disorders, including antidepressants, mood stabilizers, anticonvulsants, and antipsychotic medications, although there is a lack of randomized control trials on the use of these medications with Cluster B disorders (Blagov et al., 2007; Levy et al., 2007).

Similar to other clusters in regard to genetic research, Cluster C personality disorders also have limited evidence suggesting heritability (Bartz et al., 2007; Bornstein, 2007; Herbert, 2007). Avoidant personality disorder appears to have the strongest evidence suggesting a genetic link, whereas dependent personality disorder and OCPD have less research support. This should not be taken to mean that no genetic link exists between relatives with these disorders, but rather that more research is needed to determine a relationship, if one does indeed exist. Medication treatments for OCPD often include anticonvulsants to reduce hostility and irritability, whereas for avoidant personality disorder antidepressants have been demonstrated to be promising, and medication research is virtually absent for dependent personality disorder (Bartz et al., 2007; Ripoll et al., 2011). Clinicians often tend to treat the symptoms of comorbid disorders, hoping for a reduction of disordered personality features in the process (Ripoll et al., 2011). It should be noted that the function of psychotropic medications is primarily to target specific symptoms, rather than personalities, which are more global and pervasive, and as a result, medications used to treat personality disorders belonging to all three clusters are likely to only bring about partial improvement (Ripoll et al., 2011).

Psychological Theories and Treatments of Personality Disorders

Because personality domains are considered to be relatively stable and enduring, theories have focused on development over the life span, rather than situational causes, and many treatments have aimed more at improving life skills than at remission, yet a wide variety of explanations have been given for the development of the various personality disorders. In many cases, individuals with personality disorders had a parent with disordered personality features or other mental health problems, which both increases risk of abuse and neglect, as well as exposure to dysfunctional parenting and aberrant coping and behavioral patterns (Bradley et al., 2007).

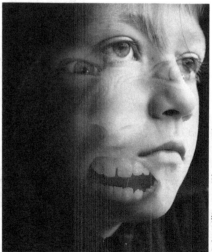

In 1921, Kraepelin differentiated three types of paranoid conditions, roughly comprising what we today call paranoid personality disorder (PDP), paranoid schizophrenia, and delusional disorder (Bernstein & Useda, 2007). Some research has demonstrated that individuals with PDP and other Cluster A personality disorders have experienced higher rates of traumatic childhood events, such as neglect and abuse, which are generally associated with increased aggression in kids (Bernstein & Useda, 2007). Psychoanalytic theories of PDP have suggested that individuals with the disorder tended to unconsciously reject their aggressive drives and to project these feelings onto the world and other people, thereby constantly feeling unsafe (Bernstein & Useda, 2007). Cognitive theories have suggested that people with PDP have core beliefs about the world and people as harmful and untrustworthy, combined with lack of self-confidence (Beck et al., 1990). Imagine working as a therapist with an

Psychodynamic theories have suggested that individuals with paranoid personality features have rejected their own aggressiveness and projected it externally.

individual who has paranoid personality tendencies, and trying to challenge problematic ideation that you clearly understand to be inaccurate. As you might expect, the client is not likely to respond well to this challenge! Due to these paranoid personality features, individuals with PDP usually only seek treatment when they are in states of increased distress, and therapists are then tasked with developing a strong therapeutic relationship and non-confrontational therapeutic approach during a particularly high stress period (Bernstein & Useda, 2007).

Social withdrawal is characteristic of Cluster A disorders, often beginning in early childhood.

Schizotypal personality disorder research suggests similar etiological roots to schizophrenia, possibly including prenatal and/or perinatal complications, diathesis-stress notions suggesting that environmental stressors (e.g., excessive criticism and negative emotional expression) may trigger the development of the disorder, and social withdrawal and cognitive maladjustment beginning in early childhood (Bollini & Walker, 2007). Similar to paranoid personality disorder, individuals with schizoid and schizotypal personality disorders are not particularly inclined to seek out treatment, and when they do seek treatment it tends to be discontinued shortly thereafter. A dearth of research-based evidence exists for what might be most effective in working with these individuals, though some theorists have suggested social skills training, psychoeducation, and providing a supportive environment, with some applicable evidence regarding schizophrenia suggesting that Cognitive-Behavioral Therapy (CBT) may be beneficial (Beck et al., 1990; Bollini & Walker, 2007).

Many personality disorders have been linked to neglectful and abusive childhood experiences.

Cluster B personality disorders tend to be strongly linked to disordered and abusive parenting patterns. Individuals with antisocial personality disorder (ASPD) appear to more likely have experienced early childhood abuse than the general population, and to have peer friendships with others who participate in deviant behaviors (Patrick, 2007). Some theorists suggest two developmental pathways for individuals with antisocial personality disorder, with some developing these personality traits due to innate impulse control problems and others due to these social-environmental experiences (Patrick, 2007). Interestingly, poor experiences with parents may have led to decreased experiences of bonding, typically associated with the production of Oxytocin. Timmermann et al. (2017) recently demonstrated with a small sample that intranasal Oxytocin may improve the facial emotion recognition of individuals with ASPD, though the relationship between developmental experiences, Oxytocin, and treatment is far from clear.

Narcissistic personality disorders are theorized to be more closely linked to experiences of being rejected, undervalued, and emotionally invalidated by one's parents, who tend to be neglectful, cold, harsh, and dismissive (Levy et al., 2007). The first conceptualizations of narcissism come from ancient Greek myths of Narcissus, who was portrayed as being so in love with his own image that he died from the longing for his image to love him back, which was of course unrequited (Levy et al., 2007). Havelock Ellis (1898) was the first modern researcher to apply this myth to a case study, conceptualizing a patient who excessively masturbated as having become "the object of his own sexual desire," and Freud followed these suggestions, coining the term "narcissistic" to describe individuals who chose sexual partners with qualities like unto themselves (Levy et al., 2007, p. 232). Cognitive-behavioral researchers have suggested that three maladaptive schemas of core beliefs may be at the root of narcissistic personality disorders, including beliefs of oneself as defective, entitled, or having been emotionally deprived, and these conceptions are closely related to psychodynamic theories suggesting an underlying "weak ego," as well as research on the cold and distant parenting styles in which these individuals tend to develop (Levy et al., 2007). Individuals with antisocial and narcissistic personality disorders rarely seek treatment, which has generally been described as difficult, with poor or mixed research outcomes for the few studies that do exist.

Cluster B disorders appear to have a strong connection with abusive or tragic childhood experiences.

Individuals with borderline personality disorder (BPD) have been found to more frequently experience poor attachment due to loss or separation, and a sexually or physically abusive childhood environment (Bradley et al., 2007). Similarly, individuals with histrionic personality disorder (HPD) have been theorized to have a strong desire for parental attention that was unmet in childhood, possibly due to abuse or neglect (Blagov et al., 2007). The interaction of genes and environment may be particularly poignant in regard to the development of these disorders, as having a parent with emotional instability due to BPD or HPD increases the chances of a plethora of risks, such as abuse and neglect, abandonment of children for long periods of time, disordered parenting patterns (e.g., increased parental conflict, poorly enforced household rules and boundaries), and even early parental death due to a parent's impulsivity, risk-taking, and other disordered behaviors (Bradley et al., 2007).

Cumulative Trauma Hypothesis

Hypothesis suggesting that the accumulation of traumatic events, rather than a singular trauma, leads to the development of certain mental disorders

Some researchers suggest a cumulative trauma hypothesis for the development of Borderline Personality Disorder, characterized by repeated trauma over the course of one's development, rather than simply a single tragic event (Bradley et al., 2007). Treatments for BPD have more research support than other personality disorders, and particularly Dialectical Behavioral Therapy (DBT) and Psychodynamic therapies have been found to be effective for the treatment of BPD (Cristea et al., 2017; Linehan, 2018). DBT is a mindfulness-based therapy emphasizing emotion regulation, distress tolerance, and skills training, which have been found to reduce suicidal and self-harming behaviors, as well as to reduce the likelihood of hospitalization (Bradley et al., 2007; Linehan, Armstrong, et al., 1991; Linehan, Heard, & Armstrong, 1993). Some research also exists for the effectiveness of psychodynamic, mentalization-based, schema-focused, and transference-focused therapies in the treatment of BPD (Bradley et al., 2007). Table 16.2 displays various psychological treatments for BPD recognized by APA Division 12 (Klonsky, 2013).

Emotion Regulation

A dynamic psychological process of feeling an emotion, and regulating that emotion by inhibiting or adjusting one's response

Distress Tolerance

The ability to regulate one's emotions well during significantly distressing events and to respond purposefully, rather than react to these events

TABLE 16.2 Empirically Supported Psychological Treatments for BPD

Psychological Treatment	Borderline Personality Disorder
Dialectical Behavioral Therapy	Strong
Mentalization-Based Treatment	Modest
Schema-Focused Therapy	Modest
Transference-Focused Therapy	Strong/Controversial

*Table based on information from Klonsky (2013).

Cluster C personality disorders have been theorized to be closely connected with overbearing and excessively critical parenting, which leads individuals to develop behavioral patterns to protect themselves from potential harm. Specifically, avoidant personality disorder is theorized to develop in relation to parenting styles that are overly worried or anxious, and which emphasize an intense concern over paying attention to how other people think about and evaluate oneself, parental overprotection, excessive criticism, and a severe authoritarian parenting style (Herbert, 2007). Dependent personality disorder (DPD) has roots in Freud's concept of oral fixation and problems with the development of trust during the earliest years of life; other psychodynamic theories, such as object relations theories, have suggested that individuals with DPD have internalized a sense of self as incapable and weak, leading them to cling tightly to others (Bornstein, 2007). Obsessive-compulsive personality disorder (OCPD) also has roots in Freud's (1959) theories, albeit in the concept of a person becoming anal retentive as a result of excessive parental criticism and control, especially during the potty training years (Bartz et al., 2007). Similarly, interpersonal theories have suggested that individuals with OCPD seek order, are afraid of being at fault, and initiate harsh, rigid criticism and discipline on themselves and others as an outgrowth of learning to relate to distant and highly controlling caregivers during their childhood (Bartz et al., 2007).

Object Relations

Psychoanalytic theory suggesting that one's personality and even one's sense of self develops as a result of how we internalize "objects," the most important of which are the mental constructs we develop in relation to immediate caregivers during childhood

© Yuganov Konstantin/Shutterstock.com

© Yuganov Konstantin/Shutterstock.com

© Pim/Shutterstock.com

© Ono studiO/Shutterstock.com

© pathdoc/Shutterstock.com

Many of the treatments for Cluster C disorders have focused on social and interpersonal skill deficits and underlying beliefs and construction of a sense of oneself. Some research suggests that individuals with avoidant personality disorder may benefit from CBT, with a focus on social skills deficits, and particularly CBT group therapy may be beneficial in helping these individuals learn to tolerate social anxiety, overcome social avoidance, and practice new social skills in a safe, supportive environment (Herbert, 2007). Cognitive behavioral treatments have also been developed for working with individuals with dependent personality disorder, targeting automatic thoughts and core beliefs (e.g., "I'm worthless; How incompetent can I be!") that reinforce dependency (Bornstein, 2007). Statements such as these can lead to an attribution bias of oneself as weak and vulnerable, which in turn can set up a vicious cycle of helplessness and reliance on others, leading to further thoughts and beliefs about one's inability and worthlessness (Bornstein, 2007; Young, 1994). Similarly, clinicians working with individuals with OCPD must remain aware of rationalization and intellectualization defenses often used by OCPD clients to help reinforce and continue their obsessive-compulsive behaviors and personality characteristics (Bartz et al., 2007). Psychodynamic, CBT, and social skills training therapies have been found to be effective with some OCPD patients, though no large-scale randomized control trial exists to confirm these findings (Bartz et al., 2007).

Conclusion

The relative pervasiveness and endurance of personality disorders tends to make treatment particularly difficult in many cases, which have reinforced myths that individuals with these disorders are in hopeless situations. Though far more research and social support is needed to assist individuals with personality disorders to recover and/or develop the skills needed to live effectively, much has already been done, and is continuing to be done in order to figure out how best to treat these disorders. Whether one thinks of personality and personality disorders in terms of what a person *is*, or something they *have*, it is important for the culture to keep a realistic picture of personality disorders. Most individuals with personality disorders are not going to appear like we see in some movies, with a weapon in hand, though some of the depictions Hollywood has given us portray the features of these disorders quite well, reflecting the intense distress and dysfunction frequently the case with these disorders.

CHAPTER REVIEW

QUESTIONS

1. What are the three clusters of personality disorders? How are they different? Similar? Which personality disorders belong to each cluster?

2. Are all people with personality disorders violent and dangerous? Which ones may be? How might this differentially be the case for various personality disorders?

3. How would you differentiate between someone with a Cluster A disorder and someone with psychotic disorder? How about someone with a Cluster B disorder and someone with an impulse-control or conduct disorder? How about a Cluster C disorder and someone with an anxiety disorder?

4. What have theorists posited as potential causes for the development of personality disorders? What is the general focus of treatment for individuals with personality disorders? Which treatments seem to be effective for each personality disorder?

KEY TERMS

Cluster A Disorders

Cluster B Disorders

Cluster C Disorders

Cumulative Trauma

Emotion Regulation

Distress Tolerance

Object Relations

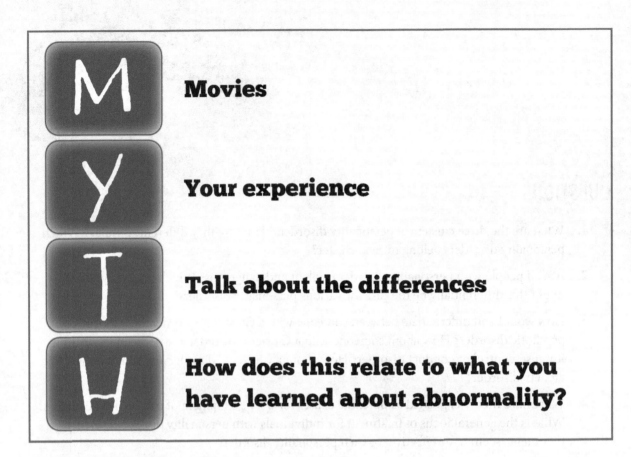

M   Movies

Y   Your experience

T   Talk about the differences

H   How does this relate to what you have learned about abnormality?

Myths in Movies Recap

American Psycho, Taxi Driver, Basic Instinct, and Seven Psychopaths

As you can guess simply from the number of movies discussed in this chapter, Hollywood has an affinity for dramatizing personality disorders. This affinity, of course, makes sense in light of the fact that many of these disorders tend toward dramatic expressions. Movies such as *American Psycho, Taxi Driver,* and *Basic Instinct* take this to an extreme by making it appear that all individuals with personality disorders are violent. While certain personality disorders do appear to predispose individuals to impulsivity and violence, the majority of individuals with personality disorders are not recurrently acting violently, and other disorders, such as intellectual deficits, may be more likely to predispose individuals to violence (Pinna et al., 2016). Additionally, while there are certain characteristics which overlap between many personality disorders, such as poor emotion regulation and self-image problems, with 10 major diagnoses across the three clusters of personality disorders, a great deal of variability exists (APA, 2013). The movie *Seven Psychopaths,* however, confuses the term psychopath with aspects of many different disorders, emphasizing excessive variability in one diagnosis, while also emphasizing the connection with violence that is a defining characteristic of Antisocial Personality Disorder, but is clearly not ubiquitous in these individuals' daily lives (APA, 2013).

Charlie and the Chocolate Factory

Charlie and the Chocolate Factory does a fantastic job demonstrating characteristics of schizotypal personality, though as previously mentioned, this is clearly dramatized in a grandiose manner, as few individuals with the disorder are going to own their own chocolate factories, or more importantly, demonstrate eccentricities of behavior to such proportions. But of course, Charlie and the Random Guy with a Cluster A Personality Disorder might not sell as many movie tickets.

American Psycho, Silence of the Lambs, and Dexter

As previously mentioned *American Psycho, Silence of the Lambs,* and *Dexter* clearly add fuel to the fire in regard to the myth that individuals with antisocial personality disorder are violent serial killers. While violence is clearly an aspect of the disorder, this should not necessarily be understood in an extreme manner. Consider that only three of the diagnostic criteria are needed for diagnosis, and these may include violating others' rights through irresponsibility, impulsivity, and deceitfulness, rather than by means of physical violence (APA, 2013). On the other hand, the lack of remorse often exhibited by individuals with this disorder is frequently off-putting for others in their life, such that characterizing them as lovable is likewise problematic, though perhaps it may lead individuals to consider the dignity and distress of those struggling with antisocial personality disorder.

Basic Instinct, Fatal Attraction, and Girl, Interrupted

Basic Instinct, Fatal Attraction, and *Girl, Interrupted* portray women with borderline personality disorders in a variety of ways. As already mentioned, the violence portrayed by the first two of these movies is clearly over-emphasized. The difference between internalized and externalized variations or aspects of the disorder may find some evidence in reality. By reviewing the diagnostic criteria of the disorder, for example, we can see that of the nine criteria, only five are needed for diagnosis, and these include externalized behaviors, such as impulsivity and displays of anger, as well as internalized behaviors, such as disturbance of identity and abandonment avoidance (APA, 2013). This variability of symptoms clearly allows for different expressions of the disorder, even if not so extreme as the difference portrayed in these films. Last of all, these three films portray borderline personality in female characters only, which could contribute to the myth that it is only a women's disorder. Research is clear that women are more frequently diagnosed with the disorder (75% of cases; APA, 2013). Why this gender difference exists is far less clear, and as our understanding of personality disorders develops, hopefully we will discover whether it is primarily a disorder found among women, or if our diagnostic categories need to be further refined.

American Beauty

In *American Beauty*, the mother of the protagonist demonstrates excessive concern for appearance and superficially wants to garnish as much attention to herself as possible, but is unstable and distressed when confronted with the fact that charimsa alone is not always enough (Wedding & Niemiec, 2014). While this film does a nice job portraying histrionic personality disorder, the excessive behaviors demonstrated should not be considered the norm, and more subtle ways of getting attention are also frequently employed. The response of the protagonist when her mother embarrasses her in public is likely to have been experienced by those close to an individual with this disorder, as they frequently will put themselves in the spotlight in ways that make many people uncomfortable.

CHAPTER SEVENTEEN

MYTHS AND CONTROVERSIES IN PRACTICE, ETHICS, AND LAW

LEARNING OBJECTIVES

- ▶ Discuss MYTHs of psychotherapists
- ▶ Explore perceptions of therapists portrayed in film
- ▶ Identify the occurrence of deception in therapy
- ▶ Explain how client deception impacts therapy
- ▶ Discuss therapist deception
- ▶ Explore ethical guidelines and standards
- ▶ Examine the ethics of therapist deception
- ▶ Consider controversies in research and practice with abortions
- ▶ Identify myths of forensic psychology
- ▶ Explain the insanity defense
- ▶ Recognize deception in the law
- ▶ Review the importance of myth-checking

CHAPTER OUTLINE

- ▶ Behind Closed Doors: Images of Psychotherapists—MYTHs
- ▶ Lying in Therapy
- ▶ Ethical Issues and Controversies
- ▶ Abnormal Psychology and Law

Behind Closed Doors: Images of Psychotherapists

When you think about practicing licensed psychologists and other mental health professionals you may have thoughts about how this is all done behind closed doors. You may have views and beliefs about practitioners based on personal experiences of seeing a therapist and other images may be influenced by movies and media. There are several movies that give various demonstrations of therapists. When thinking about the practice of licensed psychologists, psychiatrists, and other mental health providers think about the experiences and movies or other sources that have influenced your thoughts and attitudes.

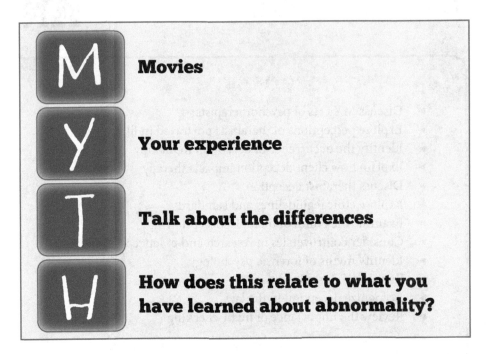

M Movies

Y Your experience

T Talk about the differences

H How does this relate to what you have learned about abnormality?

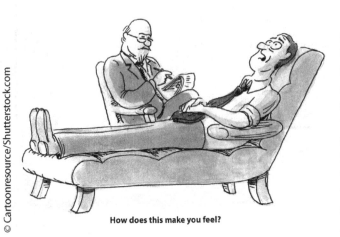

How does this make you feel?

© Cartoonresource/Shutterstock.com

Numerous images, thoughts, and myths surface when discussing the practice of psychology, specifically in psychotherapy. You may envision scenes of a client lying on a couch or sitting in a chair talking to a therapist to psychiatric facilities with people wearing straitjackets. Some people think of counseling psychotherapists as too "touchy-feely" and think of therapists synonymously with the cliché catch-phrase "How does that make you feel?" While thinking about other practitioners, such as psychiatrists, as Pez-dispensing prescribers of medications.

Sometimes therapists may be seen as always looking for some childhood trauma. Some of these images come from experience while others come from films (see Gabbard & Gabbard, 1999; Wedding & Niemiec, 2014).

Myths in Movies

WHAT ABOUT BOB and ONE FLEW OVER THE CUCKOO'S NEST

The movie *What About Bob* consists of two main characters, Bob who is a client and Dr. Leo Marvin who is Bob's therapist. The movie unravels various relational dynamics between Bob and Dr. Marvin. Bob initially seeks Dr. Marvin out for therapy in his office and then continues to pursue Dr. Marvin while he is on vacation with his family.

Scene from *What About Bob*

The classic film *One Flew Over the Cuckoo's Nest* portrays a man who has been admitted to a psychiatric institution and attempts to lead other patients in against the staff. How might these two films or other films that feature psychotherapists shape your understanding of therapists and the practice of psychology?

Scene from *One Flew Over the Cuckoo's Nest*

There are many films and television shows that illustrate various aspects of therapy and practice which informs public perceptions of therapists, therapy, and treatment. Wedding and Niemiec (2014) listed 12 misconceptions about mental illness and mental health professionals influenced from movies. Five of these misconceptions involve the practice of mental health and treatment:

- ▶ Psychiatric hospitals are harmful or unhelpful
- ▶ Treatment stifles creative thought or expression
- ▶ Stopping treatment on one's own is empowering
- ▶ Treatment often involves therapist violating interpersonal boundaries
- ▶ Diagnoses are usually made up by psychologists and patients

Another misconception to add to this list is that therapists are sometimes portrayed to have their own psychopathology. In the movie, *What About Bob*, Dr. Leo Marvin experiences acute stress and goes into a catatonic state. Other movies, such as *Clinical*, show the therapist struggling to provide therapy because she is dealing with her own PTSD. Many therapists do not suffer from psychological disorders leading to impaired competence. The American Psychological Association (2010) code of ethics suggests that psychologists refrain from activities if they are aware of personal problems that may affect their work and to take appropriate actions if personal problems affect their work.

While some films depicting mental illness are intended to be entertaining and humorous, they also shape perceptions. McDonald and Walter (2009) reviewed several films that feature electroconvulsive shock therapy (ECT), including *One Flew Over the Cuckoo's Nest*, which depicted ECT as a means of social control rather than a safe and effective treatment. Thus, films may shape public perceptions of treatment more strongly than actual scientific evidence of practice (Lilienfeld & Arkowitz, 2014).

Films also seem to shape practitioners' attitudes as well. Walter and colleagues (2002) recruited 94 medical students to test what effect watching ECT depicted in films had on attitudes toward treatment through the use of ECT. The scenes of ECT were shown from *Return to Oz, The Hudsucker Proxy, Ordinary People, One Flew Over the Cuckoo's Nest*, and *Beverly Hillbillies*. The researchers found that about 33% of participants had decreased their support of using ECT as a treatment after watching the scenes (Walter et al., 2002).

Lying in Therapy

"Everyone lies!"

—Dr. Gregory House
(Mitchell & Singer, 2004)

©VGstockstudio/Shutterstock.com

When you think of therapy you may think of lying on a couch but maybe not lying to a therapist. There is a belief that clients will enter therapy and truthfully reveal every detail of their lives with therapists. This is a myth. People do lie. As discussed in Chapter 10, people tell about two lies per day, on average (DePaulo & Bell, 1996; DePaulo & Kashy, 1998; Kashy & DePaulo, 1996; Vrij, 2000). Further, people who seek therapy will lie to their therapists (Curtis, & Hart, 2019; Kottler & Carlson, 2011). One of the reasons why people may believe that clients enter therapy with complete honesty is that people tend to have a truth bias (O'Sullivan, 2003). A truth bias is a tendency to assume that people are being honest. Holding a truth bias generally is useful due to the majority of communications being honest (Vrij, 2000). Even therapists seem to hold the belief that clients do not lie, which may be disseminated by other therapists (Curtis, 2013; Kottler & Carlson, 2011).

Truth Bias

A tendency to assume that people are being honest

What about you? Have you ever lied to a therapist or would you be willing to? Maybe in thinking about if you have ever done this you are sifting through if what you said or would say would count as a lie. Would telling a therapist that you enjoyed the session when you did not count as a lie, because it is a means to protect the therapist's feelings? What about intentionally leaving out information from the therapist because you did not want the therapist to know something about you? When discussing deception it is crucial to unpack its definition as it helps put into perspective what counts as a deception. Vrij (2008) defined deception as "a successful or unsuccessful deliberate attempt, without forewarning, to create in another a belief which the communicator considers to be untrue" (p. 15). Thus, deception involves a deliberate and intentional nature of the communicator to foster a belief in another. It does not necessarily matter if something is actually true but rather the communicator is attempting to create an opposing belief in the target of deception.

In Chapter 10, you read how people may lie to gain attention by inducing or feigning sickness (i.e., factitious disorder) or people may lie for external gain by faking symptoms (i.e., malingering). In Chapter 16, you read that one of the diagnostic criteria for antisocial personality disorder is deceitfulness (American Psychiatric Association [APA], 2013). However, not all lies that are found in therapy involve feigning symptoms or a personality disorder. People may lie to a therapist for many other reasons, which are similar to motivations for lying in other relationships (see Curtis, 2013).

Kottler and Carlson's (2011) book, *Duped*, discussed various anecdotal accounts of psychotherapists who had been deceived by their clients. Among the stories of client deceptions, one therapist discussed a 20-year-old client who lied to her about everything since the moment he entered therapy (Grzegorek, 2011). The client sought counseling services at a university counseling center presenting with concerns of loneliness, depression, and difficulties with establishing friendships (Grzegorek, 2011). Throughout months of weekly sessions the client revealed that he had been molested by a family member, he loathed himself, and reported suicidal ideation with one attempt between a therapy session (Grzegorek, 2011). After the reported suicide attempt, the concerned therapist asked the client why he seemed distant and was missing appointments and he responded by stating "I've been playing with you" (Grzegorek, 2011, p. 35). The client then proceeded to tell the therapist that he made everything up because he "like[s] to have fun with people and see if [he] could get them to do things" (Grzegorek, 2011, p. 35).

Duping Delight

A positive feeling someone experiences from lying without being caught

This client may have been after what Ekman (2009) termed as duping delight. Duping delight is a positive feeling that a person experiences when they have lied to another person without being caught. The client discussed by Grzegorek (2011) is not an example of every client who lies, as many clients may fabricate one or few things, without the intent of duping delight (see Kottler & Carlson, 2011). Although many people may have lied in therapy, this does not mean that people lie to a therapist often. One study assessed the frequencies of deception within therapy and found that a majority of people (89%) who attended psychotherapy endorsed using at least one type of lie and 86% of participants stated that they have been deceptive at least once in therapy (Curtis & Hart, 2019). Further, of those who did report lying in therapy, they indicated they lied about two times, on average, in a 50-minute therapy session (Curtis & Hart, 2019). However, zero was the most frequent response from participants, meaning that most people do not lie often in therapy but a smaller group of people tell many lies to psychotherapists (Curtis & Hart, 2019). These findings parallel the use of deception found within daily living, where people tell two lies per day on average but most people tell no lies within a day (DePaulo & Bell, 1996; DePaulo & Kashy, 1998; Kashy & DePaulo, 1996; Serota, Levine, & Boster, 2010; Serota & Levine, 2015; Vrij, 2000). In fact, another study that investigated motivations for lying in therapy compared to social situations found no statistically significant differences between participants' endorsement to use deception in either setting (Carrillo, 2016).

Kottler (2010) discussed a paradox in therapy pertaining to honesty and deception, in which the "premise of psychotherapy is that based on the idea that people are telling us things that they believe happened to them, but could very well end up being exaggerations, fabrications, or outright lies" (p. 179). This would not be a problem if people were good at detecting deception; however, this is not the case. People are slightly better than chance at their attempts to detect deception (Bond & DePaulo, 2006). Bond and DePaulo conducted a meta-analysis of 206 deception detection studies and found accuracy of detecting deception to be at 54%. Whether psychotherapists can accurately detect deception with greater accuracy has mixed findings. Vrij (2008) reported that professionals' accuracy ratings were 56% for truth detection and 56% for lie detection. However, Vrij (2008) indicated that many of these professionals were police officers. Ekman, O'Sullivan, and Frank (1999) reported that many deception detection studies assessing accuracy in professionals have been conducted in laboratories and lack external validity. Ekman, O'Sullivan, and Frank (1999) conducted a study that found clinical psychologists who had an interest in deception held a higher accuracy in detecting deception than academic psychologists. Briggs (1992) found that counselors could correctly identify honest clients with 90% accuracy and deceptive clients with 80% accuracy.

One of the reasons that detecting deception can pose a problem is that people often rely on false beliefs and myths about deception. For example, one of the most commonly held beliefs, found across 58 countries, is that people look away when they are lying (Global Deception Research Team, 2006). Gaze aversion, or looking away, is not an indicator of deception (Vrij, 2008). It would be easier to detect deception if there was one particular behavior to rely on, but "there is nothing like Pinocchio's nose" (Vrij, 2000, p. 24). Vrij (2000) meant that though there are indicators of deception, there is not one specific and consistent behavior that reveals deception. Communication is dynamic and involves multiple variables.

Gaze Aversion

Looking away, often associated with lying

Psychotherapists develop beliefs about deception too (Curtis, 2013; Curtis & Hart, 2015). Psychotherapists hold a number of incorrect beliefs about deception, including eye gaze aversion (Curtis & Hart, 2015; see Table 17.1). Curtis and Hart (2015) recruited 112 licensed psychologists and psychology interns ranging in counseling experience from 1 to 40 years and asked them to complete questionnaires assessing beliefs about indicators of deception and attitudes toward client deception. The findings revealed that psychotherapists held correct beliefs about six of the 28 indicators of deception (Curtis & Hart, 2015; see Table 17.1).

© pathdoc/Shutterstock.com

TABLE 17.1   Therapists' Beliefs About Lying-Related Changes in Behavior, Compared to a "No Change" Rating of 4.0

Deception Variable	Mean (SD)	t	Belief	Prior Research Suggests
Nonverbal Indicators				
Eye contact	3.06 (1.14)	−7.91*	Decrease	No change
Eye blinks	4.74 (0.99)	7.12*	Increase	No change
Head movements	4.29 (1.03)	2.72	No change	No change
Hand and finger movements	4.65 (1.07)	5.83*	Increase	Decrease
Arm movements	4.13 (0.89)	1.40	No change	Decrease
Leg and foot movements	4.77 (0.96)	7.68*	Increase	Decrease
Smiles	4.26 (1.01)	2.47	No change	No change
Postural shifts	5.06 (0.95)	10.77*	Increase	No change
Shrugs	4.35 (0.85)	4.00*	Increase	No change
Gestures	4.38 (0.91)	4.00*	Increase	No change
Paraverbal Indicators				
Speech interruptions	4.77 (0.93)	7.88*	Increase	No change
Pauses	4.67 (0.98)	6.54*	Increase	No change
Latency to respond	4.60 (1.15)	5.00*	Increase	Increase
Hectic speech	4.58 (0.95)	5.80*	Increase	No change
Pitch	4.71 (0.82)	8.39*	Increase	Increase
Answer length	4.69 (1.29)	5.13*	Increase	No change
Verbal Indicators				
Short simple sentences	3.42 (1.10)	−5.11*	Decrease	Increase
Plausible descriptions	4.04 (1.22)	0.34	No change	Decrease
Logical consistency	3.34 (1.05)	−6.05*	Decrease	Decrease
Detailed description	4.32 (1.35)	2.31	No change	Decrease
Unusual detail	4.72 (1.12)	6.22*	Increase	No change
Unnecessary detail	4.86 (1.15)	7.08*	Increase	No change
Description of feelings	3.46 (1.11)	−4.68*	Decrease	No change
Describe what someone said	3.95 (1.23)	−0.42	No change	Decrease
Description of interactions	3.84 (1.15)	−1.35	No change	No change
Spontaneous corrections	4.03 (1.31)	0.24	No change	Decrease
Claim lack of memory	4.74 (1.06)	6.74*	Increase	Decrease
Story contradictions	5.08 (1.01)	10.24*	Increase	No change

Further, psychotherapists' attitudes toward discovering a client's lie and toward clients who lie in therapy deception were assessed (Curtis & Hart, 2015). The findings revealed that psychotherapists held a number of negative attitudes toward clients who lie in therapy and toward discovering a client's lie (Curtis & Hart, 2015; see Table 17.2).

TABLE 17.2   Therapists' Attitudes Toward Client Lies

#	Attitude Item	n	Mean (SD)	t	Attitude Change
Discovering a Client's Lie (leads to)					
1	Liking the client	89	4.19 (0.98)	−7.823*	Decrease
2	Being angry at the client	89	5.24 (0.81)	2.741	Increase
3	Client judged as a bad person	89	4.83 (0.82)	−1.951	Decrease
4	Thinking negatively of client	87	5.31 (0.99)	2.918*	Increase
5	Judging client harshly	89	5.01 (0.96)	0.11	No change
6	Desire to interact with client	89	4.35 (1.24)	−4.942*	Decrease
7	Enthusiasm to work with client	89	4.21 (1.17)	−6.308*	Decrease
8	Judging client as a good client	89	4.35 (1.02)	−6.006*	Decrease
9	Speaking poorly of client	89	5.17 (0.93)	1.706	No change
10	Trusting the client	89	3.30 (1.14)	−14.013*	Decrease
11	Thinking positively about client	88	4.28 (0.90)	−7.493*	Decrease
12	Viewing client as sincere	89	3.43 (1.15)	−12.938*	Decrease
Clients Who Lie in Therapy (are regarded as)					
13	Successful	89	3.27 (0.88)	−7.865*	Less Successful
14	Pathological	89	4.21 (0.79)	2.549	No Difference
15	Weak	89	3.98 (0.59)	−0.363	No Difference
16	Compliant	87	3.24 (0.92)	−7.737*	Less Compliant
17	Predictable	89	3.85 (0.92)	−1.512	No Difference
18	Pleasant	89	3.69 (0.60)	−4.859*	Less Pleasant
19	Lazy	89	3.94 (0.47)	−1.149	No Difference
20	Awkward	89	4.09 (0.47)	1.812	No Difference
21	Knowledgeable	89	3.99 (0.51)	−0.207	No Difference
22	Intelligent	89	4.02 (0.40)	0.532	No Difference
23	Likable	88	3.50 (0.59)	−7.987*	Less Likable
24	Adjusted	89	3.61 (0.83)	−4.301*	Less Adjusted

International Journal for the Advancement of Counselling, "Pinnochio's Nose in Theraphy: Therapists' Beliefs and Attitudes Toward Client Deception," 37(3), 2015. © Springer Science+Business Media New York 2015. With permission of Springer.

The findings have even recently been replicated within a forensic psychotherapist sample (Dickens & Curtis, 2019). The significance of these findings for practitioners is that therapists may incorrectly assume that a client is lying if they rely on false beliefs, such as eye gaze aversion, and subsequently not like the client because the client is deemed a liar. There are many instances where nonverbal behaviors, such as eye gaze aversion may be found in therapy. A client may avert their gaze if they are nervous, thinking, or even showing respect for the therapist as an authority. Thus, these behaviors may get incorrectly interpreted as lying behaviors. If the client is deemed a liar and negative attitudes are then fostered, then therapy may be affected. Thus, it is important for therapists to be aware of their beliefs and attitudes toward clients. One recommendation for therapists is to recognize the function of a client's deception (Curtis & Hart, 2015; Kottler & Carlson, 2011). Another potential for therapist can be found in training. Therapists are provided with minimal training regarding client deception (Curtis & Hart, 2015). Training may be advantageous for therapists and therapists-in-training. Recently, a study has found promising results in using a workshop to increase correct beliefs about indicators of deception and reduce negative attitudes toward people who lie (Curtis & Dickens, 2016). Workshops such as these could be integrated into training programs to assist therapists.

Pathological Lying. What about the smaller group of people who tell numerous lies? Is there such a thing as pathological lying. While pathological lying is a term that many have probably heard or used, it is not currently a disorder in the DSM-5 (APA, 2013). However, Curtis (2019) recently put forth a theory, using the 4Fs, to better differentiate lying that is seen in the population compared to lying with excessive frequency that impairs functioning, brings pain, and can be harmful. Drawing from this theory, Curtis and Hart (in press) conducted a large-scale study with 807 participants. Their findings revealed that there is a small group of people (8 to 13%) who tell numerous lies per day (around 10 on average) and their behavior impairs functioning, specifically in relationships, and puts them at higher risk for harm. Curtis and Hart (in press) defined pathological lying as

> *A persistent, pervasive, and often compulsive pattern of excessive lying behavior leading to clinically significant impairment of functioning in social, occupational, or other areas, causing marked distress, and posing a risk to the self or others, occurring for longer than a six-month period.*

Benevolent Deception

Lying with intent to benefit another

Lies of Omission

Deception by intentionally withholding information from someone

Therapist Deception: Lying in the Other Chair. Another myth that may emerge is that therapists are always completely honest with their clients. This is not true. Deception in therapy occurs not only from clients but also from therapists. Curtis and Hart (2015) found that a majority of therapists (81%) reported lying to their clients. A greater number of therapists (96%) endorsed using benevolent deception through lies of omission (Curtis & Hart, 2015). Benevolent deception is lying with the intent to bring about a positive outcome for the target of deception. Lies of omission involve intentionally withholding information to foster a false belief in the target of the deception. Although many therapists engaged in deceiving clients, most of them do so with a good intent. Lying for the sake of others has been termed other-oriented lies, meaning that they are used for another person (DePaulo, Kashy, et al., 1996; Vrij, 2008).

Other-Oriented Lies
Deception used for another person

What is unclear is the specific deceptions that therapists may use. The outright lies or falsifications that therapists may tell to clients may range. An example of a therapist using a benevolent deception through omission may be in not telling the client that the therapist does not like the client. A therapist may choose to withhold this information because they may believe that it would be more beneficial for the client, therapeutic relationship, and therapeutic outcome to not share their feelings, if not positive. Also, note that just because many therapists have reported the use of deception, this does not imply that therapists use it frequently.

Ethical Issues and Controversies

So, do you think that lying to clients is ethical? What if a therapist lies for the sake of helping you? This issue is not addressed within the current American Psychological Association's *Ethical Principles of Psychologists and Code of Conduct* (2002; 2010). The code provides guidelines that suggest psychologists should strive for integrity, meaning they "seek to promote accuracy, honesty, and truthfulness in the science, teaching, and practice of psychology" (American Psychological Association, 2010, p. 3) Integrity is one of the five overarching principles that guide the work of psychologists. These general principles are (American Psychological Association, 2010):

- ► Beneficence and Nonmaleficence
- ► Fidelity and Responsibility
- ► Integrity
- ► Justice
- ► Respect for People's Rights and Dignity

Further, the ethics code identifies a specific ethical standard of deception within research but not within practice (American Psychological Association, 2010). Thus, psychologists unequivocally value honesty and truthfulness as a profession. On the other hand, therapists have reported being dishonest with their clients, more often with intent to do good for their clients (Curtis & Hart, 2015). This issue has been discussed within other health care professions, namely medical ethics (Hoppin, 2011; Teasdale & Kent, 1995). The source of

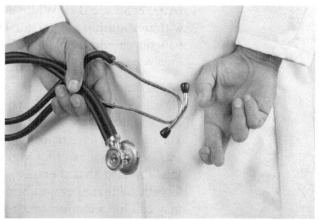

conflict is usually between principles of beneficence and integrity, in which professionals seek to bring the greatest benefits and least harm to their clients/patients and maintaining honesty. Ryan and colleagues (1995) provide a formal argument supporting lying to patients "might be represented like this:

▶ On some occasions, to tell a patient the truth will cause him harm.
▶ Doctors should not cause harm to their patients, therefore
▶ On these occasions, doctors should not tell their patients the truth" (p. 72).

Ryan and colleagues (1995) suggest that lying to a patient who experiences psychosis may bring about more benefit than harm. The idea is that a client who has delusions may have impaired judgment regarding a specific treatment or decision, which may lead to harm (Ryan et al., 1995). Thus, Ryan and colleagues suggest that this would be an example where a physician may need to deceive the patient to protect the patient from harm.

Hoppin (2011) suggested that where this dilemma is typically seen is in the use of placebos. In Chapter 4, you read about the placebo effect, in which an expectation leads to change. Placebos are essentially a deception that influences an expectation. For example, telling someone you gave them a specific drug to help treat their symptoms, while providing them with a sugar pill, would be classified as a half-truth. A half-truth is a deception in which you communicate some truth but intentionally withhold other information to create a false belief in another person (Peterson, 1996). Justification for the use of deception among nurses has been in treatment compliance (Olsen, 2012) or to protect patients or shield them from the delivery of bad news (Wolf, 2012). Some authors have suggested that it is morally acceptable and justifiable, by the principle of beneficence, for physicians to game the health care system in order to treat patients (Tavaglione, & Hurst, 2012).

Half-Truth

Communication of some truth and some lie

On the other side, authors have suggested that "the argument against deception is strong in spite of providers' beneficent intent" (Wolf, 2012, p. 17). In fact, benevolent deception, white lies, or lies told with intent to help others (Linskold & Walters, 1983), may be more harmful than people think (Argo & Shiv, 2012). White lies have been found to be negatively correlated with relationship satisfaction (Kaplar, 2006). Further, it has been argued that patients should not be lied to because there are more core medical ethics involved than just beneficence, such as autonomy (Sade, 2012).

Recently, research has investigated the ethics of therapist deception (Curtis & Kelley, 2019). Curtis and Kelley (2019) recruited 245 students and 38 therapists to assess their beliefs about the ethics of therapist deception. The study asked participants to rate how ethical a client-therapist interaction was based on a truthful vignette and six different types of lies. The findings revealed that therapists and students deemed therapist deception as less ethical than therapist honesty. The authors suggested that these findings may call for attention to a reconsideration of the American Psychological

Association's *Ethical Principles of Psychologists and Code of Conduct* (2010), to consider adding a standard related to the deception in the practice of psychology. That being said, it is important to note that even though therapists have reported using deception, they also seem to deem it as a less ethical practice than being honest with clients. Thus, it appears that therapist value honesty, aligned with their code of ethics, but may not always practice in accordance with the value. This is true of other ethical values and practice (see Pope & Vetter, 1992). Privacy and confidentiality is a standard that is explicitly addressed in the American Psychological Association's (2010) code of ethics. However, it is one of the most frequently difficult ethical areas for psychologists (Pope & Vetter, 1992). One of the reported dilemmas, involving confidentiality, from Pope and Vetter's (1992, p. 399) findings was:

> One girl underwent an abortion without the knowledge of her foster parents . . . I fully evaluated her view of the adults' inability to be supportive and agreed but worried about our relationship being damaged if I was discovered to know about the pregnancy and her action.

One of the hallmark cases that has led to much debate and heavily influenced confidentiality is the *Tarasoff* case (Koocher & Keith-Spiegel, 1998; *Tarasoff v. Board of Regents of the University of California*, 1976). The case involved a man who shot and stabbed Tatiana Tarasoff to death, which led the family of Tatiana to sue the regents of the University of California. The case moved to the Supreme Court of California, and the court ruled that therapists have a duty to warn third parties against the dangers of a patient or client (Koocher & Keith-Spiegel, 1998). The ruling based on the *Tarasoff* case is referred to as the duty to warn or protect (Koocher & Keith-Spiegel, 1998; Texas Psychological Association; TPA, 2002). Not all states have a duty to warn or protect; for example, Texas law has not established a duty to warn (TPA, 2002). Moreover, the confidentiality statue in Texas does not penalize professionals for non-disclosure of threats and it does not protect professionals from the civil liability of disclosing threats, as they make disclosures of threats at their own risk (TPA, 2002).

Tarasoff Case

A legal case that led to a duty to warn or protect ruling

Abnormal Psychology and the Law

Myths and controversies are not found only in ethics, they also are found in the context of law and forensic psychology. When you think of forensic psychology what comes to mind? Do you envision scenes from televisions shows, such as *CSI: Crime Scene Investigation*, *Criminal Minds*, or *Lie to Me*? Becoming a criminal profiler who catches serial killers has

© Couperfield/Shutterstock.com

become one of the most commonly held beliefs about those who think of forensic psychologists. There are numerous television shows that depict scenes of criminal profilers who use their understanding of human behavior to catch the bad guy. A consequence of watching these shows is that people may develop myths about forensic settings and processes, which has been termed the CSI effect (Tyler, 2006). This effect may lead jurors to expect evidence that is not often available in criminal trials (Tyler, 2006). However, others have suggested it to be a myth itself (Shelton et al., 2011). Dysart (2012) suggested that the CSI effect, while it does not have a direct effect, should be given some attention by lawyers.

What many people may have in mind when they think of forensic psychologists may be exaggerated or might even be incorrect. Many forensic psychologists engaged in practice will conduct psychological evaluations, provide testimony, and serve as expert witnesses (Van Dorsten, 2002). The work of forensic psychology is to interface psychological science in the context of the law and legal settings. This has not always been an "easy marriage" (Lilienfeld, 1994, p. 425). Due to these difficult efforts and the influence of films, there are several myths and misconceptions that develop. One of these myths that is often found in the public is the belief that psychologists label people as insane. Historically, some psychologists have used the terms sanity and insanity. If you recall from Chapter 3, Rosenhan (1973) used these terms. However, insanity is not a term that is found in the DSM-5 (APA, 2013). The common misconception is that insanity is used by psychologists, though it is a legal term and not a diagnostic term.

So, what are your thoughts about an insanity defense? Do people who commit crimes use the insanity defense to "get off" or to mitigate consequences? Surprisingly, people hold inaccurate perceptions of the insanity defense, in that people overestimate the use of an insanity plea and acquittal from the plea (Silver et al., 1994). The actual insanity plea rate is 0.9%, which is 41 times lower than the public perception estimate of 37% (Silver et al., 1994). Further, the actual acquittal rates of cases invoking insanity pleas are 26%, which is much lower than the public's perception of 44% (Silver et al., 1994). Public perception is also skewed on the consequences of acquittals, in which the public overestimates acquittees that are set free and underestimates those who are sent to a mental hospital (Silver et al., 1994).

"Acquitted. Acquitted. Acquitted. Very impressive."

Lilienfeld (1994) discussed two sides of whether the insanity defense should be maintained and clarifies that the insanity defense is formally referred to as the "not guilty by reason of insanity" defense (NGRI; p. 427). There are three rules that contribute to acquittal for the NGRI (Lilienfeld, 1994):

▶ M'Naughten Rule
▶ Durham Rule
▶ Brawner Rule

These three rules suggest that defendants are insane if they were unaware of their actions or moral consequences, have a mental disorder, and do not have the mental capacity to understand the wrongfulness of their actions (Lilienfeld, 1994). While the legal system determines the insanity, psychologists often serve in providing evaluations for these legal cases (Van Dorsten, 2002) to help determine a plea of NGRI.

Providing these services can have grave impacts on the outcomes of particular cases. Specifically, using assessments such as the Psychopathy Checklist-Revised (Hare, 2003) in capital murder trials may have fatal consequences (Edens et al., 2005). Edens and colleagues recruited 242 students, provided them with a case summary from an actual capital case that introduced psychopathy in the sentencing phase, and assessed participants' attitudes. The researchers found that psychopathy led to higher rates of supporting the death sentence (Edens et al., 2005).

Deception in the Law. Deception is not just an issue for practice and ethics but also within the law. In fact, much of the research on deception has been in its detection (Vrij, 2008; Granhag & Strömwall, 2004). Discovering techniques to discern the veracity of statements is greatly valued in forensic contexts. Being able to detect deception can be useful for police officers, interrogators, lawyers, and intelligence officers. Lying through malingering may provide clients with extrinsic gains, such as acquittals. One of the reasons that people may be fearful of the insanity defense is the idea that people may feign psychological symptoms with the intent to get set free. Using psychometrically sound instruments, such as those discussed in Chapter 3, aid inability to detect deception in these cases. Many deception detection techniques have been shown on crime shows and films. Shows such as *Lie to Me* have gained popularity through the curiosity of those with a desire to learn the secrets, tricks, and methods to unravel lies and catch criminals.

"Perhaps you would like to rephrase your last answer."

Myths in Movies

LIE TO ME

The television series *Lie to Me* depicts a consultant, Dr. Cal Lightman, who is a deception detection expert and runs a business that uses the science of emotions and microexpressions to detect deception and catch criminals. It is based on a leading researcher in deception detection.

Did you know that this show was based off of the work of Dr. Paul Ekman and his findings related to emotions and microexpressions (Ekman, 2009; Paul Ekman Group LLC, 2016)?

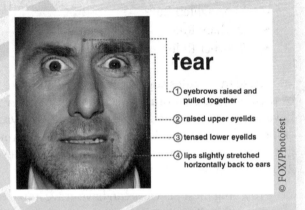

fear
1. eyebrows raised and pulled together
2. raised upper eyelids
3. tensed lower eyelids
4. lips slightly stretched horizontally back to ears

© FOX/Photofest

This show does well with portraying some of Ekman's (2009) work, even with the elements of entertainment. While the show is based off of concepts from Ekman's science (see Ekman, 2009), merely watching this will not make you better at detecting deception (Levine et al., 2010). In fact, watching the show did not increase accurate beliefs about indicators of deception, it actually promoted some inaccurate beliefs (Curtis et al., 2016). Curtis and Dickens found that participants who initially held beliefs that people decrease eye contact when lying had believed that people increase eye contact after watching the show. Therefore, shows and films that are based on science may be entertaining but may not completely convey the scientific mechanisms of phenomena or they may overemphasize the ability to accurately detect deception. As previously noted, people are not very good lie detectors (Bond & DePaulo, 2006).

Conclusion

Therapists are thought of in a variety of ways based on movies and experience. Therapists are constantly seeking to adhere to ethical guidelines and standards. Though therapists do report deceiving clients, it is not necessarily all the time, many therapists reported lying with the intent to benefit their clients, and therapists report this deception as unethical. Thus, the area of therapist deception has raised an issue of ethical standards. Practice and ethics may even merge with areas of the law and forensics. There are many myths about forensic psychology that may carry over into public perception and affect jurors in decision-making. With that, forensic psychologists do their diligence to serve as expert witnesses in a manner that promotes science and the profession. So, next time you watch a crime show, remember that most of what you see in your living room does not play out in the courtroom. These strategies will help you with myth-checking.

You now are better equipped to handle myths and misinformation from various sources. At the possible expense of ruining future films or shows for your friends (or even you), you are now more able to critically evaluate the science, practice, and research related to abnormal psychology.

CHAPTER REVIEW

QUESTIONS

1. Do therapists typically struggle with psychological problems while they are treating others?

2. Do clients lie in therapy? What are some reasons? What about therapists?

3. What is the most commonly held incorrect belief about deceptive behavior?

4. What are the five general ethical principles of psychologists?

5. What is the insanity defense and how often is it used?

6. What are the three rules that contribute to acquittal for not guilty by reason of insanity?

KEY TERMS

Truth Bias

Duping Delight

Gaze Aversion

Benevolent Deception

Lies of Omission

Other-Oriented Lies

Half-Truth

Tarasoff Case

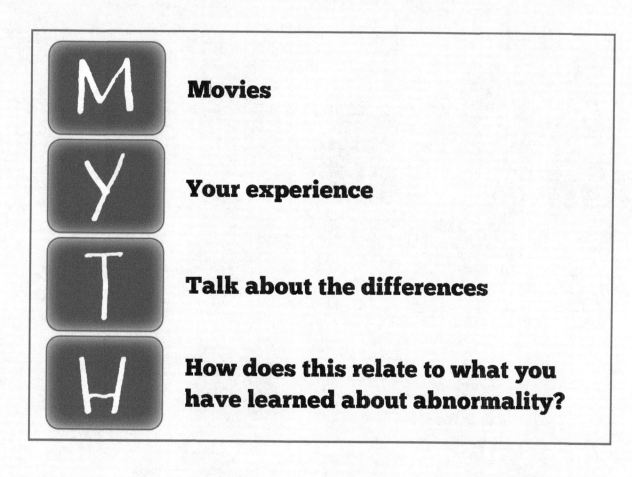

M   **Movies**

Y   **Your experience**

T   **Talk about the differences**

H   **How does this relate to what you have learned about abnormality?**

Myths in Movies Recap

What About Bob and One Flew Over the Cuckoo's Nest

Movies such as *What About Bob* depict psychological disorders as humorous. Additionally, like in other movies, the therapist is portrayed to be impaired and violates several ethical boundaries. Films such as *One Flew Over the Cuckoo's Nest* can influence perceptions of treatments, where ECT can be thought to be fearful or mechanisms of social control.

Lie to Me

Shows like *Lie to Me* can certainly perpetuate myths, such as the belief that rather than people looking away when they lie, people make more eye contact. Research (see Vrij, 2008) has revealed that eye contact is not a reliable indicator of deception.

REFERENCES

Front Matter

American Psychiatric Association. (2013). *Diagnostic and statistical manual of mental disorders* (5th ed.). American Psychiatric Association.

APA Presidential Task Force on Evidence-Based Practice. (2006). Evidence-based practice in psychology. *American Psychologist, 61,* 271–285.

Curtis, D. A. (2018, April). *Psychomythology of psychopathology.* Talk presented at the 64th Annual Southwestern Psychological Association Conference, Houston, TX.

Lilienfeld, S. O., Lynn, S. J., Ruscio, J., & Beyerstein, B. L. (2010). The top ten myths of popular psychology. *Skeptic,* (3), 36.

Wedding, D., & Niemiec, R. M. (2014). *Movies and mental illness: Using films to understand psychopathology* (4th ed.). Hogrefe Publishing.

Chapter 1

American Psychiatric Association. (2013). *Diagnostic and statistical manual of mental disorders* (5th ed.). American Psychiatric Association.

Arkowitz, H., & Lilienfeld, S. O. (2009). Lunacy and the Full Moon. *Scientific American Mind, 20*(1), 64.

Baker, D. B., & Benjamin, L. T., Jr. (2000). The affirmation of the scientist-practitioner: A look back at boulder. *American Psychologist, 55,* 241–247. doi:10.1037/0003-066X.55.2.241

Benjamin, L. T., Jr., (1997). The origin of the psychological species: History of the beginnings of APA divisions. *American Psychologist, 52,* 725–732.

Benjamin, L. T., Jr., & Baker, D. B. (2004). *From séance to science: A history of the profession of psychology in America.* Wadsworth/Thomson Learning.

Bergin, A. E. (1991). Values and religious issues in psychotherapy and mental health. *American Psychologist, 46*(4), 394–403.

Byrne, B. (2009). Why psychiatrists should watch films (or what has cinema ever done for psychiatry?). *Advances in Psychiatric Treatment, 15,* 286–296.

Curtis, D. A. (2018, April). *Psychomythology of psychopathology.* Talk presented at the 64th Annual Southwestern Psychological Association Conference, Houston, TX.

Davey, B., Gibson, M., Amin, M., & Anderson, B. (2014). *Stonehearst Asylum* [Motion picture]. United States: Icon Productions Sobini Films. http://stonehearstasylum.com/

Davison, W. P. (1983). The third-person effect in communication. *Public Opinion Quarterly, 47,* 1–15.

Engel, G. L. (1996). From biomedical to biopsychosocial: I. Being scientific in the human domain. *Families, Systems, & Health, 14*(4), 425–433. doi:10.1037/h0089973

Erikson, E. H. (1980). *Identity and the life cycle.* Norton.

Festinger, L. A. (1954). Theory of social comparison processes. *Human Relations, 7*(2), 117–140.

Frances, A. (2013). *Saving normal: An insider's revolt against out-of-control psychiatric diagnosis, DSM-5, big pharma, and the medicalization of ordinary life.* William Morrow.

Freud, S., Strachey, J., Freud, A., Rothgeb, C. L., & Richards, A. (1900). *The standard edition of the complete psychological works of Sigmund Freud.* Hogarth Press, 1953–74.

Gabbard, G. O., & Gabbard, K. (1999). *Psychiatry and the cinema* (2nd ed.). American Psychiatric Association.

Gauss, C. F., & Davis, C. H. (1963). *Theory of the motion of the heavenly bodies moving about the sun in conic sections; a translation of Theoria motus.* Dover Publications.

Gross, C. G. (1999). A hole in the head. *Neuroscientist, 5*(4), 263. doi:10.1177/107385849900500415

Hamilton, E. (1942). *Mythology: Timeless tales of gods and heroes.* Little, Brown & Company.

Haslam, N., Loughnan, S., Reynolds, C., & Wilson, S. (2007). Dehumanization: A new perspective. *Social and Personality Psychology Compass, 1*(1), 409–422.

Heider, F. (1958). *The psychology of interpersonal relations.* John Wiley & Sons Inc.

Lilienfeld, S. O. (1994). *Seeing both sides: Classic controversies in abnormal psychology.* Wadsworth Publishing.

Lilienfeld, S. O., Lynn, S. J., Ruscio, J., & Beyerstein, B. L. (2010). Busting big myths in popular psychology. *Scientific American Mind, 21*(1), 42.

Musgrave, S. (1994). *Musgrave landing: Musings on the writing life.* Stoddart.

Nolen-Hoeksema, S. (2007). Lecture 18. *What happens when things go wrong: Mental illness, Part I* (Guest Lecture by Professor Susan Nolen-Hoeksema). https://oyc.yale.edu/psychology/psyc-110/lecture-18

Nolen-Hoeksema, S. (2011). *Abnormal psychology* (5th ed.). McGraw-Hill.

Nolen-Hoeksema, S. (2014). *Abnormal psychology* (6th ed.). McGraw-Hill.

Rosenberg, T., Lucchesi, G., Boardman, P. H., Vinson, T., Flynn, B., & Derrickson, S. (2005). *The Exorcism of Emily Rose* [Motion picture]. Lakeshore Entertainment Firm Films.

Ross, L. (1977). The intuitive psychologist and his shortcomings: Distortions in the attribution process. In Berkowitz (Ed.), *Advances in experimental social psychology,* (Vol. 10, pp. 173–220). Academic Press.

Rotton, J., & Kelly, I. W. (1985). Much ado about the full moon: A meta-analysis of lunar-lunacy research. *Psychological Bulletin, 97*(2), 286–306.

Schroeder, B. L., Curtis, D. A., & Kelley, L. J. (2019, April). *Movies, psychopathology, and psychomythology.* Poster presented at the 65th Annual Southwestern Psychological Association Conference, Albuquerque, NM.

Sherif, M. (1936). *The psychology of social norms.* Harper.

Vieten, C., Scammell, S., Pierce, A., Pilato, R., Ammondson, I., Pargament, K. I., & Lukoff, D. (2016). Competencies for psychologists in the domains of religion and spirituality. *Spirituality in Clinical Practice, 3*(2), 92–114.

Wasan, A., & Edwards, R. R. (2008). Psychology, psychiatry, and brain neuroscience in pain medicine: New tools for a new science. *Pain Medicine, 9*(8), 973–974. doi:10.1111/j.1526-4637.2008.00531.x

Watson, T. S., & Eveleigh, E. (2014). Teaching psychological theories: Integration tasks and teaching strategies. *Journal of Psychology & Theology, 42*(2), 200–210.

Wedding, D., & Niemiec, R. M. (2014). *Movies and mental illness: Using films to understand psychopathology, 4th ed.* Hogrefe Publishing.

Whorf, B. L., & Carroll, J. B. (1998). *Language, thought, and reality: Selected writings of Benjamin Lee Whorf.* The MIT Press.

Zimbardo, P. G. (2007). *The Lucifer effect: Understanding how good people turn evil.* Random House, 2007.

Chapter 2

American Psychiatric Association. (2013). *Diagnostic and statistical manual of mental disorders* (5th ed.). American Psychiatric Association.

American Psychological Association. (2002). Guidelines on multicultural education, training, research, practice, and organizational change for psychologists, *American Psychologist, 58,* 377–402.

American Psychological Association. (2007). Guidelines for psychological practice with girls and women. *American Psychologist, 62,* 949–979.

Bandura, A. (1977). *Social learning theory.* Prentice-Hall.

Bandura, A., Ross, D., & Ross, S. A. (1961). Transmission of aggression through imitation of aggressive models. *Journal of Abnormal & Social Psychology, 63*(3), 575–582.

Baumeister, R. (1991). *Meanings of Life.* Guilford Press.

Beck, J. S. (1995). *Cognitive therapy: Basics and beyond.* Guilford Press.

Beck, J. S. (2011). *Cognitive Behavior Therapy: Basics and beyond* (2nd ed.). Guilford.

Becvar, D. S., & Becvar, R. J. (2009). *Family therapy: A systemic integration* (7th ed.). Allyn & Bacon.

Beeghly, M., & Tronick, E. (2011). Early resilience in the context of parent–infant relationships: A social developmental perspective. *Current Problems in Pediatric and Adolescent Health Care, 41,* 197–201.

Blankenship, K. M., & Weston, C. (2012). Syndromes of intellectual disability. In J. P. Gentile, & P. M. Gillig (Eds.), *Psychiatry of intellectual disability: A practical manual* (pp. 338–365). Wiley-Blackwell.

Book, H. E. (1997). *How to practice brief psychodynamic psychotherapy.* American Psychological Association.

Bronfenbrenner, U. (1979). *The ecology of human development: Experiments by nature and design.* Harvard University Press.

Brooks-Harris, J. E. (2008). *Integrative multitheoretical psychotherapy.* Houghton Mifflin.

Castonguay, L. G., Newman, M. G., Borkovec, T. D., Holtforth, M. G., & Maramba, G. G. (2005). Cognitive-behavioral assimilative integration. In M. R. Goldfried (Ed.), *Handbook of psychotherapy integration* (2nd ed., pp. 241–260). Oxford University Press.

Corey, G. (2009) *Theory and practice of counseling and psychotherapy* (8th ed). Brooks/Cole, Cengage Learning.

DeRubeis, R. J., Tang, T. Z., & Beck, A. T. (2001). Cognitive therapy. In K. S. Dobson (Ed.), *Handbook of cognitive–behavioral therapies* (pp. 349–392). Guilford Press.

Elliot, R., Greenberg, L. S., & Lietaer, G. (2004). Research on experiential psychotherapies. In M. J. Lambert (Ed.), *Bergin and Garfield's handbook of psychotherapy and behavior change* (5th ed., pp. 493–539). John Wiley & Sons, Inc.

Enns, C. Z. (2008). Toward a complexity paradigm for understanding gender role conflict. *The Counseling Psychologist, 35*, 446–454.

Fosha, D., & Slowiaczek, M. L. (1997). Techniques to accelerate dynamic psychotherapy. *American Journal of Psychotherapy, 51*(2), 229–251.

Frances, A. (2013). *Saving normal: An insider's revolt against out-of-control psychiatric diagnosis, DSM-5, big pharma, and the medicalization of ordinary life.* William Morrow.

Freud, A. (1936/1993). *The ego and the mechanisms of defence.* Karnac Books.

Garrett, B. (2009). *Brain and behavior: An introduction to biological psychology* (2nd ed.). Sage Publications, Inc.

Gazzaniga, M. S. (1967). The split brain in man. *Scientific American, 217*(2), 24–29.

Greenberg, L. S. (2002). *Emotion-focused therapy: Coaching clients to work through their feelings.* American Psychological Association.

Greenberg, L. S. (2011). *Emotion-focused therapy.* American Psychological Association.

Greenberg, L. S., & Paivio, S. C. (1997). *Working with emotions in psychotherapy.* The Guilford Press.

Greenberg, L. S.. & Watson, J. C. (2006). *Emotion-focused therapy for depression.* American Psychological Association.

Grissom, R. J. (1996). The magical number .7 ± .2: Meta-meta-analysis of the probability of superior outcome in comparisons involving therapy, placebo, and control. *Journal of Consulting and Clinical Psychology, 64*(5), 973–982.

Harris, J. E., Kelley, L. J., Campbell, E. L., & Hammond, E. S. (2014). Key strategies training for individual psychotherapy: An introduction to multitheoretical practice. *Journal of Psychotherapy Integration, 24*(2), 138–152. doi:10.1037/a0037056

Hyler, S. E. (1988). DSM-III at the cinema: Madness in the movies. *Comprehensive Psychiatry, 29*(2), 195–206.

Kohut, H. (1977/2009). *The restoration of the self.* University of Chicago Press.

Lambert, M. J., & Ogles, B. M. (2004). The efficacy and effectiveness of psychotherapy. In A. E. Bergin & S. L. Garfield (Eds.), *Handbook of psychotherapy and behavior change* (5th ed., pp. 139–193). John Wiley & Sons.

Levenson, H. (2010). *Brief dynamic therapy.* American Psychological Association.

Maki, P., Veijola, J., Jones, P. B., Murray, G. K., Koponen, H., Tienari, P., Miettunen, J., Paivikki, T., Wahlberg, K. E., Koskinen, J., Lauronen, E., & Ishohanni, M. (2005). Predictors of schizophrenia—A review. *British medical bulletin, 73/74*, 1–15. doi:10.1093/bmb/ldh046

Markus, H. R., & Kitayama, S. (2010). Cultures and selves: A cycle of mutual constitution. *Perspectives on Psychological Science, 5*, 420–430.

Maslow, A. H. (1943). A theory of human motivation. *Psychological Review, 50*(4), 370–396.

McCabe, D. P., & Castel, A. D. (2008). Seeing is believing: The effect of brain images on judgments of scientific reasoning. *Cognition,* 107. 343–352. https://doi.org/10.1016/j.cognition.2007.07.017

Meichenbaum, D. (1977). *Cognitive-behavior modification: An integrative approach.* Plenum Press.

Messer, S. B. (1992). A critical examination of belief structures in integrative and eclectic psychotherapy. In J. C. Norcross, M. R. Goldfried, J. C. Norcross, M. R. Goldfried (Eds.), *Handbook of psychotherapy integration* (pp. 130–165). Basic Books.

Murphy, B. P. (2010). Beyond the first episode: Candidate factors for a risk prediction model of schizophrenia. *International review of psychiatry, 22*(2), 202–223. doi:10.3109/09540261003661833

Norcross, J. C. (2005). A primer on psychotherapy integration. In J. C. Norcross, M. R. Goldfried (Eds.), *Handbook of psychotherapy integration* (2nd ed., pp. 3–23). Oxford University Press.

Norcross, J. C. & Newman, C. F. (1992). Psychotherapy integration. Setting the context. In J. C. Norcross, & M. R. Goldfried (Eds.), *Handbook of psychotherapy integration* (pp. 3–45). Basic Books.

Pagnin, D., de Queiroz, V., Pini, S., & Cassano, G. B. (2004). Efficacy of ECT in depression: A meta-analytic review. *The Journal of ECT, 20*(1), 13–20.

Paivio, S. C., & Greenberg, L. S. (1995). Resolving 'unfinished business': Efficacy of experiential therapy using empty-chair dialogue. *Journal of Consulting and Clinical Psychology, 63,* 419–425. doi:10.1037/0022-006X.63.3.419

Patil, S. T., Zhang, L., Martenyi, F., Lowe, S. L., Jackson, K. A., Andreev, B. V., Avedisova, A, S.,Bardenstein, L. M.,Gurovich, I. Y.,Morozova, M. A.,Mosolov, S. N.,Neznanov, N. G.,Reznik, A. M.,Smulevich, A. B.,Tochilov, V. A.,Johnson, B. G.,Monn, J. A., & Schoepp, D. D. (2007). Activation of mGlu2/3 receptors as a new approach to treat schizophrenia: A randomized Phase 2 clinical trial. *Nature Medicine,* (9), 1102.

PDM Task Force. (2006). *Psychodynamic diagnostic manual.* Alliance of Psychoanalytic Organizations.

Perls, F. (1973). *The Gestalt approach & eye witness to therapy.* Science & Behavior Books.

Perls, F., Hefferline, R. F., & Goodman, P. (1951). Gestalt therapy: Excitement and growth in the human personality. Delta Book/Dell.

Piaget, J. (1954). *The construction of reality in the child.* Basic Books.

Robertson, M., Rushton, P., & Wurm, C. (2008). Interpersonal psychotherapy: An overview. *Psychotherapy in Australia, 14*(3), 46–54.

Rogers, C. R. (1951). *Client-centered therapy, its current practice, implications, and theory.* Houghton Mifflin.

Rogers, C. R. (1957). The necessary and sufficient conditions of therapeutic personality change. *Journal of Consulting Psychology, 21*(2), 95–103.

Rogers, C. R. (1961). *On becoming a person; a therapist's view of psychotherapy.* Houghton Mifflin.

Rogers, C. R. (1975). Rogers' conception of the self. In R. I. Evans (Ed.), *Carl Rogers: The man and his ideas* (pp. 13–33). E. P. Dutton & Co.

Rosenzweig, S. (1936). Some implicit common factors in diverse methods of psychotherapy. *American Journal of Orthopsychiatry, 6,* 412–415.

Satel, S., & Lilienfeld, S. O. (2013). *Brainwashed: The seductive appeal of mindless neuroscience.* Basic Books.

Stahl, S. M. (2011). *Stahl's essential psychopharmacology: Neuroscientific basis and practical applications* (3rd ed.). Cambridge UP.

Summers, R. F., & Barber, J. P. (2010). *Psychodynamic therapy: A guide to evidence-based practice.* Guilford.

Tsuang, M. (2000). Schizophrenia: Genes and environment. *Biological Psychiatry, 47*(3), 210–220.

Watson, J. B., & Rayner, R. (1920). Conditioned emotional reactions. *Journal of Experimental Psychology, 3*(1), 1–14.

Wedding, D., & Niemiec, R. M. (2014). *Movies and mental illness: Using films to understand psychopathology* (4th ed.) Hogrefe Publishing.

Weissman, M. M. (2006). A brief history of interpersonal psychotherapy. *Psychiatric Annals, 36*(8), 553–557.

Yalom, I. D. (2002). *The gift of therapy.* HarperCollins Publishers.

Zuckerman, M. (1999). Diathesis-stress models. In *Vulnerability to psychopathology: A biosocial model* (pp. 3–23). American Psychological Association. doi:10.1037/10316-001

Chapter 3

American Educational Research Association, American Psychological Association, & National Council on Measurement in Education (2014). *Standards for educational and psychological testing.* American Educational Research Association.

American Psychiatric Association. (1952). *Diagnostic and statistical manual of mental disorders* (1st ed.). American Psychiatric Association.

American Psychiatric Association. (2013). *Diagnostic and statistical manual of mental disorders* (5th ed.). American Psychiatric Association.

Baker, D. B., & Benjamin, L. T., Jr. (2000). The affirmation of the scientist-practitioner: A look back at boulder. *American Psychologist, 55,* 241–247.

Blashfield, R. K., & Burgess, D. R. (2007). Classification provides an essential basis for organizing mental disorders. In S. O. Lilienfeld, W. T. O'Donohue, S. O. Lilienfeld, W. T. O'Donohue (Eds.), *The great ideas of clinical science: 17 principles that every mental health professional should understand* (pp. 93–117). Routledge/Taylor & Francis Group.

Blashfield, R. K., Keeley, J. W., Flanagan, E. H., & Miles, S. R. (2014). The cycle of classification: DSM-I through DSM-5. *Annual Review of Clinical Psychology, 10,* 25–51. doi:10.1146/annurev-clinpsy-032813-153639

Butcher, J. N., Dahlstrom, W. G., Graham, J. R., Tellegen, A., & Kaemmer, B. (1989). *The Minnesota Multiphasic Personality Inventory-2 (MMPI-2): Manual for administration and scoring.* University of Minnesota Press.

Caruso, C. (2017, February 15). Psychiatrists debate weighing in on Trump's mental health. https://www.scientificamerican.com/article/psychiatrists-debate-weighing-in-on-trumps-mental-health

Clegg, J. W. (2012). Teaching about mental health and illness through the history of the DSM. *History of Psychology, 15*(4), 364–370.

Curtis, D. A. (2018, April). *Psychomythology of psychopathology.* Talk presented at the 64th Annual Southwestern Psychological Association Conference, Houston, TX.

Exner, J. E. (2001). *A Rorschach workbook for the comprehensive system* (5th ed.) Rorshach Workshops.

Frances, A. (2013). *Saving normal: An insider's revolt against out-of-control psychiatric diagnosis, DSM-5, big pharma, and the medicalization of ordinary life.* William Morrow.

Gartner, J. D. (2017). Diagnosis: Malignant narcissism. *USA Today.* https://www.usatoday.com/story/opinion/2017/05/04/trump-malignant-narcissistic-disorder-psychiatry-column/101243584/

Goldstein, W. N., & Anthony, R. N. (1988). The diagnosis of depression and the DSMs. *American Journal of Psychotherapy, 62*(2), 180–196.

Greene, R. L. (2000). *The MMPI-2: An interpretive manual.* Allyn and Bacon.

Groth-Marnat, G. (2009). *Handbook of Psychological Assessment* (5th ed.). John Wiley & Sons, Inc.

Guthrie, R. V. (2004). *Even the rat was white: A historical view of psychology* (2nd ed.). Pearson Education.

Hathaway, S. R., & McKinley, J. C. (1940). A Multiphasic Personality Schedule (Minnesota): I. Construction of the schedule. *Journal of Psychology, 10,* 249. doi:10.1080/00223980.1940.9917000

Lilienfeld, S., Wood, J., & Garb, H. (2001). The Rorschach test is scientifically questionable. *Harvard Mental Health Letter, 18*(6), 5–6.

Lilienfeld, S., Wood, J., & Garb, H. (2012). Why questionable psychological tests remain popular. In S. O. Lilienfeld, W. T. O'Donohue (Eds.), *Great readings in clinical science: Essential selections for mental health professionals* (pp. 148–155). Pearson Education, Inc.

Louter, M. (2010). Schizophrenia: what's in a name? *Mental Health Practice, 13*(7), 28–30.

McDaniel, S. H. (2016, Nov. 1). Response to Article on Diagnosing Public Figures. http://www.apa.org/news/press/response/diagnosing-public-figures.aspx

Meehl, P. E. (1954). *Clinical versus statistical prediction: A theoretical analysis and a review of the evidence.* University of Minnesota Press.

Murray, H. A. (1943). Thematic Apperception Test manual. Harvard University Press.

Oquendo, M. A. (2017). APA remains committed to supporting Goldwater Rule. https://www.psychiatry.org/news-room/apa-blogs/apa-blog/2017/03/apa-remains-committed-to-supporting-goldwater-rule

Rosenhan, D. L. (1973). On being sane in insane places. *Science,* (4070), 250.

Ruscio, J. (2007). The clinician as subject: Practitioners are prone to the same judgment errors as everyone else. In S. O. Lilienfeld, W. T. O'Donohue, S. O. Lilienfeld, W. T. O'Donohue (Eds.), *The great ideas of clinical science: 17 principles that every mental health professional should understand* (pp. 29–47). Routledge/Taylor & Francis Group.

Von Mayrhauser, R. T. (1992). The mental testing community and validity: A prehistory. *American Psychologist, 47*(2), 244–253. doi:10.1037/0003-066X.47.2.244

Watkins, C. E., Campbell, V. L., Nieberding, R., & Hallmark, R. (1995). Contemporary practice of psychological assessment by clinical psychologists. *Professional Psychology: Research and Practice, 26,* 54–60. doi:10.1037/0735-7028.26.1.54

Wechsler, D. (2008). *Wechsler Adult Intelligence Scale-4th ed.* NCS Pearson, Inc.

Wechsler, D. (2014). *Wechsler Intelligence Scale for Children-5th ed.* NCS Pearson, Inc.

Wood J. M., Garb, H. N., & Nezworski, M. T. (2007). Psychometrics: Better measurement makes better clinicians. In S. O. Lilienfeld, W. T. O'Donohue, S. O. Lilienfeld, W. T. O'Donohue (Eds.) *The great ideas of clinical science: 17 principles that every mental health professional should understand* (pp. 77–92). Routledge/Taylor & Francis Group.

Chapter 4

Alexander, B. (2009, December 2). Dark shadows loom over 'facilitated' talk: Opening minds or telling tales? Michigan family torn apart by abuse claims. *NBC News.* http://www.nbcnews.com/id/34212528/ns/health-mental_health/t/dark-shadows-loom-over-facilitated-talk/#.VbJhytHb-KUk

American Psychiatric Association. (2013). *Diagnostic and statistical manual of mental disorders* (5th ed.). American Psychiatric Association.

American Psychological Association. (2002). Ethical principles of psychologists and code of conduct. *American Psychologist, 57,* 1060–1073.

American Psychological Association. (2010). 2010 amendments to the 2002 'Ethical principles of psychologists and code of conduct.' *American Psychologist, 65.* doi:10.1037/a0020168

American Psychological Association Task Force on Promotion and Dissemination of Psychological Procedures. (1995). Training in and dissemination of empirically validated treatments: Report and recommendations. *The Clinical Psychologist, 48,* 3–23.

Breuer, J., & Freud, S. (1957). *Studies on hysteria.* Basic Books.

Chambless, D. L., & Hollon, S. D. (1998). Defining empirically supported therapies. *Journal of Consulting and Clinical Psychology, 66,* 7–18. doi:10.1037/0022-006X.66.1.7

Crossley, R. (1992). Getting the words out: Case studies in facilitated communication training. *Topics in Language Disorders, 12,* 46–59.

Curtis, D. A., Eades, A., & Gonzales, H. C. (2014, April). *A dose of Dr. House? First day teaching demonstration for psychopathology.* Poster presented at the 10th Annual Southwest Teachers of Psychology Conference, San Antonio, TX.

Davison, G. C., & Lazarus, A. A. (2007). Clinical case studies are important in the science and practice of psychotherapy. In S. O. Lilienfeld & W. T. O'Donohue (Eds.), *The great ideas of clinical science: 17 principles that every mental health professional should understand* (pp. 149–162). Routledge/Taylor & Francis Group.

Feyerabend, P. (1975). Against method: Outline of an anarchistic theory of knowledge. NLB.

Freud, S. (1963). *Dora: An analysis of a case of hysteria.* Simon & Shuster, Inc.

Gopnik, A., Meltzoff A., & Kuhl P. (2001). *The scientist in the crib: What early learning tells us about the mind.* HarperCollins Publishers, Inc.

Green, G., & Shane, H. C. (1994). Science, reason, and facilitated communication. *Journal of the Association for Persons with Severe Handicaps, 19,* 151–199.

Haney, C., Banks, W. C., & Zimbardo, P. G. (1973). A study of prisoners and guards in a simulated prison. *Naval Research Review, 30,* 4–17.

Heinzen, T. E., Lilienfeld, S. O., & Nolan, S. A. (2015). Clever Hans. *Skeptic, 20,* 10–17.

Hersen, M. (2002). Rationale for clinical case studies: An editorial. *Clinical Case Studies, 1,* 3–5. doi:10.1177/1534650102001001001

Kendall, P. C., Holmbeck, G., & Verduin, T. (2004). Methodology, design, and evaluation in psychotherapy research. In A. E. Bergin & S. L. Garfield (Eds.), *Handbook of psychotherapy and behavior change* (5th ed., pp. 16–43). John Wiley & Sons.

Kitcher, P. (2001). *Science, truth, and democracy.* Oxford University Press.

Kottler, J. A., & Carlson, J. (2003). *The mummy at the dining room table: Eminent therapists reveal their most unusual cases and what they teach us about human behavior.* Jossey-Bass.

Kuhn, T. S. (1970). *The structure of scientific revolutions.* University of Chicago Press.

Lambert, M. J., & Ogles, B. M. (2004). The efficacy and effectiveness of psychotherapy. In A. E. Bergin & S. L. Garfield (Eds.), *Handbook of psychotherapy and behavior change* (5th ed., pp. 139–193). John Wiley & Sons.

Lilienfeld, S. O., Marshall, J., Todd, J. T., & Shane, H. C. (2014). The persistence of fad interventions in the face of negative scientific evidence: Facilitated communication for autism as a case example. *Evidence-Based Communication Assessment & Intervention, 8*(2), 62–101.

Lilienfeld, S. O., Ritschel, L. A., Lynn, S. J., Cautin, R. L., & Latzman, R. D. (2014). Why ineffective psychotherapies appear to work: A taxonomy of causes of spurious therapeutic effectiveness. *Perspectives on Psychological Science, 9,* 355–387.

Milgram, S. (1963). Behavioral study of obedience. *Journal of Abnormal & Social Psychology, 67*(4), 371.

Myers, A., & Hansen, C. (2006). *Experimental psychology* (6th ed.). Thomson Wadsworth.

O'Donohue, W. T., Lilienfeld, S. O., & Fowler, K. A. (2007). Science is an essential safeguard against human error. In S. O. Lilienfeld & W. T. O'Donohue (Eds.), *The great ideas of clinical science: 17 principles that every mental health professional should understand* (pp. 3–27). Routledge/Taylor & Francis Group.

Oltmanns, T. F., Martin, M. T., Neale, J. M., & Davison, G. C. (2012). Case studies in abnormal psychology (9th ed.). John Wiley & Sons Inc.

Pfungst, O., & Rosenthal, R. (1965). *Clever Hans, the horse of Mr. Von Osten.* Holt, Rinehart and Winston.

Popper, K. R. (1959). *The logic of scientific discovery.* Basic Books.

Rush, A. J., Beck, A. T., Kovacs, M., & Hollon, S. (1977). Comparative efficacy of cognitive therapy and pharmacotherapy in the treatment of depressed outpatients. *Cognitive Therapy and Research, 1,* 17.

Schafersman, S. D. (2012). An introduction to science: Scientific thinking and the scientific method. In S. O. Lilienfeld & W. T. O'Donohue (Eds.), *Great readings in clinical science: Essential selections for mental health professionals* (pp. 21–25). Pearson Education, Inc.

Steers, M. N., Wickham, R. E., & Acitelli, L. K. (2014). Seeing everyone else's highlight reels: How Facebook usage is linked to depressive symptoms. *Journal of Social & Clinical Psychology, 33*(8), 701–731.

Watson, J. B., & Rayner, R. (1920). Conditioned emotional reactions. *Journal of Experimental Psychology, 3,* 1–14. doi:10.1037/h0069608

Wegner, D. M., Fuller, V. A., & Sparrow, B. (2003). Clever hands: Uncontrolled intelligence in facilitated communication. *Journal of Personality and Social Psychology, 85,* 5–19. doi:10.1037/0022-3514.85.1.5

Chapter 5

AGS Publishing. (2005). *BASC: Behavior Assessment System for Children.* http://www.agsnet.com/Group.asp?nGroupInfoID=a3800

American Psychiatric Association (1987). *Diagnostic and statistical manual of mental disorders* (Rev. 3rd ed.). American Psychiatric Association.

American Psychiatric Association. (2013). *Diagnostic and statistical manual of mental disorders* (5th ed.). American Psychiatric Association.

Anastopoulos, A. D., Guevremont, D. C., Shelton, T. L., & DuPaul, G. J. (1992). Parenting stress among families of children with attention deficit hyperactivity disorder. *Journal of Abnormal Child Psychology, 20*(5), 503–520.

Barkley, R. A. (2003). Attention-deficit/hyperactivity disorder. In E. J. Mash, & R. A. Barkley (Eds). *Child Psychopathology* (2nd ed., pp. 75–143). The Guilford Press.

Barkley, R. A., Cook, E. H., Dulcan, M., Campbell, S., Prior, M., Atkins, M., Gillberg, C., Solanto-Gardner, M., Halperin, J., Bauermeister, J. J., Pliszka, S. R., Stein, M. A., Werry, J. S., Sergeant, J., Brown, R. T., Zametkin, A., Anastopoulos, A. D., McGough, J. J., DuPaul, G. J., . . . Lewandowski, L. (2002). Consensus statement on ADHD. *European Child & Adolescent Psychiatry, 11*(2), 96–98.

Barkley, R. A., Guevremont, D. C., Anastopoulos, A. D., DuPaul, G. J., & Shelton, T. L. (1993). Driving-related risks and outcomes of attention deficit hyperactivity disorder in adolescents and young adults: A 3- to 5-year follow-up survey. *Pediatrics, 92*(2), 212.

Barkley, R. A., Murphy, K., & Kwasnik, D. (1996). Psychological adjustment and adaptive impairments in young adults with ADHD. *Journal of Attention Disorders, 1*(1), 41–54.

Bird, P. D. (2015). The treatment of autism with low-dose phenytoin: A case report. *Journal of Medical Case Reports, 9*(1), 1–5.

Centers for Disease Control and Prevention. (2015a). Autism spectrum disorder. http://www.cdc.gov/ncbddd/autism/facts.html#ref

Centers for Disease Control and Prevention. (2015b). Fragile X Syndrome. http://www.cdc.gov/ncbddd/fxs/index.html

Chunzhen, X., Reid, R., & Steckelberg, A. (2002). Technology applications for children with ADHD: Assessing the empirical support. *Education & Treatment of Children, 25*(2).

Conners, C. K., Epstein, J. N., & Angold, A. (2003). Continuous Performance Test performance in a normative epidemiological sample. *Journal of Abnormal Child Psychology, 31*(5), 555–562.

Division 53 Task Forces. (2015). Retrieved March 7, 2016, from https://clinicalchildpsychology.org/TaskForces

Doyle, A., Ostrander, R., Skare, S., Crosby, R. D., & August, G. J. (1997). Convergent and criterion-related validity of the behavior assessment system for children-parent rating scale. *Journal of Clinical Child Psychology, 26*, 276–284.

Dulcan, M. K. (1985). The psychopharmacologic treatment of children and adolescents with attention deficit disorder. *Psychiatric Annals, 15*, 69–86.

Evans, S. N., Owens, J. S., & Bunford, N. (2014). Evidence-based psychosocial treatments for children and adolescents with attention-deficit/hyperactivity disorder. *Journal of Clinical Child & Adolescent Psychology, 43*(4), 527–551.

Fischer, M., Barkley, R. A., Smallish, L., & Fletcher, K. (2002). Young adult follow-up of hyperactive children: Self-reported psychiatric disorders, comorbidity, and the role of childhood conduct problems and teen CD. *Journal of Abnormal Child Psychology, 30*(5), 463–475.

Foley, D., & McCutcheon, H. (2004). Detecting pain in people with an intellectual disability. *Accident & Emergency Nursing, 12*, 196–200.

Fox, Daniel J., Tharp, David F., Fox, Lydia C. (2005). Neurofeedback: An alternative and efficacious treatment for Attention Deficit Hyperactivity Disorder. *Applied Psychophysiology and Biofeedback, 30,* 365–373.

Frye, R. E., Slattery, J., Delhey, L., Furgerson, B., Strickland, T., Tippett, M., Sailey, A., Wynne, R., Rose, S., Melnyk, S., James, S. J., Sequeira, J. M., & Quadros, E. V. (2018). Folinic acid improves verbal communication in children with autism and language impairment: A randomized double-blind placebo-controlled trial. *Molecular Psychiatry, 23*(2), 247–256.

Fuchs, T., Birbaumer, N., Lutzenberger, W., Gruzelier, J. H., & Kaiser, J. (2003). Neurofeedback treatment for attention-deficit/hyperactivity disorder in children: A comparison with methylphenidate. *Applied Psychophysiology and Biofeedback, 28,* 1–12.

Galton, D. J. (2005). Eugenics: Some lessons from the past. *Reproductive Biomedicine Online (Reproductive Healthcare Limited), 10,* 133–136.

Ghanizadeh, A., Tordjman, S., & Jaafari, N. (2015). Aripiprazole for treating irritability in children & adolescents with autism: A systematic review. *Indian Journal of Medical Research, 142*(3), 269–275.

Gharib, B., Farshadmoghadam, H., Hosseini, F., & Yaghmaie, B. (2014). Be careful of lies: A 6 year old boy with respiratory distress and decreased level of consciousness. *Acta Medica Iranica, 52*(6), 481–483.

Gillham, N. W. (2001). Sir Francis Galton and the Birth of Eugenics. *Annual Review of Genetics, 35,* 83.

Glicksman, E. (2012). Catching autism earlier. http://www.apa.org/monitor/2012/10/autism.aspx

Grandin, T. (2016). *Temple Grandin, Ph.D.* Retrieved March 13, 2016, from http://www.templegrandin.com/

Gross, L. (2009). A broken trust: Lessons from the vaccine-autism wars. *Plos Biology, 7*(5), 1–7.

Guthrie, R. V. (2004). *Even the rat was white: A historical view of psychology* (2nd ed.). Pearson Education.

Ingersoll, B., Dvortcsak, A., Whalen, C., & Sikora, D. (2005). The effects of a developmental, social-pragmatic language intervention on rate of expressive language production in young children with autistic spectrum disorders. *Focus on Autism and Other Developmental Disabilities, 20,* 213–222.

Jacobvitz, D., Sroufe, L. A., Stewart, M., & Leffert, N. (1990). Treatment of attention and hyperactivity problems in children with sympathomimetic drugs: A comprehensive review. *Journal of the American Academy of Child & Adolescent Psychiatry, 29*(5), 677–688.

Kishnani, P. S., Sommer, B. R., Handen, B. L., Seltzer, B., Capone, G. T., Spiridigliozzi, G. A., Heller, J. H., Richardson, S., & McRae, T. (2009). The efficacy, safety, and tolerability of donepezil for the treatment of young adults with Down syndrome. *American Journal of Medical Genetics. Part A, 149A*(8), 1641–1654.

Lilienfeld, S. O. (1994). *Seeing both sides: Classic controversies in abnormal psychology.* Wadsworth Publishing.

Lord, C., Rutter, M., DiLavore, P. C., Risi, S., Gotham, K., & Bishop, S. (2012). *Autism diagnostic observation schedule* (2nd ed.). Western Psychological Services.

Lubs, H. A., Stevenson, R. E., & Schwartz, C. E. (2012). Fragile X and X-linked intellectual disability: Four decades of discovery. *American Journal of Human Genetics, 90*(4), 579–590.

Lunsky, Y., Raina, P., & Burge, P. (2012). Suicidality among adults with intellectual disability. *Journal of Affective Disorders, 140*(3), 292–295.

McGough, J. J., & Barkley, R. A. (2004). Diagnostic controversies in adult attention deficit hyperactivity disorder. *American Journal of Psychiatry, 161*(11), 1948–1956.

Mckenzie, K., Smith, M., & Purcell, A. (2013). The reported expression of pain and distress by people with an intellectual disability. *Journal of Clinical Nursing, 22*(13/14), 1833–1842.

Miller, L., & Reynolds, J. (2009). Autism and vaccination—The current evidence. *Journal for Specialists in Pediatric Nursing, 14*(3), 166–172.

Monastra, V. J. (2002). The effects of stimulant therapy, EEG biofeedback, and parenting style on the primary symptoms of Attention-Deficit/Hyperactivity Disorder. *Applied Psychophysiology & Biofeedback, 27*(4), 231–249.

Monastra, V. J., Lubar, J. F., & Linden, M. (2001). The development of a quantitative electroencephalographic scanning process for attention deficit–hyperactivity disorder: Reliability and validity studies. *Neuropsychology, 15*(1), 136–144.

Monastra, V. J., Monastra, D. M., & George, S. (2002). The effects of stimulant therapy, EEG biofeedback, and parenting style on the primary symptoms of attention-deficit/hyperactivity disorder. *Appl Psychophysiol Biofeedback, 27*(4):231–249. https://doi.org/10.1023/A:1021018700609

Murphy, B. P. (2010). Beyond the first episode: Candidate factors for a risk prediction model of schizophrenia. *International review of psychiatry, 22*(2), 202–223. doi:10.3109/09540261003661833

Pandolfo, P., Machado, N. J., Köfalvi, A., Takahashi, R. N., & Cunha, R. A. (2013). Caffeine regulates frontocorticostriatal dopamine transporter density and improves attention and cognitive deficits in an animal model of attention deficit hyperactivity disorder. *European Neuropsychopharmacology, 23*(4), 317–328.

Pelham, W. E. J., Fabiano, G. A., & Massetti, G. M. (2005). Evidence-based assessment of attention deficit hyperactivity disorder in children and adolescents. *Journal of Clinical Child and Adolescent Psychology, 34*(3), 449–476.

Peterson, L., Reach, K., & Grabe, S. (2003). Health-related disorders. In E. J. Mash & R. A. Barkley (Eds). *Child Psychopathology* (2nd ed., pp. 716–749). The Guilford Press.

Reynolds, C. R., & Kamphaus, R. W. (1994). Behavior assessment system for children. *Journal of School Psychology, 32*, 419–425.

Root, R. W. I., & Resnick, R. J. (2003). An update on the diagnosis and treatment of attention-deficit/hyperactivity disorder in children. *Professional Psychology: Research and Practice, 34*, 34–41.

Scott, B. S., Atkinson, L., & Minton, H. L. (1997). Psychological distress of parents of infants with Down syndrome. *American Journal on Mental Retardation, 102*, 161–171.

Smith, T. (2011). Applied behavior analysis and early intensive intervention. In D. G. Amaral, G. Dawson, & D. H. Geschwind (Eds.), *Autism spectrum disorders* (pp. 1037–1055). Oxford University Press.

Smith, T., & Iadarola, S. (2015). Evidence base update for autism spectrum disorder. *Journal of Clinical Child and Adolescent Psychology, 44*(6), 897–922.

Stehr-Green, P., Tull, P., Stellfeld, M., Mortenson, P., & Simpson, D. (2003). Autism and thimerosal-containing vaccines: Lack of consistent evidence for an association. *American Journal of Preventive Medicine, 25*, 101.

Talwar, V., Zwaigenbaum, L., Goulden, K. J., Manji, S., Loomes, C., & Rasmussen, C. (2012). Lie-telling behavior in children with autism and its relation to false-belief understanding. *Focus On Autism & Other Developmental Disabilities, 27*(2), 122–129.

Torres, L. I., Dharamraj, R. H., Kelley, L. J., & Curtis, D. A. (Accepted, 2020, April). Myths of autism. Research presentation to be presented at the Southwestern Psychological Association Conference, Frisco, TX.

Verstraeten, D., Davis, R. L., DeStefano, F., Lieu, T. A., Rhodes, P. H., Black, S B., Shinefield, H., Chen, R. T. (2003). Safety of thimerosal-containing vaccines: A two-phased study of computerized health maintenance organization databases. *Pediatrics, 112,* 1039–1048.

Vogel, W., Young, M., & Primack, W. (1996). A survey of physician use of treatment methods for functional enuresis. *Journal of Developmental and Behavioral Pediatrics, 17*(2), 90–93.

Waterfield, J. (2009). Prescribing for incontinence and nocturnal enuresis. *Nurse Prescribing, 7*(11), 500–505.

White, E. (2014). Science, pseudoscience, and the frontline practitioner: The vaccination/autism debate. *Journal of Evidence-Based Social Work, 11*(3), 269–274.

Chapter 6

Alanen, Y. O. (2018). *Schizophrenia: Its origins and need-adapted treatment.* Routledge.

American Psychiatric Association. (1952). *Diagnostic and statistical manual of mental disorders.* American Psychiatric Association.

American Psychiatric Association. (2013). *Diagnostic and statistical manual of mental disorders* (5th ed.). American Psychiatric Association.

Arendt, M., Rosenberg, R., Foldager, L., Perto, G., & Munk-Jørgensen, P. (2005). Cannabis-induced psychosis and subsequent schizophrenia-spectrum disorders: Follow-up study of 535 incident cases. *The British Journal of Psychiatry: The Journal of Mental Science, 187,* 510–515.

Bechi, M., Bosia, M., Buonocore, M., Agostoni, G., Bosinelli, F., Silvestri, M. P., Bianchi, L., Cocchi, F., Guglielmino, C., Spangaro, M., & Cavallaro, R. (2019). Stability and generalization of combined theory of mind and cognitive remediation interventions in schizophrenia: Follow-up results. *Psychiatric Rehabilitation Journal.* https://doi.org/10.1037/prj0000379

Bjarkam, C. R., Corydon, T. J., Olsen, I. L., Pallesen, J., Nyegaard, M., Fryland, T., Mors, O., & Børglum, A. D. (2009). Further immunohistochemical characterization of BRD1 a new susceptibility gene for schizophrenia and bipolar affective disorder. *Brain Structure & Function, 214*(1), 37–47. doi:10.1007/s00429-009-0219-3

Bradley, A. J., & Dinan, T. G. (2010). A systematic review of hypothalamic-pituitary-adrenal axis function in schizophrenia: Implications for mortality. *Journal of Psychopharmacology (Oxford, England), 24*(4 Suppl), 91–118. doi:10.1177/1359786810385491

Bushe, C. J., Taylor, M., & Haukka, J. (2010). Mortality in schizophrenia: A measurable clinical endpoint. *Journal of Psychopharmacology (Oxford, England), 24*(4 Suppl), 17–25. doi:10.1177/1359786810382468

Cannon, M., Jones, P. B., & Murray, R. M. (2002). Obstetric complications and schizophrenia: Historical and meta-analytic review. *The American Journal of Psychiatry, 159*(7), 1080–1092.

Cronenwett, W. J., & Csernansky, J. (2010). Thalamic pathology in schizophrenia. *Current Topics in Behavioral Neurosciences, 4,* 509–528.

Debnath, M., Cannon, D. M., & Venkatasubramanian, G. (2013). Variation in the major histocompatibility complex [MHC] gene family in schizophrenia: Associations and functional implications. Progress in *Neuro-Psychopharmacology & Biological Psychiatry, 42*, 49–62. https://doi.org/10.1016/j.pnpbp.2012.07.009

Evans, K., McGrath, J., & Milns, R. (2003). Searching for schizophrenia in ancient Greek and Roman literature: A systematic review. *Acta Psychiatrica Scandinavica, 107*(5), 323–330.

Folsom, D., & Jeste, D. V. (2002). Schizophrenia in homeless persons: A systematic review of the literature. *Acta Psychiatrica Scandinavica, 105*(6), 404–413.

Gottesman, I. I. (1991). *Schizophrenia genesis: The origins of madness*. W. H. Freeman.

Heinrichs, R. W. (2003). Historical origins of schizophrenia: Two early madmen and their illness. *Journal of the History of the Behavioral Sciences, 39*(4), 349–363.

Hess, J. L., Tylee, D. S., Mattheisen, M., Børglum, A. D., Als, T. D., Grove, J., Werge, T., Mortensen, P. B., Mors, O., Nordentoft, M., Hougaard, D. M., Byberg-Grauholm, J., Bækvad-Hansen, M., Greenwood, T. A., Tsuang, M. T., Curtis, D., Steinberg, S., Sigurdsson, E., Stefánsson, H., … Glatt, S. J. (2019). A polygenic resilience score moderates the genetic risk for schizophrenia. *Molecular Psychiatry*. https://doi.org /10.1038/s41380-019-0463-8

Hoang, U., Stewart, R., & Goldacre, M. J. (2011). Mortality after hospital discharge for people with schizophrenia or bipolar disorder: Retrospective study of linked English hospital episode statistics, 1999–2006. *BMJ (Clinical Research Ed.), 343*, 5422. doi:10.1136/bmj.d5422

Jablensky, A. (2000). Epidemiology of schizophrenia: The global burden of disease and disability. *European Archives of Psychiatry & Clinical Neuroscience, 250*(6), 274.

Jablensky, A. (2010). The diagnostic concept of schizophrenia: Its history, evolution, and future prospects. *Dialogues in Clinical Neuroscience, 12*(3), 271–287.

Javitt, D. C., & Coyle, J. T. (2004). Decoding schizophrenia. *Scientific American, 290*(1), 48–55.

Jeste, D. V., del Carmen, R., Lohr, J. B., & Wyatt, R. J. (1985). Did schizophrenia exist before the eighteenth century? *Comprehensive Psychiatry, 26*(6), 493–503.

Karlsgodt, K. H., Sun, D., & Cannon, T. D. (2010). Structural and functional brain abnormalities in schizophrenia. *Current Directions in Psychological Science, 19*(4), 226–231.

Klonsky, E. D. (2013). Schizophrenia and other severe illnesses. http://www.div12.org/psychological-treatments/disorders/

Lichtenstein, P., Yip, B. H., Björk, C., Pawitan, Y., Cannon, T. D., Sullivan, P. F., & Hultman, C. M. (2009). Common genetic determinants of schizophrenia and bipolar disorder in Swedish families: A population-based study. *Lancet, 373*, 234–239. doi:10.1016/S0140-6736(09)60072-6

Lindberg, R., & Curtis, D. A. (2018, April). *Myths in schizophrenia*. Poster presented at the 64th Annual Southwestern Psychological Association Conference, Houston, TX.

Mäki, P., Veijola, J., Jones, P. B., Murray, G. K., Koponen, H., Tienari, P., & Isohanni, M. (2005). Predictors of schizophrenia—A review. *British Medical Bulletin, 73-741-15*.

Mamah, D., Wang, L., Barch, D., de Erausquin, G. A., Gado, M., & Csernansky, J. G. (2007). Structural analysis of the basal ganglia in schizophrenia. *Schizophrenia Research, 89*(1–3), 59–71.

McCarthy-Jones, S., Smailes, D., Corvin, A., Gill, M., Morris, D. W., Dinan, T. G., Murphy, K. C., Anthony O. N. F., Waddington, J. L., Donohoe, G., & Dudley, R. (2017). Occurrence and co-occurrence of hallucinations by modality in schizophrenia-spectrum disorders. *Psychiatry Research, 252,* 154–160. https://doi.org/10.1016/j.psychres.2017.01.102

Murphy, B. P. (2010). Beyond the first episode: Candidate factors for a risk prediction model of schizophrenia. *International Review of Psychiatry, 22*(2), 202–223.

Perrin, M. C., Opler, M. G., Harlap, S., Harkavy-Friedman, J., Kleinhaus, K., Nahon, D., Fennig, S., Susser, E. S., & Malaspina, D. (2007). Tetrachloroethylene exposure and risk of schizophrenia: Offspring of dry cleaners in a population birth cohort, preliminary findings. *Schizophrenia Research, 90*(1–3), 251–254.

Petronis, A., Gottesman, I. I., Kan, P., Kennedy, J. L., Basile, V. S., Paterson, A. D., & Popendikyte, V. (2003). Monozygotic twins exhibit numerous epigenetic differences: Clues to twin discordance? *Schizophrenia Bulletin, 29*(1), 169–178.

Prossin, A. R., McInnis, M. G., Anand, A., Heitzeg, A. H., & Zubieta, J. (2010). Tackling the Kraepelinian dichotomy: A neuroimaging review. *Psychiatric Annuls, 40*(3), 154–159.

Rector, N. A., & Beck, A. T. (2001). Cognitive Behavioral Therapy for schizophrenia: An empirical review. *The Journal of Nervous and Mental Disease, 189*(5), 278–287.

Sekar, A., Bialas, A., de Rivera, H. et al. (2016). Schizophrenia risk from complex variation of complement component 4. *Nature. 530,* 177–183. https://doi.org/10.1038/nature16549

Sommer, I. C., Diederen, K. J., Blom, J., Willems, A., Kushan, L., Slotema, K., & ... Kahn, R. S. (2008). Auditory verbal hallucinations predominantly activate the right inferior frontal area. *Brain: A Journal of Neurology, 131*(12), 3169–3177. doi:10.1093/brain/awn251

Stahl, S. M. (2011). *Stahl's essential psychopharmacology: Neuroscientific basis and practical applications* (3rd ed.). Cambridge University Press.

Valenstein, E. S. (2010). *Great and desperate cures: The rise and decline of psychosurgery and other radical treatments for mental illness.* Basic Books.

Wang, J., Jiang, Y., Tang, Y., Xia, M., Curtin, A., Li, J., Sheng, J., Zhang, T., Li, C., Hui, L., Zhu, H., Biswal, B. B., Jia, Q., Luo, C., & Wang, J. (2020). Altered functional connectivity of the thalamus induced by modified electroconvulsive therapy for schizophrenia. *Schizophrenia Research.* https://doi.org /10.1016/j.schres.2019.12.044

Waters, F., Collerton, D., Ffytche, D. H., Jardri, R., Pins, D., Dudley, R., Blom, J. D., Mosimann, U. P., Eperjesi, F., Ford, S., & Larøi, F. (2014). Visual hallucinations in the psychosis spectrum and comparative information from neurodegenerative disorders and eye disease. *Schizophrenia Bulletin, 40 Suppl 4, S233–S245.* doi:10.1093/schbul/sbu036

Weinmann, S., Read, J., & Aderhold, V. (2009). Influence of antipsychotics on mortality in schizophrenia: Systematic review. *Schizophrenia Research, 113*(1), 1–11. doi:10.1016/j.schres.2009.05.018

Yoon, J. H., Minzenberg, M. J., Raouf, S., D'Esposito, M., & Carter, C. S. (2013). Impaired prefrontal-basal ganglia functional connectivity and substantia nigra hyperactivity in schizophrenia. *Biological Psychiatry, 74*(2), 122–129. doi:10.1016/j.biopsych.2012.11.018

Chapter 7

Abramson, L. Y., Metalsky, G. I., & Lauren B. A. (1989). Hopeless depression: A theory-based subtype of depression. *Psychological Review, 96*(2), 352–372.

American Psychiatric Association. (2013). *Diagnostic and statistical manual of mental disorders* (5th ed.). American Psychiatric Association.

Beck, A. T., Rush, A. J., Shaw, B. F., & Emery, G. (1979). *Cognitive therapy of depression.* Guilford Press.

Beck, J. S. (2011). *Cognitive Behavior Therapy: Basics and beyond* (2nd ed.). Guilford.

Beitman, B. D., & Saveanu, R. V. (2005). Integrating pharmacotherapy and psychotherapy. In J. C. Norcross, & M. R. Goldfried (Eds.), *Handbook of Psychotherapy Integration* (2nd ed., pp. 417–436). Oxford.

Canetto, S. S. (2015). Suicide: Why are older men so vulnerable? *Men and Masculinities, 20*(1), 49–70. https://doi.org /10.1177/1097184X15613832

Cerullo, M. A., Adler, C. M., Delbello, M. P., & Strakowski, S. M. (2009). The functional neuroanatomy of bipolar disorder. *International Review of Psychiatry, 21*(4), 314–322. https://doi.org /10.1080/09540260902962107

de Maat, S. M., Dekker, J., Schoevers, R. A., & de Jonghe, F. (2007). Relative efficacy of psychotherapy and combined therapy in the treatment of depression: A meta-analysis. *Journal of European Psychiatry, 22*(1), 1–8.

Elkin, I., Shea, M. T., Watkins, J. T., Imber, S. D., Sotsky, S. M., Collins, J. F., Glass, D. R., Pilkonis, P. A., Leber, W. R., Docherty, J. P., Fiester, S. J. & Parloff, M. B. (1989). National Institute of Mental Health Treatment of Depression Collaborative Research Program: General effectiveness of treatments. *Arch Gen Psychiatry, 46,* 971–982.

Elliot, R., Watson, J. C., Goldman, R. N., & Greenberg, L. S. (2004). *Learning emotion-focused therapy: The process-experiential approach to change.* American Psychological Association.

Fink, M. (2001). Convulsive therapy: A review of the first 55 years. *Journal of Affective Disorders, 63,* 1–15.

Freeman, A., Mergl, R., Kohls, E., Székely, A., Gusmao, R., Arensman, E., Koburger, N., Hegerl, U., & Rummel-Kluge, C. (2017). A cross-national study on gender differences in suicide intent. *BMC Psychiatry, 17.*

Gieselman, H., & Curtis, D. A. (2018, April). *Myths in depression.* Poster presented at the 64th Annual Southwestern Psychological Association Conference, Houston, TX.

Goldstein, W. N., & Anthony, R. N. (1988). The diagnosis of depression and the DSMs. *American Journal of Psychotherapy, 62*(2), 180–196.

Green, S., Lambon Ralph, M. A., Moll, J., Deakin, J. F. W., Zahn, R. (2012). Guilt-selective functional disconnection of anterior temporal and subgenual cortices in major depressive disorder. *Archive of General Psychiatry.* doi:10.1001/archgenpsychiatry.2012.135

Hammad, T. A., Laughren, T., & Racoosin, J. (2006). Suicidality in pediatric patients treated with antidepressant drugs. *Archive of General Psychiatry, 63*(3), 332–339.

Harris, J. E., Kelley, L. J., Shepard, L. M. (2015). Multitheoretical psychotherapy for depression: Integrating strategies from evidence-based practices. *Journal of Psychotherapy Integration, 25*(4), 353–367.

Henry, M. E., Schmidt, M. E., Matochik, J. A., Stoddard, E. P., & Potter, W. Z. (2001). The effects of ECT on brain glucose: A pilot FDG PET study. *Journal of ECT, 17,* 33–40.

Horwitz, A. V. (2010). How an age of anxiety became an age of depression. *The Milbank Quarterly, 88*(1), 112–138.

Johnson, D. P., & Whisman, M. A. (2013). Gender differences in rumination: A meta-analysis. *Personality and Individual Differences, 55*(4), 367–374. https://doi.org/10.1016/j.paid.2013.03.019

Johnson, S. L., & Fulford, D. (2013). Bipolar Disorder. http://www.div12.org/psychological-treatments/disorders/

Kelley, L. J., Kuncaitis, A. J., & Curtis, D. A. (2020). *Myths of Suicide.* Unpublished manuscript.

Klein, M. (1994). Mourning and its relation to manic-depressive states. In R. V. Frankiel (Ed.), *Essential papers on object loss* (pp. 95–122). New York University Press.

Kraepelin, E. (1921). *Manic-Depressive insanity and paranoia.* R. M. Barclay (trans.). E & S Livingstone. https://archive.org/stream/manicdepressivei00kraeuoft#page/n3/mode/2up

Lam, D., Jones, S. H., & Hayward, P. (1999). *Cognitive therapy for bipolar disorder: A therapist's guide to concepts, methods and practice.* John Wiley & Sons.

Levenson, H. (2010). *Brief dynamic therapy.* American Psychological Association.

Lewis, A. J. (1938). States of depression: Their clinical and aetiological differentiation. *British Medical Journal, 2,* 875–878.

Loughlin, S. (2005). Tristitia et dolor: Does Aquinas have a robust understanding of depression? *Nova et Vetera, 3,* 761–783.

Man, V., Gruber, J., Glahn, D. C., & Cunningham, W. A. (2019). Altered amygdala circuits underlying valence processing among manic and depressed phases in bipolar adults. *Journal of Affective Disorders, 245,* 394–402. https://doi.org /10.1016/j.jad.2018.11.008

Martell, C. R., Dimidjian, S., & Herman-Dunn, R. (2010). *Behavioral activation for depression: A clinician's guide.* Guilford.

Mayberg, H. S., Lozano, A. M., Voon, V., McNeely, H. E., Seminowicz, D., Hamani, C., Schwalb, J. M., & Kennedy, S. H. (2005). Deep-brain stimulation for treatment-resistant depression. *Neuron, 45,* 651–660.

McIntyre, C. C., Savasta, M., Goff, L. K., & Vitek, J. L. (2004). Uncovering the mechanism(s) of action of deep brain stimulation: Activation, inhibition, or both. *Clinical Neurophysiology, 115,* 1239–1248.

Merikangas, K. R., Jin, R., He, J. P., Kessler, R. C., Lee, S., Sampson, N. A., Viana, M. C., Andrade, L. H., Hu, C., Karam, E. G., Ladea, M., Medina-Mora, M. E., Ono, Y., Posada-Villa, J., Sagar, R., Wells, J. E., & Zarkov, Z. (2011). Prevalence and correlates of bipolar spectrum disorder in the World Mental Health Survey Initiative. *Archives of General Psychiatry, 68*(3), 241–251.

Miller, M., Swanson, S. A., Azrael, D., Pate, V., Sturmer, T. (2014). Antidepressant dose, age, and the risk of deliberate self-harm. *JAMA Internal Medicine, 174*(6), 899–909.

National Association of School Psychologists. (2017). 13 Reasons Why Netflix series: Considerations for educators [handout]. Author.

Nock, M. K., Borges, G., Bromet, E. J., Alonso, J., Angermeyer, M., Beautrais, A., Bruffaerts, R., Chiu, W. T., Girolamo, G., Gluzman, S., de Graaf, R., Gureje, O., Haro, J. M., Huang, Y., Karam, E., Kessler, R. C., Lepine, J. P., Levinson, D., Medina-Mora, M. E., Ono, Y., Posada-Villa, J., & Williams, D. R. (2008). Cross-national prevalence and risk factors for suicidal ideation, plans and attempts. British *Journal of Psychiatry, 192,* 98–105.

Nolen-Hoeksema, S. (2014). *Abnormal psychology* (6th ed.). McGraw-Hill.

Nolen-Hoeksema, S., Wisco, B. E., & Lyubomirsky, S. (2008). Rethinking rumination. *Perspectives on Psychological Science, 3*(5), 400–424. https://doi.org/10.1111/j.1745-6924.2008.00088.x

Otto, M. W., Smits, J. A., & Reese, H. E. (2006). Combined psychotherapy and pharmacotherapy for mood and anxiety disorders in adults: Review and analysis. *Clinical Psychology: Science and Practice, 12*(1), 72–86.

Pascual-Leone, A., & Greenberg, L. S. (2007). Emotional processing in experiential therapy: Why "the only way out is through." *Journal of Consulting and Clinical Psychology, 75*(6), 875–878.

Pies, R. (2007). The historical roots of the "bipolar spectrum": Did Aristotle anticipate Kraepelin's broad concept of manic-depression? *Journal of Affective Disorders, 100*, 7–11. doi:10.1016/j.jad.2006.08.034

Rich, B. A., Schmajuk, M., Perez-Edgar, K. E., Fox, N. A., Pine, D. S., & Leibenluft, E. (2007). Different psychophysiological and behavioral responses elicited by frustration in pediatric bipolar disorder and severe mood dysregulation. *American Journal of Psychiatry, 164*, 309–317.

Robertson, M., Rushton, P., & Wurm, C. (2008). Interpersonal psychotherapy: An overview. *Psychotherapy in Australia, 14*(3), 46–54.

Sackeim, H. A., Prudic, J., Fuller, R., Keilp, J., Lavori, P. W., & Olfson, M. (2007). The cognitive effects of electroconvulsive therapy in community settings. *Neuropsychopharmachology, 32*, 244–254.

Saveanu, R. V., & Nemeroff, C. B. (2012). Etiology of depression: Genetic and environmental factors. *Psychiatric Clinics of North America, 35*, 51–71.

Shea, M. T., Elkin, S. D., Imber, S. D., Sotsky, J. T., Watkins, J. F., Collins, P. A., Pilkonis, P. A., Beckham, E., Glass, D. R., Dolan R. T., et al. (1992). Course of depressive symptoms over follow-up: Findings from the National Institute of Mental Health Treatment of Depression Collaborative Research Program. Archives of General Psychiatry, 49, 782–787.

Slotema, C. W., Blom, J. D., Hoek, H. W., & Sommer, I. E. (2010). Should we expand the toolbox of psychiatric treatment methods to include repetitive transcranial magnetic stimulation (rTMS)? A meta-analysis of the efficacy of rTMS in psychiatric disorders. *Journal of Clinical Psychiatry, 71*, 873–884.

Southwick, S. M., Vythilingam, M., & Charney, D. S. (2005). The psychobiology of depression and resilience to stress: Implications for prevention and treatment. *Annual Review of Clinical Psychology, 1*, 255–292.

Stahl, S. M. (2011). *Stahl's essential psychopharmacology: Neuroscientific basis and practical applications* (3rd ed.). Cambridge University Press.

Strunk, D. (2013). Depression. http://www.div12.org/psychological-treatments/disorders/

Waters, R. (2004). A suicide side effect? What parents aren't being told about their kids' antidepressants. *San Francisco Gate.* http://www.sfgate.com/magazine/article/A-Suicide-Side-Effect-What-parents-aren-t-2817437.php

Watson, J., Gordon, L., Stermac, L., Kalogerakos, F., & Steckley, P. (2003). Comparing the effectiveness of process-experiential with cognitive-behavioral psychotherapy in the treatment of depression. *Journal of Consulting and Clinical Psychology, 71*(4), 773–781. doi:10.1037/0022-006X.71.4.773

Wedding, D., & Niemiec, R. M. (2014). *Movies and mental illness: Using films to understand psychopathology* (4th ed.). Hogrefe Publishing.

Chapter 8

American Psychiatric Association. (2000). *Diagnostic and statistical manual of mental disorders* (4th ed., text revision). American Psychiatric Association.

American Psychiatric Association. (2013). *Diagnostic and statistical manual of mental disorders* (5th ed.). American Psychiatric Association.

APA Presidential Task Force on Evidence-Based Practice. (2006). Evidence-based practice in psychology. *American Psychologist, 61,* 271–285.

Beck, J. S. (2011). *Cognitive behavior therapy, basics and beyond* (2nd ed.). The Guilford Press.

Crerand, C. E., & Sarwer, D. B. (2010). Cosmetic treatments and body dysmorphic disorder. *Psychiatric Annals, 40*(7), 344–348.

Division 12 of the American Psychological Association. (2013). Psychological disorders and behavioral problems. http://www.div12.org/psychological-treatments/disorders/

Dobson, K. S. (1985). The relationship between anxiety and depression. *Clinical Psychology Review, 5,* 307–324.

Dwyer, K. K., & Davidson, M. M. (2012). Is public speaking really more feared than death? *Communication Research Reports, 29,* 99–107.

Hajcak, G. (2013). Panic disorder. *In Society of Clinical Psychology, Research-Supported Psychological Treatments.* http://www.div12.org/psychological-treatments/disorders/panic-disorder/

Hamilton, M. (1988). Distinguishing between anxiety and depressive disorders. In S. O. Lilienfeld (Ed.), *Seeing both sides: Classic controversies in abnormal psychology* (pp. 119–127). Wadsworth Publishing.

Harman, J. S., Veazie, P. J., & Lyness, J. M. (2006). Primary care physician office visits for depression by older Americans. *Journal of General Internal Medicine, 21*(9), 926–930.

Hayes, S. C., Follette, V. M., & Linehan, M. M. (2004). *Mindfulness and acceptance: Expanding the cognitive-behavioral tradition.* Guilford Press.

Hayes, S. C., Wilson, K. G., Gifford, E. V., Follette, V. M., & Strosahl, K. (1996). Experiential avoidance and behavioral disorders: A functional dimensional approach to diagnosis and treatment. *Journal of Consulting and Clinical Psychology, 64,* 1152–1168. doi:10.1037/0022-006X.64.6.1152

Johnson, D. P., & Whisman, M. A. (2013). Gender differences in rumination: A meta-analysis. *Personality and Individual Differences, 55,* 367–374.

Kessler, R. C., Chiu, W. T., Demler, O., & Walters, E. E. (2005). Prevalence, severity, and comorbidity of twelve-month DSM-IV disorders in the National Comorbidity Survey Replication (NCS-R). *Archives of General Psychiatry, 62,* 617–627.

Klonsky, E. D., Hajcak, G., & Starr, L. (2013). Obsessive-compulsive disorder. *In Society of Clinical Psychology, research-supported psychological treatments.* http://www.div12.org/psychological-treatments/disorders/obsessive-compulsive-disorder/

Lilienfeld, S. O. (1994). *Seeing both sides: Classic controversies in abnormal psychology.* Wadsworth Publishing.

Nolen-Hoeksema, S. (2000). The role of rumination in depressive disorders and mixed anxiety/depressive symptoms. *Journal of Abnormal Psychology, 109,* 504–511.

Quintero, M. (2016, December). 'Phone Home' Phobia. http://www.myfoxzone.com/features/phone-home-phobia/361206235

Rostand, E., & Bair, L. (1972). *Cyrano de Bergerac; heroic comedy in five acts.* New American Library.

Schatzberg, A. F. (2015). Development of new psychopharmacological agents for depression and anxiety. *Psychiatric Clinics of North America, 38,* 379–393.

Teachman, B. A. (2013). Cognitive and behavioral therapies for generalized anxiety disorder. *In Society of Clinical Psychology, research-supported psychological treatments.* http://www.psychologicaltreatments.org

Veale, D., Gournay, K., Dryden, W., Boocock, A., Shah, F., Willson, R., & Walburn, J. (1996). Body dysmorphic disorder: A cognitive behavioural model and pilot randomised controlled trial. *Behaviour Research and Therapy, 34*(9), 717–279.

Veale, D., & Riley, S. (2001). Mirror, mirror on the wall, who is the ugliest of them all? The psychopathology of mirror gazing in body dysmorphic disorder. *Behaviour Research and Therapy, 39*(12), 1381–1393.

Watson, J. B., & Rayner, R. (1920). Conditioned emotional reactions. *Journal of Experimental Psychology, 3*(1), 1–14.

Wedding, D., & Niemiec, R. M. (2014). *Movies and mental illness: Using films to understand psychopathology* (4th ed.). Hogrefe Publishing.

Westphal, C. O., & Schumacher, M. T. (1988). *Westphal's 'Die agoraphobie' with commentary: The beginnings of agoraphobia.* University Press of America.

Wittchen, H., & Fehm, L. (2003). Epidemiology and natural course of social fears and social phobia. *Acta Psychiatrica Scandinavica. Supplementum,* 1084.

Yerkes, R. M., & Dodson, J. D. (1908). The relation of strength of stimulus to rapidity of habit-formation. *Journal of Comparative Neurology & Psychology, 18*(5), 459. doi:10.1002/cne.920180503

Chapter 9

American Congress of Obstetricians and Gynecologists. (2016). http://www.acog.org/About-ACOG/News-Room/News-Releases/2009/ACOG-Issues-New-Guidelines-on-Managing-Stillbirths

American Psychiatric Association. (2013). *Diagnostic and statistical manual of mental disorders* (5th ed.). American Psychiatric Association.

American Psychological Association. (2015). *Guidelines on Trauma Competencies for Education and Training.* http://www.apa.org/ed/resources/trauma-competencies-training.pdf

Andreasen, N. C. (1985). Posttraumatic Stress Disorder. In H. I. Kaplan & B. J. Sadock (Eds.), *Comprehensive Textbook of Psychiatry* (pp. 918–924).

Blashfield, R. K., & Burgess, D. R. (2007). Classification provides an essential basis for organizing mental disorders. In S. O. Lilienfeld, W. T. O'Donohue, S. O. Lilienfeld, W. T. O'Donohue (Eds.), *The great ideas of clinical science: 17 principles that every mental health professional should understand* (pp. 93–117). Routledge/Taylor & Francis Group.

Born, L., Soares, C. N., Phillips, S., Jung, M., & Steiner, M. (2006). Women and reproductive-related trauma. *Annals of the New York Academy of Sciences, 1071,* 491–494.

Brand, B. L., Loewenstein, R. J., & Spiegel, D. (2014). Dispelling myths about dissociative identity disorder treatment: An empirically based approach. *Psychiatry: Interpersonal & Biological Processes, 77*(2), 169–189.

Briere, J., & Scott, C. (2006). *Principles of trauma therapy: A guide to symptoms, evaluation, and treatment*. Sage Publications, Inc.

Bright, D. A. (1991). Stillbirth. *The Journal of Family Practice, 32*(3), 245–256.

Cacciatore, J. (2010). Stillbirth: Patient-centered psychosocial care. *Clinical Obstetrics and Gynecology, 53*(3), 691–699.

Cacciatore, J., Rådestad, I., & Frøen, F. (2008). Effects of contact with stillborn babies on maternal anxiety and depression. *Birth: Issues in Perinatal Care, 35*(4), 313–320.

Cacciatore, J., Schnebly, S., & Frøen, J. F. (2009). The effects of social support on maternal anxiety and depression after stillbirth. *Health & Social Care in the Community, 17*(2), 167–176.

Coleman, P. K. (2011). Abortion and mental health: Quantitative synthesis and analysis of research published 1995–2009. *The British Journal of Psychiatry, 199*(3), 180–186. doi:10.1192/bjp.bp.110.077230

Coleman, P. K., Coyle, C. T., Shuping, M., & Rue, V. M. (2009). Induced abortion and anxiety, mood, and substance abuse disorders: Isolating the effects of abortion in the national comorbidity survey. *Journal of Psychiatric Research, 43*(8), 770–776. doi:10.1016/j.jpsychires.2008.10.009

Courtois, C. A., & Gold, S. N. (2009). The need for inclusion of psychological trauma in the professional curriculum: A call to action. *Psychological Trauma: Theory, Research, Practice, and Policy, 1*(1), 3–23.

Division 12 of the American Psychological Association. (2013). Psychological disorders and behavioral problems. http://www.div12.org/psychological-treatments/disorders/

Dorahy, M. J. (2001). Dissociative identity disorder and memory dysfunction: The current state of experimental research and its future directions. *Clinical Psychology Review, 21*(5), 771–795.

Hajcak, G., & Starr, L. (2013). Posttraumatic stress disorder. *In Society of Clinical Psychology, Research-supported psychological treatments.* http://www.div12.org/psychological-treatments/disorders/post-traumatic-stress-disorder/

Herman, J. L. (1997). *Trauma and recovery*. Basic Books.

Holmes, E. A., Brown, R. J., Mansell, W., Fearon, R. P., Hunter, E. M., Frasquilho, F., & Oakley, D. A. (2005). Are there two qualitatively distinct forms of dissociation? A review and some clinical implications. *Clinical Psychology Review, 25*(1), 1–23.

Hyler, S. E. (1988). DSM-III at the cinema: Madness in the movies. *Comprehensive Psychiatry, 29*, 195–206.

International Society for the Study of Trauma and Dissociation (ISSTD). (2011). Chu, J. A., Dell, P. F., Van der Hart, O., Cardeña, E., Barach, P. M., Somer, E., Loewenstein, R. J., Brand, B., Golston, J. C., Courtois, C. A., Bowman, E. S., Classen, C., Dorahy, M., Sar, V., Gelinas, D. J., Fine, C. G., Paulsen, S., Kluft, R. P., Dalenberg, C. J., . . . Twombly, J. Guidelines for treating dissociative identity disorder in adults, third revision. *Journal of Trauma & Dissociation, 12*, 115–187.

Jaffe, J., & Diamond, M. O. (2011). *Reproductive trauma: Psychotherapy with infertility and pregnancy loss clients*. American Psychological Association.

Lilienfeld, S. O. (1994). *Seeing both sides: Classic controversies in abnormal psychology*. Wadsworth Publishing.

Lilienfeld, S. O., & Arkowitz, H. (2011). Can people have multiple personalities? *Scientific American Mind, 22*(4), 64–65.

Loewenstein, R. J. (2005). Psychopharmacologic treatments for dissociative identity disorder. *Psychiatric Annals, 35*(8), 666–673.

MacIntosh, H. B. (2013). Dissociative identity disorder and the process of couple therapy. *Journal of Trauma & Dissociation, 14*(1), 84–96.

Major, B., Appelbaum, M., Beckman, L., Dutton, M., Russo, N., & West, C. (2009). Abortion and mental health: Evaluating the evidence. *American Psychologist, 64*(9), 863–890. doi:10.1037/a0017497

McCann, I. L., & Pearlman, L. A. (1990). Vicarious traumatization: A framework for understanding the psychological effects of working with victims. *Journal of Traumatic Stress, 3*(1), 131–149.

Merckelbach, H., Devilly, G. J., & Rassin, E. (2002). Alters in dissociative identity disorder. Metaphors or genuine entities? *Clinical Psychology Review, 22* 481–497.

Nathan, D. (2011). *Sybil exposed: The extraordinary story behind the famous multiple personality case.* Free Press.

Pearlman, L. A., & Mac Ian, P. S. (1995). Vicarious traumatization: An empirical study of the effects of trauma work on trauma therapists. *Professional Psychology: Research and Practice, 26*(6), 558–565.

Pearlman, L. A., & Saakvitne, K. W. (1995). Treating therapists with vicarious traumatization and secondary traumatic stress disorders. In C. R. Figley, C. R. Figley (Eds.), *Compassion fatigue: Coping with secondary traumatic stress disorder in those who treat the traumatized* (pp. 150–177). Brunner/Mazel.

Pollock, D. A., Rhodes, P., Boyle, C. A., Decoufle, P., & McGee, D. L. (1990). Estimating the number of suicides among Vietnam veterans. *The American Journal of Psychiatry, 147*(6), 772–776.

Purtle, J., Lynn, K., & Malik, M. (2016). "Calculating The Toll Of Trauma" in the headlines: Portrayals of posttraumatic stress disorder in the New York Times (1980–2015). *American Journal of Orthopsychiatry, 86*(6), 632–638.

Raison, C. L., & Miller, A. H. (2003). When not enough is too much: The role of insufficient glucocorticoid signaling in the pathophysiology of stress-related disorders. *American Journal of Psychiatry, 169*, 1554–1565.

Reinders, A. S., Willemsen, A. M., Vos, H. J., den Boer, J. A., & Nijenhuis, E. S. (2012). Fact or factitious? A psychobiological study of authentic and simulated dissociative identity states. *Plos ONE, 7*(6), 1–17.

Rind, B., Tromovitch, P., & Bauserman, R. (1998). A meta-analytic examination of assumed properties of child sexual abuse using college samples. *Psychological Bulletin, 124*(1), 22–53.

Schreiber, F. R. (1973). *Sybil.* Warner Books.

Schroeder, B. L., Curtis, D. A., & Kelley, L.J. (2019, April). *Movies, psychopathology, and psychomythology.* Poster presented at the 65th Annual Southwestern Psychological Association Conference, Albuquerque, NM.

Silver, R. M. (2007). Fetal death. *Obstetrics and Gynecology, 109*, 153–167.

Vasquez, M. T. (2012). Psychology and social justice: Why we do what we do. *American Psychologist, 67*(5), 337–346. doi:10.1037/a0029232

Waller, N., Putnam, F. W., & Carlson, E. B. (1996). Types of dissociation and dissociative types: A taxometric analysis of dissociative experiences. *Psychological Methods, 1*(3), 300–321.

Wedding, D., & Niemiec, R. M. (2014). *Movies and mental illness: Using films to understand psychopathology* (4th ed.). Hogrefe Publishing.

Woodward, J., Field, S., Davis, B., Babbin, J., Stern, S., & Petrie, D. (2006). *Sybil.* 1977.

Chapter 10

Allen, L. A., Woolfolk, R. L., Escobar, J. I., Gara, M. A., & Hamer, R. M. (2006). Cognitive-behavioral therapy for somatization disorder: A randomized controlled trial. *Archives of Internal Medicine, 166,* 1512–1518.

American Psychiatric Association (APA). (1980). *Diagnostic and Statistical Manual of Mental Disorders* (3rd ed.). American Psychiatric Association.

American Psychiatric Association (APA). (2013). *Diagnostic and statistical manual of mental disorders* (5th ed.). American Psychiatric Association.

Asher, R. (1951). Munchausen's syndrome. *Lancet, 1,* 339–341.

Bianchini, K., Etherton, J., Greve, K., Heinly, M., & Meyers, J. (2008). Classification accuracy of MMPI-2 validity scales in the detection of pain-related malingering: A known-groups study. *Assessment, 15*(4), 435–449.

Bond Jr., C. F., & DePaulo, B. M. (2006). Accuracy of deception judgments. *Personality & Social Psychology Review, 10,* 214–234. doi:10.1207/s15327957pspr1003_2

Boros, S. J., Ophoven, J. P., Andersen, R., & Brubaker, L. C. (1995). Munchausen syndrome by proxy: A profile for medical child abuse. *Australian Family Physician, 24*(5), 768.

Breuer, J., & Freud, S. (1957). *Studies on hysteria.* Basic Books, 1957.

Butcher, J. N., Dahlstrom, W. G., Graham, J. R., Tellegen, A., & Kaemmer, B. (2001). *The Minnesota Multiphasic Personality Inventory-2 (MMPI-2-revised): Manual for Administration and Scoring.* University of Minnesota Press.

Candiotti, S. (1999, October 7). Mother found guilty of child abuse, fraud for making daughter sick. *Cable News Network,* http://www.cnn.com/US/9910/07/munchausen.verdict/

DePaulo, B. M., & Bell, K. L. (1996). Truth and investment: Lies are told to those who care. *Journal of Personality and Social Psychology, 71,* 703–716. doi:10.1037/0022-3514.71.4.703

DePaulo, B. M., & Kashy, D. A. (1998). Everyday lies in close and casual relationships. *Journal of Personality and Social Psychology, 74,* 63–79. doi:10.1037/0022-3514.74.1.63

DePaulo, B. M., Kashy, D. A., Kirkendol, S. E., Wyer, M. M., & Epstein, J. A. (1996). Lying in everyday life. *Journal of Personality and Social Psychology, 70*(5): 979–995.

Ferrara, P., Vitelli, O., Bottaro, G., Gatto, A., Liberatore, P., Binetti, P., & Stabile, A. (2013). Factitious disorders and Münchausen syndrome: The tip of the iceberg. *Journal of Child Health Care, 17*(4), 366–374.

Freud, S. (1963). *Dora: An analysis of a case of hysteria.* Simon & Schuster, Inc.

Gilliam, T. (Director). (1988). *The adventures of Baron Munchausen* [Motion picture]. United Kingdom.

Greene, R. L. (2000). *The MMPI-2: An interpretive manual.* Allyn and Bacon.

Groth-Marnat, G. (2009). *Handbook of psychological assessment* (5th ed.). John Wiley & Sons, Inc.

Hagglund, L. A. (2009). Challenges in the treatment of factitious disorder: A case study. *Archives of Psychiatric Nursing, 23*(1), 58–64.

Higgins, L. (2015, April 8). Mom gets 20 years to life for poisoning son with salt. *USA Today.* http://www.usatoday.com/story/news/nation/2015/04/08/lacey-spears-to-be-sentenced-today-in-sons-death/25446521/

Jung, B., & Reidenberg, M. M. (2007). Physicians being deceived. *Pain Medicine, 8*(5), 433–437.

Kaplan, R. (2004). History O Anna: Being Bertha Pappenheim—Historiography and biography. *Australasian Psychiatry, 12*(1), 62–68.

Kashy, D. A., & DePaulo, B. M. (1996). Who lies? *Journal of Personality and Social Psychology, 70*, 1037–1051. doi:10.1037/0022-3514.70.5.1037

Komagamine, T., Kokubun, N., & Hirata, K. (2020). Battey's operation as a treatment for hysteria: A review of a series of cases in the nineteenth century. *History of Psychiatry, 31*(1), 55.

Lande, R. G., & Williams, L. B. (2013). Prevalence and characteristics of military malingering. *Military Medicine, 178*(1), 50–54.

Maines, R. P. (1998). *The technology of orgasm: Hysteria, the vibrator, and women's sexual satisfaction.* Johns Hopkins University Press.

McCoy, T. (2015, March 3). Why a woman murdered her son with salt. *The Washington Post.* https://www.washingtonpost.com/news/morning-mix/wp/2015/03/03/the-rare-disorder-experts-say-drove-lacey-spears-to-murder-her-son-with-salt/

McMahon, P. (2015, April 15). Years after case, Jennifer Bush says she wasn't a victim of Munchausen or abuse by her mom. *Sun Sentinel.* http://www.sun-sentinel.com/local/broward/fl-jennifer-bush-munchausen-20150415-story.html

Millon, T., Davis, R., Millon, C., & Grossman, S. (2009). *Millon Clinical Multiaxial Inventory-III manual* (3rd ed.). National Computer Systems.

Morrison, C. A. (1999). Cameras in hospital rooms: The Fourth Amendment to the Constitution and Munchausen syndrome by proxy. *Critical Care Nursing Quarterly, 22*(1), 65–68.

Oulis, P., Kokras, N., Papadimitriou, G. N., & Masdrakis, V. G. (2009). Adjunctive low-dose amisulpride in motor conversion disorder. *Clinical Neuropharmacology, 32*(6), 342–343.

Raspe, R. E. (2006). Surprising adventures of Baron Munchausen. In *Surprising adventures of Baron Munchausen.* Project Gutenberg Literary Archive Foundation.

Rogers, R., & Bender, S. D. (2018). *Clinical assessment of malingering and deception* (4th ed.) (R. Rogers & S. D. Bender, Eds.). The Guilford Press.

Serota, K. B., & Levine, T. R. (2015). A few prolific liars: Variation in the prevalence of lying. *Journal of Language and Social Psychology, 34*(2), 138–157.

Serota, K. B., Levine, T. R., & Boster, F. J. (2010). The prevalence of lying in America: Three studies of self-reported lies. *Human Communication Research, 36,* 2–25.

Somashekar, B., Jainer, A., & Wuntakal, B. (2013). Psychopharmacotherapy of somatic symptoms disorders. *International Review of Psychiatry, 25*(1), 107–115.

Speckens, A. E. M., Van Hemert, A. M., Spinhoven, P., Hawton, K. E., Bolk, J. H., & Rooijmans, H. M. (1995). Cognitive Behavioural Therapy for Medically Unexplained Physical Symptoms: A randomised controlled trial. *BMJ: British Medical Journal, 311,* 1328–1332.

Thompson, W. G. (2003). Factitious gastrointestinal symptoms and Münchausen syndrome. *Medicine, 31,* 115–118.

Thorne, M., & Henley, T. B. (2001). *Connections in the history and systems of psychology* (2nd ed.). Houghton Mifflin Company.

Turner, J., & Reid, S. (2002). Munchausen's syndrome. *Lancet, 359,* 346–349.

Uzuner, S., Bahali, K., Kurban, S., Erenberk, U., & Cakir, E. (2013). A pediatric case of factitious disorder with unexplained bleeding symptoms. *General Hospital Psychiatry, 35*(6), 679e7–679e8.

Vrij, A. (2000). *Detecting lies and deceit: The psychology of lying and the implications for professional practice.* John Wiley & Sons Ltd.

Wedding, D., & Niemiec, R. M. (2014). *Movies and mental illness: Using films to understand psychopathology* (4th ed.). Hogrefe Publishing.

Wiborg, J. F., Gieseler, D., Fabisch, A. B., Voigt, K., Lautenbach, A., & Löwe, B. (2013). Suicidality in primary care patients with somatoform disorders. *Psychosomatic Medicine, 75*(9), 800–806.

Woolfolk, R. L., & Allen, L. A. (2012). Cognitive behavioral therapy for somatoform disorders. In I. R. De Oliveira (Ed.), *Standard and innovative strategies in cognitive behavior therapy.* InTech. http://www.intechopen.com/books

Chapter 11

Abbate-Daga, G., Amianto, F., Delsedime, N., De-Bacco, C., & Fassino, S. (2013). Resistance to treatment and change in anorexia nervosa: A clinical overview. *BMC Psychiatry, 13*(1), 1–36.

AED Guidelines for Research-Practice Integration. (2016). AED Action Plan (www.aedweb.org). AED Data Network and Clinician Research Toolkit (www. aedweb.org).

American Psychiatric Association (APA). (2013). *Diagnostic and statistical manual of mental disorders* (5th ed.). American Psychiatric Association.

APA Presidential Task Force on Evidence-Based Practice. (2006). Evidence-based practice in psychology. *American Psychologist, 61,* 271–285.

Banker, J. D., & Klump, K. L. (2010). The research-practice gap: An enduring challenge for the eating disorders field. *Eating Disorders Review, 21,* 1.

Bemporad, J. R. (1996). Self-starvation through the ages: Reflections on the pre-history of anorexia nervosa. *International Journal of Eating Disorders, 19*(3), 217–237.

Bruch, H. (1973). *Eating disorders: Obesity, anorexia nervosa, and the person within.* Basic Books.

Chambless, D. L., Baker, M. J., Baucom, D. H., Beutler, L. E., Calhoun, K. S., Crits-Christoph, P., Daiuto, A., DeRubeis, R., Detweiler, J., Haaga, D. A. F., Bennett Johnson, S., McCurry, S., Mueser, K. T., Pope, K. S., Sanderson, W. C., Shoham, V., Stickle, T., Williams, D. A., & Woody, S. R. (1998). Update on empirically validated therapies, II. *The Clinical Psychologist, 51*(1), 3–16.

Coonley, T. D., & Ramsey, L. R. (2011). Killing us softly? Investigating portrayals of women and men in contemporary magazine advertisements. *Psychology of Women Quarterly, 35*(3), 469–478.

Farrell, C., Lee, M., & Shafran, R. (2005). Assessment of body size estimation: A review. *European Eating Disorders Review, 13*(2), 75–88.

Garner, D. M., & Bemis, K. M. (1985). Cognitive therapy for anorexia nervosa. In D. M. Garner & P. E. Garfinkel (Eds.), *Handbook of psychotherapy for anorexia nervosa & bulimia* (pp. 107–146). The Guilford Press.

Gonidakis, F., Kravvariti, V., & Varsou, E. (2015). Sexual function of women suffering from anorexia nervosa and bulimia nervosa. *Journal of Sex & Marital Therapy, 41*(4), 368–378.

Groesz, L. M., Levine, M. P., & Murnen, S. K. (2002). The effect of experimental presentation of Thin media images on body satisfaction: A meta-analytic review. *International Journal of Eating Disorders, 31*(1), 1–16.

Gull, W. W. (1874). Anorexia nervosa (apepsia hysterica, anorexia hysterica). *Transactions of the Clinical Society of London, 7*, 22–28.

Haas, H. L., & Clopton, J. R. (2003). Comparing clinical and research treatments for eating disorders. *International Journal of Eating Disorders, 33*(4), 412–420.

Harrison, K. (2000). The body electric: Thin-ideal media and eating disorders in adolescents. *Journal of Communication, 50*(3), 119.

Jhally, S., & Kilbourne, J. (2010). *Killing us softly 4: Advertising's image of women.* Media Education Foundation.

Klump, K. L., Bulik, C. M., Kaye, W. H., Treasure, J., & Tyson, E. (2009). Academy for eating disorders position paper: Eating disorders are serious mental illnesses. *International Journal of Eating Disorders, 42*, 97–103.

Lilienfeld, S. O. (2012) Bridging the gap between science and evidence-based practice. *Eating Disorders Review, 23*(4), 1.

Loeb, K. L. (2013). Eating Disorders and Obesity. Retrieved from http://www.div12.org/psychological-treatments/disorders/eating-disorders-and-obesity/

McDermott, C., & Rushford, N. (2011). Dysfunctional metacognitions in anorexia nervosa. *Eating and Weight Disorders, 16*(1), e49–e55.

Mills, M. (2007). Craving more than food: The implications of pica in pregnancy. *Nursing for Women's Health, 11*(3), 266–273.

National Institute for Health and Clinical Excellence (NICE). (2006). Nutrition support in adults oral nutrition support, enteral tube feeding and parenteral nutrition. National Collaborating Centre for Acute Care, London. Available from www.rcseng.ac.uk

Nelson, V. J. (2008, February 16). She explained her eating disorder on HBO's 'Thin.' http://articles.latimes.com/2008/feb/16/local/me-williams16

Olstad, S., Solem, S., Hjemdal, O., & Hagen, R. (2015). Metacognition in eating disorders: Comparison of women with eating disorders, self-reported history of eating disorders or psychiatric problems, and healthy controls. *Eating Behaviors, 16*, 17–22.

Peterson, C. B., Becker, C. B., Treasure, J., Shafran, R., & Bryant-Waugh, R. (2016). The three-legged stool of evidence-based practice in eating disorder treatment: Research, clinical, and patient perspectives. *BMC Medicine, 14*, 1–8.

Poulakou-Rebelakou, E., Tsiamis, C., & Ploumpidis, D. (2015). The first case of pagophagia: The Byzantine emperor Theophilus (829–842 AD). *Acta Medico-Historica Adriatica, 13*(1), 95–104.

Reese, E. D., Pollert, G. A., & Veilleux, J. C. (2016). Self-regulatory predictors of eating disorder symptoms: Understanding the contributions of action control and willpower beliefs. *Eating Behaviors, 20*, 64–69.

Schaefer, J., & Rutledge, T. (2004). *Life without Ed: How one woman declared independence from her eating disorder and how you can too.* McGraw-Hill.

Silverman, J. A. (1989). Louis-Victor Marcé, 1828–1864: Anorexia nervosa's forgotten man. *Psychological Medicine, 19*(4), 833–835.

Song, Y. J., Lee, J., & Jung, Y. (2015). Chewing and spitting out food as a compensatory behavior in patients with eating disorders. *Comprehensive Psychiatry, 62*, 147–151.

Spring, B. (2007). Evidence-based practice in clinical psychology: What it is, why it matters; what you need to know. *Journal of Clinical Psychology, 63*(7), 611–631.

Strother, E., Lemberg, R., Stanford, S. C., & Turberville, D. (2012). Eating disorders in men: Underdiagnosed, undertreated, and misunderstood. *Eating Disorders: The Journal of Treatment & Prevention, 20*(5), 346–355.

Thin [Documentary]. Greenfield, L. (Producer and Director). (2006). United States: Cinéma Vérité.

Tobin, D. L., Banker, J. D., Weisberg, L., & Bowers, W. (2007). I know what you did last summer (and it was not CBT): A factor analytic model of international psychotherapeutic practice in the eating disorders. *International Journal of Eating Disorders, 40*(8), 754–757.

Treasure, J., Claudino, A. M., & Zucker, N. (2010). Eating disorders. *The Lancet, 375*(9714), 583–593.

Wedding, D., & Niemiec, R. M. (2014). *Movies and mental illness: Using films to understand psychopathology* (4th ed.). Hogrefe Publishing.

Chapter 12

American Psychiatric Association (APA). (2013). *Diagnostic and statistical manual of mental disorders* (5th ed.). American Psychiatric Association.

Ancoli-Israel, S. (1997). Sleep problems in older adults: Putting myths to bed. *Geriatrics, 52*(1), 20–28.

APA Presidential Task Force on Evidence-Based Practice. (2006). Evidence-based practice in psychology. *American Psychologist, 61,* 271–285.

Aserinsky, E., & Kleitman, N. (1953). Regularly occurring periods of eye motility, and concomitant phenomena, during sleep. *Science, 118,* 273–274.

Bernert, R. A., & Joiner, T. E. (2007). Sleep disturbances and suicide risk: A review of the literature. *Neuropsychiatric Disease and Treatment, 3*(6), 735–743.

Bootzin, R. R., & Rider, S. P. (1997). Behavioral techniques and biofeedback for insomnia. In M. R. Pressman, W. C. Orr, M. R. Pressman, W. C. Orr (Eds.), *Understanding sleep: The evaluation and treatment of sleep disorders* (pp. 315–338). American Psychological Association.

Boyd, R. (2007). Fact or fiction?: Waking a sleepwalker may kill them: On the contrary, rousing a sleepwalker could save their life. *Scientific American.* http://www.scientificamerican.com/article/waking-a-sleepwalker-may-kill-them/

Breus, M. (2016). Sleep myths debunked. *Maclean's, 129*(17), 45.

Campbell, S. S. (1997). The basics of biological rhythms. In M. R. Pressman, W. C. Orr, M. R. Pressman, & W. C. Orr (Eds.), *Understanding sleep: The evaluation and treatment of sleep disorders* (pp. 35–56). American Psychological Association.

Clemmitt, M. (2010). The deadly impact of chronic sleep deprivation. *CQ Researcher, 20*(6), 121–144.

Clip & Save: Drug Chart. FDA-approved drugs to treat sleep disorders. (2010). *Journal of Psychosocial Nursing & Mental Health Services, 48,* 10, pp. 7–8. doi:10.3928/02793695-20100903-02

Everson, C. A., Bergmann, B. M., & Rechtschaffen, A. (1989). Sleep deprivation in the rat: III. Total sleep deprivation. *Sleep: Journal of Sleep Research & Sleep Medicine, 12*(1), 13–21.

Ferber, R. (2006). *Solve your child's sleep problems.* Fireside Book.

Foer, J. & Siffre (2008). Caveman: An interview with Michel Siffre. *Cabinet, 30.* http://www.cabinetmagazine.org/issues/30/foer.php

Gunn, S. R., & Gunn, W. S. (2006). Are we in the dark about sleepwalking's dangers?. *Cerebrum*. The Dana Foundation. http://www.dana.org/Cerebrum/2006/Are_We_in_the_Dark_About_Sleepwalking%E2%80%99s_Dangers_/

Harvey, A. G., & Payne, S. (2002). The management of unwanted pre-sleep thoughts in insomnia: Distraction with imagery versus general distraction. *Behaviour Research and Therapy, 40*, 267–277.

Hirshkowitz, M., Moore, C. A., & Minhoto, G. (1997). The basics of sleep. In M. R. Pressman, W. C. Orr, M. R. Pressman, & W. C. Orr (Eds.), *Understanding sleep: The evaluation and treatment of sleep disorders* (pp. 11–34). American Psychological Association.

Hirshkowitz, M., Whiton, K., Albert, S. M., Alessi, C., Bruni, O., DonCarlos, L., Hazen, N., Herman, J., Katz, E. S., Kheirandish-Gozal, L., Neubauer, D. N., O'Donnell, A. E., Ohayon, M., Peever, J., Rawding, R., Sachdeva, R. C., Setters, B., Vitiello, M. V., Ware, J. C., & Adams Hillard, P. J. (2015). National Sleep Foundation's sleep time duration recommendations: Methodology and results summary. *Sleep Health*, 140–143.

International Business Times. (2012, December 27). Hunger strikes and science: How long can a person go without food? *International Business Times*.

Kripke, D. F., Simons, R. N., Garfinkel, L., & Hammond, C. (1979). Short and long sleep and sleeping pills: Is increased mortality associated? *Archives of General Psychiatry, 36*(1), 103–116.

Lee, Y. J., Cho, S., Cho, I. H., & Kim, S. J. (2012). Insufficient sleep and suicidality in adolescents. *Sleep, 35*(4), 455–460.

Lieberson, A. D. (2004). How long can a person survive without food? *Scientific American. 292*, 104.

Lilienfeld, S. O., Lynn, S. J., Ruscio, J., & Beyerstein, B. L. (2010). *50 great myths of popular psychology: Shattering widespread misconceptions about human behavior*. Wiley-Blackwell.

Maslow, A. H. (1943). A theory of human motivation. *Psychological Review, 50*(4), 370–396.

Morin, C. M. (1993). *Insomnia: Psychological assessment and management*. Guilford Press.

National Institute of Neurological Disorders and Stroke (NINDS). (2016). Narcolepsy fact sheet. http://www.ninds.nih.gov/disorders/narcolepsy/detail_narcolepsy.htm

National Sleep Foundation. (2016). A time to look at some myths and facts about sleep. https://sleepfoundation.org/sleep-news/time-look-some-myths-and-facts-about-sleep/page/0/1

Pressman, M. R., & Orr, W. C. (1997). *Understanding sleep: The evaluation and treatment of sleep disorders*. American Psychological Association.

Rechtschaffen, A., Bergmann, B. M., Everson, C. A., Kushida, C. A., & Gilliland, M. A. (1989). Sleep deprivation in the rat: X. Integration and discussion of the findings. *Sleep: Journal of Sleep Research & Sleep Medicine, 12*(1), 68–87.

Rechtschaffen, A., & Kales, A. (1968). *A manual of standardized terminology, techniques and scoring system for sleep stages of human subjects* (National Institutes of Health Publications No. 204). U.S. Government Printing Office.

Ritterband, L. M., & Clerkin, E. M. (2013). Insomnia. *In Society of Clinical Psychology, research-supported psychological treatments*. http://www.psychologicaltreatments.org

Roehrs, T., & Roth, T. (1997). Hypnotics, alcohol, and caffeine: Relation to insomnia. In M. R. Pressman, W. C. Orr, M. R. Pressman, & W. C. Orr (Eds.), *Understanding sleep: The evaluation and treatment of sleep disorders* (pp. 339–355). American Psychological Association.

Roehrs, T., & Roth, T. (2001). Sleep, sleepiness, and alcohol use. *Alcohol Research & Health, 25*(2), 101–109.

Ross, J. J. (1965). Neurological findings after prolonged sleep deprivation. *Archives of Neurology, 12,* 399–403.

Rothenberg, S. A. (1997). Introduction to sleep disorders. In M. R. Pressman, W. C. Orr, M. R. Pressman, & W. C. Orr (Eds.), *Understanding sleep: The evaluation and treatment of sleep disorders* (pp. 57–72). American Psychological Association.

Saskin, P. (1997). Obstructive sleep apnea: Treatment options, efficacy, and effects. In M. R. Pressman, W. C. Orr, M. R. Pressman, & W. C. Orr (Eds.), *Understanding sleep: The evaluation and treatment of sleep disorders* (pp. 283–297). American Psychological Association.

Stahl, S. M. (2011). *Stahl's essential psychopharmacology: Neuroscientific basis and practical applications* (3rd ed.). Cambridge University Press.

Tefft, B. C., & AAA Foundation for Traffic Safety. (2014). Prevalence of motor vehicle crashes involving drowsy drivers, United States, 2009–2013. AAA Foundation for Traffic Safety. https://newsroom.aaa.com/wp-content/uploads/2014/11/AAAFoundation-DrowsyDriving-Nov2014.pdf

Wedding, D., & Boyd, M. A., & Niemiec, R. M. (2005). *Movies and mental illness: Using films to understand psychopathology.* Hogrefe & Huber.

Wheaton, A. G., Shults, R. A., Chapman, D. P., Ford, E. S., & Croft, J. B. (2014). Drowsy driving and risk behaviors—10 states and Puerto Rico, 2011–2012. *MMWR. Morbidity and Mortality Weekly Report, 63,* 557–562.

Williamson, A. M., & Feyer, A. (2000). Moderate sleep deprivation produces impairments in cognitive and motor performance equivalent to legally prescribed levels of alcohol intoxication. *Occupational and Environmental Medicine, 57,* 649–655.

Zepelin, H., & Rechtschaffen, A. (1974). Mammalian sleep, longevity, and energy metabolism. *Brain, Behavior and Evolution, 10,* 425–470.

Chapter 13

Althof, S. E., & Needle, R. B. (2013). Psychological and interpersonal dimensions of sexual function and dysfunction in women: An update. *Arab Journal of Urology, 11*(3), 299–304. https://doi.org/10.1016/j.aju.2013.04.010

American Psychiatric Association (APA). (2000). *Diagnostic and statistical manual of mental disorders* (4th ed., text revision). American Psychiatric Association.

American Psychiatric Association (APA). (2013). *Diagnostic and statistical manual of mental disorders* (5th ed.). American Psychiatric Association.

American Psychological Association. (2015). Guidelines for Psychological Practice with Transgender and Gender Nonconforming People. *American Psychologist, 70*(9), 832–864. doi: 10.1037/a0039906

American Psychological Association Task Force on Appropriate Therapeutic Responses to Sexual Orientation. (2009). *Report of the Task Force on Appropriate Therapeutic Responses to Sexual Orientation.* American Psychological Association.

Baba, T., Endo, T., Honnma, H., Kitajima, Y., Hayashi, T., Ikeda, H., Masumori, N., Kamiya, H., Moriwaka, O., & Saito, T. (2007). Association between polycystic ovary syndrome and female-to-male transsexuality. *Human Reproduction (Oxford, England), 22*(4), 1011–1016.

Barlow, D. H. (1986). Causes of sexual dysfunction: The role of anxiety and cognitive interference. *Journal of Consulting and Clinical Psychology, 54*(2), 140–148.

Basson, R., & Gilks, T. (2018). Women's sexual dysfunction associated with psychiatric disorders and their treatment. *Women's Health, 14*, 1745506518762664. https://doi.org/10.1177/1745506518762664

Berner, W., & Briken, P. (2007). [Paraphilia, sexual preference disorders. Diagnosis, etiology, epidemiology, treatment and prevention]. *Bundesgesundheitsblatt, Gesundheitsforschung, Gesundheitsschutz, 50*(1), 33–43.

Bickley, J., & Beech, A. (2001). Classifying child abusers: Its relevance to theory and clinical practice, *International Journal of Offender Therapy and Comparative Criminology, 45*(1), 51–69.

Binik, Y. M. (2010). The DSM diagnostic criteria for vaginismus. *Archives of Sexual Behavior, 39*(2), 278–291. https://doi.org/10.1007/s10508-009-9560-0

Bradford, J. M. (1999). The paraphilias, obsessive compulsive spectrum disorder, and the treatment of sexually deviant behaviour. *The Psychiatric Quarterly, 70*(3), 209–219.

Brotto, L., Atallah, S., Johnson-Agbakwu, C., Rosenbaum, T., Abdo, C., Byers, E. S., Graham, C., Nobre, P., & Wylie, K. (2016). Psychological and interpersonal dimensions of sexual function and dysfunction. *The Journal of Sexual Medicine, 13*(4), 538–571. doi:10.1016/j.jsxm.2016.01.019

Brown, J. E., Ayowa, O. B., & Brown, R. C. (1993). Dry and tight: Sexual practices and potential AIDS risk in Zaire. *Social Science & Medicine (1982), 37*(8), 989–994.

Byne, W., Bradley, S. J., Coleman, E., Eyler, A. E., Green, R., Menvielle, E., Meyer-Bahlburg, H. F. L., Pleak, R. R., & Tompkins, D. A. (2012). Treatment of gender identity disorder. *The American Journal of Psychiatry, 169*(8), 875–876. doi:10.1176/appi.ajp.2012.169.8.875

Chan, H. O., & Beauregard, E. (2015). Non-homicidal and homicidal sexual offenders: Prevalence of maladaptive personality traits and paraphilic behaviors. *Journal of Interpersonal Violence*. Retrieved from *MEDLINE with Full Text*, EBSCOhost .

Darcangelo, S. (2008). Fetishism: Psychopathology and treatment. In D. R. Laws & W. T. O'Donohue (Eds.), *Sexual deviance: Theory, assessment, and treatment* (pp. 108–119). Guilford Press.

de Alarcón, R., de la Iglesia, J. I., Casado, N. M., & Montejo, A. L. (2019). Online porn addiction: What we know and what we don't—A systematic review. *Journal of Clinical Medicine, 8*(1), 91. https://doi.org/10.3390/jcm8010091

Delizonna, L. L., Wincze, J. P., Litz, B. T., Brown, T. A., & Barlow, D. H. (2001). A comparison of subjective and physiological measures of mechanically produced and erotically produced erections (or, is an erection an erection?). *Journal of Sex & Marital Therapy, 27*(1), 21–31.

Dell'Osso, L., Carmassi, C., Carlini, M., Rucci, P., Torri, P., Cesari, D., Landi, P., Ciapparelli, A., & Maggi, M. (2009). Sexual dysfunctions and suicidality in patients with bipolar disorder and unipolar depression. *The Journal of Sexual Medicine, 6*(11), 3063–3070. doi:10.1111/j.1743-6109.2009.01455.x

Demme, J., Harris, T., & Tally, T. (1991). *The silence of the lambs* [Motion picture]. Orion Pictures.

Dhejne, C., Lichtenstein, P., Boman, M., Johansson, A. V., Långström, N., & Landén, M. (2011). Long-term follow-up of transsexual persons undergoing sex reassignment surgery: Cohort study in Sweden. *Plos One, 6*(2), e16885. doi:10.1371/journal.pone.0016885

Doran, K., & Price, J. (2014). Pornography and marriage. *Journal of Family and Economic Issues, 35*(4), 489–498. https://doi.org/10.1007/s10834-014-9391-6

Firoz, K., Nidheesh Sankar, V., Rajmohan, V., Manoj Kumar, G., & Raghuram, T. M. (2014). Treatment of fetishism with naltrexone: A case report. *Asian Journal of Psychiatry*, 867–68. doi:10.1016/j.ajp.2013.11.006

Freud, S. (1905/2011). *Three essays on the theory of sexuality*. James Strachey (trans.). Martino Publishing.

Freud, S. (1920/1990). *Beyond the pleasure principle*. Peter Gay (trans.). W. W. Norton.

Freund, K., Heasman, G., Racansky, I. G., & Glancy, G. (1984). Pedophilia and heterosexuality vs. homosexuality. *Journal of Sex & Marital Therapy, 10*(3), 193–200.

Freund, K., & Watson, R. J. (1992). The proportions of heterosexual and homosexual pedophiles among sex offenders against children: An exploratory study. *Journal of Sex & Marital Therapy, 18*(1), 34–43.

Gilliland, R., South, M., Carpenter, B. N., & Hardy, S. A. (2011). The roles of shame and guilt in hypersexual behavior. *Sexual Addiction & Compulsivity, 18*(1), 12–29. doi:10.1080/10720162.2011.551182

Green, R. (1985). Gender identity in childhood and later sexual orientation: Follow-up of 78 males. *The American Journal of Psychiatry, 142*(3), 339–341.

Greenberg, D. M., Bradford, J. M., Curry, S., & O'Rourke, A. (1996). A comparison of treatment of paraphilias with three serotonin reuptake inhibitors: A retrospective study. *The Bulletin of The American Academy of Psychiatry and the Law, 24*(4), 525–532.

Guay, D. P. (2009). Drug treatment of paraphilic and nonparaphilic sexual disorders. *Clinical Therapeutics, 31*(1), 1–31. doi:10.1016/j.clinthera.2009.01.009

Heylens, G., Elaut, E., Kreukels, B. C., Paap, M. S., Cerwenka, S., Richter-Appelt, H., & Cohen-Kettenis, P. T., Haraldsen, I. R, & De Cuypere, G. (2014). Psychiatric characteristics in transsexual individuals: Multicentre study in four European countries. *The British Journal of Psychiatry: The Journal of Mental Science, 204*(2), 151–156. doi:10.1192/bjp.bp.112.121954

Hines, M., Ahmed, S. F., & Hughes, I. A. (2003). Psychological outcomes and gender-related development in complete androgen insensitivity syndrome. *Archives of Sexual Behavior, 32*(2), 93–101.

Jenny, C., Roesler, T. A., & Poyer, K. L. (1994). Are children at risk for sexual abuse by homosexuals? *Pediatrics, 94*(1), 41–44.

Kafka, M. P. (2003). The monoamine hypothesis for the pathophysiology of paraphilic disorders: An update. *Annals of the New York Academy of Sciences, 989*, 86–94.

Kafka, M. P. (2010). Hypersexual disorder: A proposed diagnosis for DSM-V. *Archives of Sexual Behavior, 39*(2), 377–400. doi:10.1007/s10508-009-9574-7

Kafka, M. P., & Prentky, R. A. (1994). Preliminary observations of DSM-III-R axis I comorbidity in men with paraphilias and paraphilia-related disorders. *The Journal of Clinical Psychiatry, 55*(11), 481–487.

Kafka, M. P., & Prentky, R. A. (1998). Attention-deficit/hyperactivity disorder in males with paraphilias and paraphilia-related disorders: A comorbidity study. *The Journal of Clinical Psychiatry, 59*(7), 388–396.

Klein, C., & Gorzalka, B. B. (2009). Sexual functioning in transsexuals following hormone therapy and genital surgery: A review. *The Journal of Sexual Medicine, 6*(11), 2922–2939. doi:10.1111/j.1743-6109.2009.01370.x

Långström, N., & Zucker, K. J. (2005). Transvestic fetishism in the general population: Prevalence and correlates. *Journal of Sex & Marital Therapy, 31*(2), 87–95.

Lev, A. I. (2004). *Transgender emergence: Therapeutic guidelines for working with gender-variant people and their families.* Haworth Clinical Practice Press.

Lilienfeld, S. O. (Ed.). (1995). *Seeing both sides: Classic controversies in abnormal psychology.* Wadsworth.

Mannino, J. D. (1999). *Sexually speaking.* McGraw-Hill.

Marsh, P. J., Odlaug, B. L., Thomarios, N., Davis, A. A., Buchanan, S. N., Meyer, C. S., & Grant, J. E. (2010). Paraphilias in adult psychiatric inpatients. *Annals of Clinical Psychiatry: Official Journal of the American Academy of Clinical Psychiatrists, 22*(2), 129–134.

Masters, W. H., & Johnson, V. E. (1970). *Human sexual inadequacy.* Little, Brown.

McCarthy, B., & Thestrup, M. (2008). Integrating sex therapy interventions with couple therapy. *Journal of Contemporary Psychotherapy, 38*, 139–149.

McHugh, P. R. (2004). Surgical sex: Why we stopped doing sex change operations. *First Things (New York, N. Y.).* http://www.firstthings.com/article/2004/11/surgical-sex

McManus, M. A., Hargreaves, P., Rainbow, L., & Alison, L. J. (2013). Paraphilias: Definition, diagnosis and treatment. *F1000 prime reports, 36*(5), 1–6. doi:10.12703/P5-36

Megargee, E. I. (2006). Using the MMPI-2 in criminal justice and correctional settings. University of Minnesota Press.

Meyer, J. K., & Reter, D. J. (1979). Sex reassignment. Follow-up. *Archives of General Psychiatry, 36*(9), 1010–1015.

Mitchell, K. R., Jones, K. G., Wellings, K., Johnson, A. M., Graham, C. A., Datta, J., Copas, A. J., Bancroft, J., Sonnenberg, P., Macdowall, W., Field, N., & Mercer, C. H. (2015). Estimating the prevalence of sexual function problems: The impact of morbidity criteria. *Journal of Sex Research,* 1–13.

Money, J. (1981). Paraphilia and abuse-martyrdom: Exhibitionism as a paradigm for reciprocal couple counseling combined with antiandrogen. *Journal of Sex & Marital Therapy, 7*(2), 115–123.

Montgomery K. A. (2008). Sexual desire disorders. *Psychiatry, 5*(6), 50–55.

Murad, M. H., Elamin, M. B., Garcia, M. Z., Mullan, R. J., Murad, A., Erwin, P. J., & Montori, V. M. (2010). Hormonal therapy and sex reassignment: A systematic review and meta-analysis of quality of life and psychosocial outcomes. *Clinical Endocrinology, 72*(2), 214–231. doi:10.1111/j.1365-2265.2009.03625.x

Nobre, P. J., & Pinto-Gouveia, J. (2006). Emotions during sexual activity: Differences between sexually functional and dysfunctional men and women. *Archives of Sexual Behavior, 35*(4), 491–499.

Pacik, P. T., & Geletta, S. (2017). Vaginismus treatment: Clinical trials follow up 241 patients. *Sexual Medicine, 5*(2), e114–e123. https://doi.org/10.1016/j.esxm.2017.02.002

Rosen, R. C., Heiman, J. R., Long, J. S., Fisher, W. A., & Sand, M. S. (2016). Men with sexual problems and their partners: Findings from the International Survey of Relationships. *Archives of Sexual Behavior, 45*(1), 159–173. doi:10.1007/s10508-015-0568-3

Scorolli, C., Ghirlanda, S., Enquist, M., Zattoni, S., & Jannini, E. A. (2007). Relative prevalence of different fetishes. *International Journal of Impotence Research, 19*(4), 432–437.

Seftel, A. D., Mohammed, M. A., & Althof, S. E. (2004). Erectile dysfunction: Etiology, evaluation, and treatment options. *The Medical Clinics of North America, 88*(2), 387.

Seto, M. C. (2009). Pedophilia. *Annual Review of Clinical Psychology, 5*391–5407. doi:10.1146/annurev.clinpsy.032408.153618

Shifren, J. L., Braunstein, G. D., Simon, J. A., Casson, P. R., Buster, J. E., Redmond, G. P., Burki, R. E., Ginsburg, E. S., Rosen, R. C., Leiblum, S. R., Caramelli, K. E., & Mazer, N. A. (2000). Transdermal testosterone treatment in women with impaired sexual function after oophorectomy. *The New England Journal of Medicine, 343*(10), 682–688.

Simons, J. S., & Carey, M. P. (2001). Prevalence of sexual dysfunctions: Results from a decade of research. *Archives of Sexual Behavior, 30*(2), 177–219.

Singg, S. (2017) Ego-Dystonic Zoophilia: A case report with treatment plan and a critical look at the current state. Clin Case Rep Rev 2. doi:10.15761/CCRR.1000295

Soderbergh, S. (1989). *Sex, lies, and videotape* [Motion picture]. Outlaw Productions.

von Trier, L., & Asmussen, P. (1996). *Breaking the waves* [Motion picture]. Argus Film Produktie.

Zucker, K. J., & Wood, H. (2011). Assessment of gender variance in children. *Child and Adolescent Psychiatric Clinics of North America, 20*(4), 665–680. doi:10.1016/j.chc.2011.07.006

Chapter 14

American Psychiatric Association (APA). (2000). *Diagnostic and statistical manual of mental disorders* (4th ed., text revision). American Psychiatric Association.

American Psychiatric Association (APA). (2013). *Diagnostic and statistical manual of mental disorders* (5th ed.). American Psychiatric Association.

Aronofsky, D. (2000). *Requiem for a dream* [Motion picture]. Artisan Entertainment.

Biederman, J., Faraone, S. V., Milberger, S., Jetton, J. G., Chen, L., Mick, E., Greene, R. W., & Russell, R. L. (1996). Is childhood oppositional defiant disorder a precursor to adolescent conduct disorder? Findings from a four-year follow-up study of children with ADHD. *Journal of the American Academy of Child and Adolescent Psychiatry, 35*(9), 1193–1204.

Brick, J. (Ed.). (2008). *Handbook of medical consequences of alcohol and drug abuse* (2nd ed.). Haworth Press.

Burton, P. S., McNiel, D. E., & Binder, R. L. (2012). Firesetting, arson, pyromania, and the forensic mental health expert. *The Journal of The American Academy Of Psychiatry And The Law, 40*(3), 355–365.

Center for Disease Control [CDC]. (2013, July 2). *Prescription painkiller overdoses.* https://www.cdc.gov/vitalsigns/prescription-drug-overdoses.html

Chang, K. D., & Simeonova, D. I. (2004). Mood stabilizers: Use in pediatric psychopharmacology. In H. Steiner (Ed.), *Handbook of mental health intervention in children and adolescents: An integrated developmental approach* (pp. 363–412). Jossey-Bass.

Coccaro, E. F., Fanning, J. R., Phan, K. L., & Lee, R. (2015). Serotonin and impulsive aggression. *CNS Spectrums, 20*(3), 295–302. doi:10.1017/S1092852915000310

Durst, R., Katz, G., Teitelbaum, A., Zislin, J., & Dannon, P. N. (2001). Kleptomania: Diagnosis and treatment options. *CNS Drugs, 15*(3), 185–195.

Emslie, G. J., Portteus, A. M., Kumar, E. C., & Hume, J. H. (2004). Antidepressants: SSRIs and novel atypical antidepressants—An update on psychopharmacology. In H. Steiner (Ed.), *Handbook of mental health integration in children and adolescents: An integrated developmental approach* (pp. 318–362). Jossey-Bass.

Fanning, J. R., Meyerhoff, J. J., Lee, R., & Coccaro, E. F. (2014). History of childhood maltreatment in intermittent explosive disorder and suicidal behavior. *Journal of Psychiatric Research, 56,* 10–17. doi:10.1016/j.jpsychires.2014.04.012

Ford, J. D., Racusin, R., Ellis, C. G., Daviss, W. B., Reiser, J., Fleischer, A., & Thomas, J. (2000). Child maltreatment, other trauma exposure, and posttraumatic symptomatology among children with oppositional defiant and attention deficit hyperactivity disorders. *Child Maltreatment, 5*(3), 205–217.

Grant, J. E., Levine, L., Kim, D., & Potenza, M. N. (2005). Impulse control disorders in adult psychiatric inpatients. *The American Journal of Psychiatry, 162*(11), 2184–2188.

Gvion, Y., & Apter, A. (2011). Aggression, impulsivity, and suicide behavior: A review of the literature. *Archives of Suicide Research: Official Journal of the International Academy for Suicide Research, 15*(2), 93–112. doi:10.1080/13811118.2011.565265

Holden, C. (2010). Behavioral addictions debut in proposed DSM-V. *Science, 327*(5868), 935. doi:10.1126/science.327.5968.935

Jenkins, A. L., McCloskey, M. S., Kulper, D., Berman, M. E., & Coccaro, E. F. (2015). Self-harm behavior among individuals with intermittent explosive disorder and personality disorders. *Journal of Psychiatric Research, 60,* 125–131. doi:10.1016/j.jpsychires.2014.08.013

Kazdin, A. E. (1997). Practitioner review: Psychosocial treatments for conduct disorder in children. *Journal of Child Psychology and Psychiatry, and Allied Disciplines, 38*(2), 161–178.

Kelly, J. F., & Yeterian, J. D. (2015). *Outcomes research on twelve-step programs.* In M. Galanter, H. D. Kleber, & K. T. Brady (Eds.), Textbook of substance abuse treatment. (5th ed., pp. 579–593). American Psychiatric Publishing, Inc.

Lile, B. (2003). Twelve step programs: An update. *Addictive Disorders & Their Treatment, 2*(1), 19–24. https://doi.org/10.1097/00132576-200302010-00004

McCloskey, M. S., Ben-Zeev, D., Lee, R., & Coccaro, E. F. (2008). Prevalence of suicidal and self-injurious behavior among subjects with intermittent explosive disorder. *Psychiatry Research, 158*(2), 248–250. doi:10.1016/j.psychres.2007.09.011

McCloskey, M. S., Noblett, K. L., Deffenbacher, J. L., Gollan, J. K., & Coccaro, E. F. (2008). Cognitive-behavioral therapy for intermittent explosive disorder: A pilot randomized clinical trial. *Journal of Consulting and Clinical Psychology, 76*(5), 876–886. doi:10.1037/0022-006X.76.5.876

Miller, M. M. (2003). Twelve step programs: An update. *Addictive Disorders & Their Treatment, 2*(4), 157–160. https://doi.org/10.1097/00132576-200302040-00007

Najavits, L., Piotrowski, N., Brigham, G., Hampton, A., & Worley, M. (2013). *Substance and alcohol use disorders.* http://www.div12.org/psychological-treatments/disorders/

Odlaug, B. L., Grant, J. E., & Kim, S. W. (2012). Suicide attempts in 107 adolescents and adults with kleptomania. *Archives of Suicide Research: Official Journal of the International Academy for Suicide Research, 16*(4), 348–359. doi:10.1080/13811118.2013.722058

Pappadopulos, E., Woolston, S., Chait, A., Perkins, M., Connor, D. F., & Jensen, P. S. (2006). Pharmacotherapy of aggression in children and adolescents: Efficacy and effect size. *Journal of the Canadian Academy of Child and Adolescent Psychiatry, 15*(1), 27–39.

Piquet-Pessôa, M., & Fontenelle, L. F. (2016). Opioid antagonists in broadly defined behavioral addictions: A narrative review. *Expert Opinion on Pharmacotherapy, 17*(6), 835–844. doi:10.1517/14656566.2016.1145660

Riley, M., Ahmed, S., & Locke, A. (2016). Common questions about oppositional defiant disorder. *American Family Physician, 93*(7), 586–591.

Ritchey, E. C., & Huff, T. G. (1999). Psychiatric aspects of arsonists. *Journal of Forensic Science, 44*(4), 733–740.

Schneider, B. (2009). Substance use disorders and risk for completed suicide. *Archives of Suicide Research, 13*(4), 303–316.

Sher, L. (2007). The role of the hypothalamic-pituitary-adrenal axis dysfunction in the pathophysiology of alcohol misuse and suicidal behavior in adolescents. *International Journal of Adolescent Medicine and Health, 19*(1), 3–9.

Sher, K. J., Grekin, E. R., & Williams, N. A. (2005). The development of alcohol use disorders. *Annual Review of Clinical Psychology, 1*, 493–523.

Soderbergh, S. (2000). *Traffic* [Motion picture]. USA Films.

Substance Abuse and Mental Health Services Administration [SAMHSA]. (2015, Nov. 28). *Medication and counseling treatment.* http://www.samhas.gov/medication-assisted-treatment/treatment

Substance Abuse and Mental Health Services Administration [SAMHSA]. (2018). *Results from the 2018 National Survey on Drug Use and Health: Graphics from the Key Findings Report.* https://www.samhsa.gov/data/sites/default/files/cbhsq-reports/NSDUHffrBriefingSlides2018_w-final-cover.pdf

Tandon, M., Cardeli, E., Luby, J. (2009). Internalizing disorders in early childhood: A review of depression and anxiety disorders. *Child Adolesc Psychiatric Clin N Am, 13*(3), 593–610.

Wedding, D., & Boyd, M. A., & Niemiec, R. M. (2005). *Movies and mental illness: Using films to understand psychopathology.* Hogrefe & Huber.

Wong, K., & Clarke, C. (2015). The legalization of marijuana in Colorado: The impact. *Rocky Mountain High Intensity Drug Trafficking Area Investigative Support Center, 3.* www.rmhidta.org.

Chapter 15

American Psychiatric Association (APA). (2013). *Diagnostic and statistical manual of mental disorders* (5th ed.). American Psychiatric Association.

Brodaty, H., & Arasaratnam, C. (2012). Meta-analysis of nonpharmacological interventions for neuropsychiatric symptoms of dementia. *The American Journal of Psychiatry, 169*(9), 946–953. doi:10.1176/appi.ajp.2012.11101529

Brown, G. (2008). *The living end: The future of death, aging and immortality.* Macmillan.

Carpenter, B. D., Zoller, S. M., Balsis, S., Otilingam, P. G., & Gatz, M. (2011). Demographic and contextual factors related to knowledge about Alzheimer's disease. *American Journal of Alzheimer's Disease and Other Dementias, 26*(2), 121–126. doi:10.1177/1533317510394157

Cipriani, G., Lucetti, C., Danti, S., Carlesi, C., & Nuti, A. (2015). Violent and criminal manifestations in dementia patients. *Geriatrics & Gerontology International, 16*(5), 541–549. https://doi.org/10.1111/ggi.12608

Crump, C., Sundquist, K., Winkleby, M. A., & Sundquist, J. (2013). Mental disorders and risk of accidental death. *The British Journal of Psychiatry: The Journal of Mental Science, 203*(3), 297–302. doi:10.1192/bjp.bp.112.123992

Ganguli, M., Blacker, D., Blazer, D. G., Grant, I., Jeste, D. V., Paulsen, J. S., Petersen, R. C., & Sachdev, P. S. (2011). Classification of neurocognitive disorders in DSM-5: A work in progress. *The American Journal of Geriatric Psychiatry: Official Journal of the American Association for Geriatric Psychiatry, 19*(3), 205–210.

Gatz, M. (2007). Genetics, dementia, & the elderly. *Current Directions in Psychological Science, 16*, 123–127.

Gatz, M., Mortimer, J. A., Fratiglioni, L., Johansson, B., Berg, S., Andel, R., Crowe, M., Fiske, A., Reynolds, C. A., & Pedersen, N. L. (2007). Accounting for the relationship between low education and dementia: A twin study. *Physiology & Behavior, 92*(1–2), 232–237.

Gatz, M., Reynolds, C. A., Fratiglioni, L., Johansson, B., Mortimer, J. A., Berg, S., Fiske, A., & Pedersen, N. L. (2006). Role of genes and environments for explaining Alzheimer disease. *Archives of General Psychiatry, 63*(2), 168–174.

Iacono, D., Volkman, I., Nennesmo, I., Pedersen, N. L., Fratiglioni, L., Johansson, B., Karlsson, D., Winblad, B., & Gatz, M. (2014). Neuropathologic assessment of dementia markers in identical and fraternal twins. *Brain Pathology (Zurich, Switzerland), 24*(4), 317–333. doi:10.1111/bpa.12127

Iacono, D., Volkman, I., Nennesmo, I., Pedersen, N. L., Fratiglioni, L., Johansson, B., Karlsson, D., Winblad, B., & Gatz, M. (2016). Same ages, same genes: Same brains, same pathologies? Dementia timings, co-occurring brain pathologies, ApoE genotypes in Identical and fraternal age-matched twins at autopsy. *Alzheimer disease and associated disorder, 30*(2), 178–182. doi:10.1097/WAD.0000000000000114

Jackson, T. A., Wilson, D., Richardson, S., & Lord, J. M. (2016). Predicting outcome in older hospital patients with delirium: A systematic literature review. *International Journal of Geriatric Psychiatry, 31*(4), 392–399. doi:10.1002/gps.4344

Kurz, A., Wagenpfeil, S., Hallauer, J., Schneider-Schelte, H., & Jansen, S. (2010). Evaluation of a brief educational program for dementia careers: The AENEAS study. *International Journal of Geriatric Psychiatry, 25*(8), 861–869. doi:10.1002/gps.2428

Llanque, S., Savage, L., Rosenburg, N., & Caserta, M. (2016). Concept analysis: Alzheimer's caregiver stress. *Nursing Forum, 51*(1), 21–31. doi:10.1111/nuf.12090

Martorana, A., Esposito, Z., & Koch, G. (2010). Beyond the cholinergic hypothesis: Do current drugs work in Alzheimer's disease?. *CNS Neuroscience & Therapeutics, 16*(4), 235–245. doi:10.1111/j.1755-5949.2010.00175.x

Mashour, G. A., Frank, L., Batthyany, A., Kolanowski, A. M., Nahm, M., Schulman-Green, D., Greyson, B., Pakhomov, S., Karlawish, J., & Shah, R. C. (2019). Paradoxical lucidity: A potential paradigm shift for the neurobiology and treatment of severe dementias. *Alzheimer's & Dementia: The Journal of the Alzheimer's Association, 15*(8), 1107–1114. https://doi.org/10.1016/j.jalz.2019.04.002

Nahm, M., Greyson, B., Kelly, E. W., & Haraldsson, E. (2012). Terminal lucidity: A review and a case collection. Archives of *Gerontology and Geriatrics, 55*(1), 138–142. https://doi.org/10.1016/j.archger.2011.06.031

Salari, S. (2007). Patterns of intimate partner homicide suicide in later life: Strategies for prevention. *Clinical Interventions in Aging, 2*(3), 441–452.

Sharp, E. S., & Gatz, M. (2011). Relationship between education and dementia: An updated systematic review. *Alzheimer Disease and Associated Disorders, 25*(4), 289–304. doi:10.1097/WAD.0b013e318211c83c

Snowdon, D. A. (2003). Healthy aging and dementia: Findings from the Nun Study. *Annals of Internal Medicine, 139*(5 Pt 2), 450–454.

Sparks, N. (1996). *The Notebook*. Warner Books.

Tyas, S. L., Salazar, J. C., Snowdon, D. A., Desrosiers, M. F., Riley, K. P., Mendiondo, M. S., & Kryscio, R. J. (2007). Transitions to mild cognitive impairments, dementia, and death: Findings from the Nun Study. *American Journal of Epidemiology, 165*(11), 1231–1238.

van de Vorst, I. E., Koek, H. L., Bots, M. L., & Vaartjes, I. (2016). Evaluation of underlying causes of death in patients with dementia to support targeted advance care planning. *Journal of Alzheimer's Disease: JAD*.

Wedding, D., & Niemiec, R. M. (2014). *Movies and mental illness: Using films to understand psychopathology* (4th ed.). Hogrefe Publishing.

Whitehouse, P. J., & George, D. R. (2015). Is there Alzheimer's disease? *Journal of Alzheimer's Disease*. http://j-alz.com/editors-blog/posts/is-there-alzheimers-disease

Chapter 16

American Psychiatric Association (APA). (2013). *Diagnostic and statistical manual of mental disorders* (5th ed.). Arlington, VA: American Psychiatric Association.

Apter, A., King, R. A., & Kron, S. (1993). Death without warning? A clinical postmortem study of suicide in 43 Israeli adolescent males. *Archives of General Psychiatry, 50*, 138–142.

Bartz, J., Kaplan, A., & Hollander, E. (2007). Schizotypal personality disorder. In W. O'Donohue, K. A. Fowler, & S. O. Lilienfeld (Eds.), *Personality disorders: Toward the DSM-V* (pp. 325–351). CA: Sage.

Beck, A. T., Freeman, A. T., & Davis, D. D. (1990). Cognitive therapy of personality disorders. Guilford Press.

Bernstein, D. P., & Useda, J. D. (2007). Paranoid personality disorder. In W. O'Donohue, K. A. Fowler, & S. O. Lilienfeld (Eds.), *Personality disorders: Toward the DSM-V* (pp. 41–62). Sage.

Björkenstam, E., Björkenstam, C., Holm, H., Gerdin, B., & Ekselius, L. (2015). Excess cause-specific mortality in in-patient-treated individuals with personality disorder: 25-year nationwide population-based study. *The British Journal of Psychiatry: The Journal of Mental Science, 207*(4), 339–345. doi:10.1192/bjp.bp.114.149583

Blagov, P. S., Fowler, K. A., & Lilienfeld, S. O. (2007). Schizotypal personality disorder. In W. O'Donohue, K. A. Fowler, & S. O. Lilienfeld (Eds.), *Personality disorders: Toward the DSM-V* (pp. 202–232). Sage.

Bleuler, E. (1924). Textbook of psychiatry (A. A. Brill, Trans.). Macmillan.

Bollini, A. M., & Walker, E. F. (2007). Schizotypal personality disorder. In W. O'Donohue, K. A. Fowler, & S. O. Lilienfeld (Eds.), *Personality disorders: Toward the DSM-V* (pp. 80–108). CA: Sage.

Bolton, J. M., Pagura, J., Enns, M. W., Grant, B., & Sareen, J. (2010). A population-based longitudinal study of risk factors for suicide attempts in major depressive disorder. *Journal of Psychiatric Research, 44*(13), 817–826. doi:10.1016/j.jpsychires.2010.01.003

Bornstein, R. F. (2007). Dependent personality disorder. In W. O'Donohue, K. A. Fowler, & S. O. Lilienfeld (Eds.), *Personality disorders: Toward the DSM-V* (pp. 306–324). Sage.

Bradley, R., Conklin, C. Z., & Westen, D. (2007). Borderline personality disorder. In W. O'Donohue, K. A. Fowler, & S. O. Lilienfeld (Eds.), *Personality disorders: Toward the DSM-V* (pp. 167–201). Sage.

Chioqueta, A. P., & Stiles, T. C. (2004). Assessing suicide risk in Cluster C personality disorders. *Crisis, 25*(3), 128–133.

Cleckley, H. (1941). *The mask of sanity*. Mosby.

Cleckley, H. (1976). *The mask of sanity* (5th ed.). Mosby.

Cristea, I. A., Gentili, C., Cotet, C. D., Palomba, D., Barbui, C., & Cuijpers, P. (2017). Efficacy of psychotherapies for borderline personality disorder: A systematic review and meta-analysis. *JAMA Psychiatry, 74*(4), 319–328. https://doi.org /10.1001/jamapsychiatry.2016.4287

DePaulo, B. (2010) Dexter the amiable serial killer: PT bloggers and other experts show their love. *Psychology Today*. https://www.psychologytoday.com/blog/living-single/201008/dexter-the-amiable-serial-killer-pt-bloggers-and-other-experts-show-their

Ellis, H. (1898). Auto-eroticism: A psychological study. *Alienist and Neurologist, 19*, 260–299.

Fok, M. L., Hayes, R. D., Chang, C., Stewart, R., Callard, F. J., & Moran, P. (2012). Life expectancy at birth and all-cause mortality among people with personality disorder. *Journal of Psychosomatic Research, 73*(2), 104–107. doi:10.1016/j.jpsychores.2012.05.001

Fowler, K. A., O'Donohue, W., Lilienfeld, S. O. (2007). Personality disorders in perspective. In W. O'Donohue, K. A. Fowler, & S. O. Lilienfeld (Eds.), *Personality disorders: Toward the DSM-V* (pp. 1–19). Sage.

Freud, S. (1959). Character and anal eroticism. In J. Strachey (Ed. & Trans.), *The standard edition of the complete psychological works of Sigmund Freud* (pp. 169–175). Hogarth Press.

Herbert, J. D. (2007). Avoidant personality disorder. In W. O'Donohue, K. A. Fowler, & S. O. Lilienfeld (Eds.), *Personality disorders: Toward the DSM-V* (pp. 278–305). Sage.

Hopwood, C. J., Kotov, R., Krueger, R. F., Watson, D., Widiger, T. A., Althoff, R. R., Ansell, E. B., Bach, B., Bagby, R. M., Blais, M. A., Bornovalova, M. A., Chmielewski, M., Cicero, D. C., Conway, C., De Clercq, B., De Fruyt, F., Docherty, A. R., Eaton, N. R., Edens, J. F., … Zimmermann, J. (2018). The time has come for dimensional personality disorder diagnosis. *Personality and Mental Health, 12*(1), 82–86. https://doi.org /10.1002/pmh.1408

Kernberg, O. (1967). Borderline personality organization. *Journal of the American Psychoanalytic Association, 15*, 641–685.

Klonsky, E. D. (2013). *Borderline personality disorder*. http://www.div12.org/psychological-treatments/disorders/

Kraepelin, E. (1921). *Manic-depressive insanity and paranoia*. Livingstone.

Levy, K. N., Reynoso, J. S., Wasserman, R. H., & Clarkin, J. F. (2007). Narcissistic personality disorder. In W. O'Donohue, K. A. Fowler, & S. O. Lilienfeld (Eds.), *Personality disorders: Toward the DSM-V* (pp. 1–19). Sage.

Linehan, M. M. (2018). Cognitive-behavioral treatment of borderline personality disorder. Guilford Press.

Linehan, M. M., Armstrong, H. E., Suarez, A., Allmon, D., & Heard, H. L. (1991). Cognitive-behavioral treatment of chronically parasuicidal borderline patients. *Archives of General Psychiatry, 48*, 1060–1064.

Linehan, M. M., Heard, H. L., & Armstrong, H. E. (1993). Naturalistic follow-up of a behavioral treatment for chronically parasuicidal borderline patients. *Archives of General Psychiatry, 50*, 971–974.

Patrick, C. J. (2007). Antisocial personality disorder and psychopathy. In W. O'Donohue, K. A. Fowler, & S. O. Lilienfeld (Eds.), *Personality disorders: Toward the DSM-V* (pp. 109–166). Sage.

PDM Task Force. (2006). *Psychodynamic Diagnostic Manual.* Alliance of Psychoanalytic Organizations.

Pinel, P. (1801/1962). *A treatise on insanity* (Davis, Trans.). Hafner.

Pinna, F., Tusconi, M., Dessì, C., Pittaluga, G., Fiorillo, A., & Carpiniello, B. (2016). Violence and mental disorders. A retrospective study of people in charge of a community mental health center. *International Journal of Law and Psychiatry, 47,* 122–128. https://doi.org /10.1016/j.ijlp.2016.02.015

Ripoll, L. H., Triebwasser, J., & Siever, L. J. (2011). Evidence-based pharmacotherapy for personality disorders. *The International Journal of Neuropsychopharmacology / Official Scientific Journal of the Collegium Internationale Neuropsychopharmacologicum (CINP), 14*(9), 1257–1288. doi:10.1017/S1461145711000071

Skinner, B. F. (1957). *Verbal behavior.* Appleton-Century-Crofts.

Timmermann, M., Jeung, H., Schmitt, R., Boll, S., Freitag, C. M., Bertsch, K., & Herpertz, S. C. (2017). Oxytocin improves facial emotion recognition in young adults with antisocial personality disorder. *Psychoneuroendocrinology, 85,* 158–164. https://doi.org /10.1016/j.psyneuen.2017.07.483

Wedding, D., & Boyd, M. A., & Niemeic, R. M. (2005). *Movies and mental illness: Using films to understand psychopathology.* Hogrefe & Huber.

Wedding, D., & Niemiec, R. M. (2014). *Movies and mental illness: Using films to understand psychopathology* (4th ed.). Hogrefe Publishing.

Young, J. E. (1994). *Cognitive therapy for personality disorders: A schema-focused approach* (Rev. ed.). Professional Resource Press.

Zanarini, M. C., Frankenburg, F. R., Hennen, J., & Silk, K. R. (2003). The longitudinal course of borderline psychopathology: 6-year prospective follow-up of the phenomenology of borderline personality disorder. *American Journal of Psychiatry, 160*(2), 274–283.

Chapter 17

American Psychiatric Association (APA). (2013). *Diagnostic and statistical manual of mental disorders* (5th ed.). American Psychiatric Association.

American Psychological Association. (2002). Ethical principles of psychologists and code of conduct. *American Psychologist, 57,* 1060–1073.

American Psychological Association. (2010). 2010 amendments to the 2002 'Ethical principles of psychologists and code of conduct.' *American Psychologist, 65.* doi:10.1037/a0020168

Argo, J. J., & Shiv, B. (2012). Are white lies as innocuous as we think? *Journal of Consumer Research, 38*(6), 1093–1102.

Bond, C. F. Jr., & DePaulo, B. M. (2006). Accuracy of deception judgments. *Personality & Social Psychology Review, 10,* 214–234. doi:10.1207/s15327957pspr1003_2

Briggs, J. R. (1992). *Counselor assessments of honest and deceptive clients.* (Doctoral dissertation). Retrieved from http://ezproxy.twu.edu:2086/login.aspx?direct=true&db=psyh&AN=1994-71439-001&site=ehost-live. (1994-71439-001)

Carrillo, L. (2016). *Deception in therapy: Setting as a motivation* (thesis). Angelo State University, San Angelo, TX. http://hdl.handle.net/2346.1/30567

Curtis, D. A. (2013). *Therapists' beliefs and attitudes towards client deception* (Order No. 3579625). Available from ProQuest Dissertations & Theses A&I. (1508454518).

Curtis, D. A. (2019, April). *Pseudologia Phantastica-Pathological Lying: A theory.* Professional representative symposium presented at the 65th Annual Southwestern Psychological Association Conference, Albuquerque, NM.

Curtis, D. A., & Dickens, C. (2016, April). *Teach me or lie to me: Effectiveness of a deception workshop.* Poster presented at the 62nd Annual Southwestern Psychological Association Conference, Dallas, TX.

Curtis, D. A., & Hart, C. L. (2015). Pinocchio's nose in therapy: Therapists' beliefs and attitudes toward client deception. *International Journal for the Advancement of Counselling, 37*(3), 279–292.

Curtis, D. A., & Hart, C.L. (2019). Deception in psychotherapy: Frequency, typology, and relationship. *Counselling and Psychotherapy Research, 20,* 106–115. doi:10.1002/capr.12263

Curtis, D. A., & Hart, C. L. (in press). Pathological lying: Theoretical and empirical support for a diagnostic entity. *Psychiatric Research & Clinical Practice.*

Curtis, D. A., & Kelley, L. J. (2019). Ethics of psychotherapist deception. *Ethics & Behavior.* doi:10.1080/10508422.2019.1674654

DePaulo, B. M., & Bell, K. L. (1996). Truth and investment: Lies are told to those who care. *Journal of Personality and Social Psychology, 71,* 703–716. doi:10.1037/0022-3514.71.4.703

DePaulo, B. M., & Kashy, D. A. (1998). Everyday lies in close and casual relationships. *Journal of Personality and Social Psychology, 74,* 63–79. doi:10.1037/0022-3514.74.1.63

DePaulo, B. M., Kashy, D. A., Kirkendol, S. E., Wyer, M. M., & Epstein, J. A. (1996). Lying in everyday life. *Journal of Personality and Social Psychology, 70*(5), 979–995.

Dickens, C., & Curtis, D. A. (2019). Lies in the law: Therapists' beliefs and attitudes about deception. *Journal of Forensic Psychology Research and Practice, 19,* 359–375.

Dysart, K. L. (2012). Managing the CSI effect in jurors. *Trial Evidence, 20*(2), 6–10.

Edens, J. F., Colwell, L. H., Desforges, D. M., & Fernandez, K. (2005). The impact of mental health evidence on support for capital punishment: Are defendants labeled psychopathic considered more deserving of death? *Behavioral Sciences & the Law, 23*(5), 603–625.

Ekman, P. (2009). *Telling lies: Clues to deceit in the marketplace, politics, and marriage.* New York, NY: W. W. Norton & Company Inc.

Ekman, P., O'Sullivan, M., & Frank, M. G. (1999). A few can catch a liar. *Psychological Science, 10,* 263–266.

Gabbard, G. O., & Gabbard, K. (1999). *Psychiatry and the cinema* (2nd ed.). American Psychiatric Association.

Global Deception Research Team. (2006). A world of lies. *Journal of Cross-Cultural Psychology, 37,* 60–74. doi:10.1177/0022022105282295

Granhag, P. A., & Strömwall, L. A. (2004). Research on deception detection: Past and present. In P. Granhag & L. Strömwall (Eds.), *The detection of deception in forensic contexts* (pp. 3–12). Cambridge University Press.

Grzegorek, J. L. (2011). Smoke and mirrors. In J. Kottler, & J. Carlson (Eds.), *Duped: Lies and deception in psychotherapy* (pp. 33–37). Routledge/Taylor & Francis Group.

Hare, R. D. (2003). The Hare Psychopathy Checklist—Revised technical manual (2nd ed.). Multi-Health Systems.

Hoppin, S. (2011). Deception in doctor-patient communication. *International Journal of Health, Wellness & Society, 1*, 127–135.

Kaplar, M. E. (2006). *Lying happily ever after: Altruistic white lies, positive illusions, and relationship satisfaction. Dissertation Abstracts International: Section B: The Sciences and Engineering, 67*(4-B), 2281.

Kashy, D. A., & DePaulo, B. M. (1996). Who lies? *Journal of Personality and Social Psychology, 70*, 1037–1051. doi:10.1037/0022-3514.70.5.1037

Koocher, G. P., & Keith-Spiegel, P. (1998). *Ethics in psychology: Professional standards and cases* (2nd ed.). Oxford University Press.

Kottler, J. (2010). *The assassin and the therapist: An exploration of truth in psychotherapy and in life.* Routledge/Taylor & Francis Group.

Kottler, J., & Carlson, J. (2011). *Duped: Lies and deception in psychotherapy.* Routledge/Taylor & Francis Group.

Levine, T. R., Serota, K. B., & Shulman, H. C. (2010). The impact of Lie to Me on viewers' actual ability to detect deception. *Communication Research, 37*(6), 847–856.

Lilienfeld, S. O. (1994). *Seeing both sides: Classic controversies in abnormal psychology.* Wadsworth Publishing.

Lilienfeld, S. O., & Arkowitz, H. (2014). The truth about shock therapy. *Scientific American Mind, 25*(3), 70.

Lindskold, S., & Walters, P. S. (1983). Categories for acceptability of lies. *The Journal of Social Psychology, 120*(1), 129–136.

McDonald, A., & Walter, G. (2009). Hollywood and ECT. *International Review of Psychiatry, 21*(3), 200–206.

Mitchell, R. W., & Singer, B. (Producer). (2004). *Everybody lies* [DVD]. Available from http://www.housedvd.com/

Olsen, D. P. (2012). Putting the meds in the applesauce. *American Journal of Nursing, 112*, 67–69.

O'Sullivan, M. (2003). The fundamental attribution error in detecting deception: The boy-who-cried-wolf effect. *Personality and Social Psychology Bulletin, 29*, 1316–1327. doi:10.1177/0146167203254610

Paul Ekman Group LLC. (2016). *Lie to me.* http://www.paulekman.com/lie-to-me/

Peterson, C. (1996). Deception in intimate relationships. *International Journal of Psychology, 31*(6), 279–288.

Pope, K., & Vetter, V. (1992). Ethical dilemmas encountered by members of the American Psychological Association. *American Psychologist, 47*, 397–411.

Rosenhan, D. L. (1973). On being sane in insane places. *Science, 179*, 250–258.

Ryan, C. J., de Moore, G., & Patfield, M. (1995). Becoming none but tradesmen: Lies, deception and psychotic patients. *Journal of Medical Ethics, 21*, 72–76.

Sade, R. M. (2012). Why physicians should not lie for their patients. *American Journal of Bioethics, 12*, 17–19.

Serota, K. B., & Levine, T. B. (2015). A few prolific liars: Variation in the prevalence of lying. *Journal of Language and Social Psychology, 34*(2), 138–157.

Serota, K. B., Levine, T. R., & Boster, F. J. (2010). The prevalence of lying in America: Three studies of self-reported lies. *Human Communication Research, 36,* 2–25.

Shelton, D. E., Barak, G., & Kim, Y. S. (2011). Studying juror expectations for scientific evidence: A new model for looking at the CSI myth. *Court Review, 47*(1/2), 8–18.

Silver, E., Cirincione, C., & Steadman, H. J. (1994). Demythologizing inaccurate perceptions of the insanity defense. *Law and Human Behavior, 18*(1), 63–70.

Tarasoff v. Board of Regents of the University of California, 551 P. 2d 334 (Cal. Sup. Ct. 1976).

Tavaglione, N., & Hurst, S. A. (2012). Why physicians ought to lie for their patients. *American Journal of Bioethics, 12,* 4–12.

Teasdale, K., & Kent, G. (1995). The use of deception in nursing. *Journal of Medical Ethics, 77.* doi:10.2307/27717536

Texas Psychological Association (TPA). (2002). *Texas mental health law: A sourcebook for mental health practitioners.* Bayou Publishing.

Tyler, T. R. (2006). Viewing CSI and the threshold of guilt: Managing truth and justice in reality and fiction. *Yale Law Journal, 115*(5), 1050–1085.

Van Dorsten, B. (2002). *Forensic psychology: From classroom to courtroom.* Springer.

Vrij, A. (2000). *Detecting lies and deceit: The psychology of lying and the implications for professional practice.* John Wiley & Sons Ltd.

Vrij, A. (2008). *Detecting lies and deceit: Pitfalls and opportunities* (2nd ed.). John Wiley & Sons Ltd.

Walter, G., McDonald, A., Rey, J. M., & Rosen, A. (2002). Medical student knowledge and attitudes regarding ECT prior to and after viewing ECT scenes from movies. *The Journal of ECT, 18*(1), 43–46.

Wedding, D., & Niemiec, R. M. (2014). *Movies and mental illness: Using films to understand psychopathology* (4th ed.). Hogrefe Publishing.

Wolf, Z. (2012). Nursing practice breakdowns: Good and bad nursing. *MEDSURG Nursing, 21*(1), 16–36.

INDEX